CENSORED

CENSORED 2011

The Top 25 Censored Stories

Edited by
MICKEY HUFF and PETER PHILLIPS
with PROJECT CENSORED

INTRODUCTION BY KRISTINA BORJESSON
CARTOONS BY KHALIL BENDIB

Seven Stories Press

New York / London / Melbourne / Toronto

Seven Stories Press
140 Watts Street
New York, NY 10013
www.sevenstories.com

In Canada: Publishers Group Canada, 559 College Street, Suite 402, Toronto, ON
M6G 1A9

In the U.K.: Turnaround Publisher Services Ltd., Unit 3, Olympia Trading
Estate, Coburg Road, Wood Green, London N22 6TZ

In Australia: Palgrave Macmillan, 15–19 Claremont Street, South Yarra, VIC 3141

College professors may order examination copies of Seven Stories Press titles for a
free six-month trial period. To order, visit www.sevenstories.com/textbook/ or fax on
school letterhead to 212.226.1411.

ISBN 978-1-58322-920-0

ISSN 1074-5998

9 8 7 6 5 4 3 2 1

Book design by Jon Gilbert

Printed in the U.S.A.

Contents

SECTION I

Censored News and Media Analysis

SECTION II
Truth Emergency
Inside the US/NATO Military-Industrial-Media Empire

SECTION III
Project Censored International
Building Media Democracy Worldwide

In Dedication to a Great Truth Teller

Howard Zinn, PhD
1922–2010

Historian, Activist, Scholar, Playwright, Humanitarian,

and

Project Censored National Judge

Preface

by Mickey Huff and Peter Phillips

> *In the councils of government, we must guard against the acquisition of unwarranted influence, whether sought or unsought, by the military-industrial complex. The potential for the disastrous rise of misplaced power exists and will persist. We must never let the weight of this combination endanger our liberties or democratic processes. We should take nothing for granted. Only an alert and knowledgeable citizenry can compel the proper meshing of the huge industrial and military machinery of defense with our peaceful methods and goals, so that security and liberty may prosper together.*
> —UNITED STATES PRESIDENT DWIGHT D. EISENHOWER, *Farewell Address, January 17, 1961*

We approach the half-century mark since Eisenhower spoke those fateful words, warning of the supremacy of the military-industrial complex. This has most assuredly come to pass with the usurpation of the mass media and all other institutions required for the expansion and maintenance of empire. If only an alert and knowledgeable citizenry can safeguard security and liberty, then the population of the United States is in deep trouble. And indeed, we are.

Over the past decade, security and liberty have not prospered together in America. As a society, we have become more insecure and have seen our liberties disappear. Further, the income gap has widened more than at any time in our history, the economy has imploded, our ecosystems are under siege, and we are fighting two endless wars of occupation under the nebulous guise of a "war on terror." The US now spends more on its military-related programs than does the entire world combined, and has spent further trillions bailing out corrupt banks that destroyed the financial system leading to soaring foreclosures and unemployment. All this, and America still boasts among the most passive and controlled populations in the world in the midst of the country's longest war and worst economic crisis since the Great Depression. What populist angst there is seems to have been co-opted by the corporate media and elite political interests so that the causes of national frustration are blurred when not outright manufactured.

Somehow, in the US, we are still threatened by the specter of terrorism all the while not seeing things that are really destroying the republic right here at home, right in front of our eyes. Somehow, in the midst of all these crises, the corporate media has us ensconced in the non-issues and faux debates over presidential citizenship, border wars, and grandma-killing government death panels. We are immersed in dubious claims that global warming is a hoax and that government, not an unregulated private sector, is the root of all our problems (despite evidence that government is actually heavily influenced if not controlled by private sector elites—see stories #1 and #6 in *Censored 2010*).

In America, unsubstantiated opinions, rumors, and gossip surrounding important issues masquerade as real news. This is what captivates the masses in the subjects of major press conferences with America's leaders, and this is in large part what the corporate news itself entails: the creation of what philosopher Jean Baudrillard called a hyper-reality, and similar to what historian Daniel J. Boorstin called "pseudo-events" (a troubling phenomenon on the horizon of America's media landscape noted in his 1962 work, *The Image: A Guide to Pseudo-Events in America*). We live in a propaganda culture where factual information is routinely censored by degree. This is the basis of our current Truth Emergency—a lack of purity in news.

Simply put, what threatens us most is our ignorance about what is going on in the world around us. In large part, it is the corporate media, especially in the news departments, that continues to distract, misinform, disinform, and propagandize the public into misguided rages against the wrong enemies, compounding the state of our decaying republic, furthering public ignorance and apathy about things that should matter the most: the true state of the union, the causes for said state, and what we can do about it.

Two years prior to Eisenhower's prescient speech, then Senator John F. Kennedy cautioned how new technologies in media could lend themselves well to mass manipulation. In the November 14, 1959, issue of *TV Guide*, Kennedy wrote of the new medium of television:

Political success on television is not, unfortunately, limited only to those who deserve it. It is a medium which lends itself to manipulation, exploitation and gimmicks. It can be abused by demagogs [sic], by appeals to emotion and prejudice and ignorance. Political campaigns can be actually taken over by the "public relations" experts, who tell the candidate not only how to use TV but what to say, what to stand for and what "kind of person" to be.

It turns out that Ike was right, JFK sold the story of the day, and we are fifty years on from what they described in *their* time. Given the growth and dominance of what is now the military-industrial-media empire, we are currently entrenched in what can only be described as a Truth Emergency.

The theme for *Censored 2011* could be nothing other than this proverbial elephant in the room. The gap between the world Americans are shown via corporate media and the empirical reality has been steadily growing for decades, as Boorstin and others have intimated. Our democracy has reached a point of emergency. If something is not done to rectify the civil damages that have exponentially mounted since September 11, 2001, we may not be able to regain a sense of republican, participatory government (that is, if we ever really had one—see chapter 13 for more on this).

In America, sensationalism rules in virtually every quarter of society. Not just in entertainment, but in education, news, political discourse, and the private sector. As a society, we are so heavily laden with the ethos of unsustainable consumption and feckless, insatiable desire; we are so saturated by the infotainment of Junk Food News and News Abuse (see chapter 3) that we are now slaves to a system that is in fact inimical to the conditions required for democracy to even exist, let alone thrive.

Chris Hedges, most recently the author of *Empire of Illusion: The End of Literacy and the Triumph of Spectacle*, reminds us:

> A democracy survives when its citizens have access to trustworthy and impartial sources of information, when it can discern lies from truth. Take this away and a democracy dies. The fusion of news and entertainment, the rise of a class of celebrity journalists on television who define reporting by their access to the famous and the powerful, the retreat by many

readers into the ideological ghettos of the Internet and the ruth-less drive by corporations to destroy the traditional news business are leaving us deaf, dumb and blind.

And it is not just through entertainment and the news media that this is happening, as mentioned, it has also infected our educational insti-tutions, this declining interest, not to mention ability, to think critically. We have become a nation of contestants in our own media-generated, fictitious reality show that could be aptly named "American Idle," addled by pseudo-events and the hyperreal.

If all this is not enough, in another deaf, dumb, and blind moment just this past year, the Texas State Board of Education voted to rewrite US history standards for their schools by changing the history textbooks —or, more specifically, by cutting out more liberal or secular compo-nents and inserting more conservative and traditional ones, creating a grand narrative based on the narrow interests of the few politicized members of the board. This sort of decision doesn't only impact Texans, as the same publishers often provide books for other states as well. While this trend has diminished in recent years, it still raises concerns beyond Texas. Former head of the American Historical Association, Professor Eric Foner, recently wrote in the *Nation*, "Clearly, the Texas Board of Edu-cation seeks to inculcate children with a history that celebrates the achievements of our past while ignoring its shortcomings, and that largely ignores those who have struggled to make this a fairer, more equal society." We need to understand our shortcomings in terms of democratic principles if we are to rectify them. This board wants history to reflect America's greatness, its exceptionalism, while ignoring its glar-ing flaws. In short, this is an act of censorship.

George Orwell wrote in *1984*, "Those that control the present control the past. Those that control the past control the future." These board members are not just changing words in books, they are changing the framework, the very structure through which millions in subsequent generations will be taught history, which provides context for the present, which in turn impacts our future. (Perhaps the board should read James Loewen's *Lies My Teacher Told Me*). Indeed, it is just another reason we dedicated our book this year to former Project Censored national judge and historian, the late Howard Zinn. Zinn did more to change the direc-tions of American historiography in the last part of the twentieth century than most anyone else, calling for more truths to be told, more voices to be heard, more diversity and inclusiveness to be part of curriculum, and, in fact, to tell a true, uncensored People's History in all its complexity. But we also need a free press to help create that, as journalism is oft seen as the rough draft of history.

What we need is a People's Media (see section three of this volume). Without access to truthful information based on the empirically fact-based world, we have only our beliefs. We need a free press in order to meaningfully participate in our own lives. The traditional role of a free press in a democracy goes back to the days of Madison and Jefferson— before corporate and elite economic control over media in the US, when the founders assumed that information was a component of the public sphere. In large part due to the failings of the free press, our republic itself has become one of Boorstin's pseudo-events—what now constitutes our hyperreality (see chapter 3). A vibrant free press with a lack of censorship and the inclusion of all views based on all known information is the only way to reverse our course of bread and circuses.

There are, however, signs of hope. Recently, Iceland voted to create a new media haven through a proposal called the Icelandic Modern Media Initiative. The initiative "resolves to task the government with finding ways to strengthen freedoms of expression and information freedom in Iceland, as well as providing strong protections for sources and whistleblowers." This development comes on the heels of news that the Pentagon is actively seeking Austrialian journalist and Internet activist Julian Assange, founder of the whistleblower Web site Wikileaks, for releasing sensitive, classified documents. Some of the documents have revealed troubling information and videos of US war crimes. The US claims he is a threat to national security, though has not actually demonstrated that case. American whistleblower Daniel Ellsberg, who leaked the Pentagon Papers during the Vietnam War, has claimed that Assange is not a security threat, but that information leaked could be quite embarrassing for the US diplomatically, which explains the Pentagon's interest in censoring Assange's efforts, as they expose the censorship of information that should be part of democratic discourse in the determining of public policy. Time will tell the impact that the media haven initiative in Iceland will have worldwide. Nevertheless, it is clearly a step in the right direction toward protecting a free press and encouraging factual publication on delicate matters that people desperately need to know in the course of self-governance. The free press, in earnest, is meant to be a guardian of truth. Let the facts fall where they may.

And so, with the intention of seeking and speaking the truth, we now lay out this year's book. For the first time ever we have divided *Censored* into three larger, themed sections to reflect the patterns and directions of our ongoing research: Censored News and Media Analysis, Truth Emergency, and Project Censored International. We thank Kristina Borjesson for a poignant introduction that perfectly announces this volume. Her work, chronicling and criticizing mass media censorship after 9/11, is required reading for anyone wanting to understand the architecture of modern media censorship and its ramifications for our society. And we welcome back the clever editorial cartoons of Khalil Bendib. We are grateful for his creative contributions, as they embellish the text so well. We are honored to have Khalil and Kristina with us for *Censored 2011*.

Censored News and Media Analysis

Our first section, chapters 1 through 5, contains Project Censored's top 25 censored stories, Déjà vu, Junk Food News and News Abuse, Signs of Health, and Fairness & Accuracy In Reporting (FAIR)'s Fear and Favor report.

Chapter 1, as every year, features the top 25 censored stories that Project Censored's participating professors, students, and judges believe should be highlighted in order to maintain a republic and media democracy, though this year we encouraged a more thematic analysis of each story under the rubric of a Truth Emergency. We received well over three hundred story nominations, including many from our new college and university affiliates around the US and the world, and we researched, vetted, and validated every one to present what the reader will see here.

Sadly, we have just as many stories to sift through as we did over a decade ago; the problem of underreported and censored stories is still an urgent one. It is no surprise, then, that chapter 2 on Déjà vu censored stories is also alive and well. Each year this chapter holds promise: we examine previously censored stories in hopes they've seen the light of day within the mainstream media. Some stories do, though this past year, as is often the case, we also discover that some underreported stories have not only remained that way, but have disappeared even further into utter obscurity. When we quote George Santayana, who declared that those who can't remember the past are condemned to repeat it, we really do hope that the corporate media and society at large will consider that problem more seriously.

In chapter 3, Adam Bessie joins Mickey Huff and Frances A. Capell to explore what the corporate media *do* spend their precious column inches and airtime on: the top of the bottom in news coverage of the trivial and inane, with more Junk Food News and News Abuse than ever before. This year's authors dissect the increasing problem of News Abuse by studying issues of framing, language control, and propaganda that exist right in front of us all, but that often go unnoticed as we become desensitized to a hyperreal, media-landscape-generated world with a side of Junk Food News.

For the Signs of Health featured in chapter 4, we welcome our newest Media Freedom Foundation board member, Kenn Burrows. Readers often claim that the bulk of our stories cover what is wrong in our world as seen through a democratic lens, and while that may be partially true, we make sure to devote an entire chapter to the *good* news also not covered by the mainstream corporate media. Signs of Health is a real display of hope and change for the better in our world, counterbalancing the empty promises of campaign slogans. A longtime professor of holistic studies at San Francisco State University, Burrows is an expert in the field of the positive possibilities for humanity.

In chapter 5, Peter Hart of Fairness & Accuracy In Reporting rounds out the Censored News and Media Analysis section with the tenth anniversary of the Fear and Favor report. This chapter looks more closely at how decisions are made in the newsroom about what stories do and don't run in corporate media. It's an eye-opening exposé of the role fears and favors play among those determining the news.

Truth Emergency

With *Censored 2011* comes the inaugural Truth Emergency section, chapters 6 through 10. We've written about the concept of a Truth Emergency for the past several years, and here, in a section now needed more than ever, we discuss this emergency in more detail, with case studies, including a progressive institution's recent censorship of Project Censored for keeping dialogue open on specific topics that are so often marginalized, the root of this very emergency.

In this section, we showcase the work of several scholars and independent journalists who are engaged in work we believe exemplifies the ideals of a free press. Despite the constant spin from President Obama and his administration, it is just as disheartening to see so many corporate media pundits decry his messages as propaganda while having been so conspicuously silent during an earlier era, as a previous leader proclaimed, "See, in my line of work you have to keep repeating things over and over and over again for the truth to sink in, to kind of catapult the propaganda."[1] The Bush years marked some of the worst performances by the US corporate press in recent memory: from 9/11 to election fraud to WMDs, the corporate media consistently failed the public, acting like cheerleaders or stenographers to the powerful by not getting at the truth of what was going on based on the facts—facts with which other independent journalists were filling blogs, journals, and books.

We at Project Censored don't disagree that President Obama, like other politicians past and present, embarks upon many dubious communicative paths. Over the years we have written about this problem as it afflicts both major political parties, and in this volume include many critiques of Obama (see chapter 10 in *Censored 2010* for a history of this issue). Still, we reiterate: most of today's Obama critics in the corporate media were silent, some even sycophantic, during one of the most propagandistic periods of our recent past. In other words, where was the media from 2001 to 2009, the Bush years? As the late social critic and comedian George Carlin once said, "Let's not have a double standard here, one standard will do just fine."

We are entrenched in a dire and growing Truth Emergency. And so we welcome Dr. Lance deHaven-Smith, Dr. David Ray Griffin, Nora Barrows-Friedman, Dr. Robert Abele, and the return of Dr. Andrew Roth. The facts they present and argue are essential to fueling robust debate in our decaying republic. We ignore these authors and their cogent analysis at our peril.

In chapter 6, public policy professor Dr. Lance deHaven-Smith addresses the ongoing issue of state crimes against democracy (SCADs), providing a frame with which to discuss controversial matters of corruption in government and in the elite private sector, outside the realm of what is often labeled as "conspiracy theory." It is the perfect way to understand the Truth Emergency problem—especially considering the irony that Project Censored was censored when addressing ongoing SCADs in an op-ed piece. DeHaven-Smith suggests ways we can move beyond conspiracy theorist monikers and communicate more effectively about the weighty subject of SCADs, escaping labels that stifle free inquiry.

Chapter 7 is about Building 7 from the World Trade Center complex in New York. Theologian and author Dr. David Ray Griffin continues the SCAD theme, specifically applying it to the events of September 11 and the mysterious collapse of WTC 7, the third building destroyed that day after the twin towers, though it was not hit by airplanes and sustained less damage than other buildings that did not fall. The forty-seven-story skyscraper fell into its own footprint, for some time at free-fall speed. Explanations for this virtually unprecedented structural failure (besides the only other two examples in history which took place earlier that day) have been lacking, and as Griffin explains through mountains of evidence, the most plausible explanation—controlled demolition—has been attacked or ignored by government scientists in what seems to be a violation of the scientific method itself. The fact that close to half the US population has no knowledge of this building, and that the 9/11 Commission did not even mention it in its report, is testimony to the ongoing censorship of this topic (also see story #14 in chapter 1).

In chapter 8, award-winning independent journalist Nora Barrows-Friedman tells the plight of the Palestinian people that the corporate media has ignored completely, through several previously untold stories that together paint a vivid picture of the human costs of occupation tied to US support of Israel in the Middle East. To the corporate media, the mounting Palestinian civilian deaths, which far outweigh those of the occupying power, are simply invisible. Barrows-Friedman sheds light on an issue that anyone with a concern for human rights desperately needs to heed.

In chapter 9, the failures of corporate media reporting on weapons of mass destruction (WMDs) and Just War Theory are addressed in detail by philosophy professor Dr. Robert Abele. Abele's attention to detail and relentless application of logic cut through the fog of war propaganda and make it painfully clear how the failures of the so-called free press were behind the US stampede into Iraq. For Abele's expanded study on the subject, readers can see his book, *The Anatomy of a Deception: A Reconstruction and Analysis of the Decision to Invade Iraq*.

For chapter 10, former Project Censored associate director Dr. Andrew Roth returns with a study of how corporate media and the military-industrial complex merge to generate pro-military propaganda. Citing President Dwight Eisenhower's historic speech from 1961 (referenced in the epigraph of this preface), Roth looks at how the total influence of the military-industrial complex has a hegemonic influence over public debate. Given these conditions, the outcomes for citizens in a democracy are as bleak as Eisenhower had forewarned almost half a century ago. Upon the upcoming fiftieth anniversary of the Eisenhower address, it is a relevant point of reflection on our current state of affairs in the US. We thank Dr. Roth for his continued support of Project Censored.

We hope readers, regardless of the strong beliefs some may have on these subjects, will survey the often unreported or underreported facts in this controversial section with an open mind in an effort to generate public debate about these very important matters we face as a society—the impact of SCADs; actual scientific investigations regarding 9/11 issues; Israel/Palestine; mass media and mass deception in the military-industrial-media empire. We need a free press that is unafraid to report factually on these matters, regardless of the consequences for those in power or for the status quo. Democracy demands no less.

Project Censored International

The third and final section of *Censored 2011* reflects how international Project Censored has become over the past few years. Supported by our Media Freedom International Web site at www.mediafreedominternational.org, and our college and university affiliate program with participants across the US and the world, this new section displays our focus on the problems of media censorship around the globe and on what we can do to reverse these troubling trends. Here we share our vision for internationalizing media democracy research through validated independent news emanating from the grassroots where people are increasingly striving to Be the Media.

Censored 2011 co-editors Peter Phillips and Mickey Huff team up in chapter 11 to explain the evolution and trajectory of Project Censored's research methods. The authors discuss the expanding college and university affiliate program and its role in helping build a People's Media, generating Validated Independent News for the twenty-first century, in efforts to be media democracy in action.

We are pleased to have Dr. Concha Mateos, visiting scholar from Spain, discuss international problems of censorship, a framework that Project Censored has embarked upon in Germany, Japan, and parts of South America. Mateos, who will be heading up our Project Censored European affiliate program, writes chapter 12, which is exemplary of our new Project Censored International effort, providing a welcome contribution to ongoing scholarship in support of global media democracy.

Professor and activist Rob Williams of the Action Coalition for Media Education offers a primer in civics by explaining why states may need to secede while under assault from the federal government regarding constitutional rights. Chapter 13 lends significant historical and intellectual legitimacy to the international issue of regional sovereignty, to a new localism with press freedom, and to indigenous rights, themes the corporate media usually avoids discussing unless to attack or marginalize. Williams's merging of scholarship and activism are a perfect fit for the Project Censored International vision of media democracy in action.

In chapter 14, Dave Mathison, author of *Be the Media: How to Create and Accelerate Your Message . . . Your Way*, gives readers a taste of his research and lays out some problems of big media and what We the People need to do to create and control our own media systems and messages. An expert in the business of communications, and, particularly, in making communications technology work for the individual, Mathison offers sage advice regarding community-centered movement messaging strategies. In a time of rampant corporate media failures, he shows proactively how we can Be the Media.

For chapter 15, we welcome back the London-based Index on Censorship, which this year shares the censored tale of an important victory, one showing that free speech is not for sale. The case of writer and critic Simon Singh, who was legally attacked for libel after criticizing a well-heeled medical association in Britain, yielded a positive outcome for free speech, reaffirming a cornerstone principle of democratic society: the freedom of the press to criticize the powerful.

Regardless of what side one may take on the many controversial issues explored in this year's *Censored* volume, we must create an atmosphere where all topics can be discussed in a civil manner and where we can respectfully disagree on the basis of facts. As Mark Twain once said, "Get your facts first, then you can distort them as much as you please." Perhaps the second part of that notion is an inescapable reality, but the first part, getting the facts, is essential for any functioning democracy. There can be no topic that cannot be discussed. We cannot allow difficult or unpopular subjects or views to be dismissed *a priori*. In other words, we cannot tolerate the censorship of facts, ideas, or perspectives, whether we agree with them or not. To that end, we hope you not only explore the many different avenues of media studies in *Censored 2011*, but that you also join us in becoming media democracy in action as the only antidote to our current Truth Emergency.

Note
1. President George W. Bush, public speech, Rochester, New York, May 24, 2005.

Introduction

by Kristina Borjesson

> *In a time of universal deceit, telling the truth is a*
> *revolutionary act.*
> —GEORGE ORWELL

"Tell them to get the hell out of Palestine. Remember, these people [the Palestinians] are occupied and it's their land." With those words, spoken to Rabbi David Nesenoff who had asked for her comments on Israel, US press icon Helen Thomas blew up her long, distinguished career. Asked where the Israelis should go, Thomas said home to Poland, Germany and America. Former Bush White House spokesman Ari Fleischer (of weapons of mass destruction fame) immediately went on television and told *CNN Newsroom* anchor Don Lemon that she should be fired. When Thomas said that Israelis should go home to Poland, Germany, and the United States, she was obliquely referring to the fact that Palestinians are indigenous to the territories on which they live and that the Israelis took over, and that Israelis are, for the most part, European and American colonial transplants or descendants of those transplants. The horrendous fact of the Holocaust does not change this truth.

Not surprisingly, the story of continuing human rights abuses in Palestine landed on Project Censored's list of Top 25 Censored News Stories. Rare mainstream media glimpses of Israel's apartheid system, like the CBS *60 Minutes* segment "Is Peace Out of Reach?" in January 2009, air and then fade away after drawing vitriolic, selectively focused criticism. A well-oiled propaganda, censorship, and retaliation system promotes a perpetually lopsided view of Palestinians as attackers and Israelis as citizens acting in self-defense. The documentary *Peace, Propaganda & the Promised Land: U.S. Media & the Israeli-Palestinian Conflict,*[1] written and directed by Sut Jhally and Bathsheba Ratzkoff, and produced by the Media Education Foundation, shows how and when the system kicks into action.

Censorship of accurate coverage of the Israeli/Palestinian conflict is but one feature of a larger, heavily censored landscape of interconnected subjects. Looking at Project Censored's Top 25 list, one is immediately struck by the preponderance of subjects directly related to the conduct of America's Middle Eastern foreign policy and the "war on terror" that sprang from it. Eleven of the Top 25 stories share this connection directly, others to a lesser extent.

The most monumental among these is the story of unresolved 9/11 issues. Even though 9/11 took America's global war on terror into more brutal and illegal territory (like ongoing torture and extraordinary renditions—while turning the United States into a national security state almost overnight, there has been a complete mainstream press *omertà* on the discrepancies in the official story. Based on an official account full of holes, two long bloody wars are still being fought, civil liberties and the right to privacy have been lost, law enforcement on every level is being militarized, the country is being bankrupted, and everyone is a potential terrorist suspect. To me, the silence is terrifying. Mainstream corporate media's refusal to conduct ongoing investigations into events before, during, and after 9/11 means that mass hypnosis of an entire nation is not only possible but, in this case, probable.

Even independent, progressive media have been shy about covering 9/11. At the May 2010 Understanding Deep Politics Conference in Santa Cruz, California, several people asked me with desperation in their voices why Amy Goodman wasn't asking questions about 9/11. Goodman, who hosts Pacifica Radio's widely heard program *Democracy Now!*, has built a solid reputation doing ongoing, stellar reporting on a number of mainstream-censored issues, including the Israeli/Palestinian conflict. While regularly pounding away at virtually every angle of that story, Goodman has only sparsely covered 9/11. Her lack of interest is baffling, which begs the question: Why?

I had another telling experience with Jonathan Landay, McClatchy Newspapers' star national security and intelligence correspondent. After e-mailing Landay (whom I like personally and respect professionally) to request that he ask McClatchy's science correspondent to evaluate the integrity of a scientific article in the peer-reviewed *Open Chemical Physics Journal* titled "Active Thermitic Material Discovered in Dust from the 9/11 World Trade Center Catastrophe"[2] about military-grade explosive material in the 9/11 dust, I received a quick, sharp response. Landay derided wacky conspiracy theorists that seemed to believe American officials could kill thousands of their own countrymen and keep it a secret. He then directed me to the Web site Debunking911.com, which didn't mention nano-thermite at all.[3] What's key about our exchange was that I didn't offer or request an opinion on what happened on 9/11. I was simply asking Landay to extend a professional courtesy to me and give McClatchy's science reporter the article to assess whether or not proper scientific protocol had been followed. In the end, Landay dismissed me and my request with a final missive saying he had no "visibility" on the subject beyond the claims made in the article. No mention was made about passing it on to the science reporter. My journalist counterparts in Paris, where I'm writing this introduction, tell me they too are avoiding the subject. "It is the story of the century," they say, "but it smells too much." Which is exactly why everyone should be digging into it.

If 9/11 is the story of the century, other stories connected to US foreign policy in the Middle East and the so-called war on terror collectively paint a picture of ongoing corruption and brutality on mind-boggling scales. Would Americans ever see CNN's Anderson Cooper presenting a detailed account of how the US government not only helped create the Taliban but continues to fund and support this group the government itself continually identifies as one of the most significant terrorist threats to America and its interests? Would Americans ever see Fox TV's Bret Baier doing an in-depth report on the secret, illegal war their government is waging in Pakistan? Or hear him announce that charges were filed in Spain against four American presidents, including Barack Obama, for crimes against humanity and genocide? Would they see CNN's Dr. Sanjay Gupta reporting from Iraq on how the US Defense Department is the world's biggest polluter? The prospects of any of this ever happening are slim (one can always hope) to none, and the list of unreported horribles goes on and on.

In his first state of the union address, President Obama bemoaned how his government faces "a deficit of trust, deep and corrosive doubts about how Washington works that have been growing for years" and how he came to Washington to "close that credibility gap." Books such as the volume you hold in your hands right now, dear reader, provide in disturbing detail all the reasons for the existence of that credibility gap. The gap opened monstrously during George W. Bush's administration and has continued to grow. It is now so wide that Project Censored principals Mickey Huff and Peter Phillips created a whole new subject category for issues falling within it: Truth Emergency, which includes what Professor Lance deHaven-Smith calls "state crimes against democracy" (SCADs), and which are elaborated upon in chapters 6 and 7 of this volume. The issues in this category are beyond urgent. Laws institutionalizing the demise of the rule of law (i.e., the Bush administration's torture memos), the massive-scale handover of public money to huge private institutions as well as other unfettered business and election practices are turning America into a third-world nation complete with rigged electoral and judicial systems and the militarization of a vast law enforcement network to keep everyone in line as things get worse among the middle and poor classes.

Every year, the dire issues compound as the mainstream corporate media in the US and around the world persist in presenting reports based on what the global power elite want people to think. Indeed, the Truth Emergency theme of this book highlights how desperate the situation is, with so many critical subjects either remaining unreported or so tightly wrapped in propaganda that they literally make no sense. Faced with accounts that aren't helping them understand or fix their deteriorating circumstances, people are growing angry and turning to other information sources, primarily on the Internet. Project Censored's news Web site (www.projectcensored.org) and their efforts to continue globalizing their reporting network could not be more timely or necessary, and the effects that Internet news operations like that of Project Censored (www.censorednews.org) are already having are profound. In May 2010, during an extraordinarily frank lecture at the Council on Foreign Relations, President Jimmy Carter's national security advisor, Zbigniew Brzezinski, explained the new challenges to the Western power elite's vision of their small like-minded group eventually running a one-world government:

> Today the rise of the Far East has created a new but much more differentiated global leadership. . . . The other major change in international affairs is that for the first time in all of human history, mankind is politically awakened. That's a total new reality . . . people know what is generally . . . going on in the world and are consciously aware of global iniquities, inequalities, lack of respect, exploitation. Mankind is now politically awakened and staring. The combination of the two, the diversified global leadership, politically awakened masses, makes a much more difficult context for any major power including, currently, the leading world power, the United States.[4]

"The indispensable catalyst is the word, the explanatory idea," wrote noted Polish writer Ryszard Kapuscinski. "Words—uncontrolled words, circulating freely, underground, rebelliously, not gotten up in dress uniforms, uncertified—[these are what] frighten tyrants."[5] Gratifyingly frightening then, this latest Project Censored book, *Censored 2011*.

Paris, France

2010

KRISTINA BORJESSON is internationally acclaimed for her work as an investigative reporter and media critic. Borjesson has produced for major American and European television networks and published two groundbreaking books on the problems of the US press: *Into the Buzzsaw: Leading Journalists Expose the Myth of a Free Press* and *Feet to the Fire: The Media After 9/11—Top Journalists Speak Out*. Her awards include an Emmy and a Murrow Award in television, the National Press Club's Arthur Rowse Award for Press Criticism, and two Independent Publisher Book Awards for her books.

Notes

1. Watch online at http://video.google.com/videoplay?docid=-6604775898578139565#.
2. Available online at http://bentham.org/open/tocpj/openaccess2.htm.
3. The thermite-specific page is at http://www.debumking911.com/thermite.htm.
4. The video recording of Zbigniew Brzezinski's Council on Foreign Relations speech is widely available on the Internet, including at http://www.youtube.com/watch?v=oZxE8L38h6U, retrieved June 20, 2010.
5. Ryszard Kapuscinski, *Shah of Shahs* (New York: Vintage, 1992), 103.

CHAPTER I

The Top Censored Stories of 2009–10

by Trish Boreta, Mickey Huff, Peter Phillips, and Elaine Wellin with
Julie Andrzejewski, Elliot Cohen, Kevin Howley, and Project Censored

> *Censorship reflects society's lack of confidence in itself. It*
> *is a hallmark of an authoritarian regime.*
> —POTTER STEWART

WHAT IS MODERN MEDIA CENSORSHIP?

An Introduction by Mickey Huff and Project Censored

At Project Censored, we examine the coverage of news and information essential to the maintenance of a healthy and functioning democracy. We define "modern media censorship" as the subtle yet constant and sophisticated manipulation of reality in our mass media outlets. On a daily level, censorship refers to the intentional exclusion of a news story, or piece of a news story, based on anything other than a desire to tell the truth. Such manipulation can take the form of political pressure (from government officials and powerful individuals), economic pressure (from advertisers and funders), and legal pressure (the threat of lawsuits from deep-pocketed individuals, corporations, and institutions). Censorship is not only a story that was never published, it is any story that does not get widespread distribution regardless of its factual nature and significance to society and its systems of democratic government. Simply put, censorship is more than blatant and outright omission.

As political scientist and former Project Censored national judge Dr. Michael Parenti explained in his May 2001 article, "Monopoly Media Manipulation," censorship also involves framing, false balancing, attacking and labeling, preemptive assumption, face-value transition, follow-up avoidance in questioning, slighting of content, and many fallacies such as the red herring, straw person, and appeal to emotion, to name a few. Therefore, censorship is often a matter of degree, but any degree at all can obfuscate and distort any topic or story. The end result can be confusion, the arrival at non-factually supported conclusions, or the lack of total understanding, rendering one incapable of connecting the dots or seeing the bigger picture. Thus censorship is a key element of any propaganda system and is antithetical to the goals of a free press, which, according to twentieth-century journalist George Seldes, was to tell the people what was really going on in society.

Some of the stories in this chapter were slightly covered in the corporate media, and some have been covered since our vote to choose the top 25 took place. But even then, the full facts of any particular story were often still lacking in corporate media coverage, and in the rare cases that facts were adequately represented, the coverage was one or two stories in the press, not enough to gain the attention of the people at large. Consistent reporting of key stories and details, not merely passing mention, is a key component of messaging, of communicating, so we believe stories with minimal attention in corporate media still qualify as partially censored stories. Further, while there are certainly readers of alternative publications and Web sites, from where the bulk of our stories are drawn, these outlets usually do not have widespread distribution, and, even when on the Internet, people often need to know how to find them in the first place. These are all problems of accessibility and presence in our culture: because the corporate, commercial media has virtually ubiquitous access to the public eye and mind, these media entities have an extraordinary advantage over influencing the public than those that do not. And it is that unequal advantage of corporate media that accounts for many of the problems of information dissemination around the world.

On Media Accountability

The only valid justification for declining a news story in a free press system is when a medium is limited by time and space, when another news story is deemed more important to the people of the local, national, or international community. Though admittedly a subjective process, it is nonetheless a process to be undertaken by the newspeople themselves—the investigative journalists and editors—*not* by the managers and chief executive officers (CEOs) of "parent companies." A professional journalist or researcher should never have to face the destruction of his or her career (or life) simply because he or she wanted to tell the truth. While no two people will always agree on which story is more important than another, a system in which the working reporters and editors run the newsroom would at least provide a fertile environment for debate, dissent, and critical thinking.

The growth of independent media and journalism in recent years shows that people throughout the world yearn to hold not only their leaders accountable, but their media sources as well. For that reason, Project Censored continues, in its small way, to support and highlight those who tell the truth about the powerful *no matter the consequences*, and are relentless in their quest to hold corporate mass media accountable for their decisions concerning what they do and do not report.

Analysis of Story Submissions for Censored 2011
by Dr. Elaine Wellin

An analysis of the 334 articles nominated for *Censored 2011* shows that some issues tended to be ignored by mainstream media more than others—ignored mostly by the American corporate media, though the European mainstream was at fault as well. These were the sorts of stories that project participants thought necessary to uncover, and that the corporate mainstream media also deemed important to ignore or censor in some way.

▸ Nearly twenty censored stories or groups of related stories centered on the Internet.

▸ Over twenty stories described the worldwide consequences of free trade and corporate malfeasance.

▸ Over forty censored stories and groups of related stories concerned the military and war, most evidently focused on the Middle East, but also on Africa, Latin America, the United States, and elsewhere.

▸ About fifty stories and sets of related stories that did not hit the nation's dailies detailed myriad assaults on people's health, and, not surprisingly, on the consequences of lack of health care.

▸ And over sixty censored stories and groups of related stories were about the environment, reflecting persistent and growing concerns by ordinary people that continue to be ignored or covered up by corporate America and the federal government.

In summary, of the issues participating members found to be most censored, 58 percent of all nominated stories fell within five categories: the Internet, corporate malfeasance, the military, health, and the environment. Even more than in previous years, Project Censored has strived to analyze by theme, as following the connections between stories is crucial to gaining accurate and contextual knowledge about our complex global society. And so, at last, we present the top 25 censored stories for this past year.

1

Global Plans to Replace the Dollar

Sources:
Chris Hedges, "The American Empire Is Bankrupt," *Truthdig*, June 15, 2009, http://www.truthdig.com/report/item/20090614_the_american_empire_is_bankrupt/.

Michael Hudson, "De-Dollarization: Dismantling America's Financial-Military Empire: The Yekaterinburg Turning Point," *Global Research*, June 13, 2009, http://www.globalresearch.ca/PrintArticle.php?articleId=13969.

Fred Weir, "Iran and Russia Nip at US Global Dominance" *Christian Science Monitor*, June 16, 2009, http://www.csmonitor.com/2009/0616/p06s12-woeu.html.

Lyubov Pronina, "Medvedev Shows Off Sample Coin of New 'World Currency' at G-8," Bloomberg, July 10, 2009, http://www.bloomberg.com/apps/news?pid=20601087 &sid=aeFVNYQpByU4.

Edmund Conway, "UN Wants New Global Currency to Replace Dollar," *Telegraph* (UK), September 7, 2009, http://www.telegraph.co.uk/finance/currency/6152204/UN-wants-new-global-currency-to-replace-dollar.html.

Jose Arturo Cardenas, "Latin American Leftists Tackle Dollar with New Currency," Agence France-Presse, October 16, 2009, http://www.google.com/hostednews/afp/article/ ALeqM5jisHEg79Cz8uRtYfZR6WK4JmWsIg.

Student Researchers:
Nicole Fletcher (Sonoma State University)
Krystal Alexander (Indian River State College)
Bridgette Grillo (Sonoma State University)

Faculty Evaluators:
Ronald Lopez (Sonoma State University)
Elliot D. Cohen (Indian River State College)
Mickey Huff (Diablo Valley College)

Nations have reached their limit in subsidizing the United States' military adventures. During meetings in June 2009 in Yekaterinburg, Russia, world leaders such as China's President Hu Jintao, Russia's President Dmitry Medvedev, and other top officials of the six-nation Shanghai Cooperation Organisation took the first formal step to replace the dollar as the world's reserve currency. The United States was denied admission to the meetings. If the world leaders succeed, the dollar will dramatically plummet in value; the cost of imports, including oil, will skyrocket; and interest rates will climb.

Foreigners see the International Monetary Fund (IMF), the World Bank, and the World Trade Organization (WTO) as Washington surrogates in a financial system backed by US military bases and aircraft carriers encircling the globe. But this military domination is a vestige of an American empire no longer able to rule by economic strength. US military power is muscle-bound, based more on atomic weaponry and long-distance air strikes than on ground operations, which have become too politically unpopular to mount on any large scale.

As Chris Hedges wrote in June 2009, "The architects of this new global exchange realize that if they break the dollar they also break America's military domination. US military spending cannot be sustained without this cycle of heavy borrowing. The official US defense budget for fiscal year 2008 was $623 billion. The next closest national military budget was China's, at $65 billion, according to the Central Intelligence Agency."

To fund the permanent war economy, the US has been flooding the world with dollars. The foreign recipients turn the dollars over to their central banks for local currency. The central banks then have a problem. If a central bank does not spend the money in the United States, then the exchange rate against the dollar increases, penalizing exporters. This has allowed the US to print money without restraint, to buy imports and foreign companies, to fund military expansion, and to ensure that foreign nations like China continue to buy American treasury bonds.

In July 2009, President Medvedev illustrated his call for a supranational currency to replace the dollar by pulling from his pocket a sample coin of a "united future world currency." The coin, which bears the words "Unity in Diversity," was minted in Belgium and presented to the heads of G8 delegations.

In September 2009, the United Nations Conference on Trade and Development proposed creating a new artificial currency that would replace the dollar as reserve currency. The UN wants to redesign the Bretton Woods system of international exchange. Formation of this currency would be the largest monetary overhaul since World War II. China is involved in deals with Brazil and Malaysia to denominate their trade in China's yuan, while Russia promises to begin trading in the ruble and local currencies.

Additionally, nine Latin American countries have agreed on the creation of a regional currency, the sucre, aimed at scaling back the use of the US dollar. The countries, members of the Bolivarian Alliance for the Americas (ALBA), a leftist bloc conceived by Venezuela's President Hugo Chávez, met in Bolivia where they vowed to press ahead with a new currency for intraregional trade. The sucre would be rolled out beginning in 2010 in a nonpaper form. ALBA's member states are Venezuela, Bolivia, Cuba, Ecuador, Nicaragua, Dominica, Saint Vincent and the Grenadines, and Antigua and Barbuda.

The cycle supporting a permanent US war economy appears to be almost over. Once the dollar cannot flood central banks and no one buys US treasury bonds, the American global military empire collapses. The impact on daily living for the US population could be severe.

Our authors predict that in addition to increased costs, states and cities will see their pension funds drained. The government will be forced to sell off infrastructure, including roads and transport, to private corporations. People will be increasingly charged for privatized utilities that were once regulated and subsidized. Commercial and private real estate will be worth less than half its current value. The negative equity that already plagues 25 percent of American homes will expand to include nearly all property owners. It will be difficult to borrow and impossible to sell real estate unless we accept massive losses. There will be block after block of empty stores and boarded-up houses. Foreclosures will be epidemic. There will be long lines at soup kitchens and many, many homeless.

Update by Michael Hudson

Foreign countries are presently seeking to create an international monetary system in which central bank savings do *not* fund the United States' military deficit. At present, foreign "dollar holdings" take the form of US treasury bonds, used to finance the (largely military) US domestic budget deficit, a deficit that is largely due to military spending.

Russia, China, India, and Brazil have taken the lead in seeking an alternative system. But almost no information about such a system was available in the US or even the European press, except for a shorter version of my "De-Dollarization" article that I published as an op-ed in the *Financial Times* of London.

Discussions about creating an alternative monetary system have not been public. I was invited to China to discuss my views with officials there and to lecture at three universities, and was subsequently asked to write up my proposals for Premier Wen Jiabao, pending another visit just prior to this year's meetings between China, Russia, India, and Brazil, with Iran attending with visitor status. All of this signals that other countries are seeking an alternative. Now that the euro has collapsed, there's currently little alternative to the dollar as a reserve currency. This implies that there is *no* national currency that is a stable store of value for international savings.

Meanwhile, US money managers are leading the flight from the dollar to Brazil, China, and other "emerging market" countries. As matters stand, these countries are selling their resources and companies for free—as the dollars being spent to buy them end up in their central banks, to be recycled into US treasury bonds, or to be used to purchase euro debt that is plunging in international value.

The result of this conundrum is the pressure to end the postwar era of "free capital movements" and to introduce capital controls.

There has been almost no press discussion of my story or indeed of the issue itself. US and European media have successfully ignored the proposal of an alternative to the existing state of affairs.

Update by Fred Weir

This story illustrates one aspect of post–Soviet Russia's search for a place in the US-led global order—a position that would reflect that country's own distinct geopolitical interests and how it differs from the West in terms of history, culture, and level of economic development. Russia inherited from the former Soviet Union close relations with many countries that the US regards as "rogue states," including Iran, Cuba, and Venezuela. There continues to be a lot of official, public sympathy for those countries and their opposition to the US global system, even though Moscow no longer has any grand sense of anti-Western ideology or even any practical goal of mobilizing toward an "alliance" that would serve Russia's ends.

Under the George W. Bush administration, Moscow felt itself under pressure from what it viewed as Western encroachments into the post-Soviet space, what Russians term the "near abroad." This took the form of "colored revolutions," or what the Western media referred to as "pro-democracy uprisings" in Georgia, Ukraine, and Kyrgyzstan, which removed corrupt but Moscow-friendly regimes and brought to power much more outspoken and active pro-Western ones. The Kremlin, rightly or wrongly, interpreted these upheavals as US-sponsored and orchestrated attempts to reengineer the political loyalties of neighboring states with which Russia has deep historical ties. Two of those new leaders, Georgia's Mikheil Saakashvili and Ukraine's Viktor Yushchenko, sought to put their countries on a fast track to membership in the North Atlantic Treaty Organization (NATO), a prospect that Russia viewed with alarm bordering on panic. Another Bush-era initiative that engendered deep hostility in Moscow was a plan to station strategic antimissile interceptors in neighboring Poland, with associated radars in the Czech Republic. Russian military experts argued these deployments were the beginning of a strategic process that might eventually undermine Russia's own aging, Soviet-era nuclear deterrent, which is the main priority of Russia's national defense.

In response to these perceived threats, Russia seemed to sometimes go out of its way to cultivate relationships with other countries that were at odds with the US, which is the subject of this story. The Russians also held war games with the Venezuelan navy in the Caribbean, resumed cold war–era nuclear bomber patrols along the North American coast, and talked about revitalizing former Soviet air bases in Cuba.

In the past year, with substantially changed foreign policy priorities brought in by President Barack Obama, Moscow's attitude has relaxed somewhat. Obama shelved the controversial plan to station antimissile weapons in Poland, and implicitly removed from the agenda any question of inducting Ukraine and Georgia into NATO. The so-called Obama "reset" of relations between Moscow and Washington seems to be improving prospects for cooperation, even on such thorny issues as Iran, though it may be too early to draw any firm conclusions.

See below for further references to articles I have written on this topic.

Stories on Russia's overtures to Cuba and Venezuela:
http://www.csmonitor.com/World/Americas/2009/0910/p06s11-woam.html
http://www.csmonitor.com/World/Global-News/2009/0315/a-new-cuban-missile-crisis-russia-eyes-bomber-bases-in-latin-america
http://www.csmonitor.com/World/Americas/2008/1125/p01s01-woam.html
http://www.csmonitor.com/World/Europe/2008/0908/p01s06-woeu.html

Stories on Russia's relations with Iran:
http://www.csmonitor.com/World/Europe/2010/0521/Russia-sanctions-unlikely-to-delay-Iran-nuclear-power-plant
http://www.csmonitor.com/World/Global-News/2009/0921/secret-israeli-deal-to-stop-russian-s-300-missile-sale-to-iran
http://www.csmonitor.com/World/Europe/2009/0323/p06s01-woeu.html

Stories on US–Russian relations:
http://www.csmonitor.com/World/Europe/2010/0513/Leaked-Russian-document-Could-Medvedev-era-tilt-more-pro-West
http://www.csmonitor.com/World/Europe/2010/0504/NPT-Obama-reveals-size-of-US-nuclear-weapons-arsenal.-Will-Russia-respondhttp://www.csmonitor.com/World/Europe/2009/1028/p06s14-woeu.html
http://www.csmonitor.com/World/Europe/2010/0513/Leaked-Russian-document-Could-Medvedev-era-tilt-more-pro-West

2

US Department of Defense is the Worst Polluter on the Planet

Sources:
Sara Flounders, "Add Climate Havoc to War Crimes: Pentagon's Role in Global Catastrophe," International Action Center, December 18, 2009, http://www.iacenter.org/o/world/climatesummit_pentagon121809.

Mickey Z., "Can You Identify the Worst Polluter on the Planet? Here's a Hint: Shock and Awe," *Planet Green*, August 10, 2009, http://planetgreen.discovery.com/tech-transport/identify-worst-polluter-planet.html.

Julian Aguon, "Guam Residents Organize Against US Plans for $15B Military Buildup on Pacific Island," *Democracy Now!*, October 9, 2009, http://www.democracynow.org/2009/10/9/guam_residents_organize_against_us_plans.

Ian Macleod, "U.S. Plots Arctic Push," *Ottawa Citizen*, November 28, 2009, http://www.ottawacitizen.com/technology/navy+plots+Arctic+push/2278324/story.html.

Nick Turse, "Vietnam Still in Shambles after American War," *In These Times*, May 2009, http://www.inthesetimes.com/article/4363/casualties_continue_in_vietnam.

Jalal Ghazi, "Cancer—The Deadly Legacy of the Invasion of Iraq," *New America Media*, January 6, 2010, http://news.newamericamedia.org/news/view_article.html?article_id=80e260b3839daf2084fdeb0965ad31ab.

Student Researchers:
Dimitrina Semova, Joan Pedro, and Luis Luján (Complutense University of Madrid)
Ashley Jackson-Lesti, Ryan Stevens, Chris Marten, and Kristy Nelson (Sonoma State University)
Christopher Lue (Indian River State College)
Cassie Barthel (St. Cloud State University)

Faculty Evaluators:
Ana I. Segovia (Complutense University of Madrid)
Julie Flohr and Mryna Goodman (Sonoma State University)
Elliot D. Cohen (Indian River State College)
Julie Andrzejewski (St. Cloud State University)

The US military is responsible for the most egregious and widespread pollution of the planet, yet this information and accompanying documentation goes almost entirely unreported. In spite of the evidence, the environmental impact of the US military goes largely unaddressed by environmental organizations and was not the focus of any discussions or proposed restrictions at the recent UN Climate Change Conference in Copenhagen. This impact includes uninhibited use of fossil fuels, massive creation of greenhouse gases, and extensive release of radioactive and chemical contaminants into the air, water, and soil.

The extensive global operations of the US military (wars, interventions, and secret operations on over one thousand bases around the world and six thousand facilities in the United States) are not counted against US greenhouse gas limits. Sara Flounders writes, "By every measure, the Pentagon is the largest institutional user of petroleum products and energy in general. Yet the Pentagon has a blanket exemption in all international climate agreements."

While official accounts put US military usage at 320,000 barrels of

oil a day, that does not include fuel consumed by contractors, in leased or private facilities, or in the production of weapons. The US military is a major contributor of carbon dioxide, a greenhouse gas that most scientists believe is to blame for climate change. Steve Kretzmann, director of Oil Change International, reports, "The Iraq war was responsible for at least 141 million metric tons of carbon dioxide equivalent (MMTCO2e) from March 2003 through December 2007. . . . That war emits more than 60 percent that of all countries. . . . This information is not readily available . . . because military emissions abroad are exempt from national reporting requirements under US law and the UN Framework Convention on Climate Change."

According to Barry Sanders, author of *The Green Zone: The Environmental Costs of Militarism*, "the greatest single assault on the environment, on all of us around the globe, comes from one agency . . . the Armed Forces of the United States."

Throughout the long history of military preparations, actions, and wars, the US military has not been held responsible for the effects of its activities upon environments, peoples, or animals. During the Kyoto Accords negotiations in December 1997, the US demanded as a provision of signing that any and all of its military operations worldwide, including operations in participation with the UN and NATO, be exempted from measurement or reductions. After attaining this concession, the Bush administration then refused to sign the accords and the US Congress passed an explicit provision guaranteeing the US military exemption from any energy reduction or measurement.

Environmental journalist Johanna Peace reports that military activities will continue to be exempt based on an executive order signed by President Barack Obama that calls for other federal agencies to reduce their greenhouse gas emissions by 2020. Peace states, "The military accounts for a full 80 percent of the federal government's energy demand."

As it stands, the Department of Defense is the largest polluter in the world, producing more hazardous waste than the five largest US chemical companies combined. Depleted uranium, petroleum, oil, pesticides, defoliant agents such as Agent Orange, and lead, along with vast amounts of radiation from weaponry produced, tested, and used, are just some of the pollutants with which the US military is contaminating the environment. Flounders identifies key examples:

▸ Depleted uranium: Tens of thousands of pounds of microparticles of radioactive and highly toxic waste contaminate the Middle East, Central Asia, and the Balkans.

▸ US-made land mines and cluster bombs spread over wide areas of Africa, Asia, Latin America, and the Middle East continue to spread death and destruction even after wars have ceased.

▸ Thirty-five years after the Vietnam War, dioxin contamination is three hundred to four hundred times higher than "safe" levels, resulting in severe birth defects and cancers into the third generation of those affected.

▸ US military policies and wars in Iraq have created severe desertification of 90 percent of the land, changing Iraq from a food exporter into a country that imports 80 percent of its food.

▸ In the US, military bases top the Superfund list of the most polluted places, as perchlorate and trichloroethylene seep into the drinking water, aquifers, and soil.

▸ Nuclear weapons testing in the American Southwest and the South Pacific Islands has contaminated millions of acres of land and water with radiation, while uranium tailings defile Navajo reservations.

▸ Rusting barrels of chemicals and solvents and millions of rounds of ammunition are criminally abandoned by the Pentagon in bases around the world.

The United States is planning an enormous $15 billion military buildup on the Pacific island of Guam. The project would turn the thirty-mile-long island into a major hub for US military operations in the Pacific. It has been described as the largest military buildup in recent history and could bring as many as fifty thousand people to the tiny island. Chamoru civil rights attorney Julian Aguon warns that this military operation will bring irreversible social and environmental consequences to Guam. As an unincorporated territory, or colony, and of the US, the people of Guam have no right to self-determination, and no governmental means to oppose an unpopular and destructive occupation.

Between 1946 and 1958, the US dropped more than sixty nuclear weapons on the people of the Marshall Islands. The Chamoru people of Guam, being so close and downwind, still experience an alarmingly high rate of related cancer.

On Capitol Hill, the conversation has been restricted to whether the jobs expected from the military construction should go to mainland Americans, foreign workers, or Guam residents. But we rarely hear the voices and concerns of the indigenous people of Guam, who constitute over a third of the island's population.

Meanwhile, as if the US military has not contaminated enough of the world already, a new five-year strategic plan by the US Navy outlines the militarization of the Arctic to defend national security, potential undersea riches, and other maritime interests, anticipating the frozen Arctic Ocean to be open waters by the year 2030. This plan strategizes expanding fleet operations, resource development, research, and tourism, and could possibly reshape global transportation.

While the plan discusses "strong partnerships" with other nations (Canada, Norway, Denmark, and Russia have also made substantial investments in Arctic-capable military armaments), it is quite evident that the US is serious about increasing its military presence and naval combat capabilities. The US, in addition to planned naval rearmament, is stationing thirty-six F-22 Raptor stealth fighter jets, which is 20 percent of the F-22 fleet, in Anchorage, Alaska.

Some of the action items in the US Navy Arctic Roadmap document include:

▶ Assessing current and required capability to execute undersea warfare, expeditionary warfare, strike warfare, strategic sealift, and regional security cooperation.

▶ Assessing current and predicted threats in order to determine the most dangerous and most likely threats in the Arctic region in 2010, 2015, and 2025.

▶ Focusing on threats to US national security, although threats to maritime safety and security may also be considered.

Behind the public façade of international Arctic cooperation, Rob Heubert, associate director at the Centre for Military and Strategic Studies at the University of Calgary, points out, "If you read the document carefully you'll see a dual language, one where they're saying, 'We've got to start working together' . . . and [then] they start saying, 'We have to get new instrumentation for our combat officers.' . . . They're clearly understanding that the future is not nearly as nice as what all the public policy statements say."

Beyond the concerns about human conflicts in the Arctic, the consequences of militarization on the Arctic environment are not even being considered. Given the record of environmental devastation that the US military has wrought, such a silence is unacceptable.

Update by Mickey Z.

As I sit here, typing this "update," the predator drones are still flying over Afghanistan, Iraq, and Pakistan, the oil is still gushing into the Gulf of Mexico, and 53.3 percent of our tax money is still being funneled to the US military. Simply put, hope and change feels no different from shock and awe . . . but the mainstream media continues to propagate the two-party lie.

Linking the antiwar and environmental movements is a much-needed step. As Cindy Sheehan recently told me, "I think one of the best things that we can do is look into economic conversion of the defense industry into green industries, working on sustainable and renewable forms of energy, and/or connect[ing] with indigenous people who are trying to reclaim their lands from the pollution of the military industrial complex. The best thing to do would be to start on a very local level to reclaim a planet healthy for life."

It comes down to recognizing the connections, recognizing how we are manipulated into supporting wars and how those wars are killing our ecosystem. We must also recognize our connection to the natural world. For if we were to view all living things, including ourselves, as part of one collective soul, how could we not defend that collective soul by any means necessary?

We are on the brink of economic, social, and environmental collapse. In other words, this is the best time ever to be an activist.

Update by Julian Aguon

In 2010, the people of Guam are bracing themselves for a cataclysmic round of militarization with virtually no parallel in recent history. Set to formally begin this year, the military buildup comes on the heels of a decision by the United States to aggrandize its military posture in the Asia-Pacific region. At the center of the US military realignment schema is the hotly contested agreement between the United States and Japan to relocate thousands of US Marines from Okinawa to Guam. This portentous development, which is linked to the United States' perception of China as a security threat, bodes great harm to the people and environment of Guam yet remains virtually unknown to Americans and the rest of the international community.

What is happening in Guam is inherently interesting because while America trots its soldiers and its citizenry off to war to the tune of "spreading democracy" in its own proverbial backyard, an entire civilization of so-called "Americans" watch with bated breath as people thousands of miles away—people we cannot vote for—make decisions for us at ethnocidal costs. Although this military buildup marks the most volatile demographic change in recent Guam history, the people of Guam have never had an opportunity to meaningfully participate in any discussion about the buildup. To date, the scant coverage of the military buildup has centered almost exclusively around the United States and Japan. In fact, the story entitled "Guam Residents Organize Against US Plans for $15B Military Buildup on Pacific Island" on *Democracy Now!* was the first bona fide US media coverage of the military buildup since 2005 to consider, let alone privilege, the people's opposition.

The heart of this story is not so much in the finer details of the military buildup as it is in the larger political context of real-life twenty-first-century colonialism. Under US domestic law, Guam is an unincorporated territory. What this means is that Guam is a territory that belongs to the United States but is not a part of it. As an unincorporated territory, the US Constitution does not necessarily or automatically apply in Guam. Instead, the US Congress has broad powers over the unincorporated territories, including the power to choose what portions of the Constitution apply to them. In reality, Guam remains under the purview of the Office of Insular Affairs in the US Department of the Interior.

Under international law, Guam is a non-self-governing territory, or UN-recognized colony whose people have yet to exercise the fundamental right to self-determination. Article 73 of the United Nations Charter, which addresses the rights of peoples in non-self-governing territories, commands states administering them to "recognize the principle that the interests of the inhabitants are paramount." These "administering powers" accept as a "sacred trust" the obligation to develop self-government in the territories, taking due account of the political aspirations of the people. As a matter of international treaty and customary law, the colonized people of Guam have a right to self-determination under international law that the United States, at least in theory, recognizes.

The military buildup, however, reveals the United States' failure to fulfill its international legal mandate. This is particularly troubling in light of the fact that this very year, 2010, marks the formal conclusion of not one but two UN-designated international decades for the eradication of colonialism. In 1990, the UN General Assembly proclaimed 1990–2000 as the International Decade for the Eradication of Colonialism. To this end, the General Assembly adopted a detailed plan of action to expedite the unqualified end of all forms of colonialism. In 2001, citing a wholesale lack of progress during the first decade, the General Assembly proclaimed a second one to effect the same goal. The second decade has come and all but gone with only Timor-Leste, or East Timor, managing to attain independence from Indonesia in 2002.

In November 2009—one month after "Guam Residents Organize Against US Plans for $15B Military Buildup on Pacific Island" aired—the US Department of Defense released an unprecedented 11,000-page Draft Environmental Impact Statement (DEIS), detailing for the first time the true enormity of the contemplated militarization of Guam. At its peak, the military buildup will bring more than 80,000 new residents to Guam, which includes more than 8,600 US Marines and their 9,000 dependents; 7,000 so-called transient US Navy personnel; 600 to 1,000 US Army personnel; and 20,000 foreign workers on military construction contracts. This "human tsunami," as it is being called, represents a roughly 47 percent increase in Guam's total population in a four-to-six-year window. Today, the total population of Guam is roughly 178,000 people, the indigenous Chamoru people making up only 37 percent of that number. We are looking at a volatile and virtually overnight demographic change in the makeup of the island that even the US military admits will result in the political dispossession of the Chamoru people. To put the pace of this ethnocide in context, just prior to World War II, Chamorus comprised more than 90 percent of Guam's population.

At the center of the buildup are three major proposed actions: 1) the construction of permanent facilities and infrastructure to support the full spectrum of warfare training for the thousands of relocated Marines; 2) the construction of a new deep-draft wharf in the island's only harbor to provide for the passage of nuclear-powered aircraft carriers; and 3) the construction of an Army Missile Defense Task Force modeled on the Marshall Islands–based Ronald Reagan Ballistic Missile Defense Test Site, for the practice of intercepting intercontinental ballistic missiles.

In terms of adverse impact, these developments will mean, among other things, the clearing of whole limestone forests and the desecration of burial sites some 3,500 years old; the restricting of access to areas rich in plants necessary for indigenous medicinal practice; the denying of access to places of worship and traditional fishing grounds; the destroying of seventy acres of thriving coral reef, which currently serve as critical habitat for several endangered species; and the over-tapping of Guam's water system to include the drilling of twenty-two additional wells. In addition, the likelihood of military-related accidents will greatly increase. Seven crashes occurred during military training from August 2007 to July 2008, the most recent of which involved a crash of a B-52 bomber that killed the entire crew. The increased presence of US military forces in Guam also increases the island's visibility as a target for enemies of the United States.

Finally, an issue that has sparked some of the sharpest debate in Guam has been the Department of Defense's announcement that it will, if needed, forcibly condemn an additional 2,200 acres of land in Guam to support the construction of new military facilities. This potential new land grab has been met with mounting protest by island residents, mainly due to the fact that the US military already owns close to one-third of the small island, the majority of which was illegally taken after World War II.

In February 2010, upon review of the DEIS, the US Environmental Protection Agency (EPA) rated it "insufficient" and "environmentally unsatisfactory," giving it the lowest possible rating for a DEIS. Among other things, the EPA's findings suggest that Guam's water infrastructure cannot handle the population boom and that the island's fresh water resources will be at high risk for contamination. The EPA predicts that without infrastructural upgrades to the water system, the population outside the bases will experience a 13.1 million gallons of water shortage per day in 2014. The agency stated that the Pentagon's massive buildup plans for Guam "should not proceed as proposed." The people of Guam were given a mere ninety days to read through the voluminous 11,000-page document and make comments about its contents. The ninety-day comment period ended on February 17, 2010. The final EIS is scheduled for release in August 2010, with the record of decision to follow immediately thereafter.

The response to this story from the mainstream US media has been deafening silence. Since the military buildup was first announced in 2005, it was more than three years before any US media outlet picked up on the story. In fact, the October 2009 *Democracy Now!* interview was the first substantive national news coverage of the military buildup.

For more information on the military buildup:
We Are Guahan, http://www.weareguahan.com
Draft Environmental Impact Study Guam & Commonwealth of the Northern Mariana
    Islands Military Relocation, www.guambuildupeis.us
Center for Biological Diversity Response to DEIS, www.biologicaldiversity.org/news/
    center/articles/2010/los-angeles-times-02-24-2010.html
EPA Response to Guam DEIS, www.stripes.com/article.asp?section=104&article=68298

For more information on Guam's movement to resist militarization and unresolved colonialism:
The Guahan Coalition for Peace and Justice: Lisa Linda Natividad, lisanati@yahoo.com;
    Hope Cristobal, ecris64@teleguam.net; Julian Aguon, julianaguon@gmail.com;
    Michael Lujan Bevacqua, mlbasquiat@hotmail.com; Victoria-Lola Leon Guerrero,
    victoria.lola@gmail.com
We Are Guahan—We Are Guahan Public Forum: www.weareguahan.com
Famoksaiyan: Martha Duenas, martduenas@yahoo.com;
    famoksaiyanwc.wordpress.com

3

Internet Privacy and Personal Access at Risk

Sources:
Josh Silver, "Deep Packet Inspection: Telecoms Aided Iran Government to Censor Internet, Technology Widely Used in US," *Democracy Now!*, June 23, 2009, http://www.democracynow.org/2009/6/23/deep_packet_inspection_telecoms_aided_iran.

David Karvets, "Obama Sides With Bush in Spy Case," *Wired*, January 22, 2009, http://www.wired.com/threatlevel/2009/01/obama-sides-wit/.

Kim Zetter, "Deep-Packet Inspection in U.S. Scrutinized Following Iran Surveillance," *Wired*, June 29, 2009, http://www.wired.com/threatlevel/2009/06/deep-packet-inspection.

Declan McCullagh, "Bill Would Give President Emergency Control of Internet," CNET News, August 28, 2009, http://news.cnet.com/8301-13578_3-10320096-38.html?tag=mncol.

Kevin Bankston, "From EFF's Secret Files: Anatomy of a Bogus Subpoena," Electronic Frontier Foundation, November 9, 2009, http://www.eff.org/wp/anatomy-bogus-subpoena-indymedia.

Gwen Hinze, "Leaked ACTA Internet Provisions: Three Strikes and Global DMCA," Electronic Frontier Foundation, November 3, 2009, http://www.eff.org/deeplinks/2009/11/leaked-acta-internet-provisions-three-strikes-and-.

Michael Geist, "The ACTA Internet Chapter: Putting the Pieces Together," Michael Geist Blog, November 3, 2009, http://www.michaelgeist.ca/content/view/4510/125.

Tim Jones, "In Warrantless Wiretapping Case, Obama DOJ's New Arguments Are Worse Than Bush's," Electronic Frontier Foundation, April 7, 2009, http://www.eff.org/deeplinks/2009/04/obama-doj-worse-than-bush.

Steve Aquino, "Should Obama Control the Internet," Mother Jones, April 2, 2009, http://motherjones.com/politics/2009/04/should_obama_control_internet.

Noah Shachtman, "U.S. Spies Buy Stake in Firm that Monitors Blogs, Twitter," Wired, October 19, 2009, http://www.wired.com/dangerroom/2009/10/exclusive-us-spies-buy-stake-in-twitter-blog-monitoring-firm.

Noah Shachtman, "CIA Invests in Software Firm Monitoring Blogs, Twitter," Democracy Now!, October 22, 2009, http://www.democracynow.org/2009/10/22/cia_invests_in_software_firm_monitoring.

Lewis Maltby, "Your Boss Can Secretly Film You in the Bathroom—The Countless Ways You Are Losing Privacy at Work," AlterNet, March 17, 2010, http://www.alternet.org/rights/146047/your_boss_can_secretly_film_you_in_the_bathroom_—_the_countless_ways_you_are_losing_privacy_at_work.

Elliot D. Cohen, Mass Surveillance and State Control: The Total Information Awareness Project (New York: Palgrave Macmillan, 2010).

Corporate Media Sources:
Rob Pegoraro, "Copyright Overreach Goes on World Tour," Washington Post, November 5, 2009, financial sec., G01.

Student Researchers:
Lynn Demos, Ben Solomon, Steve Wojanis, Trisha Himmelein, Emily Schuler, Claire Apatoff, Erin Kielty, and Tom Rich (DePauw University)
Alyssa Auerbach, Tyler Head, Mira Patel, Andrew Nassab, and Cristina Risso (Sonoma State University)

Faculty Evaluators:
Jeff McCall, Dave Berque, Brian Howard, and Kevin Howley (DePauw University)
Jimmy Dizmang (University of San Diego)
Noel Byrne and Kelly Bucy (Sonoma State University)
Mickey Huff (Diablo Valley College)

Following in the steps of its predecessor, the Obama administration is expanding mass government surveillance of personal electronic communications. This surveillance, which includes the monitoring of the Internet as well as private (nongovernmental) computers, is proceeding with the proposal or passage of new laws granting government agencies increasingly wider latitude in their monitoring activities. At the same time, private companies and even some schools are engaging in surveillance activities that further diminish personal privacy.

In spring 2009, Senate Bill 773, the Cybersecurity Act of 2009, was proposed, which gives the president power to "declare a cyber security emergency" with respect to private computer networks, and to do with these networks what it deems necessary to diffuse the attack. In a national emergency, the president would also have the power to completely shut down the Internet in the US. The proposal requires that certain private computer systems and networks be "managed" by "cyberprofessionals" licensed by the federal government. The bill permits the president to direct the national response to the cyber threat if necessary for national defense and security; to conduct "periodic mapping" of private networks deemed to be critical to national security; and to require these companies to "share" information requested by the federal government.

Such steps toward increased control over private computer networks have been taken amid an ongoing program of mass surveillance begun by the George W. Bush administration supposedly in response to the attacks of September 11, 2001. In January 2002, the Defense Advanced Research Projects Agency (DARPA) established the Information Awareness Office (IAO) to "imagine, develop, apply, integrate, demonstrate and transition information technologies, components and prototype, closed-loop, information systems that will counter asymmetric threats by achieving *total information awareness*." Under the Bush administration, such surveillance technology was developed and subsequently deployed through major US telecommunication and Internet service providers (ISPs) to conduct mass, warrantless dragnets of all domestic and international electronic traffic passing through switches in the US. This technology includes so-called "deep packet inspection" (DPI) technology, which employs sophisticated algorithms to parse all Internet contents (data, voice, and video), searching for key words such as "rebel" or "grenade."

Presently no legislation exists that disallows use of such technology to conduct mass, warrantless surveillance. In fact, in January 2009, as David Karvets reported in *Wired*, the Obama administration sided with the Bush administration by asking a federal judge to set aside a ruling that kept alive a lawsuit challenging the Bush administration's authority to eaves-

drop on Americans without warrants. Moreover, amendments to the Foreign Intelligence Surveillance Act (FISA) passed in 2008—and voted for by then Senator Obama—had already made it possible for the federal government to conduct such information dragnets without warrants. The 2008 FISA amendments also require electronic communication service providers such as AT&T and Verizon to "immediately provide the Government with all information, facilities, or assistance necessary to accomplish the [intelligence] acquisition," while granting these companies retroactive and prospective immunity against civil suits, state investigations, and criminal prosecution.

In addition, in April 2009, the Obama Justice Department invoked the "state secrets privilege" to bar American citizens from suing the US government for illegally spying on them. It also went even further than the Bush administration by arguing that the US government is completely immune from litigation for illegal spying and can never be sued for surveillance that violates federal privacy laws.

The federal government is also presently increasing its capacity to analyze the massive sea of data on the Internet. As part of an effort to gather more "open source intelligence," the Central Intelligence Agency (CIA) is investing in Visible Technologies, a data-mining company that analyzes the content of social media Web sites. Visible Technologies, which has offices in New York, Seattle, and Boston, was created in 2005, and in 2006 it developed a partnership with WPP, a worldwide communications firm. This company has the capacity to examine over half a million sites per day.

The Federal Bureau of Investigation (FBI) has also resorted to using federal court subpoenas to try to gain access to private, online information. On January 30, 2009, IndyMedia, an alternative online news source, received a subpoena from the Southern District of Indiana Federal Court for the "IP addresses, times, and any other identifying information" of all the site's visitors on June 25, 2008. IndyMedia was then prohibited from notifying visitors of this release of otherwise private and protected information because disclosure "would impede the investigation being conducted and thereby interfere with the enforcement of the law." IndyMedia and the Electronic Frontier Foundation (EFF) challenged the order and the subpoena was eventually dropped.

The Obama administration is also currently working with a group of UN nations on the development of the Anti-Counterfeiting Trade Agreement (ACTA), "a new intellectual property enforcement treaty" to prevent illegal downloading and copying of songs, movies, pictures, and other legally protected Web content. The new law is being developed in secrecy and might allow government access to personal content on hard drives thought to be in breach of copyright. On November 3, 2009, nations participating in negotiations on the proposed law met in Seoul, South Korea, for a closed discussion of "enforcement in the digital realm." According to a leaked memo from the conference, the US is pushing for a three-strikes/graduated-response policy and proactive policing of ISPs to ensure that any digital copyright infringements are caught, stopped, and punished.

In addition to the current trend of government surveillance, private employers are also reading employees' e-mails, eavesdropping on their telephone calls, monitoring their Internet access, and watching them through the use of hidden cameras. Millions of workers carry company-issued cell phones, which are equipped with a global positioning system (GPS). The technology required to track cell phones is inexpensive (costing only five dollars per month for round-the-clock surveillance of an employee) and is readily available.

Company-issued laptops are also being monitored. Companies usually permit their employees to use such computers for personal purposes as well as for business. However, unbeknownst to the employees, all their private files (such as e-mails, photographs, and financial records) are being inspected by company techs when the computers are brought in for upgrades or repairs. Consequently, anything the techs deem questionable can be disclosed to management. Further, if the company-issued laptop has a webcam, the employer can use it to eavesdrop on the employee, even if he or she is in the bathroom.

Such clandestine use of computer webcams has not been limited to private companies spying on their employees. In one recent case, a suburban Philadelphia school district issued laptops to its students and secretly installed software that allowed school administrators to spy on the students.

As electronic surveillance technologies continue to improve, in the absence of laws to regulate their use and government watchdogs to ensure that these laws are followed, privacy in the digital age will predictably continue to decline.

Update by Liz Rose at Free Press

Deep packet inspection is a technology that gives corporations unprecedented control over Internet communications. It's the same technology that allows Iran and other countries to try to stifle Internet freedom. The use of DPI is now pervasive and has spread to next-generation wireless networks. In this country, the adoption of DPI means that the telephone and cable companies that provide Internet service can monitor, inspect, and block Internet traffic, posing a serious threat to the open Internet.

There are two major developments in this story:

1. Major telecommunications companies (including Verizon, Comcast, AT&T, RCN, and COX) have now purchased DPI technology. Because of this investment, and because the technology has now been applied to wireless communications, the industry's control over the Internet is increasing. The latest generation of DPI enables companies to monitor and ultimately to charge people for every use of an Internet connection.

Free Press filed ten pages of comments with the Federal Communications Commission (FCC) about DPI. See pages 141 to 151 of our comments in the Net Neutrality proceeding on January 14, 2010 (http://www.freepress.net/node/76101). Free Press also released a paper titled "Deep Packet Inspection: The End of the Internet as We Know It" by Josh Silver, in March 2009, before the *Democracy Now!* story, "Deep Packet Inspection: Telecoms Aided Iran Government to Censor Internet Technology Widely

Used in US," ran, and it provides evidence of the threat posed by corporations having the power to inspect, block, and choke traffic on the Internet: (see http://www.freepress.net/files/Deep_Packet_Inspection _The_End_of _the_Internet_As_We_Know_It.pdf).

2. On April 6, 2010, a federal court ruled that the FCC does not have the authority under the jurisdiction that it claimed to stop Comcast—or any company—from blocking or choking Internet traffic. So right now, there is no recourse when a company does abuse its power over online communications. The FCC has indicated that it may move ahead and try to reassert its authority to set rules of the road for the Internet, but most observers think it will be a long battle ahead over the jurisdictional issues as well as over any possible rules.

4

ICE Operates Secret Detention and Courts

Sources:

Jacqueline Stevens, "America's Secret Ice Castles," *Nation*, January 4, 2010, http://www.thenation.com/doc20100104/stevens.

Jacqueline Stevens, "ICE Agents' Ruse Operations," *Nation*, December 17, 2009, http://www.thenation.com/article/ice-agents-ruse-operations.

Jacqueline Stevens, "Secret Courts Exploit Immigrants," *Nation*, June 16, 2009, http://www.thenation.com/article/secret-courts-exploit-immigrants.

Human Rights Watch, "Locked Up Far Away, The Transfer of Immigrants to Remote Detention Centers in the United States," December 2, 2009, www.hrw.org/node/86789.

Student Researchers:

Nicole Fletcher and Amanda Olson (Sonoma State University)

Faculty Evaluator:

Ronald Lopez (Sonoma State University)

Agents of the US Immigration and Customs Enforcement (ICE) are holding thousands of US residents in unlisted and unmarked subfield offices and deporting tens of thousands in secret court hearings.

"If you don't have enough evidence to charge someone criminally but you think he's illegal, we can make him disappear." Those chilling words were spoken by James Pendergraph, then executive director of the Immigration and Customs Enforcement's Office of State and Local Coordination, at a conference of police and sheriffs in August 2008.

People are held in a vast network of more than three hundred detention facilities, located in nearly every state in the country. Only a few of these facilities are under the full operational control of ICE—the majority are jails under the control of state and local governments that subcontract with ICE to provide detention bed space. However, ICE has created a network of secret jails designed for confining individuals in transit. These 186 unlisted and unmarked subfield offices are not subject to ICE detention standards, lacking showers, beds, drinking water, soap, toothbrushes, sanitary napkins, mail, attorneys, or legal information. Many of these subfield offices are in suburban office parks or commercial spaces revealing no information about their ICE tenants—nary a sign, a marked car, or even a US flag.

In addition there is a complete lack of a real-time database tracking people in ICE custody, meaning that ICE has created a network of secret jails designed for confining individuals in transit that literally make people disappear. Immigrant detainees can be transferred away from their attorneys at any point in their immigration proceedings, and often are. Detainees can be literally "lost" by their attorneys and family members for days or even weeks after being transferred.

US residents who were held in Southern California suboffice B-18— up to one hundred on any given day—were actually in a revolving

UNDOCUMENTED PARENTS OF U.S. BORN CHILDREN ROUTINELY DEPORTED WHILE THEIR CHILDREN REMAIN IN U.S.

"NO CHILD LEFT BEHIND", MR. PRESIDENT?

WWW.MINUTEMANMEDIA.ORG

stockroom that would shuttle the same people briefly to the local jails, sometimes from 1 to 5 A.M., and then bring them back, shackled to one another, stooped and crouching in overpacked vans. These transfers made it impossible for anyone to know their location, as there would be no notice to attorneys or relatives when people were moved. At times, the B-18 occupants were left overnight, the frigid onslaught of forced air and lack of mattresses or bedding making sleep near impossible.

As one attorney who represents immigration detainees explained, "The transfers are devastating—absolutely devastating. [The detainees] are loaded onto a plane in the middle of the night. They have no idea where they are, no idea what [US] state they are in. I cannot overemphasize the psychological trauma to these people. What it does to their family members cannot be fully captured either. I have taken calls from seriously hysterical family members—incredibly traumatized people—sobbing on the phone, crying out, 'I don't know where my son or husband is!'"

ICE agents regularly impersonate civilians—Occupational Safety and Health Administration (OSHA) inspectors, insurance agents, religious workers—in order to arrest longtime US residents who have no criminal history. Guatemalans in the Boston area are seeing spies infiltrating factories, buses with tinted windows taking away unidentifiable co-workers, and men with guns grabbing their neighbors. During the summer of 2009, a woman came to the office of Marina Lowe, an attorney for the American Civil Liberties Union (ACLU) in Salt Lake City, saying she believed that ICE agents dressing as Mormon missionaries had been to her house. Lowe's client noticed that the missionaries had lacked the black name tags she'd seen others wear, and had behaved in other ways inconsistent with missionary protocol, including entering her home while her husband was absent. After she confirmed that he lived there, they left. The next day, ICE agents arrived and arrested her husband. In response to a question about whether it was consistent with government policy for ICE agents to impersonate religious workers, an anonymously written ICE e-mail explained that impersonating religious officials is part of "ruse operations" and justified this as a "tool that enhances officer safety."

You don't have to go to Iraq or North Korea to find secret courts. Detention centers across the country are restricting public access to immigration courts. The Executive Office for Immigration Review (EOIR), an agency in the Department of Justice charged with managing immigration courts, reported that its judges decided 134,117 deportation cases in 2008, of which 48 percent were for detainees. The individuals facing deportation hearings in these remote sites—far from their families, indigent, and without attorneys—are the most legally fragile population in the country.

Mark Soukup, supervisory detention and deportation officer in Eloy, Arizona, explained that ICE required a background check for anyone entering the immigration courts at Eloy, for which one would need to submit in writing, two weeks in advance, one's name, date of birth, Social Security number, home address, and the particular hearing one wanted to attend. "The problem is that anyone with a felony or misdemeanor conviction in the last five years can be prohibited to come in for security reasons," Soukup said.

Lee Gelernt, an American Civil Liberties Union attorney, found the two-week prescreening policy unacceptable: "It is critical that the public and press have access to immigration proceedings to ensure that the proceedings are conducted fairly and consistent with due process principles. It is absolutely unlawful for the DHS [Department of Homeland Security] to place unreasonable restrictions on access to immigration court."

Update by Jacqueline Stevens

I have been writing for the *Nation* magazine, as well as on my blog States Without Nations, about unlawful and largely secret detention and removal operations by agencies within the Department of Homeland Security and the Department of Justice (DOJ). My research on US citizens in ICE custody has been reported in the *San Francisco Chronicle*, the *Charlotte Observer*, CNN (online), the *Huffington Post*, and *Mother Jones*, among other publications, and I have been interviewed for National Public Radio's *Latino USA*, Public Radio International's *The World*, WNYC's *The Leonard Lopate Show*, *Democracy Now!*, and the *Henry Raines Show* in Tampa Bay, Florida.

My articles have sparked some responses among local activists as well as journalists. For instance, in January an immigrant rights group in Grand Junction, Colorado, paid a visit to an address from a list of subfield offices I obtained through a Freedom of Information Act (FOIA) request. In a memorandum, the group wrote that the building they located was "in the industrial section of Grand Junction [and] is non-descript with no signs identifying it as government office or ICE facility." (An agent said the absence of a sign was because of budget cuts.) For more on this, see http://stateswithoutnations.blogspot.com/2010/01/neighbors-visit-ice-office- in-grand.html.

One policy consequence of investigations into ICE detaining and deporting US citizens appears to be a November 2009 policy requiring agents to report claims of US citizenship to a special ICE email address. I submitted a FOIA request for this e-mail correspondence and was informed of four thousand pages of documents. I have recently received the first hundred pages and am appealing redactions. Clearly ICE's detention of US citizens continues to be a problem.

I am presently conducting research on unlawful actions taken by immigration judges. This research has proven difficult because of retaliation against me by top ICE public affairs officers Kelly Nantel and Brian Hale—they unlawfully ordered agents to block my access to ICE facilities around the country. In April, a DHS-contracted guard in Atlanta assaulted me pursuant to an order from William Cassidy, the immigration judge who deported a US citizen. (While I was in a waiting area, Mr. Cassidy told a guard to remove me from the federal building.) I have filed a misconduct complaint; in response Mr. Cassidy's cronies at the EOIR are not answering questions—documents I have received indicate a cover-up campaign is underway.

More information on these and related topics:
States Without Nations, www.stateswithoutnations.blogspot.com
Bender's Immigration Bulletin, bibdaily.com
Detention Watch Network, www.detentionwatchnetwork.org
American Civil Liberties Union Immigrant Rights, www.aclu.org/immigrant-rights

5

Blackwater (Xe): The Secret US War in Pakistan

Sources:
Jeremy Scahill, "The Secret US War in Pakistan," *Nation*, November 23, 2009, http://www.thenation.com/doc/20091207/scahill.

Jeremy Scahill, "Blackwater Wants to Surge Its Armed Force in Afghanistan," Antiwar.com, January 20, 2010, http://original.antiwar.com/scahill/2010/01/19/blackwater-wants-to-surge.

David Edwards and Muriel Kane, "Ex-employees Claim Blackwater Pimped Out Young Iraqi Girls," *Raw Story*, August 7, 2009.

Student Researchers:
Andrew Hobbs, Kelsea Arnold, and Brittney Gates (Sonoma State University)

Faculty Evaluators:
Elaine Wellin and Peter Phillips (Sonoma State University)

At a covert forward operating base run by the US Joint Special Operations Command (JSOC) in the Pakistani port city of Karachi, members of an elite division of Blackwater are at the center of a secret program in which they plan targeted assassinations of suspected Taliban and al-Qaeda operatives inside and outside Pakistan. The Blackwater operatives also gather intelligence and help direct a secret US military drone bombing campaign that runs parallel to the well-documented CIA predator strikes, according to a well-placed source within the US military intelligence apparatus.

Captain John Kirby, the spokesperson for Admiral Michael Mullen, chairman of the Joint Chiefs of Staff, told the *Nation*, "We do not discuss current operations one way or the other, regardless of their nature." Meanwhile a defense official specifically denied that Blackwater performs work on drone strikes or intelligence for JSOC in Pakistan. "We don't have any contracts to do that work for us. We don't contract that kind of work out, period," the official said. "There has not been, and are not now, contracts between JSOC and that organization for these types of services." The Pentagon has stated bluntly, "There are no US military strike operations being conducted in Pakistan."

Blackwater's founder Erik Prince contradicted this statement in an interview, telling *Vanity Fair* that Blackwater works with US Special Forces in identifying targets and planning missions, citing an operation in Syria. The magazine also published a photo of a Blackwater base near the Afghanistan–Pakistan border.

Jeremy Scahill's military intelligence source said that the previously unreported program is distinct from the CIA assassination program, which the agency's director, Leon Panetta, announced he had canceled in June 2009. "This is a parallel operation to the CIA," said the source. "They are two separate beasts." The program puts Blackwater at the epicenter of a US military operation within the borders of a nation against which the US has not declared war—knowledge that could further strain the already tense relations between the US and Pakistan. In 2006, the two countries struck a deal that authorized JSOC to enter Pakistan to hunt Osama bin Laden with the understanding that Pakistan would deny it had given permission. Officially, the US is not supposed to have any active military operations in that country.

Blackwater, which also goes by the names Xe Services and US Training Center, has denied that the company operates in Pakistan. "Xe Services has only one employee in Pakistan performing construction oversight for the US government," Blackwater spokesperson Mark Corallo said in a statement to the *Nation*, adding that the company has "no other operations of any kind in Pakistan."

A former senior executive at Blackwater confirmed the military intelligence source's claim that the company is working in Pakistan for the CIA and JSOC. He said that Blackwater is also working for the Pakistani government on a subcontract with an Islamabad-based security firm that puts US Blackwater operatives on the ground with Pakistani forces in "counterterrorism" operations, including house raids and border interdictions, in the North-West Frontier Province and elsewhere in Pakistan. This arrangement allows the Pakistani government to utilize former US Special Operations forces that now work for Blackwater while denying an official US military presence in the country. He also confirmed that Blackwater has a facility in Karachi and has personnel deployed elsewhere in Pakistan.

The covert program in Pakistan dates back to at least 2007. The current head of JSOC is Vice Admiral William McRaven, who took over the post from General Stanley McChrystal, who headed JSOC from 2003 to

2008 before being named the top US commander in Afghanistan. Blackwater's presence in Pakistan is "not really visible, and that's why nobody has cracked down on it," said Scahill's military source. Blackwater's operations in Pakistan, he adds, are not done through State Department contracts or publicly identified defense contracts. "It's Blackwater via JSOC, and it's a classified no-bid [contract] approved on a rolling basis."

Blackwater's first known contract with the CIA for operations in Afghanistan was awarded in 2002 and was for work along the Afghanistan–Pakistan border.

According to Scahill's source, Blackwater has effectively marketed itself as a company whose operatives have "conducted lethal direct action missions and now, for a price, you can have your own planning cell. JSOC just ate that up." Blackwater's Pakistan JSOC contracts are secret and are therefore shielded from public oversight, he said.

In addition to planning drone strikes and operations against suspected al-Qaeda and Taliban forces in Pakistan for both JSOC and the CIA, the Blackwater team in Karachi also helps plan missions for JSOC inside Uzbekistan against the Islamic Movement of Uzbekistan.

Since President Barack Obama was inaugurated, the United States has expanded drone-bombing raids in Pakistan. Obama first ordered a drone strike against targets in North and South Waziristan on January 23, 2009, and the strikes have been conducted consistently ever since. The number of strike orders by the Obama administration has now surpassed the number during the Bush era in Pakistan, inciting fierce criticism from Pakistan and some US lawmakers over civilian deaths.

The military intelligence source also confirmed that Blackwater continues to work for the CIA on its drone-bombing program in Pakistan, as previously reported in the *New York Times*, but added that Blackwater is working on JSOC's drone bombings as well. "It's Blackwater running the program for both CIA and JSOC," said the source. When civilians are killed, "people go, 'Oh, it's the CIA doing crazy shit again unchecked.' Well, at least 50 percent of the time, that's JSOC [hitting] somebody they've identified through HUMINT [human intelligence] or they've culled the intelligence themselves or it's been shared with them and they take that person out and that's how it works."

In addition to working on covert action planning and drone strikes, Blackwater SELECT also provides private guards to perform the sensitive task of security for secret US drone bases, JSOC camps, and Defense Intelligence Agency camps inside Pakistan.

Blackwater's ability to survive against odds by reinventing and rebranding itself is most evident in Afghanistan, where the company continues to work for the US military, the CIA, and the State Department despite intense criticism and almost weekly scandals.

6

Health Care Restrictions Cost Thousands of Lives in US

Sources:
Steffie Woolhandler, MD, David Himmelstein, MPH, and Mark Almberg, MD, "Over 2,200 Veterans Died in 2008 Due to Lack of Health Insurance," Physicians for a National Health Program, November 10, 2009, http://www.pnhp.org/news/2009/november/over_2200_veterans_.php.

Amy Goodman, "Mother Speaks Out on Insurance Giant CIGNA's Denial of Healthcare to Cancer-Stricken Twin Daughters," *Democracy Now!*, October 1, 2009, http://www.democracynow.org/2009/10/1/mother_speaks_out_on_insurance_giant.

Jason Rosenbaum, "Stacie Ritter Lost Everything. CIGNA CEO Ed Hanway Bought Another House," Health Care for America Now blog, October 1, 2009, http://blog.healthcareforamericanow.org/2009/10/01/stacie-ritter-lost-everything-cigna-ceo-ed-hanway-bought-another-house.

Ryan Grim, "When Getting Beaten By Your Husband Is A Pre-Existing Condition," *Huffington Post*, September 14, 2009, http://www.huffingtonpost.com/2009/09/14/when-getting-beaten-by-yo_n_286029.html.

Fizan Abdullah, MD, PhD, "Lack of Insurance May Have Figured in Nearly 17,000 Childhood Deaths, Study Shows," Johns Hopkins Children's Center news release, November 7, 2009, http://www.hopkinschildrens.org/Lack-of-Insurance-May-Have-Figured-In-Nearly-17000-Childhood-Deaths.aspx.

Student Researchers:
Delana Colvin, Shannon Cree, and Anna Kung (DePauw University)
Michaella Armanino, Kimberly Sullivan, and Tracena Webster (Sonoma State University)

Faculty Evaluators:
Rebecca Bordt and Kevin Howley (DePauw University)
Suzel A. Bozada-Deas, Peter Phillips, and Ben Frymer (Sonoma State University)

Despite national legislative health reform, health care in the US will remain dismal for many Americans, resulting in continuing deaths and personal tragedies. A recent Harvard research team estimates that 2,266 US military veterans died in 2008 due to lack of health insurance. The figure is more than fourteen times the number of deaths suffered by US troops in Afghanistan in 2008, and more than twice as many as have died since the war began in 2001. Harvard researchers concluded that 1.46 million working-age vets lacked health coverage, increasing their death rate. *The American Journal of Public Health* published findings demonstrating that being uninsured raises an individual's odds of dying by 40 percent.

Dr. David Himmelstein, coauthor of the analysis and associate professor of medicine at Harvard, commented, "These unnecessary deaths will continue under the new health care reform legislation. The bill would do virtually nothing for the uninsured until 2013, and leave at least 17 million uninsured over the long run."

In a related story on health care inequalities, Stacie Ritter's twin daughters were diagnosed with cancer at the age of four. They both needed stem cell transplants and other cancer treatments. The twins survived, but the glands controlling their growth were damaged beyond repair from the treatment. To continue growing, they needed doctor-recommended growth hormone injections regularly. Stacie's husband's company switched to CIGNA health insurance, and CIGNA refused to cover the hormone shots. Each time Stacie takes her daughters to the doctor for the shots, it costs her $440. The incident marked just the latest chapter in the family's ongoing troubles with the health insurance industry. Between the cancer treatment and the denied care, Stacie and

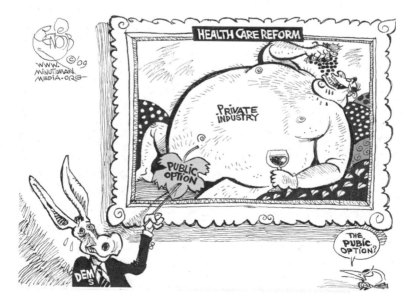

her husband had to file for bankruptcy due to their high medical expenses. Ed Hanway, CEO of CIGNA, made $12.2 million last year—$5,883 an hour.

Health insurance laws are often complicated by individual states, where health insurance is legally controlled. There are eight states, plus the District of Columbia, where insurance companies can claim that getting beaten up by your spouse is a preexisting condition for which you can be denied health insurance coverage. Victims of domestic violence are legally denied health insurance by companies that say this condition is preexisting and cannot be covered. The companies involved—Nationwide, Allstate, State Farm, Aetna, Metropolitan Life, Equitable Companies, First Colony Life, Prudential, and Principal Financial Group—were all found in 1995 to have denied or canceled coverage to women who were beaten. The states that still allow this practice are Idaho, North Dakota, South Dakota, Mississippi, North Carolina, South Carolina, Oklahoma, and Wyoming.

While the new national health care plan will remediate some of the above problems, thousands of people will continue to suffer in the US for many years to come.

Update by Steffie Woolhandler, MD

In fall 2009, as the health reform debate was roiling, we reported that 1.54 million US veterans were uninsured in 2008, and that 2,226 would be expected to die due to lack of coverage.

We based our analysis on our recently published finding (in the *American Journal of Public Health*) that being uninsured raises the odds of dying by 40 percent. Hence, lack of health insurance causes 44,798 deaths each year among the 46 million uninsured Americans. We combined this data with tabulations of the number of uninsured veterans from the Census Bureau's March 2009 Current Population Survey, which surveyed Americans about their insurance coverage and veteran status. We only classified veterans as uninsured if they neither had health insurance nor received ongoing care at Veterans Health Administration (VHA) hospitals or clinics.

We estimated that among nonelderly veterans, 2,266 deaths were associated with lack of health insurance last year. That figure is more than fourteen times the number of deaths (155) suffered by US troops in Afghanistan that year, and more than twice as many as have died since the beginning of the war.

While many Americans believe that all veterans can get care from the VHA, even combat veterans may not be able to obtain VHA care. As a rule, VHA facilities provide care for any veteran who is disabled by a condition connected to military service, and treatments for specific medical conditions acquired during military service. Low-income veterans who pass a means test are eligible for care in VHA facilities but have lower priority status (Priority 5 or Priority 7, depending upon income level). Veterans with higher incomes are classified in the lowest priority group, and are not eligible for VHA enrollment.

Like other uninsured Americans, most uninsured vets are working people—too poor to afford private coverage but not poor enough to qualify for Medicaid or means-tested VHA care. Unfortunately, lack of insurance will continue to cause deaths, despite the new health reform law. According to the Congressional Budget Office, 23 million Americans will remain uninsured in 2019, when the law is fully implemented. This will translate into about 23,000 unnecessary deaths annually. Unfortunately, Congress bowed to pressures from the insurance and drug industry, and refused to consider the reform that would have comprehensively covered all Americans—single-payer national health insurance.

For more information, visit Physicians for a National Health Program (www.pnhp.org), a research and educational organization of 17,000 doctors who support single-payer national health insurance.

Update by the Johns Hopkins Children's Center

Lack of health insurance might have led or contributed to nearly 17,000 deaths among hospitalized children in the United States in the span of less than two decades, according to research led by the Johns Hopkins Children's Center.

According to the Hopkins researchers, a study published on October 29, 2009, in the *Journal of Public Health* is one of the largest ever to look at the impact of insurance on the number of preventable deaths and the potential for saved lives among sick children in the United States.

Using more than 23 million hospital records from thirty-seven states between 1988 and 2005, the Johns Hopkins investigators compared the risk of death in children with insurance to those without. Other factors being equal, researchers found that uninsured children in the study were 60 percent more likely to die in the hospital than those with insurance. When comparing death rates by underlying disease, the uninsured appeared to have increased risk of dying regardless of their medical condition. The findings only capture deaths during hospitalization and do not reflect deaths after discharge from the hospital, nor do they count children who died without ever being hospitalized, the researchers say, which means the real death toll of uninsured children could be even higher.

"If you are a child without insurance, if you're seriously ill and end up in the hospital, you are 60 percent more likely to die than the sick child in the next room who has insurance," says lead investigator Fizan Abdullah, MD, PhD, pediatric surgeon at Johns Hopkins Children's Center.

The researchers caution that the study looked at hospital records after the fact of death so they cannot directly establish cause and effect between health insurance and risk of dying. However, because of the volume of records analyzed and because of the researchers' ability to identify and eliminate most factors that typically cloud such research, the analysis shows a powerful link between health insurance and risk of dying, they say.

"Can we say with absolute certainty that 17,000 children would have been saved if they had health insurance? Of course not," says co-investigator David Chang, PhD, MPH, MBA. "The point here is that a substantial number of children may be saved by health coverage."

"From a scientific perspective, we are confident in our finding that thousands of children likely did die because they lacked insurance or because of factors directly related to lack of insurance," he adds.

Given that more than 7 million American children in the United States remain uninsured amidst this nation's struggle with health care reform, researchers say policy makers and, indeed, society as a whole should pay heed to such findings.

"Thousands of children die needlessly each year because we lack a health system that provides them health insurance. This should not be," says co-investigator Peter Pronovost, MD, PhD, director of Critical Care Medicine at Johns Hopkins and medical director of the Center for Innovations in Quality Patient Care. "In a country as wealthy as ours, the need to provide health insurance to the millions of children who lack it is a moral, not an economic issue," he adds.

In the study, 104,520 patients died (0.47 percent) out of 22.2 million insured hospitalized children, compared to 9,468 (0.75 percent) who died among the 1.2 million uninsured ones. To find out what portion of these deaths would have been prevented by health insurance, researchers performed a statistical simulation by projecting the expected number of deaths for insured patients based on the severity of their medical conditions among other factors, and then applied this expected number of deaths to the uninsured group. In the uninsured group, there were 3,535 more deaths than expected, not explained by disease severity or other factors. Going a step further and applying the excess number of deaths to the total number of pediatric hospitalizations in the United States (117 million) for the study period, the researchers found an excess of 16,787 deaths among the nearly six million uninsured children who ended up in the hospital during that time.

Other findings from the study:

▸ More uninsured children were seen in hospitals in the Northeast and Midwest than in the South and West. However, hospitals from the Northeast had lower mortality rates than hospitals from the South, Midwest, and West.

▸ Insured children on average incurred higher hospital charges than uninsured children, most likely explained by the fact that uninsured children tend to present to the hospital at more advanced stages of their disease, which in turn gives doctors less chance for intervention and treatment, especially in terminal cases, investigators say.

▸ Uninsured patients were more likely to seek treatment through the emergency room, rather than through a referral by a doctor, likely markers of more advanced disease stage and/or delays in seeking medical attention.

▸ Insurance status did not affect how long a child spent overall in the hospital.

The research was funded by the Robert Garrett Fund for the Treatment of Children, and co-investigators in the study include Yiyi Zhang, MHS; Thomas Lardaro, BS; Marissa Black; and Paul Colombani, MD.

7
External Capitalist Forces Wreak Havoc in Africa

Sources:
John Vidal, "Food, Water Driving 21st-century African Land Grab," *Mail & Guardian*, March 7, 2010, http://www.mg.co.za/article/2010-03-07-food-water-driving-21stcentury-african-land-grab.

Paula Crossfield, "Food Security in Africa: Will Obama Let USAID's Genetically Modified Trojan Horse Ride Again?" Civil Eats, August 6, 2009, http://civileats.com/2009/08/06/will-obama-let-the-usaid-genetically-modified-trojan-horse-ride-again.

Thalif Deen, "Land Grabs for Food Production Under Fire," Inter Press Service, October 23, 2009, http://ipsnews.net/news.asp?idnews=48979.

Stephanie Hanes, "Africa: From Famine to the World's Next Breadbasket?" *Christian Science Monitor*, December 17, 2009, http://www.csmonitor.com/World/Global-Issues/2009/1231/Africa-from-famine-to-the-world-s-next-breadbasket.

Amy Goodman and Juan Gonzalez, "Massive Casualties Feared in Nigerian Military Attack on Niger Delta Villages," *Democracy Now!*, May 21, 2009, http://www.democracynow.org/2009/5/21/nigeria.

Justice in Nigeria Now, "Military Attacks Raze Niger Delta Villages Killing Civilians; Civil Society Groups Call for Immediate Ceasefire," May 21, 2009, http://uk.oneworld.net/article/view/162969/1.

OneWorld.net, "Nigeria Oil Violence Forces Thousands from Homes," May 26, 2009, http://us.oneworld.net/article/363376-new-outbreak-violence-niger-delta.

John "Ahniwanika" Schertow, "Stop Killing and Starvation of Samburu People in Kenya," *Intercontinental Cry*, November 20, 2009, http://intercontinentalcry.org/stop-killing-and-starvation-of-samburu-people-in-kenya.

Paula Palmer and Chris Allan, Kenya Human Rights Research Delegation, "When the Police are the Perpetrators: An Investigation of Human Rights Violations by Police in Samburu East and Isiolo Districts [Kenya]," *Cultural Survival*, April 20, 2010, http://www.culturalsurvival.org/files/Samburu%20Report%20Final%205-5-2010.pdf.

Shepard Daniel with Anuradha Mittal, "The Great Land Grab: Rush for World's Farmland Threatens Food Security for the Poor," Oakland Institute (Oakland, CA), www.oaklandinstitute.org.

Corporate Coverage:
Andrew Rice, "Is There Such a Thing as Agro-Imperialism?" *New York Times*, November 16, 2009, http://www.nytimes.com/2009/11/22/magazine/22land-t.html.

Student Researchers:
Amanda Olson and Michelle Sewell (Sonoma State University)
Delana Colvin, Shannon Cree, and Anna Kung (DePauw University)

Faculty Evaluators:
Mandy Henk and Kevin Howley (DePauw University)
Mickey Huff (Diablo Valley College)
Peter Phillips (Sonoma State University)

Resource exploitation in Africa is not new, but the scale of agricultural "land grabbing" in African nations is unprecedented, becoming the new colonization of the twenty-first century. State violence against Kenyan indigenous pastoralists and Nigerian civilians in oil-rich regions has heightened, leaving thousands dead as the military burns whole communities to the ground and police commit extrajudicial killings, rapes, beatings, thefts, arson, and intimidation.

The African land grab

In the midst of a severe food and economic crisis, the "land grabbing" trend has grown to an international phenomenon. The term refers to the purchase or lease of vast tracts of land by wealthier, food-insecure nations and private investors from mostly poor, developing countries in order to produce crops for export. Approximately 180 instances of such land transactions have been reported since mid-2008, as nations attempt to extend their control over food-producing lands and investors attempt to turn a profit in biofuels and soft commodities markets.

Why Africa? Because an estimated 90 percent of the world's arable land is already in use, the search for more has led to the countries least touched by development, those in Africa. The accelerating land rush has been triggered by the worldwide food shortages that followed the sharp oil price rises in 2008, growing water shortages, and the European Union's insistence that 10 percent of all transport fuel must come from plant-based biofuels by 2015. Devlin Kuyek, a Montreal-based researcher, said investing in Africa is now seen as a new food supply strategy by many governments. "Rich countries are eyeing Africa not just for a healthy return on capital, but also as an insurance policy. Food shortages and riots in twenty-eight countries in 2008, declining water supplies, climate change and huge population growth have together made land attractive. Africa has the most land and, compared with other continents, is cheap," he said.

An *Observer* investigation estimates that up to 50 million hectares of land have been acquired in the last few years or is in the process of being negotiated by governments and wealthy investors working with state subsidies. For example, Ethiopia is one of the hungriest countries in the world, with more than 13 million people needing food aid, but paradoxically the government is offering at least three million hectares of its most fertile land to rich countries and some of the world's most wealthy individuals to export food for their own populations.

The Africa-wide trend is being characterized by many as the new twenty-first-century colonization. Oromia in Ethiopia is one of the centers of the African land rush. Haile Hirpa, president of the Oromia Studies Association, said in a letter of protest to UN Secretary General Ban Ki-moon that India had acquired one million hectares; Djibouti, 10,000 hectares; Saudi Arabia, 100,000 hectares; and that Egyptian, South Korean, Chinese, Nigerian, and other Arab investors were all active in the state. "The Saudis are enjoying the rice harvest, while the Oromos are dying from man-made famine as we speak," he said.

Leading the rush are international agribusinesses, investment banks, hedge funds, commodity traders, and sovereign wealth funds, as well as UK pension funds, foundations, and individuals attracted by some of the world's cheapest land. Together they are scouring Sudan, Kenya, Nigeria, Tanzania, Malawi, Ethiopia, Congo, Zambia, Uganda, Madagascar, Zimbabwe, Mali, Sierra Leone, Ghana, and elsewhere. Ethiopia alone has approved 815 foreign-financed agricultural projects since 2007. Any land there which investors have not been able to buy is being leased for approximately one dollar per year per hectare.

Saudi Arabia, along with other Middle Eastern emirate states such as Qatar, Kuwait, and Abu Dhabi, is thought to be the biggest buyer. In 2008, the Saudi government, which was one of the Middle East's largest wheat growers, announced it would reduce its domestic cereal production by 12 percent a year to conserve its water. It earmarked $5 billion to provide loans at preferential rates to Saudi companies which wanted to invest in countries with strong agricultural potential.

A proponent of the land grabbing, Lorenzo Cotula, senior researcher with the International Institute for Environment and Development, coauthored a report on African land exchanges with the UN fund. While maintaining that well-structured deals could guarantee employment, better infrastructures, and better crop yields, he admitted that if badly handled they could cause great harm, especially if local people were excluded from decisions about allocating land and if their land rights were not protected. Indeed, the land grabbing has impacted African people's human rights. According to Kuyek, the details of the land deals—usually made among high-ranking government officials with little consultation of local peasants—are often murky. And in many cases, land that officials have said was "unused" was actually managed by local peasants in traditional ways to provide food and water for their communities.

Indian ecologist Vandana Shiva maintains that large-scale industrial agriculture not only throws people off their land but also requires chemicals, pesticides, herbicides, fertilizers, intensive water use, and large-scale transport, storage, and distribution, which together turns landscapes into enormous monocultural plantations. "We are seeing dispossession on a massive scale. It means less food is available and local people will have less. There will be more conflict and political instability and cultures will be uprooted. The small farmers of Africa are the basis of food security. The food availability of the planet will decline," she says.

To many, the land rush seems like yet another wave of African resource extraction—one that will benefit foreign governments and large corporations at the expense of Africans and small farmers. The International Institute for Sustainable Development and the World Bank have backed reports showing that "the most reasonable and most appropriate way to invest in food systems is to invest in small farmers," Kuyek says. "But here, we're just getting big industrial agriculture."

Agricultural biotechnologies

Historically, with big industrial agriculture, comes the expansion of Western agricultural biotechnologies. The introduction of genetically modified organisms (GMOs) in the US and other countries has primarily profited patent-holding companies, while creating farmer dependence on the chemical fertilizers and pesticides produced by a few US corporations and used to the detriment of human health, soil quality, and the environment.

A tangled consortium of multinational corporations, funded by taxpayer dollars via the United States Agency for International Development (USAID), seeks to further the aims of biotech abroad, especially in Africa, where Kenya, Mali, Nigeria, South Africa, Uganda, and Zambia were singled out and have been the testing grounds for this strategy. The obvious beneficiaries of such international development are the handful of corporations which own the patents and the technology, and which produce the herbicides and pesticides required by the use of such seeds. While biotechnology has been promising drought tolerance and higher yields for years without delivering, there are real answers available now—like drought-tolerant varieties, suited to certain areas, which are naturally bred; science that focuses on building the quality of the soil and the capacity for that soil to hold more water; or push-and-pull solutions that deal with pests naturally by attracting beneficial insects or planting compatible species that act as decoys for those pests.

The G8 recently pledged $20 billion in aid to promote food security in Africa, but biotech-friendly advisors in the current administration are most likely to direct those funds to multinational corporations promoting biotechnologies and land acquisition. These strategies have proven to further African resource extraction and to impoverish the real basis of food security—investment in Africa's small farmers.

Oil an underlying cause of police and military attacks on civilians in Kenya and Nigeria

Kenya: During 2009 and 2010, the Kenyan government carried out a brutal campaign of violence against the indigenous Samburu people in north-central Kenya. Kenyan police forces conducted armed assaults on at least ten Samburu pastoralist communities in Samburu East and Isiolo Districts, committing extrajudicial killings, rapes, beatings, thefts, arson, and intimidation multiple times. Their actions have caused the Samburu people to suffer death, injury, terror, displacement, economic hardship, property loss, and vulnerability to disease and famine. These crimes have been reported and protested, but no action has been taken by the government of Kenya to investigate or prosecute the offending officers or their superiors. While police say operations in Isiolo and Samburu East were intended to bring greater security to the region, unconfirmed reports that a Kenyan military officer has leaked documents that suggest this ongoing campaign is aimed at forcing the Samburu to abandon their [pastoral] way of life have surfaced. A further motive for the aggression against the Samburu was suggested when, on October 12, the Kenyan government announced that it had awarded a

$26 million lease to a Chinese firm to drill for oil fifteen miles away from Archer's Post, one of the areas most affected by the violence and cattle confiscations. It is the first of eighteen contracts the government is negotiating with Chinese firms for oil.

Nigeria: The Nigerian military has carried out helicopter and gunboat attacks by land, air, and sea on the oil-rich Niger Delta; reports indicate hundreds, possibly thousands, of Nigerian civilians may be dead. Entire villages have reportedly been burned to the ground. Nigerian military reportedly carried out attacks in the area in an effort to oust from the region groups protesting decades of environmental exploitation, destruction, and human rights violations, including the torture and execution of Ken Saro-Wiwa and eight other Nigerian activists. As many as thirty thousand civilians have been displaced without adequate food or water, and aid agencies have been barred from the region.

For years, activist groups in the Niger Delta have advocated for fair distribution of oil wealth to local communities in the impoverished region. One of the main groups in the Niger Delta, the Movement for the Emancipation of the Niger Delta (MEND), declared an oil war and threatened all international industry vessels that approach the region. Eighty percent of the oil extraction in Nigeria is in the Niger Delta. Major oil firms in the area, Shell and Chevron, have made record profits in recent years. Yet the oil-rich Niger Delta remains impoverished, with no schools, no health facilities, or basic infrastructure. Most food in the region is imported due to the decades of contamination of the water and soil by oil and gas companies operating in the region. Thus, the military blockade ultimately means starvation for thousands of people.

Update by John Schertow

In the months following this report, Kenyan police forces led two more full-scale attacks against the Samburu, one of Kenya's seven distinct indigenous peoples. These attacks, like the ones that occurred throughout 2009, were unprovoked.

For centuries, the indigenous peoples have competed with each other for scarce water resources, to replenish cattle stocks in times of drought, to covet pastures for grazing their animals, and to gain favor in their communities. But for the past fifteen years, arms traders have made weapons available to the population, turning the peoples' traditional struggle of survival and dignity into one of needless violence.

The government therefore ordered the police to get rid of the illegal weapons and restore peace and stability to the region. However, once they arrived, the police immediately criminalized the Samburu and began to attack their villages, steal their possessions, and confiscate their cattle.

"The brutal intrusion . . . [has] altered and dismantled our oral history. We shall never be the same again," states Michael Lolwerikoi, in a heartfelt letter on behalf of the Samburu to the US-based group Cultural Survival (CS).

In January 2010, CS sent a research delegation to gather evidence of the attacks. They had been receiving reports from Africa since February 2009. The research delegation was not able to verify some of the reports, including those concerning the military; but after spending two weeks in Kenya, the reason for the Samburu's "limbo state" was clear. In April 2010, they published a report on their findings: "When the Police Are the Perpetrators."

Ultimately, the organization's visit to Kenya played a key role in ending the unnecessary attacks on the Samburu. After their report was received by Kenya's Minister of Internal Security, the police were ordered to stop using force and to conduct the disarmament operation peacefully. Since then, CS says there have been no further full-scale attacks on the Samburu. However, there is still room for history to repeat. "It's something that clearly needs international pressure, because the police in Kenya continue to enjoy impunity," comments Paula Palmer, a member of the research delegation and one of the authors of the report. "[It] mirrors what occurred during the post-election violence being investigated by the International Court of Justice," she adds.

There is an equal need for international exposure—and there has never been any major coverage of these tragic events. Palmer says they have tried to reach out to journalists from the *Guardian*, the *New York Times*, and others but none of the journalists have responded.

The Samburu are asking the government to compensate them for their heavy losses. And they, along with the Borana, Rendille, Turkana, Somali, Meru, and Pokot, want to build lasting peace in the region with the help of their traditional elders. And everybody is eager to get rid of the weapons. "It's something everybody wants," says Palmer.

For more information and to learn what you can do to help, please visit www.culturalsurvival.org.

8

Massacre in Peruvian Amazon over US Free Trade Agreement

Sources:

Raúl Zibechi, "Massacre in the Amazon: The US-Peru Free Trade Agreement Sparks a Battle over Land and Resources," trans. Laura Carlson, Americas Program, Center for International Policy, June 16, 2009, http://americas.irc-online.org/am/6191.

Milagros Salazar, "'Police Are Throwing Bodies in the River,' Say Native Protesters," Inter Press Service, June 9, 2009, http://ipsnews.net/news.asp?idnews=47142.

Student Researcher:
Kelsea Arnold (Sonoma State University)

Faculty Evaluator:
Eric McGuckin (Sonoma State University)

On World Environment Day, June 5, 2009, Peruvian Amazon Indians were massacred by the government of Alán García in the latest chapter of a long war to take over common lands—a war unleashed by the signing of the Free Trade Agreement (FTA) between Peru and the United States.

Three MI-17 helicopters took off from the national police base in El Milagro, Peru, at 6 A.M. on Friday, June 5, and flew over part of the Peruvian highway that joins the jungle to the northern coast, which had been occupied for the past ten days by five thousand Awajún and Wampi indigenous peoples.

The helicopters launched tear gas on the crowd (witnesses say they also shot machine guns) while a group of agents simultaneously attacked the roadblock by ground, firing AKM rifles. An estimated five hundred police bore down on the protesters, some of whom were still sleeping, and opened fire. A hundred people were wounded by gunshot and between twenty to twenty-five were killed.

The government claimed days after the clash that eleven indigenous were dead as well as twenty-three police agents. The indigenous organizations reported fifty dead among their ranks and up to four hundred disappeared. According to witnesses, the military burned bodies and threw them into the river to hide the massacre, and also took prisoners from among the wounded in hospitals. While accounts differ, what is certain is that the government sent the armed forces to evict a peaceful protest that had been going on for fifty-seven days in five jungle regions: Amazonas, Cusco, Loreto, San Martin, and Ucayali.

The conflict began on April 9, when Amazon peoples mobilized to block the highways and gas and oil pipelines to protest the implementation of a series of decrees passed to carry out the FTA with the United States. But the situation worsened on June 4, when García's government stopped Congress from debating repeal of the decrees being challenged by the indigenous peoples and declared unconstitutional by a Constitution Commission.

The US–Peru FTA was signed on December 8, 2005, in Washington, DC, by then presidents George W. Bush and Alán García. In June 2006, it was ratified by Peru, and in December 2007 by the US Congress. On December 19, 2007, Peru's Congress gave full faculties to the government to legislate for six months by decree issues related to the FTA. Mandated by these powers, the executive drafted ninety-nine legislative decrees (LD) that are at the root of the current conflict. On February 1, 2009, the agreement went into effect.

In response to indigenous protests President García said there was "a conspiracy afoot to try to keep us from making use of our natural wealth." He was referring to the fierce opposition by the country's native peoples to ten of the ninety-nine LDs issued by his government that open up indigenous land to private investment by oil, mining, and logging companies, as well as to agribusiness, including biofuel plantations.

The most controversial of the LDs are numbers 1015 and 1073. These decrees, which were declared unconstitutional, modify the number of votes required to sell communal lands (just three votes could place community land up for sale).

LD 1083 (Promotion of Efficient Use and Conservation of Hydraulic Resources) favors the privatization of water to large consumers such as mining companies. LDs 1081, 1079, and 1020 deregulate diverse aspects of legislation in areas of mining, timber, and hydrocarbon exploitation.

It is LD 1090 (Forestry and Woodland Fauna Law), however, that is at the crux of the debate. This decree leaves 45 million hectares out of the forestry framework, that is, 64 percent of the forests of Peru, including their biodiversity in flora and fauna, making it possible to sell this vast commonwealth to transnational corporations.

Based on his logic of converting everything into merchandise, García maintained, "The first resource is the Amazon." He proposed to divide 63 million hectares into 5,000-, 10,000-, and 20,000-hectare parcels—as land sold in "large lots will attract long-term investment and high technology." He notes that one should not "deliver small lots of land to poor families that do not have a penny to invest." He makes no mention of the fact that these lands are the collective property of native communities.

On April 9, over one thousand communities agreed to start demonstrating. Prime Minister Yehude Simon called the April 18 indigenous demands "capricious." On May 5, the bishops of eight Catholic dioceses demanded that President García repeal the decrees, declaring them "a threat to the Amazon." On May 10, the government announced a state of emergency in five regions of the country where roadblocks and blockages of ports and oil pipelines were taking place.

Hugo Blanco, a well-known Peruvian activist and editor of the monthly *Lucha Indígena*, stated in his column: "After 500 years of silencing, the Amazon peoples receive the support of the peoples of Peru and the world. The greatest achievement of this campaign has been to make these nationalities visible, weaving links between diverse sectors of the country, as divided as those who dominate. By defending the Amazon we are defending the life of all of humanity; and by not ceding to the deceit of the government, they are rewriting history, recuperating for all the sense of the word dignity."

9
Human Rights Abuses Continue in Palestine

Sources:

Virginia Tilley, Human Sciences Research Council of South Africa, "Occupation, Colonialism, Apartheid," HSRC Web site, May 2009, http://www.hsrc.ac.za/Media_Release-378.phtml.

Jonathan Cook, "Israel Brings Gaza Entry Restrictions to West Bank," *Electronic Intifada*, August 18, 2009, http://electronicintifada.net/v2/article10718.shtml.

Amnesty International, "Israel Rations Palestinians to Trickle of Water," October 27, 2009, http://www.amnesty.org/en/news-and-updates/report/israel-rations-palestinians-trickle-water-20091027.

Rory McCarthy, "Non-Violent Protests Against West Bank Barrier Turn Increasingly Dangerous," *Guardian*, April 27, 2009, http://www.guardian.co.uk/world/2009/apr/27/israel-security-barrier-protests.

Electronic Intifada, "Harvard Fellow Calls for Genocidal Measures to Curb Palestinian Births," February 22, 2010, http://electronicintifada.net/v2/article11091.shtml.

Student Researchers:
Josette Canilao, Ashley Housley, Crystal Schreiner, and Ashlee Plouffe
(Sonoma State University)
Nolan Higdon and Kajal Shahali (Diablo Valley College)

Faculty Evaluators:
Andrew Roth and Heather Smith (Sonoma State University)
Mickey Huff (Diablo Valley College)

The Human Sciences Research Council of South Africa (HSRC) has released a study indicating that Israel is practicing both colonialism and apartheid in the occupied Palestinian territories. The HSRC commissioned an international team of scholars and practitioners of international public law from South Africa, the United Kingdom, Israel, and the West Bank to conduct the study.

The team found that Israel's policy and practices violate the prohibition on colonialism, which the international community developed in the 1960s in response to the great decolonization struggles in Africa and Asia. Israel's policy is demonstrably to fragment the West Bank and annex part of it permanently to Israel. Through these measures, Israel has denied the indigenous population the right to self-determination, and has indicated a clear intention to assume sovereignty over portions of its land and natural resources. The team also found that Israel's laws and policies in the Occupied Palestinian Territories (OPT) fit the definition of apartheid in the International Convention on the Suppression and Punishment of the Crime of Apartheid. Israeli law conveys privileges to Jewish settlers and disadvantages Palestinians in the same territory on the basis of their respective racial identities.

Jonathan Cook, writing for the *Electronic Intifada*—the nonprofit, independent news source covering issues stemming from Israel's forty-year occupation of Palestinian territories—reported Israel's restrictions on entry into the West Bank territory. Israel's imposed restriction denies movement between Israel and the West Bank to people with foreign passports. This restriction affects Palestinian residents as well as humanitarian aid organizations. "The new regulation is in breach of Israel's commitments under the Oslo accords to Western governments that their citizens would be given continued access to the Occupied Palestinian Territories." Despite the breach, the US has not made any attempt to correct it. The US asserts it can do nothing about Israel's restriction and, in fact, has raised no objections to it.

The restriction on entry for foreign passport holders deepens the isolation and separation Israel has imposed on the West Bank territory. The enforced regulation has created rifts and obstacles for Palestinians who have gone abroad, but settled in the West Bank territory. Thousands of Palestinians who have done this have been denied residency permits and are required to renew visas every three months in different regions. Palestinian resident Sam Bahour told reporters, "The latest rule change should be understood as one measure in a web of restrictions strangling normal Palestinian life that has been imposed by Israel, which controls the population registers for both Israelis and Palestinians." Bahour further observes that this new regulation is another attempt to forward Israel's goal to rid the territory of Palestinians.

Amnesty International has uncovered Israel's monopoly on water in the occupied West Bank. The international human rights organization has accused Israel of denying Palestinians the right to adequate water access. Israel uses over 80 percent of the Mountain Aquifer, the only quality water source for populations in the West Bank. Though Israel has various other sources of water, it also uses the Mountain Aquifer and restricts access to it, leaving Palestinians to struggle with less than enough water. "Some 180,000 to 200,000 Palestinians living in rural communities have no access to running water and the Israeli army often prevents

them from even collecting rainwater. In contrast, Israeli settlers, who live in the West Bank in violation of international law, have intensive-irrigation farms, lush gardens and swimming pools." Many Palestinians suffer from lack of water access, subsequently adjusting their life to just subsist. Water restrictions imposed by Israel have affected Palestinian farmers, and the general way of life. "Restrictions imposed by Israel on the movement of people and goods in the OPT further compound the difficulties Palestinians face when trying to carry out water and sanitation projects, or even just to distribute small quantities of water." Amnesty International has termed Israel's water restrictions in the West Bank as "discriminatory policies" that deny basic human rights to Palestinians.

The Guardian has covered violence on Palestinians while they nonviolently protest Israeli occupation. Palestinian marchers devoted to nonviolent protest have fallen under abuse by the Israeli military, who claim the protesters created a "violent and illegal riot." In an attempt to act on their concerns of occupation, Palestinians marched toward the West Bank barrier to display their opposition. On April 17, a Palestinian caught in the danger, Basem Abu Rahmeh, was a victim of the military violence and died by a tear gas canister to the chest. Another vicitim, American demonstrator Tristan Anderson, lost sight in his right eye and incurred debilitating brain damage when a tear gas canister hit him in the head. "The Bil`in [village in West Bank] demonstration was always intended to be nonviolent, although on Friday, as is often the case, there were half a dozen younger, angrier men lobbing stones at the soldiers with slingshots. The Israeli military, for its part, fires tear gas, stun grenades, rubber-coated bullets and sometimes live ammunition at the crowd."

According to the *Electronic Intifada*, Harvard University fellow Martin Kramer, who is also a member of the Washington Institute for Near East Policy (WINEP), called for the West to stop providing pro-natal subsidies to Palestine, in order to curb the births of Palestinians. Kramer's argument was that too many children lead to too many "superfluous young men" who then will become violent radicals. His views symbolize a genocidal measure. "The 1948 UN Convention on the Prevention and Punishment of the Crime of Genocide, created in the wake of the Nazi holocaust, defines genocide to include measures 'intended to prevent births within' a specific 'national, ethnic, racial or religious group.'" Kramer's view reflects a long-standing Israeli and Zionistic concern about the so-called "demographic threat" to Israel, as the Palestinians are soon to outnumber Jews in Israel and Palestine.

10

US Funds and Supports the Taliban

Sources:

Aram Roston, "How the US Funds the Taliban," *Nation*, November 20, 2009, http://www.thenation.com/doc/20091130/roston.

Ahmad Kawoosh, "Is the US Aiding the Taliban?" *Taiwan News*, October 31, 2009, opinion sec., http://www.etaiwannews.com/etn/news_content.php?id=1095689&lang=eng_news&cate_img=140.jpg&cate_rss=news_Opinion.

Ahmad Kawoosh, "Helicopter Rumor Refuses to Die," Institute for War and Peace Reporting, November 2, 2009, http://www.iwpr.net/?p=arr&s=f&o=356886.

Student Researchers:
Anne Cozad (Sonoma State University)
Nolan Higdon (Diablo Valley College)

Faculty Evaluators:
Mickey Huff (Diablo Valley College)
Peter Phillips (Sonoma State University)

In a continuous flow of money, American tax dollars end up paying members of the Taliban and funding a volatile environment in Afghanistan. Private contractors pay insurgents with the hope of attaining the very safety they are contracted to provide. Concurrently, US soldiers pay at checkpoints run by suspected insurgents in order to get safe passage. In some cases, Afghan companies run by former Taliban members, like President Hamid Karzai's cousin, are protecting the passage of American soldiers. The funding of the insurgents, along with rumors of American helicopters ferrying Taliban members in Afghanistan, has led to widespread distrust of American forces. In the meantime, the US taxpayer's dollar continues to fund insurgents to protect American troops so they can fight insurgents.

Ahmad Rate Popal is a grand example of how those who controlled Afghanistan under Taliban rule are still controlling Afghanistan today and being paid by US tax dollars. Popal, who served as interpreter at one of the ruling Taliban's last press conferences, is greatly increasing his wealth through the US war in Afghanistan. In 1988, he was charged with conspiring to import heroin into the United States. He was released from prison in 1997. Popal's cousin is Afghanistan's President Karzai. Popal and his brother Rashid (who pleaded guilty in 1996 to a separate heroin charge) control the Watan Group in Afghanistan, which is a consortium engaged in many different fields of business. One of Watan's enterprises is to protect convoys of Afghan trucks heading from Kabul to Kandahar, carrying American supplies. Popal is one example of the virtual carnival of improbable characters and shady connections, with former CIA officials and ex-military officers in Afghanistan joining hands with former Taliban members and *mujahideen* to collect US government funds in the name of the war effort.

US security contractors as well as countless other private American corporations cannot provide the safety that they are paid to offer. So US military contractors in Afghanistan pay suspected insurgents to protect the US supply routes they were contracted to protect. A war-torn country such as Afghanistan has plenty of impoverished citizens, and, as a result, it is not hard for private contractors to find individuals willing to take money to protect supply routes.

Thus, an estimated 10 percent of the Pentagon's logistics contracts worth hundreds of millions of dollars are paid to insurgents as the US government funds the very forces American troops are fighting.

An example of these contracts are those granted to the NCL Holdings in Afghanistan run by Hamed Wardak, the young American son of Afghanistan's current defense minister, General Abdul Rahim Wardak. NCL is a small firm that was awarded a US military logistics contract worth hundreds of millions of dollars. Despite the fact that the firm only operates in Afghanistan, Wardak incorporated NCL in the United States early in 2007, due to his connections there.

On NCL's advisory board is Milton Bearden, a well-known former CIA officer who in 2009 was introduced by Senator John Kerry as "a legendary former CIA case officer and a clearheaded thinker and writer." Bearden is an incredible asset to a small defense contracting firm. Wardak was able to get a contract for Host Nation Trucking despite having no apparent trucking experience. The contract is aimed at handling the bulk of US trucking in Afghanistan, bringing supplies to bases and remote outposts throughout Afghanistan. At first the contract was small, but very quickly it expanded by 600 percent, making it a gargantuan contract worth $360 million. NCL had struck pure contracting gold. These profits, which only go to a very select and well-connected portion of the Afghan people, build a large amount of distrust from Afghan citizens toward American troops and those connected to them.

It is persistently rumored in Afghanistan that US forces are using their helicopters to ferry Taliban fighters. The rumor is strongly denied by the military. However, the helicopter rumors heard in many areas are feeding mistrust of the forces that are supposed to be bringing order to the country. The international troops deny that they are supporting the insurgents. "This entire business with the helicopters is just a rumor," said Brigadier General Jüergen Setzer, recently appointed commander for the International Security Assistance Force (ISAF) in northern Afghanistan. "It has no basis in reality, according to our investigations." But the persistent rumors that foreign helicopters have been sighted assisting the Taliban in northern Afghanistan were given an unexpected boost in mid-October 2009 by President Karzai, who told the media that his administration was investigating similar reports that "unknown" helicopters were ferrying the insurgents from the Helmand province in the south to the Baghlan, Kunduz, and Samangan provinces in the north.

Update

On June 6, the *New York Times* reported that the House National Security Subcommittee, whose chair is John Tierney (D-MA), is holding hearings on this issue. In a March 2010 *Washington Post* article, Congressman Tierney cited the article in the *Nation* as the reason he began the investigation.

Since our initial search of corporate media coverage on this issue in February 2010, finding zero coverage at that time, both the *New York Times* and the *Washington Post* have covered part of the story on their front pages. Both mentioned President Hamid Karzai's cousin, and both acknowledged that in all likelihood money is making its way to the Taliban. Neither paper mentioned the US connection, Milton Bearden. The *Washington Post* covered the story on March 29, 2010, and mentioned the *Nation* magazine article. *The New York Times* story came out on June 6, 2010, acknowledging the corruption, but included the news that President Obama was addressing the issue with President Karzai. That the two stories came out two months apart, and that the US links are left out, led to the decision at Project Censored to keep this important story in the top censored stories list for the year.

11

The H1N1 Swine Flu Pandemic: Manipulating Data to Enrich Drug Companies

Source:

Michel Chossudovsky, "The H1N1 Swine Flu Pandemic: Manipulating the Data to Justify a Worldwide Public Health Emergency," *Global Research*, August 25, 2009, http://www.globalresearch.ca/PrintArticle.php?articleId=14901.

Student Researchers:

Nolan Higdon and Michael Smith (Diablo Valley College)

Faculty Evaluator:

Mickey Huff (Diablo Valley College)

The H1N1 virus has spawned widespread panic and fear throughout the world. However, upon closer examination, many of the claims made by the World Health Organization (WHO) seem to be based on weak and incomplete data. The Atlanta-based Centers for Disease Control and Prevention (CDC) has created and used data to grossly exaggerate the need for an expensive and unnecessary vaccine aimed at creating profits for the pharmaceutical industry—not protecting Americans.

The WHO claimed that a worldwide public health emergency had unfolded on an unprecedented scale in 2009, and 4.9 billion doses of H1N1 swine flu vaccine were needed to stop the spread. Very soon thereafter countries all around the globe began preparation for the inoculation of millions of people in accordance with WHO recommendations. In some countries the WHO recommended that the H1N1 vaccination be mandatory. However, most people were unaware that the data used by the WHO was faulty at best.

In the US, both federal and state governments began preparation for the pandemic. State governments are generally responsible for these preparations, in coordination with federal agencies. President Obama's Council of Advisors on Science and Technology released a report that "considered the H1N1 pandemic 'a serious health threat' to the US—not as serious as the 1918 Spanish flu pandemic but worse than the swine flu outbreak of 1976." Responding to such terrifying language, Massachusetts's legislation introduced hefty fines and prison sentences for those who refused to be vaccinated. The US military was expected to have an active role in this health emergency.

There was no uniform system for collecting data on suspected swine flu victims in the US, which led to confusion in the absence of accurate statistics. The CDC acknowledged that the figures being collected on "confirmed and probable cases" in the US contained no separation between "confirmed" and "probable." In fact, only a small percentage of the reported cases were "confirmed" by laboratory tests. This faulty data and much more like it from around the globe was given to the WHO, who in turn used the numbers to justify a pandemic.

The need for a perfected method of diagnosing and counting infected people was demonstrated when the WHO's "data" caused a wave of inaccurate conclusions as to the severity of the flu and the distance it had spread.

The WHO declared a Phase 4 level of severity on April 27. Just two days later (April 29), without corroborating evidence, the pandemic was raised to Phase 5. Just over a month later (June 11) it was raised again to Phase 6, the level of an actual pandemic. The abrupt change in numbers should have been a wake-up call to the WHO that something had gone wrong in its data collection. Yet despite the suspicious changes, there was no attempt to improve the process of data collection in terms of laboratory confirmation. In fact quite the opposite occurred. Following the Phase 6 pandemic announcement, the CDC decided that data collection of individual confirmed and probable cases was no longer necessary to determine the spread of swine flu. The WHO ignored the change in data collection and that same month predicted with authority that "as many as 2 billion people could become infected over the next two years—nearly one-third of the world population." The report created an atmosphere of fear and insecurity.

By August 2009, the WHO casually acknowledged that the underlying symptoms were moderate and that "most people will recover from swine flu within a week, just as they would from seasonal forms of influenza."

The inaccurate data collection exaggerated numbers of infected people due to the CDC's quantitative model created in July 2009. From April 15 to July 24, 2009, states reported a total of 43,771 confirmed and probable cases of novel influenza A (H1N1) infection. Of these reported cases, 5,011 people were hospitalized and 302 died.

On July 24, 2009, counts were discontinued by the CDC. Instead of collecting data that could have provided empirical backing for assessments of how the H1N1 virus was spreading, the CDC announced that it had developed its model to determine the true number of novel H1N1 flu cases in the United States.

The CDC further stated, "The model took the number of cases reported by states and adjusted the figure to account for known sources of underestimation," such as accounting for people who never reported their illness, despite no proof that these infected people existed. These estimations caused an inaccurate and basically made-up figure of infections. The CDC recognized early in the outbreak that, once the disease was widespread, it would be more valuable to transition to standard surveillance systems to monitor illness, hospitalizations, and deaths.

The CDC's data was then used to justify massive vaccinations, which created huge profits for the pharmaceutical industry. The CDC posits that the data sent to them by the states is "underestimated." The CDC then inflates figures of "unconfirmed" cases, many of which are cases of seasonal influenza. The "corrected figures" are then inserted into the model. Using the CDC model approach, it is estimated that more than one million people became ill with novel H1N1 flu between April and June 2009 in the United States. Since these estimates are not based on confirmed illness, the numbers can grow and shrink at the whim of those controlling the model. The CDC's model simulations and predictions of the spread of H1N1 swine flu are then used to plan the implementation of a nationwide vaccination program. Based on the model's "predictions," mass vaccination of half of the US population is required, with the possible provision for quarantines under civilian and/or military jurisdiction.

According to reports, the US government expected to have 85 million doses of the vaccine by the end of October 2009. The US government had ordered 195 million doses from the pharmaceutical companies. On July 29, 2009, the Advisory Committee on Immunization Practices (ACIP)—an advisory committee to the CDC—recommended that novel H1N1 flu vaccine be made available first to priority groups; these groups together would equal approximately 159 million individuals. The Agence France-Presse reported that the United States put in orders for the vaccine that would cover between 30 and 78 percent of Americans. As a result, the pharmaceutical industry gained massive profits from Americans who purchased an unnecessary and potentially dangerous vaccine in large quantities.

It is essential that physicians, epidemiologists, and health workers speak out through their respective associations and refute the government officials who are acting on behalf of the pharmaceutical industry, as well as denounce the manipulation of data. An accurate method of counting infected people has to be created in time for the next pandemic, should one hit, in order to better serve the needs of the public. It is also important to warn the public on the dangers of untested H1N1 flu vaccines. The WHO cannot accurately serve the people it claims to serve without the cooperation of groups like the CDC. Sadly, the CDC is not protecting humanity because it is too busy expanding the bottom line of the pharmaceutical industry.

12

Cuba Provided the Greatest Medical Aid to Haiti after the Earthquake

Sources:
Ernesto Wong Maestre, "Haití y el Paradigma Cubano de Solidaridad" (Haiti and the Cuban Paradigm of Solidarity), *Rebelión*, January 24, 2010, http://www.rebelion.org/noticia.php?id=99233.

Tom Fawthrop, "Cuba's Aid Ignored By The Media?" Al Jazeera English, February 16, 2010, http://english.aljazeera.net/focus/2010/01/201013195514870782.html.

Emilio González López, "La Otra Realidad de Haití y la Ayuda de 400 Médicos Cubanos" (Haiti's Other Reality and the Aid from 400 Cuban Doctors), *Público* (Madrid), February 7, 2010, letter to the editor, http://rreloj.wordpress.com/2010/01/15/intensa-actividad-de-los-medicos-cubanos-en-haiti.

Radio Santa Cruz, "La Oficina Panamericana de la Salud Califica de 'excelente' la Ayuda Médica Cubana a Haití" (The Pan American Heath Organization Evaluates the Cuban Aid to Haiti as "Excellent"), January 25, 2010, http://www.radiosantacruz.icrt.cu/noticias/internacionales/califica-excelente-ops-ayuda-medica-cubana-haiti.htm.

Al Ritmo de los Tiempos, "EEUU Olvidó la Inmensa Ayuda de Médicos Cubanos a Haití," (USA Forgets Cuban Doctors' Massive Help to Haiti), January 18, 2010, http://actualidad.rt.com/actualidad/america_latina/issue_3106.html.

Student Researcher:
Sarah Maddox (Sonoma State University)

Faculty Evaluators:
José Manuel Pestano Rodríguez and José Manuel de Pablos Coello (University of La Laguna, Canary Islands)
William Du Bois (Southwest Minnesota State University)

Cuba was the first to come into Haiti with medical aid when the January 12, 2010, earthquake struck. Among the many donor nations, Cuba and its medical teams have played a major role in treating Haiti's earthquake victims. Public health experts say the Cubans were the first to set up medical facilities among the debris and to revamp hospitals immediately after the earthquake struck. Their pivotal work in the health sector has, however, received scant media coverage. "It is striking that there has been virtually no mention in the media of the fact that Cuba had several hundred health personnel on the ground before any other country," said David Sanders, professor of public health from Western Cape University in South Africa.

The Cuban team coordinator in Haiti, Dr. Carlos Alberto Garcia, said the Cuban doctors, nurses, and other health personnel worked nonstop, day and night, with operating rooms open eighteen hours a day. During a visit to La Paz Hospital in the Haitian capital Port-au-Prince, Dr. Mirta Roses, director of the Pan American Health Organization, which is in charge of medical coordination between the Cuban doctors, the International Committee of the Red Cross (ICRC), and a host of health sector nongovernmental organizations (NGOs), described the aid provided by Cuban doctors as "excellent and marvelous."

Haiti and Cuba signed a medical cooperation agreement in 1998. Before the earthquake struck, 344 Cuban health professionals were already present in Haiti, providing primary care and obstetrical services as well as operating to restore the sight of Haitians blinded by eye diseases. More doctors were flown in shortly after the earthquake as part of the rapid response. "In the case of Cuban doctors, they are rapid responders to disasters, because disaster management is an integral part of their training," explains Maria Hamlin Zúniga, a public health specialist from Nicaragua. Cuban doctors have been organizing medical facilities in three revamped hospitals, five field hospitals, and five diagnostic centers, with a total of twenty-two different care posts aided by financial support from Venezuela. They are also operating nine rehabilitation centers staffed by nearly seventy Cuban physical therapists and rehabilitation specialists, in addition to Haitian medical personnel. The Cuban team has been assisted by one hundred specialists from Venezuela, Chile, Spain, Mexico, Colombia, and Canada, as well as seventeen nuns.

However, in reporting on the international aid effort, Western media have generally not ranked Cuba high on the list of donor nations. One major international news agency's list of donor nations credited Cuba with sending over thirty doctors to Haiti, whereas the real figure stands at more than 350, including 280 young Haitian doctors who graduated from Cuba. A combined total of 930 Cuban health professionals make Cuba's the largest medical contingent on the ground in Haiti. Another batch of 200 Cuban-trained doctors from twenty-four countries in Africa and Latin American, and a dozen American doctors who graduated from medical schools in Havana, went to Haiti to provide reinforcement to existing Cuban medical teams. By comparison, the internationally renowned Médecins Sans Frontières (MSF or Doctors without Borders) has approximately 269 health professionals working in Haiti. MSF is much better funded and has far more extensive medical supplies than the Cuban team.

But while representatives from MSF and the ICRC are frequently in front of television cameras discussing health priorities and medical needs, the Cuban medical teams are missing in the media coverage. Richard Gott, the *Guardian*'s former foreign editor and a Latin America specialist, explains, "Western media are programmed to be indifferent to aid that comes from unexpected places. In the Haitian case, the media have ignored not just the Cuban contribution, but also the efforts made by other Latin American countries." Brazil is providing $70 million in funding for ten urgent care units, fifty mobile units for emergency care, a laboratory, and a hospital, among other health services. Venezuela has canceled all of Haiti's debt and has promised to supply oil, free of charge, until the country has recovered from the disaster. Western NGOs employ media officers to ensure that the world knows what they are doing. According to Gott, the

Western media has grown accustomed to dealing with such NGOs, enabling a relationship of mutual assistance to develop. Cuban medical teams, however, are outside this predominantly Western humanitarian-media loop and are therefore only likely to receive attention from Latin American media and Spanish language broadcasters and print media.

There have, however, been notable exceptions to this reporting syndrome. On January 19, a CNN reporter broke the silence on the Cuban role in Haiti with a report on Cuban doctors at La Paz Hospital. Cuban doctors received global praise for their humanitarian aid in Indonesia. When the US requested that their military planes be allowed to fly through Cuban airspace for the purpose of evacuating Haitians to hospitals in Florida, Cuba immediately agreed despite almost fifty years of animosity between the two countries.

Although Cuba is a poor, developing country, their wealth of human resources—doctors, engineers, and disaster management experts—has enabled this small Caribbean nation to play a global role in health care and humanitarian aid alongside the far-richer nations of the west. Cuban medical teams played a key role in the wake of the Indian Ocean tsunami and stayed the longest among international medical teams treating the victims of the 2006 Indonesian earthquake. They also provided the largest contingent of doctors after the 2005 earthquake in Pakistan. In the Pakistan relief operation, the US and Europe also dispatched medical teams. Each had a base camp with most doctors deployed for a month. The Cubans, however, deployed seven major base camps, operated thirty-two field hospitals, and stayed for six months.

A Montreal summit of twenty donor nations agreed to hold a major conference on Haiti's future at the United Nations in March 2010. Some analysts see Haiti's rehabilitation as a potential opportunity for the US and Cuba to bypass their ideological differences and combine their resources—the US has the logistics while Cuba has the human resources—to help Haiti. "Potential US-Cuban cooperation could go a long way toward meeting Haiti's needs," says Dr. Julie Feinsilver, author of *Healing the Masses,* a book about Cuban health diplomacy, who argues that maximum cooperation is urgently needed. Feinsilver is convinced that "Cuba should be given a seat at the table with all other nations and multilateral organizations and agencies in any and all meetings to discuss, plan and coordinate aid efforts for Haiti's reconstruction." In late January 2010, Secretary of State Hillary Clinton thanked Cuba for its efforts in Haiti and welcomed further assistance and cooperation. In

Haiti's grand reconstruction plan, Feinsilver argues, "There can be no imposition of systems from any country, agency or institution. The Haitian people themselves, through what remains of their government and NGOs, must provide the policy direction, and Cuba has been and should continue to be a key player in the health sector in Haiti."

13

Obama Cuts Domestic Spending and Increases Military Corporate Welfare

Sources:

Tom Engelhardt, "Weapons Makers as 'Welfare Queens,'" *TomDispatch*, March 18, 2010, http://www.commondreams.org/view/2010/03/19.

William J. Astore, "The Pentagon Church Militant and Us: The Top Five Questions We Should Ask the Pentagon," *TomDispatch*, March 18, 2010, http://www.tomdispatch.com/blog/175219/tomgram%3A_william_astore,_you_have_no_say_about_your_military.

Sam Husseini and David Zupan, "Obama: Cut Domestic, Increase Military," Institute of Public Accuracy, January 26, 2010, http://www.commondreams.org/newswire/2010/01/26-14.

Carl Conetta, "The Pentagon's Runaway Budget," Antiwar.com, March 3, 2010, http://original.antiwar.com/carl-conetta/2010/03/03/the-pentagons-runaway-budget.

Jeremy Scahill, "US War Privatization Results in Billions Lost in Fraud, Waste and Abuse," *RebelReports*, June 10, 2009, http://rebelreports.com/post/121172812/u-s-war-privatization-results-in-billions-lost-in.

Student Researchers:
Molly Lipinski and Meghan Brandts (St. Cloud State University)

Faculty Evaluator:
Julie Andrzejewski (St. Cloud State University)

President Obama's decision to increase military spending this year and in the future will result in the greatest administrative military spending since World War II. This decision is being made in spite of continued evidence of extreme waste, fraud, abuse, and corporate welfare in the military budget. At the same time, spending on "non-security" domestic programs such as education, nutrition, energy, and transportation will be frozen, resulting in inflationary cuts to essential services for the US public over the upcoming years.

While these domestic programs constitute only 17 percent of the total federal spending, they will sustain all of the proposed cuts. Jo Comer-

ANOTHER BUSY DAY IN THE OVAL OFFICE

ford, executive director of the National Priorities Project, states, "[Obama's] proposal caps non-security spending at $447 billion for each of the next three fiscal years. During that time, inflation will erode the purchasing power of that total; requiring cuts in services in each successive year." The consequences of cutting domestic spending will result in a further increase in the gap between the rich and the poor.

In contrast, military spending is roughly 55 percent of the discretionary spending in the current fiscal year, and will increase even more next year. According to the Office of Management and Budget's projections, the military budget will increase an additional $522 billion over the next decade. Tom Engelhardt points out, "Here's an American reality: the Pentagon is our true welfare state, the weapons makers are our real 'welfare queens,' and we never stop shoveling money their way."

There is widespread and continuous waste, fraud, and abuse by the Pentagon and by military contractors resulting in welfare for the rich. William Astore, a retired lieutenant colonel with the US Air Force, concludes, "When it comes to our nation's military affairs, ignorance is not bliss. What's remarkable then, given the permanent state of war in which we find ourselves, is how many Americans seem content not to know."

The public never hears about war spending in the corporate media and how much everything actually costs. Several examples highlight the extent of abuse.

▸ A single future weapons system is now estimated to cost the American taxpayer almost one-third of what the Obama administration's health care plan is expected to cost over a decade. Originally expected to cost $50 million, the estimated cost today just for one F-35 plane is $113 million. The marines, the air force, and the navy are planning to buy a combined 2,450 of F-35s, which would cost more than $323 billion.

▸ A recent hearing of the federal Commission on Wartime Contracting in Iraq and Afghanistan addressed a 111-page report on its "initial investigations of the nation's heavy reliance on contractors." According to a release on the hearing, "More than 240,000 contractor employees, about 80 percent of them foreign nationals, are working in Iraq and Afghanistan to support operations and projects of the US military, the Department of State, and the US Agency for International Development. Contractor employees outnumber US troops in the region. While contractors provide vital services, the Commission believes their use has also entailed billions of dollars lost to waste, fraud, and abuse due to inadequate planning, poor contract drafting, limited competition, understaffed oversight functions, and other problems." Jeremy Scahill notes that while the wartime commission is charged with revealing the scope of corruption, it includes members who are either pro-war or have worked for major war contractors.

▸ According to Kathy Kelly, author of *Tough Minds, Tender Hearts*, "The US government devotes massive resources and much sophistication to killing in Afghanistan. Would that it would spend a little to realize that its policies are creating anger. . . . It costs about $1 million a year for a US soldier—boots on the ground—in Afghanistan. Imagine what good that money could do if spent to help the Afghan people. A governor in Afghanistan makes about $1,000 a year."

President Obama is continuing the process of reinflating the Pentagon that began in late 1998—fully three years before the 9/11 attacks. The rise in national defense spending since 1998 is as large as the Kennedy-Johnson surge (43 percent) and the Reagan increases (57 percent) put together. The Department of Defense has been given about $7.2 trillion since 1998, which is when the post–cold war decline in defense spending ended. Current spending is above the peak years of the Vietnam War era and the Reagan years, and the Pentagon plans to remain there at this point. The radical increase in military spending now, compared to the cold war and World War II, is justified by the wars in Iraq and Afghanistan. However, even if today's wars are taken out of the picture, there has still been a 54 percent increase since 1998.

Last year innumerable public hearings were held on health care reform. Constant news and debate by the public, corporations, the media, and Congress continued for months. The health care program, in ten years, will cost the American people as much as defense and homeland security cost in a single year. Yet runaway defense budgets get passed each year without a single "town hall" meeting, next to no media coverage, and virtually no debate in Congress.

The taxpayer, forced to pay about one trillion dollars yearly to fund the military, national security infrastructure, and wars, remains ignorant of the real costs. Reasons for the lack of public knowledge about military spending include: lack of corporate media coverage altogether; media employing retired military officers as "experts," thus presenting only one side; inculcated civilian deference toward military leaders (leave it to the experts in uniform); and secrecy and "black budgets" obscuring military spending. Among the questions William J. Astore poses about the US military, a key one is: why is the military immune from the painful budgetary belt tightening faced by the rest of America?

Astore concludes, "It's true that the world is a dangerous place. The problem is that the Pentagon is part of that danger. Our military has grown so strong and so dominates our government, including its foreign policy and even aspects of our culture, that there's no effective counterweight to its closeted, conflict-centered style of thinking." This dominance is costing the US public enormous sums of money, is a major contributor to the economic crisis, and will continue to erode desperately needed public support programs now and in the future.

14

Increased Tensions with Unresolved 9/11 Issues

Sources:
PR News Wire, "1,000 Architects & Engineers Call for New 9/11 Investigation: Cite Evidence of Explosive Demolition at Three World Trade Center Towers," February 19, 2009, http://www.prnewswire.com/news-releases/1000-architects—engineers-call-for-new-911-investigation-84768402.html.

Shawn Hamilton, "Over 1,000 Architects and Engineers Have Signed Petition to Reinvestigate 9-11 Destruction," Examiner.com, February 23, 2010, http://www.examiner.com/x-36199-Conspiracy-Examiner.

Architects & Engineers for 911 Truth, "1,000+ Architects & Engineers Officially Demand New 9/11 Investigation," Infowars.com, January 18, 2010, http://www.infowars.com/1000-architects-engineers-officially-demand-new-911-investigation.

Global Research, "1,000 Architects & Engineers Call for a Real 9/11 Investigation," January 25, 2010, http://www.globalresearch.ca/index.php?context=va&aid=17507.

Sue Reid, "Has Osama bin Laden Been Dead for Seven Years—And Are the US and Britain Covering It Up to Continue War on Terror?" Daily Mail (UK), September 1, 2009, http://www.dailymail.co.uk/news/article-1212851/Has-Osama-Bin-Laden-dead-seven-years—U-S-Britain-covering-continue-war-terror.html.

Daniel Tencer, "Obama Staffer Wants 'Cognitive Infiltration' of 9/11 Conspiracy Groups," RawStory, January 13, 2010, http://rawstory.com/2010/01/obama-staffer-infiltration-911-groups.

Student Researchers:
Mike Smith, Nolan Higdon, and Sy Cowie (Diablo Valley College)
Mikey Hemkens, Ryan Huffman, and Colin Doran (DePauw University)
Greg Bernardi (Sonoma State University)

Faculty Evaluators:
Mickey Huff (Diablo Valley College)
Andrea Sununu and Kevin Howley (DePauw University)
Rick Luttmann and Peter Phillips (Sonoma State University)

Several contentious issues still plague the US government and their version of the events of September 11, 2001. Those in political power along with media elites would like to see the ongoing grassroots debates surrounding unanswered 9/11 questions and discrepancies disappear, despite the mountains of evidence that suggest that American citizens were told little about the truth of the biggest single-day attack on their homeland in history. Nearly ten years after the events, many unanswered questions still exist: How did Building 7 fall? What caused the destruction of the twin towers? Where is Osama bin Laden? Are people that question the official story of 9/11 dangerous conspiracy theorists?

The academics and intellectuals who have tried to answer these questions have been ignored or derided by corporate mainstream (and even some progressive leftist) media, political pundits, and government officials who clearly intend to silence the so-called 9/11 Truth Movement, or anyone who questions the officially sanctioned government stance on the matter. However, the questions will not go away and increasingly beg for answers.

As of spring 2010, over 1,200 architects and engineers are calling for a new investigation into the events of 9/11. These building professionals and academics are motivated by the fact that the 9/11 Commission Report has been proven erroneous on multiple counts, scientific explanations have been flawed and contradictory, and the American people deserve a more fact-based explanation.

At the same time, new evidence of explosives that can be used in controlled demolition has been found in the dust traces of the World Trade Center (WTC) towers and Building 7 of the WTC complex. After careful examination of the official story about 9/11 (in which the commission never even mentioned Building 7), along with the forensic data omitted from official reports, these professionals have concluded that a new independent and transparent investigation into these massive and mysterious structural failures is needed.

Richard Gage, a San Francisco–based architect and founder of Architects & Engineers for 9/11 Truth, states, "The official Federal Emergency Management Agency (FEMA) and National Institute of Standards and Technologies (NIST) reports provide insufficient and fraudulent accounts of the circumstances of the towers' destruction." Gage, along with other architects and engineers, attacked NIST's first reports such that NIST eventually changed their conclusions, addressed new evidence, and released a new draft report in 2008. In the thirty days after the 2008 draft report was released, NIST took public questions on the report. Gage's group sent a letter that covered myriad inconsistencies and omissions in the 2008 report. However, the final report released later in 2008 addressed almost none of the concerns raised. The scientific method was not adhered to in this study.

Gage and Architects & Engineers for 9/11 Truth's actions pushed NIST to recognize that Building 7, a forty-seven-story skyscraper that was *not* hit by an aircraft, did come down at free fall acceleration for more than one hundred feet. An explanation as to how or why it fell at free fall speed was not provided by NIST. NIST continues to state that looking at the thermitic materials found at Ground Zero noted in the demolition theory "would not necessarily have been conclusive." Despite their own claim that evidence of demolition is inconclusive, they decided not to test or address it at all, as if this could not and/or did not happen (see chapter 7 of this book for more details). Again, the scientific method was not fully followed by government agencies.

In other 9/11 related matters, there is the ongoing mystery regarding the whereabouts of the alleged perpetrator, Osama bin Laden. Even though bin Laden did not take credit for the incident (he in fact claimed the contrary, nor is the Federal Bureau of Investigation (FBI) holding him as a suspect in those crimes due to lack of evidence) government officials of both parties regularly refer to bin Laden as the one responsible for the 9/11 attacks (see story #16 in *Censored 2008*).

Furthermore, Dr. David Ray Griffin, a former professor at California's Claremont School of Theology and author of numerous books on 9/11 issues, suggests that Osama bin Laden has been dead for nearly nine years. He argues that bin Laden died on December 13, 2001, of kidney failure or a kidney-related illness. There are records of bin Laden being treated in an American hospital in Dubai for a urinary infection, often linked with kidney disease, and a related order for a mobile dialysis machine, essential to his survival, that was shipped to Afghanistan. Griffin, along with doctors that he cites, says it would be impossible for bin Laden to survive in a cave with that machine for any substantial period of time. Griffin goes on to note that the US and British governments are aware of bin Laden's death, and have been covering it up to continue the war on terror. (See Griffin's book on the subject, *Osama bin Laden: Dead or Alive?*).

In other ongoing tension concerning 9/11 on the home front, President Obama's appointee to head the Office of Information and Regulatory Affairs (OIRA), Harvard law professor Cass Sunstein, claims that the United States government should infiltrate and discredit activist groups.

Sunstein's call to discredit groups includes those who challenge the official views of the 9/11 attacks, the so-called 9/11 'truthers.' Sunstein acknowledges that the US government has been involved in conspiracies in the past, but he confidently believes that this is no longer a problem. (See the Truth Emergency section of this volume for more on this issue, especially chapter 6.) He claims that groups that question the events of 9/11 are dangerous and could lead some people to violence (while presenting no concrete evidence to prove this).

Sunstein maintains that refuting these groups in public is not productive. He suggests that the most effective method of refute is to infiltrate and cogitatively discredit their internal sources. Sunstein is essentially calling for a return of the Counter Intelligence Program (COINTELPRO) from the cold war days when agents of the US government covertly infiltrated antiwar and civil rights groups with the intent to disrupt and discredit their activities—provoking violence or planning illegal acts themselves in order to bring groups up on criminal charges.

Sunstein's call for infiltration of private citizen groups plays to the very concerns of many 9/11 activists—concerns that they may be targeted or infiltrated, tried on some trumped up terrorist or criminal charges, and then may not get a fair public hearing. (For more on this, see story #6 in *Censored 2009*, and story #20 in *Censored 2008*.)

Such a climate of fear and intimidation does not bode well for First Amendment rights, nor for academic freedom in the US, let alone the possibility of discovering the truth about what really happened on September 11.

Update by Shawn Hamilton

Over one thousand architects and engineers have signed a petition to reinvestigate the 9/11 destruction.

When I went to San Francisco to cover the Architects and Engineers for 9/11 Truth (AE911Truth) press conference, I didn't tell the news department with which I am most closely allied; I was afraid I'd be told not to do the story. This may not surprise anyone considering mainstream media's deafening silence on 9/11 issues, but this wasn't an organ of mainstream media; it was an alternative radio station founded on principles that encourage coverage of underreported stories. To be fair, no news director said I *couldn't* cover the story, and the story ran that weekend. The point is that I had felt constrained by the prevailing atmosphere of suspicion and fear surrounding media reception of 9/11 topics generally—including at this "progressive" station where people are sharply divided on the issue. I've never seen such general weirdness surrounding media coverage of an issue except for the Kennedy assassination. In the 1970s people mocked those few who suggested Lee Harvey Oswald didn't act alone, branding them "conspiracy nuts," just as 9/11 activists now are labeled "truthers," which sounds like "flat earthers." Some of these activists have embraced the "truther" tag, but I suggest they should refrain. The term is not meant to be a compliment.

I asked theologian David Ray Griffin, who spoke at the conference, why he thought the media was acting so bizarrely towards 9/11 issues. Griffin pointed out how the terms "conspiracy theory" and "conspiracy theorist" are manipulated to make reporters fear losing their reputations and jobs. "You know how it works. Everybody in the media knows how it works," he said. "Nobody has to be explicitly threatened; they just know the rules."

The press conference was a newsworthy story whether or not anything the group claims is true. It's a valid story because so many citizens are questioning the official explanations for the tragedy of September 11, 2001. The fact that over a thousand licensed architects and engineers are demanding a new investigation increases that relevance. If what they say is even partly true, the implications are profound, but either way, there's a legitimate story. I don't expect news agencies to endorse the views of groups like AE911Truth; that's not their proper role. I do expect them not to run for cover when they hear those unsettling words: "9/11." Democracy is not served by reporters fearing to cover sensitive stories.

As of summer 2010, AE911Truth (ae911truth.org) has gotten more than 1,200 building professionals to sign its petition to Congress demanding a truly independent investigation, and a new group has formed called Firefighters for 9-11 Truth (firefightersfor911truth.org) that challenges official reports and public misconceptions of what occurred on September 11. A group called New York City Coalition for Accountability Now (nyccan.org) is attempting to convince the New York City Council to investigate the anomalous circumstances surrounding the collapse of World Trade Center Building 7 (ae911truth.org/index.php/news/41-articles/286-nyccan-ae911truth-ask-ny-city-council.html). All the Web sites I've mentioned have links to some of the more credible 9/11 Web sites. The AE911Truth links page is a good place to start. I will be following related issues on this Web site as well: examiner.com/x-36199-Conspiracy-Examiner. My email address is lesseroftwoevils@rocketmail.com.

Update by Daniel Tencer

In May 2010, the *New York Times Magazine* ran a comprehensive profile of Cass Sunstein, the first such profile to be found in the mainstream media since the law professor took over as head of the White House's Office of Information and Regulatory Affairs (OIRA). The article's title— "Cass Sunstein Wants to Nudge Us"—is an understatement given the views Sunstein has expressed over the years, but it at least heads in the right thematic direction: that much of Sunstein's academic writing has been focused on social control and government control over information.

Not surprisingly, the article treated Sunstein with kid gloves and largely glossed over the more controversial elements of his ideas. It focused on him as one of the leading proponents of the concept of "libertarian paternalism," a burgeoning new field of study that blends behavioral psychology with free-market economics and posits that people can be "nudged" into making the right choices (i.e., the government's desired choices) not by laws and regulations, but by making the "right" choice seem more psychologically appealing.

Writing at the *Huffington Post*, Russ Baker criticized the *New York Times* for "burying" Sunstein's more controversial assertions thirty-five paragraphs into the story, where we are finally told that he advocated for the "cognitive infiltration" of conspiracy theory groups. The *Times* then quotes Sunstein suggesting that, as a government official, he would not execute the more radical or experimental elements of his academic ideas. But, as Baker points out, that comment was made in the fall of 2009—before Sunstein's paper on conspiracy theories came to light in the media. What appears in the *Times* to be Sunstein backing off his more controversial ideas is, in actuality, no such thing.

Understanding Cass Sunstein and his effect on government and society is made difficult by two things. The first is that he is a political chimera who has supporters and detractors on both sides of the political spectrum. Among conservative critics, the populists have come out against him, while the intellectuals appear to have thrown their weight behind him. Even as Glenn Beck declared Sunstein to be "more powerful than the Fed" and desirous of "controlling your every move," columnist George F. Will declared that his ideas would lead to better, smaller government and would "have the additional virtue of annoying those busybody, nanny-state liberals." In the UK, Sunstein's works are "required reading for aspiring Conservative MPs," reports the *Daily Telegraph*.

The second element making it difficult to understand Sunstein is that his position inside the government deals primarily with dry, bureaucratic issues that fail to capture the imaginations of either the mainstream press or the alternative media. As head of OIRA, Sunstein is responsible for reviewing all new government regulations. Yet thus far his decisions—those that we know of—have been on a small scale and largely technical, such as his call to streamline the process of naming and writing regulations so that citizens have better access to them.

Sunstein did, however, manage to anger environmentalists recently when he blocked a new Environmental Protection Agency (EPA) regulation that would list coal ash as a dangerous carcinogen. Environmentalists accused him of caving to the coal industry, which doesn't want to see its coal ash disposal costs rise under the new rule.

So where is Sunstein headed? Is he likely to attempt the sort of information control programs that he has advocated in the past? Even if he does, it's likely the mainstream media will support at least some of his efforts to push the political debate towards an "acceptable" center. In a 2009 *New Yorker* review of his book *On Rumors*, Sunstein is given credit for predicting the circumstances that would lead to the rise of Internet rumors such as the "birther" claim that President Obama wasn't born in the US, and the "death panel" allegation about health care reform. He is then cast as the hero fighting against these trends. Given the existing precedent, it's likely that any attempt Sunstein makes at shaping the content of public information will likely find a positive hearing in the old guard media.

15

Bhopal Water Still Toxic Twenty-five Years After Deadly Gas Leak

Sources:
Randeep Ramesh, "Bhopal Water Still Toxic 25 Years After Deadly Gas Leak, Study Finds," *Guardian*, December 1, 2009, http://www.guardian.co.uk/world/2009/dec/01/bhopal-chemical-studies-toxic-levels.

Randeep Ramesh, "Bhopal Marks 25th Anniversary of Union Carbide Gas Disaster," *Guardian*, December 3, 2009, http://www.guardian.co.uk/world/2009/dec/03/bhopal-anniversary-union-carbide-gas#history-link-box.

Indra Sinha, "Bhopal: 25 Years of Poison," *Guardian*, December 3, 2009, http://www.guardian.co.uk/world/2009/dec/03/bhopal-anniversary-union-carbide-gas#history-link-box.

George Monbiot, "Bhopal Being Poisoned All Over Again," *Guardian*, September 28, 2009, http://www.guardian.co.uk/environment/georgemonbiot/2009/sep/27/bhopal-poison.

"Indian Court Issues Arrest Warrant for Warren Anderson, the Former Head of Union Carbide, in Bhopal Gas Leak Case," *Guardian*, July 31, 2009, http://www.guardian.co.uk/world/2009/jul/31/warren-anderson-arrest-warrant.

"Bhopal 1984 Until Today," Bhopal Medical Appeal, December 1, 2009, http://www.bhopal.org/index.php?id=155.

"'That Night,'" Bhopal Medical Appeal, December 1, 2009, http://www.bhopal.org/index.php?id=30.

"Bhopal's Secret Disaster," Bhopal Medical Appeal, December 1, 2009, http://www.bhopal.org/index.php?id=29.

"Health Issues," Bhopal Medical Appeal, December 1, 2009, http://www.bhopal.org/index.php?id=100.

"Poisoned Water," Bhopal Medical Appeal, December 1, 2009,
http://www.bhopal.org/index.php?id=111.

Student Researchers:
Abbey Wilson and Jillian Harbin (DePauw University)

Faculty Evaluators:
Tim Cope and Kevin Howley (DePauw University)

Around midnight on December 2, 1984, the citizens of Bhopal, India, a city of over 500,000 people in central India, were poisoned by approximately forty tons of toxic gases pouring into the night air from a largely abandoned chemical insecticide plant owned by the US-owned Union Carbide Corporation (UCC). The long-predicted gas leak at UCC was, and remains today, the worst industrial disaster in history.

Released by faulty and neglected equipment, methyl isocyanate, phosgene and other highly toxic gases killed an estimated 8,000 people immediately. The death toll attributed to "that night" in the following weeks and months eventually rose to 20,000 people. Hundreds of thousands of others were harmed, in many cases permanently, with lung, liver, kidney, and immune system damages, and blindness. The Indian Council of Medical Research (ICMR) concluded that over 520,000 exposed persons had poisons circulating in their bloodstream causing different degrees of damage to almost all systems in the body.

The 1984 disaster may have faded in the world's memory, but in Bhopal, the damaged births continue today. The very same factory that spewed out poison gas has been leaking deadly chemicals into the drinking water of about 30,000 people. In affected communities, there are epidemics of kidney disease and cancer, with hundreds of damaged children.

Indra Sinha, a Booker Prize nominee for his book on the Bhopal disaster, *Animal's People*, explained why the gas leak that killed 20,000 people twenty-five years ago—and continues to create health problems for countless more—is still a national scandal: "After the night of horror, the factory was locked up. Thousands of tons of pesticides and waste remained inside. UCC never bothered to clean it. The chemicals were abandoned in warehouses open to wind and rain. Twenty-four monsoons have rusted and rotted the death factory. The rains wash the poisons deep into the soil. They enter the groundwater and seep into wells and bore pipes. They gush from taps and enter people's bodies. They burn stomachs, corrode skin, damage organs and flow into wombs where they go to work on the unborn. If babies make it into the world alive, the poisons are waiting in their mothers' milk."

A Greenpeace survey found substantial and, in some locations, severe contamination of land and water supplies with heavy metals and chlorinated chemicals. From their samples, groundwater from wells around the site showed high levels of chlorinated chemicals including chloroform and carbon tetrachloride, indicative of long-term contamination. Additionally, lead, nickel, copper, chromium, hexachlorocyclohexane, and chlorobenzenes were found in soil samples. Overall contamination of the site and immediate surroundings is due both to routine spills and accidents during the operation of the factory, and to the continued releases of chemicals from the toxic wastes that remain on site.

According to New Delhi's Centre for Science and the Environment, water found two miles from the factory contains pesticides at levels forty times higher than the Indian safety standard. In a second study, the UK-based Bhopal Medical Appeal (BMA) found a chemical cocktail in the local drinking water—with one carcinogen, carbon tetrafluoride, present at 2,400 times the World Health Organization's guidelines.

Union Carbide Corporation—now the Dow Chemical Company (Dow), following a February 2001 merger—continues to claim over sixty years of research (including research on human "volunteers") on methyl isocyanate (the gas that leaked from the Bhopal pesticide plant) as "trade secrets." There is more than enough research to suggest that by withholding information, propagating misinformation and the withdrawal of funds meant for medical care, Dow–UCC has impeded the efforts of the victims to help themselves. The ICMR has in turn stopped all research into the health effects of the gas in 1994 and has yet to publish the findings of the twenty-four research studies it had carried out up to that point involving over 80,000 survivors. The alarming rise in cancers, tuberculosis, reproductive difficulties, and growth retardation among children born after the disaster remains undocumented. The official agency for monitoring deaths has been closed since 1992.

The local, BMA-funded Sambhavna clinic claims that one in twenty-five—a rate ten times higher than the national average—are born with severe birth defects including lameness and twisted or missing limbs, deaf-mute, brain-damage, hare-lips and cleft palates, webbed fingers, cerebral palsy, and tumors where eyes should be. Multiple generations are now affected; one victim, Mohini Devi, claims her children and grandchildren have experienced birth defects. "My real worry is my grandchildren. Already some have been born without eyes. Why is nobody doing anything for us?" she said.

In the absence of medical information, no treatment protocols specific to exposure-induced multi-systemic problems exist. Instead, in many places, ineffective and sometimes kidney-damaging drugs are prescribed to the thousands seeking relief and medical treatment. One exception is the Sambhavna Clinic, which in 1996 began offering survivors a combination of free modern medicine, ayurvedic herbal treatments, yoga, and massage.

While today tons of poisonous pesticides and other hazardous wastes remain scattered and abandoned on the Dow–UCC factory premises, insidiously poisoning the ground water and contaminating the land, the company and its former CEO Warren Anderson have distanced themselves from the "Indian-managed company," eventually blaming employee sabotage. As a result, the disaster has done little to affect Dow–UCC. In February 1989, after forcing a paltry compensation settlement—$470 million as opposed to $3 billion demanded by the government of India—UCC's share price jumped 44 cents and they went back to business as usual. Survivors in Bhopal received meager compensation. Most of them got a 25,000-rupee check (about US$500) for a lifetime of suffering caused by damage to their lungs, liver, kidneys, and the immune system.

Given the hundreds of thousands of victims dead and injured, the settlement worked out to less than 9 cents a day—only enough for one cup of tea each day—for nearly twenty years of unimaginable suffering. None of the thousands since born with gas-related congenital defects or illnesses from current water contamination have received help. When Dow acquired UCC, it denied further responsibility for the disaster. A Dow public relations official maintained that the settlement was "plenty good for an Indian."

Union Carbide Corporation and Warren Anderson, then CEO of UCC, were charged with culpable homicide or manslaughter and proclaimed absconders by the Bhopal Court in 1992, after failing repeatedly to honor the summons of the court. Warren Anderson was arrested briefly in 1984 and then fled the country. Anderson's whereabouts were considered unknown despite the fact that his residences, one in the Hamptons, an upscale New York suburb, are publicly listed. Neither the Indian government nor the US government is willing to support the warrants for Anderson's arrest or Dow–UCC's responsibilities. In fact,

Indian campaigners working to hold UCC responsible for its actions claim that their government has called the now-closed factory "safe" and "open for the public to tour." The Bhopal government also allegedly neglected to work toward any sort of allegations against UCC, and simply left the plant to continue leaking chemicals.

Now, Satinath Sarangi, of the Sambhavna clinic in Bhopal, says the government is working to strike a contract with Dow, which would yield a $1 billion investment, and would allegedly allow Union Carbide to overlook its obligations to clean up their spill. "This is all about the money. Politicians in India would rather do this than fight for people who suffered," Sarangi said.

16

US Presidents Charged with Crimes Against Humanity as Universal Jurisdiction Dies in Spain

Sources:

Glen Ford, "Four U.S. Presidents and Four UK Prime Ministers Charged With Genocide," *Black Agenda Report*, October 13, 2009, http://www.blackagendareport.com/?q=content/four-us-presidents-and-four-uk-prime-ministers-charged-genocide.

"Justice for Iraq: Legal Case Filed U.S. Presidents and UK Prime Ministers," *Brussels Tribune*, October 7, 2009, http://axisoflogic.com/artman/publish/printer_57154.shtml.

Center for Constitutional Rights, "CCR Seeks to Intervene in Spanish Court's Investigations into Bush Administration's Torture Program," press release, April 27, 2010, http://ccrjustice.org/newsroom/press-releases/ccr-seeks-intervene-spanish-court%E2%80%99s-investigations-bush-administration%E2%80%99s-tor.

Student Researcher:
Crystal Schreiner (Sonoma State University)

Faculty Evaluator:
Mickey Huff (Diablo Valley College)

In October 2009, under great pressure from the United States, the government of Spain decided to limit its own jurisdiction in cases of genocide and crimes against humanity, thus closing one of the last windows of accountability for the most serious crimes committed by the most powerful nations on Earth. Under international law, such crimes fall under the universal jurisdiction of any nation, whether one's own citizens are victims or not. The logic is that crimes against humanity are offenses against every member of the human species—a crime against all.

Spain had been a venue for bringing high crimes charges against human rights violators in Guatemala, Argentina, China, Israel, and elsewhere. Most of the lawsuits have been against individuals linked to the untouchable political right, such as Chile's Augusto Pinochet, the Argentine military officer Adolfo Scilingo, former US secretary of state Henry Kissinger, Italian prime minister Silvio Berlusconi, former Israeli prime minister Ariel Sharon and six of his senior advisors, and most recently, former George W. Bush administration officials.

Calls to reign in the judges increased when Spanish magistrates announced probes involving Israel and the United States.

In January 2009, Spanish National Court Judge Fernando Andreu announced he would investigate seven current or former Israeli officials over a 2002 air attack in Gaza that killed a top member of Hamas and fourteen other people. In March 2009, Baltasar Garzón, Spain's most high-profile judge, invoked the principle of universal jurisdiction when he sought to investigate six former Bush administration officials for giving legal cover to torture in the American prison at Guantánamo Bay, Cuba. And in May 2009, another Spanish high-court judge, Santiago Pedraz, declared he would charge three US soldiers with crimes against humanity for the April 2003 deaths of a Spanish television cameraman and a Ukrainian journalist. The men were killed when a US tank crew shelled their Baghdad hotel.

Activist judges like Garzón, Andreu, and Pedraz have created a big diplomatic headache for the Zapatero government. China has warned Spain that bilateral relations could be damaged over a case regarding Tibet, and Israel's Prime Minister Benjamin Netanyahu has told Spain that it risks being sidelined in the Middle East peace process.

But the Spanish government is most worried about the negative impact the Guantánamo probe may have on relations with the United States. Zapatero has raised expectations of Spanish voters with the promise he can forge warm ties to the Obama administration. Indeed, other European leaders have distanced themselves from the Spanish position, fearful of jeopardizing future relations with Washington.

Reporter Glen Ford noted that the world's biggest potential defendant for war crimes and crimes against humanity is the United States, whose record of direct and indirect involvement in torture and mass killings has been unmatched by any other nation since at least World War II. It was primarily US pressure that forced Spain to close off its courts from international jurisdiction cases.

A motion separate from Judge Garzón's was filed on April 27, 2010, by the New York–based Center for Constitutional Rights (CCR), which is seeking to intervene as a party in the criminal investigation currently pending into the US torture program in Guantánamo. The investigation focuses on the torture and abuse of four former Guantánamo detainees with strong ties to Spain. CCR determines that, because of the nature of the alleged crimes and Spain's obligations as a signatory to the Geneva Conventions, the Convention Against Torture in particular, Spain should retain jurisdiction over this case.

"For eight long years we have fought to redress the brutal, inhumane and illegal acts perpetrated against our clients but have been blocked at every turn by both the Bush and Obama administrations," said CCR President Michael Ratner, who filed the first habeas corpus petition brought on behalf of a Guantánamo detainee in 2002. "We come to Spain in pursuit of nothing less than justice, which, sadly, is not available in the United States."

One day before the change in Spanish law, a number of members of the B *Russells* Tribunal, acting under the umbrella of the International Initiative to Prosecute US Genocide in Iraq, filed charges of crimes against humanity and genocide against four presidents of the United States and four prime ministers of Great Britain. The charges cite 1.5 million Iraqi deaths over the course of nineteen years of American and British attacks, including two full-scale wars of aggression, the "most draconian sanctions regime ever designed," and subsequent occupation of Iraq. Half a million of the dead, according to the charges, were children.

In parallel, Iraq's rich heritage and unique cultural and archaeological patrimony has been wantonly destroyed. In order to render Iraq dependent on US and UK strategic designs, successive US and UK governments have attempted to partition Iraq and to establish by military force a pro-occupation Iraqi government and political system. They have promoted and engaged in the massive plunder of Iraqi natural resources, attempting to privatize the property and wealth of the Iraqi nation. So massive and systematic were the assaults on Iraq, stretching for roughly a generation, the accusers charge the US and the UK with the deliberate destruction of a nation.

The defendants are George Herbert Walker Bush, William J. Clinton, George W. Bush, Barack Hussein Obama, Margaret Thatcher, John Major, Anthony Blair, and Gordon Brown. The suit holds that each has played a key role in Iraq's intended destruction—that they instigated, supported, condoned, rationalized, executed and/or perpetuated, or excused this destruction based on lies and narrow strategic and economic interests, and against the will of their own people. The B*Russels* Tribunal asserts that allowing those responsible to escape accountability means such actions could be repeated elsewhere.

The global clearinghouse for war crimes, crimes against humanity, and genocide is the International Criminal Court. However Ford notes that in recent years that court has prosecuted no one but Africans and is increasingly exposed as a tool of Western hegemony. The United States refuses to join the International Criminal Court, and thus claims immunity from prosecution.

Update by Glen Ford

Lawless United States has been offered a job as International Court enforcer. The impunity with which the United States and Britain caused the deaths of 1.5 million Iraqis and the displacement of 4.7 million more during two decades of uninterrupted aggression (1990 to present), is eclipsed in scale of slaughter by the genocide in the eastern Democratic Republic of Congo (DRC). An estimated 6 million Congolese have died since the main US proxies in the region, Uganda's dictator Yoweri Museveni and Rwanda's ruling Tutsi military, poured across the DRC's borders in pursuit of approximately 1 million Rwandan Hutus displaced in the 1994 Rwandan civil war, including the defeated Hutu militia.

Ugandan and Rwandan military commanders quickly established control over mining operations in the mineral-rich region, providing raw materials to US- and Europe-based extraction corporations—a mutually profitable business relationship that thrives in an environment of terror and massacre. Despite the fact that their activities in eastern Congo have resulted in a holocaust equal to that under the Nazis, Rwanda and Uganda enjoy impunity as Washington's most loyal clients in Black Africa. US corporate media, led by their collective noses by the US State Department, find *genocidaires* lurking everywhere in Africa *except* among the US proxies in Kampala and Kigali.

Having failed to prosecute anyone but Africans since its creation in 2002, the International Criminal Court (ICC) now actively woos the US, the world's most prolific perpetrator and sponsor of war crimes, crimes against humanity, and genocide, as global enforcer of ICC indictments. The US refuses to join the ICC, for fear it might be prosecuted for its own crimes (only the 111 nations that have ratified the treaty fall under its jurisdiction). Yet ICC chief prosecutor Luis Moreno-Ocampo openly lobbies for the US to head up a "coalition of the willing" to deploy "special forces" as the enforcement arm of the Hague-based court.

Moreno-Ocampo apparently believes the global quest for justice would be empowered by access to the "rare and expensive capabilities" of the world's most active war-maker, as reported by scholar-journalists Adam Branch and Samar Al-Bulushi in the African journal *Pambazuka*. The US also sees no contradiction in acting as enforcer of international laws it neither respects nor recognizes as binding. Stephen Rapp, US ambassador at large for war crimes, said Washington "can support this court constructively when it works in our interest. And so far in the cases it is taking on, they are in our interests and in the interest of all of humankind."

The US was the center of attention, although officially only an observer, at the ICC's latest conference (May 31–June 11) in Kamala, Uganda. "It's hard to emphasize how happy countries are to see us here," said State Department legal adviser Harold Koh. "They felt very distressed at the period of US hostility to the court." Washington remains, of course, unalterably opposed to any limits on its superpower prerogatives, but welcomes Moreno-Ocampo's invitation to enforce the ICC's highly selective indictments.

The world's biggest bully—a nation that proudly proclaims that the law ends where its own interests begin—is being offered the marshal's badge. Justice cannot possibly be served.

Update by Ad Hoc Committee For Justice For Iraq

In October 2009, we filed in Madrid—on behalf of Iraqi victims—a legal case against four US presidents and four UK prime ministers under laws of universal jurisdiction for war crimes, crimes against humanity, and genocide in Iraq. Our case spans nineteen years, including thirteen years of sanctions proven to have an overwhelmingly destructive impact on Iraqi public health, and the launching of an illegal war of aggression against Iraq based on deliberate falsification and systematic efforts to hide from the general public, in the US, the UK, and elsewhere, the true objectives of the war. Sanctions led to an estimated 1.5 million excess Iraqi deaths, including 500,000 children under five. To date, estimates of violent deaths among Iraqis post-2003 run to 1.2 million. Some 5 million Iraqis have been displaced inside and outside the country—a fifth of the entire population.

Despite the enormity of the crimes, the high profile of those accused, and a full press campaign on the case, the filing got zero publicity in the mainstream English-speaking media. In Spain, it was reported once in the margins. Only the alternative media carried our press releases, and only those who listen to alternative media heard of the case. The mainstream continued to propagate the lie—supposedly a criticism—that the US-led foray into Iraq was a blunder. But it was not a blunder. Nor did the US wander blind into a quagmire. Our case charts the synchronicity of crimes committed—including the destruction of civil infrastructure, indiscriminate bombing and use of depleted uranium, and promotion of sectarianism and corruption, destruction of state institutions, urbicide, plunder, promotion of torture—all leading to, and resulting in, the intended destruction of the Iraqi state and nation. The humanitarian disaster that is present-day Iraq was an end in itself. This is what the mainstream media cannot say and conceals.

We knew when we filed our case that public pressure would be instrumental. Based on years of research and analysis, our case was filed one day before the Spanish Senate voted, under external pressure, to radically circumscribe the practice of universal jurisdiction in Spain. The silence of the mainstream media surely contributed to the result. The new law, imposed retroactively, led to the closing of our case and others. Though Spanish courts had been open to hearing human rights grievances from those unable to find redress in their own countries or by other means, and though Spain had been taking a lead role in efforts to address impunity in international affairs, that window closed, virtually without comment. In real terms, our case was censored. But not only our case that was censored: in effect, Iraq, too, has been censored.

How important is this failure of the mainstream media? The war on Iraq is not only an attack on a sovereign country, it is a frontal attack on international law. If the destruction of Iraq goes unaccounted for, what is happening to Iraq could happen anywhere. Thus we remain committed to working toward the prosecution of crimes in Iraq perpetrated by the US and the UK. Though Spain had been the clearest route for legal redress, new routes can be opened. Just as we look for allies in this work, we are ready to assist similar initiatives taken up by others.

For more information, visit www.USgenocide.org.

17

Nanotech Particles Pose Serious DNA Risks to Humans and the Environment

Sources:

Carole Bass, "Tiny Troubles: Nanoparticles are Changing Everything From our Sunscreen to our Supplements," *E Magazine*, July/August 2009, http://www.emagazine .com/view/?4723.

Janet Raloff, "Nanoparticles' Indirect Threat to DNA," *Science News*, November 5, 2009,http://www.sciencenews.org/view/generic/id/49191/title/Science_%2B_the _Public__Nanoparticles_indirect_threat_to_DNA.

L. Geranio, M. Heuberger, and B. Nowack, "The Behavior of Silver Nanotextiles During Washing," *Environmental Science & Technology*, September 24, 2009, http://pubs.acs .org/doi/abs/10.1021/es9018332.

Paul Eugib, DVM, and Wendy Hessler, "Silver Migrates From Treated Fabrics," *Environmental Health News*, January 7, 2010, http://www.environmentalhealthnews .org/ehs/newscience/silver-migrates-from-nanoparticle-treated-fabrics.

David Rejeski, "Nanotech-enabled Consumer Products Top the 1,000 Mark," *Project on Emerging Nanotechnologies*, August 25, 2009, http://www.nanotechproject.org/ news/archive/8277.

Y. Song, X. Li, and X. Du, "Exposure to Nanoparticles Is Related to Pleural Effusion, Pulmonary Fibrosis and Granuloma," *European Respiratory Journal*, August, 20, 2009, http://www.erj.ersjournals.com/cgi/content/abstract/34/3/559.

Science Daily Staff, "Health Risks of Nanotechnology: How Nanoparticles Can Cause Lung Damage, and How the Damage Can Be Blocked," *Science Daily*, June 11, 2009, http://www.sciencedaily.com/releases/2009/06/090610192431.htm.

Science and Technology Committee, "Nanotechnologies and Food, House of Lords Media Notice," January 8, 2010, http://www.parliament.uk/parliamentary_committees/ lords_press_notices/pn080110st.cfm.

Ian Sample, "Attack of the Tiny Nano Particles—Be Slightly Afraid," Organic Consumers Association, November 15, 2008, http://www.organicconsumers.org/ articles/article_15621.cfm.

George John, "Silver Nanoparticles Deadly to Bacteria," Physorg.com, March 10, 2008, http://physorg.com/print124376552.html.

Nanowerk Spotlight, "Problematic New Findings Regarding Toxicity of Silver Nanoparticles," Nanowerk.com, June 6, 2008, http://www.nanowerk.com/ spotlight/spotid=5966.php.

R. J. Aitken et al., "Nanoparticles: An Occupational Hygiene Review," Institute of Occupational Medicine, Health and Safety Executive (Edinburgh), 2004, http://www.hse.gov.uk/research/rrhtm/rr274.htm (accessed November 2006).

Student Researchers:
Jody Lempa, Tina Shaerban, Katherine Tellez, and Jillian Wolande (DePaul University)

Faculty Evaluator:
Marla Donato (DePaul University)

Personal products you may use daily and think are harmless—cosmetics, suntan lotion, socks, and sports clothes—may all contain atom-sized nanotech particles, some of which have been shown to sicken and kill workers in plants using nanotechnology. Known human health risks include severe and permanent lung damage. Cell studies indicate genetic DNA damage. Extremely toxic to aquatic wildlife, nanoparticles pose clear risks to many species and threaten the global food chain.

Nanotech particles have been embraced by industry as the wonder ingredient in personal hygiene products, food packaging, paints, medical procedures and pharmaceuticals, even tires and auto parts, among burgeoning numbers of other consumer products. Cosmetic companies add titanium dioxide nanoparticles to sun creams to make them transparent on the skin. Sports clothing firms have introduced odor-free garments containing nanosilver particles that are twice as toxic to bacteria than bleach. Auto industry companies have added carbon nanofibers to tires and body panels to strengthen them.

According to the Project on Emerging Nanotechnologies (PEN), health and fitness items continue to dominate available nanotech products, representing 60 percent of products listed. More products are based on nanoscale silver—used for its antimicrobial properties—than any other nanomaterial; 259 products (26 percent) use silver nanoparticles. PEN's updated inventory represents products from over twenty-four countries, including the US, China, Canada, and Germany.

Yet, nanomaterials are so poorly understood that scientists are unable to predict how they will behave and are unsure of how to check their safety. Over one thousand consumer products made with nanoparticles, which can be one hundred times smaller than a virus, are already on the market, despite an almost complete lack of knowledge of the dangers they pose to human health and the environment. And while these atomic-sized particles may be beneficial in certain medical applications, scientists and environmentalists are calling for more studies. Until now, few adverse effects have been found for this virtually unregulated technology. Yet, that may simply be due to the relatively few studies that have been done in the rush to find ever more and profitable nanotech applications.

Nanotechnology, the science of the extremely tiny, is an important emerging industry with a projected annual market of around one trillion dollars by 2015. It involves manipulating or building new materials from atoms and molecules; silver and carbon are now the most important building blocks.

The nanomaterials are far smaller than a human hair and can only be seen with powerful microscopes. A nanometer is a billionth of a meter, while a human hair is about eighty thousand nanometers wide. An atom is roughly one-third of a nanometer across, and nanoparticles are groups of atoms that are typically smaller than one hundred nanometers. The tiny-sized materials often have unique properties that differ from the properties of their larger scaled versions. Nanoparticles lend their success to the extraordinary, and sometimes highly unusual, properties they have. For example, tennis rackets made with carbon nanotubes are incredibly strong, while the larger pieces of graphite easily shear apart. The medical industry is investing heavily in nanoparticles to create precision drugs that can target specific tissues, such as cancer cells. While some of these new materials may have beneficial applications in medical procedures, wound dressings, and pharmaceuticals, concerns are growing that they may have toxic effects. In particular, nanoparticles have been linked to lung and genetic damage.

In a new British study, researchers discovered an unforeseen process, dubbed "toxic gossip," by which metal nanoparticles inflict genetic damage to DNA, even through walls of tissue that were not physically breached. Researchers called the finding "a huge surprise," particularly since the billionth-of-a-meter-scale particles appear to have wreaked their havoc indirectly.

Now, for the first time, a scientific study has established a clear and causal relationship between human contact with nanoparticles and serious health damage. According to an article published in the *European Respiratory Journal* by a group of Chinese researchers headed by Yuguo Song, from the Department of Occupational Medicine and Clinical Toxicology at the Beijing Chaoyang Hospital, seven young female workers fell seriously ill after working in a paint factory that used nanotechnology. The workers suffered severe and permanent lung damage, and face and arm eruptions. Two of them died, while the other five have not improved after several years.

Around five hundred studies have shown nanotechnology toxicity in animal studies, in human cells, and in the environment. Although

Song's article finds evidence of clinical toxicity in human beings for the first time, according to researcher Silvia Ribeiro, this finding could be only the tip of the iceberg of an extremely risky industry.

Nanoparticles behave unlike lumps of the same materials—stronger, more toxic, and with radically different properties. What makes them so useful also makes their safety so uncertain. Immediate, further research into nanoparticle toxicities and its dissemination is needed. Effects on human health and the environment result from nanoparticles reaching waterways through wastewater treatment and disposal sites, affecting the organisms that live in the water and the people who drink and cook with water.

Three types of nanoparticles are of particular concern: nanosilver particles; carbon nanofibers; and "buckyballs," or microscopic, football-shaped cages of carbon.

Nanosilver is known to be highly toxic to aquatic life. While silver is safer for people than other toxics such as lead and chromium, for aquatic organisms, the story is quite different. Silver is more toxic to many fresh- and salt-water organisms, ranging from phytoplankton (at the bottom of the food chain) to marine invertebrates—such as oysters and snails—to different types of fish, especially in their immature stages. Many species of fish and shellfish, as well as their food, are susceptible; widespread exposure to silver impacts and disrupts ecosystem health. Nanosilver is significantly more toxic than lumps of silver because the tiny particles' huge surface area increases their ability to interact with the environment. Nanosilver has been shown to break down and leach into water systems when, for example, sports garments incorporating silver nanoparticles for odor control are agitated in washing machines. In one study of silver nanoparticles used as antimicrobials in fabrics, of seven nanoparticle fabrics tested, four of them lost 20 percent to 35 percent of their silver in the first wash, and one brand lost half of its silver content in just two washings—all of which drained directly into the environment. Many waterways are just recovering from high levels of silver introduced by the photography industry during the twentieth century. New silver nanoparticle products may result in highly toxic levels of silver being reintroduced into rivers and lakes through water treatment facilities.

Carbon nanofibers, which are added to tires and woven into clothing to produce different colors without using dyes, are also likely to be shed where they can be inhaled and cause lung damage. In a study published in the *Journal of Molecular Cell Biology*, Chinese researchers discovered that a class of nanoparticles being widely developed in medicine—ploy-amidoamine dendrimers (PAMAMs)—cause lung damage by triggering a type of programmed cell death known as autophagic cell death. And finally, carbon-based "buckyballs" have shown to be absorbed by simple organisms, raising concerns that toxicities contaminate the food chain at the most damaging lower levels.

Today, according to PEN, over one thousand nanotechnology-enabled products have been made available to consumers around the world. The most recent update to the group's three-and-a-half-year-old inventory reflects the increasing use of the tiny particles in everything from conventional products like non-stick cookware and lighter, stronger tennis racquets, to more unique items such as wearable sensors that monitor posture.

"The use of nanotechnology in consumer products continues to grow rapidly," says PEN director David Rejeski. "When we launched the inventory in March 2006 we only had 212 products. If the introduction of new products continues at the present rate, the number of products listed in the inventory will reach close to 1,600 within the next two years. This will provide significant oversight challenges for agencies like the Food and Drug Administration and Consumer Product Safety Commission, which often lack any mechanisms to identify nanotech products before they enter the marketplace."

More information on nanotechnology:
www.fda.gov/ScienceResearch/SpecialTopics/Nanotechnology/FrequentlyAskedQuestions/default.htm.

Nanotech products listing:
www.nanotechproject.org/inventories/consumer/browse/products.

Update by Paul Eubig and Wendy Hessler, *Environmental Health News*

We found this story interesting because the research is an initial step toward defining how much consumer products contribute to silver nanoparticles in the environment. Knowing the amount of a chemical entering the environment is a necessary step in estimating the risk the contaminant poses to the environment and to human health. On a larger scale, this story also intrigued us because the questions it raises reflect unanswered concerns about nanotechnology in general.

This story was not widely reported. Short write-ups appeared in the *New York Times* and *Chemical & Engineering News*. *Environmental Health News* reported on an interesting follow-up in *Particle and Fibre Toxicology*, which found that silver nanoparticles are released from nanoparticle-treated fabrics when exposed to artificial human sweat. So a picture is emerging of silver nanoparticles exiting consumer products, exposing humans and entering wastewater to a greater extent than may have been intended. Meanwhile, in articles in *Environmental Health Perspectives* and *Small*, other researchers have demonstrated the adverse effects of silver nanoparticles on developing nerve cells and fish embryos, respectively.

The intent is not to target silver nanoparticles but rather bring attention to a broader topic: the safety of nanotechnology. The great potential of nanotechnology to revolutionize a broad array of fields—including energy production and management, health care, and manufacturing—is gradually being realized.

Yet, nanotechnology also provides great challenges in safety assessment. The composition, size and structure of nanoparticles are some of the numerous factors that influence how they act in the body or in the environment. Additionally, nanoparticles of a particular type, such as silver, do not necessarily act as individual molecules or atoms of the same substance, such as free, ionic silver.

Unfortunately, regulatory agencies have been slow to contend with the rapid emergence of nanotechnology in the workplace and in the home, as well as in the environment in a broader sense, resulting in a dizzying catch-up game in which the applications of nanotechnology continue to multiply while the regulatory playing field has still not been established. Current debate centers on whether existing safety data is sufficient for nanoparticle-containing products, or whether further assessment of the impacts on human and environmental health needs to be performed.

The past century provides numerous examples of chemicals—lead, dichlorodiphenyltrichloroethane (DDT), and polychlorinated biphenyls (PCBs) to name a few—that were considered a great boon initially, but were later shown to have adverse effects on human or environmental health that outweighed their benefits. Our reporting aspires to help society remember the lessons of the past and to exercise caution as it embraces the promise of the future.

Additional Resources:

O. Bar-Ilan et al., "Toxicity Assessments of Multisized Gold and Silver Nanoparticles in Zebrafish Embryos," *Small* 5, no.16 (2009): 1897–1910 [doi:10.1002/smll.200801716], www.environmentalhealthnews.org/ehs/news/nanosilver.

K. Kulthong et al., "Determination of Silver Nanoparticle Release From Antibacterial Fabrics into Artificial Sweat," *Particle and Fibre Toxicology* 7, no. 1 (2010): 8 [doi:10.1186/1743-8977-7-8], http://www.environmentalhealthnews.org/ehs/newscience/fabrics-release-silver-nanoparticles-into-artificial-sweat.

C. M. Powers et al., "Silver Impairs Neurodevelopment: Studies in PC12 Cells," *Environmental Health Perspectives* 118, no. 1 (2009): 73–79 [doi:10.1289/ehp.0901149], http://www.environmentalhealthnews.org/ehs/newscience/silver-is-potent-neurotoxicant.

A. Halperin, "Nanosilver: Do We Know the Risks?" *New Haven Independent*, March 17, 2010, http://newhavenindependent.org/index.php/archives/entry/regulating_nanosilver_a_very_small_puzzle/id_24412.

National Nanotechnology Initiative FAQs: http://www.nano.gov/html/facts/home_facts.html

US Environmental Protection Agency's Fact Sheet for Nanotechnology Under the Toxic Substances Control Act: http://www.epa.gov/oppt/nano/nano-facts.htm

US Environmental Protection Agency's Nanotechnology White Paper, EPA 100/B-07/001 (February 15, 2007): http://www.epa.gov/OSA/nanotech.htm

US Food and Drug Administration's Nanotechnology Web site: http://www.fda.gov/ScienceResearch/SpecialTopics/Nanotechnology/default.htm

Researcher who studies the environmental, health, and safety impacts of nanotechnology: Stacey L. Harper, Oregon State University, 1007 ALS, Corvallis Oregon 97331, (541) 737-2791, stacey.harper@oregonstate.edu

18

The True Cost of Chevron

Source:
Antonia Juhasz, "The True Cost of Chevron: An Alternative Annual Report," True Cost of Chevron, May 27, 2009, http://truecostofchevron.com/report.html.

Student Researcher:
Kelley Zaino (Sonoma State University)

Faculty Evaluators:
Stephanie Dyer and Sascha von Meier (Sonoma State University)

Chevron's 2008 annual report to its shareholders is a glossy celebration heralding the company's most profitable year in its history. Profits of $24 billion catapulted Chevron past General Electric to become the second most profitable corporation in the United States. The oil company's

2007 revenues were larger than the gross domestic product (GDP) of 150 nations.

What Chevron's annual report does not reveal is the true cost paid for those financial returns: lives lost, wars fought, communities destroyed, environments decimated, livelihoods ruined, and political voices silenced. Nor does it describe the global resistance movement gaining voice and strength against these operations.

Thus, the communities, and their allies, who bear the consequences of Chevron's oil and natural gas production, refineries, depots, pipelines, exploration, offshore drilling rigs, coal fields, chemical plants, political control, consumer abuse, false promises, and much more, have prepared an Alternative Annual Report for Chevron.

The alternative account reveals the true impact of just a handful of Chevron's operations in the US in communities across Alaska, California, Colorado, the District of Columbia, Florida, the Gulf Coast, Mississippi, New Jersey, New York, Utah, and Wyoming; and internationally across Angola, Burma, Canada, Chad, Cameroon, Ecuador, Iraq, Kazakhstan, Nigeria, and the Philippines. These accounts are demonstrative, not inclusive. We would need one hundred reports to document all such impacts. These accounts include active lawsuits against the company from around the world, totaling in the tens of billions of dollars, which threaten its vaulted financial gains—for when a company operates in blatant disregard for the health, security, livelihood, safety, and environment of the communities within which it operates, there can be real financial repercussions.

Chevron buys political influence and control at the local and national levels at each of its operational sites, in order to circumvent or trump laws that would protect people and environments from the company's destructive practices.

In California, Chevron is the state's largest corporation and the dominant oil industry force before the state legislature, led by chief lobbyist Jack Coffey, and with the support of the Western States Petroleum Association. As Coffey explained, Chevron's money is spent "to be sure our business opportunities can continue in the way we want them to continue." As one of the major players in what is increasingly recognized as a rogue industry, above any government control, Chevron buys assurances that government representatives will look the other way as the health of communities and environments around the planet are destroyed.

This alternative report shows Chevron's pattern of hiring harsh military "protection" against local residents, evidenced in Iraq, the Niger Delta, Chad, Cameroon, Angola, and Burma, where massive increases in military presence and widespread abuses of human rights—including forced labor, murder, rape, forced relocation of villages, and more—are ongoing against communities living in and around Chevron projects.

In Cabinda, the heart of Angola's oil production, twenty-four-hour oil operations are, as lawyer and journalist Daphne Eviatar wrote, "what financed the government's army during a civil war. . . . And they're the most obvious sign of the West's relentless tentacles reaching into Angola today." Like in other Chevron "company towns" around the world, extractive industry practices in Cabinda only stress and deepen poverty levels as Chevron pollutes and destroys the environment, accentuates social injustice, stops development, and sows frustration. The report quoted Angola resident Agostinho Chicaia: "The solution? Discontinue Chevron's oil exploration in Cabinda, as it is the mother of our disgrace, bringing poverty, environmental problems, and armed conflict."

Chevron's Chad–Cameroon project has fueled violence, impoverished people in the oil fields and along the pipeline route, exacerbated pressures on indigenous peoples, and created enormous environmental problems. The money from the oil has paid for arms that have fueled Chad's civil war and the associated conflict in neighboring Darfur.

In what is likely the Earth's most oil damaged region, the Niger Delta, Chevron continues to employ the notoriously brutal Nigerian military to provide it with security services. The military is known to violently repress peaceful protest by villagers from the Delta communities.

In Ecuador, Texaco (now Chevron) oil production has irreversibly altered and degraded an environment that people have called home for millennia. Indigenous peoples who knew the forest intimately and lived sustainably off its resources for countless generations have found themselves forced into dire poverty, unable to make a living in their traditional ways when the now toxic rivers and forests are empty of fish and game. The physical ailments they suffer from oil pollution are accentuated by the cultural impoverishment that the oil industry has brought to the region, in many cases amounting to the almost total loss of ancient traditions and wisdom.

As affected Amazon residents battle Chevron for accountability, Chevron has engaged in repeated attempts to subvert the judicial process, ranging from the use of deceptive sampling techniques in scientific studies of the contamination, to lobbying efforts in Washington to tie the renewal of Ecuador's trade privileges to its dismissal of the case.

In Iraq, one invasion and seven years of occupation later, Chevron negotiated for two oil fields. Iraq's five trade union federations released a statement rejecting "the handing of control over oil to foreign companies, which would undermine the sovereignty of the state and the dignity of the Iraqi people." A confidential intelligence report on the Iraq Oil Law prepared for US officials and leaked to ABC News concluded that "if major foreign oil companies were going to go to work in Iraq, they would need to be heavily underwritten by the US government." The report further concluded that if and when US oil companies got to work in Iraq they would require protection—most likely that of the US military.

The world sits on a precipice. Oil is running out. The oil that is left is found in more environmentally, socially, and politically sensitive areas and is more hotly contested. Chevron contended in its 2008 annual report that "meeting future demand will be one of the world's great challenges—but one that Chevron is convinced can be met in an environmentally responsible way." Nothing in the report actually supports such a contention. Nor does it indicate that Chevron is seeking to do so in a manner that protects social, political, or human rights.

While spending, at best, less than 3 percent of its capital and exploratory budget on green energy in 2008, Chevron marketed itself as an "alternative energy" company that is "part of the solution," but few truly believe the hype. Rather, the movements to embrace real energy alternatives and to hold Chevron fully accountable for its disastrous actions is gaining far greater currency than the company's billions can ultimately withstand.

Update by True Cost of Chevron Authors

In April 2010, Chevron released its 2009 annual report. It would not take long for the cover design—Chevron's Gulf of Mexico ultra-deepwater drillship, the *Discoverer Clear Leader*—to seem a terribly poor choice.

Just days prior to publication, 18,000 gallons of crude oil spilled from a Chevron-operated pipeline in the Delta National Wildlife Refuge in southeastern Louisiana.

A far worse disaster struck less than two weeks later. The largest blowout in thirty years of an oil and gas well in the Gulf of Mexico killed eleven people and saturated the surrounding areas in a blanket of oily destruction. The rig was owned and operated by Transocean, the same company with which Chevron has a five-year contract to operate the *Discoverer Clear Leader*, among other Chevron offshore rigs.

While the cover image of Chevron's annual report features a pristine rig, perhaps the more appropriate photo for Chevron will prove to be the image on page two: the sun setting on the Chevron Way.

Chevron's 2009 annual report celebrated 130 years of Chevron operations. In it, the company declared that the "values of the Chevron Way" include operating "with the highest standards of integrity and respect for human rights," a deep commitment "to safe and efficient operations and to conducting our business in an environmentally sound manner," and the building of "strong partnerships to produce energy and support communities."

We—the communities and our allies who bear the consequences of Chevron's offshore drilling rigs, oil and natural gas production, coal fields, refineries, depots, pipelines, exploration, chemical plants, political control, consumer abuse, false promises, and much more—have a very different account to offer. Thus, we have once again prepared the Alternative Annual Report for Chevron.

Written by dozens of community leaders from sixteen countries and ten states across the US where Chevron operates, the sixty-page report encompasses the full range of Chevron's activities, from coal to chemicals, offshore to onshore production, pipelines to refineries, natural gas to toxic waste, lobbying and campaign contributions to greenwashing.

On May 25, 2010, forty authors of the alternative report authors appeared at a press conference in Houston to address the true cost of Chevron's operations in their communities. On May 26, they delivered the report directly to Chevron inside the company's annual general meeting (AGM) while supporters rallied outside. Chevron had five protesters arrested from the site, including the report's lead author and editor, Antonia Juhasz. Chevron also refused entry to another two dozen people from Chevron-affected countries around the world, like Nigeria, Ecuador, and Burma. Those denied entry held legal shareholder proxies.

See the 2010 Alternative Report at www.TrueCostofChevron.com.

19

Obama Administration Assures World Bank and International Monetary Fund a Free Reign of Abuse

Sources:

Lori Wallach, "Report: US-Initiated WTO Rules Could Undermine Regulatory Overhaul of Global Finance," *Democracy Now!*, September 25, 2009, www.democracynow.org/2009/9/25/report_us_initiated_wto_rules_could.

Public Citizen, Global Trade Watch, "New Report: No Meaningful Safeguards for Prudential Measures in WTO Financial Service Deregulation Agreements," Public Citizen, September 23, 2009, http://www.citizen.org/hot_issues/issue.cfm?ID=2374.

Michael O'Brien, "Obama Issues Signing Statement on $106B War Bill," *Hill*, June 26, 2009, http://thehill.com/homenews/administration/48019-obama-issues-signing-statement-on-106b-war-bill.

Maggie Jaruzel Potter, "NGO to G-20 Leaders: 'World Bank and IMF Ideology Has Failed,'" Charles Stewart Mott Foundation Web site, April 24, 2009, http://www.mott.org/news/news/2009/G20.aspx.

Student Researchers:
Meg Carlucci and Marissa Warfield (Sonoma State University)
Abbey Wilson and Jillian Harbin (DePauw University)

Faculty Evaluators:
Laurie Dawson and Elaine Wellin (Sonoma State University)
Tim Cope and Kevin Howley (DePauw University)

On April 24, 2009, US Treasury Secretary Timothy Geithner hosted meetings with finance ministers from the world's top economies to discuss increased oversight of the global financial system in the wake of the meltdown. The meetings preceded semi-annual gatherings of the International Monetary Fund (IMF) and World Bank in Washington, DC.

The April G20 meeting in London secured a lot of positive media attention after world leaders announced a global package of $1.1 trillion for economic recovery and reform, mostly for the IMF. The plan, however, did not include specific information about the much needed operational reforms to the IMF and the World Bank.

Speaking five months later on the eve of the September 2009 G20 summit, Geithner called for higher regulatory standards:

> As you know, the United States Congress has a very aggressive schedule to legislate sweeping changes to our financial system that are going to make—provide greater protection for consumers and investors to create a more stable financial system and to try to make sure that taxpayers are no longer on the hook in the future to bear the burdens of financial crises. But we can't do this alone. If we continue to allow risk and leverage to migrate where standards are weakest, the entire US global financial system will be less stable in the future. We need to see competition for stronger standards, not weaker standards.

How far will the G20 go on the regulation of financial markets? A September 2009 report from Public Citizen's Global Trade Watch emphasized that the World Trade Organization (WTO) has long advanced extreme financial deregulation under the guise of trade agreements that will undermine the current professed push for increasing regulation.

Lori Wallach of Public Citizen warned of the incredible contradiction: "While the summit communiqué is going to, on one hand, talk about regulating finance, at the same time, they're going to talk about adopting the Doha WTO expansion, and a huge part of that agreement is deregulating finance." Wallach continued, "The problem is that the G20 commitments aren't binding. It's a commitment of faith on the countries about what they're going to do domestically. But the WTO rules are very binding and enforceable by sanctions. And so, it's hard to know if it's ignorance or it's cynicism, but if the Doha round goes into place, all of the world's countries will have a commitment not only to keep in place the existing WTO deregulation dictates on finance, but to deregulate further, right in the midst of what seems to be a global commitment to re-regulate."

The WTO has an agreement called the Financial Services Agreement that explicitly applies to over a hundred countries and mandates major deregulation. For instance, it has a rule that you cannot have a domestic law that limits the size of a financial service firm—insurance, banking, securities—even if it applies equally to foreign and domestic companies. So while everyone talks about putting into place rules regarding being "too big to fail," there is a WTO dictate that forbids such regulation.

In short, these binding WTO rules require countries to maintain the same policies that led to the financial crisis. This agreement was never brought to a vote in any Congress.

Jesse Griffiths, coordinator of the London-based Bretton Woods Project, under the International Finance for Sustainability program of the Mott Foundation's environmental division, said, "The ideology of the IMF and World Bank has failed and the accompanying structures have failed." He added, "In addition to the current enormous economic instability, the system has failed to create equity and eradicate poverty; it has failed to ensure that human rights are protected, and it has failed to address environmental issues."

The failures of these global entities have not prevented President Obama from allowing their relatively free reign in relation to the US government. In June 2009, President Obama used his sixth signing statement to negate provisions of US legislation that would have compelled the World Bank to strengthen labor and environmental standards. When signing the $106 billion war-spending bill into law, Obama included a five-paragraph signing statement with the bill in which he also refused to require the Treasury Department to report to Congress on the activities of the World Bank and the IMF.

The sections rejected by Obama would have required his administration to direct its World Bank representatives to pressure that institution into using metrics that "fairly represent the value of internationally recognized workers" rights. Organized labor groups had pushed for a revision of those standards.

Another section rejected by Obama would have pushed the World Bank to account for the cost of greenhouse gas in pricing projects and to more fully disclose operating budgets.

Yet another section rejected by Obama in this signing statement would have required Geithner to develop a report with the heads of the World Bank and IMF, "detailing the steps taken to coordinate the activities of the World Bank and the Fund," to eliminate overlap between the two.

Obama said in a statement that "provisions of this bill . . . would interfere with my constitutional authority to conduct foreign relations by directing the Executive to take certain positions in negotiating or discussions with international organizations and foreign governments." He added, "I will not treat these provisions as limiting my ability to engage in foreign diplomacy or negotiations."

20

Obama's Charter School Policies Spread Segregation and Undermine Unions

Sources:
E. Frankenberg, G. Siegel-Hawley, and J. Wang, "Choice without Equity: Charter School Segregation and the Need for Civil Rights Standards," Civil Rights Project/Proyecto Derechos Civiles, University of California–Los Angeles, http://www.civilrightsproject .ucla.edu/news/pressreleases/pressrelease20100204-report.html.

Danny Weil, "Obama and Duncan's Education Policy: Like Bush's, Only Worse," *CounterPunch*, August 24, 2009, http://counterpunch.org/weil08242009.html.

Michelle Chen, "Equity and Access in Charter School Systems," *Race Wire*, August 19, 2009, http://www.racewire.org/archives/2009/08/special_education_equity_and_a_1.html.

Paul Abowd, "Teacher Reformers Prepare for Battle Over Public Education," *Labor Notes*, October 13, 2009, http://www.labornotes.org/node/2472.

Student Researchers:
Kelsey Harris and Gina R. Sarpy (Sonoma State University)

Faculty Evaluators:
Laura Watt and Sheila Katz (Sonoma State University)

Charter schools continue to stratify students by race, class, and sometimes language, and are more racially isolated than traditional public schools in virtually every state and large metropolitan area in the country.

Charter schools are often marketed as incubators of educational innovation, and they form a key feature of the Obama administration's school reform agenda. But in some urban communities, they may be fueling *de facto* school segregation and undermining public education.

A University of California–Los Angeles (UCLA) Civil Rights Project study, "Choice without Equity: Charter School Segregation and the Need for Civil Rights Standards," reported that charter schools, particularly those in the western United States, are havens for white re-segregation from public schools. "The charter movement has flourished in a period of retreat on civil rights," stated UCLA professor Gary Orfield, co-director of the project.

In many charter schools, 90 to 100 percent of the population is minority students, close to twice the rate of traditional public schools. But even a charter school with a social mission of promoting economic and racial equity still runs up against the limits posed by selectivity and exclusion.

Obama's national education policy supports the expansion of charter schools to undermine public education and schoolteacher labor unions. Obama wants to tie teachers' pay to student performance, which would be measured through test scores. Merit pay based on performance is strongly opposed by teachers' unions nationwide. Teachers want equal pay for equal work and assurances that funding for low-income schools will be fair. Charters are known for resisting teacher unions, which means they drive segregation not only in the student population but in the school workforce as well.

As a junior senator from Illinois, Obama doubled the number of charter schools in his state, despite reservations from teachers, community leaders, and unions. Obama seems to have latched onto the ideological rhetoric that charter schools are somehow engines of innovation that promise to raise all public schools performance, even though, in actuality, the expansion of charter schools is a process of privatizing public schools. Some argue that this is not improving schools but rather replacing public schools with non-union for-profit and nonprofit private institutions. Charter schools are often accused of "cherry picking students" to build higher test scores, leaving low-income and difficult-to-teach students in inadequately funded public systems. Obama's secretary of education, Arne Duncan, closed seventy neighborhood schools while he was Superintendent of Schools in Chicago, resulting in a loss of six thousand Chicago teachers' union members.

On July 30, 2009, the US Senate Appropriations Committee voted for a $40 million increase in federal charter school program (CSP) funding, bringing the total to $256 million for fiscal year 2010. Also included in the bill were significant educational reform investments strongly

aligned with the Obama administration's priorities. The unprecedented payout takes a bead on the teachers unions: money will flow to districts that alter pay and seniority provisions in union contracts and states that roll out the carpet for (mostly non-union) charter schools.

Public schools will now be forced to choose stimulus money over policy, a form of economic extortion and increased federal and corporate control over decision making, especially at a time when many of these states are financial insolvent. Nonprofit and private charter school operators stand to make big gains from the federal incentive package. Several states have already amended their laws to expand charter schools, which are publicly funded but privately managed.

The Obama administration's actions, in tandem with Secretary of Education Arne Duncan, is part and parcel of typical neoliberal policy making: wielding federal stimulus funds as a financial weapon to force all states to increase the number of charter schools they host, as well as to force states that do not have them to pass legislation authorizing their creation. Through financial arm-twisting at a time of disastrous economic crisis, the Obama administration plans to use the power of the federal government to create a much larger national market for charter school providers, be they for profit or nonprofit, virtual charters, educational management organizations (EMOs), or single operators.

Using government to create market opportunities for business interests is at the heart of neoliberal economic policies; as a result, market adherents both need and relish government for its role in legislating and unleashing favorable public policies that benefit businesses' ability to maximize private capital while charging private costs to the public.

The real story and prospects for the nation's future education policy can be best revealed by Arne Duncan's historical involvement in support of neoliberal policies created in Chicago under the Renaissance 2010 project. Renaissance 2010 is a corporate project to reform both the city and its public schools, with the intent of creating schools and geographical spaces that serve to attract the professionals believed to be needed in a twenty-first-century global city. Renaissance 2010 places public schooling under the control of corporate leaders who aim to convert public schools to charter and contract schools, breaking the power of unions and handing over the administration of the newly created charter schools to "providers" beholden to corporations, philanthropists, and business interests. Duncan, as the former CEO of the Chicago public schools (CPS), was an efficient manager for the neoliberal policies and legislative necessities dictated by the corporate elite corporations and their political representatives.

Duncan personally oversaw the attempted closure of twenty Chicago public schools in low-income neighborhoods of color in 2004. He did so with little or no community input—managing, at least for a time, to snub the meddlesome outsiders, like parents and their children, who might have raised objections to the CEO's plans for the schools, or at the very least offer suggestions in the spirit of community decision making.

In fact, rapid increases in military programs in Chicago public schools actually did occur largely under Duncan's tenure as CEO of CPS. The Chicago public school system has five military high schools, more than any city in the nation, and twenty-one "middle school cadet corps" programs. The military high schools teach military history and have military-style discipline. Students wear military uniforms, perform military drills, and participate in summer boot camps. The hierarchical authority structure mirrors the army, navy, and marines, with new students ("cadets") under the command of senior students who had worked their way up and require obedience from those in "lower ranks." All but one of the military high schools are in African-American communities, and all the middle school cadet programs are in overwhelmingly black or Latino schools. (See the honorable mentions in chapter 1, *Censored 2010*.)

The charter school takeover has been achieved quietly in Detroit and Washington DC, where around half the school kids in each city are now enrolled in charters. Under the emergency control of a state-appointed manager, Detroit opened twenty-nine fewer schools in fall 2009 and put many high schools under the control of private management groups. The next target is the teachers' contract. In late August 2009, thousands of Detroit teachers protested proposed 10 percent wage cuts, elimination of step increases, and increased fines for work stoppages from $250 to $7,500 per day.

The Obama education policy hardly differs from the Bush administration's policy of hitching student and teacher performance to what many in the educational community and beyond call inauthentic assessments, which force teachers to teach to the test and do little to encourage critical thinking or collaborative problem solving. The Obama policy is also quite similar to Bush's in its goals for the rapid expansion of charter school networks and nonprofit with for-profit providers to run them.

Update by Danny Weil

When I wrote "Obama and Duncan's Education Policy: Like Bush's, Only Worse" for *CounterPunch* back in August of 2009, it was obvious that a corporate takeover of education was ginned up, triggered, and in process. The insidious experiment was initially fully launched in New Orleans after Hurricane Katrina in 2005, under the tutelage of Paul T. Hill's "Diverse Strategies" model. Since the publication of the *CounterPunch* article, the corporatization of education has continued at rapid speeds, with public school closures occurring daily and student and teacher dislocation becoming the norm.

"Race to the Top," the new brand name for No Child Left Behind conjured up by Secretary of Education Arne Duncan, is now cannibalizing urban areas in the same way venture capitalists descended on New Orleans and privatized the educational system after the hurricane. Arne Duncan—along with his philanthropic friends who make up the Department of Education (DOE) and the business entrepreneurs who are anxious to get their greedy hands on the 5.6 percent of the national economy that education represents—is simply mouthing the same themes enunciated more than twenty-five years ago in the Reagan administration's 1983 report, A Nation at Risk: The Imperative for Educational Reform, and for many of the same reasons.

They say the US cannot compete globally without an educated workforce; they tell us that America is falling behind in the economic global race to the top; they say US competition is failing and thus the entire enterprise of America stands held hostage to the unforgiving failures of American public education that can be pinned on the teacher's unions.

The American public is now witnessing the wholesale privatization of education as cities, municipalities, and states are suffering from budget woes caused by the pillage and social failures of financial monopoly capitalism and its devastating policies that are intent on privatizing everything public, from schools, to the military, to health care, to public housing. With the public sector virtually bankrupt, Race to the Top is now forcing states to bend their knees and adopt the "four assurances" that underlie the radical new program Duncan is proposing, or close to their public schools and face massive losses of revenues and the denial of public services to children and decent, livable wages to teachers.

For states to be eligible for the $4.3 billion that Duncan has pocketed in federal funds to dole out to states that meet his criteria, they must show they are progressing toward meeting the four assurances. If they do not, then the states will not qualify for the funds and their political representatives will be forced to tell their constituencies that there are no monies for education and face the wrath of voters. As a result, many states are clamoring to meet Duncan's "standards" and are doing all they can to become victims of Duncan's extortion demands.

To begin with, teachers and schools must accept and "assure" what are called "high quality standards and assessments," as explained by the International Center for Leadership and Education.

These standards and assessments are not the product of teachers' collaborative thinking, but are instead the progeny of the well-heeled Wall Street bankers and their "turnaround" artists who have decided what our children should learn and how teachers must teach. The standards are inauthentic and laced to the vicious No Child Left Behind law inherited from the bipartisan Congress, signed into law by the Bush administration, and now chest held by the Obama administration. Although Obama blasted the tests as no way to measure student performance, as I indicated in the piece for *CounterPunch*, this was mere rhetoric designed to fool the public, as the standards and assessments are now the providence of private companies who work with the DOE.

Certainly charter chains would prefer national standards; that is why they look to the government to assure they have a highly profitable landscape to scrape up the contracts. This would allow them to use prepackaged curricula across their charter outlets no matter the location—it's highly conducive to expanding their "market share," for dummied down, standardized curricula keep costs down, and the dispensation is formulaic and repetitive. This is the Wal-Mart model of education.

The second assurance that states must meet to qualify for the federal monies is to tie teaching to material incentives for the purposes of what Duncan calls "teaching effectiveness." Nowhere can this be seen more clearly and directly than in the merit pay schemes being flown as trial balloons in many cities in an effort to destroy teacher unions and collective bargaining.

The third assurance is "turning around low performing schools," which means opening up the floodgate for charter schools, state by state, by forcing states to either initiate charter legislation and/or to raise the caps on the number of charter schools that can be opened in their states without being in violation of state law. In other words, using government legislation as a fulcrum to assure that the financial monopoly class has the ability to start "charter retail chains" without any blockage by meddlesome state laws or unions limiting their opening and expansion.

It also means closing public schools, city by city. According to a survey conducted last fall by the school administrators' association, nationally 6 percent of districts closed or consolidated schools for the 2009–10 school year, double the number from the 2008–09 school year. The ranks of public school closures are expected to grow to 11 percent for the 2010–11 school year.

Closing schools is good news for privatizers looking to make a buck, for it actually increases the school system's ability to qualify for state construction dollars that can be turned over to private corporations. As a result, the contracts to build new schools are given to Wall Street corporate financial interests and developers who profit off the devastation left by the Wall Street crash and theft of public funds. This sordid "assurance" is all bundled up as "school choice," the favored language of the educational prevaricators.

It is important to understand that Arne Duncan and the Obama administration have bought the notion of public school choice and corporate education as a panacea for what ails public education. Like his predecessor under George W. Bush, former secretary of education Margaret Spellings, Arne Duncan and President Obama espouse the common rationale given for neoliberal educational reforms: competition provides the best or most efficient motor for change and reform. The contention is similar to the private voucher argument that traditional public schools (TPS) can be best improved by competitive market mechanisms.

Like private choice, the public choice rationale maintains that all public schools, and student learning in general, improve when schools have to compete for students, when students and their parents have the right to choose. Such an environment sends the message to teachers that they too need to compete, and then values such as solidarity, diversity appreciation, equity and equal opportunity, and participatory democracy all go out the window. They are not valued in the new "scheme of things."

Race to the Top embraces a new but old business language, the language of competition rather than the language of collaboration, until what is posited is a scarcity environment: of winners and losers, no one in between.

Finally, the fourth assurance is to adopt "data systems to inform instruction." These data systems come in the form of longitudinal testing and tracking systems for students, from kindergarten to workforce. This assurance is now moving rapidly, galloping across the educational terrain as testing companies see a virtual bonanza in preparing and selling tests, training teachers and students for the state tests with privatized for-profit test prep kits, as well as using the tests as Wall Street rating devices pointing to exciting new privatized educational opportunities and "best practices."

Sadly, the results of the new national and state testing regime will be fed into an expanded data system used to evaluate teachers, to see if they are meeting the "measured outcomes," the free-market "targets" they have been hired to accomplish. Reduced to "clerks in the classroom," teachers could expect to devote themselves to "professional development" days, to be told by corporate spokespeople how to use the data kits, computer-generated graphs, tables, and more to figure out if their students are meeting the mandatory measured outcomes under No Child Left Behind.

It is now time to resist this regimented individualism through as combination of understanding, solidarity among working people, critical dialogue, and direct collective action. Otherwise, we will look to a society inhabited by more war, militarism, regimentation, authoritarianism, competition, penalty, and social decline. We will hollow out the moral body of our citizenry by forcing them to feed at the trough of illegitimate learning—a body blow to the body politic. It is time to stand up for public education, no matter the level of the educator, for as solidarity tells us, we are all in this together, and if the bridge goes down we all go down. The good news is that the responses to my article and many more like it are having a compelling effect.

Public schools in Detroit, Washington, DC, throughout New Jersey, and many other diverse cities and states across the nation are struggling back with high school and middle school student walkouts—16,000 in New Jersey alone. Student leaders are emerging, and their presence will no doubt increase as shown in the occupation of Governor Jennifer Granholm's office in Detroit.

Also in Detroit, students defeated a plan by Wal-Mart; the retailer attempted to worm its way into four high schools by offering "internships" for course credit. Students will be at the forefront of the battles that will take place as the unfavorable policies go forward and the economy continues to affect the population, especially Latinos and Blacks in urban centers throughout the nation.

Corporate news coverage of the events is virtually nonexistent. Surreptitiously each day, Arne Duncan and his close allies on Wall Street continue to collect tax dollars under the radar of most citizens who are too busy trying to cope with a deracinated economic and social landscape that has left them bereft of any public safety net during a time of economic meltdown and job loss. Reportage of the carnage caused by Race to the Top and the new corporate model for education has been left to progressive reporting online or through organizational organizing and efforts by such groups as By Any Means Necessary, and any others who are fighting privatization and the destruction of educational opportunities for our nation's youth.

We can only hope further education regarding the new corporate educational model will lead to stiff resistance and block the plans of the "turnaround" artists, venture capitalists, and Wall Street money makers. If not, then education will be reduced to training and teachers reorganized as "at-will" associates in the long march toward corporatocracy and the Walmartization of Education.

References:

By Any Means Necessary Web site, www.bamn.com.

A. Duncan, "Elevating the Teaching Profession," *American Educator* 33, no. 4 (Winter 2009–10).

A. Greenblatt, "Schools Across US Grapple With Closures," National Public Radio,

March 11, 2010, http://www.kpbs.org/news/2010/mar/11/schools-across-us-grapple-closures.

Barbara Martinez, "D.C. Deal Puts Merit Pay for Teachers on the Syllabus," *Wall Street Journal*, April 8, 2010, http://online.wsj.com/article/SB10001424052702303 591204575170280501458008.html?mod=WSJ_newsreel_us.

D. Simmons, "DC Teacher Contract Includes Merit Pay," *Washington Times*, April 8, 2010, http://www.washingtontimes.com/news/2010/apr/08/merit-pay-deal-included-in-dc-teacher-contract.

K. Spak, "D.C. Teacher's Union Agrees to Merit Pay," April 9, 2010, http://www.newser.com/story/85502/dc-teachers-union-agrees-to-merit-pay.html.

International Center for Leadership in Education, "The Impact of the Four Assurances on Classrooms and Schools, Getting to the finish line in Race to the Top," April 2, 2010, www.leadered.com/pdf/Race to theTop4.2.10.pdf.

D. Weil, "On the Future of Education if Bill Gates and Arne Duncan Get Their Way," *CounterPunch*, January 1, 2009.

D. Weil, "Tenure, Merit Pay and Teachers: Washington D.C. and Florida Set to Lose Tenure, Adopt Merit Pay and Create At-will Employees Just Like Wal-Mart's Greeters," April 10, 2010, http://dailycensored.com/2010/04/10/tneure-merit-pay-washington-d-c-and-forida.

D. Weil, "New Jersey Students Walk Out of Public Schools," April 29, 2010, http://dailycensored.com/2010/04/29/new-jersey-students-walk-out-of-public-schools.

D. Weil, "Pass It On! Students and Activists Arrested at Governor of Michigan, Jennifer Granholm's Office Over the Decimation of Public Education in Detroit," May 12, 2010, http://dailycensored.com/2010/05/12/students-and-activists-arrested-at-governor-of-michigan-jennifer-granholms-office-over-the-decimation-of-public-education.

D. Weil, "Yvette Felarca Must Replace the Current American Federation of Teachers (AFT) President Randi Weingarten," June 5, 2010, http://dailycensored.com/2010/06/05/yvette-felarca-must-replace-the-current-american-federation-of-teachers-aft-president-randi-weingarten.

Update by Paul Abowd

President Obama has made good on another one of those campaign promises that many progressives had wishfully chalked up to an electoral strategy of "playing to the center." It turns out that Obama's vision for public education goes way beyond electioneering, and has turned into an aggressive federal schools initiative revealing the administration's abiding faith in market principles to resolve issues of public concern.

Obama's Race to the Top contest has awarded only two states thus far, but has compelled nearly every state to alter its education code in anticipation of winning a piece of the several billion dollar federal aid package.

While the federal plan proceeds apace, resistance to it has grown—most notably in Chicago. A progressive slate of teachers is poised to take over the third largest teachers' union in the country this summer. In an effort to connect the union with a broader community movement to revitalize public education, the Chicago teachers are putting up perhaps the most promising opposition to the privatization of public education—in the city where Obama's education plan was hatched.

In Detroit, a foundation-funded schools manager appointed by the governor is finding community resistance and a legal challenge to his school closure plan, while DC teacher reformers are knocking on the door in union elections. In Los Angeles, teachers won their first battle against the city's attempt to put public schools up for bid. Parents' and teachers' proposals for union-run schools beat out charter operators for control of dozens of contested campuses.

The summer 2009 national meeting of teacher reformers in Los Angeles was important in coalescing a national strategy for opposing Obama's schools plan—and it has produced significant victories along the way. However, unions are still scrambling to find a unified response to attacks from a president they wholeheartedly supported. Because now, the work of saving public schools is not only about resisting and reacting, but proactively putting forth an alternative—lest teachers' unions face charges of obstructing progress that the mainstream media is all too ready to level against them.

Luckily, the blogosphere is becoming a valuable resource as battles over public education continue. Current and former teachers themselves are broadcasting their experiences, their insider knowledge, and the dirty tricks of administrators and corrupt union officials alike. Some recommended blogs and independent news outlets on education include the Web sites for NYC Educator, Education Notes, Substance News, the Washington Teacher, and the Caucus of Rank and File Educators.

21

Western Lifestyle Continues Environmental Footprint

Sources:

James Randerson, "Western Lifestyle Unsustainable, Says Climate Expert Rajendra Pachauri," *Guardian*, November 29, 2009, http://www.guardian.co.uk/environment/2009/nov/29/rajendra-pachauri-climate-warning-copenhagen.

Bobbie Johnson, San Francisco bureau, "Web Providers Must Limit Internet's Carbon Footprint, Say Experts," *Guardian*, May 3, 2009, http://www.guardian.co.uk/technology/2009/may/03/internet-carbon-footprint.

Jeremy Page, "Scientist's Himalayan Mission Provides Unwelcome Proof: Glaciers Are Dying," *Times* (UK), December 5, 2009, http://www.timesonline.co.uk/tol/news/environment/copenhagen/article6945249.ece.

Dan Joling, "Global Warming Threatens Alaska's Waters with Acidification," AlterNet, September 9, 2009, http://www.alternet.org/water.

Student Researchers:
Abbey Wilson and Jillian Harbin (DePauw University)
Anne Cozza (Sonoma State University)

Faculty Evaluators:
Tim Cope and Kevin Howley (DePauw University)
Buzz Kellogg (Sonoma State University)

Speaking in advance of the climate summit in Copenhagen, Rajendra Pachauri, the United Nation's leading climate scientist, warned that Western society must enact radical changes and reform measures if it is to avoid the worst effects of climate change. Pachauri, chair of the Intergovernmental Panel on Climate Change (IPCC), told the *Observer* that Western society urgently needs to develop a new value system of "sustainable consumption." The Nobel Prize winner stated, "Today we have reached the point where consumption and people's desire to consume has grown out of proportion." "The reality is that our lifestyles are unsustainable."

Pachauri offered a wide-ranging proposal—including legal requirements, economic disincentives, and government subsidies—to lead Western society toward a more sustainable future. Among Pachauri's suggestions is that hotels be held accountable for the energy use of their guests. The energy consumed by guests in hotels could be metered and then charged to guests' bills. Pachauri's proposal also includes measures to regulate travel by land and air. For instance, Pachauri argues that automobile travel could be "curbed" through pricing schemes that discourage the use of private transportation. Likewise, Pachauri suggests that governments tax air travel to encourage citizens to travel by rail—a mode of transportation that is significantly lower in cost and environmental impact.

Travel and tourism are but one feature of an increasingly unsustainable Western lifestyle. As the Internet becomes an indispensable feature of modern life, the costs and environmental impact associated with Internet usage is on the rise. According to recent estimates, there are over 1.5 billion people online around the world. As a result, the Internet's energy footprint is growing at a rate of more than 10 percent each year. As the Net's appetite for electricity grows, Internet companies like Google are having a hard time managing the costs associated with delivering Web pages, video, audio, and data files. This situation not only threatens the bottom line of Web firms, but may compromise the long-term viability of the Internet. According to Subodh Bapat, vice president of Sun Microsystems, a leading manufacturer of computer servers, "In an energy-constrained world, we cannot continue to grow the footprint of the Internet . . . we need to rein in the energy consumption."

Energy consumption associated with Western lifestyles has been linked with melting glaciers around the world. Dr. Shresth Tayal of The Energy and Resources Institute (TERI), India's leading environmental institute, selected three of approximately eighteen thousand glaciers in the Himalayas as benchmarks to measure the rate of the glaciers' retreat. According to Dr. Tayal, the glaciers, which feed rivers across India and China, providing fresh water to more than two billion people during the dry season, are disappearing at an alarming rate. As Dr. Tayal bluntly assessed in the *Times*, "The glacier is dying." Tayal's findings support the contention made in 2007 by the IPCC that glaciers could disappear by 2035. The IPCC warns that a shortage of fresh water will cause "famine, water wars and hundreds of millions of climate change refugees."

Climate change is also taking a toll on the quality of Alaska's marine waters, where cooler oceans absorb and hold more gas than do warmer waters. Jeremy Mathis, a chemical oceanographer at the University of Alaska–Fairbanks, found that Alaskan waters are turning acidic from the absorption of greenhouse gases. Increased levels of carbon dioxide in the atmosphere lead to ocean acidification, as nearly 30 percent of greenhouse gases emitted by humans gets absorbed into the ocean each year.

According to Mathis, the same qualities that make Alaskan waters some of the most productive in the world—cold, shallow depths and an abundance of marine life—make them especially vulnerable to acidification. Mathis notes that ocean acidification stunts the growth, development, and reproductive health of some species of crabs and fish. This situation has enormous implications, not only for marine life in Alaskan waters, but for the broader Alaskan ecosystem, and the state's $4.6 billion fishing industry.

Despite growing evidence that Western lifestyles contribute to global climate change, it may take a generation before the new value system Pachauri calls for takes hold. Nevertheless, Pachauri believes that young people will recognize the need to adopt some of the radical changes he recommends. "I think they will be far more sensitive than adults, who have been corrupted by the ways we have been following for years."

Update by Bobbie Johnson

It is nearly impossible to calculate the impact the Internet has had on the world over the decades since it was first created. With more than a quarter of the global population now online, it has become a central part of the lives of millions of people around the planet, revolutionizing everything from communication and retail to our day-to-day social lives along the way.

This growth, combined with the power demands of Internet data centers, convinced me that more attention needed to be paid to the issue. After all, the most voracious of the Internet's energy demands are the parts of the Internet that are usually hidden from the sight of ordinary Web surfers. My story, titled "Web Providers Must Limit Internet's Carbon Footprint, Say Experts," was largely intended to highlight the question of the Internet's energy footprint, and to act as a corrective to some of the misinformed and confusing reports published in the past. The article elicited a direct response from Google—somewhat unusual for an issue of this kind—but the mainstream press remained fairly ambivalent to it, preferring to focus on the next big product launch or another overhyped Internet start-up.

Experts suggest that the Internet's energy footprint continues to grow at least 10 percent each year, and major companies continue to build vast new server farms at a rapid clip. Indeed, just upriver from Google's plant in The Dalles, Oregon, Amazon is hard at work on a $100 million, one hundred thousand-square-feet monster of a data center. And Facebook, now the world's second-largest Web site, announced in January that it was breaking ground on its first custom data center—also in Oregon. It will, surely, be the first of many.

And on top of this expansion comes the even more chilling realization that this is not a problem that can be solved merely through national regulation or even agreement between the Internet's most powerful companies. Thanks to the speedy expansion of the Internet population in countries like China and India, hordes of corporations are building new data centers that have fewer rules intended to keep their power usage in check.

It's a looming crisis everywhere—and despite the valiant attempts on all sides to ignore the issue, our desire to be more connected than ever means that the Internet's appetite for electricity is not a problem that will be going away any time soon.

22

1.2 Billion People in India to be Given Biometric ID Cards

Sources:
Randeep Ramesh, "1.2 Billion People in India to be Given Biometric ID Cards," *Guardian*, September 16, 2009, http://www.guardian.co.uk/world/2009/sep/16/india-population-biometric-id-cards.

Anjana Pasricha, "India Begins Project to Issue Biometric Identity Cards to All Citizens," *Voice of America News*, September 24, 2009, http://www1.voanews.com/english/news/a-13-2009-09-24-voa18-68709357.html.

Corporate Media Source:
Rama Lakshmi, "Biometric Identity Project in India Aims to Provide for Poor, End Corruption," *Washington Post*, March 28, 2010, A8.

Student Researcher:
Danielle Caruso (Sonoma State University)

Faculty Evaluator:
Rashmi Singh (Sonoma State University)

India's 1.2 billion citizens are to be issued biometric identification cards. The cards will hold the person's name, age, and birth date, as well as fingerprints or iris scans, though no caste or religious identification. Within the next five years a giant computer will hold the personal details of at least 600 million citizens, making this new information technology system the largest in the world. The project will cost an estimated $3.5 billion. The 600 million Indians will receive a sixteen-digit identity number by 2014 in the first phase of the project.

India's red tape is legendary: citizens have dozens of types of identity verification, ranging from electoral rolls to ration cards, yet almost none can be used universally. The new system will be a national proof of identity, effective for everything, from welfare benefits to updating land records. Forty-two percent of India's population is below the poverty line and citizens frequently move in search of jobs. The government believes the ID system will help citizens because they will no longer have a problem identifying themselves. The biometric identity number will be entered every time someone accesses services from government departments, driver's license offices, and hospitals, as well as insurance, credit card, telecom, and banking companies. By bringing more people into the banking system, Indian officials also hope to raise the number of people paying income taxes; currently, less than 5 percent of the population pays income taxes.

The head of Oxfam India, Nisha Agarwal, says a lack of identity verification is a major problem, especially for urban migrants. As a result, they are excluded from dozens of government programs, which offer cheaper food, jobs, and other benefits for poor people. "They remain treated as temporary migrants and, without that piece of paper, some form of identification, they are not able to access many of these government schemes that exist now, that have large funds behind them and could actually make a huge difference in poor people's lives."

The scheme is the brainchild of Nandan Nilekani, one of India's best-known software tycoons and now head of the government's Unique Identification Authority. "We are going to have to build something on the scale of Google, but it will change the country . . . every person for first time [will] be able to prove who he or she is. . . . We are not profiling a billion people. This will provide an ID database which government can access online. There will be checks and balances to protect identities," said Nilekani, who has also been in talks to create a personalized carbon account so that all Indians might buy "green technologies" using a government subsidy.

The government also plans to use the database to monitor bank transactions, cell phone purchases, and the movements of individuals and groups suspected of fomenting terrorism. In January 2010, the Ministry of Home Affairs began collecting biometric details of people in coastal villages to boost security; the gunmen in the 2008 Mumbai attacks, which killed 165 people, sneaked into the country from the sea.

Critics say the project will turn India into an Orwellian police state that will spy on citizens' private lives. "We do not want an intrusive, surveillance state in India," said Usha Ramanathan, a lawyer who has written and lobbied against the project. "Information about people will be shared with intelligence agencies, banks and companies, and we will have no idea how our information is interpreted and used." Civil liberty campaigners fear the ID card will become a tool of repression. Nandita Haskar, a human rights lawyer, said, "There is already no accountability in regards to violations of human and civil rights. In this atmosphere, what are the oversight mechanisms for this kind of surveillance?"

India's plunge into biometric identification comes as countries around the globe are making similar moves. In 2006, Britain approved a mandatory national ID system with fingerprints for its citizens before public opposition prompted the government to scale back plans for a voluntary pilot program beginning in Manchester. United States senators have proposed requiring all citizens and immigrants who want to work in the country to carry a new high-tech social security card linked to fingerprints as part of an immigration overhaul.

23

Afghan War: Largest Military Coalition in History

Source:
Rick Rozoff, "Afghan War: NATO Builds History's First Global Army," *Global Research*, August 9, 2009, http://www.globalresearch.ca/index.php?context=va&aid=14707.

Student Researcher:
Dani Wright (Sonoma State University)

Faculty Evaluator:
Peter Phillips (Sonoma State University)

The North Atlantic Treaty Organization (NATO) has become history's first global army. Never before have soldiers from so many states served in the same war theater, much less the same country. At the eighth anniversary of the United States' invasion of Afghanistan, the world is witness to a twenty-first-century armed conflict waged by the largest military coalition in history.

With recent announcements that troops from such diverse nations as Colombia, Mongolia, Armenia, Japan, South Korea, Ukraine, and Montenegro are to join those of some forty-five other countries serving under the command of the NATO-led International Security Assistance Force (ISAF), there will soon be military personnel from fifty nations and five continents serving under a unified command structure.

NATO's fiftieth anniversary summit in Washington DC in 1999 welcomed the first expansion of the world's only military bloc in the post–cold war era, absorbing former Warsaw Pact members such as the Czech Republic, Hungary, and Poland. Two years later, after the 9/11 attacks in New York City and Washington DC, NATO activated Article 5—in which the "Parties agree that an armed attack against one or more of them in Europe or North America shall be considered an attack against them all."

The main purpose of invoking NATO's mutual military assistance clause was to rally the then nineteen-member military bloc for the invasion and occupation of Afghanistan and the stationing of troops, warplanes, and bases throughout South and Central Asia, including Kyrgyzstan, Pakistan, Tajikistan, and Uzbekistan. Flyover rights were also arranged with Kazakhstan and Turkmenistan, and newly acquired airbases in Bulgaria and Romania have since been used for the transit of troops and weapons to the Afghan war zone.

The 1999 war against Yugoslavia was NATO's first "out of area" operation—that is, outside of North America and those parts of Europe in the alliance. The war in Afghanistan, however, marked NATO's transformation into a global war fighting machine. NATO officials now employ such terms as global, expeditionary, and twenty-first century to describe NATO and its operations.

NATO members who have deployed troops to Afghanistan include Bulgaria, the Czech Republic, Estonia, Latvia, Lithuania, Poland, Romania, Armenia, Azerbaijan, Belarus, Georgia, Kazakhstan, Kyrgyzstan, Moldova, Tajikistan, Turkmenistan, Ukraine, and Uzbekistan, as well as ten European nations that had never before been part of a military bloc— Austria, Bosnia, Finland, the Republic of Ireland, Macedonia, Malta, Montenegro, Serbia, Sweden, and Switzerland. The twenty-eight full original NATO members all have troops there as well.

All of the new members were prepared for full NATO accession under the Partnership for Peace (PfP) program, which demands weapons interoperability (scrapping contemporary Russian and old Warsaw Pact arms in favor of Western ones); increasing future members' military spending to 2 percent of their national budget no matter how hard-hit that nation is economically; purging of "politically unreliable" personnel from military, defense, and security posts; training abroad in NATO military academies; hosting US Alliance military exercises; and instructing the officer corps in a common language—English—for joint overseas operations.

In calendar year nine of the war in Afghanistan, and now with the expansion into Pakistan, NATO has built upon previous and current joint military deployments in Bosnia, Albania, Kosovo, Macedonia, Djibouti, Iraq, Kuwait, Jordan, Sudan, and off the coast of Somalia. In Camp Lemonier in Djibouti, NATO has conducted maritime surveillance and boarding operations, and in the autumn of 2009, NATO deployed its first naval task force off the coast of Somalia.

At the 2004 NATO summit in Istanbul, Turkey, NATO upgraded its Mediterranean Dialogue, whose partners are Algeria, Egypt, Israel, Jordan, Mauritania, Morocco, and Tunisia, with the so-called Istanbul Cooperation Initiative, which also laid the groundwork for the military integration of the six members of the Gulf Cooperation Council, Bahrain, Kuwait, Oman, Qatar, Saudi Arabia, and the United Arab Emirates. The last named is the only Arab state with troops in Afghanistan to date.

The Afghan war has also led to another category of NATO partnership, that of Contact Countries, which so far officially include Australia, Japan, New Zealand, and South Korea.

NATO also has a Tripartite Commission with Afghanistan and Pakistan for the prosecution of the dangerously expanding war in South Asia, and defense, military, and political leaders from both nations are regularly summoned to NATO headquarters in Belgium for meetings and directives. Afghan and Pakistani soldiers are trained at NATO bases in Europe, and from July 20 to 24, 2009, senior leaders of the American and Pakistani armed forces met in Atlanta, Georgia, at a counterinsurgency seminar. The director of the US Army and Marine Corps Counterinsurgency Center, Colonel Daniel Roper, said of the proceedings: "This week we presented some lessons learned in counterinsurgency. We used those lessons to stimulate conversation and took our previous experiences in Iraq and applied them to our current status. We exchanged our viewpoints on the challenges in Afghanistan, Pakistan and South Asia at large." South Asia at large includes not only Afghanistan and Pakistan, but also India, Nepal, Bangladesh, and Sri Lanka.

Included in the West's Greater Afghan war is not only "South Asia at large," but also Central Asia and the Caspian Sea Basin. In both instances nations already involved in providing bases for US and NATO forces (Kyrgyzstan, Tajikistan, Uzbekistan) and those supplying troops and ancillary services are being pulled deeper into the NATO web. On August 7, 2009, Pentagon chief Robert Gates expressed his gratification that Kyrgyzstan, which earlier that year evicted US and NATO troops from the air base at Manas, had proven susceptible to bribery and allowed the US military to conduct transit again through the same base. The new arrangement "will enable the US and Kyrgyzstan to continue their highly productive military relations created earlier."

Additionally, the penetration of Kazakhstan, a member of NATO's Partnership for Peace, by the Pentagon and NATO would simultaneously insert a hostile Western military presence onto both Russia's and China's borders.

In Kazakhstan's Caspian neighbor to the south, Turkmenistan, the Pentagon has been no less active of late. At the end of July, Under Secretary of State for Political Affairs William Burns announced plans for what was described as an intergovernmental commission for regular consultations with Turkmenistan which "marks progress in . . . the contribution to stability in Afghanistan and across the region." Turkmenistan is quietly developing into a major transport hub for the northern supply network, which is being used to relay nonlethal supplies to US and NATO forces in Afghanistan.

It was recently announced that Mongolia was sending an initial contingent of 130 troops to serve under NATO in Afghanistan. Mongolia's involvement in Iraq and Afghanistan has helped cement its alliance with the United States. The South Asian war is being exploited by Washington and Brussels to intrude their military structures into Mongolia and other nations neighboring Russia and China, such as Kazakhstan, Uzbekistan, Kyrgyzstan, Tajikistan, and Turkmenistan, to further encircle two of the West's main competitors in that region and the world.

The Afghan war is no ordinary war. The German army has engaged in its first combat operations since the defeat of the Third Reich in 1945. Finnish soldiers have engaged in combat for the first time since World War II, and Swedish forces for the first time in almost 200 years. The only beneficiary of this conflagration is a rapidly emerging global NATO.

24

War Crimes of General Stanley McChrystal

Sources:

Seymour Hersh, "Secret US Forces Carried Out Assassinations in a Dozen Countries, Including in Latin America," *Democracy Now!*, March 31, 2009, http://www.democracynow.org/2009/3/31/seymour_hersh_secret_us_forces_carried.

Seymour Hersh, "You Can't Authorise Murder," interview with Abbas Al Lawati, *Gulf News*, May 12, 2009, http://gulfnews.com/news/region/palestinian-territories/you-can-t-authorise-murder-hersh-1.68504.

PressTV, "McChrystal Was Cheney's Chief Assassin," May 16, 2009, http://www.presstv.ir/detail.aspx?id=94884&sectionid=3510203.

Student Researcher:
Cristina Risso (Sonoma State University)

Faculty Evaluator:
Elaine Wellin (Sonoma State University)

A little more than a year before he was fired on June 23, 2010, for making potentially insubordinate remarks in a *Rolling Stone* profile, General Stanley McChrystal was appointed by President Barack Obama as commander in charge of the war in Afghanistan. He had been formerly in charge of the Joint Special Operations Command (JSOC) headed by former Vice President Dick Cheney. Most of what General McChrystal has done over a thirty-three-year career remains classified, including service between 2003 and 2008 as commander of the JSOC, a special black operations commando unit of the Navy SEALS and Delta Force so clandestine that the Pentagon for years refused to acknowledge its existence.

Pulitzer Prize–winning journalist Seymour Hersh claims that the Bush administration ran an executive assassination ring that reported directly to former Vice President Dick Cheney, and that Congress had no oversight of it whatsoever. The JSOC team would go into countries, without talking to the ambassador or to the CIA station chief, find people on a to-be-killed list, execute them, and leave. There was an ongoing list of targeted people, cleared by Vice President Cheney's office, who had committed acts of war or were suspected of planning operations of war against the United States. Hersh asserts that there have been assassinations in a dozen countries in the Middle East and Latin America. "There's an executive order, signed by President Ford, in the '70s, forbidding such action. It's not only contrary—it's illegal, it's immoral, it's counterproductive," he added.

JSOC was also involved in war crimes, including the torture of prisoners in secret "ghost" detention sites. Camp Nama in Iraq was one such "ghost" facility hidden from the International Committee of the Red Cross (ICRC), the international body charged under international law with monitoring compliance with the Geneva Conventions, and given the right to inspect all facilities where people are detained in a country that is at war or under military occupation. On July 22, 2006, Human Rights Watch issued a report, titled "No Blood, No Foul," about American torture practices at three facilities in Iraq. One of them was Camp Nama, accused of some of the worst acts of torture, and operated by JSOC, under the direction of McChrystal. McChrystal, then a Major General, was officially based at Fort Bragg in North Carolina, but he was a frequent visitor to Camp Nama and other bases in Iraq and Afghanistan under his command.

An interrogator at Camp Nama described locking prisoners in shipping containers for twenty-four hours at a time in extreme heat, exposing them to extreme cold with periodic soaking in cold water, bombardment with bright lights and loud music, sleep deprivation, and severe beatings. When he and other interrogators went to the colonel in charge and expressed concern that this kind of treatment was not legal, and that they might be investigated by the military's Criminal Investigation Division or the ICRC, the colonel told them he had "this directly from General McChrystal and the Pentagon that there's no way that the Red Cross could get in." The interrogator said that he did see McChrystal visiting the Nama facility on several occasions. "I saw him a couple of times. I know what he looks like."

In describing why no other press had covered the story, Hersh stated, "My colleagues at the press corps often don't follow up, not because they don't want to but because they don't know who to call. If I'm writing something on the Joint Special Operations Command, which is an ostensibly classified unit, how do they find it out? The government will tell them everything I write is wrong or that they can't comment. It's easy for those stories to be dismissed. I do think the relationship with JSOC is changing under Obama. It's more under control now."

However, according to Press TV, the decision by Obama's administration to appoint General McChrystal as the new commander in charge of the war in Afghanistan, as well as the continuation of the military commission for the detainees held in the Guantánamo Bay prison, are unfortunately examples of the Obama administration continuing to walk in Bush's footsteps.

Update

Rock Creek Free Press reported in their June 2010 issue that Seymour Hersh, speaking at the Global Investigative Journalism conference in Geneva in April 2010, had criticized President Barack Obama and alleged that US forces are engaged in "battlefield executions." "Those we capture in Afghanistan are being executed on the battlefield," Hersh claimed.

25

Prisoners Still Brutalized at Gitmo

Sources:

Jeremy Scahill, "Little Known Military Thug Squad Still Brutalizing Prisoners at Gitmo Under Obama," *AlterNet*, May 15, 2009, http://www.alternet.org/story/140022.

Andrew Wander, "Guantanamo Conditions 'Deteriorate,'" *Al Jazeera English*, November 10, 2009, http://www.commondreams.org/headline/2009/11/10-0.

Student Researcher:
Scott Macky (Sonoma State University)

Faculty Evaluator:
Peter Phillips (Sonoma State University)

In Guantánamo, the notorious but seldom-discussed thug squad, officially known as the Immediate Reaction Force (IRF), deployed by the US military remains very much active. Inside the walls of Guantánamo, the prisoners know the squad as the Extreme Repression Force.

In reality, IRF is an extrajudicial terror squad, the existence of which has been documented since the early days of Guantánamo. IRF has rarely been mentioned in the United States media or in congressional inquiries into torture. On paper, IRF teams are made up of five military police officers who are on constant standby to respond to emergencies. "The IRF team is intended to be used primarily as a forced-extraction team, specializing in the extraction of a detainee who is combative, resistive, or if [there is] the possibility of a weapon . . . in the cell at the time of the extraction," according to a declassified copy of the Standard Operating Procedures (SOP) for Camp Delta at Guantánamo. The document

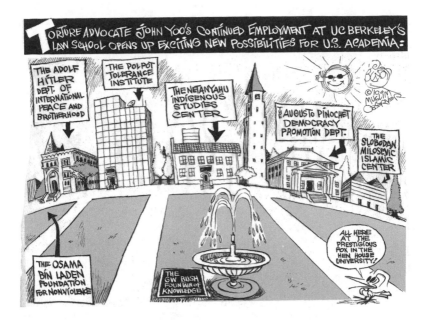

was signed on March 27, 2003, by Major General Geoffrey Miller, the man credited with eventually "Gitmoizing" Abu Ghraib and other US-run prisons.

When an IRF team is called in, its members are dressed in full riot gear, which some prisoners and their attorneys have compared to "Darth Vader" suits. Each officer is assigned a body part of the prisoner to restrain: head, right arm, left arm, left leg, right leg. According to the SOP document, the teams are to give verbal warnings to prisoners before storming the cell: "Prior to the use of the IRF team, an interpreter will be used to tell the detainee of the discipline measures to be taken against him and ask whether he intends to resist. Regardless of his answer, his recent behavior and demeanor should be taken into account in determining the validity of his answer." The IRF team is authorized to spray the detainee in the face with mace twice before entering the cell.

David Hicks, an Australian citizen held at Guantánamo, said in a sworn affidavit, "I have witnessed the activities of the IRF, which consists of a squad of soldiers that enter a detainee's cell and brutalize him with the aid of an attack dog. . . . I have seen detainees suffer serious injuries as a result of being IRF'ed. I have seen detainees IRF'ed while they were praying, or for refusing medication."

Binyam Mohamed, released in February 2009, has also described an IRF assault: "They nearly broke my back. The guy on top was twisting me one way, the guys on my legs the other. They marched me out of the cell to the fingerprint room, still cuffed. I clenched my fists behind me so they couldn't take prints, so they tried to take them by force. The guy at my head sticks his fingers up my nose and wrenches my head back, jerking it around by the nostrils. Then he put his fingers in my eyes. It felt as if he was trying to gouge them out. Another guy was punching my ribs, and another was squeezing my testicles. Finally, I couldn't take it any more. I let them take the prints."

On January 22, 2009, newly inaugurated President Obama issued an executive order requiring the closure of Guantánamo within a year, and also ordered a review of the status of the prisoners held there, requiring "humane standards of confinement" in accordance with the Geneva Conventions. But one month later, the Center for Constitutional Rights (CCR) released a report titled "Conditions of Confinement at Guantánamo: Still In Violation of the Law," which found that abuses continued. In fact, one Guantánamo lawyer, Ahmed Ghappour, said that his clients were reporting "a ramping up in abuse" since Obama was elected, including "beatings, the dislocation of limbs, spraying of pepper spray into closed cells, applying pepper spray to toilet paper and over-force-feeding detainees who are on hunger strike."

A year after Obama's election win, Al Jazeera reports that despite the new president's pledge to close the prison and improve the conditions of detainees held by the US military, prisoners believe that their treatment has deteriorated on his watch. While the dominant media coverage of the US torture apparatus has portrayed these tactics as part of a "Bush-era" system that Obama has now ended, when it comes to the IRF teams that is simply not true. "Detainees live in constant fear of physical violence. Frequent attacks by IRF teams heighten this anxiety and reinforce that violence can be inflicted by the guards at any moment for any perceived infraction, or sometimes without provocation or explanation," according to the CCR.

The CCR has called on the Obama administration to immediately end the use of the IRF teams at Guantánamo. However, the abuse continues, and the White House and powerful congressional leaders from both parties fiercely resist the appointment of an independent special prosecutor to investigate the abuses.

Ahmed Ghappour, who represents several Guantánamo prisoners, has lodged several requests to initiate investigations since President Obama took office. "I have requested four investigations regarding prisoner abuse just this past year," he said. "The military responded to my first request indicating that they would investigate, but have been radio silent since then."

Released after a federal court found him to be entirely innocent, Mohammed el Gharani is now adjusting to life outside prison. He reports that the allegations made by current inmates match his experience of Guantánamo during the months leading up to his release. "I recognize all of this," he said. "There are still more than two hundred people in Guantánamo. Since Obama became president, less than twenty have been released. I don't know why, but he has broken his promises."

RUNNERS UP FOR CENSORED 2011

We are pleased to announce that all nominations for the *Censored* yearbooks are now placed online year-round for public comment and discussion. These stories are researched, fact-checked by faculty and students, investigated for corporate media coverage in the LexisNexis database, and written up as what we call Validated Independent News. Below are short briefs on the top runners-up for this year. Please visit our Media Freedom International Web site at www.mediafreedominternational.org for more information on these stories and new nominations from our worldwide affiliate colleges and universities.

Copenhagen Climate Summit Ends in Discord

Martin Khor, "Copenhagen Climate Summit Ends in Discord," *Third World Resurgence* 233 (January 2010), http://www.twnside.org.sg/title2/resurgence/2010/233/cover01.htm.

Third World Demands Climate Responsibility

Naomi Klein, "Climate Rage: The Only Way to Stop Global Warming Is for Rich Nations to Pay for the Damage They've Done—or Face the Consequences," *Rolling Stone*, November 11, 2009, http://www.rollingstone.com/politics/story/30841581/climate_rage.

US Initiated WTO Rules Undermine Regulation of Global Finance

Lori Wallach, "Report: US-Initiated WTO Rules Could Undermine Regulatory Overhaul of Global Finance," *Democracy Now!*, September 25, 2009, www.democracynow.org/2009/9/25/report_us_initiated_wto_rules_could.

Public Citizen, "New Report: No Meaningful Safeguards for Prudential Measures in WTO Financial Service Deregulation Agreements," September 23, 2009, http://www.citizen.org/hot_issues/issue.cfm?ID=2374.

EPA's Secret Plan to Raise Exposure Limits after Nuke Accidents

"EPA's Secret Plan to Raise Public Radiation Exposure Levels Challenged," *Environment News Service*, October 29, 2009, http://www.ens-newswire.com/ens/oct2009/2009-10-29-091.asp.

Rape in the Ranks: The Enemy Within

Ann Wright, "Rape in the Ranks: The Enemy Within," *Op Ed News*, October 27, 2009, http://www.opednews.com/articles/Rape-in-the-Ranks-The-Ene-by-Ann-Wright-091027-923.html.

Arms Trade Watch Dogs Disappear in Air France Crash

Andrew McLeod, "Key Figures in Global Battle Against Illegal Arms Trade Lost in Air France Crash," *Herald Scotland*, June 7, 2009, http://www.heraldscotland.com/key-figures-in-global-battle-against-illegal-arms-trade-lost-in-air-france-crash-1.829372.

India's Children Crippled by Uranium Waste

Gethin Chamberlain, "India's Generation of Children Crippled by Uranium Waste," *Guardian*, August 30, 2009, http://www.guardian.co.uk/world/2009/aug/30/india-punjab-children-uranium-pollution.

In US, 90 Percent of Black Children Will Be Fed by Food Stamps

Agence France-Presse, "Study: In US, 90 Percent of Black Children Will Be Fed by Food Stamps," *Raw Story*, November 2, 2009, http://rawstory.com/2009/2009/11/study-90-percent-black-children-fed-food-stamps.

Madagascar: Poverty Forces 2 Million Children into Hard Labor

Fanja Saholiarisoa, "Poverty Forces 2 Million Children into Hard Labor," Inter Press Service, September 22, 2009, http://www.ipsnews.net/news.asp?idnews=48552.

The Dark Side of Dairies: A Broken System that Leaves Workers Invisible—and in Danger

Rebecca Clarren, "The Dark Side of Dairies: A Broken System Leaves Immigrant

Workers Invisible—and in Danger," *High Country News*, August 31, 2009, http://www.hcn.org/issues/41.15/the-dark-side-of-dairies.

Human Rights Abuses Exacerbating Poverty In Afghanistan

United Nations Office of the High Commissioner for Human Rights, Human Rights Dimensions of Poverty in Afghanistan (Kabul: UNOHCHR, March 2010), http://www.scribd.com/doc/29203806/Poverty-Report-30-March-2010-English-1.

According to UN Committee Against Torture, the Spanish State's Incommunicado Detention Violates Human Rights; UN Calls for its Abolition

Committee Against Torture, *Convention Against Torture and Other Cruel, Inhuman or Degrading Treatment of Punishment*, 43rd sess., November 2–20, 2009, http://www2.ohchr.org/english/bodies/cat/docs/co/CAT-C-ESP-CO-5_sp.doc (Español) or http://www2.ohchr.org/english/bodies/cat/docs/co/CAT-C-ESP-CO-5.doc (English).

Alvar Chalmeta, "El Comité Contra la Tortura de la ONU Pide Abolir la Incomunicación," Diagonal 115, http://www.diagonalperiodico.net/El-Comite-contra-la-Tortura-de-la.html.

Iratxe Urizar, "¿No les parece que ya se les ha repetido suficientemente?" Diagonal 115, http://www.diagonalperiodico.net/El-Comite-contra-la-Tortura-de-la.html.

The US Chamber of Commerce: A Record of Obstruction on Climate Action

Shaun Goho, "The US Chamber of Commerce: A Record of Obstruction on Climate Action," *Yale Environment 360*, February 26, 2010, http://www.commondreams.org/headline/2010/02/26-2.

Obama Administration's Housing Initiative Benefits the Banks

Center for Economic and Policy Research, "Economist Who Foretold First Housing Bubble Says, 'Beware,'" press release, March 26, 2010, http://www.commondreams.org/headline/2010/03/26-10.

America's Secret Afghan Prisons: Investigation Unearths New US Torture Site, Abuse Allegations in Afghanistan

Amy Goodman, "America's Secret Afghan Prisons: Investigation Unearths New US Torture Site, Abuse Allegations in Afghanistan," *Democracy Now!*, February 2, 2010, http://www.democracynow.org/2010/2/2/americas_secret_afghan_prisons_investigation_unearths.

Andan Gopal, "America's Secret Afghan Prisons," *Nation*, January 28, 2010, http://www.thenation.com/doc/20100215/gopal.

Haitian Aid Racket—NGOs Profiting from Grave Situation

Ashley Smith, "The Aid Racket," *Socialist Worker*, February 24, 2010, http://socialistworker.org/2010/02/24/the-aid-racket.

Israel Criticized for Nuclear Weapons

David Morrison, "The Elephant in the Room: Israel's Nuclear Weapons," *Common Dreams*, June 29, 2009, http://www.commondreams.org/view/2009/06/29-8.

Associated Press, "Nuclear Conference Criticizes Israeli Nukes," MSNBC.com, September 8, 2009, http://www.google.com/hostednews/ap/article/ALeqM5hnEzom45RpoqPwIeSBA9sQLziV8QD9APSNP00.

US Special Forces Murder Family in Syria

Reese Erlich and Peter Coyote, "The Murders at al-Sukariya," Vanity Fair, October 27, 2008, http://www.vanityfair.com/politics/features/2009/10/al-sukariya-200910.

Genetic Manipulation in Farm Animals

Wayne Pacelle, "Frankenfurters: Genetic Engineering of Farm Animals," *Huffington Post*, October 15, 2009, http://www.huffingtonpost.com/wayne-pacelle/frankenfurters-genetic-en_b_321969.html.

Michael Gregor, "Trait Selection and Welfare of Genetically Engineered Animals In Agriculture," Journal of Animal Science 88:811–814, http://jas.fass.org/cgi/content/abstract/jas.2009-2043v1; http://www.hsus.org/farm/news/ournews/genetic_manipulation_farm_animal_suffering_101409.html.

The Oath Keepers and the Rise of Radical Patriotism

Justine Sharrock, "Oath Keepers and the Age of Treason," *Mother Jones*, March/April 2010, http://motherjones.com/politics/2010/03/oath-keepers.

Secret Fundamentalist "Family"—Beyond C Street

Amy Goodman and Jeff Sharlet, "The Family: The Secret Fundamentalism at the Heart of American Power," *Democracy Now!*, May 6, 2009, http://www.democracynow.org/2009/8/12/sharlet.

Microloans = Mega-Profits, Not Development

Sara Flounders, "Microloans = Mega-profits, Not Development," *Workers World*, February 24, 2010, http://www.workers.org/2010/world/microloans_0304/index.html.

Obama Backs DNA Test for All Arrests in the US

Josh Gerstein, "Obama Backs DNA Test in Arrests," Politico, March 9, 2010, http://www.politico.com/news/stories/0310/34097.html.

Venezuela Strengthens National Health System and Lessens Poverty

Edward Ellis, "Venezuela Strengthens National Health System, Marks Advance in Fight Against Poverty," *Venezuela News Analysis*, March 4, 2010, http://www.venezuelanalysis .com/news/5173.

Obama Executive Order Expands US Military Control over State National Guards

Tom Burghardt, "Obama Executive Order Seeks to 'Synchronize and Integrate,'" *Dissident Voice*, January 16, 2010, http://dissidentvoice.org/2010/01/obama-executive-order-seeks-to-synchronize-and-integrate-state-and-federal-military-forces.

Obama Sells Ambassadorships

Michael Beckel, Center for Responsive Politics, "Obama Elevates Three More Bundlers & Big Donors in Latest Ambassador Picks," Open Secrets Web site, August 7, 2009, blog section, http://www.opensecrets.org/news/2009/08/obamas-elevates-three-more-big.html.

Wealthy Petition for Tax Increase

Katrina Vanden Heuvel, "Wealth for the Common Good," Nation, July 30, 2009, http://www.thenation.com/blogs/edcut/457403/wealth_for_the_common_good.

Was the Iranian Election Stolen?

Mark Weisbrot, "Was the Iranian Election Stolen? Does It Matter?" *Washington Post*, June 26, 2009, http://www.cepr.net/index.php/op-eds-&-columns/op-eds-&-columns/was-the-iranian-election-stolen.

James Petras, "Iranian Elections: The 'Stolen Elections' Hoax," Global Research, June 18, 2009, http://www.globalresearch.ca/index.php?context=va&aid=14018.

PROJECT CENSORED GERMANY'S TOP 10 CENSORED NEWS STORIES FROM 2009

Published on January 30, 2010,
by Initiative Nachrichtenaufklärung / Initiative News Enlightenment

1. Hospital Emergency: Patients in Need Are Left Alone

In Germany, there are half a million people who are dependent on professional caregivers in their daily lives. During hospital stays, they have to do without this help. Moreover, German clinics, with their severe shortage of nursing staff, are not equipped to deal with the needs of chronically ill or disabled patients. As a results, meals are cleared away too early and unacceptable behaviour is treated with tranquilizers. Social organizations have been fighting for years to put an end to this deplorable state of affairs. As a result of their pressure, a law was passed in the summer of 2009, which has, however, only solved the problem for very few patients. This nursing shortage predicament has not been covered by the media.

2. Psychiatric Hospitals: German Laws Violate UN Convention

In Germany, people who medical experts think present a danger either to themselves or to others can be forced to go into psychiatric clinics. However, the UN Convention on the Rights of Persons with Disabilities requires compulsory hospitalization and treatment only if someone violates criminal law. The convention has been valid in Germany since 2009 but at this point, has wrongfully been put into national law with the intention of maintaining practice. This behaviour has been criticized by human rights lawyers and patient interest groups. The media has shown no interest in the subject.

3. War Reporting Diverts Attention from Civilian Measures for Conflict Resolution

Civilian measures for dealing with conflicts, as an alternative to military intervention, are rarely a matter for discussion in the media, although these measures often bring peace to areas of crisis. Good examples of this are the Nepal conflict and the Baltic States' process for leaving the Soviet Union. As Germany commits itself more and more frequently to military actions worldwide in areas of crisis, the civilian alternatives should also be made public.

4. Illegal Police Violence

Even in Germany, a state of law, there can be violent police attacks on people. These cases are rarely made public, as the culprits are investigated by their own colleagues: most court cases are abandoned because policemen do not testify against each other and, apart from the victim, are often the only witnesses. The media reports isolated cases but fails to point out the lack of an independent investigative committee.

5. Church Finances Not Controlled

Religious institutions under public jurisdiction—as in the case of many Catholic monasteries in Bavaria without an affiliated business—are exempt from tax and are therefore not controlled by the tax office. They are automatically considered trustworthy. This makes it possible to use faked donation receipts and evade tax without anyone noticing. The media tends to ignore the lack of financial supervision and these potential tax loopholes.

6. Iodine Additives Not Always Declared

The strong lobbying by salt and pharmacy companies propagates iodine additives in food. Nevertheless, approximately 10 percent of Germans suffer from iodine intolerance, while sicknesses induced by the lack of iodine are declining. It is also suspected that too much iodine has a worsening effect on autoimmune diseases of the thyroid gland. Often, the addition of iodine does not have to be declared on food packaging, which makes the ingredient difficult to avoid. The media rarely reports on this lack of consumer choice.

7. Patents for Human Genes and Gene Sequences

Decoded human genes, and gene sequences such as those that contribute to high blood pressure or breast cancer, may be patented. The monopoly of individual patent owners hinders competing firms in the development of their own pharmaceutics and makes independent research expensive. There can also be disadvantages for patients, as forms of treatment not requiring a license are preferred by the medical insurance companies for economic reasons. Comprehensive reporting on the chances, risks and consequences of gene patenting does not take place.

8. Rejection of Sign Language in Schools for the Deaf

Sign language is taught in very few German schools for the deaf. Around eighty thousand Germans are deaf. Scientists have been arguing for decades about whether the deaf should learn their own language system or not. Most teachers of the deaf assume that the mastery and use of sign language excludes their pupils from society. Critics, on the other hand, fear that without the use of sign language the deaf could be inhibited in their mental development, as only 30 percent of spoken language can be lip read. Very few people even know of the existence of this debate.

9. Germany Is a Leading Power in Exporting Arms

For many years, Germany has been one of the world's biggest exporters of weapons and armaments. In spite of an allegedly restrictive licensing practice, armed conflicts make use of German weapons. They are delivered to countries with problematic human rights statuses such as Georgia, Darfur, and Afghanistan. Only in exceptional cases do the media embark on the painstaking research into this complex and elusive subject.

10. Building and Renovation of Houses Without Waste Disposal Problems

Even after the prohibition of the cancer-inducing building material asbestos, many materials are still used in building and renovation, which presents a problem for human beings and for the environment. Many chemicals in floor and wall insulations, for example, cause allergic reactions. For many synthetic insulation materials such as polystyrene, there are natural alternatives like flax, hemp, or wool. People are encouraged to insulate their houses without any public discussion about long-term consequences caused by synthetic materials. The disposal problem of these is, at best, analyzed in the specialist media or in special supplements.

INITIATIVE NACHRICHTENAUFKLÄRUNG / INITIATIVE NEWS ENLIGHTENMENT is based at Jacobs University under the leadership of Professor Peter Ludes: p.ludes@jacobs-university.de

CHAPTER 2

Déjà vu
What Happens to *Censored* Stories from Years Past?

by Mickey Huff and Josette Canilao, with Nolan Higdon, Mike Smith, Kajal Shahali, Sy Cowie, Kira McDonough, and Ryan Shehee (with special thanks to Carl Jensen)

> *It's like déjà vu all over again.*
> —YOGI BERRA

> *Those who cannot remember the past are condemned to repeat it.*
> —GEORGE SANTAYANA

Each year, Project Censored looks back on its past in an effort to discover what may have become of some of its previous years' stories. Have they seen the light of day in the corporate media? Have they been reported and explored in detail and become part of public discourse in democratic society? If so, how and to what degree? Further, why does this matter? Let's examine some of last year's top stories, as well as a few of the more significant ones from years past, to see if there truly are déjà vu moments in terms of media revelation—or continued censorship.

Censored 2010 #1

US Congress Sells Out to Wall Street

Federal lawmakers responsible for overseeing the US economy have received millions of dollars from Wall Street firms. Since 2001, eight of the most troubled firms have donated $64.2 million to congressional candidates, presidential candidates, and the Republican and Democratic parties. As senators, Barack Obama and John McCain received a combined total of $3.1 million. The donors include investment bankers Bear Stearns, Goldman Sachs, Lehman Brothers, Merrill Lynch, Morgan Stanley, insurer American International Group (AIG), and mortgage giants Fannie Mae and Freddie Mac.

Some of the top recipients of contributions from companies receiving Troubled Assets Relief Program (TARP) money are the same members of Congress who chair committees charged with regulating the financial sector and overseeing the effectiveness of this unprecedented government program. In total, members of the Senate Committee on Banking, Housing and Urban Affairs, Senate Finance Committee, and House Financial Services Committee received $5.2 million from TARP recipients in the 2007–08 election cycle. President Obama collected at least $4.3 million from employees at these companies for his presidential campaign.

Original Sources: Greg Gordon, "Lax Oversight? Maybe $64 Million to DC Pols Explain it," *Truthout,* October 2, 2008; Lindsay Renick Mayer, "Congressmen Hear from TARP Recipients Who Funded Their Campaigns," Capital Eye blog, February 10, 2009; Matt Taibbi, "The Big Takeover," *Rolling Stone,* March 19, 2009.

Update: Though there has been mainstream corporate media coverage on Congress selling out to Wall Street, there has been no specific coverage about members of Congress receiving contributions from the main banks that were awarded TARP funds. Publications in the corporate press that did cover the issue were *Newsweek* and the *Washington Post.* Both mentioned the cycle of funds occurring between political officials and bailout beneficiaries.

Open Secrets, the Web site for the Center for Responsive Politics (CRP), has continued to update and expose the issue, reporting that the CRP, which tracks how money affects and is used in US politics, found that "companies that have been awarded taxpayers' money from Congress's bailout bill spent $77 million on lobbying and $37 million on federal campaign contributions. . . . The return on investment: 258,449 percent." In turn, "some of the top recipients of contributions from companies receiving TARP money are the same members of Congress who chair committees charged with regulating the financial sector and overseeing the effectiveness of this unprecedented government program." In other words, the banks that are receiving the bailout money are awarded that aid by the same political officials they finance. Despite a few reports, this has gone seemingly unnoticed in much of the corporate media.

Corporate Media Sources: Michael Isikoff, "Follow the Bailout Cash," *Newsweek*, March 29, 2009, http://www.newsweek.com/2009/03/20/follow-the-bailout-cash.html; Dan Eggen, "Firms Infused With Rescue Cash Find Money to Fund Lobbying," *Washington Post*, April 22, 2009, http://www.washingtonpost.com/wp-dyn/content/article/2009/04/21/AR2009042101788.html.

Source: Center for Responsive Politics, "TARP Recipients Paid Out $114 Million for Politicking Last Year," Open Secrets, February 4, 2009, http://www.opensecrets.org/news/2009/02/tarp-recipients-paid-out-114-m.html.

Censored 2010 #2

US Schools are More Segregated Today than in the 1950s

Schools in the United States are more segregated today than they have been in more than four decades. Millions of nonwhite students are locked into "dropout factory" high schools, where huge percentages do not graduate, and few are well prepared for college or a future in the US economy.

Our nation's segregated schools result from decades of systematic neglect of civil rights policy and related educational and community reforms. According to a University of California–Los Angeles (UCLA) report, what is needed are leaders who recognize that we have a common destiny in an America where our children grow up together, knowing and respecting each other, and are all given the educational tools that prepare them for success in our society. The author maintains that if we are to continue along a path of deepening separation and entrenched inequality, it will only diminish our common potential.

Original Source: Gary Orfield, "Reviving the Goal of an Integrated Society: A 21st Century Challenge," The Civil Rights Project, University of California–Los Angeles, January 2009.

Update: Since *Censored 2010*, the conversation about segregation, along with the UCLA findings, has become more public. In particular, California has received the harshest criticism from commentators regarding

segregation. But the inability of Americans to see the connection between racial and economic segregation has caused a laissez-faire attitude toward solving the problem. Commentators and critics have not drawn a clear picture of how poorly funded schools offer a less rigorous education and under-equipped staffs, and the coverage is chock-full of blame and finger pointing without possible solutions.

The 2009 UCLA study concluded that segregation is the worst in the West, a finding affirmed by a 2010 national report card that found that three of the five states to tie for the lowest reading scores in the nation came from the western United States, including California. San Francisco responded; the *New York Times* reported in 2010 that the San Francisco Unified School District planned to revamp and fix its student-assignment system in an attempt to relieve segregation. Critics of the proposed plan, though, noted that economic segregation could grow worse if San Francisco's districts were divided to stop racial divide while ignoring economic factors.

In early 2009, Sonoma State University (SSU) professor Dr. Peter Phillips also released a faculty report that lambasted SSU for its application process, which has led to segregation along both racial and economic lines. The report demonstrated how SSU's attempt to create an upper-class and wealthy college has resulted in "the whitest college" in the California State system. Meanwhile, SSU administrators have continued to assert that its campus is very diverse despite information to the contrary.

Students have not been blind to the growing problem in public education; on March 4, 2010, they protested across the US in opposition to nationwide budget cuts. Sadly, the US will never be able to thoroughly discuss these issues unless government and community leaders begin a dialogue aimed at explaining that education is a right as important as any other. Education should be granted to all Americans in the best possible—and most equal—fashion no matter what the cost, as the cost of ignorance and illiteracy is simply too high.

This topic has been highlighted in the mainstream corporate media, especially in California, the area noted as specifically segregated, and it has also been covered by the independent press. But the debate about what to do must continue, with particular attention paid to the right of all people—including those most disenfranchised—to be educated.

Corporate Sources: Jesse McKinley, "New Plan on School Selection, but Still Discontent," *New York Times*, February 21, 2010; Jill Tucker, "Charter schools split by race, study finds," *San Francisco Chronicle*, February 5, 2010; "The Bay Area is bucking a national trend of racial segregation in charter schools, according to a new national study," *Oakland Tribune*, February 17, 2010; Jill Tucker, "State shares rock bottom in U.S. reading scores," *San Francisco Chronicle*, March 25, 2010, http:/www.sfgate.com/ cgi-bin/article.cgi?f=/ c/a/2010/03/24/MNCHiCKMAA.DTL; Connie Llanos, "Charter schools too segregated," *Daily News Los Angeles*, February 4, 2010, http://www .dailynews.com/ci_14338318.

Sources: Connie Llanos, "Charter schools too segregated," *Inland Valley Daily Bulletin*, February 4, 2010; Sonja Sharp, "Charter Schools Segregated Just Like Public Schools," *Mother Jones*, February 5, 2010, http://motherjones.com/mojo/2010/02/charter-schools-segregated-just-public-schools; David Moltz, "Not So White Noise About Diversity," *Inside Higher Education*, February 25, 2009, http://www.insidehighered .com/news/2009/02/25/sonoma; "Iraq War Spending vs. Education Spending," *Education Portal*, July 16, 2007, http://education-portal.com/articles/Iraq_War_Spending_vs._Education_Spending.html; Peter Phillips, "Building a Public Ivy," http://www.projectcensored.org/ articles/story/building-a-public-ivy.

Toxic Waste Behind Somali Pirates

The international community has come out in force to condemn and declare war on the Somali fishermen pirates, while discreetly protecting the illegal, unreported, and unregulated (IUU) fleets from around the world that have been poaching and dumping toxic waste in Somali waters since the fall of the Somali government eighteen years ago.

According to the High Seas Task Force (HSTF), there were over 800 IUU fishing vessels in Somali waters at one time in 2005, taking advantage of Somalia's inability to police and control its own waters and fishing grounds. The IUUs poach an estimated $450 million in seafood from Somali waters annually. In so doing, they steal an invaluable protein source from some of the world's poorest people and ruin the livelihoods of legitimate fishermen.

Original Sources: Najad Abdullahi, "Toxic waste behind Somali piracy," Al Jazeera English, October 11, 2008; Johann Hari, "You are being lied to about pirates," *Huffington Post*, January 4, 2009; Mohamed Abshir Waldo, "The Two Piracies in Somalia: Why the World Ignores the Other," *WardheerNews*, January 8, 2009.

Update: Since this story was featured in *Censored 2010*, there have been no changes in the way the mainstream media covers the actions of Somalia's fishermen. Though the *Washington Post* did manage to touch on the issue, most mainstream corporate media continues to deem Somali fishermen as "pirates." Described as a "17th-century crime" by Secretary of State Hillary Clinton, these fishermen have been protecting Somalia's natural resources and providing national defense since the government's collapse and subsequent civil war almost two decades ago. Yet, despite international attention after attacks on the merchant vessels *Maersk Alabama* and *Liberty Sun* in spring 2009, the corporate media remains one-sided, continually ignoring the root cause of the problem (exploitation by European and Asian companies in the wake of a collapsed Somali government with no coast guard or navy to protect the coast) and highlighting only the Somalis' misdeeds. Certainly the taking of hostages is unjustifiable, but it remains the corporate mainstream media's sole point of interest regarding Somalia and its people.

Likewise, there have been no changes in the situation in which these fishermen find themselves. Illegal poaching and toxic waste dumping along Africa's longest (and largely unprotected) coastline have ruined Somali lives. These people continue to be demonized in much of the Western press, even after a 2004 tsunami uncovered frightening amounts of toxic waste, which produced illness among the coastal population and posed an ongoing environmental hazard. The United Nations continues to ignore appeals and instead encourages military aggression against these "pirates"; Nicholas Kralev of the *Washington Times* reports "unprecedented military cooperation among NATO forces, Russia, China and other countries" in order to "decrease the number of pirate attacks" in the Gulf of Aden.

Finally, there have been no changes in the way Somalis themselves view these "pirates." Although the majority of the world views them as criminals, therefore justifying military protection of an integral waterway in the world's oil supply and economy, many Somalis see them as protectors against the illegal actions of foreign nations that are threatening Somalia's sovereignty.

Corporate Source: Nicholas Kralev, "Multinational policing curbs piracy off Somalia," *Washington Times*, February 19, 2010.

Source: Firoz Osman, "For many Somalis, these 'pirates' are marine police," *Star* (South Africa), June 30, 2009.

Censored 2010 #4

Nuclear Waste Pools in North Carolina

One of the most lethal patches of ground in North America is located in the backwoods of North Carolina, where Shearon Harris nuclear plant is housed and owned by Progress Energy. The plant contains the largest radioactive waste storage pools in the country. It is not just a nuclear-power-generating station, but also a repository for highly radioactive spent fuel rods from two other nuclear plants. The spent fuel rods are transported by rail and stored in four densely packed pools filled with circulating cold water to keep the waste from heating. The Department of Homeland Security has marked Shearon Harris as one of the most vulnerable terrorist targets in the nation.

The threat exists, however, without the speculation of terrorist attack. Should the cooling system malfunction, the resulting fire would be virtually unquenchable and could trigger a nuclear meltdown, putting more than 200 million residents of this rapidly growing section of North Carolina in extreme peril. A recent study by Brookhaven Lab estimates that a pool fire could cause 140,000 cancers, contaminate thousands of square miles of land, and cause over $500 billion in off-site property damage.

Original Source: Jeffrey St. Clair, "Pools of Fire," *CounterPunch*, August 9, 2008, http://www.counterpunch.org/stclair08092008.html.

Update: In May 2010, officials from five different local governments around the Shearon Harris nuclear plant asked for an investigation into possible wrongdoing by the Nuclear Regulatory Commission (NRC), involving the top safety issue at the nation's reactors. Along with three watchdog groups, the local governments say that the NRC is ignoring its own regulations; it is also under criticism from numerous fire science experts. Thus far, the Common Dreams Web site had been one of the only media outlets to report on the safety issues at Shearon Harris and its waste storage pools, in an attempt to raise awareness and concern, though in May, after the investigation request, the Web site for the local television station WRAL reported that the NRC wants to hear from neighbors of Shearon Harris. The NRC has scheduled a meeting, which will include a question-and-answer session. Outside of these two small outlets, there has been no coverage on Shearon Harris, its nuclear waste pools, or the safety issues that continue to affect the plant. No mainstream corporate media coverage has exposed the hazards present at Shearon Harris.

Sources: "Feds Duck Nagging Problems with #1 Safety Rule at U.S. Nuclear Plants," Common Dreams, May 5, 2010; "Nuke regulators talk to Shearon Harris neighbors," WRAL Web site, May 18, 2010, http://www.wral.com/news/news_briefs/story/7619700.

Business Booms for Lobbyists

According to a study by the Center for Responsive Politics (CRP), special interests paid Washington lobbyists $3.2 billion in 2008—more than any other year on record. This was a 13.7 percent increase from 2007 (which broke the record by 7.7 percent over 2006).

The CRP calculates that interest groups spent $17.4 million on lobbying for every day Congress was in session in 2008, or $32,523 per legislator per day. Center director Sheila Krumholz says, "The federal government is handing out billions of dollars by the day, and that translates into job security for lobbyists who can help companies and industries get a piece of the payout."

Original Source: Center for Responsive Politics, "Washington Lobbying Grew to $3.2 Billion Last Year, Despite Economy," Open Secrets, http://www.opensecrets.org/news/2009/01/washington-lobbying-grew-to-32.html.

Update: In 2009, the CPR reported that special interests paid Washington lobbyists around $3.47 billion; this breaks the record set the previous year, at $3.2 billion. This record has been set and broken each year since 2006. CPR also calculates that special interests spend $19 million per day in Washington when Congress is in session.

The first quarter of 2010 doesn't bring any better news from the lobbyist front; so far, $903 million has been spent, compared to last year's first quarter at $811 million. This is an 11 percent increase from the first quarters of the previous two years. The total in the first quarter of 2010 is a 7 percent decrease from that of the final quarter of 2009, which was $970 million. The overall total for 2010, considering the amount in only the first quarter, is likely to shatter the previous record set in 2009.

Despite the current recession, businesses, health interests, energy companies, and Wall Street firms invested more than $123 million in the first quarter of 2010. The business sector spent $139 million, winning first place; a close second was the health sector, which spent $138 million. The top three spenders in the health sector are Pharmaceutical Research and Manufacturers of America (PhRMA) ($7,010,000), American Medical Association ($6,360,000), and Pfizer Inc. ($4,340,000).

The energy and natural resource sector is the third highest spender at $128 million; this sector's top three spenders are PG&E Corporation ($25,820,000), ConocoPhillips ($6,408,978), and Edison Electric Institute ($4,160,000). Last but not least is the finance, insurance, and real estate sector at $123 million; the highest payer is the National Association of Realtors ($4,320,000). The highest spending organization overall is the US Chamber of Commerce at $30,897,500.

Outside of the Open Secrets Web site, which posted the CPR's study, there is little mainstream coverage of the increasing amount spent on Washington lobbyists. Dan Eggen, journalist for the *Washington Post*, mentioned this rise in two articles published within the first two weeks of April 2009. Though lobbyist spending broke a record in 2009, and 2010 is on a path toward beating it, Eggen's were the last articles to report on this issue.

Source: Center for Responsive Politics, "Lobbying Database," Open Secrets, http://opensecrets.org/lobby.

Censored 2010 #8

Bailed-Out Banks and America's Wealthiest Cheat IRS Out of Billions

Story #8 in *Censored 2010* covered the use of offshore tax havens, to evade taxation, by top US companies who had received TARP funds by financial institutions such as Goldman Sachs, American International Group (AIG), Bank of America, and Citigroup use offshore subsidiaries in places like the Cayman Islands, Luxembourg, and Hong Kong to hide their profits from the US government and cheat the Internal Revenue Service (IRS). Corporations sell products and/or services to offshore subsidiaries at reduced rates, then use the subsidiaries to resell these products and/or services to customers for actual market rates. Thus, these corporations make their profits in a tax-free or low-tax environment. In addition, corporations can record losses from these deals by selling to their subsidiaries at below cost, allowing them to write off the loss in the US, thus avoiding the taxes that would be levied on the parent company's profits.

Original Sources: Christine Harper, "Goldman Sachs's Tax Rate Drops to 1% or $14 Million," Bloomberg, December 16, 2008; Thomas B. Edsall,

"Gimme Shelter: Tax Evasion and the Obama Administration," *Huffington Post*, February 23, 2009.

Update: Panama is one of the largest tax havens in the world with over 350,000 foreign-registered companies. Corporations that have received TARP funds—such as Morgan Stanley, Citigroup, and AIG—have subsidiaries in Panama, where they can avoid paying their US taxes.

The Panama Trade Promotion Agreement (PTPA), which is awaiting approval by the US Congress, is a North American Free Trade Agreement (NAFTA)–style trade agreement that would allow these subsidiary companies to file suit against the US government for the loss of notional future profits incurred as a result of regulatory action, or the imposition of new regulation, in the US. The loss of notional future profits is referred to in these trade agreements as "indirect expropriation." Protocols governing compensation for indirect expropriation are now a standard part of trade agreements.

According to a report put out by Public Citizen, a nonprofit consumer rights advocacy organization, the PTPA would prevent the US from treating Panama and Panamanian financial services differently from nontax havens, in terms of regulation of financial interactions and trade. The proposed agreement would prevent limitations on financial transactions (except in a few special circumstances), limitations that are an essential tool for preventing tax evasion and money laundering. PTPA would secure market access in the US for banks and other entities based in Panama. This would limit the US government's ability to regulate its financial system. It would also put a system into place that would allow foreign investors and subsidiaries of multinationals based in Panama to challenge US regulation of goods and services passing between the two nations, a provision that could stall regulation of US markets for as long as the challenge process takes. It could ultimately cause the overall derailment of US regulatory action, which stems from the collapse of the financial markets, by the very entities that caused the financial collapse—without any input by the taxpayers that bailed out said entities. No updates on PTPA bailouts and other key aspects of this issue have gone unreported by corporate mainstream press.

Source: "Panama FTA would undermine U.S. efforts to stop offshore tax-haven abuse and regulate risky financial behavior," Public Citizen, April 2009, http://www.citizen.org/documents/PanamaTaxEvasionReport April2009-FINAL.pdf.

US Arms Used for War Crimes in Gaza; Private Corporations Profit from the Occupation of Palestine

Stories #9 and #11 both covered the ongoing controversies regarding the Israeli occupation of Palestine. Story #9, specifically, focused on the Israeli firepower that was unleashed largely on Palestinian civilians in Gaza during the three-week attack starting December 27, 2008, and which was fueled by US-supplied weapons and paid for with US tax dollars. Washington provided F-16 fighter planes, Apache helicopters, tactical missiles, and a wide array of munitions, including (illegal) white phosphorus and dense inert metal explosive (DIME). The weapons required for the Israeli assault were decided upon in June 2008, and the transfer of 1,000 bunker-buster GPS-guided Small Diameter Bombs (GBU-39s) were approved by Congress in September. The GBU-39 bombs were delivered to Israel in November (prior to any claims of Hamas cease-fire violation) for use in the initial air raids on Gaza.

Story #11 is largely about how Israeli and international corporations are directly involved in, and profiting from, the occupation of Palestine. Along with various political, religious and national interests, the Israeli occupation of the West Bank, Gaza, East Jerusalem, and the Golan Heights is fueled by corporate interests. These occupying companies and corporations lead real estate deals, develop the Israeli colonies and infrastructure, and contribute to the construction and operation of an ethnic separation system, including checkpoints, walls, and roads—in other words, an apartheid system. They also design and supply equipment and tools used in the control and repression of the civilian population under occupation.

Original Sources: Fred Abrahams, "White Phosphorus Use Evidence of War Crimes Report: Rain of Fire: Israel's Unlawful Use of White Phosphorus in Gaza," Human Rights Watch, March 25, 2009; Rory McCarthy, "Suspend Military Aid to Israel, Amnesty Urges Obama after Detailing US Weapons Used in Gaza," *Guardian*, February 23, 2009; Thalif Deen, "US Weaponry Facilitates Killings in Gaza," Inter Press Service, January 8, 2009; Saed Bannoura, "US military re-supplying Israel with ammunition through Greece," International Middle East

Media Center News, January 8, 2009; Jeremy R. Hammond, "US Senate Endorses Israel's War on Gaza," *Foreign Policy Journal*, January 9, 2009; Coalition of Women for Peace, "Who Profits? Exposing the Israeli Occupation Industry," WhoProfits.org; "US Tax Breaks Support Israeli Settlers," Palestine News Network, August 26, 2008; Sara Flounders, "The Tunnels of Gaza: An underground economy and resistance symbol," *Workers World Newspaper*, February 9, 2009, and Global Research, February 11, 2009; Ann Wright, "Can Gaza Be Rebuilt Through Tunnels? The Blockade Continues—No Supplies, No Rebuilding," Common Dreams, February 24, 2009.

Update: On December 27, 2008, the Israeli military campaign "Operation Cast Lead" left 1,387 Palestinians dead, 773 of whom were civilians. The Israelis lost four civilians and ten soldiers. In September 2009, the United Nations Fact Finding Mission on the Gaza Conflict, led by former South African judge Richard Goldstone, concluded that both Hamas and Israel committed crimes against humanity, though these crimes were disproportionate. Goldstone very meticulously looked at Israel's aggressions and based his recommendations for international investigations on the testimonies and the destruction inside Gaza. Hamas—and other political groups—fired rockets and killed four civilians. Of the nine soldiers killed, five were by friendly fire attacks. The Israeli response to this, as indicated, was massive.

US Representatives Howard Berman (D-CA) and Ileana Ros-Lehtinen (R-FL) introduced H.Res.876 "calling upon the president and the secretary of state to oppose unequivocally any endorsement or further consideration" of the Goldstone report. The resolution was passed by the House under "suspension of the rules" on November 3, 2009. Simultaneously, Israel continued to deny any firing of white phosphorus, and the United States was never questioned or implicated by the corporate media regarding its involvement in the distribution of weapons to Israel. In early 2010, Israel admitted using white phosphorus in the Gaza War, blaming two officers for "exceeding their authorities," though with no mention of the United States' role in the attacks.

There has been little coverage of US corporations profiting from the occupation of Palestine in the corporate media, with only minor coverage free of in-depth analysis in early 2010. In protest of the Israeli occupation of Palestine, University of California (UC)–Berkeley students attempted to have a campus bill approved, to divest from two US companies—General Electric, which manufactures helicopter engines, and United Technologies, which manufactures Sikorsky helicopters and F-16 aircraft engines. The bill looked further into responsible investment for the UC system. The initial divestment bill passed by a 16–4 vote in the student senate, but Will Smelko, UC president of the student union, vetoed the bill a week later, after pro-Israel groups and Washington lobby groups such as the American Israel Public Affairs Committee (AIPAC)) became involved in an aggressive campaign to equate the bill with "anti-Semitism" to therefore delegitimize its intent.

In February 2010, independent journalist Nora Barrows-Friedman wrote in *Truthout* that the Obama administration had doubled its previous commitment to store American weapons stockpiles on Israeli soil, with the caveat that "Israel, after approval from the US government, would be able to access the American weapon and ammunition stockpile in case of a military 'emergency.'" The terms and definition of such an "emergency," including against whom the weaponry could be used, remained unclear.

Barrows-Friedman wrote that this agreement came on the heels of

> Obama's recent signing of a $30 billion, ten-year agreement for an expanded military aid package to the Israeli government. The first installment of the aid package, $2.775 billion, was signed over in December [2009] by President Obama, and was earmarked completely for Israel's military budget instead of the prior allocation to both civilian and military infrastructure. This massive military package is over and above the annual $3.1 billion in loan guarantees to Israel that the Obama administration plans to continue.

She revealed, "As a part of the ten-year agreement, Israel is required to contract 75 percent of the package toward the purchase of American-made military equipment and ammunition, intended to further subsidize US weapons manufacturers."

For more on Barrows-Friedman's coverage of Palestine, see chapter 8 of this volume.

Sources: Omer, M. "Life Upside Down: One Year After Israel's Winter War on Gaza," *Washington Report on Middle East Affairs* 29 (2): 16–17; "In Voting to Condemn Goldstone Report, 344 House Members Pass AIPAC

'Litmus Test,'" *Washington Report on Middle East Affairs*, 29 (1): 18–19, 22; Prusher, Ilene R. "Israel says white phosphorus use in Gaza 'exceeded authority,'" *Christian Science Monitor*, February 1, 2010, http://www.csmonitor.com/World/Middle-East/2010/0201/Israel-says-white-phosphorus-use-in-Gaza-exceeded-authority; "UC Berkeley Student Senate Approves Bill To Divest from General Electric and United Technologies," *UC Rebel Radio*, March 20, 2010, http://ucrebelradio.wordpress.com/2010/03/20/uc-berkeley-student-senate-approves-bill-to-divest-from-general-electric-and-united-technologies; Nora Barrows-Friedman, "US' Expanded Weapons Stockpiling in Israel," *Truthout*, February 10, 2010, http://www.truthout.org/us-expanded-weapons-stockpiling-israel56700.

Censored 2010 #13

Katrina's Hidden Race War

A shocking report in the *Nation* magazine exposes how white vigilante groups patrolled the streets of New Orleans after Hurricane Katrina, shooting at least eleven African-American men. While the media portrayed African Americans as looters and thugs, it is now clear that the most serious crimes were committed by gun-toting white males.

Democracy Now! footage showed that dead bodies were left, sometimes for weeks, to rot in full view of Homeland Security, state troopers, army personnel, private security guards, and police who "secured" the streets of New Orleans in the aftermath of Katrina.

Original Sources: A. C. Thompson, "Katrina's Hidden Race War," *Nation*, December 17, 2008; A. C. Thompson, "Body of Evidence," *Nation*, December 18, 2008; "Katrina's Hidden Race War: In Aftermath of Storm, White Vigilante Groups Shot 11 African Americans in New Orleans," *Democracy Now!*, December 19, 2008.

Update: In late summer 2009, London's the *Guardian* wrote of journalists' unwillingness to expose the murders of black citizens by the New Orleans Police Department and white vigilante groups in the aftermath of Hurricane Katrina. *The New York Times*, however, soon ran the headline "New Orleans Police Facing Katrina Investigations." The article included a report that police opened fire on the Danziger Bridge, wounding six and killing two, including a mentally challenged man. Dozens of officers were under investigation by the FBI for murder, including for the murder of Henry Glover, who was shot by vigilantes and brought to police by passerby William Tanner. It was Tanner who was then handcuffed and beaten. His car was confiscated by police, then was later discovered burned, with Glover's charred remains inside. The story remains under investigation.

In February 2010, the *New York Times* published the story "First Charge in U.S. Inquiry into New Orleans Police Shootings after Katrina," reporting that Lt. Michael Lohman was charged with one count of conspiring to obstruct justice when an investigation determined that he was involved in a police coverup—planting a gun on the Danziger Bridge to make the police shootings appear justified. In April 2010, *USA Today* reported that the US Justice Department was considering suing New Orleans to force changes within the police department after another former New Orleans police officer, Michael Hunter, plead guilty to obstruction of justice, among other charges, during the aftermath of Hurricane Katrina. *The Times-Picayune* (New Orleans), *Frontline*, and ProPublica have also been collaborating on the project "Law and Disorder," which follows up on the police shootings of black citizens in the hurricane's aftermath.

Since the *Censored 2010* story, mainstream corporate media outlets have covered the race war following Katrina. They have worked to expose the injustice apparent in last year's story, though more widespread reporting is still needed.

Corporate Sources: Campbell Robertson, "New Orleans Police Facing Katrina Investigations," *New York Times*, October 9, 2009; Campbell Robertson, "First Charge in U.S. Inquiry into New Orleans Police Shootings after Katrina," *New York Times*, February 25, 2010; Rick Jervis, "Feds may force changes at NOPD; In face of at least eight cases alleging police misconduct, Justice Dept. might sue New Orleans," *USA Today*, April 14, 2010; Elizabeth Redman, "ProPublica, Frontline and Times-Picayune investigate New Orleans police department," *Times-Picayune*, February 16, 2010.

Source: Rebecca Solnit, "Comment & Debate: Four years on, Katrina remains cursed by rumour, cliché, lies and racism: Ordinary people mostly behaved well. Those in power panicked, spread fear and fiction, and showed eagerness to kill," *Guardian*, August 28, 2009.

Secret Control of the Presidential Debates

The Obama and McCain campaigns jointly negotiated a detailed secret contract dictating the terms of the 2008 debates. This included who got to participate, what topics were to be raised, and the structure of the debate formats.

Since 1987, a private corporation created by and for the Republican and Democratic parties called the Commission on Presidential Debates (CPD) has sponsored the US presidential debates and implemented debate contracts. In order to shield the major party candidates from criticism, CPD has refused to release debate contract information to the public. In 1986, the Republican and Democratic National Committees ratified an agreement "to take over the presidential debates" from the nonpartisan League of Women Voters. Fifteen months later, then–Republican Party chair Frank Fahrenkopf and then–Democratic Party chair Paul Kirk incorporated the Commission on Presidential Debates. Fahrenkopf and Kirk still co-chair the Commission on Presidential Debates, and every four years it implements and conceals contracts jointly drafted by the Republican and Democratic nominees.

Original Sources: George Farah, "Pro-democratic Groups Call on Debate Commission to Make Secret Contract Public," Open Debates, September 18, 2008; George Farah, "No Debate: How the Republican and Democratic Parties Secretly Control the Presidential Debates," *Democracy Now!*, October 2, 2008.

Update: Other than the aforementioned sources and a few other alternative media outlets, nothing new has been reported on the secrecy of the CPD and the 2008 election cycle. This is an ongoing and important issue because control of presidential debates is held by a corporation that is private, lacks transparency and public oversight, and is not nonpartisan (it is bipartisan, which excludes many other political entities)—all of which is disturbing for democracy. Prior to the last presidential election, these stories were published and aired by some independent media, but were not picked up by the mainstream corporate media, which, in fact, still has not covered the issue: no stories of the secrecy of the CPD can be readily found through mainstream news outlets. It is the role of the free press to inform the public, particularly in political matters, and especially regarding candidates' views around election time. These reports about the corruption of the CPD contain crucial information that the public ought to know and understand if we are to participate more meaningfully in the next presidential election.

Censored 2010 #7 & #22

Obama's Military Appointments Have Corrupt Past; Obama's Trilateral Commission Team— "Change" Rhetoric Rings Hollow

Stories #7 and #22 both covered President Barack Obama's appointments, some of which have a questionable impact on his platform for change. Story #7 focused especially on Obama's retention of Robert Gates as secretary of defense, making Gates the first appointment from an outgoing administration of the opposing party to be kept in the position. Over the last two years of the previous administration, Gates was a key implementer of Bush's Iraq War "surge" after he replaced Defense Secretary Donald Rumsfeld, who had opposed the escalation.

Story #22 covered Obama's appointment of eleven members of the Trilateral Commission to top-level and key positions in his administration within his first ten days in office. This represents a very narrow source of international leadership inside the Obama administration, with a core agenda that is not necessarily in support of working people in the United States, and is inconsistent with Obama's campaign mantra of "change."

Original Sources: Robert Parry, "The Danger of Keeping Robert Gates," ConsortiumNews.com, November 13, 2008; Andrew Hughes, "Obama's Defense Department Appointees: The 3.4 Trillion Dollar Question," Global Research, February 13, 2009; Allan Nairn, "Obama Nominee Admiral Dennis Blair Aided perpetrators of 1999 church Killings in East Timor," Democracy Now!, January 7, 2009; Roxana Tiron, "Ties to Chevron, Boeing Raise Concern on Possible NSA Pick," The Hill, November 24, 2008; Patrick Wood, "Obama: Trilateral Commission Endgame," August Review, January 30, 2009, http://www.augustre-

view.com/news_commentary/trilateral_commission/obama_trilateral
_commission_endgame_update_1_20090127110.

Update: The mainstream corporate media has continued to use obfus-
catory "change candidate" terminology when referring to Barack
Obama's presidency, while ignoring that his cabinet is filled with the
same faces who oversaw, in past administrations, arguably disastrous
military and economic policies that often exacerbated situations rather
than yielded stated goals or solutions.

No corporate media outlets have been willing to discuss the connection between Obama's cabinet and the Trilateral Commission, which
dates back to 1973, because recognizing a connection would strip Obama
of his title as the "change candidate." The information necessary to
report on these connections exists: the commission's Web site releases
a mission statement along with its members' information, and Trilateralist co-founder and key Obama advisor Zbigniew Brzezinski has
released books on his stance on global politics. In the introduction to
Censored 2011, the quote from Brzezinski is instrumental to understanding Trilateral interests in strategically maintaining US global
control (as is his 1998 book, *The Grand Chessboard: American Primacy
And Its Geostrategic Imperatives*).

The corporate media continues to ignore the contradiction of
Obama's claims that Trilateralists in his cabinet, such as Paul Volcker,
give a "fresh perspective." In the Ronald Reagan era, Volcker presided
over an economy in which the top 1 percent controlled nearly 50 percent
of financial wealth. Trilateralist and Deputy Secretary of State James
Steinberg wrote Obama's AIPAC speech, which asked for continued
funding and support of the Israeli military—all while the Israeli military
illegally used white phosphorus against Palestinian civilians. This is not
a break in US policy on the Israeli/Palestinian issue.

Further, Secretary of the Treasury Timothy Geithner is connected to
the commission through his "informal group of advisors," which
includes E. Gerald Corrigan, Paul Volcker, Alan Greenspan, and Peter
G. Peterson—all Trilateralists. Brent Scowcroft, also a Trilateralist, has
been an unofficial advisor to Obama and was a mentor to Defense Secretary Robert Gates. Secretary of State Hillary Clinton is married to
former president Bill Clinton, a commission member, and a close political ally and confidante. The director of the White House National
Economic Council, Larry Summers, is also a Trilateralist who served as

treasury secretary in the Clinton and George W. Bush administrations. With these usual suspects come many of the same ideas dating back to the Carter administration. These people close to Obama do not represent the change he seemed to promise on the campaign trail.

Defense Secretary Robert Gates's past involvement with failed and corrupt military policy and the CIA has gone virtually unmentioned by the corporate mainstream press. Gates's past—namely his involvement in the Iran–Contra scandal from the Reagan years—has been mentioned only briefly, and he continues to preside over the failed, secret "terrorist" war that he oversaw in the George W. Bush administration. William Lynn, Robert Hale, and Dennis Blair—also mentioned in the *Censored 2010* stories—have had their military-industrial complex and lobbyist pasts almost completely ignored by the corporate press. In fact, the day after Obama signed an ethics pledge attempting to end the appearance of a revolving-door conflict of interest pattern between the public and private sector, he appointed William Lynn, a prominent member of the major defense contractor Raytheon, to the number two slot at the Pentagon. These aforementioned people all serve at Obama's side under the banner of change, even though it appears business as usual is alive and well in Washington, DC.

Obama also appointed Harvard lawyer Cass Sunstein to head the Office of Information and Regulatory Affairs, despite Sunstein's contradictory stance on the civil liberties he is appointed to protect. Sunstein called for the United States government to infiltrate and discredit private citizen groups that question and dispute the accepted, official accounts of recent historical events, particularly surrounding 9/11. Such an act directly conflicts with the responsibilities of his appointed position, which entails "overseeing policies relating to privacy, information quality . . ." This is also not a major change from the previous administration, which often violated civil liberty protections and had members of the Department of Homeland Security work with local law enforcement to infiltrate and attempt to disrupt lawful peace groups, in what can only be classified as a return to the days of COINTELPRO. (For more background, see story #14 in chapter 1 of this volume; as well as stories #1, #2, and #20 of *Censored 2008*; and stories #3, #5, #6, and #8 of *Censored 2009*.)

Robert Rubin, champion of ending the Glass–Steagall Act from the Clinton years, is a very important voice in Obama's cabinet as he keeps alive the revolving-door pattern in fiscal affairs, between the private sector and government, advocating for the deregulation of banks and the creation of conditions that eventually led to the economic collapse of 2008. Rubin, associated with both Citigroup (where he was forced out after economic implosion) and Goldman Sachs, meets regularly with Treasury Secretary Tim Geithner. Another prime example of the lack of change in Obama's cabinet, Rubin's past has gone largely unmentioned by the corporate press.

The mainstream corporate press, and thus the public at large, have failed to recognize that Obama is not a candidate of change. Though some corporate media outlets have addressed the issue of his appointees, they fail to expose, with adequate context and thoroughness, how his current administration is carrying on long-standing global dominance and pro-business agendas. The stripping of civil liberties and the continuation of war were issues Obama was elected to change. He has, however, maintained and expanded many previous policies with help from key figures from the past, with little mention in the corporate press.

Corporate Sources: "Trial and Error," *New York Times*, March 5, 2010; Elizabeth Bumiller, "Gates Experiences Fallout From Dysfunctional U.S. Relationship With Pakistan," *New York Times*, January 24, 2010.

Sources: Eamons Javers, "Robert Rubin Returns Common dreams," Common Dreams, April 8, 2010, http://commondreams.org/headline/2010/04/08-0; Michael B. Farrell, "Obama signs Patriot Act extension without reforms," *Christian Science Monitor*, March 1, 2010; Daniel Tencer, "Obama staffer wants 'cognitive infiltration' of 9/11 conspiracy groups," Raw Story, January 15, 2010, http://rawstory.com/2010/01/obama-staffer-infiltration-911-groups; William G. Domhoff, "Wealth, Income, and Power," September 1, 2005, http://sociology.ucsc.edu/whorulesamerica/power/wealth.html.

Censored 2007 #18

Physicist Challenges Official 9-11 Story

Research into the events of September 11, 2001, by (now former) Brigham Young University (BYU) physics professor Steven E. Jones, concluded that the official explanation for the collapse of the World Trade Center (WTC) buildings is implausible according to laws of physics. Jones is still calling for an independent, international scientific investigation "guided not by politicized notions and constraints but rather by observations and calculations."

Original Sources: Elaine Jarvik, "Y. Professor Thinks Bombs, Not Planes, Toppled WTC," *Deseret Morning News*, November 10, 2005; Steven E. Jones, "Why Indeed Did the WTC Buildings Collapse?" Brigham Young University Web site, winter 2005; Elaine Jarvik, "BYU professor's group accuses U.S. officials of lying about 9/11," *Deseret Morning News*, January 26, 2006.

Update: This story originally appeared in *Censored 2007*, and the subject has been revisited by Project Censored many times in all subsequent Déjà vu chapters, and additionally in chapter 7 of *Censored 2008*; in story #24 of chapter 1, as well as chapters 11 and 14, of *Censored 2009*; in chapters 5 and 10 of *Censored 2010*; and in story #15 of chapter 1, as well as chapters 6, 7, and 11, of this work, *Censored 2011*. However, despite several opportunities over the years, the mainstream corporate media has failed to address these and later findings in detail.

In proposing a hypothesis of explosive demolition, Dr. Jones first presented his objections to the official theory at a seminar on September 22, 2005, at BYU, a private research university owned by the Mormon church and located an hour's drive from Salt Lake City. The earliest coverage of this story came from local news on November 10, 2005: the *Deseret Morning News*, a Salt Lake City newspaper, and KUTV News, a television station serving the greater Salt Lake City metro area. Early national coverage came primarily from MSNBC's *The Situation with Tucker Carlson* on November 16, 2005, with further coverage less than a week later in the *Pittsburgh Tribune-Review* and the *Vermont Guardian*.

Less than a year later, in September 2006—after controversy over a paper hosted on BYU's Web site, in which Jones expressed his views—the university asked the professor to remove his paper and placed him on paid leave before his "retirement" in October (he was given an ultimatum by the university and chose to leave so he could continue his research). Yet, despite Jones's own admittance that the hypothesis supported by these findings can be "proven wrong," he and his colleagues' results remain largely unchallenged by the scientific community and altogether unmentioned by the mainstream corporate media (as reported in *Censored 2007*).

In 2008 and 2009, Dr. Jones participated in several peer-reviewed studies, including papers in the *Open Civil Engineering Journal*, the *Environmentalist*, and the *Open Chemical Physics Journal*. The latter offers additional support for the explosive demolition hypothesis, as it publishes the discovery of a highly energetic explosive material amid WTC debris that could have been used to quickly remove the lower floors and allow the near free-fall speeds observed (as reported in *Censored 2010*).

In July 2009, Richard Gage—a member of the American Institute of Architects, a practicing architect for more than twenty years, and the founder of Architects & Engineers for 9/11 Truth—included this evidence in a series of public events and meetings with congressional representatives in Washington, DC. In February 2010, a column in the *Concord Monitor* mentioned this and other evidence as being the reason for asking New Hampshire's congressional delegation to push for a reexamination of the events of September 11. Still, these stories, and others like them, continue to be ignored by the mainstream corporate media, and even by most alternative and progressive-leaning publications, in which academics and researchers that dare to ask these difficult questions are derided as "conspiracy theorists" in an effort to dismiss and attack them without actually looking at all the evidence. A truly free press would welcome such inquiry and debate—not ignore, ridicule, or shut it down.

Sources: Tad Walch, "BYU's Jones denies bias," *Deseret Morning News*, September 14, 2006; Niels H. Harrit, et al., "Active Thermitic Material Discovered in Dust from the 9/11 World Trade Center Catastrophe," *Open Chemical Physics Journal*, February 2009; "Architect to Speak in D.C. on 9/11 World Trade Center Destruction," U.S. Newswire, June 30, 2009; Ray Duckler, "9/11 conspiracy makes it onto town warrant," *Concord Monitor*, February 19, 2010.

Déjà Vu Stories from Years Long Past Remain Relevant

Project Censored founder Dr. Carl Jensen still posts occasionally on the Project's blog, the Daily Censored. This past year, Jensen wrote about a number of Déjà vu stories and followed them all the way to the present; clearly, some stories remain censored for a very long time. Some highlights (or lowlights) include "America's Secret Police Network," dating back from 1978; "Censored Stories on Haiti," from 1994; and "The Continuing Censorship of the Nuclear Issue," from 1980. For more on these significant yet censored stories throughout the past few decades, visit www.dailycensored.com/category/censored-deja-vu. We at Project Censored hope the corporate media will begin more factual reporting on the issues that affect society the most. Until that time, there is much work to be done and we must not rely on a failing corporate media system when there are so many valuable independent voices in journalism that are increasingly accessible.

The very fact that some stories remain in the dark for so long further illustrates the problems of censorship in a supposed free press culture. Journalism is oft considered the rough draft of history. Problems do not only exist in the present; much is rooted in the past, and the continued censorship of socially and politically relevant issues impacts how history is recorded, remembered, and ultimately interpreted. Where the public record becomes distorted on the most crucial matters for a society, the truth remains elusive and understanding obfuscated.

With that in mind, perhaps George Santayana was right: "Those who cannot remember the past are condemned to repeat it." So, let us all get busy: not just remembering the past, but remembering more accurately and inclusively, so we can act more intelligently, and in a more egalitarian fashion, in the present. Our democracy and the vision of freedom and equality promised by America's founders depend upon a true, vibrant, and unfettered free press. Let the facts be known and the truth telling begin.

MICKEY HUFF is the director of Project Censored, an associate professor of history at Diablo Valley College, and a member of the board of directors of the Media Freedom Foundation.

JOSETTE CANILAO is a senior in communications at Sonoma State University and a summer intern with Project Censored.

CARL JENSEN is the founder of Project Censored.

NOLAN HIGDON, MIKE SMITH, KAJAL SHAHALI, SY COWIE, KIRA MCDONOUGH, and RYAN SHEHEE are present or former students at Diablo Valley College and interns with Project Censored.

CHAPTER 3

Manufacturing Distraction
Junk Food News and News Abuse on a Feed to Know Basis

by Mickey Huff, Frances A. Capell, and Adam Bessie

> *Our politics, religion, news, athletics, education and com-*
> *merce have been transformed into congenial adjuncts of*
> *show business, largely without protest or even much pop-*
> *ular notice. The result is that we are a people on the verge*
> *of amusing ourselves to death.*
> ——NEIL POSTMAN, Amusing Ourselves to Death[1]

It has been no real surprise for those paying a whit of attention that the corporate media in the United States is not in the business of news. For the past few decades, tripe has increasingly dominated the dwindling pages of newspapers, fearmongering has filled the hot airwaves of radio, and the cheap, tawdry, and bawdy now rule the 24/7 cable news broadcasts. The so-called "Most Trusted Name in News" and "Fair & Balanced" networks have become self-parodies on the verge of succumbing to their own propaganda.

This troublesome trend has been documented by Project Censored for almost three decades as well as by numerous other academics, independent journalists, and activists who have focused on what could be argued is the most problematic subject of our time: the sorry state of the supposed free press.[2] There are many facets to this issue facing democracy. The former dean of the Graduate School of Journalism at the University of California–Berkeley, Ben Bagdikian, tripped the alarm concerning conglomerates, consolidation brought about by deregulation, and the potential negative impact on news reporting in *The Media Monopoly* in 1983.[3] Lo and behold, like a sage, his predictions turned out to be quite accurate, even underestimated.

The problems Bagdikian addressed are not, however, the only problems associated with the corporate news media. Today we have more outlets for information than ever before, yet fewer owners and producers of mass media. Further, a vast majority of Americans watch television for their news (virtually a corporate and commercially dominated medium). What is reported in the most viewed news sources matters, because it helps to shape the public mindset. Control of information and censorship of sensitive yet important topics come in many guises. It is not just *what* the corporate media are not reporting that matters, it is also what they *do* report and *how* they report it. Much of this content amounts to what is called Junk Food News and News Abuse.[4]

Since Project Censored founder Dr. Carl Jensen coined the term Junk Food News almost thirty years ago, Americans have seen their news diet consistently filled with tripe and fluff, creating a news-deficient society. Junk Food News stories are inane, trivial tales that amuse and distract the masses (deridingly referred to as the "Booboisie" by early twentieth-century essayist and critic H. L. Mencken). However, it is not merely junk and distraction that Americans are treated to on their daily news menus, but also News Abuse, the reporting of important stories and issues, for all the wrong reasons and with numerous dubious detours that result in spin, distortion, and even falsehood.[5] In fact, News Abuse helps create a state where people can no longer discern between the real and unreal—hyperreality.[6]

Around the same time that Jensen was noting the increasingly disturbing trend of Junk Food News, New York University media scholar Neil Postman warned that America was fast becoming a culture more reminiscent of Aldous Huxley's *Brave New World* rather than George Orwell's *1984*.[7] The American media landscape was a world where inanity, desire, and consumerism were fast becoming the order of the day. Said Postman in the preface of his now-classic 1985 work, *Amusing Ourselves to Death: Public Discourse in the Age of Show Business*,

> What Orwell feared were those who would ban books. What Huxley feared was that there would be no reason to ban a book, for there would be no one who wanted to read one. Orwell feared those who would deprive us of information. Huxley feared those who would give us so much that we would be reduced to passivity and egoism. Orwell feared that the truth would be concealed from us. Huxley feared the truth would be drowned in a sea of irrelevance. Orwell feared we would become a captive culture. Huxley feared we would become a trivial culture, preoccupied with some equivalent of the feelies, the orgy

porgy, and the centrifugal bumblepuppy . . . In short, Orwell feared that what we hate will ruin us. Huxley feared that what we love will ruin us.[8]

"This book," Postman then concluded in the preface, "is about the possibility that Huxley, not Orwell, was right."[9] Frighteningly, that prescient passage lays the framework for our present hyperreality. This chapter explores the most significant and timely examples of Junk Food News and News Abuse in 2009–10, and examines what becomes of a culture consumed by infotainment disseminated by a corporate media hell-bent on manufacturing distraction, and suggests what we can do to change the trend of Junk Food News and News Abuse in order to realize not only a true free press, but a functioning and egalitarian democracy.

THE YEAR OF THE TIGER: SEX STILL SELLS AS JUNK FOOD NEWS

Just Do It.
——NIKE AD SLOGAN

The only stories corporate media seem to love more than those with titillating sexual or violent details are stories in which such details are wedded to scandalous exploits of celebrities. For corporate news, 2010 has indeed turned out to be the Year of the Tiger. The Tiger Woods infidelity scandal appeared on twenty consecutive covers of the *New York Post*, officially surpassing the tabloid's coverage of the events of 9/11.[10] Troubling as this may be, the recurrence of the story in tabloid pages is overshadowed by a far more upsetting trend in contemporary journalism. While the newsworthiness of the recent unraveling of the celebrity golfer's public image is surely questionable, the methods the corporate media employed in reporting the story deserve immediate attention. Just as the boundary between "junk" news and real news has become increasingly blurred, in the case of Tiger Woods the line between the media's treatment of facts and lurid, unverified gossip has almost entirely disappeared.

Not to be outdone by the clever headline "What a Dope" for last year's top Junk Food News story involving Michael Phelps's momentous bong load, British tabloid *News of the World* ran a salacious piece about a

Florida restaurant manager Mindy Lawton's alleged affair with Woods titled "Tiger Had Me in the Rough."[11] The article contained all the necessary elements for a sensational tabloid story: Tiger's "favourite breakfast," "saucy" red underpants, and detailed accounts of "frantic" garage sex.[12] While the story was packed with tawdry accusations, it was entirely lacking in credibility. As Paul Farhi pointed out in the *American Journalism Review* article "Lost in the Woods," the *News of the World* item contained no incriminating text messages, e-mails, voicemails, or even one eyewitness to corroborate it. "Most suspicious were some of Lawton's direct quotes," wrote Farhi. "She referred to Woods as a 'sportsman' and a parking lot as a 'car park,' British locutions unlikely to have been uttered by a Florida restaurant manager."

These questions of validity did not, however, prevent dozens of *real* news outlets from retelling the tabloid tall tale. The *Chicago Sun-Times*, the *Miami Herald*, and NBC's *Today Show* all reported on the supposed affair despite the story's shady origins. "The thrust of *Today*'s reporting on the scandal was to report what others had reported," said Farhi. "In a single news report on December 7, for instance, [Peter] Alexander cited TMZ twice, *News of the World*'s story about Mindy Lawton, *Saturday Night Live*, and the *Daily Beast*'s report about Woods's alleged addiction to prescription drugs."[13]

Though many corroborated allegations of infidelity and vague yet nonetheless guilty admissions from Tiger Woods himself would keep the story afloat, the unnecessary attention granted by the media did not go unnoticed. In the UK, when the BBC ran Tiger's public apology as their top story on the same day that 1,600 workers lost their jobs when a large steel plant was shut down, the news corporation received 283 formal complaints. "To have this Tiger Woods item as the main item was an insult to those 1,600 people going home tonight in Redcar jobless, while our main news provider concentrated on a multi-millionaire golfer who's been unfaithful to his wife," wrote one viewer. Protested another, "Our economy is in tatters, our children are dying in Afghanistan, at least 1,600 jobs are going in Teesside . . . I pay my license fee for much better than this."[14]

An article in the *Christian Science Monitor* titled "Yahoo! loves Tiger Woods" pointed out that while Woods's sponsors and fans were suffering in the midst of the scandal, the outpouring of public interest in the story meant profit for many others. "God bless Tiger. This week we got a huge uplift: Front Page, News, Sports, Gossip. He just filtered through the whole place," Yahoo! Chief Executive Officer (CEO) Carol Bartz told attendees of the UBS Global Media and Communications Conference on December 8, 2009. The increased traffic for Yahoo! thanks to Tiger's "transgressions" meant a huge increase in ad revenue for the company. "[This] is better than Michael Jackson dying," Bartz joked, "it is kind of hard to put an ad next to a funeral."[15] Maybe so, but funerals aside, there was plenty of media money to be made in the business of celebrity deaths, as will be examined in the next section.

As if the Year of the Tiger escapades were not enough, the sex scandals of the past year also involved a handful of political figures. Widespread media attention was given to the fact that former senator John Edwards had fathered a child in an extramarital affair with his aide Rielle Hunter during the democratic primaries. Though the *National Enquirer* ran stories on the affair in 2007, it was conveniently seized upon elsewhere in the media well after Edwards had ended his campaign. On June 16, 2009, Republican Senator John Ensign admitted to having an extramarital affair. The woman in question was Cynthia Hampton, the wife of one of his top aides. A few days later the mysterious disappearance of Republican Governor Mark Sanford was reported. Sanford initially claimed that he had been hiking in the Appalachian trail. He then admitted that he had instead been with his mistress in Argentina. Luckily for these two, immediately after their stories broke the death of Michael Jackson eclipsed their affairs in terms of media coverage.[16]

One of the most amusing aspects of the reporting of these political sex scandals comes from Fox News's coverage of Sanford. The network's on-screen graphic while the Republican governor confessed to the affair labeled him as a Democrat. Fox had previously given ample attention to Sanford's opposition to Obama's stimulus package, when the governor was correctly identified as a Republican. The graphic could have been more readily dismissed as a mistake, had Fox not also done the same thing to former Republican Congressman Mark Foley after his notorious scandal involving male, teenage congressional pages.[17]

While the sensationalizing of sex scandal stories does little in the way of developing properly informed and empowered members of society, the relative prioritizing of these stories is indicative of a warped sense of what the public really needs to know. On December 12, 2009, a *Saturday Night Live* skit delivered poignant commentary on the matter. The opening to the show depicted Sanford, Ensign, and Edwards critiquing the media's overcoverage of the Woods scandal. "Like Tiger Woods, we have broken our marriage vows, but in addition, as elected officials, we have also violated the public trust," says the Ensign character. He later adds, "If I may, let me make a point here. Many of Tiger's girlfriends were meaningless one-night stands. He barely spent any time with them. Certainly not enough to affect his work, unlike us."[18] And in the end, it seems the late-night laughs are on us.

GRIEF PORN: POSTMORTEM VOYEURISM AS POSTMODERN CAUSE CÉLÈBRE

No one ever went broke underestimating the taste of the American public.
——H. L. MENCKEN

When Michael Jackson died suddenly on June 25, 2009, coverage of his passing consumed mainstream media coverage like a raging wildfire. His death accounted for 18 percent of the news during the week of his death, and 17 percent for the following two weeks, according to the Pew Research Center's Project for Excellence in Journalism. The loss of the beloved King of Pop equaled huge financial gains for news corporations. The Magazine Information Network estimated that in the two months following Jackson's untimely death, the magazine industry pulled in an extra $55 million.[19] The Pew Research Center also observed that 93 percent of cable coverage studied on the Thursday and Friday following the death was about Jackson.[20] His eighteen-hour memorial appeared live on eighteen cable and broadcast networks including ABC, NBC, and CNN, and drew in 31.1 million viewers.[21] The Internet was also heavily impacted as word of Jackson's demise began to spread, so much so that Google went into malware-defense mode. Searches related to Michael Jackson generated a response of: "We're sorry, but your query looks similar to automated requests from a computer virus or spyware application." One article went so far as to suggest in its title, "Jackson Dies, Almost Takes Internet with Him."[22]

Microblogging service Twitter was among the Web sites that crashed as a result of Jackson's death. Before the crash, TweetVolume had recorded that "Michael Jackson" appeared in more than 66,500 Twitter updates. On the afternoon of June 25, according to data from Trendrr, a service that tracks social media sites, Twitter posts containing "Michael

Jackson" reached more than 100,000 per hour.[23] Twitter user FoieGrasie observed: "Irony: The protesters in Iran using Twitter as com are unable to get online because of all the posts of 'Michael Jackson RIP.'"[24] The Pew Research Center found that Iran and its turbulent elections made up for 19 percent of news for the week of June 22–28, and despite Jackson's death occurring midweek, his passing accounted for only 1 percent less for the entire week.[25] Even in death, it seemed that the Michael Jackson brand, media icon and juggernaut, could not be stopped and was set to overshadow any other newsworthy events.

The 1970s actress and pinup star Farrah Fawcett died just a few hours before the King of Pop after a long battle with cancer. Before commercial breaks on CNN, the channel was flashing photos of Mark Sanford and Fawcett to keep the audience engaged. Perspectives on the *Charlie's Angels* star were promised to occupy the evening's time slots.[26] That all changed when word of Jackson's death hit the airwaves, and Fawcett's name joined others on a list of celebrities *New York Magazine* calls the "Eclipsed Celebrity Death Club." Fawcett herself was posthumously eclipsing another recent celebrity death, that of David Carradine (best known from the television series *Kung Fu*), though given the circumstances surrounding his death (speculated as caused by autoerotic asphyxiation), Carradine would likely have been pleased about the death of Fawcett and then Jackson, as they helped kick him off the front page, where media had been ensconced in the lurid details of his own death for weeks.[27] Historically, another member of this so-called club is Groucho Marx, who died the same week as Elvis Presley.[28] It is interesting to note that when Presley died in 1977, *CBS News* was criticized for *not* choosing to lead their newscast with the celebrity's death.[29] Times have clearly changed.

The death of Michael Jackson harkens back to another sensationalized death from over a decade ago, that of Princess Diana. The news coverage and public response to her passing inspired writer Mick Hume to coin the term "mourning sickness" to describe the collective condition of "recreational grieving" by individuals at the death of a celebrity.[30] According to Patrick West, author of a pamphlet called *Conspicuous Compassion*, these public displays of mourning for strangers, also known as "grief porn" or "grief-lite," have become an "enjoyable event, much like going to a football match or the last night of the proms." The hyper-attentive, intrusive, and voyeuristic media coverage surrounding celebrity deaths results in a massive "inflation" of the traditional moment of silence, rendering it virtually meaningless.[31]

HOAX OPERA: CURTAIN CALL FOR THE INANE

Newspapers are unable, seemingly to discriminate between
a bicycle accident and the collapse of civilization.
—GEORGE BERNARD SHAW

As the saga of Falcon "Balloon Boy" Heene unfolded on October 15, 2009, the corporate media dragged the public afloat with him. "A 6-year-old boy climbed into a homemade balloon aircraft and floated away Thursday," read the opening lines to Associated Press (AP) stories and updates, "forcing officials to scramble to figure out how to rescue the boy."[32] This was widely reported by press and news agencies despite the fact that the only witness was a sibling who supposedly watched him climb inside. There was little discussion of whether or not such a balloon could actually take off and float the way that it did with a fifty-pound child inside. Only after the balloon touched down and was revealed to be empty did TV hosts stress that reports of Falcon being inside were "unverified" and began alluding to a possible hoax.[33] "The authorities, and the media, believed they had a credible report that the kid had climbed aboard this weird balloon rocket that his family had constructed . . . It seemed to be a life-and-death drama as the balloon was buffeted by the winds," wrote *Washington Post* media critic Howard Kurtz in defense of the excessive coverage.[34]

"We are not going to show impact. We will be on a delay," CNN assured the public, and then proceeded to air the balloon crash live.[35] "Not only did cable news programmers make a risky decision in covering this story live," wrote *Mediaite's* Colby Hall, "they may have inadvertently aired his death."[36] However, Falcon was discovered to be hiding in a box in the family's attic, and suspicions were raised when he admitted during a CNN interview with Wolf Blitzer, "We did this for the show."[37] Furthermore, only after the boy was found safe was attention turned to the fact that the boy's father, spotlight-hungry Richard Heene, had an affinity for hoaxes. Heene, who had appeared on the program *Wife Swap*, had unsuccessfully tried to participate in other reality shows, and posted online videos depicting a fake terror attack on the US Capitol and discussions of shapeshifting and Hillary Clinton as a human-reptile being.[38] Perhaps if these things had been looked into a bit earlier, i.e., while a horrified public followed the balloon's flight with bated breath, the sensational story could have been dismissed in lieu of actual news. Instead, from October 15 to 18, the Balloon Boy story was the top news story, according to the Pew Research Center. Falcon Heene was the number two item of news for the entire week, second only to President Obama.[39] "With record home foreclosures, the announcement that seniors would receive no cost-of-living increase in Social Security (the first time since 1975), and an Arctic ice cap now forecast to be completely melted in ten to twenty years," wrote Janet Loughrey in a piece for the independent online *OpEd News*, "there was plenty to talk about . . . real journalism and real news reporting has been all but discarded."[40]

A little over a month later, fame-seekers dominated news headlines once again as Washington, DC couple Tareq and Michaele Salahi were admitted to a state dinner at the White House on November 24, 2009, despite not being on the guest list, and successfully hobnobbed with the elite. The Secret Service only caught on after Michaele Salahi posted pictures of herself at the event on her Facebook page. The whole ordeal lead to scrutiny of Social Secretary Desirée Rogers, who later resigned from her position.[41] During the week of November 30 to December 6, the party crashers occupied 18 percent of morning news airtime studied by the Pew Research Center. Coverage often centered around the quirky couple rather than matters of White House security.[42] Soon after, it was reported that the pair was vying for a spot on Bravo's *The Real Housewives of DC* and that the show's cameras had even captured some of the incident. Despite the fact that the couple is still under federal investigation for their gate-crashing antics, they are ultimately being rewarded with the media attention they crave.[43] The Salahis appeared on the *Today Show* with Matt Lauer and David Letterman's *Tonight Show* on May 25, 2010. It appears Michaele will star on *The Real Housewives of DC*, and the couple is writing a tell-all book.[44] With publicity stunts like those of the Salahis and the Heenes gobbling up legitimate news airtime, we can only dread the next sensational hoax that will take fame-seekers from America's attics and turn them into America's sweethearts.

MEANWHILE: THE CONSEQUENCES OF JUNK FOOD NEWS COVERAGE

While corporate media lavish attention on these Junk Food News subjects and their casts, real news goes underreported and largely unnoticed.[45] This could have a catastrophic impact on human affairs; that which we do not know can indeed affect us all.

Regardless of the plenitude of significant news stories to cover, Junk Food News remains alive and well in corporate media and continues to engorge the American populace with a high-calorie, no-news diet while it eats away at the nation's already emaciated attention span. If this type of reporting was the most egregious among the failings of the free press, perhaps it could be more easily rectified. However, another serious problem afflicting major newsrooms is far more insidious: the propensity for News Abuse.

NEWS ABUSE: THE PERILS AND POSSIBILITIES OF NETWORKED NEWS

A newspaper is a device for making the ignorant more ignorant and the crazy crazier.
—H. L. MENCKEN

News Abuse is not the same as Junk Food News, which Project Censored founder Carl Jensen called "junk food for the brain." The category became part of the Project's scope early in the new millennium when then-director Peter Phillips expanded the idea of Junk Food News to include News Abuse. This involves the actual coverage of important news stories, not fluff. However, it is the way in which corporate media go about covering a particular story that can transform an otherwise straightforward, factual news story into a form of propaganda through spin, obfuscation, distortion, omission, and even outright prevarication. Of course, corporate media outlets can then claim a particular story or topic has been reported, and that it has not been censored. Yet, upon deeper examination, one often discovers that the facts in a particular story in question have been abused, transformed into something other than what the original report encompassed, perhaps something more distracting or titillating, or more confusing. Hence, the need for the category of analysis called News Abuse. Along with the proliferation of Junk Food News, this growing problem can be much harder to detect. News Abuse must be more carefully deconstructed so the public can become aware of the levels of deception that are afoot in the corporate press. The following provides a framework from which to understand the significance and many guises of News Abuse.

We Are the Corporate Media

The scene is set. A perfectly coifed evening anchor sits in a generic corporate news studio prepared to deliver BREAKING NEWS—this news, however, is not breaking from the teleprompter, but comes from a Tweet fresh off a smartphone that the anchor is staring at, rather than the camera. With Walter Cronkite–esque gravitas, the anchor solemnly proclaims, "Your friend can't decide which sandwich to eat for lunch." After a dramatic pause, as if to let the "news" soak in, the anchor stares into the camera with a well-polished parody of melodramatic reporterly ethos, announcing that this program is "Giving you the news that *matters* to you."

While CNN has not taken to reading a friend's lunch habits on the air—not yet, at least—this Motorola advertisement captures the darker side of the new participatory media landscape, one in which people use their newfound power to "be the media," not to question the Junk Food News that is sold, but to collude with corporate media in the creation and distribution of it through social networks. With the rise of participatory media, are people now no longer consumers, but also peddlers of Junk Food News, and more broadly, the ideological spin of corporate news? Are We the People now active participants in a News Abuse cycle? And if so, what does this mean in terms of a free press?

Perils of Parody Meet Reality

We have passed through the age of network news, where information was transmitted directly from media source to the consumer, and have entered the age of Networked News, in which our social networks are integral to how we experience news. In their March 2010 report, "How Internet and Cell Phone Users Have Turned News Into a Social Experience," the Pew Research Center's Project for Excellence in Journalism shows that rather than simply wait for the evening news, we "hunt and gather" from TV, Internet, radio, and, although less so now, newspapers, across multiple sources. We are now more diverse in our informational habits—and through our social networks, we share this information with friends, family, colleagues, and acquaintances across the world. Nearly three-quarters of those online get news from friends through e-mail or social networking. Additionally, we are not just passively passing news along, but are becoming more engaged with that news. Nearly 40 percent of those who use the net "have contributed to the creation of news, commented about it, or disseminated it via postings on social media sites like Facebook or Twitter." In the age of Networked News, we don't just listen to the news—we are actively involved in discussing and distributing it.[46]

As a part of the Networked News, we are now no longer merely consumers, but participants in the fourth estate. While this presents a new opportunity to publicly question Junk Food News, misinformation, and spin, we also become complicit in spreading Junk Food News and News Abuse, becoming de facto, unpaid employees of the corporate media machine. Or as "Wolf Blitzer" in a *Saturday Night Live* parody of CNN's *Situation Room* tells us, "Send us your updates, send us your photos . . . In other words, do our job for us."[47]

Junk Food News Feed

The sad truth is that we no longer need corporate media channels to provide us with distracting gossip in the guise of news. On Facebook and Twitter, nowhere else is the banal minutiae of life more celebrated than on "news feeds," such as "What sandwich should I eat for lunch?" Rather than follow celebrity gossip, rather than settling to only follow the trials and travails of Tiger Woods, we can now follow each other, becoming our own tabloids, creating Junk Food News out of our own lives, which we then post to our social network's news feed.[48] In this way, Networked News becomes an imitation—a simulacrum—of our network news, simply another avenue in which to immerse ourselves in gossip.[49]

That is not to say, however, that we have forgotten celebrities, as noted previously. After all, Americans talked about Tiger Woods's car accident as much as they discussed Obama's decision to begin pulling troops out of Afghanistan.[50] Yet, interestingly, during the same period, Afghanistan received considerably more media coverage than Woods.[51] In other words, the public actively amplified Woods's tasty adventures—and through the power of social networking, had a megaphone by which to permeate our media atmosphere with his story. Networked News, in this way, is not only imitating, but actively distributing network news gossip. Perhaps, as the adage goes, we have become what we eat—after years of consuming Junk Food News, it is all we know how to serve.

Say What You Really Meme

Networked News, while composed of individuals, appears to have a mind of its own. Just as a news story will dominate all the major corporate out-lets, so do stories appear to take over news feeds. The Red Cross's response to the January 2010 earthquake in Haiti, which raised $30 mil-lion through text messages, is a perfect example of this phenomenon.[52] In the days following the earthquake, a message advising people to donate ten dollars by texting to a number spread not through ads, but virally through Facebook and other social networks, popping up on news feeds, and through e-mails and text messages. In early February, as the viral philanthropy for Haiti appeared to begin declining, a new virus caught on—that of "celebrity doppelganger week," in which the fad of changing one's profile picture to a celebrity's photo quickly spread.[53]

The viral nature of these trends, which spread so quickly through social networks, can be explained by famed scientist, controversial atheist, and "enthusiastic Darwinian" Richard Dawkins and his theory of the "meme," or "unit of cultural transmission." The Haiti text message philanthropy and celebrity doppelganger fads are both examples of memes, as are "tunes, ideas, catch-phrases, clothes fashions, ways of making pots or of building arches." A meme, in short, is any idea that can be passed from one person to another. "Just as genes propagate themselves in the gene pool by leaping from body to body via sperm or eggs," Dawkins writes, explaining the concept via analogy, "so memes propagate themselves in the meme pool by leaping from brain to brain via a process which, in the broad sense, can be called imitation." Much more simply, Dawkins thinks that culture works like our genes—just as genes replicate themselves, so does culture, and so do ideas. Thus, "if a scientist hears, or reads about, a good idea, he passes it on to his colleagues and students. . . . If the idea catches on, it can be said to propagate itself, spreading from brain to brain." In other words, Dawkins believes, ideas have a life of their own, using each of us to make copies of themselves in new people, who in turn do the same—spreading ideas virally.[54] The strong ideas thrive and propagate, like a species of mice, and the weak ones adapt or die out. As Dan Fletcher writes in *Time* of the celebrity doppelganger trend, "These are grass-roots memes that spread virally throughout the site, making them difficult to trace back to an origin with any certainty."[55] According to this theory, then, trends—memes—develop organically, as if from everywhere and nowhere, with no real author, no real creator but the crowd itself.

In Networked News, information spreads quickly from brain to brain regardless of substance or accuracy. As one can see, the memes of phi-lanthropy and celebrity worship appear to spread at the same rate, consuming social networks. Truth and falsehood spread at the same speed. A telling illustration of this phenomenon can be found in a study published in the *American Journal of Infection Control*. The authors studied the discussion of antibiotics on Twitter updates, finding that both accurate and inaccurate information on antibiotic use was being disseminated.[56] And just as the public can spread misinformation on antibiotics through social media, so can they spread spin and create a hyperreality, the inability to distinguish between what is real and not.[57] Networked News provides another potential forum to disseminate corporate or ideological spin, sensationalism, and misrepresentation—further propagating News Abuse.

The following News Abuse story themes show how corporate media coverage of otherwise serious issues are distorted and routinely propagandized, resulting in the censorship of ideas and the stunting of critical discourse that ultimately harm democracy.

Obama is Hitler: Vile Goes Viral

"At 11:09 Eastern Standard Time, Barack Obama is Hitler," jokes late-night comedian Jon Stewart in a November 2008 segment of *The Daily Show*. Stewart had just shown a clip from Fox News in which Republican Representative Paul Broun equated President Barack Obama with the infamous Nazi leader Adolf Hitler.[58] Stewart, along with Senior Absolutely Reasonable Hitler Comparison Analyst John Oliver, satirically relates the inept nature of such hyperbolic comparison. Broun's sensationalist analogy, however, wasn't a one-time gaffe, a simple slip of the tongue revealing the strange mindset of a single representative.[59]

Rather, comparing Obama to Hitler has become a "standard right-wing trope,"[60] not only among the conservative talkers—Rush Limbaugh, Michael Savage, Glenn Beck—but in Networked News as well. In summer 2008, two videos comparing Obama to Hitler hit YouTube, garnering over a million hits over two years.[61] Later that summer, at a town hall meeting for Democratic Representative Barney Frank, a woman made a comment drawing a similar comparison. The clip spread like wildfire across the news and the Internet. This woman was not a lone extremist, as the Obama=Hitler analogy has continued to surface at Tea Party protests.[62] The image itself has been so viral and suggestive that the notion of Obama as Orwellian Big Brother even graces the cover of this book, calling attention to how propaganda works via imagery.

The Obama=Hitler meme appears not only surprisingly popular

among many of the politically disaffected on the right, but also exceptionally tenacious, as evidenced in a spring 2010 Facebook page with over a million members praying for Obama's death.[63] Around the same time former Republican Speaker of the House Newt Gingrich released a book in which he claimed the current progressive agenda "represents as great a threat to America as Nazi Germany or the Soviet Union once did." This statement was broadcast via corporate media both on the *Today Show*[64] and Fox News.[65]

The Obama=Hitler meme presents a case study of Networked News Abuse, in which the social networks work in collusion with the corporate media and its ideological interests to cultivate, maintain, and disseminate a sensationalist, paranoid hyperreality, which obfuscates any real discussion of Obama's policies. More simply, network news and Networked News act as a hyperbolic echo chamber, in which extreme overstatement overshadows substantive democratic dialogue. (Obama has strangely been called everything from a fascist to a socialist and anywhere in between, further illustrating the absence of intellectual sobriety in the political media climate when discussing the president or his administration's policies.)

In 1946, George Orwell observed, "Fascism has now no meaning except in so far as it signifies 'something not desirable.'"[66] And while literally meaningless except to express extreme distaste, the emotionally powerful term has persisted in political dialogue for well over a half century. Indeed, in the more recent past the Hitler meme has not only been used by the right. During the 2004 presidential election, the liberal group MoveOn featured a user-generated anti-Bush ad online that compared Bush to Hitler. In response, Republican National Committee Chairman Ed Gillespie said on Fox News that the ad was "the worst and most vile form of political hate speech,"[67] a sentiment echoed by MSNBC's Joe Scarborough, who also referred to the ad as "political hate speech." Members at MoveOn apparently agreed that the comparison was egregious, and the organization subsequently distanced itself from the ad, which never officially aired.[68]

With the election of America's first black president, Barack Obama, "political hate speech" has resurfaced with a vengeance, this time cultivated in the corporate media by right-wing ideologues. In the last two years, numerous high-profile right-wing commentators have used Hitler or Nazism to refer to select Democrats and/or progressive policies or people, across a wide swath of corporate media outlets. Noah Lederman of the media watchdog Fairness and Accuracy In Reporting (FAIR) observed the return of the Hitler analogy, this time in the corporate press in reference to Obama.[69] Widely watched Fox News commentator Glenn Beck has been particularly glib in evoking the Hitler meme. Beck's recurrent use of the Nazi analogy prompted Lewis Black, the permanently outraged comedic pundit, to diagnose Beck with a case of "Nazi Tourette's" while on *The Daily Show*.[70]

While Beck may be the most vocal of the political epithet-hurling crowd, he did not create the Obama=Hitler meme. Rather, the genesis of the analogy originates with the conservative magazine *National Review* and three fellows at Stanford's powerful right-wing think-tank Hoover Institution. Two years before Glenn Beck's fascist tirades began, *National Review* writer and Hoover Institution fellow Thomas Sowell was one of the first to pose the Liberal–Nazi connection, writing, "Not since the days of the Hitler Youth have young people been subjected to more propaganda on more politically correct issues."[71] Yet, it wasn't until a year later, in January 2008, that the idea took hold, with *National Review* editor, Hoover Institution media fellow,[72] and Fox News contributor Jonah Goldberg's book *Liberal Fascism: The Secret History of the American Left, From Mussolini to the Politics of Meaning* (published by an imprint of the international multimedia conglomerate Bertelsmann AG).[73] Ten days after the release of the book (which ultimately reached number one on the *New York Times* bestseller list), Goldberg was interviewed on MSNBC with Joe Scarborough, claiming "I'm not saying that today's liberalism is the son of Nazism or the son of Italian fascism. I'm saying it's sort of like the great-grandniece once removed. . . . They have some common DNA, some common themes, some family resemblances that come up."[74] Four years after the fact, Scarborough appeared to have forgotten that he himself once called any such comparison "political hate speech"; a week later, Scarborough even stated, "I love Jonah Goldberg."

This "political hate speech" is now a part of mainstream political discourse surrounding Obama. In the following months, the meme took off as the right-wing crowd took on the comparison: Ann Coulter, Ben Stein, and Rush Limbaugh used the Nazi comparison after Goldberg, all in corporate media forums. Glenn Beck claimed that Goldberg's book "began to open his eyes" (his Nazi Tourette's syndrome was apparently a side effect). Further, according to FAIR's Lederman, Goldberg had been on Beck's show a whopping seventeen times.[75] With millions of viewers and readers, Beck has a powerful Networked News force, having garnered 900,000 Facebook friends and 240,000 followers on Twitter, who then redistribute Goldberg's "political hate speech" across their own individual social networks (in much the same way as information about antibiotics spread on Twitter). In August 2009, wrapping up his "Liberal Fascism" blog on the *National Review,* Goldberg claimed he regretted the continued use of the term "fascist." Goldberg lamented, "As I've said many times, one naïve hope I had for my book was that it would remove the word 'fascist' from popular discourse, not expand its franchise. Alas, on that score the book is a complete failure."[76] Given the title of Goldberg's book that seems an odd expectation.

Six months after Goldberg wrapped up press for his book, another Hoover Institution fellow was featured on the same corporate outlets repeating the same claims. Newt Gingrich, with a million more followers on Twitter than Beck, was keeping the comparison alive and well in the public mind with his book, *To Save America: Stopping Obama's Secular-Socialist Machine.*[77] Gingrich and Beck have their own Networked News, their own audiences, who, through social networks, have their own audiences, and so on. The Obama=Hitler meme passes from pundits through corporate outlets with their own online presence, through social networks, and into the political arena, becoming like a growing brand, accepted, if not agreed upon, and ultimately mainstreamed. So goes the hyperreality propaganda machine on the Obama=Hitler meme: News Abuse writ large.

The grassroots nature of the Networked News may be something of an illusion, with all the appearance of a grassroots movement but with none of the substance—an Astroturf hyperreality. In this example, we see a top-down model still operating within Networked News, where powerful ideological and corporate interests dictate not only the terms of the debate, but also the terms used *in* the debate. While the protestor using the Nazi analogy at Representative Barney Frank's town hall meeting appeared to be part of a grassroots uprising of the people, she in fact borrowed terms and ways of thinking cultivated and broadcast in the right-wing, corporate media. It is doubtful this woman received marching orders from anyone, but rather took the ideas and language in the culture—the memes—to form and express her frustration. Because the clip of this protestor was replayed again and again on corporate news and YouTube, the Obama=Hitler meme spread even farther, to others who continue to use it with little thought of the comparison's historical roots. Recycling through the news and through viral means across Networked News, the image of this protester—and her language—has become a template for others to utilize. Even if Gingrich and Beck did not give this protester direct orders, even if she never listened to either commentator, nor read Goldberg's *Liberal Fascism*, nor heard of the Hoover Institution, she is nonetheless a participant in spreading their point of view, which then permeates the media environment. While we have focused on the media infrastructure that propagated this right-wing extremist spin, this case study illustrates the potential of any powerful ideological, religious, and/or corporate interests to hijack social networks, spread spin, and stymie authentic democratic debate. In this way, Networked News serves to further confuse genuine discourse, further amplifying paranoia and sensationalism over trust and substance.

(B)LATANT (P)ROPAGANDA: FRAMING AS NEWS ABUSE AND CENSORSHIP

But if thought corrupts language, language can also corrupt thought.
—GEORGE ORWELL, Politics and the English Language[78]

Immediately following the disastrous malfunction of British Petroleum's (BP) oil rig and the ensuing flood of oil pouring into the Gulf of Mexico, a battle began—not only to stop and capture the flow of oil, but as Paul Farhi of the *Washington Post* astutely observed, to publicly name the man-made disaster. Farhi notes, "The name of a disaster can be critical, both as a historic matter and the more immediate matters of image, public relations and legal liability."[79]

In other words, the labels affixed to the catastrophe would compete to influence the public's perception, and as a result, impact the consequences for BP, the Environmental Protection Agency, and the Obama administration (and as we write, this is an ongoing battle for the public mind). BP is the fourth-largest corporation in the world. For it to preserve its image, keep business flowing and lawsuits down, they would need the right name to stick in the public consciousness (like oil to pelicans), and thus, the right frame of mind (not like oil to pelicans). From day one, BP attempted to linguistically wriggle from responsibility by calling the incident the "Gulf of Mexico Response."[80] President Obama, wanting to distance himself from responsibility and appear tough on corporate malfeasance, deemed it the "BP Oil Spill" (this despite, according to *Politico*, the president's status as "the biggest recipient of BP cash").[81] By contrast, conservative radio commentator Rush Limbaugh used the disaster to pin blame on the president, calling it "Obama's Katrina."[82] BP, Obama, and Limbaugh were doing their best to win the battle for the public mind, each vying to use their label to frame the event in the public consciousness. These parties were all trying to influence news of the event, not necessarily to get at the truth.

As Orwell observed in the epigraph above, the ways we speak and use language not only reflect upon our thinking, but can alter it—our language can help us see reality more clearly, or it can corrupt our thinking, obscuring reality. The words we use, and the language that media use, matter—as the media have the power to conceal or reveal, to censor or shed light, to control thought or liberate it.

We cannot, as cognitive linguist George Lakoff observes, avoid frames that are "among the cognitive structure[s] we think with."[83] Whenever we hear any word, a frame of associated words and concepts jumps into our mind, whether we like it or not. Lakoff demonstrates this theory through the title of his *New York Times* bestseller, *Don't Think of an Elephant! Know Your Values and Frame the Debate*. His point—even if he tells you not to think of one, your brain will still produce an image of the enormous mammal, with associated concepts and words: tusks, stampeding, republicans.[84] When Limbaugh calls the ecological disaster in Louisiana "Obama's Katrina," and others in media echo the phrase, we can't help but imagine the horrors of Katrina and link them to the devastation currently happening, and to Obama as well—even if we disagree with the connection. Similarly, when Obama uses "BP Oil Spill," he does so purposely, to highlight the corporation's responsibility, and, perhaps, to downplay the responsibility inherent in his administration's response. When BP representatives leave their name out of the frame altogether, and even omit the fact that there was any sort of "spill," they are trying to downplay their role and responsibility, and perhaps the idea that anything even happened at all. The phrases most repeated in the public sphere push us to think about the event in specific ways, which can serve to illuminate the reality of what happened, or to confuse it. Lakoff theorizes, "If we hear the same language over and over, we will think more and more in terms of the frames . . . activated by that language." Whatever phrase prevails will likely determine how the public interprets the event overall, and how they refer to it in person, and on Networked News.[85] This influences the dominant narrative of the event and how it will be recorded in history (and possibly in oral testimony and eventually collective memory). Censorship and distortion can be preserved, instead of a narrative based on empirical facts.

Language engineers such as Lakoff and "Word Doctor" Frank Luntz, who encouraged Republicans to use the terms "death tax," "tax relief," "climate change," and "war on terror," actively shape the words which evoke the "right" frames and ideas. Luntz, a contributor to Fox News, is also a professional *framer* for major corporations: McDonald's, NBC, Twentieth Century Fox, Boeing, Disney, General Motors, Lockheed Martin, and many others.[86] "If words are weapons," a *Time* magazine writer opines, "Frank Luntz is a samurai."[87] His most famous method, touted on his Web site and demonstrated in the PBS documentary *The Persuaders*, is Instant Response, in which he measures audience response to specific words or phrases to see how positively they react. The audience holds a dial in which they can instantly register positive and negative responses to parts of a speech, which Luntz carefully analyzes. He pitches the method for potential clients: "*We can draft* and analyze a wide array of language, *so you will know* down to the very word or phrase what resonates most. Whether it's hours of speeches, reels of advertisements, or clip after clip of *your* spokesperson on national TV, we can test anything that you can tape. We even test language *live* as it is happening. That's the 'instant' in instant response."[88]

Luntz ascertains the language that suits his clients' interests, what language best "resonates" with the public, what best registers in their minds to create a positive impression. Then, based on this data, he encourages his clients to use the proposed words and phrases repetitively to invoke the most positive impression possible. This language, developed in a laboratory setting, is sent to the public through press releases and corporate spokespersons as frequently as possible, in an effort to create a positive frame. More simply, what Luntz is trying to do is create language memes, or ways of talking about a corporation, politician, policy, or event, which then become "normalized" through everyday conversation. Once the words of spin doctors become normalized and spread through network news and Networked News, the frames themselves become normalized. Note how this process, this memetic engineering, bears no resemblance to traditional journalistic standards of fact-based reporting or truth telling.

It is a very sophisticated form of propaganda. It amounts to censorship and manipulation of the public perception of reality. In short, it is thought control and deception peddling.

In this light, BP's language engineers are currently winning the battle to minimize the scope of the disaster and their role in it (while losing the battle to actually stop the gushing oil). Although no major media outlets appear to be using BP's official language, very few sources are using language that emphasizes the real ecological devastation caused, nor their corporate responsibility for it. Like Obama, the Associated Press,[89] the *Christian Science Monitor*,[90] and *Democracy Now!*[91] have all used the phrase "BP Oil Spill," which emphasizes BP's responsibility. On the other hand, the phrase "spill" dramatically understates what is physically happening in the Gulf of Mexico: the oil is gushing from the seabed, not spilling, as BP's own live video feed clearly shows. This seemingly slight difference in phrasing, repeated again and again, conceals what is in reality a volcanic, gushing flow of oil spewing into the Gulf of Mexico, to the tune of several millions of gallons a day (up to 4.2 million gallons a day by some estimates).[92] This makes it the worst oil "spill" disaster in US history. Still, many of the references don't even attach BP's name to the oil gushing from their facility (leased from Transocean), hiding the long-term scope of their responsibility. Among the most frequently used phrases in the corporate media include "Gulf Oil Spill" or "Gulf of Mexico Oil Spill." BP's name, and responsibility, is absent in what are actually empirical misnomers—that is, propaganda.

Some progressive media and environmental groups, even when railing against BP, also employed misnomers, including the *Huffington Post*,[93] the *Socialist Equality Party*,[94] and *Earth First*.[95] Although the Sierra Club called it the "BP Oil Disaster" in the *Washington Post*, they used the innocuous term "Gulf Oil Spill" on their own Web site.[96] Similarly, *OnEarth* magazine, an outgrowth of the Natural Resources Defense Council, has used the term "BP Oil Disaster," but also frequently uses "Gulf Coast Oil Spill."[97] This innocuous way of speaking about the gusher in the Gulf is seeping into our social networks as well. A Facebook group that is supported by the *Mississippi Press*, the *Times-Picayune*, and other newspapers in the Gulf region calls itself "Save the Gulf," leaving BP out of the title entirely.[98] Thus, as these groups try to critique BP and encourage the enraged public to take action, by using BP's neutered language they serve to reinforce BP's spin. "It doesn't matter if you are negating words or questioning them," Lakoff writes, "the same frames . . . will be activated and hence strengthened."[99] The more the critics, the media, and each member of Networked News uses the corporate language, which mitigates BP's responsibility and minimizes the disaster, the more we unwittingly become BP's proxy public relations (PR) agents.

Phrases like the "Gulf Oil Spill" and "Obama=Hitler" are real, though diluted forms of what George Orwell called "Newspeak," from the archetypal dystopia of 1984. The language engineers of the Party (Ingsoc, or English Socialism) created Newspeak, the official language of the totalitarian nation Oceania, "not only to provide a medium of expression for the world-view and mental habits proper to the devotees of Ingsoc, but to make all other modes of thought impossible." By constructing language, the Party could control thought; they could privilege frames that reinforced their ideology. And Newspeak, of course, was designed as a mechanism of control, not to "extend but to diminish the range of thought."[100] Corporate media and public relations firms operate in much the same way by employing tactics that yield News Abuse.

In Orwell's nightmare world of 1984, language is an instrument to censor, suppress, and corrupt thought. Clearly, powerful interests—like BP, owners of the corporate media, or political parties—are best served by Newspeak, by a language, a way of speaking that bolsters their image at the expense of reality, and thus at the expense of We the People. BP recently spent $50 million on a PR campaign designed to shape the way the public thinks and speaks about their company.[101] Part of BP's campaign included the purchasing of oil spill–related search terms on Google, which ensured more people were directed in Web searches about the Gulf incident to BP's pages, BP's Newspeak language, and BP's frames.[102]

If reporters, critics, and citizens choose to use language unreflectively rather than thoughtfully, we may all succumb to the easiest language, the language we see the most, the language that has the most money behind it, that appears across the corporate media, and that now appears across our social media. The result is that we use the most powerful and prevalent words or frames in the "meme pool," rather than those that best express reality. Without thinking about the words we use and the frames we construct, we unwittingly promote spin, giving greater currency, legitimacy, and normalcy to visions of the world that may be entirely hyperreal.

Fortunately, unlike in Orwell's Oceania, we can still choose our own words, and construct our own public frames. We must do so in an effort to actualize a society not only capable of imagining a free press, free speech, and protection of the commons, but of achieving these ideals as well.

SHATTERING THE ILLUSIONS: WHAT WE CAN DO TO COMBAT JUNK FOOD NEWS AND NEWS ABUSE

You are what you Tweet.
—DAVID MATHISON, *author of* Be the Media[103]

As much as what has been outlined here clearly fits into Orwellian constructs of language and thought control, or outright propaganda and distraction, it is indeed important that we return to the notion put forth by Neil Postman at the outset proposing that Aldous Huxley prevails over Orwell as an overall frame for the American mindset. It is one thing to be duped, deceived, mislead, lied to, manipulated, and cajoled, but it is quite another that a people allow this continued pattern to prevail (dare we suggest some among us may enjoy living in the dark), especially when we now have at our fingertips the knowledge and power to dismantle the master's house with the master's tools. Postman aptly noted, "[M]ost of our daily news is inert, consisting of information that gives us something to talk about but cannot lead to any meaningful action."[104] We can demand more than that. We can change how we get our information and not only insist upon truthful reporting, but help to create it and support it where it already exists.[105]

We can use the Internet, Facebook, and Twitter to further social justice, to inform each other about truthful news items that affect all of our communities, and to proactively engage in democratic participatory arenas, or we can be part of the News Abuse cycle. We can deny PR spin and demand factual reporting and just civil proceedings. We can also proclaim that Hitler is not among us in the public arena. It's a choice. Postman remarked that, "Technology always has unforeseen consequences, and it is not always clear, at the beginning, who or what will win, and who or what will lose."[106] In other words, it is not too late.

We can be the media, we can build citizen journalism to serve the public good, we can utilize our public educational system of colleges and universities and libraries to research and produce accurate news.[107] We can influence the direction we take as a democratic society, and refuse to be lead by rogues of one political stripe preying upon our commons or wolves in sheep's clothing of another stripe peddling faux elixirs like "hope and change." We have to be the change, we cannot rely on elites from political parties or corporate boardrooms to give us hope. We are hope and we can manifest our ideals in a democratic culture that we create, with our own media, our own frames—not BP's, not CNN's or Fox's, not Bush's or Obama's, or Beck's: the People's.

One thing that is certain: Americans cannot rely on the corporate media to report the truth about the most crucial matters at hand. In his recent book, *The Empire of Illusion: The End of Literacy and the Triumph of Spectacle*, Chris Hedges clearly lays out the case against the televised corporate news media, with their fusion of Junk Food News and News Abuse:

> Television journalism is largely a farce. Celebrity reporters, masquerading as journalists, who make millions a year give a platform to the powerful and the famous so they can spin, equivocate, and lie. Sitting in a studio, putting on makeup, and chatting with Joe Biden, Hillary Clinton, or Lawrence Summers has little to do with journalism. If you are a true journalist, you should start to worry if you make $5 million a year. No journalist has a comfortable, cozy relationship with the powerful. No journalist believes that serving the powerful is a primary part of his or her calling. Those in power fear and dislike journalists—and they should.[108]

Hedges expands, "We are cleverly entertained during our descent. We have our own version of ancient Rome's bread and circuses with our ubiquitous and elaborate spectacles, sporting events, celebrity gossip and television reality shows."[109] In other words, as Huxley implied, we will come to enjoy our servitude, and in fact rely upon it, mistaking the stability of a consistent and relative intellectual and democratic decline for progress.

Make no mistake: the mendacity of paid corporate media shills that masquerade as journalists and propagate Junk Food News and News Abuse stories night and day, week in and week out, around the clock, knows no bounds and will not stop. They cannot be reformed. It is their job, their role in the technocratic, mass media, privatized, for profit, corporate propaganda machine. It is our job, our role, as a free people, as responsible individuals acting in concert, and as citizens, to safeguard and realize a truly independent and free press. Such a press is the life's blood of republican government. Our future depends upon it.

MICKEY HUFF is the director of Project Censored, an associate professor of history at Diablo Valley College, and a member of the board of directors at the Media Freedom Foundation. He has co-edited and coauthored two volumes of *Censored* yearbooks with Dr. Peter Phillips.

FRANCES A. CAPELL is a senior creative writing major at San Francisco State University, a Project Censored intern, and the student representative on the board of the Media Freedom Foundation. She coauthored "Infotainment Society: Junk Food News and News Abuse for 2008–2009" with Mickey Huff in *Censored 2010*.

ADAM BESSIE is an assistant professor of English at Diablo Valley College, where he teaches composition, reading, and critical thinking. His scholarship on metaphor and the mind is being used by Robert Wallerstein, MD, former president of the International Pyschoanalytical Association, in an upcoming major journal article. He regularly publishes essays on language, education, and culture on diverse, independent media Web sites, including the Daily Censored and OpEd News.

Special thanks to NOLAN HIGDON, Project Censored intern, for research assistance and formatting of this article, and to MEG HUFF, for editing and inspiration.

Notes

1. Neil Postman, *Amusing Ourselves to Death: Public Discourse in the Age of Show Business* (New York: Penguin, 1985), 3–4.
2. For more information about Project Censored see our Web site at www.projectcensored.org; and for more of an overview and background about what the Project has done over the years, see Peter Phillips, Charlene Jones, Sandy Murphy, Carl Jensen, and Project Censored, "Thirty Years of Censored News" in *Censored 2007*, eds. Peter Phillips and Project Censored (New York: Seven Stories Press, 2006), 159–69 (these are remarks on the founding and history of the Project by Dr. Carl Jensen); and see Peter Phillips and Mickey Huff, "Analysis of Project Censored: Are We a Left-Leaning, Conspiracy-Oriented Organization?" in *Censored 2010*, eds. Peter Phillips, Mickey Huff, and Project Censored (New York: Seven Stories Press, 2009), 261–90.
3. Ben Bagdikian, *The Media Monopoly* (Boston, MA: Beacon Press, 1983). The work has now gone through seven editions and illustrates the ongoing impact of conglomerates in media ownership; whereas in the US there used to be over fifty corporations in mass media ownership, today there are fewer than ten major players. For a primer on problems of mass media and propaganda issues in the US, see Noam Chomsky and Edward Herman's classic work *Manufacturing Consent: The Political Economy of Mass Media* (New York: Pantheon, 1988).
4. For more on the history of Project Censored's Junk Food News (started in 1984) and News Abuse (started in 2001), see Mickey Huff and Frances A. Capell, "Infotainment Society: Junk Food News and News Abuse for 2008–2009," in *Censored 2010*, 147–74.

The late New York University media scholar Neil Postman once said about America, "We are the best entertained least informed society in the world." Since the mid-1980s, Project Censored has examined this phenomenon in the culture of the 24/7 television news cycle. Looking beyond what the corporate news media undercover or ignore, Project Censored surveys what they do spend precious airtime and column inches on while not covering the top censored stories or others in the public interest. Which types of news stories have been found consistently by such surveys in this so-called information age? "Junk Food News," said Project Censored founder Dr. Carl Jensen. "It's like a Twinkie, not very nourishing for the consumer." This is how Jensen described it back in 1984 when he first began looking at how tabloid sensationalism had inundated the nightly news with the "Where's the Beef" campaign. Jensen still considers Junk Food News a major problem in journalism and corporate media, particularly on today's cable and television news.

While the News Abuse category may be confusing in relation to Junk Food News, one distinction is that News Abuse stories are about serious issues or are genuinely newsworthy items. However, they are misrepresented in the corporate press, and have been manipulated, trivialized, distorted, personalized, or, more aptly, tabloidized. News Abuse stories are transformed from potentially newsworthy items into far more titillating yet irrelevant distractions as a result.

5. Ibid.
6. Hyperreality is a term often associated with the French philosopher Jean Baudrillard, among others. It refers to a condition in which one cannot distinguish between what is real and what is not and is often linked causally to a media-saturated culture. A common example given for this is Disneyland. See Jean Baudrillard, "Simulacra and Simulations," in *Jean Baudrillard: Selected Writings*, ed. Mark Poster (Stanford: Stanford University Press, 1988), 166–84; and John Tiffin and Nobuyoshi Terashima, eds., *Hyperreality: Paradigm For The Third Millennium* (New York: Routledge, 2001). Historian Daniel Boorstin also addressed this issue and associated it with the rise of advertising in *The Image: A Guide to Pseudo-Events in America* (originally published 1961). Also, for more on the application of the term hyperreality in media studies see Andrew Hobbs and Peter Phillips, "The Hyperreality of a Failing Corporate Media System," in *Censored 2010*, 251–59 (also online at http://www.projectcensored.org/top-stories/articles/the-hyperreality-of-a-failing-corporate-media-system).
7. Aldous Huxley, *Brave New World* (New York: Harper & Brothers, 1932); and George Orwell, *1984* (New York: Harcourt Brace Jovanovich, 1949).
8. Postman, *Amusing Ourselves to Death*, vii–viii.
9. Ibid.
10. Frank Rich, "Tiger Woods, Person of the Year," *New York Times*, December 19, 2009, http://www.nytimes.com/2009/12/20/opinion/20rich.html.
11. James Desborough, "Tiger Had Me in the Rough," *News of the World*, December 6, 2009, http://www.newsoftheworld.co.uk/news/631528/Tiger-had-me-in-the-rough-Mindy-Lawtons-frantic-sex-with-Tiger-Woods.html.
12. Ibid.
13. Paul Farhi, "Lost in the Woods," *American Journalism Review* (March 2010), http://www.ajr.org/article.asp?id=4856.
14. Liz Thomas, "BBC's News Coverage of Tiger Woods' Apology Sparks 'Dumbing Down' Backlash," *Mail Online*, February 25, 2010, http://www.dailymail.co.uk/news/article-1253598/BBCs-news-coverage-Tiger-Woods-apology-sparks-dumbing-backlash.html.

15. Jimmy Orr, "Yahoo! Loves Tiger Woods," *Christian Science Monitor*, December 9, 2009, http://www.csmonitor.com/Innovation/Horizons/2009/1209/yahoo-loves-tiger-woods-god-bless-tiger-says-yahoo-ceo.

16. John Ridley, "Mark Sanford Gets Lucky. Again." *Huffington Post*, June 26, 2009, http://www.huffingtonpost.com/john-ridley/mark-sanford-gets-lucky-a_b_221673.html.

17. *Politicususa*, "Fox News Disowns Mark Sanford," June 24, 2010, http://www.politicususa.com/en/FNC-Sanford.

18. *The State*, "Video: 'SNL' Pokes Fun at Tiger Media Coverage, via Mark Sanford," December 13, 2009, http://www.thestate.com/2009/12/13/1069736/video-snl-pokes-fun-at-tiger-media.html.

19. Lauren Streib, "Dead Celebrities Are Good For Dying Media Industry," *Forbes*, October 27, 2009, http://www.forbes.com/2009/10/27/dead-celebrities-good-for-magazines-dead-celebs-09-magazines.html.

20. Tom Rosenstiel, Paul Hitlin, and Mahvish Shahid Khan, "Media Swing from Protests in Iran to the Passing of the King of Pop," *Pew Research Center's Project for Excellence in Journalism*, June 22–28, 2009, http://www.journalism.org/index_report/pej_news_coverage_index_june_22_28_2009.

21. Ibid.

22. Linnie Rawlinson and Nick Hunt, "Jackson Dies, Almost Takes Internet with Him," *CNN*, June 26, 2009, http://www.cnn.com/2009/TECH/06/26/michael.jackson.internet/index.html.

23. Maggie Shiels, "Web Slows after Jackson's Death," *BBC News*, June 26, 2009, http://news.bbc.co.uk/2/hi/8120324.stm.

24. Rawlinson and Hunt, "Jackson Dies, Almost Takes Internet with Him."

25. Rosenstiel, Hitlin, and Khan, "Media Swing from Protests in Iran to the Passing of the King of Pop."

26. Ibid.

27. See Russell Goldman, "Police: Carradine's Death Likely Sex Accident," *ABC News*, June 5, 2009, http://abcnews.go.com/Entertainment/story?id=7763422&page=1.

28. Christopher Bonanos, "The Eclipsed Celebrity Death Club," *New York Magazine*, June 26, 2009, http://nymag.com/daily/intel/2009/06/the_eclipsed_celebrity_death_c.html.

29. Rosenstiel, Hitlin, and Khan, "Media Swing from Protests in Iran to the Passing of the King of Pop."

30. Mick Hume, *Televictims: Emotional Correctness in the Media AD (After Diana)* (UK: InformInc [LM] Ltd, 1998).

31. Patrick West, *Conspicuous Compassion: Why Sometimes It Really Is Cruel To Be Kind* (UK: Civitas, 2004); and BBC News, "'Mourning Sickness Is a Religion,'" February 23, 2004, http://news.bbc.co.uk/2/hi/uk_news/3512447.stm.

32. Associated Press, "Colorado Boy Said to Have Floated Off in Balloon Found Safe," WJBF-TV (ABC), October 15, 2009, http://www2.wjbf.com/news/2009/oct/15/6-year-old_boy_floats_away_in_flying_saucer-shaped-ar-226969.

33. Jason Linkins, "Media's Balloon Boy Coverage Filled With More Hot Air Than Actual Balloon," *Huffington Post*, October 16, 2009, http://www.huffingtonpost.com/2009/10/16/medias-balloon-boy-covera_n_323780.html.

34. Mark Jurkowitz, "Balloon Boy Takes Media for a Ride," *Pew Research Center Publications*, October 20, 2009, http://pewresearch.org/pubs/1384/media-coverage-of-balloon-boy.

35. Linkins, "Media's Balloon Boy Coverage Filled With More Hot Air Than Actual Balloon."

36. Colby Hall, "This Was Still Wrong: Boy Found Alive Didn't Change The Risks," *Mediaite*, October 15, 2009, http://www.mediaite.com/online/this-was-still-wrong-balloon-landing-empty-didnt-change-risk.

37. *CNN*, "Balloon Boy Incident Raises More Questions, Officials Say," October 16, 2009, http://www.cnn.com/2009/US/10/16/colorado.balloon.boy/index.html.

38. Linkins, "Media's Balloon Boy Coverage Filled With More Hot Air Than Actual Balloon."

39. Jurkowitz, "Balloon Boy Takes Media for a Ride."

40. Janet Loughrey, "Balloon Boy: Is Mainstream Media Purposely Distracting Us?" *OpEd News*, October 17, 2009, http://www.opednews.com/articles/Mainstream-Media-Madness-by-Janet-Loughrey-091016-566.html. Given how many real news stories are not covered as a result of covering Junk Food News, it seems the answer to the question in Loughrey's title is yes. Some of these stories the corporate media missed are listed later in the notes of this piece.

41. Corky Siemaszko, "White House Party Crasher Michaele Salahi Cast on Bravo's Reality TV Series, 'Real Housewives of DC,'" *New York Daily News*, March 26, 2010, http://www.nydailynews.com/gossip/2010/03/26/2010-03-26_white_house_party_crasher_michaele_salahi_cast_on_reality_tv_series_real_housewi.html.

42. Mark Jurkowitz, "Afghanistan Dominates While Two Scandals Fascinate," *Pew Research Center's Project for Excellence in Journalism*, November 30–December 6, 2009, http://www.journalism.org/index_report/pej_news_coverage_index_november_30december_6_2009.

43. Siemaszko, "White House Party Crasher Michaele Salahi Cast on Bravo's Reality TV Series, 'Real Housewives of DC.'"

44. Ibid. Also see *Huffington Post*, "Michaele And Tareq Salahi, Accused State Dinner Party Crashers, Crash Letterman Monologue (VIDEO)," May 26, 2010, http://www.huffingtonpost.com/2010/05/26/michaele-and-tareq-salahi_n_589867.html.

45. Here is a brief listing of stories the corporate media could have been covering more during the Tiger Woods debacle of November 27–28 and just after: Pamela Hess, "Saddam Was Telling Truth in Missing Gulf War Pilot," *Associated Press*, November 29, 2009, http://www.commondreams.org/headline/2009/11/29-4; James Randerson, "Western Lifestyle Unsustainable, Says Climate Expert Rajendra Pachauri," *The Observer*, November 29, 2009, http://www.guardian.co.uk/environment/2009/nov/29/rajendra-pachauri-climate-warning-copenhagen; Nina Lakhani, "Bhopal: The Victims Are Still Being Born," *The Independent*, November 29, 2009, http://www.independent.co.uk/news/world/asia/bhopal-the-victims-are-still-being-born1830516.html; and Sean D. Naylor, "Trigger-happy Security Complicates Convoys," *Army Times*, December 2, 2009, http://www.armytimes.com/news/2009/11/army_convoy_security_112909w/.

    Stories the corporate media could have been covering after the death of David Carradine, from June 17 on: Jeff Mason, "US Climate Report Details Energy, Agriculture Harm," *Reuters*, June 17, 2009, http://www.commondreams.org/headline/2009/06/17-0; Bruce A. Dixon, "Teachers File Racial Discrimination Suit Against Obama Administration's School 'Turnaround' Plan," *Black Agenda Report*. June 17, 2009, http://www.blackagendareport.com/?q=content/teachers-file-racial-discrimination-suit-against-obama-administrations-school-%E2%80%9Cturnaround%E2%80%9D-p; and *Environment News Service.*, "EPA Declares Public Health Emergency in Asbestos-Ridden Libby, Montana," June 18, 2009, http://www.commondreams.org/headline/2009/06/18-1.

    Stories the corporate media could have been covering during Governor Sanford scandal, from June 24 on: Kate Devlin, "Chemicals In Shampoos and Toys 'Could Lead to Low Birth Weight,'" *The Telegraph*, June 25, 2009, http://www.telegraph.co.uk/health/health-news/5624161/Chemicals-in-shampoos-and-toys-could-lead-to-low-birth-weight.html; and Elizabeth Bluemink, "Court Allows Gold Mine To Dump Waste In Lake," *Anchorage Daily News*, June 22, 2009 (modified June 23, 2009), http://www.adn.com/2009/06/22/840031/court-allows-gold-mine-to-dump.html.

Stories the corporate media could have given more attention to after the death of Michael Jackson, from June 25 on: Sharon Cohen, "Did Toxic Chemical in Iraq Sicken GIs?" *Associated Press*, June 28, 2009, http://www.commondreams.org/headline/2009/06/28; and Dafna Linzer and Peter Finn, "White House Is Drafting Executive Order to Allow Indefinite Detention; Move Would Bypass Congress," *Pro Publica,* June 26, 2009, http://www.propublica.org/feature/white-house-drafts-executive-order-to-allow-indefinite-detention-626.

Stories the corporate media could have been covering during the Balloon Boy incident, from October 15 on: Graham Bowley, "Bailout Helps Fuel a New Era of Wall Street Wealth," *Common Dreams,* October 17, 2009, http://www.commondreams.org/ headline/2009/10/17-0; Thalif Deen, "US Berated for Shielding Israel on Gaza Killings," *Inter Press Service*, October 14, 2009, http://www.ipsnews.net/ news.asp?idnews=48864; and Ben Webster, "The Arctic Will Be Ice-Free in Summer within 20 Years, Research Says," *Times* (London), October 15, 2009, http://www.timesonline.co.uk/tol/news/science/earth-environment/article6875260.ece.

Stories the corporate media could have been covering during the Salahi Gate Crashers incident, from November 30 on: Sue Sturgis, "The Campaign Cash Behind the Afghanistan Escalation," *Facing South*, December 1, 2009, http://www.southern-studies.org/2009/12/the-campaign-cash-behind-the-afghanistan-escalation.html; Yara Bayoumy, "UN: Rape in Afghanistan a Human Rights Problem of 'Profound Proportions,'" *Reuters*, November 30, 2009, http://www.commondreams.org/headline/2009/11/30-8; Ryan Grim, "Senate Bill Contains A Gift For Big Banks," *Huffington Post*, November 30, 2009, http://www.huffingtonpost.com/2009/11/30/senate-bill-contains-a-gi_n_373962.html; Richard Norton-Taylor, "Iraq Inquiry: Blair Told Bush He Was Willing To Join, 11 Months Before War," *Guardian*, November 30, 2009, http://www.guardian.co.uk/uk/2009/nov/30/iraq-inquiry-david-manning.

46. Kristen Purcell, et al., "Understanding the Participatory News Consumer: How Internet and Cell Phone Uses Have Turned News into a Social Experience," *Pew Research Center's Project for Excellence in Journalism*, March 1, 2010, http://journalism.org/analysis_report/understanding_participatory_news_consumer.

47. "CNN Reports," *Saturday Night Live*, March 6, 2010, http://hulu.com/watch/132877/saturday-night-live-cnn-reports.

48. Thanks to Allison Levitsky from Adam Bessie's English 122 course at Diablo Valley College for the insightful phrase "tabloids of ourselves."

49. Jean Baudrillard's groundbreaking definition of the term "simulacrum" essentially means a "simulation." He argues that today's reality is mass-produced, or simulated, by powerful social forces. "It is the map," Baudrillard writes, "that precedes the territory." In other words, we use the map to shape the territory, not just to represent it. The map does not depict what exists, but creates what exists. An example might be a pre-planned suburb, in which the developers attempt to recreate a "rustic landscape," thus shaping the actual landscape into their vision. The residents, then, are living in a simulation of a rustic landscape, in the vision created by what developers thought rustic should look like. The simulation becomes reality. In much the same way, what we argue here is that corporate news has essentially provided a map, a blueprint, for how we report news on our on social networks. Celebrity culture, which we are awash in, becomes the model—the map—on which we create our own media culture. Thus,

our social networks become a photocopy, a simulation, of what we see on network news. In our own lives, we often mime what we see in the major media. For more detail on the concept of "simulacrum," see Baudrillard, "The Procession of Simulacra," in *The Norton Anthology of Theory and Criticism*, eds. Vincent B. Leitch, et al. (New York: Norton, 2001), 1729–1741. Also, the excerpt from this book on which our theory is built is available online at http://www.stanford.edu/dept/HPS/Baudrillard/Baudrillard_Simulacra.html.

50. *Pew Research Center Publications*, "Public Follows War, Talks Tiger," December 10, 2009, http://pewresearch.org/pubs/1435/public-interest-afghanistan-tiger-woodssalahis.

51. Jurkowitz, "Afghanistan Dominates While Two Scandals Fascinate."

52. Timothy Ogden, "How Texting is Changing Philanthropy," *Harvard Business Review*, March 24, 2010, blogs section, http://blogs.hbr.org/cs/2010/03/how_texting_is _changing_philan.html.

53. Andrew Heining, "Facebook Celebrity Doppleganger Week: What You Need to Know," *Christian Science Monitor*, February 2, 2010, http://www.csmonitor.com/Innovation/Horizons/2010/0202/Facebook-Celebrity-Doppelganger-Week-What-you-need-to-know.

54. Richard Dawkins, *The Selfish Gene* (Oxford University Press, 1976). See the chapter which coined the term "meme," and the field of memetics, "Memes: The New Replicators," available at http://www.rubinghscience.org/memetics/dawkinsmemes.html.

55. Dan Fletcher, "Facebook's Doppelganger Week is Viral Groupthink," *Time*, February 5, 2010, http://www.time.com/time/business/article/0,8599,1960458,00.html#ixzz0nMDqtCPB.

56. Daniel Scanfeld, Vanessa Scanfeld, and Elaine Larson, "Dissemination of Health Information Through Social Networks: Twitter and Antibiotics," *American Journal of Infection Control* 38, no. 3, http://download.journals.elsevierhealth.com/pdfs/journals/0196-6553/PIIS0196655310000349.pdf.

57. For a more thorough discussion of hyperreality, see Andrew Hobbs and Peter Phillips, "The Hyperreality of a Failing Corporate Media System," in *Censored 2010*, 251-259; also see endnote numbers 6 and 46 of this article, specifically regarding Jean Baudrillard.

58. *Daily Show*, "Baracknophobia," November 13, 2008, http://www.thedailyshow.com/ watch/thu-november-13-2008/obama-and-hitler.

59. Adam Bessie "Obama is Hitler? WTF?" *OpEd News*, December 1, 2008, http://www.opednews.com/articles/Obama-is-Hitler-WTF-by-Adam-Bessie-081130755.html.

60. Noah Lederman, "Playing the Nazi Card: Comparing Obama to Hitler Becomes a Standard Right-Wing Trope," *Fairness and Accuracy in Reporting (FAIR)*, March 2010, http://www.fair.org/index.php?page=4022. It should also be noted that in the Bush years, the corporate media criticized Hitler comparisons made by the left, while under Obama they treat them as potentially serious critiques from the right.

61. "Obama=Hitler," posted on *YouTube* by cyclon85912, October 4, 2008, http://youtube .com/watch?v=eS2rJP-udUs&feature=related. It is unclear if the poster is the author of the video, or if this is the original date it hit *YouTube*. Such is the nature of social networking—it is not known at the time of writing who produced this video nor who funded it.

62. Lederman, "Playing the Nazi Card."

63. Bianca Bosker, "Facebook Group 'Praying' For President Obama's Death Passes One Million Members," *Huffington Post*, April 28, 2010, http://www.huffingtonpost .com/2010/04/28/facebook-group-praying-fo_n_555227.html.

64. *Today Show*, "Gingrich: Left Redefining 'American'," MSNBC, May 18, 2010, http://today.msnbc.msn.com/id/37194394/ns/today-today_books/.

65. Newt Gingrich, interview by Chris Wallace, "Transcript: Newt Gingrich on 'FNS,'" *Fox News*, May 17, 2010, aired on May 16, 2010, http://www.foxnews.com/story/0,2933,592990,00.html.

66. George Orwell, "Politics and the English Language," 1946. Read the essay online at http://www.mtholyoke.edu/acad/intrel/orwell46.htm.

67. Carl Cameron and Liza Porteus, "Ad Comparing Bush to Hitler Gets Heat," *Fox News*, January 6, 2004, http://www.foxnews.com/story/0,2933,107426,00.html.

68. Glen Greenwald, "GOP Political Tactics and Media Inanity in a Nutshell," *Salon*, August 6, 2009, http://www.salon.com/news/opinion/glenn_greenwald/2009/08/06/republicans.

69. Lederman, "Playing the Nazi Card."

70. Lewis Black, "Back in Black: Glenn Beck's Nazi Tourette's," *Daily Show*, May 12, 2010, http://www.thedailyshow.com/watch/wed-may-12-2010/back-in-black---glenn-beck-s-nazi-tourette-s.

71. Thomas Sowell, "Premature Politics," *National Review Online*, March 6, 2007, http://article.nationalreview.com/307516/premature-politics/thomas-sowell.

72. "The William and Barbara Edwards Media Fellows Program," *Hoover Institution*, Stanford University, http://media.hoover.org/fellows/by-title/media-fellows. This site provides a comprehensive list of Hoover's media fellows.

73. *Columbia Journalism Review*, "Who Owns What," http://cjr.org/resources/index.php?c=bertelsmann. Readers can research the complex network of media ownership here, along with contact information for each corporation. For a history of this issue, see Bagdikian's classic *The Media Monopoly*, now in its seventh edition.

74. *Media Matters*, "On MSNBC, Jonah Goldberg Claimed 'You Can Draw a Clear Line' from Mussolini to Clinton and Obama," January 10, 2008, http://mediamatters.org/research/200801100016.

75. Lederman, "Playing the Nazi Card."

76. Jonah Goldberg, "Liberal Fascism: The Blog," *National Review Online*, August 25, 2009, http://liberalfascism.nationalreview.com.

77. See @newtgingrich, Newt Gingrich's Twitter account, at http://twitter.com/NewtGingrich. Readers can search public figures, Twitter followers, and who they follow by opening a Twitter account at http://twitter.com.

78. Orwell, "Politics and the English Language."

79. Paul Farhi, "BP Touts Itself As 'Green,' But Faces PR Disaster with 'BP Oil Spill,'" *Washington Post*, May 6, 2010, http://www.washingtonpost.com/wp-dyn/content/article/2010/05/05/AR2010050505022_pf.html.

80. Ibid.

81. Erica Lovley, "Obama Biggest Recipient of BP Cash," *Politico*, May 5, 2010, http://www.politico.com/news/stories/0510/36783.html.

82. *Media Matters*, "Media absurdly claim oil spill is 'Obama's Katrina,'" April 30, 2010, http://mediamatters.org/research/201004300034.

83. George Lakoff, *The Political Mind: A Cognitive Scientist's Guide To Your Brain and it's Politics* (New York: Penguin Books, 2008), 22.

84. George Lakoff, *Don't Think Of An Elephant! Know Your Values and Frame the Debate* (Vermont: Chelsea Green Publishing, 2004).

85. Lakoff, *The Political Mind*, 15.

86. See Frank Luntz's Web site, The Word Doctors, at http://www.theworddoctors.com. See http://www.theworddoctors.com/clients-corporate.html for a list of corporate clients.

87. Randy James, "Pollster Frank Luntz, Warrior with Words," *Time*, September 21, 2009, http://www.time.com/time/nation/article/0,8599,1925066,00.html.

88. See Luntz's own description of the method online at http://www.theworddoctors.com/instant-response.html.

89. *Media Matters*, "Media absurdly claim oil spill is 'Obama's Katrina.'"

90. Pete Spotts, "BP Oil Spill Could Make Gulf Hurricane Season 'Devasting,'" *Christian Science Monitor*, June 1, 2010, http://www.csmonitor.com/USA/2010/0601/BP-oil-spill-could-make-Gulf-hurricane-season-devastating.

91. *Democracy Now!*, "Headlines for June 1, 2010," June 1, 2010, http://www.democracynow.org/shows/2010/6/1.

92. Mark Guarino, "Gulf Oil Spill: 'Top Kill' Could Be Last Best Chance To Stop Leak," *Christian Science Monitor*, May 19, 2010, http://www.csmonitor.com/USA/2010/0519/Gulf-oil-spill-top-kill-could-be-last-best-chance-to-stop-leak. Says Guarino, "Despite BP and Coast Guard estimates that about 210,000 gallons, or 5,000 barrels, of oil are escaping, independent sources are reporting that number is greatly conservative, saying the real discharge is estimated between 3.9 million to 4.2 million gallons a day." Also reported by Amy Goodman, "Government Doubles Oil Spill Size Estimate," *Democracy Now!*, June 11, 2010, http://www.democracynow.org/2010/6/11/headlines. Another common media obfuscation involves switching oil amounts from barrels to gallons, given the fact that many people do not immediately realize that there are 42 gallons in a barrel. So, saying there are 4.2 million gallons gushing from the Gulf a day sounds worse than saying there are 100,000 barrels leaking or spilling, even though it is basically the same amount. The use of different terms with shifting measurements acts to shape perception, not reality.

93. Jason Linkins, "Oil Spill Response: If Relief Well Drilling Is Only Guaranteed Option, Why Not Make It Mandatory?" *Huffington Post*, June 1, 2010, http://www.huffingtonpost.com/2010/06/01/oil-spill-response-if-rel_n_596142.html.

94. *Socialist Equality Party*, "The Gulf Coast Oil Spill," May 28, 2010, http://socialequality.com/gulfoilspill.

95. *Earth First!*, "Gulf Oil Spill Hits Day 40 With No End In Sight," May 29, 2010, news section, http://www.enn.com/wildlife/article/41375/print. *Earth First!* linked to the *Environmental News Network* who in turn linked to a *Reuters* article. Additionally, even the *Revolution* newspaper (of the Revolutionary Communist Party) continued to use terms describing the BP-induced disaster without invoking the company's name in their headlines, despite being contacted by this chapter's coauthor Mickey Huff explaining to them how they were furthering the corporate line on the issue. Given the anticapitalist nature of the organization, it illustrates how these memes or frames in the corporate media infiltrate social networks and potentially corrupt language to such an extent that groups adopt language that is contrary to their own ideological principles (*Revolution*'s Facebook updates also often left BP out of the headlines and even adopted the term "spill" which does not empirically describe what is happening in the Gulf as a result of BP's failures). As of June 15, 2010, *Revolution*'s Web site, http://www.rwor.org, had for the most part left BP out of any headline on the issue that they called the "oil catastrophe."

96. "The Gulf Oil Spill and the case for socialism," *Socialist Equality Party*, June 8, 2010, http://www.wsws.org/articles/2010/jun2010/pers-j08.shtml.

97. For example, Osha Gray Davidson, "BP Oil Disaster Threatens Survival of the 'Gulf's Sea Turtle,'" *OnEarth*, May 4, 2010, http://www.onearth.org/article/bp-oil-disaster-threatens-survival-of-the-"gulf's-sea-turtle"; and various articles linked from "Disaster in the Gulf," *OnEarth*, http://www.onearth.org/gulfspill (accessed July 7, 2010).

98. "Save the Gulf of Mexico," Facebook, http://www.facebook.com/SaveTheGulfOfMex-ico?ref=ts. This is a Facebook group with about 80,000 people that "like it" as of June 8, 2010. That said, in terms of framing, we also found more popular, explicitly anti-BP Facebook pages such as "Stop the Oil Spill by Stuffing BP Executives Into the Leak," with over 250,000 fans as of the same date, http://www.facebook.com/stoptheoilspill?ref=ts, and another called "Boycott BP" with over 620,000 fans as of June 15, 2010, http://www.facebook.com/?ref=logo#!/pages/Boycott-BP/119101198107726?ref=ts. Being aware of different frames is the key point.

99. Lakoff, *The Political Mind*, 15.

100. George Orwell, *1984* (New York: Signet Classic, 1984), 246–56.

101. Alex Brownsell, "BP Chief Hayward Vows Not To Quit Ahead of New Ad Campaigns," *Marketing*, June 7, 2010, http://www.marketingmagazine.co.uk/News/MostEmailed/1008151/BP-chief-Hayward-vows-not-quit-ahead-new-ad-campaigns.

102. Hibah Yousuf, "BP Buys Google, Yahoo Oil Spill Search Terms," *CNN Money*, June 7, 2010, http://money.cnn.com/2010/06/07/news/companies/BP_search_terms/index.htm. Here, BP is even attempting to skew public research. It should be noted that other corporate news outlets also reported on this phenomenon, further illustrating that the medium is not operating completely outside free press standards of journalism, but it is so often complicit in Junk Food News and News Abuse that extreme vigilance is required, ultimately making corporate media an untrustworthy and inconsistent source of accurate information.

103. David Mathison, *Be the Media* (Tiburon, CA: natural E creative Group, LLC, 2009); see http://bethemedia.com. For more about Mathison, see chapter fourteen of this volume.

104. Postman, *Amusing Ourselves to Death*, 68. On page 68–69, Postman goes on to say this phenomenon has come about since the invention of the telegraph. He stated, "By generating an abundance of irrelevant information, it dramatically altered what may be called the 'information ratio.'" The creation of later communications technologies exacerbated this and "made the relationship between information and action both abstract and remote." Postman concluded, "for the first time in human history, people were faced with the problem of information glut, which means that simultaneously they were faced with the problem of a diminished social and political potency. . . . [W]e have here a great loop of impotence: the news elicits from you a variety of opinions about which you can do nothing except to offer them as more news, about which you can do nothing." Bear in mind Postman was writing all this before the Internet. That is both a scary thought as well as a promising one depending upon if we choose to use new technology proactively rather than be used by it passively.

105. See Project Censored's "Daily Independent News Feeds We Trust" at http://www.censorednews.org.

106. Neil Postman, speech given at a meeting of the German Informatics Society (Gesellschaft fuer Informatik), sponsored by IBM-Germany, October 11, 1990, Stuttgart, Germany http://courses.eserver.org/s03/tc599/readings/informing_ourse%E2%80%A6_to_death.txt.

107. See chapter eleven of this volume for more on this issue.

108. Chris Hedges, *The Empire of Illusion: The End of Literacy and the Triumph of Spectacle* (New York: Nation Books, 2009), 169. Hedges expands on the themes of Postman, Boorstin, and others cited in this article throughout his book.

109. Chris Hedges, "Bad Days for Newsrooms—and Democracy," *In These Times*, July 24, 2008, http://www.inthesetimes.com/article/3828/bad_days_for_newsrooms_and_democracy.

CHAPTER 4

Signs of Health
Stories of Hope and Creative Change from 2009 and 2010

by Kenn Burrows

> *The strange paradox of the news business is that on any aver-age day the world's best papers and radio and television stations are not covering the best stories. The media's atten-tion is focused on loss, failure, deceit, murder and war. In short: on everything that's going wrong. . . . The choice to tell a better story does not mean denying or hiding from misery and abuse. Better stories change the world. . . . They promote progress, inspire the recipients and fulfill the messengers.*
> —JURRIAAN KAMP, *veteran newsman and co-founder,* Ode *magazine*

The world is full of complex problems and much suffering. Add a con-stant stream of bad news from the commercial media, and reality can seem mean and dangerous. It is easy to feel discouraged, disengaged, and afraid. Discouragement and fear are powerful forces; some people respond by becoming cynical, some by giving up and some by taking sides and fighting. These reactions take a real toll on us and don't seem to help in solving the problems that concern us.

Now contrast the above predicaments with those moments when you get a glimpse of something new, a promise of something that signals a whole different understanding. This is what "good news" does. It gives us a sense of possibilities that you had not imagined before . . . and things seem different. Good news is not about feel-good stories that mask the challenges of life; it's about inspiring solutions and creative insight that don't make the problem-oriented headlines. We need a reg-ular dose of this inspiration and hope to maintain a healthy balance with today's challenges. Yet, this is just what gets left out of the news. War, crime, and big business are news, yet love, peace, and spirituality are not. The things that are deeply important typically lie outside the scope of conventional news.

The rest of this chapter explores solution-based stories from this last year—healing stories that embrace real change and new possibilities. These "better stories" suggest that when ordinary people use their imagination and work together, they can do extraordinary things. This news of creative accomplishment is organized into four areas: 1) Community Solutions, 2) Environmental Solutions, 3) Economic Solutions, and 4) Psychological Solutions. Each of these four areas has a unique role to play in the multidimensional reality of local and global change. These stories suggest that a better world is both possible and practical and that every day, all over the world, people are solving problems. The message is simple: stop fighting and lamenting existing reality—be an innovator and help create something better. Pass it on . . .

COMMUNITY SOLUTIONS

These stories are about using collaborative processes within communities in order to recognize, support, and act upon common needs and justice-related issues.

Coalition of Peace Groups Permanently Shuts Down Army Experience Center

A coalition of thirty peace groups triumphed in their goal of shutting down the Army Experience Center (AEC) in a suburban shopping mall in Philadelphia. In June 2010, the *Philadelphia Inquirer* reported that the army plans to permanently close the $13-million, 14,500–square foot facility stationed at Franklin Mills Mall, which housed dozens of video game computers and Xbox video game consoles simulating interactive, military-style shooting games.

Former United States Army Sergeant Jesse Hamilton stated, "By portraying war as a game, the AEC glorified violence to our children. As a combat veteran, nothing makes me happier than to know that the AEC will no longer have the ability to corrupt our children's minds and disrespect our deceased war heroes." Teamwork among the peace groups led to the coalition's success in shutting down the center.

Sources: "Peace Groups Permanently Shut Down Army Experience Center in Philadelphia," Shut Down the Army Experience Center, press

release, June 10, 2010, http://shutdowntheaec.net/?p=398; Edward Col-
imore and Nicole Lockley, "Army Experience Center in Northeast will
close," *Philadelphia Inquirer*, June 10, 2010, http://www.philly.com/
philly/news/local/96031939.html.

Local Food Comes to a Neighborhood Near You

Communities across the United States are turning to local food to
improve health and combat obesity, strengthen the local economy, and
bring fresh foods to those living in food deserts. While some school cafe-
terias, such as those in Boulder, Colorado, already incorporate fresh,
regional produce in their menus, others have much work ahead of them,
such as the University of California students who have launched a movement to serve 20 percent "real" food on campus by 2020, referring to
products that are local, fairly traded, and environmentally sound. In
Savannah, Georgia, the Southeastern African-American Farmers
Organic Network regularly hosts farmers markets at historic Forsyth
Park—a location African Americans were excluded from just decades
ago. Cities like Seattle and Minneapolis fund the creation of community
gardens on vacant land, and San Francisco requires that all farmers markets accept food stamps. Community gardening has even gone cyber;
Web site Hyperlocavore connects "landless gardeners with land hosts" to
involve everyone in the movement.

Sources: Ellen Mahoney, "Smarter School Lunches," *Yes! Magazine*, January
12, 2010, http://www.yesmagazine.org/happiness/smarter-school-lunches;
Berit Anderson, "People We Love: Hai Vo," *Yes! Magazine*, April 13, 2010,
http://www.yesmagazine.org/issues/america-the-remix/people-we-love-hai-
vo; Mark Winne, "African American Farmers Go Organic," *Yes! Magazine*,
March 5, 2010, http://www.yesmagazine.org/planet/african-american-
farmers-go-organic-bring-healthy-food-to-georgia-community;   Pamela
O'Malley Chang, "Yard for Share: My Hyperlocavore Garden," *Yes! Magazine*, April 13, 2010, http://www.ycsmagazinc.org/blogs/pamela-omalley-
chang/yard-for-share-my-hyperlocavore-garden.

Outrage Turns to Action Over Supreme Court Decision on Corporate Elections Funding

Seldom since the Dred Scott decision in 1857 has a Supreme Court ruling been so clarifying, yet viewed by so many as so wrong . Just as Dred

Scott caused outrage by declaring that black people could not enjoy full constitutional rights, the Citizens' United case is causing outrage with the declaration that corporations have the constitutional rights of people and can spend unlimited amounts of money on elections. Across the political spectrum, polls show that people oppose the decision and are getting organized to protect the rights of real people, to elect the representatives of their choice, free of the outsized influence of corporate treasuries.

Source: Doug Pibel, "Real People v. Corporate 'People': The Fight is On," *Yes! Magazine*, Summer 2010.

Ranchers and Tribes Agree to Protect Critical Salmon River

For years, ranchers, farmers, environmentalists, and fishermen had been at loggerheads over one of the West Coast's most important salmon rivers, the Klamath River. In 2010, all the parties reached an agreement to protect the salmon on the Klamath River, following the intervention of the peoples who claim to speak for the salmon—the tribes of the Klamath Valley.

Source: "Western Showdown: Saving the Klamath," *Yes! Magazine*, Summer 2010, http://www.yesmagazine.org/issues/water-solutions/western-showdown-saving-the-klamath.

Paraguayan Farmers Mobilize for Agrarian Reform

Marching through the streets of Paraguay's capital city, Asunción, thousands of farmers raised signs and fists demanding that President Fernando Lugo follow through on his campaign promises for agrarian reform, including the distribution of land to poor farmers, and access to health care, education, and better homes and roads for rural communities. These various farmer organizations were motivated to voice their concerns after President Lugo had failed to meet promised demands after a year and a half in office.

Source: Benjamin Dangl, "Paraguayan Farmers Mobilize for Agrarian Reform," *Toward Freedom*, March 29, 2010, http://towardfreedom.com/home/content/view/1903/1.

It's Not a Silent War: Israel's Blockade of Gaza

In response to the current blockade in Gaza, an international group of fifteen hundred men and women from forty-two nations traveled to Egypt over the New Year (2009–10) to join a Freedom March. Marchers protested the fact that a year after the attack by Israeli armed forces—destroying most of Gaza's homes, hospitals, schools, and other structures—residents have no possibility of rebuilding because their borders are closed. In addition to mobilizing communities in solidarity, some independent media, including the documentary *Roadmap to Apartheid*, has garnered awareness and supportive action for this tragic human crisis.

Sources: "The Silent War: Israel's Blockade on Gaza," World News, May 25, 2010, http://article.wn.com/view/2010/06/14/Gaza_blockade_to _be_eased_within_days_declares_Tony_Blair; Ana Nogueria, *Roadmap to Apartheid*, http://www.grittv.org/2009/03/01/got-docs-roadmap-to-apartheid; "Never Before Campaign," Window into Palestine, http://windowintopalestine.blogspot.com/2009/02/never-before-campaign.html; "Roger Waters Records New Version of 'We Shall Overcome,'" Musicians for Freedom, http://musicians4freedom.com/ ?p=8597.

ENVIRONMENTAL SOLUTIONS

We cannot be healthy if our environment is sick. Here are news stories of efforts to align culture with nature, including strategies to reduce environmental degradation caused by human activity and to restore the earth to a sound and healthy state—thereby enhancing everyone's future.

Permaculture—Greening the Desert

This year's winner of the Buckminster Fuller Challenge—Allan Savory for Operation Hope—demonstrated that it is possible to apply whole-systems thinking and permaculture design principles to reverse the desertification of the world's savannas and grasslands, thereby contributing enormously to mitigating climate change, biomass burning, drought, flood, drying of rivers and underground waters, and disappearing wildlife, and, in turn, massive poverty, social breakdown, violence, and genocide.

Educator and consultant Geoff Lawton has also cultivated permaculture on the salted land of the Dead Sea Valley, designing a strategy to harvest every drop of rain that fell onto a ten-acre area. Using man-made ditches called swales, mulch from nearby fields and micro-irrigation, he reduced the evaporation of water then planted trees. Afterward, he planted fruit trees. The bountiful harvest produced four months later proved that the desalination of the soil had been successful.

Sources: "Buckminster Fuller Challenge: Operation Hope: Permanent Water and Food Security for Africa's Improverished Millions,"Buckminster Filler Challenge Web site, http://challenge.bfi.org/winner_2010; Geoff Lawton, "Greening the Desert Project—Outcomes Profiled," February 2010, http://www.growvideos.com/video/2264/Permaculture-in-Action—Greening-The-Desert, http://www.permacultureusa.org/2009/01/29/greening-the-desert-project-outcomes-profiled.

California Bans Free Plastic Bags

The California State Assembly passed Assembly Bill 1998, banning single-use carryout plastic bags at large retail establishments. California Governor Arnold Schwarzenegger publicly stated his support, applauding assembly member Julia Brownley (D-Santa Monica) for her efforts in passing the bill. In accordance with new regulations, plastic bags will no longer be available to the customer, though paper bags may be purchased for a nickel each. Californians use 19 billion plastic bags every year, or about 552 per person. These bags are a major contributor to marine debris, which is responsible for the deaths of large volumes of marine life. With the implementation of this bill, there will be not only less plastic waste in our water, but also less in our landfills.

Sources: Brian Merchant, "California is Banning Plastic Bags," *Treehugger*, June 7, 2010, http://www.treehugger.com/files/2010/06/california-ban-plastic-bags.php; "60,000 Plastic Bags are Being Used This Second: Help Slow it Down," http://planetgreen.discovery.com/home-garden/plastic-bag-facts.html.

Town Bans Bottled Water Sales

The town of Concord, Massachusetts, has banned the sale of bottled drinking water to take effect at the beginning of 2011. Under the measure, refillable water containers would still be delivered and sold in town; only non-reusable plastic bottles would be banned. Supporters claim that the production of plastic water bottles uses 17 million barrels of oil each year. The beverage industry opposes the measure.

Source: "Town Bans Bottled Water Sales," WCVB (ABC) TV, May 1, 2010, www.thebostonchannel.com/news/23320994/detail.html.

Returning to the Soil

For every unit of food we consume using conventional agricultural methods employed in the United States, six times that amount of topsoil is lost. According to the US Food and Drug Administration, the average person eats one ton of food each year, necessitating twelve thousand pounds of topsoil. Topsoil, or dirt, is the product of the decomposition of dead organic matter and the waste products of living animals. When this material is not circulated back into the natural cycle, the soil suffers erosion and nutrient runoff, leaving the next season of plants—and those that consume them—less healthy than before. At the forefront of the movement to reduce the soil footprint of humankind is John Jeavons, who asserts that all farming on the planet takes more than it gives. With composting at the center of his system, he recommends that gardeners devote 60 percent of planting space to growing crops whose primary purpose is to add biomass to compost piles. By putting this and other strategies into practice, Jeavons says his system can increase the productivity of food and dirt sixtyfold.

Source: Larry Gallagher, "The Joy of Dirt," *Ode*, March 2010, http://www.odemagazine.com/doc/69/dirt.

Mail In Your Old Cell Phone and Support the Planting of Trees

Plant My Phone is a new company designed to reduce the large number of old cell phones occupying landfills. The idea is both simple and potentially far-reaching: cell phone users may send in old, unwanted cell phones using postage-paid bags available in cities like Chicago, San Francisco, and New Orleans, or on the Internet. The mailed phones are recycled, and their materials are sold to fund tree planting. According to the company's Web site, mailing in an average two-year-old phone will result in the planting of fifteen trees. A first generation Apple iPhone in good condition equates to the planting of seventy-nine trees. Cell phones contain heavy metals, which are toxic to the environment when not disposed of properly, thus recycling them is important because "of the 140 million old cell phones each year, only 10 percent get recycled."

Source: Jake Richardson, "Plant Trees by Mailing In Old Cell Phones," *Care2*, June 3, 2010, http://www.care2.com/greenliving/plant-trees-by-mailing-in-old-cell-phones.html.

A Win for Grid Innovation and Green Power

Despite a massive $46 million campaign, Proposition 16—a California ballot measure, backed by Pacific Gas & Electric Company (PG&E), that attempted to block local governments from creating or growing their own municipal utilities—failed to pass in a June 2010 election. The measure's failure is a major victory for its opponents—including the Sierra Club, the American Association of Retired Persons (AARP), and local sites. Opposition voters claimed that PG&E was actively working against the incorporation of renewable forms of energy and was insincere in its arguments.

As the largest electric corporation in the United States, PG&E is often held up as an example with its activities capable of setting precedents for the hundreds of other corporate utilities across the country. Because many smaller utilities look to the company for guidance, the results of Proposition 16 have national consequences.

Sources: Camille Ricketts, "PG&E Loses $46M Prop. 16—A Win for Grid Innovation," *Beat*, June 9, 2010, http://green.venturebeat.com/2010/06/09/pge-loses-its-46m-prop-16-battle-in-california-a-win-for-grid-innovation; Kevin Drum, "Prop 16 and Ratepayer Rage," *Mother Jones*, June 10, 2010, http://motherjones.com/kevin-drum/2010/06/prop-16-and-ratepayer-rage.

Bacteria May Help Oil Spill Cleanup—Bioremediation

The greatest environmental disaster that has ever occurred to the US is looming a few miles offshore in the Gulf of Mexico. Given the amount of oil already spilled and the undetermined amount of oil still flowing up from a mile under the sea, it is impossible for the upper areas of the Gulf of Mexico to survive as we know it. There is a simple and natural solution: oil-eating microbes. Microbes occur in nature—in fact, humans have over a pound of microbes in their bodies—and each type performs certain tasks. Some decompose plant matter, while others help break down toxins. In the last twenty years, scientists have discovered and "harvested" naturally occurring microbes from around the world so that trillions are now available to help us!

Commercially available, these microbes have been tested successfully on large oil spills around the world. The microbes are simply mixed with water and sprayed on the oil as it reaches the calmer waters near shore or onshore itself. Once applied to the oil, the microbes eat it—leaving a natural waste product that is harmless to marine life. The process can completely clean an area of oil in just a few weeks—not years. NY3, a new form of a bacteria developed at Oregon State University, may help to break down oil even faster and safer. The bacteria produce rhamno-lipids, a natural, nontoxic, and biodegradable substance that breaks down oil before it has a chance to hurt ecosystems. Discovered years ago in China, researchers have made a new form that produces ten times the amount of rhamnolipids, which are safe to all life and break down naturally.

So far, British Petroleum has decided not to use microbes to clean up the Gulf Oil Spill. The Gulf Oil Spill Bioremediation Industry Alliance has been formed to bring the top bioremediation companies and their scientists together to create an implementation plan, with hope they will be called in.

Sources: QMI Agency, "New Bacteria May Help Oil Spill Cleanup," *Toronto Sun*, June 13, 2010, http://www.torontosun.com/news/world/2010/06/13/14372716.html;
"Spill Fighters Posts," Spillfighters, June 7–10, 2010, http://spillfighters.com/category/recent-posts *Biomediation*; Environmental Inquiry, http://ei.cornell.edu/biodeg/bioremed.

Worldwide Climate Movement Flexes Its Muscles

The December 2009 United Nations climate talks in Copenhagen did not produce a binding treaty, but they did galvanize a united international movement of people calling for solutions to stop runaway climate change. The movement builds on years of political organizing in Europe, the United States, and around the world: in Europe and Australia, civil disobedience training camps have blockaded and shut down coal-fired power plants, and in the United States, rural conservatives have joined young people to protest mountaintop removal mining. On October 24, 2009, citizens in 181 countries staged demonstrations during a global day of climate action coordinated by the group 350.org, founded by author and activist Bill McKibben. In December, climate activists delivered a petition calling for an ambitious climate treaty to the United Nations with 10 million signatures.

When negotiations broke down and leaders failed to agree on a binding deal, civil society groups and countries from the Global South stepped forward to propose their own solutions. A climate conference held in May 2010 in Cochabamba, Bolivia, drew thirty thousand people. The gatherers drew up a "People's Agreement," which demands that wealthy nations slash their carbon emissions and pay for the damages that climate change will cause to developing nations.

Sources: Mark Engler, "Rise People: The Climate Justice Movement Breaks Through," *Yes! Magazine*, Winter 2010; Jim Schultz, "Climate Talks End With People's Agreement," *Yes! Magazine*, Summer 2010; Richard Graves, "10 Million People Petition for Climate Action," *Yes! Magazine*, December 8, 2010, www.yesmagazine.org/blogs/copenhagen/10-million-people-petition-for-climate-action.

ECONOMIC SOLUTIONS

With the dollar no longer the global reserve currency it was designed to be after World War II, economic uncertainties fill the air. And few people understand the nature of money and finance. The average American lives in a web of debt and a state of servitude to a mortgage, taxes, and a job. These news stories explore alternative systems of banking, currency, and work exchange, and call for the monetary and financial literacy necessary for a better tomorrow.

Wall Street Banking Crisis Spurs Development of State Banks

At a time of state budget crises, North Dakota has a sizable budget surplus, and while other states are cutting back on essential services and jobs, North Dakota is adding jobs. How is it different than other states?

North Dakota is the only state in the United States that owns its own bank. Now, other states are taking notice. Massachusetts, Washington, Illinois, Michigan, and Virginia have bills introduced in their legislatures, and state leaders in Missouri, New Mexico, Hawaii, and Vermont are also calling for the study and development of state banks.

Sources: Ellen Brown, "More States May Create Public Banks," *Yes! Magazine*, Summer 2010, http://www.yesmagazine.org/issues/water-solutions/more-states-may-create-public-banks; Ellen Brown, "Whose Bank? Public Investment, Not Private Debt," *Yes! Magazine*, February 19, 2010, http://www.yesmagazine.org/new-economy/campaign-for-state-owned-banks; Josh Harkinson, "How the Nation's Only State-Owned Bank Became the Envy of Wall Street," *Mother Jones*, March 27, 2009.

Time Banks Thrive in the Midst of the Recession

We use money to pay for services, but what if we paid for services with services? This is precisely what is being done among people who participate in "time banks," which are online systems that people can use to record the barter hours they earn: "Spend an hour doing something for somebody else; deposit an hour into your time bank account as a time dollar. You now have one time dollar to spend on having someone do something for you."

The idea is that a time bank—such as Hour Exchange Portland (HEP) of Portland, Maine—provides the vehicle for a community to come together and work directly for each other without the need of traditional currency. With traditional currency, such as Federal Reserve notes, one earns money from an employer; but with time banks, one earns "time dollars" by directly engaging with members of the community. In addition to the benefit of fostering cooperation and communication within communities, time-banking helps people though difficult financial times such as recessions and market collapse. Time banking is a new way of increasing the efficiency and practicality of simple barter systems, and may be one of the key ideas needed to strengthen the cohesion, trust, and stability that many communities desire.

Source: Leah Dobkin and Carmel Wroth, "Time Banks Thrive in the Midst of the Recession," *Ode*, September/October, 2009.

Happiness, Not Economic Growth, Is Becoming the Goal

Increasing numbers of people are recognizing that growth-at-all-costs policies can't continue: growth-based policies may increase wealth for the already rich but have failed to result in broad well-being. And fast-growing economies are hitting up against limits to the planet's natural resources (like energy) and sinks for wastes (like the atmosphere). Global surveys confirm that the happiest people are not those living in countries with the highest growth rates or the most wealth, but those with the most equity, "social solidarity," work-life balance, and strong safety nets. Happiness is emerging as a substitute goal among researchers and leading policy makers in the European Union, in the Kingdom of Bhutan, within the Organisation for Economic Co-operation and Development (OECD), and, increasingly, in the United States.

Sources: John de Graaf, "Putting the Science of Happiness Into Practice," December 6, 2009, http://www.yesmagazine.org/happiness/putting-the-science-of-happiness-into-practice; Richard Wilkinson and Brooke Jarvis, "Want the Good Life? Your Neighbors Need It, Too," *Yes! Magazine*, March 4, 2010, http://www.yesmagazine.org/happiness/want-the-good-life-your-neighbors-need-it-too.

Altruism and Economics

In order to bridge a municipal budget deficit, the City of Yonkers, New York, planned to terminate six of its firefighters. The men and women of the Yonkers Fire Department, however, saw another possibility to overcoming their city's economic crisis: by a 75 percent majority, they chose to work without pay enough time, over six months, to save the city the money needed to save their fellow firefighters' jobs.

The president of the local firefighter's union, Patrick Brady, stated that the firefighter's union "banded together and voted to save our brethren." By cooperating in partnership and solidarity, the firefighters of the City of Yonkers were not only able to save the jobs of six of their colleagues, they likewise contributed to the overall safety of their community, and demonstrated the strength of altruism over personal material gain. This story is an illustration of how an economic problem can be addressed with new ways of thinking about economics, such as realizing the long-term value of fostering harmonious group and community dynamics, rather than merely cutting jobs so that the money comes out "right."

Source: Jeremy Mercer, "The Altruism in Economics," *Ode*, May 2009.

Worker Ownership Burgeoning in the United States

Corporate outsourcing and trade policies that encourage the movement of production to the world's lowest-wage countries had already created long-term unemployment and community decline before the 2008 economic crash. But in the last two years, these trends have only gotten worse. Those facts are well covered in the media, but what is unreported is the growth of cooperatives, which are creating the sorts of jobs that can't pick up and move overseas, while helping some communities make a green economic recovery. Worker-owned co-ops are just one segment of the 30,000 cooperative business in the US generating $500 billion in revenue.

Sources: J. Trimarco and Jill Bamburg, "Worker Co-ops: Green and Just Jobs You Can Own," *Yes! Magazine*, Summer 2009; Ted Howard, Steve Dubb, and Gar Alperovitz, "Cleveland's Worker-Owned Boom," *Yes! Magazine*, Summer 2009.

These cooperatives are among the many inspired by the Mondragon cooperatives in the Basque region of Spain: Georgia Kelly and Shaula Massena, "When Worker-Owners Decide How to Ride Out a Downturn," *Yes! Magazine*, Summer 2009.

Citizen Budgeting Comes to the US

Born in Porto Alegre, Brazil, participatory budgeting has come to Chicago's 49th Ward, the first place in the United States to adopt the practice that allows taxpayers to directly decide how to spend public money. Over 1,600 community members got involved in the process: proposing project ideas, planning budgets, and voting on what they felt was most important. Participatory budgeting has already spread to cities throughout Latin American and Europe, where the process keeps government spending transparent, adapts governmental priorities to people's needs, and makes democracy palpable.

Sources: J. Lerner and M. Antieau, "Chicago's $1.3 Million Experiment in Democracy," *Yes! Magazine*, April 20, 2010, http://www.yesmagazine.org/people-power/chicagos-1.3-million-experiment-in-democracy; Jeff Raderstrong, "Chicago Ward Tries Citizen Budgeting," *Yes! Magazine*, Spring 2010.

PSYCHOLOGICAL SOLUTIONS

These news stories emphasize the importance of our state of mind, of the beliefs and views we hold, and show how we can expand these limited perspectives. And when we do expand our perspectives, everything else seems to change—notably our health, and our capacity to create, relate, and succeed.

The Power of Hope

Any experience of utter powerlessness—whether a serious illness, a robbery, or a rape—leaves emotional scars. If persistent, these feelings of powerlessness and despair can weaken our body's natural defense systems, leaving us more vulnerable to the very illnesses we fear. A study from University of California–Berkeley has suggested the power that negative thinking holds by analyzing patients' answers to two questions: "Do you feel it is impossible for you to achieve the goals you've set yourself?" and "Do you get the feeling your future is hopeless and is it difficult to believe things will get better for you?" Participants who replied "yes" to both questions were three times more likely to develop cancer in the six years thereafter, and four times more likely to suffer from cardiovascular disease such as heart attack or brain hemorrhage. Awareness of the power of hope is the first step in regaining some measure of control over our body and our emotions.

Source: David Servan-Schreiber, "The Power of Hope," *Ode*, April/May 2010, http://www.odemagazine.com/doc/70/The-power-of-hope.

Change Your Mind in Troubled Times—Try Good News and Intelligent Optimism

Tired of the focus on doom and gloom that surrounds us these days? *Ode* magazine sheds light on people solving problems and on the positive things being reported around the world.

Every January, *Ode* raises awareness of good news by honoring twenty-five "Intelligent Optimists"—leaders and change agents who are changing the world with their creativity and commitment. If you know someone who is making a big difference, make a nomination.

Sign up to receive good news daily via e-mail: http://www.odemagazine .com/p/good-news.

Source: "Intelligent Optimists," *Ode*, January 2010, http://www .odemagazine.com/intelligent_optimists.

Art and Imagination—Creating Comics for the Middle East

Jordanian comic book artist Suleiman Bakhit explains why Superman, Spiderman, and Batman, are not fit for Middle Eastern youth: "We cannot relate to these Western heroes, because they're so out of tune with our cultural values and our daily experiences." Bakhit says that a Middle Eastern superhero would not "leap tall buildings in a single bound," but rather would provide youth with the "inspiration to deal with the challenges of their daily lives." And, he continues, "there are few if any public leaders that youth can relate to."

Bakhit was studying at an American university at the time of the 9/11 attacks and recalled feeling attacked himself by others who judged him based on his appearance. The negativity he felt from others spurred his attention to "reducing people's fear of Muslims and the Middle East." He spoke at elementary schools and answered questions from the children. When one child asked him what the Arab superheroes look like, he began drawing comics to give the youth of the Middle East the heroes and role models they were lacking. "[Middle Eastern youth] were always told what to read and what to believe," he says. "That needs to change, and it's already changing." Bakhit plans to post his comic books online in Arabic and English.

Source: Marco Visscher, "Creating Comics for the Middle East," *Ode*, May 2009.

Cultivating Worldview Literacy—High School Pilot Program

Globalization, technology, and urbanization have sparked a need for an adapted curriculum that emphasizes creativity and learning from a range of perspectives beginning early in one's educational career. To address this need, the Institute of Noetic Sciences has begun the Worldview Literacy Project, a large-scale initiative dubbed Seeds of Change, which aims to promote awareness by celebrating diverse outlooks in California classrooms. The program, which began as a curriculum created for students from kindergarten to twelfth grade, facilitates learning through a systems level of understanding—how everyone and everything is interconnected and valuable. It consists of fifteen lessons, with disciplines ranging from science to poetry, using paired dialogue, small group processes, and class discussions to explore the unique beliefs, attitudes, and assumptions of the students.

Over the past several months, Seeds of Change has been piloted at Bay Area high schools. High school–age students who had felt disconnected from both the curriculum and the idea of working with classmates on a more intimate level showed a noticeable change in disposition after eight weeks. They began incorporating new students into discussions, sitting together, and saving room in their circles for any late arrivals. Students once uninterested in school became noticeably enthusiastic about the learning that was taking place through interactions with fellow classmates. "Consciousness is all it takes for one to transform and transcend the obstacles we face in life and really see the beauty of life that surrounds us," one student said of her experience in the program. "I am learning how to know myself and recognize all that's meaningful and authentic to me."

Sources: Liz Miller, "Cultivating Worldview Wisdom," *Noetic Post*, Fall/Winter 2009–10, www.noetic.org; Liz Miller, "'IONS' Worldview Literacy Program: Notes from the Field," *Noetic Post*, Fall/Winter 2009–10.

ACKNOWLEDGMENTS

Thanks to the San Francisco State University students who helped in editing and preparing this chapter: Amanda Epstein, Kali Cheung, and Justin Francis. And thanks to Josette Canilao of Sonoma State University.

A special thanks to the people of *Yes! Magazine*, who contributed the majority of stories, and especially to Executive Editor Sarah Van Gelder for her good ideas and caring support. *Yes! Magazine* is an award-winning, ad-free, nonprofit publication that supports people's active engagement in building a just and sustainable world.

Thanks to Marco Visscher, managing editor of *Ode* magazine. *Ode* is a print and online publication about positive news, featuring the people and ideas that are changing our world for the better.

To further your exploration of creative solutions, integrative thinking, and an expanded definition of health and activism, see the Web site for the Holistic Health Learning Center, San Francisco State University, with its extensive set of links and articles: http://www.sfsu.edu/~holistic/Links.html.

KENN BURROWS has been an educator and consultant for over thirty years, teaching holistic health studies at San Francisco State University since 1991. He is founder and director of the SF State Holistic Health Learning Center, an unusual library and community action center staffed by student volunteers, and he is also the producer and director of the biennial conference The Future of Health Care. Prior to coming to SF State, he taught for twelve years at Foothill College (Los Altos Hills, California) and operated Stress-Care, a corporate training and consulting company. For fifteen years, he has taught the popular course Holistic Health, Human Nature & Global Perspectives. He serves as an advisor to four different student clubs, including the SF State affiliate of Project Censored, and is a member of the board of the Media Freedom Foundation.

Fear & Favor
10th Annual Report
Hidden Interference in the Newsroom

by Peter Hart

By now, this much should be obvious: a corporate media system heavily dependent on commercial advertising and controlled by sprawling conglomerates has structural deficiencies.

Dramatic reductions in advertising and subscription revenue in recent years mean news outlets are even less likely to push back against commercial intrusions in the functioning of the newsroom. Journalists trying to hold onto their jobs in a shrinking newsroom are less likely to speak up about interference from owners or other powerful interests. The examples of non-journalistic interference in the newsroom—which Fairness & Accuracy in Reporting (FAIR) has been compiling for the past decade—are emblematic of a media system trying to find new ways to serve advertisers and marketers, in a desperate effort to increase revenue any way it can.

The conflicts this will surely create were starkly illustrated when the news Web site *Politico* revealed in July 2009 that *Washington Post* publisher Katharine Weymouth was to have a dozen off-the-record "salons" at her home, bringing together lobbyists, politicians, and key *Post* reporters and editors. The get-togethers were to be "underwritten" by corporations with a financial stake in public policy—starting with a discussion of health care paid for by health giant Kaiser Permanente.[1] As the promotional literature put it, such underwriters would be able to "build crucial relationships with *Washington Post* news executives in a neutral and informal setting."[2]

The *Post*'s plans collapsed in the wake of negative publicity, but the paper's willingness to compromise its independence was plain to see. Other media outlets have engineered similar gatherings; *Newsweek* magazine, for example, has partnered with Shell to present discussions on energy.[3]

As FAIR notes every year, the anecdotes gathered here are a sampling of incidents that have been reported in one venue or another, and do not represent a full accounting of the problems in the media business.

▶ Journalists working for owners with interests other than news gathering are usually aware of their owner's ties to commercial ventures or civic campaigns. A memo dated December 2, 2009, from newspaper publisher David Thompson to his staff at the *Oklahoman*, offered the chance to volunteer to work on a campaign for a bond initiative called MAPS 3 (Metropolitan Area Projects), which the paper was supporting:

> As we have said all along, OPUBCO [Oklahoma Publishing Company] employees should feel free to vote as they please next Tuesday, but if you are in favor of MAPS 3 and would like an opportunity to earn paid Volunteer Leave to support this initiative, this is a worthy opportunity for you!

▶ Sometimes the owner's interests directly affect what's printed in the paper. In August 2009, the *New York Times* reported that Long Island paper *Newsday*, which was bought by Cablevision in 2008, decided it would no longer accept advertising from Verizon—whose FiOS television service is a Cablevision competitor. As the *Times* noted, this was not the first time there were questions about the way Cablevision was running *Newsday*:

> In January, the top three editors at *Newsday* did not report for work for a few days amid reports that they had been fired or had resigned in a dispute with Cablevision over the paper's coverage of the New York Knicks basketball team, which is also owned by the company. The editors returned to duty, and neither they nor the company offered a full explanation of what had happened.[4]

▶ A newspaper that owns a cable company and a local sports franchise is certainly a conflicted source of news. But what happens when the local paper is owned by a powerful church? The Church of Jesus Christ of Latter-day Saints owns the Utah-based *Deseret News*, and the conflict inherent in that connection was obvious when the Mormon church's donations to an anti-gay marriage ballot initiative in California received national media scrutiny.

As *Columbia Journalism Review* (*CJR*) reported in May 2009, "the *Deseret News* gave short shrift to the allegations, only quoting sources who defended the Church, whereas the competing *Salt Lake Tribune*, and other publications, published several articles on the topic that let both sides express their positions."[5] The editorial independence of the *Deseret News* has come under scrutiny in the last few years, as Editor in Chief Joe Cannon has sought to bring the paper in line with the church's mission—an effort to make it "more Mormon." *CJR* noted that these efforts included reassigning two editors, which sparked a newsroom protest and a byline strike on February 25, 2009.

▸ A *New York Times* report on August 1, 2009, revealed an example of corporate interference involving two of cable television's most prominent foes.[6] Fox News Channel star Bill O'Reilly and MSNBC's Keith Olbermann have spent several years trading criticism and taunts. At MSNBC, executives at parent company General Electric (GE) were specifically concerned about O'Reilly's criticism of GE's business; according to the *Times*, executives from the rival companies met in May 2009 to hash out some sort of "cease-fire" agreement.

As the *Times* reported, MSNBC President Phil Griffin "told producers that he wanted the channel's other programs to follow Mr. Olbermann's lead and restrain from criticizing Fox directly, according to two employees." While Olbermann told the paper that he was "party to no deal," other MSNBC sources indicated otherwise. *Salon's* Glenn Greenwald reported that one regular MSNBC guest "was recently told by a segment producer that explicit mentions of Fox News were prohibited," and that "there has been talk among MSNBC employees ever since the GE edict was issued about ways to protest it and to stand up for their journalistic freedom."[7]

The "truce" seemed to vanish after the *Times* story was printed. But Olbermann's bosses at GE offered little in the way of explanation, which raised obvious concerns about the independence of journalists working for the company. If a star at MSNBC can be convinced to rein in the kind of commentary that made his show successful, would journalists further down the corporate food chain be able to resist such pressure?

▸ Sometimes it's a boss's personal relationship that needs to be protected. In June 2009, when *Newsweek* posted a Web interview with MSNBC's *Morning Joe* host Joe Scarborough, it mentioned up top that

Scarborough had been a defense attorney for an anti-abortion murderer.[8] With the murder of abortion provider George Tiller in the news, the mention made journalistic sense.

That's when *Newsweek* Editor Jon Meacham intervened. Saying that he was contacted by "a member of Scarborough's team," Meacham had the discomfiting detail removed from the top of the story.[9] When the subject is a friend who regularly invites you on his television program, the journalistic rules can be bent.

▸ Other times, bosses themselves make news. On December 8, 2009, Bloomberg reported that a Chicago underwriting company called Mesirow Financial had mishandled a municipal bond, potentially costing the city millions of dollars.[10] As Michael Miner noted in the *Chicago Reader*, Mesirow's chief executive officer is Jim Tyree, who also happens to lead the group of investors that owns the Chicago Sun-Times Media Group.[11]

So how did the *Sun-Times* newspaper play the news about the boss's botched bond deal? As Miner noted, the Bloomberg piece—originally more than 1,800 words—was cut to 259 in the *Sun-Times*, with enough space reserved for Tyree to respond. Did Tyree give the paper any pointers on how to cover his business deals? "Not on this nor on anything else," he said. But how much guidance is really needed for a journalist or editor interested in keeping a job?

IN ADVERTISERS WE TRUST

▸ Reminders that advertisers have undue influence on the news business are constant, and that message can be sent any number of ways. In December 2009, a *Dallas Morning News* memo from Editor Bob Mong and Senior Vice President of Sales Cyndy Carr announced a change in policy to employees of the A. H. Belo Corporation: some editors would henceforth report directly to the company's sales managers.[12] The sales team would "be working closely with news leadership in product and content development." The memo caused "uneasiness" among some news staffers, according to Mong, but others were, well, at ease—one editor was "excited about the idea of working with a business partner on an arts and entertainment segment." The memo itself called the rearrangement "one of several key strategies we have implemented this year to better serve our advertising clients."

▶ These blurry lines between advertising and news seem to be getting ever blurrier. In the past year, NBC Universal sought to make special advertising packages tied to specific "causes." One example—Campbell's Soup would sponsor health segments on the *Today* show.[13]

▶ When Glenn Greenwald exposed that former *Newsweek* reporter Richard Wolffe was making appearances on MSNBC without disclosing his new job at a public relations outfit, Wolffe was unusually direct about his former profession: "The idea that journalists are somehow not engaged in corporate activities is not really in touch with what's going on. Every conversation with journalists is about business models and advertisers." Wolffe also recounted that, on the day after the 2008 election, *Newsweek* sent him to Detroit to deliver a speech to advertisers. "You tell me where the line is between business and journalism," he said.[14]

▶ That attitude is commonplace in news media these days. The panelists on MSNBC's *Morning Joe* always rather conspicuously consumed Starbucks drinks on the air, and at some point decided to make that arrangement official—and profitable. As *New York Times* reporter Brian Stelter put it, host Joe Scarborough "sips Frappuccinos on camera so often that some viewers have wondered whether it is a form of product placement, paid for by the coffee company. Starting Monday, it will be." The $10 million deal included "Starbucks graphics and mentions during each hour" of the show.[15]

Would the arrangement cause any sort of conflict? MSNBC President Phil Griffin assured the *Times* that the show "would continue to cover Starbucks as a news item if warranted. 'They understand that we have standards.'" One such "standard" involved interviewing the CEO of the company soon after the deal was reached.[16]

▶ On April 9, 2009, the *Los Angeles Times* ran a front-page advertisement for the NBC drama *Southland* that was made to look like a news article; careful readers saw an NBC logo and the small label "Advertisement." Worse, it was revealed that the concept for the ad came not from NBC but from the paper's advertising department.[17] NBC official Adam Stotsky sounded ecstatic: "What was great about this ad unit is it gave us a quote-unquote 'editorial voice.'"

LA Times readers left queasy about the arrangement hardly had time to recover; three days later, the *New York Times* reported that the LA paper's entertainment section was "accompanied by a four-page advertisement for the movie 'The Soloist' that is laid out like a news section."[18] The "ad" included an interview with a columnist from the paper, whose work inspired the film. Like the front-page ad, the concept was developed by the paper. For what it's worth, the advertising arrangements seem to have offended many of the journalists at the *LA Times*; the *Soloist* ad ran despite the objections of the paper's editor, and one hundred reporters wrote a letter of protest.[19]

▸ Making news decisions with an eye toward the needs of advertisers was the subject of a November 2009 *Wall Street Journal* report about actions at the *Detroit Free Press*.[20] Upon learning that insurance company Humana Inc. was interested in advertising alongside any reporting about a Medicare open-enrollment period, the paper decided to do a special section on the topic, giving Humana the kind of marketing opportunity it apparently craved. That the news staff got wind of Humana's interest was no accident; as the *Journal* reported, the *Free Press* has a "Client Solutions Group" that was established "in part to act as a liaison between the business and news staffs."

The *Journal* also noted that the *Free Press* had run consecutive education features in its Sunday editions in late September—stories that appeared above ads for the retail giant Target, touting the company's education initiatives. That arrangement seemed to be similar to the Humana deal, though the precise nature of the deal is somewhat murky. Not so murky, on the other hand, was a comment from *Detroit Free Press* editor and publisher Paul Anger: "One of the things I think newsrooms have to realize . . . is we're here to cover the news in an unvarnished way, but we're also here to facilitate commerce."

▸ How far such facilitation might go remains a concern. Las Vegas TV station KVBC filed a Federal Communications Commission (FCC) complaint against three of its rivals (KVVU, KLAS, and KTNV) in October 2009, "charging that the stations sold airtime to an advertiser inside their newscasts and used reporters to conduct interviews presented as objective news stories without disclosing that the segments were purchased."[21] The complaint alleges that the stations conducted interviews that were essentially paid for—dressing up advertisements as news. The station seemingly learned of this when advertising staffers were told that they needed to "guarantee the news coverage" the same way its rivals were apparently doing.

▶ An example of the blending of TV advertising and news was reported in the *Tulsa World* in April 2009, thanks to a deal that Oklahoma television company Griffin Communications made with the state government insurance provider Insure Oklahoma.[22] The $3 million deal resulted in promotional spots airing within the newscasts on two Griffin-owned stations that looked exactly like news segments; they even hired a former newscaster from the station to appear in the spots. There is disclosure—of a sort, according to the *World*: "After the stories, the news anchor typically reads a disclosure statement informing viewers that the segment is sponsored by the station's parent company, Griffin Communications, and the Oklahoma Health Care Authority." Griffin CEO David Griffin told the paper, "We don't sell the news. We never have, and we never will. . . . The spots that run match up to our commitment to Insure Oklahoma."

▶ Of course, the clearest lesson a reporter might learn about not offending an important advertiser is one that ends in that reporter being out of a job. In December 2009, Colorado journalist Bob Berwyn was fired from the *Summit Daily News* days after writing a column critical of local ski resorts.[23] The column did not sit well with Vail Resorts CEO Rob Katz, who apparently warned that it might reconsider its advertising relationship with the paper.

▶ As *Hartford Courant* consumer columnist, George Gombossy alleged that he was fired from his paper after forty years of experience for writing critically about the Sleepy's mattress company in August 2009. Officials at the paper deny the allegation, but a *New York Times* report recalled some troubling backstory: Gombossy said he'd been previously ordered to meet with a company he had criticized—a company that happened to be an advertiser.[24] The *Courant* acknowledged that it was standard policy to alert major advertisers in advance of critical reporting.

CONCLUSION

FAIR began compiling these Fear & Favor reports ten years ago. The project was borne out of a desire to collect the scattered anecdotes about pressures on journalists from owners, advertisers, and other powerful interests. It's been noted that, over this time, some practices that were once considered "over the line"—an advertisement on the front page of a newspaper, for example—are much more common and now hardly elicit moral or ethical judgment.

The collapse of some aspects of the corporate media's business model has only placed additional pressure on managers and publishers to find new sources of revenue—which will likely further undermine the independence of journalism within the commercial system. In old and new media alike, the lines between editorial content and advertising are blurrier than ever—more evidence, if any was required, that a media system based on commercial advertising and dominated by profit-seeking conglomerates cannot deliver what citizens in a democracy require.

PETER HART is the activism director at Fairness & Accuracy in Reporting. He writes for FAIR's magazine, *Extra!*, and is a co-host and producer of FAIR's syndicated radio show, *CounterSpin*. He is the author of *The Oh Really? Factor: Unspinning Fox New Channel's Bill O'Reilly* (Seven Stories Press, 2003).

NOLAN HIGDON, Project Censored intern, formatted the notes in this piece for publication in this volume.

Notes

1. Michael Calderone and Mike Allen, "Washington Post cancels lobbyist event amid uproar," *Politico*, July 3, 2009, http://www.politico.com/news/stories/0709/24441.html.
2. Andrew Alexander, "A Sponsorship Scandal at The Post," *Washington Post*, July 12, 2009, http://www.washingtonpost.com/wp-dyn/content/article/2009/07/11/AR2009071100290.html.
3. Peter Hart, "Journalistic Reputations for Sale Pay to play at the Post . . . and elsewhere," *Extra!*, September 2009, http://www.fair.org/index.php?page=3943.
4. Richard Perez-Pena, "Newsday Rejects Ads by Verizon, Now a Rival," *New York Times*, August 30, 2009, http://www.nytimes.com/2009/08/31/business/media/31newsday.html.
5. Katia Bachko, "Darts & Laurels," *Columbia Journalism Review*, May/June 2009, http://www.cjr.org/darts_and_laurels/darts_laurels_1.php.
6. Brian Stelter, "Voices From Above Silence a Cable TV Feud," *New York Times*, July 31, 2009, http://www.nytimes.com/2009/08/01/business/media/01feud.html.
7. Glenn Greenwald, "The scope—and dangers—of GE's control of NBC and MSNBC," *Salon*, August 3, 2009, http://www.salon.com/news/opinion/glenn_greenwald/2009/08/03/general_ele ctric/.
8. Johnnie L. Roberts, "Can Republicans Survive?" *Newsweek*, June 5, 2009, http://www.newsweek.com/id/200691; and John Cook, "Joe Scarborough's "Team" Asks for, Receives Special Treatment from *Newsweek*," *Gawker*, June 9, 2009, http://gawker.com/5284507/joe-scarboroughsteam-asks-for-receives-special-treatment-from-newsweek.

9. John Cook, "Joe Scarborough's 'Team,'" June 9, 2009.

10. Michael Quint and John McCormick, "Hedge Funds Win on Chicago Sewer Debt at Public Cost (Update1)," Bloomberg, December 8, 2009, http://www.bloomberg.com/apps/news?pid=206 01103&sid=a6VIlkHPwGKM.

11. Michael Miner, "The $8 Million Business Brief," Blog, Chicago Reader, December 11, 2009, http://www.chicagoreader.com/TheBlog/archives/2009/12/10/the-8-million-news-brief.

12. Robert Wilonsky, "At The Dallas News, a New 'Bold Strategy': Section Editors Reporting to Sales Managers," Dallas Observer, December 3, 2009, http://blogs.dallasobserver.com/unfairpark/2009/12/at_the_dallas_news_the_latest.php.

13. Suzanne Vranica, "NBC Universal Tees Up Cause-Related Shows," Wall Street Journal, October 19, 2009, http://online.wsj.com/article/SB10001424052748704112904574477872926288910.htm.

14. Glenn Greenwald, "GE's silencing of Olbermann and MSNBC's sleazy use of Richard Wolffe," Salon, August 1, 2009, http://www.salon.com/news/opinion/glenn_greenwald/2009/08/01/ge.

15. Brian Stelter, "Starbucks Is Now the Official Joe of 'Morning Joe,'" New York Times, May 31, 2009, http://www.nytimes.com/2009/06/01/business/media/01joe.html.

16. New York Times, "Starbucks pays for product placement on MSNBC's 'Morning Joe.'" Seattle Times, June 1, 2009, http://seattletimes.nwsource.com/html/businesstechnology/2009284441_starbucks01.html.

17. Stephanie Clifford, "Front of Los Angeles Times Has an NBC 'Article.'" New York Times, April 9, 2009, http://www.nytimes.com/2009/04/10/business/media/10adco.html.

18. Stephanie Clifford, "Another Los Angeles Times Advertisement Draws Fire." New York Times, April 10, 2009, http://www.nytimes.com/2009/04/11/business/media/11paper.html.

19. Maureen Dowd, "Slouching Towards Oblivion," Los Angeles Times, April 25, 2009, http://www.nytimes.com/2009/04/26/opinion/26dowd.html.

20. Russell Adams, "Major Detroit Newspaper Takes Cues From Advertisers," Wall Street Journal, November 2, 2009, http://online.wsj.com/article/SB100014240527487047463045747506010958046446.html.

21. Steve Bornfield, "KVBC-TV sues three rivals: Station alleges competitors crossed line between news, advertising," Las Vegas Review, October 9, 2009, http://www.lvrj.com/news/kvbc-tv-sues-three-rivals-63835707.html.

22. Kim Archer, "Media company airing TV ad spots as part of state contract," Tulsa World, April 5, 2009, http://mobile.tulsaworld.com/article.aspx?articleid=20090405_17_A1_Thesta922572&sort=new.

23. Stan Bush, "Journalist Fired After Critical Report Published," CBS 4 Denver, December 10, 2009, http://cbs4denver.com/local/summit.county.ski.2.1363449.html.

24. Stephanie Clifford, "Losing Job, Consumer Columnist Cries Foul," New York Times, August 17, 2009, http://www.nytimes.com/2009/08/18/business/media/18courant.html.

SECTION II

Truth Emergency
Inside the US/NATO Military-Industrial-Media Empire

Facts do not cease to exist because they are ignored.
—*Aldous Huxley,* Proper Studies

*There is nothing so strong or safe in an emergency of
life as the simple truth.*
—*Charles Dickens*

The Times of London reported on June 5, 2010, that American troops are now operating in seventy-five countries. It seems that President Barack Obama has secretly sanctioned a huge increase in the number of United States Special Forces carrying out search-and-destroy missions against al-Qaeda around the world. This increase is far in excess of the special forces operations that took place under George W. Bush and reflects how aggressively Obama is pursuing al-Qaeda despite his public rhetoric of global engagement and diplomacy. Somehow this information didn't make it into the American corporate media.[1]

The United States, in cooperation with the North Atlantic Treaty Organization (NATO) (see story #23 in chapter 1), is building global occupation forces for the control of international resources, and all for Trilaterialist—US, Europe, Japan—corporate profits. The empire's objectives are laid bare in a June 2010 *New York Times* report on the availability of a trillion dollars' worth of mineral wealth in Afghanistan,[2] on top of the need for an oil/gas pipeline from the Caspian Sea.

Jim Lobe of Inter Press Service writes:

> The timing of the publication of a major *New York Times* story on the vast untapped mineral wealth that lies beneath Afghanistan's soil is raising major questions about the intent of the Pentagon. . . .
>
> As noted by Blake Hounshell, managing editor at *Foreign Policy* magazine, the US Geological Survey (USGS)

already published a comprehensive inventory of Afghanistan's non-oil mineral resources on the Internet in 2007, as did the British Geological Survey. Much of their work was based on explorations and surveys undertaken by the Soviet Union during its occupation of Afghanistan during the 1980s.[3]

Thus, there is nothing new about Afghanistan's resources that the Pentagon and US multinational corporations didn't already know. Instead, we should recognize that the emergence of this resources story is a managed-news press release by the Pentagon being revealed at a sensitive time concerning NATO's mission in Afghanistan. A deliberate news insertion such as this is designed to distract the public from—or to create support among the public for—the US/NATO global empire agenda.

On the other hand, we are *not* informed of the continuing privatization of this global empire war. Independent journalists such as Jeremy Scahill, however, do just that: in the *Nation* magazine, he discusses how Blackwater (Xe) operatives in the Pakistani port city of Karachi are gathering intelligence to help direct a secret US military drone bombing campaign in that country.[4] There has been similarly little coverage on the US's new capabilities for cyber warfare, announced recently by Secretary of Defense Robert Gates as the activation of the Pentagon's first computer command and the world's first comprehensive, multiservice military cyber-operation. CYBERCOM is based at Fort Meade, Maryland, which also is home to the National Security Agency (NSA).[5]

Truth Emergency arises as an important issue inside the US/NATO military-industrial-media complex, as there are deliberate news management efforts undermining the freedom of information on the doings of the powerful military and corporate elites though overt censorship, mass distractions (see chapter 3), and artificial news—stories timed for release to influence public opinion (i.e., propaganda).

Truth Emergency is the lack of purity in news brought about by such propaganda and distraction. It is the state in which people—despite potentially being awash in a sea of information—lack the power of discernment, creating a paucity of understanding about what it all means. In short, we are living at a time when people do not know whom to trust for accurate information and thus yearn for the truth.

Efforts to address the crimes and conspiracies of the powerful can go unreleased even by seemingly progressive media groups. The following article excerpted below was one of over fifty op-ed pieces written by Project Censored over the past several years for Minuteman Media. The articles were released weekly to about fifteen hundred small-town and college newspapers, accompanied by the insightful cartoons of Khalil Bendib also used in this book. The Minuteman Media op-ed release process was transferred to the progressive Institute for Policy Studies (IPS) based in Washington, DC, in fall 2009. Our first op-ed under IPS, entitled "Thank the Rich for the Higher Education Fiscal Crisis," was well received and published in several venues. Our second op-ed, submitted in late February 2010, ran into some difficulties. It is reprinted below, with sources in the endnotes.

NEW ACADEMIC RESEARCH ON STATE CRIMES AGAINST DEMOCRACY
BY PETER PHILLIPS AND MICKEY HUFF

New research in the journal *American Behavioral Scientist* (Sage Publications, February 2010) addresses the concept of "State Crimes Against Democracy" (SCAD). Professor Lance deHaven-Smith from Florida State University writes that SCADs involve high-level government officials, often in combination with private interests, that engage in covert activities for political advantages and power. Proven SCADs since World War II include McCarthyism (fabrication of evidence of a communist infiltration), Gulf of Tonkin Resolution (President Johnson and Robert McNamara falsely claimed North Vietnam attacked a US ship), burglary of the office of Daniel Ellsberg's psychiatrist, the Watergate break-in, Iran-Contra, Florida's 2000 Election (felon disenfranchisement program), and fixed intelligence on WMDs to justify the Iraq War.[6]

Other suspected SCADs include the assassination of Lee Harvey Oswald, the shooting of George Wallace, the October Surprise near the end of the Carter presidency, military grade anthrax mailed to Senators Tom Daschle and Patrick Leahy, Martin Luther King's assassination, and the collapse of World Trade Center Building 7 on September 11, 2001. The proven SCADs have a long trail of congressional hearings, public records, and academic research establishing the truth of the activities. The suspected SCADs listed above have substantial evidence of covert actions with countervailing deniability that tends to leave the facts in dispute.[7]

The term "conspiracy theory" is often used to denigrate and discredit inquiry into the veracity of suspected SCADs. Labeling SCAD research as "conspiracy theory" is an effective method of preventing ongoing investigations from being reported in the corporate media and will keep such issues outside of broader public scrutiny. Psychologist Laurie Manwell, University of Guelph, addresses the psychological advantage that SCAD actors hold in the public sphere. Manwell, writing in *American Behavioral Scientist* (Sage 2010) states, "research shows that people are far less willing to examine information that disputes, rather than confirms, their beliefs . . . pre-existing beliefs can interfere with SCADs inquiry, especially in regards to September 11, 2001."[8]

New academic research goes largely unreported when the work contradicts prevailing public understandings. A specific case of uncovered academic research is the peer reviewed journal article from *Open Chemical Physics Journal* (Volume 2, 2009), entitled "Active Thermitic Material Discovered in Dust for the 9/11 World Trade Center Catastrophe." In the abstract the authors write, "We have discovered distinctive red/gray chips in all the samples. The properties of these chips were analyzed using optical microscopy, scanning electron microscopy (SEM), X-ray energy dispersive spectroscopy (XEDS), and differential scanning calorimetry (DSC). The red portion of these chips is found to be an unreacted thermitic material and highly energetic." Thermite is a pyrotechnic composition of a metal powder and a metal oxide, which produces an aluminothermic reaction known as a thermite reaction, and may be used in controlled demolitions of buildings.[9]

National Medal of Science recipient (1999) Professor Lynn Margulis from the Department of Geosciences at the University of Massachusetts at Amherst is one of many academics who supports further open investigative research in the collapse of the World Trade Center towers. Margulis recently wrote in *Rock Creek Free Press*, "All three buildings were destroyed by carefully planned, orchestrated and executed controlled demolition."[10]

Richard Gage, AIA, architect and founder of the non-profit Architects & Engineers for 9/11 Truth, Inc. (AE911Truth), announced a decisive milestone February 19, 2010, at a press conference in San Francisco, CA. More than 1,000 architects and engineers worldwide now support the call for a new investigation into the destruction of the Twin Towers and Building 7 at the World Trade Center complex on September 11, 2001.[11]

Credible scientific evidence brings into question the possibility that some aspects of the events of 9/11 involved State Crimes Against Democracy. Psychologically this is hard concept for most Americans to consider. However, ignoring the issue in the context of multiple proven SCADs since World War II seems far more dangerous for democracy than the consequences of future scientific inquiry.[12]

We consider this op-ed absolutely academic and within the tradition of the questioning of the powerful that we had been publishing for several years. However, some of the staff at IPS felt differently, and after trying to reject it on contract grounds (which we did not violate) they completely rejected—in other words, censored—the piece. An e-mail from Emily Schwartz Greco, op-ed manager at IPS, on February 22, 2010, asked, "Is this by 9-11 'truthers'? If so, I'd prefer a different topic."[13] We immediately contacted Ms. Greco by telephone to question the decision. Her response was that she didn't want to "encourage truthers," and that they were "disruptive people who hurt the peace movement." A follow-up e-mail from Ms. Greco on February 26 stated, "I had concerns about the topic in general before I saw the text. Now that I've seen the text, I'm also certain that the writing style is inappropriate for a general audience."[14]

We were completely taken back by this deliberate censorship of not just a single written article, but a complete topic of discussion regarding the events of September 11, 2001. How can a free press have topics it simply will not cover?

We had known this to be true of various subjects within the corporate media, including impeachment during the Bush administration, election fraud in 2004, lies about weapons of mass destruction (WMD) before the Iraq invasion, and one million dead Iraqi civilians (see chapter 7 in *Censored 2008*). And we had known that a number of progressive, leftist media outlets have been shy on 9/11 issues, but we were astonished to learn that an entire topic is unacceptable to the long established progressive Institute for Policy Studies (see story #14 in chapter 1 for more ongoing censorship surrounding 9/11 issues).

We pushed the issues with the higher-ups at IPS, receiving no responses but a terse, "Your op-eds will no longer be needed." So not only was 9/11 as a topic totally rejected, but Project Censored has been permanently banned as an op-ed writing group by IPS as well. The irony is most astounding.

Thanks to the Internet, our SCADs op-ed was published on over forty Web sites and print publications worldwide, starting at *Global Research*, including on the front page of a local, independent monthly paper in Washington, DC, the *Rock Creek Press*, which believes that there is no topic beyond discussion. We at Project Censored continue to receive thousands of views a day on our various news and opinion sites linked from www.projectcensored.org. If only the corporate—and even some progressive—purportedly muckraking media in America would catch on to the meaning of a free press and deal with all topics factually, regardless of their potential controversial nature. This is not about agreeing with particular conclusions on controversial subjects, it's about agreeing to have an open, transparent, factual, public dialogue about the most crucial issues our society faces. It's an invitation to a conversation, one that the corporate media and even many progressive media outlets apparently do not want to have (as mentioned in this volume's introduction by Kristina Borjesson). At Project Censored, we believe this to be antithetical to a free press system. And it is our duty to fight censorship in any form, even, or especially, when it comes from those we may respect the most.

The experience with IPS led us to build this section of the *Censored 2011* yearbook, to address the ongoing global Truth Emergency in an open and specific way. First reinforcing the notions expressed in our op-ed, and, second, expanding upon the ongoing censorship and deliberate news management by the global US/NATO military-industrial-media empire, we offer this section as an antidote to the Truth Emergency.

For our inaugural Truth Emergency section, comprising chapters six through ten, we welcome the work of Dr. Lance deHaven-Smith on state crimes against democracy (SCADs), referenced in our censored op-ed piece; Dr. David Ray Griffin on unresolved 9/11 issues, particularly regarding Building 7 in the framework of a potential SCAD; journalist Nora Barrows-Friedman on the underreported stories from Israeli-occupied Palestine; Dr. Robert Abele on corporate media failures on WMDs, and the failed debate on Just War Theory, that led to the ongoing Iraqi occupation; and Dr. Andrew Roth with a recent case study on the connection between media propaganda and the military-industrial complex. All of these subjects deserve the attention of the American public. No matter where one stands on these topics, these studies should be part of a vibrant dialogue in the free press of any democratic society.[15] Anything less is simply a matter of censorship.

—Mickey Huff and Peter Phillips

Notes

1. Tim Reid and Michael Evans, Washington bureau, "Obama Secretly Deploys US Special Forces to 75 Countries Across World," *Times* (London), June 5, 2010.
2. James Risen, "U.S. Identifies Vast Mineral Riches in Afghanistan," *New York Times*, June 13, 2010, http://www.nytimes.com/2010/06/14/world/asia/14minerals.html?_r=1.
3. Jim Lobe, "Timing of Leak of Afghan Mineral Wealth Evokes Skepticism," Inter Press Service, June 15, 2010.
4. Jeremy Scahill, "The Secret US War in Pakistan," *Nation*, November 23, 2009.
5. Rick Rozoff , "U.S. Cyber Command: Waging War In The World's Fifth Battlespace," *Global Research*, May 27, 2010, http://www.globalresearch.ca/index.php?context=va&aid=19360.
6. Source notes within original op-ed piece: Lance deHaven-Smith, "Beyond Conspiracy Theory: Patterns of High Crime in American Government," *American Behavioral Scientist* 53, no. 6 (February 2010), 795–825. For more studies on SCADs and related issues see all articles for *American Behavioral Scientist*, Sage Publications 53, no. 6 (February 2010), http://abs.sagepub.com/content/vol53/issue6/. For more background reading on this subject with specifics on the controversial cases mentioned in this paragraph, see the following scholarly works: Robert P. Abele, *The Anatomy of a Deception: A Reconstruction and Analysis of the Decision to Invade Iraq* (New York: University Press of America, 2010); Bob Coen and Eric Nadler, *Dead Silence: Fear and Terror on the Anthrax Trail* (Berkeley, CA: Counterpoint, 2009); Daniel Ellsberg, *Secrets: A Memoir of Vietnam and the Pentagon Papers* (New York: Viking Adult, 2002); Steve Freeman and Joel Bleifuss, *Was the 2004 Election Stolen? Exit Polls, Election Fraud, and the Official Count* (New York: Seven Stories Press, 2006); Robert Griffith, *The Politics of Fear: Joseph R. McCarthy and the Senate* (Amherst, MA: University of Massachusetts Press, 1987); David Ray Griffin, *The Mysterious Collapse of World Trade Center 7: Why the Final Official Report About 9/11 Is Unscientific and False* (New York: Olive Branch Press, 2008); Mark Crispin Miller, *Loser Take All: Election Fraud and the Subversion of Democracy, 2000–2008* (New York: Ig Publishing, 2008); Kenneth O'Reilly, *Hoover and the Un-Americans: The FBI, HUAC, and the Red Menace* (Philadelphia: Temple University Press, 1983); Robert Parry, *Trick or Treason: The October Surprise Mystery* (New York: Sheridan Square Press, 1993); William Pepper, *An Act of State: The Execution of Marin Luther King* updated ed. (New York: Verso, 2008); Shel-

don Rampton and John Stauber, *Weapons of Mass Deception: The Uses of Propaganda in Bush's War on Iraq* (New York: Tarcher, 2003); selected works of Peter Dale Scott, including *Deep Politics and the Death of JFK* (Berkeley, CA: University of California Press, 1993, 1996), *Drugs, Oil, and War: The United States in Afghanistan, Colombia, and Indochina* (Lanham, MD: Rowman and Littlefield, 2003), *The Road to 9/11: Wealth, Empire, and the Future of America* (Berkeley: University of California Press, 2008), and *The War Conspiracy: JFK, 9/11, and the Deep Politics of War* (Ipswich, MA: Mary Ferrell Foundation Press, 2008); Norman Solomon, *War Made Easy: How Presidents and Pundits Keep Spinning Us to Death* (New Jersey: John Wiley and Sons, 2005); Lawrence E. Walsh, *Firewall: The Iran-Contra Conspiracy and Cover-up* (New York: W.W. Norton & Company, 1997); Gary Webb, *Dark Alliance: The CIA, The Contras, and the Crack Cocaine Explosion*, 2nd edition (New York: Seven Stories Press, 2003).

7. Ibid.

8. Source notes within original op-ed piece: *American Behavioral Scientist* 53, no. 6 (February 2010), Sage Publications, http://abs.sagepub.com/content/vol53/issue6/. Specifically, see Laurie A. Manwell, "In Denial of Democracy: Social Psychological Implications for Public Discourse on State Crimes Against Democracy Post-9/11," *American Behavioral Scientist* 53, no. 6, (February, 2010), 848–84.

9. Source note within original op-ed piece: Niels H. Harrit, et al., "Active Thermitic Material Discovered in Dust from the 9/11 World Trade Center Catastrophe," *Open Chemical Physics Journal* 2 (April 3, 2009), 7–31, http://www.bentham.org/open/tocpj/openaccess2.htm.

10. Source note within original op-ed piece: Lynn Margulis, "Two Hit, Three Down, the Biggest Lie," *Rock Creek Press* 4, no. 2 (February 2010), 6, http://rockcreekfreepress.tumblr.com/post/353434420/two-hit-three-down-the-biggest-lie.

11. Source notes for original op-ed piece: Richard Gage, AIA, Architects and Engineers for 911 Truth, Press Conference (San Francisco, California), February 19, 2010, http://www.ae911truth.org/info/160. See the conference announcement video at http://www.youtube.com/ae911truth#p/c/891B0945A34D98F7/0/R35O_QQP8Vw. The piece can also be seen in its original form at *Global Research*, http://www.globalresearch.ca/index.php?context=va&aid=17922.

12. This article was eventually published by several Web sites, with the addition of following paragraph and notes:

    "Professor Steven Hoffman, visiting scholar at the University of Buffalo, recently acknowledged this phenomenon in a study 'There Must Be a Reason: Osama, Saddam and Inferred Justification.' Hoffman concluded, 'Our data shows substantial support for a cognitive theory known as "motivated reasoning," which suggests that rather than search rationally for information that either confirms or disconfirms a particular belief, people actually seek out information that confirms what they already believe. In fact, for the most part people completely ignore contrary information.'"

    Source notes within original op-ed piece: "How We Support Our False Beliefs," *Science Daily*, August 23, 2009, http://www.sciencedaily.com/releases/2009/08/090821135020.htm. For the full study, see Steven Hoffman, PhD, et al., "There Must Be a Reason: Osama, Saddam and Inferred Justification," *Sociological Inquiry* 79, no. 2 (2009), 142–62.

    For more on issues of media censorship see Peter Phillips, Mickey Huff, and Project Censored, eds., *Censored 2010: The Top 25 Censored Stories of 2008–09* (New York: Seven Stories Press, 2009).

13. E-mail from Emily Schwartz Greco, February 22, 2010, on file at Media Freedom Foundation.

14. E-mail from Emily Schwartz Greco, February 26, 2010, on file at Media Freedom Foundation.

15. For more on the Truth Emergency topic, see Peter Phillips and Mickey Huff, "Inside the Military Industrial Media Empire," in *Censored 2010: The Top 25 Censored Stories of 2008–09*; Peter Phillips, Mickey Huff, et al., "Truth Emergency Meets Media Reform," in *Censored 2009: The Top 25 Censored Stories of 2007–09*, ed. Peter Phillips, Andrew Roth, and Project Censored (New York: Seven Stories Press, 2008); and the Web site for the Truth Emergency Conference held in Santa Cruz, California, in 2008, http://truthemergency.us.

CHAPTER 6

Beyond Conspiracy Theory
Patterns of High Crime in American Government

by Lance deHaven-Smith

INTRODUCTION

This article explores the conceptual, methodological, and practical implications of research on state crimes against democracy (SCADs). In
contrast to conspiracy theories, which speculate about each suspicious
event in isolation, the SCAD construct delineates a general category of
criminality and calls for crimes that fit this category to be examined com-
paratively. Using this approach, an analysis of post–World War II SCADs
and suspected SCADs highlights a number of commonalities in SCAD
targets, timing, and policy consequences. SCADs often appear where
presidential politics and foreign policy intersect. SCADs differ from earlier forms of political corruption in that they frequently involve political,
military, and/or economic elites at the very highest levels of the social
and political order. The article concludes by suggesting statutory and
constitutional reforms to improve SCAD prevention and detection.

Antidemocratic conspiracies among high-ranking public officials in the
United States and other representative democracies constitute a sensitive and potentially controversial topic for behavioral research. This may
explain why, until recently, social scientists have focused, instead, on
graft, bribery, embezzlement, and other forms of government corruption where the aim is personal enrichment rather than social control,
partisan advantage, or political power. In any event, the topic is sensitive
because it raises questions about the ethics of top leaders and suggests
that American democracy may be in thrall to behind-the-scenes manipulations. Even if research on the issue were to discredit various
conspiracy theories, it could fuel mass cynicism and undermine civility
in public discourse simply by making conspiracy theories a legitimate
subject for public consideration. McCarthyism quite clearly demon-

strated the dangers posed to democracy by unbridled, runaway accusations of conspiratorial suspicions.

On the other hand, antidemocratic conspiracies in high office do, in fact, happen. The congressional hearings on Watergate, the Church Committee's discoveries about illegal domestic surveillance, and the special prosecutors' investigations of Oliver North and Scooter Libby revealed that public officials at the highest levels of American government can and sometimes do engage in conspiracies to manipulate elections, wiretap and smear critics, mislead Congress and the public, and in other ways subvert popular sovereignty. Certainly, such crimes and the criminogenic circumstances surrounding them warrant scientific inquiry, not only to better understand elite politics but also to identify institutional vulnerabilities so that protections can be established or strengthened. The challenge for scholars is to engage in serious, unblinkered study of the subject without contributing to mass paranoia or elite incivility.

The popular conspiracy theory literature contributes to mass cynicism because it presents a variety of conflicting suspicions about numerous, seemingly unrelated events, leaving the impression that elite political crime is widespread but unpredictable and therefore incapable of being understood and managed. This article examines the conceptual foundations, political context, and practical implications of research on state crimes against democracy (SCADs). The SCAD construct is designed to move beyond the debilitating, slipshod, and scattershot speculation of conspiracy theories by focusing inquiry on patterns in elite political criminality that reveal systemic weaknesses, institutional rivalries, and illicit networks.

The article is divided into five sections. The first section defines SCADs and contrasts the SCAD construct with ordinary conspiratorial theorizing. The second section identifies a number of patterns in post–World War II SCADs that suggest SCADs are being committed by military and military-industrial elites. The third section compares SCADs to earlier forms of political corruption and explains why SCADs have proliferated in recent decades. The fourth section focuses on the SCAD-conducive circumstances that arise at the intersection of presidential politics and national security policy making. The article concludes by considering the implications of SCAD theory and research for SCAD detection and prevention.

CONCEPTUALIZING HIGH CRIMINALITY

SCADs

SCADs are concerted actions or inactions by government insiders intended to manipulate democratic processes and undermine popular sovereignty.[1] By definition, SCADs differ from other forms of political criminality in their potential to subvert political institutions and entire governments or branches of government. They are high crimes that attack democracy itself.

Although only a few SCADs in US history have ever been officially corroborated, evidence indicates that at least since World War II American democracy has become quite vulnerable to subversion from within. Examples of SCADs that have been officially proven include the Watergate break-ins and cover-up,[2] the secret wars in Laos and Cambodia,[3] the illegal arms sales and covert operations in Iran-Contra,[4] and the effort to discredit Joseph Wilson by revealing his wife's status as an intelligence agent.[5]

Many other political crimes in which involvement by high officials is suspected have gone uninvestigated or unpunished. Examples of suspected SCADs include the fabricated attacks on US ships in the Gulf of Tonkin in 1964,[6] the "October Surprises" in the presidential elections of 1968[7] and 1980,[8] the assassinations of John Kennedy and Robert Kennedy,[9] the election breakdowns in 2000 and 2004,[10] the numerous defense failures on September 11, 2001,[11] and the misrepresentation of intelligence to justify the invasion and occupation of Iraq.[12]

The Conspiracy Theory Label

The concept of SCADs was developed, in part, to replace the term *conspiracy theory*, which, since the 1960s, has been associated with paranoia[13] and harebrained speculation.[14] Considered as a label, the phrase *conspiracy theory* does a poor job of characterizing speculations about political intrigue, yet the label remains popular because it functions normatively to protect political elites from mass doubts about their motives and tactics.[15] Although not immediately apparent, this function becomes evident when the label's surface meaning is compared to its meaning in use. On the surface, the term *conspiracy theory* refers to a suspicion that some troubling event was the result of a secret plot, but the term's usage implies something else.

Not every theory that alleges a secret plot qualifies as a conspiracy theory in the common sense of the term. The official account of 9/11 claims that the twin towers were brought down by a team of Muslims who conspired to highjack planes and fly them into buildings. The theory posits a conspiracy, but the theory is not what most people would call a "conspiracy theory." Conspiracy theories of 9/11 claim more than that the attacks were secretly planned and executed by an organized team. Most conspiracy theories of 9/11 allege that the US government itself carried out the attacks or that officials knew the attacks were coming and allowed them to succeed.[16]

Still, a conspiracy theory is not simply a theory about a government plot. No one considers the (now) accepted accounts of the Watergate scandal or Iran-Contra affair as conspiracy theories. Conspiracy theories in the pejorative sense of the term are always *counter*theories: that is, they are always posed in opposition to official accounts of suspicious events. Today's most popular conspiracy theories involve the assassinations of John Kennedy, Robert Kennedy, and Martin Luther King; the October Surprise of 1980; the defense failures on 9/11; and the anthrax mailings in 2001. Conspiracy theorists argue that official accounts of these events ignore important evidence, contain anomalies and inconsistencies, and are tendentious in their exoneration of public officials

Thus, the conspiracy theory label, as it is applied in public discourse, does not disparage conspiratorial thinking or analysis in general, even though this is what the term suggests. Rather, the broad-brush "conspiracy theory" disparages inquiry and questioning that challenge official accounts of troubling political events in which public officials themselves may have had a hand. Deployed in public discourse to discredit and silence those who express suspicions of elite criminality, the label functions, rhetorically, to shield political elites from public interrogation.

The Politics of Silence

The problem with the conspiracy theory label is that it is overly broad in its condemnation of speculation about political intrigue. The label provides no basis for distinguishing groundless smears from reasonable suspicions warranting investigation. History has shown all too clearly that public trust in high officials is sometimes misplaced.

The normative force of the conspiracy theory label comes in part from the principle in American jurisprudence that suspects are considered innocent until proven guilty. However, the presumption of innocence was never intended to outlaw suspicions. Rather, it calls for suspicions to be tested with thorough and fair investigations grounded by procedural rules for procuring and presenting evidence. In contrast, the conspiracy theory label is applied not to categorize a position that will actually be considered but to shut off argumentation before it begins. As a practical matter, the label condemns as hysterical and pernicious almost all speculations about the possible complicity of political elites in suspicions events.

Given that US elites themselves could become the targets of assassination plots, illegal surveillance, and other conspiracies by their domestic political opponents, their blanket hostility to conspiracy theories seems irrational, for it encourages them to dismiss real dangers and to deny reasonable concerns. It also silences those who believe they have been victims. George Wallace suspected, with good reason, that the attempt on his life during the 1972 presidential campaign had been engineered by Richard Nixon.[17] Wallace never expressed this suspicion publicly, but this is why he withdrew his support from Nixon during the Watergate hearings. Similarly, by 1968, Robert Kennedy was convinced that JFK's assassination had been the work of a conspiracy involving the CIA, but he did not voice his suspicions publicly while running for president because he feared it would discredit him politically or get him killed.[18] Hence, a useful axiom for scholarly consideration may conjecture that norms against conspiratorial speculations in public discourse sacrifice the safety of individual political elites to protect the legitimacy of political elites *as a class*.

Still, although thus understandable as an elite defense mechanism, norms against conspiratorial theorizing make little sense conceptually. In disparaging speculation about possible elite criminality, the conspiracy theory label posits as given what actually needs to be falsified empirically, namely, whether democratic processes are being improperly and systematically manipulated by strategically placed insiders. In the post-WWII era, official investigations have attributed assassinations, election fiascos, defense failures, and other suspicious events to such unpredictable, idiosyncratic forces as lone gunmen, antiquated voting equipment, bureaucratic bumbling, and innocent mistakes, all of which suspend numerous and accumulating *cui bono* questions. In effect, political elites have answered *conspiracy* theories with *coincidence* theories.

Conspiracy theorists have contributed to this disjunctive dispute because they have focused on each suspicious event in isolation. Amateur investigators have developed a large popular literature on the assassination of President Kennedy and a number of other political crimes in which state complicity is suspected or alleged. The research has discredited official accounts of many incidents, thus casting suspicion on the government. But such ad hoc research has failed to actually solve the crimes under analysis or even to identify the agencies and officials most likely to have been the perpetrators.

SCAD PATTERNS

SCAD Research

By delineating a specific form of political criminality, the SCAD concept allows inquiry to move beyond incident-specific theories of government plots and to examine, instead, the general phenomenon of elite political criminality. Similar to research on white-collar crime, domestic violence, serial murder, and other crime categories, SCAD research seeks to identify patterns in SCAD victims, tactics, timing, those who benefit, and other SCAD characteristics. These patterns offer clues about the motives, institutional location, skills, and resources of SCAD perpetrators. In turn, as SCAD research brings SCAD perpetrators into focus, it provides a basis for understanding and mitigating the criminogenic circumstances in which SCADs arise.

For research purposes, the universe of SCADs must include not only those that have been officially investigated and confirmed but also suspected SCADs corroborated by evidence that is credible but unofficial. Although including the latter bring some risk of error, excluding them would mean accepting the judgment of individuals and institutions whose rectitude and culpability are at issue. Public officials are usually quite reluctant to allow independent investigations into questions about their own actions or those of their close associates. For over a year after 9/11, the Bush–Cheney administration resisted and dodged demands for a 9/11 Commission before finally acceding to pressures from the victims' families, at which point the administration gave the commission a very small budget and placed it under unrealistic deadlines.[19] The crimes for which Richard Nixon was forced from office were not the Watergate break-ins but his efforts to obstruct the FBI's investigation. Nixon also tried to preempt congressional inquiries by issuing a superficial study from the White House,[20] as did Ronald Reagan when the Iran-Contra scandal first surfaced in the media.[21]

Even when purportedly independent investigations are undertaken, they are almost invariably compromised by conflicts of interest. Investigating officers and commissions of inquiry usually include or are appointed by the very officials who should be considered prime suspects. The Warren Commission, for example, was appointed by Lyndon Johnson, who was one of the primary beneficiaries of President Kennedy's assassination. Also, a key member of the Warren Commission was Allen Dulles, the former head of the Central Intelligence Agency whom Kennedy had fired after the Bay of Pigs. The 9/11 Commission was similarly compromised.[22] All of its members were government insiders, and none was a vocal critic of the Bush administration. Moreover, the Commission's executive director, Philip Zelikow, had previously served on George W. Bush's presidential transition team, had been appointed by Bush to the president's Foreign Intelligence Advisory Board, and had drafted America's national security strategy following the events of 9/11.[23] Both the commission's chair and its executive director had to recuse themselves from parts of the inquiry because of conflicts of interest.[24]

Conflicts of interest also plague agencies that are typically charged with assisting investigations into suspected SCADs. Such agencies usually bear some blame or have some connection to the events in question. Hence, personnel in these agencies are inevitably tempted to conceal evidence that would implicate or embarrass the agencies or their top managers. Both the FBI and the CIA concealed evidence of their contacts with Lee Harvey Oswald and Jack Ruby.[25] Likewise, the Department of Defense appears to have withheld from the 9/11 Commission evidence that military intelligence agents had uncovered the 9/11 hijackers' activities well in advance of September 2001.[26]

SCAD Targets and Tactics

A variety of SCADs and suspected SCADs have occurred in the United States since World War II. Table 1 contains a list of 15 known SCADs and other counterdemocratic crimes, tragedies, and suspicious incidents for which strong evidence of US government involvement has been uncovered. For each SCAD or alleged SCAD in the list, the table includes a brief description of the crime or suspicious event; information about timing, suspects, motives, investigations, and political circumstances; bibliographical references; and a summary assessment of the extent to which allegations of state complicity have been verified.

TABLE 1. CRIMES AGAINST AMERICAN DEMOCRACY COMMITTED OR ALLEGEDLY COMMITTED BY ELEMENTS OF THE U.S. GOVERNMENT

Crime or Suspicious Event, Time Frame, and Modus Operandi	Perpetrator Motive or Policy Implication	Suspected or Confirmed Perpetrator	Degree of Confirmation of Government Role
McCarthyism (fabricating evidence of Soviet infiltration), 1950-1955. FALSE INFO RE: DEFENSE	Large scale purge of leftists from government and business. POLITICAL OPPORTUNISM	Joseph McCarthy, with others. Although his tactics were not investigated, they were discredited in Senate hearings, and a Democratic Senate censured the Republican Senator.	High (Fried, 1990; H. Johnson, 2005)
Assassination of President Kennedy. 1963. ASSASSINATION	Lyndon Johnson's presidency; escalation of the Vietnam War. CONTROL WAR POLICY	Probably right-wing elements in CIA, FBI, and Secret Service. Possible involvement of Johnson and/or Nixon.	Medium (Fetzer, 2000; Garrison, 1988; Groden, 1993; Lane, 1966; Scott, 1993; White, 1998)
Assassination of Lee Harvey Oswald. 1963. ASSASSINATION	Oswald's ties to the CIA remain hidden. A trial of Oswald is avoided. CONCEAL CRIME	Jack Ruby, who has ties to the CIA and organized crime. Part of overall JFK assassination plot.	Medium (Scott, 1993)
Gulf of Tonkin Resolution. 1964. PLANNED INTERNATIONAL EVENT	Large expansion of military resources committed to the Vietnam conflict. CONTROL WAR POLICY	President Johnson and Secretary of Defense McNamara falsely claimed that North Vietnam attacked a U.S. military ship in neutral waters.	High (Ellsberg, 2002, pp. 7-20)
Assassination of Senator Robert Kennedy. 1968. ASSASSINATION	Weak Democratic nominee (Humphrey); election of Nixon; no further investigation of JFK assassination; continued escalation of Vietnam conflict. CONTROL WAR POLICY	Right-wing elements in the CIA and FBI, with likely involvement of Nixon. Suspicions of government involvement are based largely on number of bullets shot and failure to fully investigate.	Low (Pease, 2003)

Event	Perpetrators / Evidence	Outcome / Motivation	Likelihood
Burglary of the office of Daniel Ellsberg's psychiatrist. 1968. BURGLARY	President Nixon, White House staff, and CIA operatives or former operatives. The crime was discovered during Ellsberg's trial, not in an investigation of the break-in.	Discredit Ellsberg. Exposure of the break-in prevented use of the stolen information. CONTROL WAR POLICY	High (Ellsberg, 2002)
Attempted assassination of George Wallace. 1972. ASSASSINATION	Arthur Bremer. Much circumstantial evidence points to the involvement of Nixon via the plumbers. Evidence includes comments of Nixon.	Wallace taken out of 1972 election and Nixon reelected. Wallace was likely to win seven southern states, forcing the election to be decided by a Democratically controlled Congress. POLITICAL OPPORTUNISM	Medium (Bernstein & Woodward, 1974, pp. 324–330; Carter, 2000)
Watergate break-in. 1972. BURGLARY	President Nixon, White House staff, and CIA operatives or former operatives.	Weak Democratic nominee (McGovern) and reelection of Nixon. POLITICAL OPPORTUNISM	High (Bernstein & Woodward, 1974)
Attempted assassination of Ronald Reagan. 1981. ASSASSINATION	John Hinckley. Evidence shows connections between Hinckley's family and the family of VP Bush.	VP Bush's role in the administration is strengthened, especially in relation to covert operations in the Mideast and Latin America. CONTROL WAR POLICY	Low (Bowen, 1991; Wiese & Downing, 1981)
Iran-Contra. 1984–1986. FALSE INFO RE: DEFENSE	President Reagan, VP Bush, CIA, military	Release of hostages; civil war in Nicaragua. CONTROL WAR POLICY	High (Kornbluh & Byrne, 1993; Martin, 2001; Parry, 1993)
Florida's disputed 2000 presidential election. 2000. ELECTION TAMPERING	Jeb Bush and Katherine Harris developed flawed felon disenfranchisement program. Jeb Bush, Harris, and Tom Feeney colluded to block recount. Harris facilitated counting of fraudulent overseas military ballots.	Legally mandated recount is blocked; G. W. Bush becomes president through U.S. Supreme Court decision. POLITICAL OPPORTUNISM	High (Barstow & Van Natta, 2001; deHaven-Smith, 2005)

Crime or Suspicious Event, Time Frame, and Modus Operandi	Perpetrator Motive or Policy Implication	Suspected or Confirmed Perpetrator	Degree of Confirmation of Government Role
9/11 terrorist attacks. 2001. PLANNED INTERNATIONAL EVENT	Bush popularity rises; defense spending increases; Republicans gain in off-year elections; military invasion of Afghanistan; pretext for invasion of Iraq. CONTROL WAR POLICY	President G. W. Bush and VP Cheney arrange for a "stand down" of the military, or the attacks were actually committed by U.S. intelligence operatives.	Medium (Griffin, 2004, 2005; Hufschmid, 2002; Paul & Hoffman, 2004; Tarpley, 2005)
Attempted assassination of Senators Tom Daschle and Patrick Leahy. 2001. ASSASSINATION	Heightened fears of terrorism. If successful, would have given Republicans control of Senate. CONTROL WAR POLICY	Military and/or intelligence operatives. The anthrax has been traced to a strain developed by the U.S. military. Circumstantial evidence of cover-up.	Medium (Tarpley, 2005)
Assassination of Senator Wellstone. 2002. ASSASSINATION	Republicans regain control of the Senate after Wellstone's replacement. CONTROL WAR POLICY	Intelligence operatives.	Low
Iraq-gate. 2003. FALSE INFO RE: DEFENSE	U.S. gains control of Iraq oil production; Iran surrounded by U.S. armies; other Mideast nations intimidated. CONTROL WAR POLICY	President Bush, VP Cheney, CIA director fix intelligence to justify war. Bush misrepresents intelligence to Congress in State of Union address. CIA officer Valerie Plame is outed in an attempt to discredit Joseph Wilson.	High (Clarke, 2004; Dean, 2004; Wilson, 2004; Woodward, 2006)
Disputed 2004 presidential election. 2004. ELECTION TAMPERING	Bush wins electoral college vote with a 118,000 vote margin in Ohio. POLITICAL OPPORTUNISM	White House uses terror alerts to rally support; Republican election officials impede voting in Democratic precincts.	High (Hall, 2005; Miller, 2005; Tarpley, 2005)

In the list of SCADs in Table 1, several patterns stand out. First, many SCADs are associated with foreign policy and international conflict. Such SCADs include the Gulf of Tonkin incident, the burglary of Daniel Ellsberg's psychiatrist's office, Iran-Contra, 9/11, Iraq-gate, the assassinations of John Kennedy and Robert Kennedy, and the attempted assassinations of Patrick Leahy and Tom Daschle. All of these SCADs contributed to the initiation or continuation of military conflicts.

Second, SCADs are fairly limited in their modus operandi (MO). The most common SCAD MOs are assassinations (six) and mass deceptions related to foreign policy (three). Other MOs include election tampering (two), planned international conflict events (two), and burglaries (two). With the possible exception of election tampering, all of these MOs are indicative of groups with expertise in the skills of espionage and covert, paramilitary operations.

Third, many SCADs in the post-WWII era indicate direct and nested connections to two presidents: Richard Nixon and George W. Bush. Not only was Nixon responsible for Watergate and the illegal surveillance of Daniel Ellsberg, he also alone benefited from all three of the suspicious attacks on political candidates in the 1960s and 1970s: the assassinations of John Kennedy and Bobby Kennedy and the attempted assassination of George Wallace. If JFK and RFK had not been killed, Nixon would not have been elected president in 1968, and if Wallace had not been shot, Nixon would probably not have been reelected in 1972. The SCADs that benefited Bush include the election-administration problems in 2000, the defense failures on 9/11, the (US defense grade) anthrax attacks on top Senate Democrats in October 2001, Iraqgate, and the multiple and specious terror alerts that rallied support for Bush before the 2004 presidential election.[27]

Assassinations

The relatively large number of assassinations in the post-WWII era permits analysis of variation within this MO. Several patterns contradict the conclusion from official inquiries that political assassinations in the United States have been random, with no connections to one another and no involvement of political elites. First, the range of officials targeted for assassination is limited to those most directly associated with foreign policy: presidents and senators. Most other high-ranking officials in the federal government have seldom been murdered, even though many have attracted widespread hostility and opposition. No vice presidents have been assassinated, nor have any members of the US House of Representatives or the US Supreme Court. If lone gunmen have been roaming the country in search of political victims, it is difficult to understand why they have not struck more widely, especially given that most officials receive no Secret Service protection. Why did no assassins go after Joe McCarthy when he became notorious for his accusations about communists, or Earle Warren after the Supreme Court's decisions requiring school desegregation, or Spiro Agnew after he attacked the motives of antiwar protestors, or Janet Reno after she authorized the FBI's raid on the Branch Davidians in Waco?

A second pattern has to do with the particular presidents and senators who have been targeted for elimination, as opposed to the many who have not. Presidents and senators have been targeted only when their elimination would benefit military and prowar interests. Because a president who is killed or dies in office is automatically succeeded by the vice president, a presidential assassination would benefit military interests only if the vice president's background or policy positions were dramatically better for the military than the president's. This situation has existed only twice since 1960—during the presidencies of John F. Kennedy and Ronald Reagan. Unlike Kennedy, who was trying to end the cold war, Lyndon Johnson was a well-known hawk and pentagon supporter. Similarly, although Reagan and George H. W. Bush had similar positions on the cold war, Bush's background as former director of the CIA gave him much closer ties than Reagan to the military establishment.

Assassinations and assassination attempts have been carried out against US senators only under similar circumstances. The Senate is more important to foreign policy than the House because it must confirm cabinet appointments and approve international treaties. However, the death of a single US senator would almost never cause significant shifts in military action or defense policy because individual senators are seldom that powerful. Hence, if the aim were to affect foreign policy, a senator would be targeted for assassination only in rare instances. This has indeed been the case. Just one senator is known to have been assassinated since 1960, despite the large number of available targets and the absence of bodyguards. Senator Robert F. Kennedy was murdered after he had denounced the Vietnam War and had become the Democratic Party's frontrunner for the 1968 presidential nomination. Given the high probability that RFK would have been elected, his murder was, in effect, a preemptive assassination of a president-to-be.

The only other senatorial assassinations or attempted assassinations in the post-WWII era occurred in 2001 when Democrats controlled the Senate by virtue of a one-vote advantage over Republicans. In May 2001, just four months after George W. Bush gained the presidency in a SCAD-ridden disputed election, Republican Jim Jeffords left the party to become an independent, and the Senate shifted to Democratic control for the first time since 1994. Five months later, on October 9, 2001, letters laced with anthrax were used in an unsuccessful attempt to assassinate two leading Senate Democrats, Majority Leader Tom Daschle and Judiciary Committee Chairman Patrick Leahy. The anthrax in the letters came from what is known as the "Ames strain," which was developed and distributed to biomedical research laboratories by the US Army.[28] Thus, aside from the assassination of Robert Kennedy, the only other time since WWII that senators have been targeted for death was when a war was about to be fought for dubious reasons and the death of a single senator could shift control of the Senate to the political party pushing for war.[29]

These patterns in assassinations, as well as the patterns across SCADs in general, point to likely suspects and criminogenic circumstances. SCADs frequently involve presidents as either victims or principals, benefit military and military-industrial elites, and employ the skills of intelligence and paramilitary operatives. Conditions conducive to SCADs include periods of warfare or heightened international tensions, administrations with prowar vice presidents, and Senates closely divided along partisan lines. SCADs often appear where presidential politics and foreign policy intersect. This policy locus could mean that the nation's civilian leadership is being targeted by military and intelligence elites or that military and intelligence assets and capabilities are being politicized by the civilian leadership, or both.

POLITICAL CORRUPTION IN AMERICAN HISTORY

Forms of Political Corruption

In addition to directing attention to the general phenomenon of elite political criminality, the SCAD concept allows this particular type of political corruption to be compared to others and placed in historical context. In modern representative democracy, political corruption has taken two principal forms.[30] One involves misuse of office for personal material gain, as in graft, nepotism, embezzlement, and kickbacks. The other form of political corruption occurs when democratic processes for arriving at collectively binding decisions are subverted, either to benefit the interests of a ruling faction or class or to violate the rights of minority factions or individuals. Examples here include election tampering, assassination, malicious prosecution, voter disenfranchisement, and unlawful incarceration. These forms of corruption are not mutually exclusive, but they are sufficiently distinct to permit analysis of corrupt behavior in terms of its origins and aims.

As explained in *The Federalist Papers*, the US Constitution was designed to protect "the spirit and form of popular government" against the dangers of both pecuniary corruption and antidemocratic corruption."[31] Pecuniary corruption, or what the Constitution's framers referred to as "perfidious" and "mercenary" public officials, was to be impeded by elections,[32] loyalty oaths,[33] and the threat of impeachment.[34] Antidemocratic corruption, which the framers described as "oppressive factions," was to be impeded by federalism, divided powers, and checks and balances.[35] In the Constitution, both forms of corruption are captured by the term *high crimes and misdemeanors*.[36]

Over the course of American history, the modal form of political corruption has fluctuated between pecuniary and antidemocratic corruption, requiring in each instance significant reforms to counter new kinds of threats and abuses. The main eras of corruption and subsequent reform are listed and described in Table 2. Because reforms have never been totally effective, vulnerabilities from earlier eras continue to be problematic even though they have been mitigated. In this sense, the form and scope of political corruption have expanded over time. SCADs are a new or more sophisticated type of corruption that combines antidemocratic and pecuniary motives of an extreme nature. SCADs have yet to be adequately targeted for detection and prevention, although some limited reforms were instituted after Watergate and Iran-Contra.[37]

Political Parties

As the framers themselves soon recognized, America's constitutional framework was vulnerable from the beginning to manipulation by elite conspiracies. Alliances could be formed between officials in the different offices and branches of government to undercut the system of checks

TABLE 2. ERAS OF CORRUPTION AND REFORM IN AMERICAN HISTORY

Time Period	Vehicle of Corruption	Form of Corruption	Specific Type of Corruption	Example	Reforms
1796–1830	Political Parties	Primarily antidemocratic	Oppressive faction: Antidemocratic legislation to suppress dissent, opposition, or unwanted advocacy or inquiry	The Alien and Sedition Acts	Procedures for partisan competition that protect minority rights.
1890–1946					Professionalizing public administration
1830–1890	Political "machines"	Primarily pecuniary	Perfidious and mercenary officials: Misuse of administrative resources for electoral advantage	The spoils system	
1890–1946	Iron triangles	Primarily pecuniary	Special-interest manipulation: Insider manipulation of legislative and administrative technicalities, usually for economic gain	The conspiracy theory of the Fourteenth Amendment; Teapot Dome	Regulation of stakeholder–government relations, i.e., restrictions on campaign finance, lobbying, government rule making, etc.
1946–	Political-economic complexes	Both antidemocratic and pecuniary	State crimes against democracy: Conspiracies by high officials to commit fraud, treason, murderer, etc., usually for a combination of ideological, economic, and bureaucratic reasons	Watergate; Iran-Contra; assassinations of JFK and RFK	Restricting presidential powers, e.g., the War Powers Act and the Federal Intelligence Surveillance Act

and balances. Once an enduring alliance of legislative, executive, and/or judicial powers was in place, many procedural limits on oppressive majorities would be deactivated, and public officials who represented the dominant faction could then employ the coercive organs of government to suppress opponents, conceal information, and in other ways handicap the electorate's ability to hold representatives accountable.

The archetype of multibranch alliances in American government is the political party, which is essentially an organization dedicated to gaining control of the political system as a whole so that a program can be legislated, executed, and judicially sustained. As George Washington pointed out in his farewell address, such parties not only weaken the system of checks and balances by placing the reins of legislative, executive, and/or judicial powers in the hands of a single group but also tend, by their very nature, to inspire a certain "team spirit" that blurs the distinctions among legitimate political action, unprincipled political tactics, and political criminality. This became apparent soon after the first national political party, the Federalists, was organized and gained control of the legislative and executive branches in the election of 1796. The Federalists enacted the Alien and Sedition Acts, which ignored the Constitution's guarantees of free speech and made it a crime to criticize public officials.

Thomas Jefferson, who in 1796 had campaigned against the Federalists and had been elected vice president, was so troubled by this development that he left Washington and returned home for the duration of his term. The remedy subsequently crafted by Jefferson and Madison to address the Federalist Party was a counteralliance—the Democratic Republican Party—which carried Jefferson to the presidency in 1800. Over the next several decades, the parties developed rules and procedures to regulate the majority and protect the minority's ability to be heard. Although partisan competition did not restore the full vigor of checks and balances to the constitutional system, it did prevent any majority, oppressive or otherwise, from permanently evading electoral accountability.

Political Machines and Administrative Corruption

Still, although partisan competition prevented majorities from escaping the criticism and blocking the electoral appeals of their opponents, it did not totally foreclose the possibility of untoward coordination between constitutionally separated powers. Rather, it drove factions to search for indirect· routes to the same end. Officials in the executive branch of government at all levels began to use the powers of their offices to entrench themselves and their parties throughout the political system. Their main objective was to capture and distribute government jobs and other resources. Political machines proliferated until, toward the end of the nineteenth century, public administration scholars and practitioners professionalized American government by instituting professional civil service requirements, prohibiting the use of government resources in political campaigns, and moving to the council-manager system in local government.

The reforms of the Progressive Era succeeded in partially restoring integrity to elections and emerging principles to US public administration, but they also brought organizational changes that weakened the system of checks and balances in new ways. A new instrument of government, the independent regulatory commission, which combined legislative, executive, and judicial powers in a single unit, was introduced. By creating what became in effect self-contained minigovernments, such commissions opened the door to a cartelization of the political system, whereby public power and resources were divvied up and distributed to various economic, social, and geographic constituencies.[38] This pattern was repeated with the vast expansion of federal grants in aid to states and localities under the New Deal and the Great Society. Policy making and administration were fragmented into a plethora of separate and distinct arenas where public and private "stakeholders" could work out mutually acceptable compromises more or less independent of the larger political process. The resulting political-economic conglomerates have been described variously as "iron triangles," "whirlpools," "subsystems," and "subgovernments."[39]

The proliferation of iron triangles was accompanied by a new type of pecuniary corruption in which stakeholders in a given policy arena colluded to manipulate legal and procedural technicalities for the benefit of special interests. Frequently, the stakeholders in question were corporations and industrial interests—especially railroads, electric utilities, and oil companies—that were suspected of bribing, hoodwinking, or otherwise influencing policy makers to gain legal and financial advantages at the public's expense. The earliest example of a suspected manipulation of this sort was described by Charles and Mary Beard in their "conspiracy theory of the Fourteenth Amendment."[40] (This, incidentally, is where the term "conspiracy theory" originated.) According to Beard, legal experts for the railroad industry pushed for and obtained wording that led the courts to apply the legal guarantees of the Fourteenth Amendment not only to individual citizens but also to corporations.[41] Eventually, concerns about the growing potential for these kinds of special-interest abuses in America's increasingly fragmented and technical system of government were addressed with restrictions on campaign contributions and lobbying, financial disclosure requirements for public officials, public records and open meeting laws, and other reforms to reduce improper influences in policy making and administration.

SCADs

The most recent corruption-related development in American government has been the rise of political-economic complexes with the ability to affect the political priorities of the political system as a whole. For the first half of the twentieth century, American government's increasing fragmentation was seen by scholars and practitioners as a positive development that allowed popular participation in policy making while at the same time preventing majority tyranny.[42] The assumption was that oppressive factions could not exert control over the government as a whole because power, although less well divided in terms of function (legislation, execution, adjudication) than it had been before independent commissions and grants in aid, was now splintered into numerous substantive domains or topics. In keeping with James Madison's theory of faction, with each policy arena dominated by different factions, no faction or combination of factions would be able to control the government as a whole, and national priorities would have to emerge incrementally from "partisan mutual adjustment" among diverse power blocks.

By midcentury, however, scholars and practitioners began to realize that not all policy arenas and stakeholders are equal. Among stakeholders, corporate business interests were predominant because they were active and influential in virtually all policy areas, giving US public policy in general a decidedly procapital cast relative to labor, consumers, the environment, and other interests.[43] Congruently, policy making about national defense and military action had risen in importance and now influenced all other policy areas as well. As President Eisenhower warned in his farewell address, military leaders and armament manufacturers had become a "military-industrial complex" capable of influencing the entire direction of American government.[44]

Since Eisenhower's day, the military-industrial complex has expanded while other, related complexes have formed. Energy, finance, and pharmaceutical interests have grown in influence not simply because of their vast economic assets but also because of their strategic importance to globalizing societies.[45] Complexes differ from iron triangles in their command over resources that affect overall societal conditions, mass perceptions, and political priorities. Falling energy prices can help save a presidency, as they did in 2004. Military threats can rally support for the party in power, as happened after 9/11. Fears of epidemics and biological weapons can fuel militarism and restrictions on civil liberties, as they did after the anthrax mailings in 2001.

This ramifying quality heralds a morphologically new type of threat to American governing institutions. Unlike iron triangles, which typically involve narrow economic interests and midlevel policy makers, complexes pose moral hazards for the highest offices of government because their assets can be used to wield dominant control over the national political agenda. The same moral hazards exist for the corporate and industrial interests that compose the economic side of political-economic complexes because the national political agenda is the primary factor affecting the income, importance, and long-term prospects of the corporations involved.

Anticorruption Policies

Although they need to be strengthened and better enforced, policies for preventing pecuniary corruption are already in place. In recent years, the main threats from these forms of corruption have come from innovative schemes to circumvent existing controls. A good example is how the savings and loan industry was looted in the 1980s. Corporate leaders who were engaged in far-flung conspiracies to commit fraud finagled changes in regulatory policies and enforcement that allowed their frauds to go undetected until their banks had been plundered.[46] This special-interest corruption in the finance and banking industry was repeated little more than a decade later when Enron used its tight connections with the Bush–Cheney administration to evade controls on energy pricing and asset accounting.[47] The collapse of Enron and other financial conglomerates led policy makers to strengthen regulations for monitoring corporate accounting and holding corporate officers responsible for their companies' actions.

Another example of a resurgent type of pecuniary corruption is the new spoils system that has developed around privatization and outsourcing.

Much of the waste and incompetence of military contractors in Iraq have been attributed to politicization of the contracting process. In many cases, companies were selected solely on the basis of their ties to the Republican Party.[48] Similarly, in the system of influence peddling by members of Congress, including Representatives Cunningham, Ney, and Delay, large government contracts and specific legislation were traded for cash payments, campaign contributions, jobs for relatives, and access to corporate planes. Although additional reforms are needed, the procedures for government contracting, accounting, and earmarking were tightened after voters gave Democrats a majority in both the House and Senate in 2006.

These examples suggest that once particular types of vulnerabilities have been recognized, the system of checks and balances will eventually be activated if schemes are devised to attack the same weak points in a new way. It may be difficult to detect fraud in corporate accounting, cronyism in government contracting, and influence peddling in legislative earmarking, but no one doubts that such crimes are possible and that regulators, investigators, and legislators need to guard against them.

In contrast, the political system's vulnerability to the newest and deadliest type of antidemocratic corruption—conspiracies in high office to undermine popular sovereignty, often by manipulating national circumstances or priorities—has yet to be widely recognized, much less targeted for corrective action. When suspicious incidents occur that alter the nation's objectives, disrupt presidential elections, provoke military action, or otherwise affect the national agenda, Americans tend to accept the self-serving accounts of public officials, seldom considering the possibility that such incidents might have been initiated or facilitated by the officials themselves. The role and function of the universally understood concept of "agent provocateur" is grossly neglected in the idiom of American political discourse. This mass gullibility, which itself invites SCADs, is unlikely to change until SCAD detection and prosecution are improved.

SCADS AND THE POLITICS OF NATIONAL SECURITY

The National Security Apparatus

The connection among SCADs, presidential politics, and the military-industrial complex calls for inquiry into national security policy making. National security policy is developed and implemented by what can be called the "National Security Apparatus." The apparatus is composed of all those persons who gather and interpret intelligence, carry out covert, invisible operations,[49] develop secret military capabilities, are involved in regime change around the world, and formulate and communicate America's foreign policies. This includes the offices of the president and the vice president, the diplomatic corps, the nation's intelligence agencies (notably, the CIA, NSA, and FBI), top leaders in the military, private research organizations (such as the RAND Corporation), and certain military and intelligence contractors. Significantly, intelligence contractors are estimated to now account for 70 percent of America's intelligence expenditures,[50] leading some observers to speak of an "intelligence-industrial complex."[51]

The apparatus originated in World War II and played a critical role in the war effort, particularly with the Manhattan Project, which developed the first atomic bombs. The advent of nuclear weapons and the cold war made espionage and counterintelligence a national priority. From the beginning, the apparatus had a presence internationally through the diplomatic corps and affiliations with the intelligence agencies of US allies. But its international reach has been greatly expanded in recent decades because of America's growing number of foreign military bases and its land- and space-based equipment for surveillance. The United States has 725 foreign military bases, and its forces are stationed in 153 foreign nations,[52] in addition to an untold number of espionage bases.

The organs of national security policy are an "apparatus" in the sense that they are compartmented and disjointed by design.[53] Organizing national security functions in the aftermath of World War II, officials at the highest levels of the national government recognized the dangers that agencies, shielded by secrecy and armed with lethal capabilities, posed to representative democracy. Most of the nation's offices for intelligence gathering and covert operations were removed from the armed services and placed under civilian control. The functions and purviews of different offices, even those within a single agency, were strictly delineated and separated in order that each office would have only a partial picture of the nation's aims, tactics, weapons, and operations. This administrative compartmentalization was intended to protect secrecy and to prevent policy interests, especially those of the armed services, from distorting intelligence. However, compartmentalization also facilitates the misuse of apparatus assets for purposes of domestic politics because it leaves each component of an operation ignorant of the operation's principals and overall purpose.

SCADs and National Security Capabilities

In the first decades after World War II, SCAD targets and tactics evolved in tandem with the skills and techniques of the National Security Apparatus. The first covert operations of the apparatus were undertaken immediately after the end of World War II. In the late 1940s, the CIA made secret financial contributions to anticommunist political parties in Italy, France, and Japan. In Italy, it also bought Mafia help in keeping communists out of the dock workers' union. In the 1950s, it became actively involved in coups against democratically elected regimes. After these coups, the apparatus instructed and aided its coup partners in the use of state terrorism for quelling unrest and opposition.[54]

During this period, isolated elements in the apparatus—notably the FBI—began to surreptitiously intervene into domestic political processes to strengthen the public's resolve in the cold war. Tape recordings of Richard Nixon in the White House reveal that the FBI colluded with Nixon to frame Alger Hiss.[55] Hiss was probably guilty of espionage, but the FBI lacked proof, so Hoover tapped Nixon to interrogate Hiss in Senate hearings. The FBI then forged documents to match Hiss's typewriter, and the documents were sufficient to convict Hiss of perjury. The FBI also fed secret information to Joseph McCarthy, whose attacks on alleged communists and communist sympathizers terrorized more-liberal public administrators, intellectuals, artists, and others.

Not long before the Kennedy assassination, the covert activities of the apparatus had reached a new scale. In 1961, the apparatus planned and executed an unsuccessful invasion of Cuba by Cuban expatriates it had trained and equipped. After the invasion failed, the apparatus began working with bosses in the American Mafia to engineer the assassination of Fidel Castro. In 1963, the apparatus directed a coup in Vietnam that resulted in the murder of President Diem, who had previously been installed with the help of the CIA. From these initiatives, it would have been only a small step for the assassination capabilities of the apparatus to be directed at a domestic target. In any event, as the apparatus was learning how to organize conspiracies to murder foreign leaders, the United States experienced an unprecedented rash of political assassinations and attempted assassinations. The targets included John Kennedy, Lee Harvey Oswald, Robert Kennedy, Martin Luther King, Malcolm X, George Wallace, Gerald Ford, and Ronald Reagan.

In the late 1960s and early 1970s, the apparatus began to establish profit-making enterprises, which gave it financial resources beyond the knowledge and control of Congress. Many of these enterprises were legitimate businesses. Perhaps the best example is Air America, which was the proprietary airline of the CIA. By the end of the Vietnam War, Air America had become the largest airline in the world. The CIA also had front companies or "cutouts" in many other industries related to its covert operations, especially public relations, telecommunications, energy, and publishing.

Other enterprises, such as drug dealing, were illegal or extralegal. The CIA first became involved in the drug trade during the Vietnam War. Profits from the illicit activity were used to support paramilitary operations in Laos and Cambodia that Congress had not authorized and about which it was unaware.

In 1980 if not sooner, these newly developed business skills of the apparatus began to be used in domestic politics. An example is the so-called October Surprise in the 1980 presidential election, where the Reagan–Bush campaign is alleged to have made a deal to sell arms to Iran in return for Iran delaying the release of the hostages until after Election Day.[56] The principals who secretly negotiated the arrangement in Paris reportedly included vice presidential candidate George H. W. Bush and former intelligence officers Bill Casey (Reagan's campaign manager) and Robert Gates. After the Reagan administration took office, Casey became director of the CIA and Gates became assistant director.

The special prosecutor's investigation of Iran-Contra was precluded by its enabling legislation from revisiting the 1980 October Surprise, which had previously been investigated by Congress. The congressional investigation had cleared Casey and Bush after they produced alibis for the alleged date of the meeting in Paris, but these alibis were later brought into question. Given what is now known about Iran-Contra, it appears likely that the Iran-Contra operation grew out of the October Surprise agreement. At the direction of President Reagan and with the direct involvement of Vice President Bush, the apparatus began selling arms to Iran at highly inflated prices and funneling the profits to the Contras. The Contras were also brought into the drug trade and were given assistance in smuggling cocaine into the United States.[57]

The Crimes of Watergate

The Watergate scandal offers the most detailed picture available of how, why, and by whom the National Security Apparatus can become involved in presidential politics. The Watergate prosecutions, congressional investigations, and presidential tape recordings provide a thorough account of the break-ins and of the efforts by the president and others to cover-up Watergate's connection to the administration. This official record has also been supplemented by the books of several investigative journalists and by the memoirs of Nixon's chief of staff Bob Haldeman[58] and Watergate burglars Howard Hunt,[59] Gordon Liddy,[60] and James McCord.[61] Watergate suggests that SCADs are not so much aberrations within the apparatus as they are predictable turns taken when national security initiatives intersect with domestic presidential politics.

Nixon considered espionage against partisan opponents to be a normal part of American politics, and he saw nothing wrong with using government resources for this purpose. After all, he knew that the government had targeted him in the 1968 election. After he became president, FBI director Hoover informed him that, at the instructions of President Johnson, the FBI had placed wiretaps on the phones in Nixon's airplane.[62] President Johnson's action in this regard implies that he, too, considered such espionage legitimate. That Johnson and Nixon were from different parties but were both able to use the FBI for political espionage indicates that, by the late 1960s, apparatus capabilities were seen by the president, the FBI director, and probably others at their level to be resources appropriate for use in domestic politics.

Nixon and his close advisors believed that the antiwar movement was an attack on the American form of government and that leaking secret or sensitive information to the press, as Daniel Ellsberg had done with the Pentagon Papers, amounted to a treasonous assault on national security. After the FBI refused to wiretap reporters, Nixon and his team established the Special Investigative Unit in the White House to stop information from "leaking." This is why the White House staff referred to Howard Hunt and Gordon Liddy as the "plumbers." Wiretaps were placed on the telephones of reporters as well as administration officials. Among the latter was Henry Kissinger, who was discovered to be one of the media's sources.

The plumbers engaged in a variety of operations before the Watergate break-ins. They followed Ted Kennedy and tried to discover evidence that would embarrass or discredit him. They burglarized the office of Daniel Ellsberg's psychiatrist, Lewis Fielding. They recruited thugs to attack protestors and instigate unrest at antiwar demonstrations. Finally, as the 1972 election approached, Hunt and Liddy were brought into Nixon's reelection campaign to handle the campaign's security and intelligence activities. Hunt and Liddy prepared an extensive plan for, among other things, infiltrating the primary and general election campaigns of the Democrats, disrupting the Democratic National Convention, and luring convention delegates into compromising liaisons with prostitutes. Also part of this plan was placing wiretaps on two telephones in the headquarters of the National Democratic Party and searching through the files in the office of the Democratic Party Chairman. The plan was recognized at the time to be risky and illegal, but it was approved by top officials in the White House and by the Committee to Re-elect the President.

Although Watergate is remembered as simply a single, botched burglary almost entirely unrelated to the CIA and FBI, it was more plausibly part of a much larger initiative involving various apparatus components. When the Watergate break-in was being investigated by Congress, staff found reports of more than 100 burglaries in the DC area that were similar to Hunt and Liddy's operation against Daniel Ellsberg's psychiatrist.[63] The plumbers had broken into Fielding's office in search of information needed by CIA profilers for preparing an analysis of how to "break" Ellsberg emotionally. The other burglaries in the DC area similarly targeted the offices of physicians and psychiatrists whose patients were Nixon's opponents or their wives. This MO is consistent with one of various forms of psychological warfare practiced by the apparatus, which had conducted years of psychological research to learn how to psychoanalyze people from a distance, identify their psychological conflicts, and create pressures in their lives to produce emotional breakdowns.[64] Hunt and Liddy may have been just one compartment in a larger assemblage of operatives who were conducting psychological warfare against many of Nixon's "enemies." This would explain why "Deep Throat" (deputy director of the FBI Mark Felt) told Bob Woodward that almost the entire law enforcement wing of the national government was involved in the Watergate operation and coverup and that bugs had been placed in the homes of Woodward, Bernstein, and *Washington Post* editor Ben Bradlee.

Nor were Nixon's political crimes necessarily limited to burglaries, wiretaps, and dirty tricks. Nixon's surrogates may have also murdered US citizens on US soil. Charles Colson, one of Nixon's main political advisors in the White House, hinted as much in taped conversations with the president.[65] Furthermore, Liddy reports in his memoirs that in 1972 Colson instructed Hunt and him to prepare a plan for assassinating Jack Anderson, an investigative journalist.[66] Although Anderson's murder was called off, Hunt and Liddy were quite willing to perform the operation and viewed it as a reasonable assignment. For that matter, shortly after the Watergate burglars were arrested, Liddy told John Dean that he would understand if he, Liddy, were slated to be killed; he asked only that the hit occur someplace other than at his home, where his wife and children might come to harm.[67] One death that a grand jury suspected had been arranged by the White House was that of Dorothy Hunt, Howard Hunt's wife, who was killed in an airplane crash not long after she had begun blackmailing Nixon to provide financial support for the Watergate burglars during their incarceration.[68]

Limited Reforms After Watergate

Ironically, Watergate revealed not only how national security operations can become enmeshed in presidential politics but also how reluctant public officials are to acknowledge and confront the conditions that permit this. The Watergate investigations exposed the crimes of high-ranking public officials, and a number of officials went to jail. But few changes were made to the organization, procedures, or oversight of national security agencies even though they had been quite willing to go along with Nixon's crimes. In the aftermath of Nixon's resignation, the Church Committee hearings on the CIA uncovered many illegal and illegitimate activities by the apparatus, including assassinations of foreign leaders, coups, collaboration among state agents with criminal organizations, illegal domestic surveillance, and more. They also turned up evidence of CIA and FBI involvement in US domestic politics, including not just Watergate and the dirty tricks of Donald Segretti but also the secret provision of funds to a wide range of civic organizations and the use of illegal wiretaps and agent provocateurs against the civil rights and antiwar movements.[69]

Nevertheless, the congressional investigators and special prosecutors never seriously considered the possibility that the National Security Apparatus was engaging in domestic assassinations and other high crimes. The suspicion was voiced by others; for example, Bernstein and Woodward speculated in their book on Watergate that Nixon might have been behind the attempted assassination of George Wallace.[70] But public officials were seemingly unwilling to take their suspicions this far; the post-Watergate reforms targeted isolated abuses of power rather than the general problem of elite political criminality in the national security state.

This allowed criminal tendencies revealed by Watergate to continue developing. Even as Nixon was departing, he drew additional politicians and intelligence professionals into his network of unprincipled partisans. Alexander Haig became Nixon's chief of staff, and he brokered the deal between Nixon and Gerald Ford for Nixon's pardon.[71] Haig later played a role in Iran-Contra when he approved weapons sales to Iran not long after Ronald Reagan's inauguration.[72] George H. W. Bush had been a frequent visitor to the Nixon White House after Nixon had picked him to be chairman of the Republican National Party. Ford appointed Bush as the director of the CIA despite Senator Church's strong objection to a politician serving in that position. Although Bush was CIA director for only one year, he became enormously popular in the apparatus because he kept the CIA's secrets and protected the CIA professionals from exposure and prosecution in the aftermath of Watergate.[73]

When Bush pardoned the Iran-Contra conspirators after losing his reelection bid in 1992, he effectively condoned the apparatus's growing criminality. In fact, less than a decade later, many of the people implicated in Iran-Contra returned to positions of power in the Bush–Cheney administration. Cheney himself had been indirectly involved in Iran-Contra. In the 1980s, Cheney was a member of Congress. Serving on the House Intelligence Committee, he had been briefed on aspects of the Contra program, and he had been a vocal defender of the Iran-Contra project when it was first investigated by Congress (before an independent prosecutor was appointed). Others directly involved or associated with Iran-Contra who returned to power with Bush–Cheney included Robert Gates, Elliot Abrams, John Poindexter, Otto Reich, Richard Armitage, and John Negraponte.

The Bush–Cheney Administration

Another SCAD besides Watergate where national security considerations became enmeshed with presidential politics was the "outing" of CIA agent Valerie Plame.[74] Shortly before the 2003 invasion of Iraq, the president changed longstanding policy to allow the vice president to declassify state secrets.[75] A few months later, after Joseph Wilson challenged the administration's claims about Iraq seeking to acquire uranium in Africa, the vice president informed his aid Scooter Libby of Plame's status. Libby then leaked this information to the press and to others in the administration who also leaked it to the press. These circumstances suggest that Libby was following the orders of the president and the vice president, but Libby alone was indicted, and only then for committing perjury when he denied having leaked Plame's identity to reporters. Without a confession from Libby implicating Cheney and Bush, no one was willing to take action against either the president or the vice president, both of whom appear to have been part of a criminal conspiracy to expose the identity of a covert agent in a time of war.

In any event, the circumstances and White House actions in Plamegate are very similar to those in the Nixon administration's efforts to discredit Daniel Ellsberg. In both cases, the presidents were misleading the public about their foreign policy motives and initiatives, their credibility was threatened by whistleblowers who took their stories to the *New York Times*, they responded by using national security assets (operatives for Nixon, and information for Bush) in an effort to undermine the whistleblowers' credibility, and when the underlings who had carried out their criminal schemes were apprehended and prosecuted, they put their reelections ahead of all considerations of loyalty and culpability, denied all knowledge and involvement in the crimes, and let their minions take the full blame.

The criminality of the Bush–Cheney administration is also similar to Nixon's in another respect. Just as the Watergate break-ins were simply the tip of Nixon's criminal iceberg, Plamegate was only one small element in a much larger pattern of political lawlessness. Much evidence indicates that, in addition to outing Valerie Plame, the Bush–Cheney administration manipulated and distorted intelligence to concoct a pretext for invading Iraq,[76] fired federal prosecutors who refused to target Democratic officials,[77] sought to intimidate and silence civilian and military career public administration professionals who arrived at conclusions contradicting the administration's claims or premises,[78] conducted domestic electronic surveillance without first obtaining court orders,[79] periodically raised terrorist threat levels to rally electoral support for the president,[80] and countenanced cruel and inhumane treatment of suspected terrorists.[81]

There is also circumstantial evidence that the Bush–Cheney administration may have somehow been involved in 9/11. The administration ignored many warning signs that the 9/11 terrorist attack was imminent and that the attack might include hijackings;[82] the CIA had a working relationship with bin Laden and provided weapons, money, and technical support to Islamist terrorists in Afghanistan during the Soviet occupation;[83] some officials appear to have received warnings not to fly on 9/11;[84] the twin towers and Building 7, which collapsed at near free-fall speed, are suspected of having been brought down by controlled demolition;[85] chemical tests have found traces of thermite (an incendiary used in demolishing steel skyscrapers) in steel from the Trade Center site;[86] and, as is usual with most SCADs, the twin towers crime scene was cleaned up quickly and given only a superficial investigation.[87] Evidence also indicates that the Pentagon was hit by a missile rather than a passenger plane and that Flight 93 was exploded at high altitude.[88]

SCAD DETECTION AND PREVENTION

The first step toward SCAD detection and prevention is facing up to the nature and magnitude of the threat. Recently, many mainstream scholars and journalists have concluded that American democracy is becoming increasingly corporatist, imperialistic, and undemocratic.[89] However, mainstream authors have seldom considered the possibility that authoritarian tendencies in American politics are being systemically engineered by top-ranking civilian and military officials. Rather than thinking in terms of high crimes, their diagnoses have blamed abstract institutional weaknesses or isolated failures of leadership.[90]

In contrast, the upshot of the foregoing analysis is that SCADs are surface indications of a deeper, invisible level of politics[91] in which officials at the highest levels of government use deception, conspiracy, and violence to shape national policies and priorities. This sub-rosa manipulation of domestic politics is an extension of America's duplicity in foreign affairs and draws on the nation's well-developed skills in covert operations. Through its experience with covert actions, the National Security Apparatus has developed a wide range of skills and tactics for subverting and overthrowing regimes, manipulating international tensions, and disrupting ideological movements. The United States, or more specifically presidential administrations, uses these skills in combination with visible foreign policies to maximize the impact of both the visible and invisible sides of their efforts.

To the extent that policy makers are called to justify their covert actions and other deceptions, they do so by asserting that public opinion, both domestic and international, is a critical battlefront in conflicts between democratic capitalism and its ideological and military opponents. Although the implications of this policy for popular control of government are seldom examined, the policy itself was and is no secret. As an assistant secretary of defense said in response to claims that public opinion had been manipulated during the Cuban missile crisis,

News generated by actions of the government as to content and timing are part of the arsenal of weaponry that a president has in application of military force and related forces to the solution of political problems, or to the application of international political pressure.[92] Richard Nixon put it more bluntly. In claiming that the president has the power to break the law when protecting national security, he said, "Well, when the president does it that means that it is not illegal."[93]

US capabilities for covert operations enter the nation's domestic politics as SCADs in at least two ways. Sometimes, the process is rather haphazard. In Watergate, for example, the Nixon administration was using covert-action skills domestically in legitimate matters of national security when it diverted these skills, first, to attack Daniel Ellsberg and perhaps other political enemies and, subsequently, to gain advantage in the 1972 presidential election. Generalizing from this example, covert-action capabilities can end up being exploited for SCADs because the officials who control these capabilities are operating in an intensely political environment, and they occasionally succumb to temptations to use their national security powers for personal or partisan advantage. The idea that SCADs are opportunistic gambits in presidential politics was the conclusion reached in the official investigations of both Watergate and Iran-Contra.

On the other hand, several SCADs for which evidence of government involvement is unofficial but nevertheless credible point to elaborate planning by enduring networks of strategically placed insiders pursuing a combination of bureaucratic, ideological, and economic objectives. The assassinations of John and Robert Kennedy, and the attempted assassination of George Wallace, all benefited Richard Nixon and served the interests of military and military-industrial elites. Furthermore, arranging these shootings and pinning them on patsies would have required many operatives, extensive resources, and a variety of skills. Similarly, if the attacks of 9/11 were executed or somehow facilitated by US public officials—as much evidence suggests—a number of agencies would have had to have been involved, including elements of the Department of Defense, the CIA, and the FBI.

Reforms for SCAD prevention and detection should address both of these etiological scenarios. The potential for SCADs to be committed opportunistically in presidential politics can be reduced statutorily by mandating procedures for investigating election problems, defense failures, assassinations, and similar incidents. As it stands, events with profound implications for the nation and the world are left to be investigated on an ad hoc basis; procedures for controlling crime scenes, inventorying evidence, interviewing suspects, interpreting evidence, overseeing the investigative process, and reporting findings are developed on the spot in the aftermath of the tragedies, when the nation is in shock and the perpetrators may be covering their trail. Public officials or their agents lost, discarded, or destroyed critical evidence in the World Trade Center destruction,[94] the anthrax mailings in October 2001,[95] the disputed presidential elections of 2000 and 2004,[96] the assassinations of JFK, RFK, and Martin Luther King,[97] and the attempted assassination of George Wallace.[98]

Reducing American democracy's vulnerability to manipulation by military and intelligence elites will require amendments to the US Constitution to strengthen the role of Congress and the public in national security policy making. In particular, revisions are needed to the constitutional procedures for declaring, fighting, and ending wars.[99] SCADs usually draw on the skills of covert action and are often connected to secret foreign-policy objectives, from discrediting dissidents and stopping leaks to fabricating intelligence and provoking wars. The United States has become extensively involved in covert operations overseas because the nation's leadership is no longer adhering to the Constitution's requirements governing military action. The last military action for which Congress issued a declaration of war was World War II. Since then, the introduction of nuclear weapons has made Congress reluctant to authorize the kind of uninhibited aggression that a declaration of war might unleash. However, the Constitution contains no process for authorizing limited wars or for ensuring that Congress can end such wars at its discretion. In large part this is why the role of Congress and the president became so muddled during the Vietnam War. The failure of the War Powers Act to correct this situation was demonstrated all too clearly after 2006 by legislative–executive conflict over the occupation of Iraq.

Social science can play a critical role in furthering this reform agenda by bringing behavioral research to bear on antidemocratic corruption in American government. The potential for SCADs is large because elite political conspiracies are difficult to detect and investigations are in the hands of the very people who actually need to be scrutinized. However, social scientists have the requisite conceptual resources, methodological skills, and scholarly independence to make antidemocratic corruption visible. Once it is rendered visible, it will no longer be tolerated.

This chapter was originally published in *American Behavioral Scientist* 53 (6): 795–825. © 2010 SAGE Publications. Reprinted with permission from Sage Publications.

LANCE DEHAVEN-SMITH is a professor in the Reubin Askew School of Public Administration and Policy at Florida State University in Tallahassee.

Notes

1. L. deHaven-Smith, "When Political Crimes Are Inside Jobs: Detecting State Crimes Against Democracy," *Administrative Theory & Praxis* 28, no. 3:330–55.

2. C. Bernstein and B. Woodward, B, *All The President's Men* (New York: Simon & Schuster, 1974); L. P. Gray, *In Nixon's Web: A Year in the Crosshairs of Watergate* (New York: Henry Holt, 2008); S. I. Kutler, *The Wars of Watergate: The Last Crisis of Richard Nixon* (New York: Norton, 1990); and A. Summers, *The Arrogance of Power: The Secret World of Richard Nixon* (New York: Viking, 2000).

3. D. Ellsberg, *Secrets: A Memoir of Vietnam and the Pentagon Papers* (London: Penguin, 2002).

4. P. Kornbluh and M. Byrne, eds., *The Iran-Contra Scandal: The Classified History* (New York: New Press, 1993); A. Martin, *The Conspirators: Secrets of an Iran-Contra Insider* (Pray, MT: National Liberty Press, 2001); and R. Parry, *Trick or Treason: The October Surprise Mystery* (New York: Sheridan Square Press, 1993).

5. M. Isikoff and D. Corn, *Hubris: The Inside Story of Spin, Scandal, and the Selling of the Iraq War* (New York: Crown, 2006); F. Rich, *The Greatest Story Ever Sold* (New York: Penguin, 2006); F. Rich, "When the Vice President Does It, That Means It's Not Illegal," *New York Times*, July 1, 2007, http://select.nytimes.com/2007/07/01/opinion/01rich.html?scp=1&sq=&st=nyt (accessed July 1, 2007); and J. Wilson, *The Politics of Truth: Inside the Lies that Led to War and Betrayed My Wife's CIA Identity* (New York: Carroll & Graf Publishers, 2004).

6. Ellsberg, *Secrets*, 7–20.

7. Summers, *The Arrogance of Power*, 298–308.

8. Parry, *Trick or Treason*; and G. Sick, *October Surprise: America's Hostages in Iran and the Election of Ronald Reagan* (New York: Random House, 1991).

9. J. H. Fetzer, "Smoking Guns and the Death of JFK," in *Murder in Dealey Plaza: What We Know that We Didn't Know Then About the Death of JFK*, ed. J. H. Fetzer, 1–16 (Chicago: Catfeet Press, 2000); J. Garrison, *On the Trail of the Assassins: My Investigation and Prosecution of the Murder of President Kennedy* (New York: Sheridan Square Press, 1988); R. J. Groden, *The Killing of a President: The Complete Photographic Record of the JFK Assassination, the Conspiracy, and the Cover-up* (New York: Penguin, 1993); M. Lane, *Rush to Judgment: A Critique of the Warren Commission's Inquiry into the Murders of President John F. Kennedy, Officer J. D. Tippit, and Lee Harvey Oswald* (New York: Holt, Rinehart, & Winston, 1966); P. D. Scott, *Deep Politics and the Death of JFK* (Berkeley: University of California Press, 1993); and R. F. White, "Apologists and Critics of the Lone Gunman Theory: Assassination Science and Experts in Post-modern America," in *Assassination Science: Experts Speak Out on the Death of JFK*, ed. J. H. Fetzer, 377–413 (Chicago: Catfeet Press, 1998).

10. L. deHaven-Smith, *The Battle for Florida* (Gainesville: University Press of Florida, 2005); and A. Miller, ed., *What Went Wrong in Ohio: The Conyers' Report on the 2004 Presidential Election* (Chicago: Academy Publishers, 2005).

11. N. F. Ahmed, *The War on Truth: 9/11, Disinformation, and the Anatomy of Terrorism* (Northampton, MA: Olive Branch Press, 2005); D. R. Griffin, *The New Pearl Harbor: Disturbing Questions About the Bush Administration and 9/11* (Northampton, MA: Olive Branch Press, 2004); D. R. Griffin, *The 9/11 Commission Report: Omissions and Distortions* (Northampton, MA: Olive Branch Press, 2005); E. Hufschmid, *Painful Questions: An Analysis of the September 11th Attack* (Goleta, CA: Endpoint Software, 2002); D. Paul and J. Hoffman, *Waking Up from Our Nightmare: The 9/11/01 Crimes in New York City* (San Francisco: Irresistible/Revolutionary, 2004); and W. G. Tarpley, *9/11 Synthetic Terror* (Joshua Tree, CA: Progressive Press, 2005).

12. Isikoff and Corn, *Hubris*; and Rich, *The Greatest Story Ever Sold.*

13. G. E. Marcus, ed., *Paranoia Within Reason: A Casebook on Conspiracy as Explanation* (Chicago: University of Chicago Press, 1999).

14. J. Parish and M. Parker, *The Age of Anxiety: Conspiracy Theory and the Human Sciences* (Oxford, UK: Blackwell, 2001); and T. Sanders and H. G. West, "Power Revealed and Concealed in the New World Order," in *Transparency and conspiracy: Ethnographies of suspicion in the new world order*, eds. H. G. West and T. Sanders, 1–37 (Durham, NC: Duke University Press, 2003).

15. See L. A. Manwell, "In Denial of Democracy: Social Psychological Implications for Public Discourse on State Crimes Against Democracy Post-9/11," *American Behavioral Scientist* 53, no. 6:848–84.

16. Griffin, *The New Pearl Harbor*; Hufschmid, *Painful Questions*; and J. Marrs, *The Terror Conspiracy: Deception, 9/11 and the Loss of Liberty* (New York: Disinformation, 2006).

17. Summers, *The Arrogance of Power*, 406, 473, 526.

18. J. W. Douglass, *JFK and the Unspeakable: Why He Died and Why It Matters* (Maryknoll, NY: Orbis Books, 2008); and D. Talbot, *Brothers: The Hidden History of the Kennedy Years* (New York: Free Press, 2007).

19. P. Shenon, *The Commission: The Uncensored History of the 9/11 Investigation* (New York: Twelve, 2008), 25, 29–31, 36–38.

20. S. I. Kutler, *Abuse of Power: The New Nixon Tapes* (New York: Touchstone, 1997).

21. C. L. Hinson, "Negative Information Action: Danger for Democracy," *American Behavioral Scientist* 53, no. 6:826–47.

22. Griffin, *The 9/11 Commission Report*; and Shenon, *The Commission.*

23. Shenon, *The Commission*, 43–44.

24. Ibid., 171.

25. Douglass, *JFK and the Unspeakable*, 40–41, 65–66, 144–45, 333–34, 363–68; and Talbot, *Brothers.*

26. Ahmed, *The War on Truth*; and C. Weldon, *Countdown to Terror* (Washington, DC: Regnery, 2005).

27. M. Hall, "Ridge Reveals Clashes on Alerts," *USA Today*, May 10, 2005, http://www.usatoday.com/news/washington/2005-05-10-ridge-alerts_x.htm (accessed May 10, 2008); and R. Suskind, *The One Percent Doctrine: Deep Inside America's Pursuit of Its Enemies Since 9/11* (New York: Simon & Schuster, 2006).

28. Tarpley, *9/11 Synthetic Terror*, 311–18.

29. Also suspicious was the death, a year later, of Democrat Paul Wellstone, one of the few senators to criticize the congressional authorization for military action against Iraq. Wellstone was killed in an airplane crash. See F. Arrows and J. Fetzer, *American Assassination: The Strange Death of Senator Paul Wellstone* (Brooklyn, NY: Vox Pop, 2004).

30. A. A. Rogow and H. D. Lasswell, *Power, Corruption, and Lies* (Englewood Cliffs, NJ: Prentice Hall, 1963).

31. M. Diamond, "The Federalist," in *History of Political Philosophy*, eds. L. Strauss and J. Cropsey, 659–79 (Chicago: University of Chicago Press, 1987); and *The Federalist* 10.
32. *The Federalist* 28, 57.
33. Ibid. 29, 44.
34. Ibid. 38, 47, 64, 65, 66, 77, 84.
35. Ibid. 9, 11, 47, 51.
36. Ibid. 69.
37. See Hinson, "Negative Information Action."
38. T. Lowi, *The end of liberalism* (New York: Norton, 1969).
39. L. deHaven-Smith and C. E. Van Horn, "Subgovernment Conflict in Public Policy," *Policy Studies Journal* 12 no. 4:627–42.
40. C. A. Beard and M. R. Beard, *The Rise of American Civilization* (New York: Macmillan, 1927).
41. Ibid., 111–14.
42. See, e.g., R. Dahl and C. E. Lindblom, *Politics, Economics, and Welfare* (New Haven, CT: Yale University Press, 1946).
43. P. Bachrach and M. S. Baratz, "Two Faces of Power," *American Political Science Review* 56, no. 4:947–52.
44. D. D. Eisenhower, *Farewell Address*, http://www.eisenhower.archives.gov/ (accessed January 17, 2008).
45. N. Klein, *The Shock Doctrine: The Rise of Disaster Capitalism* (New York: Allen Lane/Penguin, 2007).
46. W. K. Black, *The Best Way to Rob a Bank Is to Own One* (Austin: University of Texas Press, 2005); and K. Calavita, H. Pontell, and R. Tillman, *Big Money Crime: Fraud and Politics in the Savings and Loan Crisis* (Berkeley: University of California Press, 1999).
47. R. Munson, *From Edison to Enron: The Business of Power and What It Means For the Future of Electricity* (Westport, CT: Praeger, 2005).
48. See J. Scahill, *Blackwater: The Rise of the World's Most Powerful Mercenary Army* (London: Serpent's Tail, 2007).
49. K. Thorne and A. Kouzmin, "The USA PATRIOT Acts (et al.): Convergent Legislation and Oligarchic Isomorphism in the "Politics of Fear" and State Crime(s) Against Democracy (SCADs)," *American Behavioral Scientist* 53, no. 6:885–920.
50. T. Shorrock, *Spies For Hire: The Secret World of Intelligence Outsourcing* (New York: Simon & Schuster, 2008), 19–20.
51. Ibid., 12–13, 90, 162, 166, 168.
52. C. Johnson, *The Sorrows of Empire: Militarism, Secrecy, and the End of the Republic* (New York: Henry Holt, 2004).
53. M. A. Goodman, *The Failure of Intelligence: The Decline and Fall of the CIA* (New York: Rowman and Littlefield, 2008), 1–29; and D. Wise and T. B. Ross, *The Invisible Government* (New York: Random House, 1964), 91–128.
54. See W. K. Blum, *Killing Hope: U.S. Military and C.I.A. Interventions Since World War II* (Monroe, ME: Common Courage Press, 2004); and Klein, *The Shock Doctrine*.
55. Summers, *The Arrogance of Power*, 70–75.
56. Parry, *Trick or Treason*; and Sick, *October Surprise*.
57. M. C. Ruppert, *Crossing the Rubicon: The Decline of the American Empire at the End of the Age of Oil* (Gabriola Island, Canada: New Society, 2004); and G. Webb, *Dark Alliance: The CIA, the Contras, and the Crack Cocaine Explosion* (New York: Seven Stories Press, 1998).
58. H. R. Haldeman, *The Ends of Power* (New York: Times Books, 1978).
59. E. H. Hunt, *Undercover: Memoirs of an American Secret Agent* (New York: G. P. Putnam, 1974).
60. G. G. Liddy, *Will: The Autobiography of G. Gordon Liddy* (New York: St. Martin's, 1980).

61. J. W. McCord, Jr., *A Piece of Tape: The Watergate Story, Fact and Fiction* (Rockville, MD: Washington Media Services, 1974).

62. Gray, *In Nixon's Web*, 161–62.

63. Summers, *The Arrogance of Power*, 392, 524n22.

64. J. Marks, *The Search for the Manchurian Candidate: The CIA and Mind Control* (New York: Norton, 1979).

65. Kutler, *Abuse of Power*, 194.

66. Liddy, *Will*, 207–210.

67. Ibid., 257–58.

68. Kutler, *Abuse of Power*, 474.

69. Johnson, *The Sorrows of Empire*; H. Wilford, *The Mighty Wurlitzer: How the CIA Played America* (Cambridge, MA: Harvard University Press, 2008); and D. Wise, *The American Police State: The Government Against the People* (New York: Vintage, 1976).

70. Bernstein and Woodward, *All the President's Men*.

71. B. Woodward, "Closing the Chapter on Watergate Wasn't Done Lightly," *Washington Post*, December 28, 2006, A5.

72. Kornbluh and Byrne, *The Iran-Contra Scandal*.

73. R. S. Bowen, *The Immaculate Deception: The Bush Crime Family Exposed* (Chicago: Global Insights, 1991), 41–58.

74. M. Wheeler, *Anatomy of Deceit: How the Bush Administration Used the Media to Sell the Iraq War and Out a Spy* (Berkeley, CA: Vaster Books, 2007).

75. Rich, "When the Vice President Does It, That Means It's Not Illegal."

76. Isikoff and Corn, *Hubris*; and Rich, *The Greatest Story Ever Sold*.

77. S. Horton, "Political Profiling: The Smoking Gun," *Harpers*, April 13, 2007, http://www.harpers.org/archive/2007/04/horton-political-profiling (accessed April 30, 2007).

78. C. Savage, *Takeover: The Return of the Imperial Presidency and the Subversion of American Democracy* (New York: Little, Brown, 2007), 279–307.

79. Suskind, *The One Percent Doctrine*.

80. M. Hall, "Ridge Reveals Clashes on Alerts," *USA Today*, May 10, 2005, http://www.usatoday.com/news/washington/2005-05-10-ridge-alerts_x.htm (accessed May 10, 2008).

81. J. Goldsmith, *The Terror Presidency: Law and Judgment Inside the Bush Administration* (New York: Norton, 2007); G. Greenwald, *A Tragic Legacy: How a Good vs. Evil Mentality Destroyed the Bush Presidency* (New York: Crown, 2007); and J. Mayer, *The Dark Side: The Inside Story of How the War on Terror Turned into a War on American Ideals* (New York: Doubleday, 2008).

82. R. A. Clarke, *Against All Enemies: Inside America's War on Terror* (New York: Free Press, 2004).

83. Blum, *Killing Hope*, 338–52.

84. Griffin, *The New Pearl Harbor*, 72–73; and E. Thomas and M. Hosenball, "Bush: 'We are at war,'" *Newsweek*, September 24, 2001, http://www.newsweek.com/id/76065 (accessed November 15, 2007).

85. Hufschmid, *Painful Questions*, 73–80; and K. R. Ryan, J. R. Gourley, and S. E. Jones, "Environmental Anomalies at the World Trade Center: Evidence for Energetic Materials," *Environmentalist* 29:56–63, http://www.springerlink.com/content/f67q6272583h86n4/fulltext.pdf (accessed Ocotber 21, 2008).

86. Ryan et al., "Environmental Anomalies at the World Trade Center."

87. R. Morgan and I. Henshall, *9/11 Revealed: The Unanswered Questions* (New York: Carroll & Graff, 2005), 94–98.

88. A large and growing literature challenges official accounts of the events of 9/11. See, e.g., Griffin, *The New Pearl Harbor*; Griffin, *The 9/11 Commission Report*; Hufschmid, *Painful Questions*; Paul and Hoffman, *Waking Up From Our Nightmare*; and Tarpley, *9/11 Synthetic Terror*. There is also a "9/11 Truth Movement," which is producing detailed studies of 9/11 issues and anomalies; see www.911truth.org, www.911scholars.org, and www.911essentials.com.

89. A. J. Bacevich, *The New American Militarism: How Americans Are Seduced by War* (Oxford, UK: Oxford University Press, 2005); J. W. Dean, *Broken Government: How Republican Rule Destroyed the Legislative, Executive, and Judicial Branches* (New York: Viking, 2007); Goldsmith, *The Terror Presidency*; Greenwald, *A Tragic Legacy*; Johnson, *The Sorrows of Empire*; Klein, *The Shock Doctrine*; Mayer, *The Dark Side*; Savage, *Takeover*; Shorrock, *Spies For Hire*; and S. Wolin, *Democracy Incorporated: Managed Democracy and the Specter of Inverted Totalitarianism* (Princeton, NJ: Princeton University Press, 2008).

90. Institutional weaknesses that have been cited include the large role of lobbyists and corporations in campaign finance, increasing partisanship because of an evenly divided electorate, gradual growth of the US military presence around the world, and the superficial character of television as a medium for public discourse. Leadership failures that have been blamed include opportunistic responses by political elites to terrorist threats, exaggerated fears of terrorist attacks, and politicization of intelligence gathering and interpretation to support ideological positions. An important exception to this mainstream failure to think in terms of high crimes is Wolin, who argues that American democracy is becoming deeply corrupt (Wolin, *Democracy Incorporated*). But even in Wolin's account, America's corruption is more moral than criminal. He says that elites and masses alike have lost sight of democratic values because they have become preoccupied with material rewards and imperial ambitions. Hence, Wolin calls for a renewed ethics of democratic citizenship, not heightened vigilance against criminal conspiracies in high office.

91. Thorne and Kouzmin, *The USA PATRIOT Acts*.

92. Wise and Ross, *The Invisible Government*, 297–98.

93. D. Frost, "The Third Nixon-Frost Interview," *New York Times*, May 20, 1977, A16.

94. Griffin, *The New Pearl Harbor*; and Hufschmid, *Painful Questions*.

95. W. J. Broad, D. Johnston, J. Miller, and P. Zielbauer, "Anthrax Probe Hampered by FBI Blunders," *New York Times*, November 9, 2001, http://www.sfgate.com/cgi-bin/article.cgi?f=/chronicle/archive/2001/11/09/MN153227.DTL (accessed on March 25, 2008).

96. D. Barstow and D. Van Natta, Jr., "How Bush Took Florida: Mining the Overseas Absentee Vote," *New York Times*, July 15, 2001, A1; deHaven-Smith, *The Battle for Florida*; and Miller, *What Went Wrong in Ohio*.

97. Groden, *The Killing of a President*; Pease, *The RFK Plot*; and D. Weldon, "The Kennedy Limousine: Dallas 1963," in *Murder in Dealey Plaza: What We Know Now That We Didn't Know Then About the Death of JFK*, ed. J. H. Fetzer. (Chicago: Catfeet Press, 2000), 129–58.

98. Hunt, *Undercover*, 216; and Summers, *The Arrogance of Power*.

99. Bacevich, *The New American Militarism*; R. C. Byrd, *Losing America: Confronting a Reckless and Arrogant Presidency* (New York: Norton, 2004); Dean, *Broken Government*; and L. Fisher, "The Way We Go To War: The Iraq Resolution," in *Considering the Bush Presidency*, eds. G. L. Gregg and M. J. Rozell (New York: Oxford University Press, 2004), 107–24.

CHAPTER 7

Building What?
How State Crimes Against Democracy (SCADs) Can Be Hidden in Plain Sight

by David Ray Griffin

At 5:21 PM on 9/11, Building 7 of the World Trade Center collapsed, even though it had not been hit by a plane—a fact that is important because of the widespread acceptance of the idea, in spite of its scientific absurdity, that the twin towers collapsed because of the combined effect of the impact of the airplanes plus the ensuing jet fuel–fed fires. The collapse of World Trade Center 7 (WTC 7) thereby challenges the official account of the destruction of the World Trade Center by al-Qaeda hijackers, even if one accepts the government's scientifically impossible account of the collapse of the twin towers. This fact was recently stressed in the title of a book review by National Medal of Science–winner Lynn Margulis, reviewing my book on the subject, *The Mysterious Collapse of World Trade Center 7: Why the Final Official Report about 9/11 Is Unscientific and False:*[1] "Two Hit, Three Down—The Biggest Lie."[2]

1. WHY THE COLLAPSE OF WTC 7 CREATED AN EXTRAORDINARY PROBLEM

An Unprecedented Occurrence

One explanation for why WTC 7 poses such a problem for the official account of how the towers collapsed is that this account states that, for the first time, a steel-framed high-rise building was brought down by fire, and science looks askance at claims of unprecedented occurrences regarding physical phenomena. *New York Times* writer James Glanz, who also has a PhD in physics, wrote: "[E]xperts said no building like it, a modern, steel-reinforced high-rise, had ever collapsed because of an uncontrolled fire." Glanz then quoted a structural engineer as saying: "[W]ithin the structural engineering community, [WTC 7] is considered to be much more important to understand [than the twin towers]," because engineers had no answer to the question, "[W]hy did 7 come down?"[3]

Visual Evidence of Implosion

The mere fact that the building came down was extraordinary, but equally remarkable was the way it collapsed: straight down, in virtual free fall, making it appear to be an example of the type of controlled demolition known as "implosion," in which explosives and/or incendiaries are used to slice the building's steel support columns in such a way as to cause the building to collapse into its own footprint. CBS anchor Dan Rather, not one to let a remarkable fact go unremarked, said:

> [I]t's reminiscent of those pictures we've all seen . . . on television . . . , where a building was deliberately destroyed by well-placed dynamite to knock it down.[4]

Dan Rather was not the only reporter to make such a comment. Al Jones, a reporter for WINS NYC News Radio, said: "I turned in time to see what looked like a skyscraper implosion—looked like it had been done by a demolition crew."[5]

Moreover, whereas Jones and Rather, being laymen in these matters, merely said that the collapse of Building 7 *looked like* a controlled demolition, experts, upon seeing the video, could tell immediately that it *actually was* a controlled demolition. In 2006, for example, a Dutch filmmaker asked Danny Jowenko, the owner of a controlled demolition company in the Netherlands, to comment on a video of the collapse of WTC 7 without telling him what it was. (Jowenko had been unaware that a third building had collapsed on 9/11.) After viewing the video, Jowenko said: "They simply blew up columns, and the rest caved in afterwards. . . . This is controlled demolition." When asked if he was certain, he replied: "Absolutely, it's been imploded. This was a hired job. A team of experts did this."[6]

Testimonies about Explosions

In addition to the very appearance of the collapse of Building 7 implying that it had been brought down by explosives, there were also testimonies about explosions in the building.

Michael Hess, New York City's corporation counsel and a close friend of Mayor Rudy Giuliani, provided one of these testimonies. While on his way back to City Hall on 9/11, Hess was stopped for an interview at 11:57 AM, during which he said:

> I was up in the emergency management center on the twenty-third floor [of WTC 7], and when all the power went out in the building, another gentleman and I walked down to the eighth floor [sic] where there was an explosion and we were trapped on the eighth floor with smoke, thick smoke, all around us, for about an hour and a half. But the New York Fire Department . . . just came and got us out.[7]

Hess thus reported a midmorning explosion in WTC 7.

The other gentleman in the quote, Barry Jennings of the New York City Housing Authority, reported the same thing during another on-the-street interview, reporting that he and "Mr. Hess" had been walking down the stairs when they were trapped by a "big explosion."[8] Jennings, in fact, said that explosions continued going off while they were waiting to be rescued.[9]

There were also reports of explosions in the late afternoon, just as WTC 7 started coming down. Reporter Peter Demarco of the *New York Daily News* said:

> [T]here was a rumble. The building's top row of windows popped out. Then all the windows on the thirty-ninth floor popped out. Then the thirty-eighth floor. Pop! pop! pop! was all you heard until the building sunk into a rising cloud of gray.[10]

NYPD officer Craig Bartmer gave the following report:

> I was real close to Building 7 when it fell down. . . . That didn't sound like just a building falling down to me. . . . There's a lot of eyewitness testimony down there of hearing explosions. . . . [A]ll of a sudden . . . I looked up, and . . . [t]he thing started pealing in on itself. . . . I started running . . . and the whole time you're hearing "boom, boom, boom, boom, boom."[11]

A New York University medical student, who had been serving as an emergency medical worker that day, gave this report:

[W]e heard this sound that sounded like a clap of thunder. . . .
[T]urned around—we were shocked. . . . [I]t looked like there
was a shockwave ripping through the building and the windows
all busted out. . . . [A]bout a second later the bottom floor caved
out and the building followed after that.[12]

Physical Evidence

In addition to the visual and testimonial evidence, there was clear physical evidence that WTC 7 was brought down by explosives.

Swiss Cheese Steel: Within a few months of 9/11, three professors from
Worcester Polytechnic Institute had issued a report about a piece of steel
from Building 7 that was described in a *New York Times* story by James
Glanz and Eric Lipton as "[p]erhaps the deepest mystery uncovered in
the investigation."[13] Part of the mystery was the fact that the steel was
"extremely thin," indicating that the steel had "melted away," even
though "no fire in any of the buildings was believed to be hot enough to
melt steel outright."[14]

Describing this mysterious piece of steel more fully, an article entitled "The 'Deep Mystery' of Melted Steel" in the Worcester Polytechnic
Institute's magazine, said:

> "[S]teel—which has a melting point of 2,800 degrees Fahren-
> heit—may weaken and bend, but does not melt during an
> ordinary office fire. Yet . . . [a] one-inch column has been
> reduced to half-inch thickness. Its edges—which are curled like
> a paper scroll—have been thinned to almost razor sharpness.
> Gaping holes—some larger than a silver dollar—let light shine
> through a formerly solid steel flange. This Swiss cheese appear-
> ance shocked all of the fire-wise professors, who expected to see
> distortion and bending—but not holes."[15]

Indeed, the thinning and the holes suggested that the steel had vaporized. Explaining as early as November 2001 why fire could not account
for this mysterious steel, Glanz paraphrased one of the three professors
as saying that it "appear[ed] to have been partly evaporated in extraordinarily high temperatures."[16]

Another *New York Times* story reported that the same phenomenon
was reported by Professor Abolhassan Astaneh-Asl of the University of

California, Berkeley, who had received a National Science Foundation grant to spend two weeks at Ground Zero studying steel from the buildings. According to reporter Kenneth Change, Professor Astaneh-Asl, speaking of a horizontal I-beam from WTC 7, said: "Parts of the flat top of the I, once five-eighths of an inch thick, had vaporized."[17]

These reports clearly showed that something other than fire had caused the damage and the collapse, because the fires in the building could not possibly have been higher than 1800 degrees Fahrenheit, while the boiling point of steel is roughly the same as that of iron, or 5182°F.[18] Even if the steel had simply melted, it would still have been remarkable, as the melting point of steel is only a little less than that of iron (2800°F).[19]

Evidence in Plain Sight

Therefore, clear evidence against the official account of WTC 7, that it was brought down by fire, existed in the form of videos of the collapse, published testimonies about explosions in the building, and physical evidence reported in the *New York Times*. The reasonable inference to draw from this evidence—namely, that the official account is false, because explosives must have been used—was reinforced by the first official report on the building's collapse, which was issued in 2002 by the Federal Emergency Management Agency (FEMA). In addition to including as an appendix the report by the three professors at Worcester Polytechnic Institute on the Swiss-cheese steel, the scientists who wrote the report for FEMA admitted that their "best hypothesis" about why WTC 7 collapsed had "only a low probability of occurrence"[20]—which is science-speak for, "We don't have a clue."

Failure to Become Well Known

WTC 7 was a very big building, forty-seven stories high. Although it was dwarfed by the 110-story twin towers, it would have been the tallest building in half of the states in the nation. For all of these reasons, the collapse of this building should have become one of the best-known facts about 9/11. But it did not.

2. WIDESPREAD IGNORANCE ABOUT WTC 7

A Zogby poll in May 2006 found that 43 percent of the American people were unaware that WTC 7 had collapsed,[21] and that same year, as mentioned earlier, Danny Jowenko of the Netherlands still did not know about it, even though controlled demolition was his field.

A dramatic example of the fact that this building's collapse has not been prominent in the public consciousness was provided in a New York City courtroom in September 2009. Judge Edward Lehner was hearing arguments about a petition sponsored by NYC CAN to allow residents to vote on whether New York City should have its own investigation of the World Trade Center attacks. After Judge Lehner had observed that the 9/11 Commission had carried out an investigation and issued a report, Dennis McMahon, a lawyer for NYC CAN, said that this report left many unanswered questions. "One of the biggest questions," he added, "is why did Building 7 come down"—at which point Judge Lehner said: "Building what?" McMahon replied: "World Trade Center Seven. There were three buildings that came down." When the judge, continuing to illustrate his ignorance about the building, asked if it was owned by the Port Authority of New York and New Jersey, McMahon replied that it was owned by Larry Silverstein.[22]

Judge Lehner, it should be emphasized, was not simply an ordinary American citizen. In addition to being a judge presiding in New York City, he had been assigned to a case involving the 9/11 attacks. His ignorance about WTC 7 should be surprising; and yet, it was typical. With his query— "Building what?"—Judge Lehner expressed the ignorance manifested in 2006 by controlled demolition expert Danny Jowenko and almost half of the American people. How can we account for this ignorance?

Abnormal Circumstances

In a *New York Times* story in November 2001, James Glanz wrote that the collapse of WTC 7 was "a mystery that under normal circumstances would probably have captured the attention of the city and the world."[23] Clearly these were not normal circumstances.

Part of the abnormality was the fact that WTC 7, although huge, was overshadowed by the twin towers, which were over twice as tall. However, as Glanz pointed out, knowledgeable people had said right away that the collapse of WTC 7 should have been the bigger story. Why was it not?

Deliberate Suppression

The answer seems to be that it was a deliberately suppressed story. This conclusion is supported by the following facts:

First, after 9/11, our television networks played videos of the Twin towers being hit by planes, and then coming down, over and over, but the collapse of WTC 7 was seldom if ever shown.

Second, when *The 9/11 Commission Report* was issued in 2004, it did not even mention that WTC 7 collapsed.

 Third, after NIST—the National Institute for Standards and Technology—took over from FEMA the task of explaining the destruction of the World Trade Center, it repeatedly delayed its report on WTC 7. In 2003, NIST said that this report would be issued along with its report on the twin towers, the draft of which was to appear in September 2004.[24] However, even though NIST's report on the twin towers did not actually appear until 2005, the promised report on WTC 7 was not included; NIST said that it would appear in 2006. But in August 2006, NIST said, "It is anticipated that a draft report [on WTC 7] will be released by early 2007."[25] However, it was not released in 2007—either early or late in the year. NIST instead "projected" that it would release draft reports on July 8, 2008, followed by final reports on August 8, 2008.[26] Instead, the draft report for public comment did not appear until August, and the final report not until November of that year—when the Bush-Cheney administration was about to leave office.

Moreover, when in 2008 NIST was accused of having deliberately delayed its report on WTC 7 (which the 9/11 Truth Movement had long considered the "Achilles' heel" or "smoking gun" of the official account of 9/11[27]), NIST lied, saying that it had worked on the report only since 2005 and hence for only three years—the same length of time it had worked on its twin towers report. However, NIST had filed progress reports on WTC 7 in December 2002 and May 2003;[28] it published an "Interim Report on WTC 7" in June 2004;[29] and in April 2005, NIST released another preliminary report on WTC 7.[30] Then, after ceasing work on this building until after the report on the twin towers was issued in October 2005, NIST reported, "the investigation of the WTC 7 collapse resumed."[31] In truth, therefore, NIST had worked on its report on WTC 7 for almost six years, not merely three. There was good reason to suspect that this report had been deliberately delayed.

3. NIST'S DRAFT FOR PUBLIC COMMENT: MYSTERY SOLVED?

In any case, when the Draft for Public Comment on the collapse of WTC

7 did finally appear in August 2008, it was announced at a press conference with much bravado. S. Shyam Sunder, NIST's lead investigator for its World Trade Center projects, said:

> Our take-home message today is that the reason for the collapse of World Trade Center 7 is no longer a mystery. WTC 7 collapsed because of fires fueled by office furnishings. It did not collapse from explosives.[32]

The mainstream media for the most part simply repeated Sunder's claims. For example, an Associated Press story entitled "Report: Fire, Not Bombs, Leveled WTC 7 Building," began by saying: "Federal investigators said Thursday they have solved a mystery of the Sept. 11, 2001, attacks: the collapse of World Trade Center building 7, a source of long-running conspiracy theories." Then, after reinforcing this message by quoting Sunder's assurance that "the reason for the collapse of World Trade Center 7 is no longer a mystery," this story concluded by quoting Sunder's claim that the science behind NIST's findings is "incredibly conclusive," so that "[t]he public should really recognize that science is really behind what we have said."[33]

Reporters, however, could easily have discovered that this was not so. They could have seen, in fact, that NIST's WTC 7 report committed scientific fraud, as defined by the National Science Foundation.

4. NIST FALSIFICATION OF EVIDENCE

One type of fraud is falsification, which includes "omitting data."[34] While claiming that it "found no evidence of a . . . controlled demolition event,"[35] NIST simply omitted an enormous amount of evidence that explosions had brought WTC 7 down.

Omitting Testimonial Evidence

NIST failed, for example, to mention any of the testimonial evidence for explosions. NIST claimed that the event described as a midmorning explosion by Michael Hess and Barry Jennings was simply the impact of debris from the collapse of the North Tower—which occurred at 10:28 AM and hence about an hour later than the explosion they had described—and also failed to mention any of the reports of explosions just as the building started to come down.

Omitting Physical Evidence

NIST's report on this building also omitted various types of physical evidence, such as the piece of Swiss cheese steel reported by the Worcester Polytechnic Institute professors in the appendix of the 2002 FEMA report.

The Swiss Cheese Steel: After describing this piece of steel, the professors said: "A detailed study into the mechanisms of this phenomenon is needed."[36] When NIST took over the responsibility of issuing the official reports on the World Trade Center from FEMA, NIST's director promised that its reports would address "all major recommendations contained in the [FEMA] report."[37] However, when NIST's report on WTC 7 appeared in 2008, it did not mention the piece of Swiss cheese steel, let alone explain how it had been produced. NIST even claimed that no recovered steel from this building had been identified.[38]

Melted Iron: Deutsche Bank, which owned a building close to the World Trade Center that was contaminated with dust, hired the RJ Lee Group, a scientific research organization, to prove to its insurance company that the dust contaminating its building was not ordinary building dust, as the insurance company claimed, but had resulted from the destruction of the World Trade Center. Reports issued by the RJ Lee Group proved that the dust was indeed WTC dust, with a unique chemical signature. Part of this signature was "[s]pherical iron . . . particles,"[39] and this meant, the RJ Lee Group pointed out, that iron had "melted during the WTC Event, producing spherical metallic particles."[40]

The RJ Lee Group reports, which were issued in 2003 and 2004, thereby provided additional evidence that temperatures had been reached that significantly exceeded those that could have been produced by fire. These reports, which were made known in an article published in January 2008 by a group of scientists led by physicist Steven Jones,[41] were ignored by NIST.

Melted Molybdenum: Another study, carried out by scientists at the US Geological Survey (USGS), also found iron particles. In addition, these scientists determined that something had melted molybdenum[42]— which has an extremely high melting point of 4,753°F.[43] Although these USGS scientists failed to mention this discovery in the published version of their report, the Steven Jones group, having obtained the USGS team's data through a Freedom of Information Act (FOIA) request, reported evidence that this team had devoted serious study to "a molybdenum-rich spherule."[44] NIST, however, failed to mention this discovery by the US Geological Survey, although it is another federal agency.

Nanothermite: A report by Jones and several other scientists, including University of Copenhagen chemist Niels Harrit, showed that the WTC dust contained unreacted nanothermite. Unlike ordinary thermite, which is an incendiary, nanothermite is highly explosive.

This report by Harrit, Jones, and their colleagues did not appear until 2009,[45] so it could not have been mentioned in NIST's final report, which came out at the end of November 2008. But NIST, given the standard guidelines for the investigation of building fires, should have tested the WTC dust for signs of incendiaries, such as ordinary thermite, and explosives, such as nanothermite.[46]

When asked whether it did test for such substances, however, NIST said that it had not.[47] When reporter Jennifer Abel of the *Hartford Advocate* asked NIST spokesman Michael Newman why it had not done such testing, he replied: "[B]ecause there was no evidence of that." When she asked the obvious follow-up question, "How can you know there's no evidence if you don't look for it first?" Newman replied: "If you're looking for something that isn't there, you're wasting your time . . . and the taxpayers' money."[48]

5. NIST'S FABRICATION OF EVIDENCE

In addition to omitting and otherwise falsifying evidence, NIST also committed the type of scientific fraud called fabrication, or "making up results."[49]

No Girder Shear Studs

In offering its explanation as to how fire caused WTC 7 to collapse, NIST said that the culprit was thermal expansion, meaning that the fire heated up the steel, thereby causing it to expand. Expanding steel beams on the thirteenth floor, NIST claims, caused a steel girder connecting columns forty-four and seventy-nine to break loose. Having lost its support, column seventy-nine failed, starting a chain reaction in which the other eighty-one columns all failed.[50]

Leaving aside the question of whether this is even remotely possible, let us simply ask: Why did that girder fail? NIST's answer was that it was not connected to the floor slab with sheer studs. NIST wrote: "In WTC 7, no studs were installed on the girders."[51] In another passage, NIST said: "Floor beams . . . had shear studs, but the girders that supported the floor beams did not have shear studs."[52]

However, NIST's *Interim Report on WTC 7*, which it published in 2004, before it had developed its girder-failure theory, said shear studs were used to anchor "[m]ost of the beams and girders," including the girder in question.[53]

A Raging Twelfth Floor Fire at 5:00 pm

Although in its 2004 *Interim Report on WTC 7*, NIST said that by 4:45 PM, "the fire on Floor 12 was burned out,"[54] it claimed in its 2008 report that at 5:00 PM, just twenty-one minutes before the building collapsed, the fire on this floor was still going strong.[55]

6. NIST'S FINAL REPORT: AFFIRMING A MIRACLE

NIST's final report on WTC 7, which appeared in November 2008, was for the most part identical to its Draft Report, which had appeared in August. But NIST did add one new element: the affirmation of a miracle, a violation of basic laws of physics.

This issue is treated in a cartoon in which a physics professor has written a proof on a chalkboard. Most of the steps consist of mathematical equations, but one of them simply says: "Then a miracle happens."[56] This is humorous because one thing scientists absolutely cannot do in their scientific work is appeal to miracles, even implicitly. And yet that is what NIST does.

NIST's August Denial of Free Fall

Members of the 9/11 Truth Movement had long been pointing out that WTC 7 came down at the same rate as a free-falling object, or at least virtually so. But in NIST's Draft for Public Comment, issued in August 2008, it denied this, saying that the time it took for the upper floors—the only floors that are visible on the videos—to come down "was approximately 40 percent longer than the computed free fall time and was consistent with physical principles."[57]

As this statement implies, any assertion that the building *did* come down in free fall would *not* be consistent with physical principles— meaning the laws of physics. Explaining this during a "WTC 7 Technical Briefing" on August 26, 2008, S. Shyam Sunder said:

> [A] free fall time would be [the fall time of] an object that has no structural components below it. . . . [T]he . . . time that it took . . . for those seventeen floors to disappear [was roughly 40 percent longer than free fall]. And that is not at all unusual, because there was structural resistance that was provided in this particular case. And you had a sequence of structural failures that had to take place. Everything was not instantaneous.[58]

In saying this, Sunder was, of course, presupposing NIST's rejection of controlled demolition—which *could* have produced a free-fall collapse by causing all eighty-two columns to fail simultaneously—in favor of NIST's fire theory, which necessitated a theory of *progressive* collapse.

Chandler's Challenge and NIST's November Admission of Free Fall

In response, high school physics teacher David Chandler, who was present at this briefing, challenged Sunder's denial of free fall, stating that Sunder's "40 percent" claim contradicted "a publicly visible, easily measurable quantity."[59] Chandler then placed a video on the Internet showing that, by measuring this publicly visible quantity, anyone knowing elementary physics could see that "for about two and a half seconds. . . . the acceleration of the building is indistinguishable from free fall."[60]

Amazingly, in NIST's final report, which came out in November 2008, it admitted free fall. Dividing the building's descent into three stages, NIST described the second phase as "a free fall descent over approximately eight stories at gravitational acceleration for approximately 2.25 s[econds]."[61] So, after presenting over six hundred pages of descriptions, photographs, testimonies, graphs, analyses, explanations, and mathematical formulae, NIST says, in effect: "Then a miracle happens."

Chandler, explaining why this second phase of WTC 7's collapse would be a miracle, said: "Free fall can only be achieved if there is zero resistance to the motion."[62] In other words, the upper portion of WTC 7 could have come down in free fall only if something had suddenly removed all the steel and concrete in the lower part of the building, which would have otherwise provided resistance. If everything had not been removed and the upper floors had come down in free fall anyway, even for only 2.25 seconds, a miracle—meaning a violation of the laws of physics—would have happened.

That was what Sunder himself had explained the previous August, saying that a free-falling object would be one "that has no structural components below it" to offer resistance. But in November, while still defending its fire theory, NIST agreed that, as an empirical fact, free fall happened. For a period of 2.25 seconds, NIST admitted, the descent of WTC 7 was characterized by "gravitational acceleration (free fall)."[63]

Knowing that it had thereby affirmed a miracle, NIST no longer claimed that its analysis was consistent with the laws of physics. In its August draft, in which it said that the collapse occurred 40 percent slower than free fall, NIST had repeatedly said that its analysis was "consistent with physical principles." One encountered this phrase time and time again.[64] In the final report, however, every instance of this phrase had been removed. NIST thereby almost explicitly admitted that its report on WTC 7, admitting free fall while continuing to deny that explosives were used, is *not* consistent with the principles of physics.

Implications

If, according to physics, free fall in the absence of explosives is impossible, then NIST's final report necessarily implies that explosives were used to bring down WTC 7; this would suggest the same about the twin towers, because the collapses of these buildings manifested many of the same telltale signs of controlled demolition as did WTC 7, as well as additional signs such as the horizontal ejection of sections of steel columns, weighing many thousands of pounds, more than 500 feet from the towers.[65]

And with this implicit admission that explosives were used in the collapse of the World Trade Center Buildings, NIST undermined the al-Qaeda theory of 9/11.

For one thing, the straight-down nature of the collapse of the twin towers and WTC 7 means that the buildings were subjected to the type of controlled demolition known as implosion, which is, in the words of a controlled demolition Web site, "by far the trickiest type of explosive project," which "only a handful of blasting companies in the world . . . possess enough experience . . . to perform."[66] Al-Qaeda terrorists would most likely not have had this kind of expertise.

Second, the only reason to go to the trouble of bringing a building straight down is to avoid damaging nearby buildings. Had the World Trade Center buildings toppled over sideways, they would have caused massive destruction in Lower Manhattan, crushing dozens of other buildings and killing tens of thousands of people. If al-Qaeda operatives had had the expertise to make the buildings come straight down, would they have done so?

Lastly, if foreign terrorists had indeed wanted to induce implosion, they could not have obtained access to the buildings for all the amount of time needed to plant explosives. Only insiders could have done this.[67]

7. EXPLAINING THE IGNORANCE ABOUT WTC 7

NIST's admission that WTC 7 came down in free fall for over two seconds should have been front-page news. The same is true, moreover, of the various other things I have reported—NIST's fabrications; NIST's omission and distortion of testimonial evidence; NIST's omissions of physical evidence, such as the Swiss cheese steel and the particles showing that iron and molybdenum had been melted; and the later discovery of nanothermite particles in the WTC dust. Especially given the fact that the collapse of WTC 7 had been declared a mystery from the outset, the world should have been waiting with bated breath for every new clue as to why this forty-seven-story building had collapsed. Upon hearing WTC 7 mentioned, nobody in the world with access to CNN should have replied, "Building what?" How do we explain the fact that five and even nine years after the mysterious collapse of this building, ignorance about it was and is still widespread?

To begin answering this question, let us return to James Glanz's statement that the collapse of WTC 7 was "a mystery that under normal circumstances would probably have captured the attention of the city and the world."[68] As I stated before, the abnormality seems to have been such that the fact of this building's collapse, and especially videos of this collapse, were deliberately suppressed. What was this abnormality?

SCADS

A symposium in the February 2010 issue of *American Behavioral Scientist*, one of the leading social science journals, argues that social scientists need to develop a scientific approach to studying an increasingly important type of criminality: state crimes against democracy, abbreviated SCADs,[69] understood as "concerted actions . . . by government insiders intended to manipulate democratic processes and undermine popular sovereignty." Having the "potential to subvert political institutions and entire governments . . . [SCADs] are high crimes that attack democracy itself."[70]

Distinguishing between SCADs that have been officially proven, such as "the Watergate break-ins and cover-up . . . , the secret wars in Laos and Cambodia . . . , the illegal arms sales and covert operations in Iran-Contra . . . , and the effort to discredit Joseph Wilson by revealing his wife's status as an intelligence agent," on the one hand, and suspected SCADs for which there is good evidence, on the other, the symposium authors include in the latter category "the fabricated attacks on US ships in the Gulf of Tonkin in 1964 . . . , the 'October Surprises' in the presidential elections of 1968 . . . and 1980 . . . , the assassinations of John Kennedy and Robert Kennedy . . . , the election breakdowns in 2000 and 2004 . . . , the numerous defense failures on September 11, 2001 . . . , and the misrepresentation of intelligence to justify the invasion and occupation of Iraq."[71]

Moreover, above and beyond regarding the 9/11 attacks as one of the suspected SCADs for which there is good evidence, this symposium treats it as its primary example. The abstract for the introductory essay begins by asserting: "The ellipses of due diligence riddling the official account of the 9/11 incidents continue being ignored by scholars of policy and public administration."[72] The symposium's final essay, criticizing the majority of the academic world for its "blithe dismissal of more than one law of thermodynamics," which are violated by the official theory of the World Trade Center collapse, also criticizes the academy for its failure to protest when "Professor Steven Jones found himself forced out of tenured position for merely reminding the world that physical laws, about which *there is no dissent whatsoever*, contradict the official theory of the World Trade Center Towers' collapse."[73]

HIDING THE MOST OBVIOUS EVIDENCE THAT 9/11 WAS A SCAD

If 9/11 was a SCAD, then we would understand the full extent to which the destruction of the World Trade Center occurred under abnormal circumstances, and we would thereby be in position to understand why the collapse of WTC 7, which "under normal circumstances would probably have captured the attention of the city and the world," did not do so.

It was not allowed to become well known, for reasons mentioned earlier. Unlike the twin towers, it was not hit by a plane; because of this, there was no jet fuel to spread big fires to many floors; and its collapse, unlike that of each of the twin towers, looked exactly like a classic implosion, in which the collapse begins from the bottom and the building folds in upon itself, ending up almost entirely in its own footprint. That WTC 7 was brought down by explosives was, therefore, much more obvious.

This greater likelihood is illustrated not only by Danny Jowenko's response to seeing WTC 7 collapse, but also by the many engineers and scientists who joined the 9/11 Truth Movement only after viewing the footage. For example, Daniel Hofnung, an engineer in Paris, wrote:

In the years after the 9/11 events, I thought that all I read in professional reviews and French newspapers was true. The first time I understood that it was impossible was when I saw a film about the collapse of WTC 7.[74]

Likewise, civil engineer Chester Gearhart wrote:

I have watched the construction of many large buildings and also have personally witnessed 5 controlled demolitions in Kansas City. When I saw the towers fall on 9/11, I knew something was wrong and my first instinct was that it was impossible. When I saw building 7 fall, I *knew* it was a controlled demolition.[75]

The video was decisive even for University of Copenhagen chemist Niels Harrit, who later became the first author of the nanothermite paper. When asked how he became involved with these issues, he replied:

It all started when I saw the collapse of Building 7, the third skyscraper. It collapsed seven hours after the Twin Towers. And there were only two airplanes. When you see a 47-story building, 186 meters tall, collapse in 6.5 seconds, and you are a scientist, you think, "What?" I had to watch it again . . . and again. I hit the button ten times, and my jaw dropped lower and lower. Firstly, I had never heard of that building before. And there was no visible reason why it should collapse in that way, straight down, in 6.5 seconds. I have had no rest since that day.[76]

Given these reactions, it is obvious why, if 9/11 was a state crime against democracy, the fact of WTC 7's collapse and especially the video of this collapse had to be suppressed as much as possible.

WTC 7 AS A DUD

Having made this point, I need to respond to an obvious objection: If those who were responsible for bringing down Building 7 were going to need to suppress the video of its collapse, why did they wait until late in the afternoon to bring it down, when the air was clean and cameras would be trained on this building, with the consequence that we have perfectly clear videos of the collapse of this building from various angles, each one showing its straight-down free-fall descent? Why did they not bring it down in the morning, shortly after one of the twin towers had collapsed, when the resulting dust cloud would have made any images impossible? After the collapse of the North Tower at 10:28 AM, for example, visibility did not return sufficiently for film crews to come back to the area, NIST reported, until 11:00 AM.[77] Had WTC 7 been imploded at, say, 10:45 AM, we would not have these videos clearly showing it coming straight down in free fall.

There are many reasons, as I showed in an appendix to *The Mysterious Collapse of World Trade Center 7*, to believe that this had indeed been the plan, but that this building was, as one researcher put it, "a dud"[78]— meaning that "the demolition system in WTC 7 simply did not respond as intended and the building defiantly remained intact."[79] As a result, agents had to be sent into the building to set fires, so that the cover story that fires had brought the building down would be plausible—a hypothesis that would explain why, although the fires in WTC 7 were supposedly started by flaming debris from the North Tower's collapse at 10:28 AM, no flames were visible in this building, NIST admits, until after noon.[80]

In any case, had the demolition system worked as intended, WTC 7's collapse would still have been mysterious, but there would have been no videos showing that it had come straight down and, for over two seconds, in absolute free fall.

I have emphasized this likelihood—that the destruction of WTC 7 was a botched operation—because if true it provides the clearest possible illustration of the theme of this essay, namely, that SCADs can be hidden in plain sight. There are literally dozens of contradictions in the official account of 9/11 that demonstrate that it could have been an inside job. But the clearest proof of this is provided by the video of this enormous building coming straight down in absolute free fall. And yet even though such proof has existed in plain sight for all these years, this state crime against democracy has remained a hidden fact, at least in the sense that it is not part of the public conversation. If the destruction of WTC 7 was a botched operation, then the cover-up of 9/11 as a SCAD is even more impressive. How has this concealment been achieved?

HIDING SCADS: THE ROLE OF THE MAINSTREAM MEDIA

Peter Dale Scott, discussing the erosion of the US constitution in recent times, suggests that "this erosion has been achieved in part through a series of important deep events in [post-World-War-II] American history—events aspects of which . . . will be ignored or suppressed in the mainstream media."[81] Indeed, Scott adds:

> [T]he mainstream US media . . . have become so implicated in past protective lies . . . that they, as well as the government, have now a demonstrated interest in preventing the truth about *any* of these events from coming out. This means that the current threat to constitutional rights does not derive from the deep state alone. . . . [T]he problem is a global dominance *mindset* that prevails not only inside the Washington Beltway but also in the mainstream media . . . , one which has come to accept recent inroads on constitutional liberties, and stigmatizes, or at least responds with silence to, those who are alarmed by them. . . . [A]cceptance of this mindset's notions of decorum has increasingly become a condition for participation in mainstream public life.[82]

Referring to events such as the JFK assassination, the Tonkin Gulf hoax, and 9/11, by "deep events" Scott means the same types of events called SCADs by the authors of the symposium on that topic. Indeed, one of those authors explicitly cites Scott's writings, treating his "deep events" as examples of SCADs and quoting his statements about the complicity of the mainstream media in covering up the truth about these events.[83]

Authors at the symposium also make the same point themselves, remarking that "the US government's account of 9/11 [is] parroted by the mainstream media"[84] and commenting on "the profound disavowal of still burning, molten questions originating at 9/11 Ground Zero gone begging by the American media."[85]

In addition to repeating the government's account of 9/11 and stigmatizing those who provide alternative accounts with the discrediting label of "conspiracy theorist," how has America's mainstream media kept the truth about WTC 7 hidden from the majority of the American people? Through various means:

First, by never replaying the statements by Dan Rather and other reporters about how the collapse of WTC 7 looked just like a controlled demolition.

Second, by seldom if ever replaying the video of this building's collapse.

Third, by never mentioning credible critiques of the official account. For example, *The Mysterious Collapse of World Trade Center 7*, which has been endorsed by prestigious scientists and engineers, has never been reviewed in the mainstream media, even though my previous 9/11 book, *The New Pearl Harbor Revisited*, was a *Publishers Weekly* "Web pick of the week" in 2008.[86]

Fourth, by never mentioning, except for one story that apparently slipped through,[87] the existence of an organization called Architects and Engineers for 9/11, which by now has over 1200 licensed and/or degreed members calling for a new investigation of WTC 7 as well as the twin towers.

Fifth, by never reporting scientific evidence contradicting the official account of the World Trade Center collapses, such as the reported discovery of nanothermite in the WTC dust.

Sixth, by overlooking the fact that NIST's report on WTC 7 omitted an enormous amount of evidence showing that explosives must have been used. For example, after calling the piece of Swiss cheese steel recovered from this building "the deepest mystery uncovered in the investigation," the *New York Times* did not issue a peep when NIST's report on WTC 7 failed to mention it, and even claimed that no steel from the building had been recovered.

Seventh, by reporting NIST's August press briefing announcing the

Draft for Public Comment, in which S. Shyam Sunder announced with great bravado that the "the reason for the collapse of World Trade Center 7 is no longer a mystery" and that "science is really behind what we have said," but then *not* reporting NIST's final report in November, in which it almost explicitly admitted that science *contradicts* its theory of WTC 7's collapse.

CONCLUSION AND PROPOSAL

Through these and related means, the truth about the collapse of WTC 7 has been effectively hidden, even though it has existed in plain sight for all these years. Even the bare fact of the collapse itself has been so effectively hidden that in 2006 over 40 percent of the American public did not know that it had occurred, and in 2009 a New York City judge, upon hearing its name, could ask: "Building what?"

I offer this essay as a case study in the power of those behind SCADs or "deep events" to hide things that exist in plain sight, because if they can hide the straight-down free-fall collapse of a forty-seven-story building captured on video in broad daylight, they can hide almost anything.

I say this, however, not to instill despair, but to point to the seriousness of the problem, and also to pave the way for making a proposal. Recognizing the high correlation between those who know about the collapse of WTC 7 and those who believe that a new—or rather *real*—9/11 investigation is needed, I propose that the 9/11 Truth Movement initiate, starting this September, a worldwide, year-long "Building What?" campaign. Through this campaign, we would seek to make as many people in the world as possible aware of the collapse of World Trade Center 7 by the tenth anniversary of 9/11. May it never again be known as "Building What?"

DAVID RAY GRIFFIN is emeritus professor of philosophy of religion and theology at Claremont School of Theology and Claremont Graduate University in Claremont, California, where he remains a co-director of the Center for Process Studies, which is oriented around the science-based philosophy of Alfred North Whitehead. In addition to co-editing the corrected edition of Whitehead's major work, *Process and Reality*, he has published thirty-six other books. Most of these are on philosophy, philosophy of science, philosophy of religion, and theology, but ten of them are about 9/11 and its effects. One of these, *Debunking 9/11 Debunking: An Answer to Popular Mechanics and Other Defenders of the Offi-*

cial Conspiracy Theory, was awarded a Bronze Medal in the 2008 Independent Publisher Book Awards. Another, *The New Pearl Harbor Revisited: 9/11, the Cover-Up, and the Exposé*, was named "Pick of the Week" by *Publishers Weekly* in November 2008. His most recent books are *The Mysterious Collapse of World Trade Center 7: Why the Final Official Report about 9/11 is Unscientific and False* (2009) and *Cognitive Infiltration: An Obama Appointee's Plan to Undermine the 9/11 Conspiracy Theory* (2010).

Notes

1. David Ray Griffin, *The Mysterious Collapse of World Trade Center 7: Why the Final Official Report about 9/11 Is Unscientific and False* (Northampton, MA: Olive Branch [Interlink Books], 2009).
2. Lynn Margulis, "Two Hit, Three Down—The Biggest Lie," *Rock Creek Free Press*, January 24, 2010, http://rockcreekfreepress.tumblr.com/post/353434420/two-hit-three-down-the-biggest-lie.
3. James Glanz, "Engineers Have a Culprit in the Strange Collapse of 7 World Trade Center: Diesel Fuel," *New York Times*, November 29, 2001, http://www.nytimes.com/2001/11/29/nyregion/nation-challenged-site-engineers-have-culprit-strange-collapse-7-world-trade.html.
4. "Dan Rather says that WTC Collapses Look Like Demolitions," YouTube.com, March 3, 2007, http://www.youtube.com/watch?v=Nvx904dAw00.
5. *911 Eyewitness*, http://video.google.com/videoplay?docid=65460757734339444, 28:25.
6. "Danny Jowenko on WTC 7 Controlled Demolition," YouTube.com, June 3, 2007, http://www.youtube.com/watch?v=877gr6xtQIc; for more of the interview, see "Jowenko WTC 7 Demolition Interviews," YouTube.com, September 24, 2006, http://www.youtube.com/watch?v=k3DRhwRNo6I&feature=related.
7. "Michael Hess, WTC7 Explosion Witness," YouTube.com, September 19, 2008, http://www.youtube.com/watch?v=BUfiLbXMa64. Hess should have said "down to the sixth floor." As Barry Jennings later clarified, the explosion that blocked their descent occurred when they reached the sixth floor, after which they walked back up to the eighth floor, where they waited to be rescued; see "Barry Jennings—9/11 WTC7 Full Uncut Interview—1 of 2," YouTube.com, http://www.youtube.com/watch?v=VQY-ksiuwKU, 2:00–2:02 and 5:56–6:18; and "Barry Jennings—9/11 WTC7 Full Uncut Interview—2 of 2," YouTube.com, July 10, 2008, http://www.youtube.com/watch?v=kxUj6UgPODo, 5:08–5:33.
8. "Barry Jennings—9/11 Early Afternoon ABC 7 Interview," YouTube.com, July 10, 2008, http://www.youtube.com/watch?v=5LO5V2CJpzI.
9. "Barry Jennings—9/11 WTC7 Full Uncut Interview," Part 1, 3:57-4:05.
10. Quoted in Chris Bull and Sam Erman, eds., *At Ground Zero: Young Reporters Who Were There Tell Their Stories* (New York: Thunder's Mouth Press, 2002), 97.
11. Bartmer's statement is quoted in Paul Joseph Watson, "NYPD Officer Heard Building 7 Bombs," *PrisonPlanet.com*, February 10, 2007, http://www.prisonplanet.com/articles/february2007/100207hcardbombs.htm).
12. This unnamed medical student can be seen making this statement in *911 Eyewitness*, 31:30.
13. James Glanz and Eric Lipton, "A Search for Clues in Towers' Collapse; Engineers Volunteer to Examine Steel Debris Taken to Scrapyards," *New York Times*, February 2, 2002, http://query.nytimes.com/gst/fullpage.html?res=9C04E0DE153DF931A35751C0A9649C8B63.
14. Ibid.

15. Joan Killough-Miller, "The 'Deep Mystery' of Melted Steel," *WPI Transformations* (Spring 2002), http://www.wpi.edu/News/Transformations/2002Spring/steel.html.

16. James Glanz, "Engineers Suspect Diesel Fuel in Collapse of 7 World Trade Center," *New York Times*, November 29, 2001, http://www.nytimes.com/2001/11/29/nyregion/29TOWE.html. I have here quoted Glanz's paraphrase of Barnett's statement.

17. Kenneth Change, "Scarred Steel Holds Clues, And Remedies," *New York Times*, October 2, 2001, http://query.nytimes.com/gst/fullpage.html?res=9B05E6DC123DF931A35753C1A9 679C8B63.

18. WebElements: The Periodic Table on the Web, "Iron," http://www.webelements.com/ iron/physics.html.

19. Ibid.

20. FEMA, "Probable Collapse Sequence," *World Trade Center Building Performance Study*, 31, http://www.fema.gov/pdf/library/fema403_ch5.pdf.

21. Zogby International, "A Word about Our Poll of American Thinking Toward the 9/11 Terrorist Attacks," May 24, 2006, http://www.zogby.com/features/features.dbm?ID=231.

22. In the ensuing exchange, Judge Lehner showed that he was not completely unaware of this building's destruction, asking if it was "the one that has been rebuilt." Shortly thereafter, however, the judge confused this building with the twin towers. See "Proceedings, Christopher Burke et al, Petitioners. vs. Michael McSweeney as City Clerk of New York and Clerk of the City Council of New York and the Board of Elections in the City of New York, before Honorable Edward H. Lehner, J. S. C., Supreme Court of the State of New York, September 29, 2009," 16–19.

23. Glanz, "Engineers Have a Culprit in the Strange Collapse of 7 World Trade Center: Diesel Fuel."

24. National Construction Safety Team Advisory Committee, "2003 Report to Congress of the National Construction Safety Team Advisory Committee," http://wtc.nist.gov/ media/NCSTAC2003ReporttoCongressFinal.pdf, 4.

25. National Institute of Standards and Technology (NIST), "Answers to Frequently Asked Questions," August 30, 2006, http://wtc.nist.gov/pubs/factsheets/faqs_8_2006.htm, Question 14.

26. NIST, "WTC Investigation Overview," December 18, 2007, http://wtc.nist.gov/media/ NCSTAC_December18(Sunder).pdf.

27. See "WTC 7: The Smoking Gun of 9/11," YouTube.com, September 26, 2007, http://www.youtube.com/watch?v=MwSc7NPn8Ok; and Paul Joseph Watson, "BBC's 9/11 Yellow Journalism Backfires: Building 7 Becomes the Achilles Heel of the Official Conspiracy Theory," *PrisonPlanet.com*, March 5, 2007, http://infowars.wordpress .com/2007/03/05/bbcs-911-yellow-journalism-backfires.

28. NIST, "Progress Report on the NIST Building and Fire Investigation into the World Trade Center Disaster," December 9, 2002, http://www.fire.nist.gov/bfrlpubs/ build03/PDF/b03040.pdf; NIST, "Progress Report on the Federal Building and Fire Safety Investigation of the World Trade Center Disaster," May 2003, http://wtc.nist.gov/pubs/MediaUpdate%20_FINAL_ProgressReport051303.pdf.

29. NIST, "Interim Report on WTC 7," June 2004, http://wtc.nist.gov/progress_report _june04/appendixl.pdf.

30. NIST, "WTC 7 Collapse," April 5, 2005, http://wtc.nist.gov/pubs/WTC%20Part%20 IIC%20-%20WTC%207%20Collapse%20Final.pdf.

31. NIST, "Answers to Frequently Asked Questions," Question 14.

32. S. Shyam Sunder, "Opening Statement," NIST Press Briefing: Report on the Collapse of World Trade Center Building 7, August 21, 2008, http://wtc.nist.gov/media/opening_remarks_082108.html.

33. *USA Today*, "Report: Fire, Not Bombs, Leveled WTC 7 Building," August 21, 2008, http://www.usatoday.com/news/nation/2008-08-21-wtc-nist_N.htm.

34. Peggy Fischer, Office of Inspector General, National Science Foundation, "What is Research Misconduct?" in *New Research Misconduct Policies*, http://www.nsf.gov/oig/session.pdf. This document is undated, but internal evidence suggests that it was published in 2001.

35. NIST NCSTAR 1-9, *Structural Fire Response and Probable Collapse Sequence of World Trade Center Building 7*, vol. 1, Draft for Public Comment, November 2008, wtc.nist.gov/NCSTAR1/PDF/NCSTAR%201-9%20Vol%201.pdf, 324.

36. Jonathan Barnett, Ronald R. Biederman, and Richard D. Sisson Jr., "Appendix C: Limited Metallurgical Examination," *World Trade Center Building Performance Study*, Federal Emergency Management Agency (FEMA), May 2002, 13, http://wtc.nist.gov/media/AppendixC-fema403_apc.pdf.

37. House Science Committee, *Hearing on "The Investigation of the World Trade Center Collapse,"* testimony of Dr. Arden L Bement Jr., Director of NIST, May 1, 2002, http://911research.wtc7.net/cache/wtc/official/nist/bement.htm. In the quoted statement, the name "FEMA" replaces "BPAT," which is the abbreviation for "Building Performance Assessment Team," the name of the American Society of Civil Engineers (ASCE) team that prepared this report for FEMA.

38. NIST, "Questions and Answers about the NIST WTC 7 Investigation," April 21, 2009, http://www.nist.gov/public_affairs/factsheet/wtc_qa_082108.cfm.

39. RJ Lee Group, "Expert Report: WTC Dust Signature," May 2004, 11, http://www.nyenvirolaw.org/WTC/130%20Liberty%20Street/Mike%20Davis%20LMDC%20130%20Liberty%20Documents/Signature%20of%20WTC%20dust/WTCDustSignature_ExpertReport.051304.1646.mp.pdf.

40. RJ Lee Group, "WTC Dust Signature Report: Composition and Morphology," December 2003, 17, http://www.nyenvirolaw.org/WTC/130%20Liberty%20Street/Mike%20Davis%20LMDC%20130%20Liberty%20Documents/Signature%20of%20WTC%20dust/WTC%20Dust%20Signature.Composition%20and%20Morphology.Final.pdf. This earlier (2003) version of the RJ Lee Group report contained much more information about melted iron than the 2004 version. For discussion, see Griffin, *The Mysterious Collapse*, 40–42.

41. Steven E. Jones et al., "Extremely High Temperatures during the World Trade Center Destruction," *Journal of 9/11 Studies* (January 2008): 8, http://journalof911studies.com/articles/WTCHighTemp2.pdf.

42. Ibid., 4–5.

43. WebElements: The Periodic Table on the Web, http://www.webelements.com/molybdenum/physics.html.

44. Jones et al., "Extremely High Temperatures," 4.

45. Niels H. Harrit et al., "Active Thermitic Material Observed in Dust from the 9/11 World Trade Center Catastrophe," *The Open Chemical Physics Journal*, 2 (2009): 7–31, http://www.bentham.org/open/tocpj/openaccess2.htm.

46. According to the *Guide for Fire and Explosion Investigations*, put out by the National Fire Protection Association, investigators should, in seeking to determine the cause of a fire, look for evidence of *accelerants*, which are any substances that could be used to ignite a fire or accelerate its progress (National Fire Protection Association [NFPA], *NFPA 921: Guide for Fire and Explosion Investigations*, 1998 ed., section 12-2.4, http://www.interfire.org/res_file/92112m.asp), and thermite mixtures are explicitly classified as accelerants (*NFPA 921*, section 19-2.4).

47. NIST, "Answers to Frequently Asked Questions," Question 12.

48. Jennifer Abel, "Theories of 9/11," *Hartford Advocate*, January 29, 2008, http://www.ae911truth.org/press/23.

49. Fischer, "What is Research Misconduct?"

50. See Griffin, *The Mysterious Collapse*, 150–55.

51. NIST NCSTAR 1-9, *Structural Fire Response*, vol. 1, 346.

52. NIST NCSTAR 1-9, *Structural Fire Response and Probable Collapse Sequence of World Trade Center Building 7*, vol. 2, Draft for Public Comment, November 2008, 462, http://wtc.nist.gov/NCSTAR1/PDF/NCSTAR%201-9%20Vol%202.pdf.

53. See NIST, "Interim Report on WTC 7," section L.6.7, and Griffin, *The Mysterious Collapse*, 212–15.

54. NIST, "Interim Report on WTC 7," section L.26. This contradiction is pointed out in a video, "NIST Report on WTC7 Debunked and Exposed!" YouTube, http://www.youtube.com/watch?v=qFpbZ-aLDLY, 0:45–1:57.

55. NIST NCSTAR 1-9, *Structural Fire Response*, vol. 2, 384.

56. This cartoon can be seen on the Internet at http://www.sciencecartoonsplus.com/pages/gallery.php.

57. NIST NCSTAR 1-9, *Structural Fire Response*, vol. 2, 595–96.

58. NIST, "WTC 7 Technical Briefing," August 26, 2008. NIST has evidently removed this video and the accompanying transcript from the Internet. However, the transcript, entitled "NIST Technical Briefing on Its Final Draft Report on WTC 7 for Public Comment," can be read at David Chandler's Web site, http://911speakout.org/NIST_Tech_Briefing_Transcript.pdf.

59. Ibid.

60. David Chandler, "WTC7 in Freefall: No Longer Controversial," YouTube.com, February 12, 2010, http://www.youtube.com/watch?v=rVCDpL4Ax7I, 2:45.

61. NIST NCSTAR 1-9, *Structural Fire Response*, vol. 2, 607.

62. Chandler, "WTC7 in Freefall: No Longer Controversial," at 3:27.

63. NIST, "Questions and Answers about the NIST WTC 7 Investigation."

64. NIST NCSTAR 1-9, *Structural Fire Response*, vol. 2, 595–96, 596, 610.

65. See David Ray Griffin, *The New Pearl Harbor Revisited: 9/11, the Cover-Up, and the Exposé* (Northampton, MA: Olive Branch, 2008), 30–31.

66. ImplosionWorld.com, "The Myth of 'Implosion,'" *Did You Know?* http://www.implosionworld.com/dyk2.html.

67. As to how *domestic* terrorists could have gotten access, if we are aware that Larry Silverstein, who owned WTC 7 and had recently taken out a lease on the rest of the World Trade Center, stood to make several billion dollars if it was destroyed in a terrorist attack, and that a brother and cousin of George W. Bush were principals of a company that handled security for the World Trade Center, we might arrive at a possible answer; see David Ray Griffin, *Debunking 9/11 Debunking: An Answer to Popular Mechanics and Other Defenders of the Official Conspiracy Theory* (Northampton, MA: Olive Branch, 2007), 111.

68. Glanz, "Engineers Have a Culprit in the Strange Collapse of 7 World Trade Center."

69. Symposium on State Crimes Against Democracy, special issue, *American Behavioral Scientist* 53 (February 2010): 783–939, http://abs.sagepub.com/content/vol53/issue6.

70. Lance deHaven-Smith, "Beyond Conspiracy Theory: Patterns of High Crime in American Government," *American Behavioral Scientist* 53 (February 2010): 796, http://abs.sagepub.com/content/vol53/issue6.

71. Ibid., 797.

72. Ibid., 783.

73. Matthew T. Witt, "Pretending Not to See or Hear, Refusing to Signify: The Farce and Tragedy of Geocentric Public Affairs Scholarship," *American Behavioral Scientist* 53 (Feb-

ruary 2010): 935, http://abs.sagepub.com/content/vol53/issue6 (emphasis in original). Steven Jones was the physicist who, with a group of scientists, published the RJ Lee Group and the US Geological Survey findings that iron and molybdenum, respectively, had melted in the World Trade Center building collapses.

74. Daniel Hofnung, "Statement in Support of Architects and Engineers Petition," in *Engineers and Architects Question the 9/11 Commission Report*, PatriotsQuestion9/11.com, http://patriotsquestion911.com/engineers.html#Dhofnung.

75. Chester W. Gearhart, "Statement in Support of Architects and Engineers Petition," in *Engineers and Architects Question the 9/11 Commission Report*, PatriotsQuestion9/11.com, http://patriotsquestion911.com/engineers.html#Gearhart.

76. "Danish Scientist Niels Harrit, on Nanothermite in the WTC Dust (English subtitles)," YouTube, April 10, 2009, http://www.youtube.com/watch?v=8_tf25lx_30.

77. NIST NCSTAR 1A, *Final Report on the Collapse of World Trade Center Building 7*, November 2008, 51, http://wtc.nist.gov/NCSTAR1/PDF/NCSTAR%201A.pdf; NIST NCSTAR 1-9, *Structural Fire Response*, vol. 1, 119.

78. Jeremy Baker, "Was WTC 7 a Dud?" *Serendipity.com*, 2005, http://www.serendipity.li/wot/wtc7_dud.htm.

79. Jeremy Baker, "Last Building Standing," *Serendipity.com*, 2007, http://www.serendipity.li/wot/last_building_standing.pdf. This is a revised and updated version of Baker, "Was WTC 7 a Dud?"

80. NIST NCSTAR 1-9, *Structural Fire Response*, vol. 1, 194.

81. Peter Dale Scott, "9/11, Deep State Violence and the Hope of Internet Politics," *GlobalResearch.ca*, June 11, 2008, http://www.globalresearch.ca/index.php?context=va&aid=9289.

82. Ibid.

83. Laurie A. Manwell, "In Denial of Democracy: Social Psychological Implications for Public Discourse on State Crimes Against Democracy Post-9/11," *American Behavioral Scientist* 53 (February 2010): 867–70, http://abs.sagepub.com/content/vol53/issue6.

84. Ibid., 863.

85. Matthew T. Witt and Alexander Kouzmin, "Sense Making Under 'Holographic' Conditions: Framing SCAD Research," *American Behavioral Scientist* 53 (February 2010): 789, http://abs.sagepub.com/content/vol53/issue6.

86. "Web Pick of the Week," *Publishers Weekly*, November 24, 2008, http://www.publishersweekly.com/pw/by-topic/1-legacy/15-web-exclusive-book-reviews/article/6017-web-exclusive-reviews-week-of-11-24-2008-.html.

87. Jennifer Harper, "Explosive News," *Washington Times*, February 22, 2010, http://www.washingtontimes.com/news/2010/feb/22/inside-the-beltway-70128635/?feat=home_columns.

CHAPTER 8

Invisible Victims
US Corporate Media Censorship of Israeli International Law Violations in Palestine

by Nora Barrows-Friedman

> *We lock the doors. We lock the windows. We have nothing with which to protect our family and our neighbors from the soldiers or the settlers. If a Palestinian kidnapped and beat and jailed an Israeli child, the whole world would be up in arms about it. It would be all over the media. But the Israelis, they come into our communities with jeeps and tanks and bulldozers, they take our children and throw them into prison, and no one cares.*
> —FADEL MOHTASSEB, *father of two young boys who were arrested, detained, interrogated, imprisoned, and beaten by Israeli soldiers, March 2010, Hebron (West Bank)*[1]

The Mohtasseb family's story is one of countless censored and silenced testimonies that punctuate daily life under Israeli occupation—and that never make it to the front pages of the news. As a Palestinian father who watched his two sons, aged ten and twelve, suffer at the hands of Israeli soldiers, Fadel Mohtasseb asserts that there is an entrenched double standard in the Western media against the Palestinian experience under Israeli military occupation—an assertion that is neither emotional hyperbole nor a new phenomenon.

These types of stories have been omitted from the headlines within the American corporate establishment media structure for decades. Even as Palestine/Israel remains a heavily saturated news feature, there is a long-standing bias in the media favoring Israel's actions—a paradigm in which contextual and historical lenses have been removed. And as the pro-Israel lobbies in the United States work hard to keep the sanitized news slant in place; as they apply pressure to lawmakers and US administration officials to keep the yearly aid package of three billion to six billion dollars flowing uninterrupted to the Israeli government; and as they wantonly label critics of Israeli policy "anti-Semites" in absurd attempts to crush debate, the work of independent journalists is critically important in documenting the real human impact of Israeli policies on the ground.

Palestinian journalists, however, face more than just censorship. Since 2000, according to the Committee to Protect Journalists, ten Palestinian reporters (and two foreign reporters) have been killed by the Israeli military. And on a regular basis, local Palestinian journalists are assaulted, harassed, arrested, or beaten by Israeli forces when covering the story from their own backyards.[2]

Whether it's the message or the messenger, the attacks on the truth about Palestine continue unabated, either by brute military force or by simple elimination of proportionate sources and context within the American corporate media.

What's happening to Palestinians is deeply biased. Israel, with the fourth-largest military in the world, weaponized and financed by the United States, is an illegal occupier and has—as I discuss later in this chapter—legalized racial and religious discrimination in favor of its Jewish population. Palestinians, however, are confined to desperate ghettos and broken treaties, forced to endure hundreds of checkpoints and the daily theft of land. They have no military, no economic or administrative sovereignty, and no United Nations veto power. But the corporate media establishment consistently and disproportionately favors the Israeli side of the story, relinquishing the mantra of "objectivity" in reporting—thus shifting the bias toward the side of the empowered oppressor.

Words and nuances are extremely powerful. We are told that the land Israel occupies is "disputed territory,"[3] as the *New York Times* calls it. Euphemistic terms become weapons to discredit legitimate circumstances—what the *Times* calls "disputed," Amnesty International and the United Nations rightly call "occupied." What's to dispute? When you look at the facts, and what historians and international legal bodies classify as legitimate terms, why do the *New York Times*, Fox News [sic], and even National Public Radio get it so wrong, even though it's nicely packaged and sounds informative?

Most journalists, faced with this entrenched Palestine/Israel formulaic slant, self-censor if they want to get their story published in a mainstream outlet. If one covers a story that exposes Palestinian experience under Israeli occupation, editors may worry that it could be viewed as "too political" (as though this was a dangerous act). This notion enforces the culture of censorship. Independent journalists are then pushed into the margins of alternative online, radio, and print media, for the most part preaching to a choir that is already informed and settled on their positions.

As Fadel Mohtasseb—and countless other Palestinians I've encountered in my years on the ground there—said, if mainstream Americans knew about what's really happening in Palestine/Israel, Israel's occupation and its apartheid regime would end. The incessant violence to which Palestinians are subjected would not exist with an informed and critical American public majority—especially when so much of our tax dollars support it.

The subchapters that follow reveal small glimpses of this daily life—stories culled from the refugee camps in the West Bank and Gaza, to villages inside the State of Israel itself, where Jim Crow–style segregation and discrimination run rampant against its Palestinian citizens. As corporate media continues to strangle the truth when it comes to Palestine/Israel, these types of stories become ammunition on the frontlines of the information war.

CHILDREN IN THE CROSSHAIRS

Acting within what Israeli historian Ilan Pappé says are parameters of a "genocide in slow-motion," fundamentalist Jewish settlers, the Israeli military, and Israeli police are working together to terrorize children—the most vulnerable segments of any society—in order to force entire communities into leaving.

From January through March 2010 alone, community leaders in the al-Bustan neighborhood of the village of Silwan in occupied East Jerusalem reported that thirty-three children—some as young as nine years old—had been arrested, detained, and interrogated by Israeli police. The mother of a ten-year-old boy whom I interviewed told me that after his arrest at four o'clock in the morning in early March, he had regular hallucinations of police and soldiers lurking outside of his bedroom window. The mother said that the children in her community try to lead normal lives, but the ongoing threats and intimidation by the police, the military, and the settlers have left a permanent psychological scar on the entire neighborhood.

Nearly half of all of Israel's home demolition orders are taking place inside the neighborhoods of occupied East Jerusalem, as Israeli police and the Jewish settler movements—Israelis, Americans, and Europeans empowered and protected by an Israeli administration intent on expanding the settlement colonies against international law—launch these daily attacks.

In the West Bank, inside areas such as Hebron, where settlement colonies are expanding within the city limits or in the "seam zone" areas up against the 1967 Green Line borders, not only are people losing their homes and livelihoods due to aggressive evictions and house demolitions, but children are also being subjected to extreme violence, imprisonment, and torture.

When the two young Mohtasseb brothers walked one day in late February 2010, from their modest flat in the old city of Hebron to their aunt's home, they had to cross a street that is heavily saturated with Israeli soldiers. Without provocation, for no reason other than their presence, the boys were grabbed by two soldiers, handcuffed, and thrown in the back of two separate jeeps. The jeeps took them to the nearby Kiryat Arba Jewish settlement colony, where there is a military detention center housed inside.

For approximately the next ten hours, both brothers were separately subjected to severe interrogation tactics meted out by border police and armed soldiers. In testimonies I gathered from each of the boys, they were handcuffed and blindfolded, forced to sit the entire time in chairs with barking dogs next to them, as Israeli forces told them they may not see their families ever again. Amir, the ten-year-old, asked if he could use the bathroom at one point and was refused. He was humiliated and terrified, and wet himself.

Meanwhile, their father, Fadel Mohtasseb, informed by eyewitness neighbors that his sons were abducted by soldiers, was made to wait outside the settlement colony until Israeli soldiers permitted him to enter the detention facility to recover Amir and Hasan. But only Amir was let go—Hasan, he was told, had already been transferred to Ofer, an adult prison near Ramallah.

In the week that followed their detention and Hasan's transfer to Ofer, the Mohtasseb family was distraught, outraged, and frustrated at their disempowerment. Fadel told me that the boys never threw stones at the military—there were no witnesses to corroborate this story of which the soldiers had accused the boys. His sons were, as he put it, in the wrong place at the wrong time—the wrong place being their own neighborhood where they had grown up; the wrong time being every waking moment a Palestinian child languishes under a severe military occupation.

Hasan would spend a week in Ofer before an Israeli military judge acknowledged that the court was breaking the state's own law in holding a child in an adult prison. But he didn't let Hasan off the hook completely: Hasan's release was on condition that he'd have to appear back in court at an arbitrary future date—for a crime he did not commit and was never formally charged with.

Amir, however, would suffer an even more egregious turn of events. Hours after the first interview I did with the family, four days after the brothers' arrests, and while Hasan was still in prison, Israeli soldiers from the same unit that had arrested and interrogated the boys invaded the family's home in the middle of the night. They broke down the front door, ransacked the apartment, beat Fadel and his wife, snatched Amir from his bed, and took him under the stairwell of the apartment building. They beat him with their rifles for fifteen minutes.

His parents—after being restrained and threatened with American-made M16 rifles pointed at their heads as they tried to protect their ten-year-old son—found Amir unconscious on the floor, bleeding from the nose and mouth.

Amir had internal bleeding in his abdomen, which necessitated a hospital stay. He wouldn't speak for a day and a half afterward, in extreme post-traumatic shock. His mother told me he'd need a lifetime of psychological care.

Today, approximately 350 children are languishing inside Israeli prisons and detention camps, enduring interrogation, torture, and indefinite sentences, sometimes without charge. The number fluctuates constantly, but several thousand Palestinian children between the ages of twelve and sixteen have moved through the Israeli military judicial system over the past decade since the outbreak of the second Palestinian intifada.

I spoke to Abed Jamal, a researcher at Defense for Children International's Palestine office in Hebron. He said that several international laws were being violated here, including the United Nations Convention on the Rights of the Child and Article 13 of Part II of the Fourth Geneva Convention.

Israel designates eighteen as the age of adulthood for its own citizens, but through a military order, and against international law, Israel mandates sixteen as the age of adulthood for Palestinians. Additionally, Israel has special military orders (#1644 and #132) to be able to arrest and judge Palestinian children—termed "juvenile delinquents"—as young as twelve years old. "This way, they have a 'legal' cover for what they are doing, even though this is against international laws," Jamal said. "However, in Amir's case, they broke even their own laws by arresting and detaining him as a ten-year-old boy. These laws are obviously changeable according to Israel's whim. We have yet to see a prosecution for crimes such as these."[4]

And, of course, we have yet to see the American corporate media take a modicum of interest in this issue. Imagine, as Fadel Mohtasseb urged Americans to do, if Amir and Hasan were young Jewish Israeli boys, arrested, detained, interrogated, imprisoned, and beaten by Palestinians. The world would be up in arms, and Fox News [sic] would give it nonstop coverage.

There is something seriously wrong with this equation.

GAZA DE-DEVELOPED AS BLOCKADE CONTINUES

Since the 2008–09 US-subsidized and US-armed Israeli attacks on Gaza, which killed nearly 1,400 Palestinians and wounded over 5,000 in a three-week bloodbath, Israel has continued to silently kill Palestinians within the parameters of a suffocating blockade. The state's campaign of deliberate privation of basic aid, goods, medicine, and rebuilding equipment has forced Gaza into a premeditated social and humanitarian catastrophe, and the corporate American media has censored the excruciating details.

Since the 2006 democratic elections that resulted in the Hamas party's victory, Israel has enforced measures of collective punishment against the 1.5 million Palestinians sealed inside the strip. In June 2007, the Israeli government slapped a draconian blockade against Gaza, restricting a multitude of essential items from reaching people inside. Israel's "banned-items list" remains in place three years later, with goods and products being added to and deleted from the list at arbitrary whim. "Sometimes, shampoo is allowed in," said Rami al-Meghari, a journalist in Gaza's Magazi refugee camp. "Sometimes, it's not. This week, almonds may make it inside. Next week, Israel could decide that they're not necessary."

Al-Meghari explained that even when Israel allows a select number of trucks into Gaza, garnering a modicum of media interest, many of the items inside the truckloads have already expired (if the contents are food or medicine); or have been damaged in storage during the three-year waiting period. "Recently, the Israelis approved a shipment of shoes to be allowed into Gaza," al-Meghari said. "But there are 8,000 other items that are waiting in 600 truckloads stuck on the border." He remarked that these technicalities are not even mentioned in the mainstream press—all they focus on, he said, are Israel's small token gestures. In Gaza, the real story remains untold.

Though those shoes and some clothes have made it into Gaza, jam, chocolate, books, musical instruments, ink, paper, canned fruit, rebuilding materials, medical equipment and life-saving medicines remain on the banned-items list. In a cynical move, the Israeli government casually admitted that it actually estimated the daily caloric need of Gazans, and disregarded the notion that the information could be used in "policy-making."[5] This statement was a troubling but relevant echo of then–Israeli Prime Minister Ehud Olmert's advisor, Dov Weisglass, who remarked in 2006 that "the idea is to put the Palestinians on a diet, but not to make them die of hunger," referring to Israel's merciless determination to force Palestinians in Gaza to turn against Hamas.

Nearly two years after the attacks, thousands of Palestinians are still living in tent camps, or are forced to live in homes halfway demolished from the unscrupulous bombings. Since housing materials—including cement, glass, rebar, and nails—have been denied entry into Gaza, Palestinians are building entire homes out of mud and materials scavenged from rubble, which is all-too omnipresent across the tiny strip of coastal land.

Hundreds of Palestinians, including infants, toddlers, and the elderly, have died—or, more to the point, have been killed—directly because of the blockade. Israel restricts not only the import of essential medicines needed for cancer, kidney problems, and diabetes treatment, but the state has also prevented the freedom of movement out of Gaza for patients seeing medical treatment in Egypt or elsewhere abroad. Children are dying from easily treatable illnesses due to the lack of medicine in Gazan hospitals and clinics. Gaza is, for all intents and purposes, an open-air prison; it is a testing ground for new weapons technology; it is an experiment in deliberate, calculated calamity.

In an interview with Inter Press Service in March 2010, Mahmoud Abu Rahma, a leading figure in the Palestinian human rights group Al Mezan in Gaza, explained the nature of Israel's policies of methodical humanitarian erosion in the strip. "What we see in Gaza," said Abu

Rahma, "is a continuous process of de-development. All the sectors are going backwards. The economy is in its worst situation ever. The environment is in a very bad shape because the sanitation system has not been rehabilitated for a long time. Pollution is leaking into the aquifer because of the kind of weapons that have been used. Poverty is increasing, so is unemployment. And the siege continues. So the situation is dramatically worse than it was last year."[6]

Israel's systematic stranglehold on the Gaza Strip, and the 2008–09 attacks that killed so many Palestinians, has caught the attention of millions of activists around the world—but the international community still fails to act. In 2009, the publication of the Goldstone report (authored by former South African Judge Richard Goldstone, a special investigator for the United Nations on the issue of what exactly happened in Gaza), drew widespread acclaim across Palestine and the Arab world, and—not surprisingly—searing condemnation from Israel and the United States. For Palestinians, the report was viewed as a corroborating documentation of their suffering through an international legal and human rights lens. However, as Israel and the US continue to pressure the United Nations and hold major veto power within the institution, the report has yet to impact policy and hold Israeli officials legally accountable.

Paragraph 75 of the Goldstone report asserts that the treatment of Palestinians in Gaza amounts to persecution. Again, Abu Rahma responded to the Goldstone report and its conclusions about the siege:

> Most people think that the siege of Gaza, the blockade, started in June 2007. But I would say that the blockade started in June 1967. The first Israeli military order after the Six-Day War announced that the Gaza Strip was a unit and the West Bank was another unit and that they were two closed military zones. No one was allowed to leave or to enter these zones without a special permit from the Israeli military authorities. Now, this has not changed. I came here, with a special permit from the Israeli authorities. So it still applies.
>
> It is true that in June 2007, Israel announced that Gaza was a hostile entity. They canceled what is known as the custom code, so no imports can go directly to Gaza. We don't exist anymore on the economic map. The siege has been stepped up since then and it is hitting the population very hard.

This paragraph [in the Goldstone report] took note of the consequences of the Israeli policy of siege and blockade on Gaza. It particularly found that there are a series of violations of economic, social, cultural and political rights that are very complex, that do not allow people to move freely but also not to access life-saving services or goods. This has created a very complex situation for the entire population. People who were hit by it were not allowed proper legal remedy in Israel. If a state has a policy and civilians are affected, there should be some kind of recourse for these people. But this has been denied as the Israeli high court has tended to take the side of the Israeli government. The report found that the massive human rights violations, together with the denial to civilians of any legal remedy, amount to persecution. Persecution is a war against humanity. Goldstone went even farther than that and said this could warrant forming a special tribunal to investigate this particular issue.

What is unfortunate is that most of the United Nations and human rights organizations have not focused on this, although the siege on Gaza is a very immediate priority.[7]

Professor and historian Norman Finkelstein pointed out in his 2010 book, *This Time We Went Too Far: Truth & Consequences of the Gaza Invasion*, that American corporate media has consistently and mistakenly referred to the Israeli massacres as a "war." Yet how can one categorize a bloodbath as a war? This was not a conflict between two militaries. Finkelstein said that not one US-made Israeli helicopter gunship, not one F-16 or F-15 fighter jet, was downed or damaged during the invasion. He mentioned that Palestinian-fired homemade rockets were Gaza's only means of defense against Israel's enormous, relentless, and high-tech assaults.

Israel besieged the Gaza Strip using weapons such as white phosphorus, which burned flesh to the bone, and dense inert metal explosive (DIME) shells—developed in conjunction with the US Air Force and Lawrence Livermore National Laboratory in the San Francisco Bay Area—to literally shred civilians to bits. Schools, mosques, hospitals, United Nations buildings, media offices, ambulances, and thousands of homes and apartment buildings were bombed by the Israeli military.

Of the thirteen Israeli deaths, ten were soldiers—five of them killed in friendly-fire incidents. Page after page of Israeli soldier testimonies following the massacres revealed that there were no fierce ground battles between soldiers and Palestinian guerrilla fighters. This was a genocidal act, according to the president of the United Nations General Assembly Miguel d'Escoto Brockmann. If we do the math, for every Israeli civilian killed, there were over 460 Palestinian deaths.

A war? Hardly. And those Palestinians in Gaza, nameless and faceless in the American corporate media, remain at Israel's interminable whim.

ETHNIC CLEANSING AND DISPLACEMENT INSIDE ISRAEL AGAINST PALESTINIAN/BEDOUIN COMMUNITIES

As home demolitions, racist policies, and discrimination within the occupied West Bank and East Jerusalem continue apace, corporate establishment media—in both the West and inside Israel—has been mute on similar violations happening within the State of Israel itself.

Since Israel was established in 1948, when 800,000 indigenous Palestinians were forced to flee—becoming refugees in their own land or in the larger diaspora—the indigenous minority that remained inside the state have been subjected to decades of subjugation, discrimination, and institutionalized racism. Israel's representatives effusively describe the state as a democracy for all of its citizens, yet if one peels back the layers just a tiny bit, an entirely different narrative becomes clear.

Israel's internal segregation policies, evoking disturbing echoes of the Jim Crow American South, are rarely revealed in the American corporate media. The indigenous communities pay taxes, speak Arabic and Hebrew, and are afforded the same civil rights as Jewish Israelis in theory, but exist as a subjugated second-class minority in practice as the state inflicts draconian policies usually thought to be confined to the occupied territories.

British journalist Jonathan Cook, who lives in Nazareth, has documented the silent war being waged on Israel's Palestinian citizens in exquisite detail. He wrote in March 2010 in the *National*:

> Israel has nationalized 93 per cent of the country's territory, confining most of its 1.3 million Arab citizens, one-fifth of the population, to 120 or so communities that existed at the time of the state's creation in 1948.

Meanwhile, more than 700 rural communities . . . have remained exclusively Jewish by requiring that anyone who wants to buy a home applies to local vetting committees, which have been used to weed out Arab applicants.[8]

Cook documented widespread institutionalized racism and apartheid practices within the Israeli educational system as well. In August 2009, he wrote in *CounterPunch*:

Instances of Arab children being denied places at Jewish kindergartens and junior schools have become more common in recent years, especially in the country's handful of mixed cities.

Yousef Jabareen, head of Dirasat, a Nazareth-based organization monitoring education issues, said when parents tried to switch their children to Jewish schools it was because of the poor conditions in Arab education institutions.

[Jabareen says,] "In Jewish schools Arab children are not taught their language, culture or history. Their Arab identity has to be sacrificed for them to receive a decent education."

A report published in March revealed that the government invested $1,100 in each Jewish pupil's education compared to $190 for each Arab pupil. . . .

There is also an official shortfall of more than 1,000 classrooms for Arab children, said Mr. Jabareen, though Arab organizations believe the problem is in reality much worse. In addition, a significant proportion of existing Arab school buildings have been judged unsafe or dangerous to children's health.[9]

Rawia abu Rabia—a Palestinian–Bedouin lawyer from Beer Saba' (Beersheba), a large city in the northern Naqab/Negev region—said that along with a lack of basic services in these "unrecognized villages," and regular home demolitions across the state, there exists a long-standing structure of legalized racism and discrimination against the indigenous communities of Israel. For example, abu Rabia pointed out, if a Palestinian citizen of Israel wanted to marry a Palestinian from the West Bank, the West Banker would be prohibited from attaining Israeli citizenship and they could not live together. Moreover, it would be virtually impossible for either of the two people to physically meet—Palestinians from the West Bank cannot cross into Israel; and it is illegal for Israeli citizens to enter the West Bank (except, of course, if one lives inside a settlement colony). It would be easier for them to be together in Paris than it would for them to be together in Jerusalem.

But if a Jewish person wanted to marry another Jewish person from anywhere in the world, they could both easily enjoy citizenship in Israel. Israel employs its "law of return" that guarantees immediate citizenship to any Jew, but the Palestinian right of return—the United Nations Resolution 194, mandated in 1947 and vetoed every year since by the US and Israel—to come back to the land from which they were expelled in 1948 and 1967 is being ignored and violated.

"Israel is a democracy for its Jewish citizens, but a Jewish state for its Palestinian citizens," abu Rabia said. "This is a discriminatory reality."

Along with educational and ethnic discrimination, Israel has implemented frequent home demolitions against indigenous communities in areas where Jewish housing is expanding. Abu Rabia reported that in 2009, 254 homes were demolished in "unrecognized villages" across the country.

A prime example: On April 13, 2010, in the Naqab/Negev Desert, Israeli police invaded the Bedouin village of al-Araqib, destroying three houses. At the same time, Israeli forces once again razed to the ground all tents, huts, and water collection containers in Twail abu Jarwal, in a move that a spokesperson for the Regional Council of Unrecognized Villages in the Negev said was the "fortieth time . . . in the last few years" that these homes and structures have been destroyed.

Abu Rabia said:

> The state of Israel and the officials ignore these people's existence. They are invisible citizens under the eyes of the law. As a result, the Bedouins are not entitled and are not afforded the same rights as the Jewish citizens. Land laws do not mention Bedouin communities. If people in these villages want to build houses, they are refused permits by the planning authorities to do so. Under this policy, they are deprived the basic human right of housing, and the state doesn't provide an alternative. This institutionalized discrimination is written into the law in order to criminalize the Bedouins and make them illegal.

As Bedouins in the Naqab/Negev Desert continue to fight to stay on their land, Palestinians in the more urban areas remain at the mercy of lengthy and tedious court rulings to keep their houses intact. I reported from the "unrecognized village" of Dhammash, near Tel Aviv, where thirteen home demolition orders were handed out by Israeli police to Palestinian homeowners—many who have lived there since before the State of Israel was established.

Dhammash community spokesman Arafat Ahmed Ismayil explained, "We don't have sewage systems or adequate electricity and water services. We've had to go to court several times to have the government provide our children with school buses."

Other community organizers said, while we walked through Dhammash village, that open agricultural land had been strategically destroyed and made barren by the Israeli authorities to implement a toxifying, open-air scrap metal processing center in the middle of the village. "That, now, is the only place where people can find a job in Dhammash," one of the organizers said.

Ismayil said that the local municipality wants the Dhammash land to build a Jewish-only condominium complex. "That's why they want us to leave as soon as possible," he explained.

He asserted that home demolition policies forced upon Palestinians inside Israel are exactly the same as those in the occupied West Bank, including East Jerusalem, and the Gaza Strip. "When they want to destroy a house, they impose a curfew, they close the area, and they bring hundreds of police and soldiers with dogs. Helicopters hover overhead. They bring busloads of Jewish extremist settlers with them to empty furniture from the houses, and arrest people who refuse to be evicted.

"We experience the same policies of apartheid here in Israel as those that are in effect in the occupied territories," Ismayil added. "People on the outside think that we're enjoying Israel's gift of democracy. But we're in the exact same situation. There is no peace, no democracy here."[10]

MASSIVE MILITARY STOCKPILING AGREEMENTS BETWEEN THE US AND ISRAEL CONTINUE UNDER THE OBAMA ADMINISTRATION

When it comes to Palestine (or Pakistan, or Afghanistan, or Iraq, for that matter), the Obama administration has continued the status quo–foreign policy positions of its predecessors. The Israel lobbies enjoy their

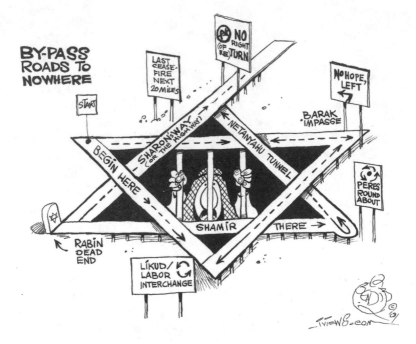

BY-PASS ROADS TO NOWHERE

START

LAST CEASE-FIRE NEXT 20 MILES

NO RIGHT (OF RE)TURN

NO HOPE LEFT?

BARAK IMPASSE

BEGIN HERE

SHARON'S WAY (OR THE HIGHWAY)

NETANYAHU TUNNEL

PERES' ROUND ABOUT

SHAMIR

THERE →

RABIN DEAD END

LIKUD/ LABOR INTERCHANGE

close alliances with US politicians and policy makers, and the money keeps flowing from our tax coffers to the Israeli government and its occupation military.

The American corporate media reports these types of stories in the financial or business sections of newspapers, stating the facts and values of these agreements, but fails to inform the public about the policies between both governments that impede international law and create human rights catastrophes on the ground.

A prime example came a year after the 2008–09 Gaza massacres, when Israel and the United States agreed to a weapons stockpiling deal to store $800 million worth of US-made arms and military equipment on Israeli soil.

Reported early on by Israeli liberal newspaper *Haaretz*, Israelis discussed the steadfast policies toward their country by the new American administration, but in the US, this specific story was buried in mainstream American sources.

In January 2010, I reported on the details of this agreement in *Truthout*, an important online independent news service. According to a January 11, 2010, report in the weekly paper *Defense News*, the Obama administration previously mapped out a plan that would place $400 million worth of military arsenal in Israel, but that project was exactly doubled after a meeting in December 2009 between the Israeli military's technology and logistics branch, and Rear Adm. Andy Brown, director of logistics for the US Army European Command.

Included in this agreement is the caveat that Israel, after approval from the US government, would be able to access the American weapons and ammunitions stockpile in case of a military "emergency." The terms and definition of such an "emergency," including against whom the weaponry could be used, remain unclear. Barbara Opall-Rome reported that "wartime emergencies warranting Israeli use of such weaponry typically require Israel to reimburse Washington under foreign military sales procedures," though conveniently for Israel, "reimbursement costs are funded through annual US military grant aid to Israel."[11]

During the election campaign and over this last year in office, the Obama administration has repeatedly demonstrated its commitment to what it calls "Israel's security."

An anonymous US defense official stated that Washington believes that "[American] economics and inflation were taking their toll on the Israel-based prepositioning," thereby limiting—in relative terms—the procurement of weapons caches by the Israeli government, up until this point.

Missiles, armored vehicles, aerial ammunition, and artillery ordnance have already been stockpiled in Israel since the US Congress began expanding their "forward basing" program in 1990.

Opall-Rome wrote that American stockpile value in Israel began with "a starting ceiling of $100 million that quickly grew to $300 million following the 1991 war in Iraq. . . . Under the new agreement, Israel not only gains access to more US stockpiles, but enjoys greater latitude in the categories and specific types of weaponry it can request for in-country storage."

I interviewed Ohio Democratic Congressman Dennis Kucinich, who said that there is no oversight process for which specific weapons will be part of stockpiling deals with Israel. He noted that these weapons stockpiling agreements send a worrisome message to the people in the region. "What's troubling is the pullback from serious diplomatic initiatives. . . . and the reliance on weapons to solve what are really diplomatic issues. There's no doubt that there is some strategic consideration at work. And there is the fact that several US administrations now have failed to enforce the Arms Export Control Act. The policies are not consonant with peace," he continued. "They're consonant with war."

Frida Berrigan, of the US Arms Trade Resource Center at the World Policy Institute in New York, noted that the US State Department originally raised questions about Israel's use of cluster bomb munitions during the 2006 Lebanon assault. Berrigan pointed out that the State Department said it was concerned about the amount of bomblets that were dropped. "But after a year of its own investigation," Berrigan said, "the results were officially 'inconclusive.' A report was forwarded to the US Congress, and that's where it ended. If Israel uses these [US-made] weapons, it is defined under 'defense' as far as Congress is concerned. Because under the Arms Export Controls Act, there are no set terms of activities, no definition of what 'defense' really means."

Berrigan said that, although Congress routinely questions other weapons packages to allied countries, military aid to Israel is rarely, if ever, challenged. "There is a fast-track mechanism [for Israel] in place," she added.

This move to double American weaponry and military equipment stockpiles on Israeli soil comes on the heels of Obama's recent signing of a $30 billion, ten-year agreement for an expanded military aid package to the Israeli government. The first installment of the aid package, $2.775 billion, was signed over in December 2009 by President Obama, and was earmarked completely for Israel's military budget instead of the prior allocation to both civilian and military infrastructure. This massive military package is over and above the annual $3.1 billion in loan guarantees to Israel that the Obama administration plans to continue.

As a part of the ten-year agreement, Israel is required to contract 75 percent of the package toward the purchase of American-made military equipment and ammunition, intended to further subsidize US weapons manufacturers. This arrangement was conceived by the Bush administration and former Israeli Prime Minister Ehud Olmert, and was designed, Berrigan explained, to "lock in" the US–Israeli military relationship, tying the hands of the forthcoming US administration. "This benefits only the American weapons manufacturers," she said, "and it sets the Obama administration up with a solid framework which Israel sought out and insisted on ahead of time. Once again, the United States was eager to comply."

Sameh Habeeb, a journalist friend from Gaza, watched torrents of missiles and white phosphorus rain down on his neighborhood during the Israeli attacks. He said he remains extremely worried about the expanded weapons proliferation agreements between the US and Israel. "Israel already has enough weapons to destroy the whole world," he said. "As a Palestinian, I thought Obama would send us the results of his change, which was peace. Instead, we get missiles."[12]

The tens of billions of dollars offered unconditionally to Israel by the Obama administration, as the US dives deeper into economic collapse, should warrant clear scrutiny by a free press. Sameh Habeeb's fear of Gaza's further destruction should warrant the same as well.

PALESTINIAN AUTHORITY'S COLLUSION WITH AMERICAN "COUNTERTERRORISM" UNITS

When I returned to the occupied West Bank in 2010, conversations with colleagues and community leaders were focused on the state of internal politics and their growing distrust of the Fatah-led Palestinian Authority (PA)'s motives in the sociopolitical spectrum. The PA's close relationship with both the United States and the Israeli government, each connected through their common discomfort for political opposition in Palestine, has provoked many people to call what's happening on the ground in the West Bank a second, subcontracted occupation.

The Obama administration and Israel's government have finally found willing "partners for peace" in the Palestinian Authority—and most of the American corporate media has fallen in line. What we're not hearing about, as these talks drag on, is how the US is actively working to undermine Palestinian democracy on the ground and increasing the political factionalization. David Rose of *Vanity Fair* wrote an excellent piece around the end of the Bush administration's term about this undermining effort, a plan that he aptly called "Iran-Contra 2.0."[13]

While PA officials abide by the deceptive and laborious "peace process" with US and Israeli leaders, American counterterrorism specialists in Jordan are working with PA security services armed and trained by a unit led by decorated US Army official Lieutenant-General Keith Dayton. Dayton-trained hit squads use this schooling—and the weapons—to arrest, imprison, torture, and even kill members of political parties that oppose Fatah, such as Hamas and the communist Popular Front for the Liberation of Palestine.

On street corners and near the Green Line borders, I watched heavily armed Palestinian Authority police harass and intimidate their Palestinian brethren. During one instance in Bethlehem, I witnessed several PA security jeeps protect an armed Israeli military convoy as it wound its way through the narrow streets. Needless to say, people watching this were not impressed with the West Bank government's forces providing cover for an illegally occupying military unit.

Independent Canadian journalist Jon Elmer has written extensively on this internal upheaval pulled by external strings, and documented the unraveling of security on the ground for al-Jazeera in February 2010. Except for that in-depth article in *Vanity Fair* in early 2008, this story continues to receive scant attention in the US.

Elmer wrote:

> Abu Abdullah has never been charged with a crime, but he has been arrested by Palestinian security forces so many times in the past two years that he has lost count.
>
> He has been arrested at work, in the market, on the street, and, more than once, during violent raids by masked men who burst into his home and seized him in front of his family.
>
> Deep in the heart of the Deheishe refugee camp on the outskirts of Bethlehem, Abu Abdullah describes in detail the beatings he has endured in custody, the numerous cold, sleepless nights in cramped and filthy cells, the prolonged periods bound in painful stress positions, and the long hours of aggressive questioning.
>
> "The interrogations always begin the same way," Abu Abdullah explains. "They demand to know who I voted for in the last election."
>
> Abu Abdullah is not alone. Since Palestinian Prime Minister Salam Fayyad's caretaker government took power in Ramallah in June 2007, stories like Abu Abdullah's have become commonplace in the West Bank. The arrests are part of a wider plan being executed by Palestinian security forces—trained and funded by American and European backers—to crush opposition and consolidate the Fatah-led government's grip on power in the West Bank.

The government of Mahmoud Abbas, the Palestinian president, is bolstered by thousands of newly trained police and security forces whose stated aim is to eliminate Islamist groups that may pose a threat to its power—namely Hamas and their supporters. Under the auspices of Lieutenant-General Keith Dayton, the US security coordinator, these security forces receive hands-on training from Canadian, British and Turkish military personnel at a desert training center in Jordan. The program has been carefully coordinated with Israeli security officials. Since 2007, the Jordan International Police Training Center has trained and deployed five Palestinian National Security Force battalions in the West Bank. By the end of Dayton's appointment in 2011, the $261 million project will see ten new security battalions, one for each of the nine West Bank governorates and one unit in reserve.

Their aim is clear. Speaking before a House of Representatives subcommittee in 2007, Dayton described the project as "truly important to advance our national interests, deliver security to Palestinians, and preserve and protect the interests of the State of Israel."

Others are even more explicit about what the force is for. When Nahum Barnea, a senior Israeli defense correspondent, sat in on a top-level coordinating meeting between Palestinian and Israeli commanders in 2008, he said he was stunned by what he heard.

"Hamas is the enemy, and we have decided to wage an all-out war," Barnea quoted Majid Faraj, then the head of Palestinian military intelligence, as telling the Israeli commanders. "We are taking care of every Hamas institution in accordance with your instructions."[14]

CONCLUSION

Imagine if mainstream America were told these stories—in their deserved context—on the nightly news, in the top-fold of the *New York Times*; on Clear Channel radio stations. Imagine if we knew the names and ages of all of the Palestinians who were killed under decades of Israel's occupation the same way we know the Israelis who were killed in horrific suicide bombings.

Not only is the mainstream press heavily slanted in its general editorial bias in favor of Israel, but it has become clear that, sometimes, those disseminating the (mis)information are personally invested in keeping the slant in place.

Independent journalists have not only taken on the task of truthtelling about Palestine, but have also confronted those in the corporate media who fail to disclose their own personal proclivity in their reporting. Take, for example, the work that the *Electronic Intifada* (*EI*) did in exposing the story of how the *New York Times* failed to publicly disclose a major conflict of interest with its Jerusalem bureau chief, Ethan Bronner. Acting on a tip that Bronner's son had recently been inducted into the Israeli military as a soldier protecting and carrying out the government's illegal occupation, *EI* launched an investigation of the *Times'* editorial staff and duly called out their double standards on this issue.

On January 25, 2010, *EI*'s staff wrote:

> Bronner, as bureau chief, has primary responsibility for his paper's reporting on all aspects of the Palestine/Israel conflict, and on the Israeli army, whose official name is the "Israel Defense Forces."
>
> On 23 January, Bronner published a lengthy article on Israel's efforts to refute allegations contained in the UN-commissioned Goldstone report of war crimes and crimes against humanity during its attack on Gaza last winter ("Israel Poised to Challenge a UN Report on Gaza"). . . . [15]
>
> *The New York Times'* own "Company policy on Ethics in Journalism" acknowledges that the activities of a journalist's family member may constitute a conflict of interest. It includes as an example, "A brother or a daughter in a high-profile job on Wall Street might produce the appearance of conflict for a business reporter or editor." Such conflicts may on occasion require the staff member "to withdraw from certain coverage."
>
> After Israel's invasion of Gaza last winter, Israeli military censors banned local media from printing the names of individual officers who participated in the attack for fear that this could assist international efforts to bring war crimes suspects to justice. This followed the publication of a number of soldiers' personal testimonies in the Israeli press describing atrocities they had seen committed by the Israeli army in Gaza.
>
> *The Times'* treatment of Bronner sets an interesting precedent. Would the newspaper's policy be the same if a reporter in its Jerusalem bureau had an immediate family member who faced Bronner's son across the battlefield, as a member of a Palestinian or Lebanese resistance organization?
>
> It would appear that despite the highly sensitive nature of

Palestine/Israel coverage, and the very high personal stakes for Bronner and his son that could result from full and open coverage of the Israeli army's abuses of Palestinians, the *New York Times* does not consider this situation to be a problematic case. It had not even disclosed the situation to its readers—until now.[16]

After independent media "outed" Ethan Bronner's clear conflict of interest in his duties as bureau chief, the *Times* was forced to acknowledge its double standard—however, Bronner continues reporting from Jerusalem as if nothing had happened.

As the American corporate media places gag orders on the reality unfolding in Palestine/Israel, people are moved to discover the truth from alternative, non-corporate journalism structures. The work that courageous journalists on the ground in Palestine and in the West do, feeding stories to independent outlets and letting Palestinians speak for themselves, has undoubtedly contributed to the widening call for justice and international condemnation of Israeli policies in Palestine.

We need to strengthen these voices and these outlets. In making the corporate media's entrenched and unjust slant on Palestine obsolete, Israeli policies are sure to follow.

NORA BARROWS-FRIEDMAN is an award-winning independent journalist and writer. She was the senior producer and co-host of *Flashpoints* on KPFA/Pacifica Radio for seven years, where she covered Palestine issues for national and international audiences. Since 2004, Nora has reported from Palestine, where she has worked alongside Palestinian refugee youth, leading workshops in digital media arts, journalism, and photography. Nora is currently working as a special correspondent with the *Electronic Intifada*, and contributes to Inter Press Service and *Truthout*, among many other news outlets, magazines, and online media sources. She is the recipient of a 2009 Media Freedom Award from Project Censored and the Media Freedom Foundation, and was named a Top 20 Global Media Figure by Pulse Media.

Notes

1. Nora Barrows-Friedman, "Amir, Ten Years Old, Abducted by Israeli Soldiers from His Bed," *Electronic Intifada*, March 8, 2010, http://electronicintifada.net/v2/article11120 .shtml.
2. Committee to Protect Journalists, "10 Journalists Killed in Israel and the Occupied Territory since 1992/Motive confirmed," http://cpj.org/killed/mideast/israel-and-the-occupied-palestinian-territory/.
3. Editorial, "Diplomacy 102," *New York Times*, March 10, 2010, Opinion section.

4. Nora Barrows-Friedman, "Amir, Ten Years Old, Abducted by Israeli Soldiers from His Bed," *Electronic Intifada*, March 8, 2010, http://electronicintifada.net/v2/article11120.shtml.

5. Tim Franks, "Details of Gaza Blockade Revealed in Court Case," BBC News, May 3, 2010, http://news.bbc.co.uk/2/hi/8654337.stm.

6. David Cronin, "Israeli Siege Causing De-Development of Gaza," Inter Press Service, March 8, 2010, http://ipsnews.net/news.asp?idnews=50587.

7. Ibid.

8. Jonathan Cook, "Arab Family Denied Right to Rent Home," *National*, March 21, 2010, http://www.thenational.ae/apps/pbcs.dll/article?AID=/20100321/FOREIGN/703209910&SearchID=7339046507691.

9. Jonathan Cook, "Israeli School Apartheid," August 10, 2009, *CounterPunch*, http://www.counterpunch.org/cook08102009.html.

10. Nora Barrows-Friedman, "In the Eyes of the State, We Don't Exist Here," *Electronic Intifada*, April 16, 2010, http://electronicintifada.net/v2/article11213.shtml.

11. Nora Barrows-Friedman, "US' Expanded Weapons Stockpiling in Israel," *Truthout*, February 10, 2010, http://www.truthout.org/us-expanded-weapons-stockpiling-israel56700.

12. Ibid.

13. David Rose, "The Gaza Bombshell," *Vanity Fair*, April 2008.

14. Jon Elmer, "A Prescription for Civil War," Al-Jazeera (English), February 8, 2010, http://english.aljazeera.net/focus/2009/12/2009121311331278355.html.

15. Ethan Bronner, "Israel Poised to Challenge a U.N. Report on Gaza," *New York Times*, January 23, 2010, Middle East section.

16. Staff, "New York Times Fails to Disclose Jerusalem Bureau Chief's Conflict of Interest," *Electronic Intifada*, January 25, 2010, http://electronicintifada.net/v2/article11031.shtml.

CHAPTER 9

How Not to Be Fooled Again
An Analysis of Mainstream Media Arguments Supporting the Invasion of Iraq

by Robert Abele

It is a fact beyond dispute that the majority of articles and commentaries prior to the invasion of Iraq in 2003 in the mainstream media outlets spotlighted those who beat on the war drum.[1] Although this slanted media coverage alone makes a fairly clear case that the government-media complex was engaging in classical conditioning (i.e. propaganda) of its populous to reach a pre-determined conclusion concerning US hegemony in the world, there is another aspect to the "media megaphone syndrome" that must be addressed, for we see it again in President Obama's bellicose decisions thus far in his presidency. This aspect concerns the decided lack of critical reasoning and the ignoring of ethical principles in making the case to go to war.

In the Iraq phase of the ongoing attempt to provide the US with complete dominance in the Middle East, there was some room given to antiwar voices in the mainstream media. Perhaps of all the anti-invasion articles written, former president Jimmy Carter's was among the most articulate,[2] utilizing the philosophical theory of the "Just War," a centuries-old structure of a series of individually necessary and jointly sufficient ethical conditions for going to war and for ethically measuring one's conduct in war. While there are various problems that have been raised concerning some of these criteria, they generally suffice for a solid ethical examination of the decision to go to war. In fact, notable requirements of the international laws of war are predicated on Just War Theory principles. So let us follow the line of Mr. Carter and ask: Can the invasion and subsequent occupation of Iraq be justified in terms of the Just War tradition?

THE JUST WAR THEORY AND IRAQ: PRO AND CON ARGUMENTS CONCERNING THE INVASION

Some of the more spirited defenses of the Bush proposal concerning Iraq came from Thomas M. Nichols, Chairman of the Department of Strategy and Policy at the US Naval War College, and author and literary critic Christopher Hitchens, a regular contributor to neoconservative publications such as the *Weekly Standard*. Since these commentators were accorded repeated opportunities to justify the invasion of Iraq, they will be used as paradigm cases in the following analysis.

1. Just Cause

This is arguably the most critical aspect of an ethical justification for going to war. By this, it is generally meant that an attack from another nation is either occurring or imminent.

Pro Argument. Thomas M. Nichols, in an article published in *Ethics & International Affairs*, crafted the listing of events to support the Bush rationale that the cause for military action against Iraq was just:

> Iraq has shown itself to be a serial aggressor led by a dictator willing to run imprudent risks, including an attack on the civilians of a noncombatant nation during the Persian Gulf War; a supreme enemy of human rights that has already used weapons of mass destruction against civilians; a consistent violator of both UN resolutions and the terms of the 1991 cease-fire treaty, to say nothing of the laws of armed conflict and the Geneva Conventions before and since the Persian Gulf War; a terrorist entity that has attempted to reach beyond its own borders to support and engage in illegal activities that have included the attempted assassination of a former US president; and most important, a state that has relentlessly sought nuclear arms against all international demands that it cease such efforts.[3]

The conclusion Nichols draws from this impressive list of Saddam Hussein's crimes is that *"any one* of these would be sufficient cause to remove Saddam and his regime . . . but taken together they are a brief for what can only be considered a just war."[4]

Adding to the just cause, for Nichols, is the fact that Saddam had not only "repeatedly" violated the 1991 cease-fire agreement (i.e., United Nations Security Council Resolution [UNSCR] 687), but had done so in "blatant and contemptuous" fashion. Nichols does not elaborate on what these "contemptuous" violations were. He merely asserts that "violation of a cease-fire treaty has long been accepted as one of the clearest moments allowing the renewal of hostilities."[5]

In addition, Nichols lists Iraq's "repeated acts of aggression": not accepting the no-fly zones and firing on over seven hundred US flights over the zones, and attempting to assassinate former President George H. W. Bush.

Nichols concludes by stating that the only two choices we face are to invade Iraq or let Saddam "command an arsenal of the most deadly materials on earth . . . there is no third choice."[6]

Con Argument. Not to be outdone, Christopher Hitchens adds his own evidence for why going to war with Iraq was just by compiling the following list of Saddam's crimes: he "committed genocide on [Iraq's] own soil, harbored and nurtured international thugs and killers, and flouted every provision of the Non-Proliferation Treaty. . . . Meanwhile, every species of gangster from the hero of the Achille Lauro hijacking to Abu Musab al Zarqawi was finding hospitality under Saddam's crumbling roof."[7]

In addition, Hitchens proffers the following evidence supporting Iraq's weapons of mass destruction program: that Abdul Rahman Yasin, "who mixed the chemicals for the World Trade Center attack in 1993, subsequently found refuge in Baghdad; that Dr. Mahdi Obeidi, Saddam's senior physicist, was able to lead American soldiers to nuclear centrifuge parts and a blueprint for a complete centrifuge . . . that Saddam's agents were in Damascus as late as February 2003, negotiating to purchase missiles off the shelf from North Korea . . . that Rolf Ekeus, the great Swedish socialist . . . was offered a $2 million bribe in a face-to-face meeting with Tariq Aziz."[8]

One can also find, as part of the case for war made by Hitchens, an interesting argument that the US must invade Iraq as a humanitarian intervention. Hitchens argues that because Iraq has been "maimed and beggared by three decades of war and fascism," then "in logic and morality, one must therefore compare the current state of the country with the likely or probable state of it" if the US does not invade. "All of the alternatives would have been infinitely worse," asserts Hitchens, as he goes on to paint a doomsday scenario in which Turkey, Iran, and Saudi Arabia invade Iraq to stop Saddam Hussein, followed by American involvement to clean up, after "a more costly and bloody intervention" than the one planned by President Bush.

Analysis of the Nichols Argument. The list of studies from the United Nations, the US State Department, the Central Intelligence Agency (CIA), the Federal Bureau of Information (FBI), and other agencies should be enough to demonstrate clearly that the claims Nichols makes are very broad and general in the first instance (e.g., "a terrorist entity that has attempted to reach beyond its own borders to support and engage in illegal activities"), unsupported or untrue in other instances (e.g., Hussein has "relentlessly sought nuclear arms against all international demands that [Iraq] cease such efforts"; he has been "a consistent violator of both UN resolutions and the terms of the 1991 cease-fire treaty"), and insufficient in law or morality to support a preemptive attack on another nation, e.g., the "attack on the civilians of a noncombatant nation during the Persian Gulf War" and the assertion that Saddam "has already used weapons of mass destruction against civilians." Both happened during the Gulf War of 1991, and thus are not legitimate pretexts for a 2003 invasion. This would be the moral equivalent of double jeopardy.

Nichols is also incorrect to assert that "*any one* of these would be sufficient cause to remove Saddam and his regime . . . but taken together they are a brief for what can only be considered a just war." In fact, none of the items listed are by themselves a sufficient condition for a preemptive war, if that in fact is what the US was attempting to do. We will support and examine this assertion in more detail below. For now, it will suffice to say that none of these issues taken singly allows for a definition of "imminent threat" to be fulfilled.

Perhaps worst of all, Nichols commits the logical fallacy of false dilemma when he argues that the only options we face are to invade Iraq or let Saddam have weapons of mass destruction (WMDs) and use them. There are quite obviously other routes to take short of military action. The inspections were certainly working, as demonstrated by the conclusion Dr. Hans Blix made in January 2003 that "more weapons of mass destruction were destroyed under [the disarmament process] than were destroyed during the Gulf War."9 That is strong evidence that there is a working alternative to invasion.

Analysis of the Hitchens Argument. First of all, assuming the veracity of Hitchen's evidence, it is still not enough to make the case for invasion of another country when the United States is not directly or imminently threatened. His examples are only circumstantial, and thus are insufficient in law or morality to make the hard case that one nation must invade and occupy another. For instance, he hyperbolically accuses Saddam of harboring "every species of gangster from the hero of the Achille Lauro hijacking to Abu Musab al Zarqawi," but then presents only one case to support it. This commits the logical fallacy of hasty generalization. Even if he had added the names of the two terrorists William Safire alleged were given safe harbor by Saddam, invasion is still not justified as the proper response. A just cause for a full-scale war requires imminent threat of military invasion by another country, not the fact that a country harbors a few known terrorists.

Critically, the evidence Hitchens provides is false. For example, Kenneth Pollack, who at the time worked in the State Department, stated that there was no CIA information tying Abdul Rahman Yasin one of the "terrorists" Hitchens uses as a *casus belli*, to the 1993 World Trade Center bombing. In May 2002, on the CBS program *60 Minutes*, Leslie Stahl interviewed Yasin from an Iraqi prison and found him in handcuffs and prison clothes.[10] Furthermore, on the news program *Democracy Now!* on September 16, 2003, it was reported that Iraq had attempted to hand Yasin over to the US in exchange for a lifting of sanctions. The US refused to negotiate.[11]

Hitchens uses the statements of Rolf Ekeus, executive chairman of the United Nations Special Commission (UNSCOM) on Iraq from 1991 to 1997, as evidence to justify war with Iraq. However, Ekeus interviewed General Hussein Kamel, Saddam Hussein's son-in-law, in 1995, who testified that "all weapons, biological, chemical, missile, nuclear, were destroyed."[12]

Finally, the implied humanitarian intervention in the argument Hitchens uses to support a US invasion is a red herring. First, in 2003, Saddam Hussein was not involved—and had not been involved for the previous decade—in homogenizing the Iraqi population. The only possible exception to this would be the Kurds, and as they had a relatively safe haven in the northern "no-fly zone" of Iraq, Saddam could not reach them easily, and has not done so to any significant degree. So although Saddam was a brutal dictator, the ethnic cleansing that would justify an American humanitarian invasion was not part of the current crimes that he had been accused of.

Given the flimsy evidence and the lack of logic that went into Hitchens's arguments, it is safe to say that Hitchens reached his conclusion first, and then "grasped at straws" to find the evidence to support it. At best, his argument is based on premises of US unilateralism and self-interest, and it follows pragmatic and utilitarian reasoning without adding a sustained moral or legal analysis.

Analysis of the Method of Nichols and Hitchens. Note that neither Nichols nor Hitchens make a single reference to Just War Theory, international laws of aggression, or to general moral principles and arguments. Both writers argue strictly from the perspective of national interests, using a utilitarian analysis and concluding that the invasion is legitimate from that point of view. For them, if the consequences will be good and the man to be deposed bad, then the just cause criterion is satisfied. This is especially true for Hitchens, who lists all the "positive accounting" of the invasion, and justifies it on the grounds of the good consequences to come from it. But a utilitarian argument does not make for a normative argument, which must engage moral principles to determine if an invasion is to be "justified."

The value assumptions of Nichols and Hitchens. The assumption made in both the arguments of Nichols and Hitchens is that a certain number of instances of bad international behavior on the part of the leader of a nation justifies an invasion of that nation. This is insufficient without adding a normative premise. Hitchens's compiling of particular instances in no way allows him to logically reach his value conclusion concerning the justifiability of the invasion of Iraq without the assumed value premise that "*many* violations of international law or UN mandates morally justify an invasion of Iraq."

Similarly, Nichols states explicitly that "any one of" the examples of Saddam Hussein's bad behavior is a sufficient condition for invading Iraq. Again, this cannot be true without the value premise that "*any* violation of international law or UN mandates morally justifies an invasion of Iraq."

Now, the value premise in Hitchens's argument is vague, and in Nichols's argument it is absurd. Nichols's normative premise is absurd because, if true, then any country may be invaded for a single violation of law or UN mandate. Without assigning weight to violations that range from unintentional to gross, his conclusion is a *non sequitur*. Nichols's conclusion requires the following assumption: any generally recognized or agreed upon significant violation of international law is a pretext for invasion by the world collective. However, this remains absurd as a normative principle, for then it is still the case that numerous countries may invade other countries for singular acts, such as the violation of a UN mandate. Surely this is not what Nichols wants. If it is, then the US should have invaded Israel, for instance, before it invaded Iraq, since Israel has ignored far more UN mandates concerning its nuclear weapons and its treatment of the Palestinians than has Iraq concerning weapons pursuits.

The argument Hitchens makes, with the use of jointly sufficient premises and a weaker moral principle, is a stronger argument. Still, when the criterion of universality is applied, it results in consequences unacceptable to the argument Hitchens is making. In other words, if a certain number of violations of international law or mandate is sufficient for invasion by the world, it is sufficient for any nation to be susceptible to intervention upon reaching a(n unknown) critical mass of violations. This application of the normative principle opens the US to precisely such attacks, for the US has violated not just one, but many world mandates.

For example, the Central American terrorist Luis Posada Carriles resides comfortably in Miami, Florida, after blowing up a Cuban plane carrying seventy-three people and also engaging in illegal work for the US government in Central America, even though Venezuela has sought to extradict Carriles to face charges for the plane bombing. President George H. W. Bush pardoned Orlando Bosch, another terrorist who worked with the US government.[13] In addition, the Bush administration, in direct violation of the Nuclear Non-Proliferation Treaty, armed India with nuclear weapons. The United States has also ignored the judgments of the World Court concerning its actions in Nicaragua, and has consistently rejected international law and claimed for itself alone the use of unilateral military attacks.[14]

An objective moral analysis would suggest that these actions on the part of the United States are equal in importance to Saddam Hussein's above-mentioned actions. But neither Nichols nor Hitchens would allow the conclusion that the Central American countries, or any others, would be justified in invading and occupying the US. Therefore, their moral arguments each fail the test of the universality of moral norms, and may be safely rejected.

A cynical response to this would reject the requirement that normative principles be applied consistently, and appeal instead to the Thucydidean principle that "the strong do as they can." However, it is important to keep in mind that Hitchens, Nichols, and others were attempting to make the *moral* case for invading Iraq.

Hitchens argues that the invasion of Iraq is justified on humanitarian grounds, due to Iraq's ethnic cleansing policies over a decade earlier and the years of war under Saddam. But humanitarian intervention is justified at the time it is needed, not over a decade later. This makes his argument *post hoc* and thus irrelevant to the issue of a 2003 invasion. There is also something quite disingenuous about using Saddam's genocidal policies as a pretext for invasion when the US provided the military means and the political support for it. When Saddam used poison gas against the Kurds in 1988, the Reagan administration not only turned a blind eye to it, but they also prevented the international community from condemning it.[15] To suddenly turn on Saddam for doing what the US allowed him to do makes for a contradictory argument. Finally, Hitchens' assertion that Iraq has been "maimed and beggared" is due in part to the US-sponsored sanctions against Iraq, not just Saddam's bellicosity. Hitchens is guilty of suppressing evidence in this regard.

Because of the significant requirements for proof of pretext for a pre-emptive war, and because, as we have seen, the proof simply did not exist to take such drastic action, the war against Iraq cannot be morally justified. "In the absence of a just cause, there can be no just war."[16]

2. Proper Intention

Intention deals with the goals of contemplated action. What did the Bush administration intend to be the outcome of the war against Iraq? St. Augustine and the Just War Theory in general refer to the *status quo ante* in their analysis of intention. This includes such considerations as the restoration of stolen property, territorial integrity, and most of all, peace. As Augustine puts it, "Peace, then, is the purpose of waging war; and this is true even of men who have a passion for the exercise of military prowess as rulers and commanders."[17]

So what was the intention of the president and his cabinet in going to war in 2003? Was it simply to rid Iraq of Saddam Hussein? That would in no way be permitted by Just War Theory, not only because uprooting a nation's leader would not be justified in this case (as we have seen), but also because such an action would violate the political sovereignty and territorial integrity of Iraq. The only way to justify the invasion by proper intention is if Saddam had actually done something directly or imminently threatening to the peace and the security of the United States.[18] Short of that, there was no moral reason for military action, and thus no proper intention.

Was it to rid Iraq of WMDs, which threatened peace? The UN reports completed and released prior to the invasion clearly show that inspections under threat of invasion were working, but they were ignored by the Bush administration. Had their intention been to restore peace or *status quo ante*, they would have adopted the working, ongoing peaceful means of eliminating the weapons they asserted Iraq possessed.

Was it to establish democracy in the Middle East? That intention was never stated as the Bush administration made its case for invading Iraq. Instead, it came as a *post hoc* reason, after the invasion was already underway. Nonetheless, as a singular intention for war, it would be immoral, given the requirements of just cause for preventive attacks.

Was the invasion for the cause of peace? One sees no direct statement of this intention in the case for war made by the Bush administration and its supporters. It might be assumed to be the case. Ridding the world of Saddam Hussein and reducing WMDs can only help the cause of peace. There are two things to note here. First, as Augustine states, just cause requires the intention of peace *status quo ante*, not the peace that "might" "someday" be disrupted by a menace. Second, if the peace is one of *Pax Americana*, then it is an unstable peace, because someone else's imposed conditions of peace will not be taken lightly by those imposed upon, whether the goal is democracy or not. Those so imposed upon will always seek ways of exploiting the vulnerabilities of the holder of the *Pax*, when it is from outside the culture or state. Such is the origin of terrorism. So *Pax Americana* is a temporary and always uncertain peace, not peace in the sense of mutually recognized coexistence between states.

Exercising the philosophical principle of charity, let us assume that each of the Bush reasons were individually necessary and jointly sufficient conditions of the justification for the invasion. Thus, if there is a possibility that each of the conditions is false, then the case for proper intention fails on logical grounds as well as moral grounds.

3. Proper Authority

There had been great animus toward the UN on the part of the Bush administration and the American writers who supported the war. They had made it clear that they did not believe that the US needed UN authorization to pursue preventive war. However, simultaneously and in contradictory fashion, they all likewise stated that in attacking Iraq the US was enforcing UNSCR 687 and 1441. This contradictory argument was nowhere more clearly seen than in the argument provided by the Heritage Foundation, and used by many mainstream media outlets. In its position paper, the Foundation attempted to support their conclusion that the US did not need UN authorization on the basis of four arguments, three of which will be analyzed here.[19]

Argument One: Self-Defense. This argument invokes UN Charter Article 51, which guarantees the right of every country to self-defense. It rightly applies this to the notion of imminent threat, and then adds that Saddam Hussein is an imminent threat because "he seeks to develop" WMDs.

Analysis. This argument uses "imminent threat," which is defined as an immediately forthcoming military action on the part of another state (i.e., an aggression). There are two ways to understand the term "imminent threat"; one is conceptual, the other is legal. The conceptual definition has been solidified by Michael Walzer in his classic text *Just and Unjust Wars*. Here Walzer makes a distinction between imminent threat and sufficient threat, stating that the legitimacy of a preemptive strike is based not on the former but on the latter. He makes the following claim concerning sufficient threat that has been widely accepted in the literature on war since: "I mean it to cover three things: a manifest intent to injure, a degree of active preparation that makes that intent a positive danger, and a general situation in which waiting, or doing anything other than fighting, greatly magnifies the risk."[20]

In terms of international law, the precedent-setting definition of imminent threat was given by American Secretary of State Daniel Webster in his rejection of the British explanation for their boarding of and attack on the ship *Caroline*. As quoted by the Nuremberg Tribunal, "preventive action in foreign territory is justified only in case of 'an instant and overwhelming necessity for self-defense, leaving no choice of means, and no moment of deliberation.'"[21]

By neither definition was an attack on Iraq justified. Furthermore, the self-defense argument betrays its weakness when it states that Hussein "seeks" WMDs. That means that he does not possess them, nor is he threatening to use them. Seeking weapons is not the same as an extant threat. Again, even if possession does mean threat, it is only so in the widest possible sense of the word. It certainly does not mean that an attack is imminent. Imminence contains within it a notion of immediacy, a definitional criterion not met by Iraq's supposed threat. Furthermore, a threat requires an objective act or statement of intention to cause immediate injury to another. Again, Michael Walzer puts it best when he says that a "sufficient threat" requires, among other things, "actual preparation for [a] war [with another nation]."[22] Additionally, the danger must be immediate for the threat to be imminent or sufficient. This in no way applied to Saddam Hussein in 2003.

Argument Two: The US Constitution. This Heritage argument rests on the claim of authority given to the president "as commander in chief of the armed forces" by the United States Constitution. The argument simply stipulates that, "no treaty, including the UN Charter, can redistribute this authority."

Analysis. There are at least two problems with this argument. First, the argument does not mention where the Constitution might give the president the power to override other treaties, including the UN Charter. This leads to the second point: this argument does not mention Article VI of the Constitution, which states explicitly that all treaties made by the US become US law.[23] Given this, the only plausible reason the president would have to violate his oath to uphold the Constitution would presumably be in the case of self-defense of the nation. Thus, the Heritage argument invoking the supreme authority of the Constitution is contradictory to their first argument, which rests upon the UN Charter's Article 51. One cannot appeal to the UN Charter and then deny the Charter's authority over the US Constitution.

Argument Three: UNSCR 678. Existing UN Security Council Resolution 678, passed in 1990, allowed "member states co-operating with the Government of Kuwait . . . to use all necessary means" to expel Iraq from occupying Kuwait and to "restore international peace and security in the area."[24] Because this second part of the resolution has never been completed, the Heritage argument concludes, the US has UN authorization to enforce this UN resolution.

Analysis. First, an appeal to a thirteen-year-old resolution, even if it "has not been rescinded," is problematic in the sense that it is time-specific.

The resolution never stated that it was intended to be a general mandate of the UN Security Council. Further, note the specificity of the resolution. It was intended for those states working with Kuwait to expel Iraq, not for dealing with Iraq in general. One has to stretch the meaning of the second part of the resolution in order to make the resolution a universal and ongoing mission of the UN states. Creating such ongoing goals is something the Charter does, not a particular UN resolution. Equally important, when the Security Council authorizes force, it does so quite clearly, usually by using the phrase "all necessary means." It did not do so on any other resolution concerning Iraq, not even the oft-cited Resolution 1441, in which it threatens "serious consequences" of any "material breach" of past resolutions by Iraq.[25] The United States took it upon itself to judge the UNSCR 678 ongoing in order to justify its attack on Iraq, and that is beyond its proper authority.[26]

Further, the idea that the US can bypass international bodies and use only its own authority to send its military into another country presumes that unilateralism trumps international law. It allows one nation to determine what is best for both itself and the world and then to act upon that determination, whether or not it is in concert with the rest of the world. Because this excludes dialogue and more importantly the demands of universality of principle required by ethics, it has no place in a moral analysis of war.

Finally, a violation of the UN Charter is concomitantly a violation of Article VI of the US Constitution, which states that "all Treaties made . . . under the Authority of the United States, shall be the supreme Law of the Land . . ."[27]

Therefore, the proper authority criterion is not met by the arguments in support of the invasion of Iraq, as asserted by the Heritage Foundation.

4. Last Resort

Thomas M. Nichols states the case for invasion under this category quite bluntly: "There is no longer a credible way to envision any peaceful road to Iraqi disarmament," because Saddam has violated his word to open his weapons caches to UN inspectors. When he did begin to follow through on his promise, he reneged, which he will no doubt do again. Nichols asserts that because of this lying, "dictators like Saddam forfeit the right to demand further negation and make military action . . . the only reliable and permanent means of ending their nuclear and other lethal aspirations."[28]

Contrarily, the condition of last resort was clearly unmet by the Bush administration. UN reports clearly state that although there were many problems, the inspection process was producing results; the US went to war anyway. When there is progress over disputed issues, one cannot put an end to dialogue by claiming that no further negotiations are possible. These are contradictory notions. Nichols's statement that Saddam has no right to demand further negotiation is at sharp odds with both ethical prescriptions and reality. From the start, the Bush position was "no negotiations."[29]

5. Probability of Success and Proportionality

The final necessary conditions for having a just cause for war are a sufficient probability of success, and a calculation that the overall good that would come from the war outweighs the harm that it might cause. Prior to the invasion, there were many assertions by the Bush administration that the invasion would be "a cakewalk"[30] and the Iraqi people would greet the invading US military as "liberators."[31] Even authors like Father John Langan, S. J., professor of Catholic Social Thought at Georgetown University, argued that the US had "technologically sophisticated and physically overwhelming resources" that guaranteed success in the invasion.[32]

So what are the conceivable projected results from an invasion of Iraq, and do these positive results outweigh any negative consequences that might exist? These issues were dealt with quite thoroughly in two studies, both produced in 2002. First, the American Academy of Arts and Sciences (AAAS) Committee on International Security Studies (CISS) produced an impressively detailed and well-documented analysis[33] of the conceivable consequences of a US invasion of Iraq, all of which both individually and collectively call into question the probability of a successful outcome. Rather than elaborate on these speculated consequences, a quick listing of them will suffice. We will begin with the plausible positive outcomes enumerated by the report:

▸ Saddam's reign of brutal tyranny would come to an end.
▸ The Iraqi people would be liberated.
▸ The spread of democracy in the Middle East would begin.
▸ Respect for US military power would be restored.
▸ Future threats would be reduced as a consequence of potential foes observing US military power and resolve.
▸ The stability of a democratic Iraq and the end of an evil dictator would demonstrate US morality and leadership to the world.

In addition to these possible positive outcomes, the report elaborates on other, gloomier consequences:

▶ Costs of US involvement in Iraq could mount if the war becomes too bloody or prolonged.

▶ Iraq could set their own oil fields ablaze, which would result in billions of dollars in economic losses.

▶ Iraq could disrupt the flow of oil delivery from the Persian Gulf.

▶ Fighting in Iraq could be urban and guerilla in style, prolonging the war.

▶ Iraq could attack other nations in the region.

▶ Saddam could preempt the preventive war by attacking ports, sinking tankers, etc.

▶ The war on terror launched by President Bush would be thwarted. An invasion of Iraq would certainly divert attention and resources away from Afghanistan, where the focus on al-Qaeda was and should be.

▶ It could undermine international cooperation on fighting terrorism. "The global war on terrorism depends on the extensive collaboration among intelligence services, policing agencies, militaries, and so on."[34]

▶ Attacking Iraq in preventive fashion could lead to the loss of "hearts and minds" in the Arab world, which already harbors hatred toward America and which would no doubt see this as yet another insult of American imperialism.

▶ Invading Iraq could bring a change in world order, from American cooperation with other nations to unilateralism and self-interest alone.

▶ The preventive war could set a precedent for other countries to do the same.

▶ The war could damage America's reputation in the world.

▶ It could undermine US relationships with friends and allies.

▶ It could undermine America's position as a moral leader in the world.

▶ US relations with the Arab world may be damaged.

▶ Saddam's absence could reduce or even eliminate the need of other Arab nations to have a US presence in the Middle East for protection, thus complicating the US presence in the region.

▶ The war could drive other nations to the conclusion that possession of WMDs is necessary in order to deter American aggression.

▸ The war could inflame anti-American sentiment in Pakistan, thus changing the cooperative role the US and Pakistan have had since 9/11.

▸ An upsurge of Kurdish nationalism could damage US-Turkey relations.

▸ The US could get bogged down in Baghdad, both economically and militarily. Even Dick Cheney said this in 1991, defending the decision of President George H. W. Bush to not invade Iraq after expelling Saddam from Kuwait.

▸ US forces in Iraq could be subject to regular attacks.

An Oxford Research Group report makes many of the same observations.[35] As such, it seems that a successful invasion of Iraq would be improbable in the face of the numerous negative consequences that would also result from such an invasion. Additionally, if establishing democracy was part of the United States' true intention for going to war, then the probability of success is even lower. Iraq has never had experience with democracy. The chances of imposing a form of democracy alien to both people and leaders, and doing so by violent means, when there is already suspicion in many Arab minds about US intentions, is a recipe for disaster, not success.

As for proportionality, it takes only a cursory examination of these conceivable outcomes to see that the negative outcomes outweigh the positive ones in a utilitarian calculation. The potential consequences of the invasion are more negative than positive; thus, the criterion of proportionality would argue against the morality of an invasion of Iraq.

CONCLUSION

This brief analysis of the two paradigms of pro-war arguments demonstrates not only that they are radically insufficient on logical, ethical, and legal grounds, but that this insufficiency could have been shown *at the time they were being made*, as well as in retrospect. The power of propaganda, the media as government megaphone, a compliant and complicit Congress, and an apathetic and ill-informed public are all to be blamed for allowing the invasion to occur on such flimsy premises. These problems continue, as President Obama has now expanded the number of forces in Afghanistan and moved the war into Pakistan and Yemen, and very few have made a significant objection. It is the aim of organizations like Project Censored to see to it that the American public doesn't get fooled again in the future.

This chapter is an excerpt adapted from Robert Abele's book *The Anatomy of a Deception: A Reconstruction and Analysis of the Decision to Invade Iraq* (Lanham, MD: University Press of America, 2009).

ROBERT ABELE holds a PhD in philosophy from Marquette University and MA degrees in theology and divinity. Dr. Abele is an instructor of philosophy at Diablo Valley College, located in Pleasant Hill, California, and is the recipient of numerous scholarships and fellowships, including the National Endowment for the Humanities Fellowship to the US Naval Academy for the study of war and morality (2004) and the Illinois Council of Humanities Scholarship for his work on the issues of freedom and democracy (2003). He is the author of three books, *A User's Guide to the USA PATRIOT Act and Beyond* (2004), *The Anatomy of a Deception: A Reconstruction and Analysis of the Decision to Invade Iraq* (2009), and *Democracy Gone: A Chronicle of the Last Chapters of the Great American Democratic Experiment* (2009), and numerous articles on politics and US foreign and domestic policies. His latest articles on political theory and war will be published in the forthcoming *Encyclopedia of Global Justice*.

Notes

1. See Fairness & Accuracy in Reporting (FAIR), "In Iraq Crisis, Networks are Megaphones for Official Views," March 18, 2003.
2. Jimmy Carter, "Just War—or a Just War?" *New York Times*, March 9, 2003.
3. Thomas M. Nichols, "Just War, Not Prevention," *Ethics & International Affairs* 17, no. 1 (Spring 2003).
4. Ibid.
5. Ibid.
6. Ibid.
7. Christopher Hitchens, "A War to be Proud Of," *Weekly Standard* 10, no. 47. While this article was a post-invasion contribution, it summarizes and recapitulates the arguments Hitchens had made prior to the invasion, and thus is more convenient than collating his previous contributions.
8. Ibid.
9. Hans Blix, "An Update on Inspection," speech to the United Nations Security Council, January 27, 2003, http://www.un.org/Depts/unmovic/recent%20items.html.
10. Mike Sims, "Transcript: The Yasin Interview," interview by Leslie Stahl, *60 Minutes*, CBS, http://www.cbsnews.com/stories/2002/06/02/60minutes/main510847.shtml.
11. Amy Goodman, transcript of "Cheney Suggests Iraq Is Linked To '93 WTC Bombing Through Wanted Iraqi-American," *Democracy Now!*, September 16, 2003, http://www.democracynow.org/2003/9/16/cheney_suggests_iraq_is_linked_to#transcript.
12. United Nations Special Commission (UNSCOM)/International Atomic Energy Agency (IAEA), "UNSCOM/IAEA Sensitive." This is an internal document made public by FAIR; it can be seen at http://www.fair.org/press-releases/kamel.pdf.
13. Noam Chomsky, *Failed States: The Abuse of Power and the Assault on Democracy* (New York: Metropolitan Books, 2006), 5–6.

14. Ibid, 85–86.
15. See Jon Wiener, "America's Complicity in Saddam's Crimes," *Nation*, December 30, 2006. See also the Human Rights Watch report on this issue in 1993.
16. John Langan, S. J., "Is There a Just Cause for War Against Iraq?" *State of the Nation* 4, no. 1 (Winter/Spring 2003).
17. St. Augustine, Book XIX, in *City of God* (New York: Penguin Classics, 1984), 12.
18. The use of the term "directly threatening" refers to the imminence of the threat. As we have seen, there was no imminent threat from Saddam Hussein.
19. Heritage Foundation, http://www.heritage.org/.
20. Michael Walzer, *Just and Unjust Wars* (New York: Basic Books, 1977), 81.
21. Quoted in Duncan E.J. Currie, "'Preventive War' and International Law after Iraq," www.Globelaw.com, May 22, 2003. The interior quote is from Daniel Webster, http://www.globelaw.com/Iraq/Preventive%20War%20After%20Iraq.pdf.
22. Walzer, *Just and Unjust Wars*, 81.
23. U.S. Constitution Online, http://www.usconstitution.net/const.html#Article6. In full, Article VI says: "All Debts contracted and Engagements entered into, before the Adoption of this Constitution, shall be as valid against the United States under this Constitution, as under the Confederation.

    "This Constitution, and the Laws of the United States which shall be made in Pursuance thereof; and all Treaties made, or which shall be made, under the Authority of the United States, shall be the supreme Law of the Land; and the Judges in every State shall be bound thereby, any Thing in the Constitution or Laws of any State to the Contrary notwithstanding.

    "The Senators and Representatives before mentioned, and the Members of the several State Legislatures, and all executive and judicial Officers, both of the United States and of the several States, shall be bound by Oath or Affirmation, to support this Constitution; but no religious Test shall ever be required as a Qualification to any Office or public Trust under the United States."
24. United Nations Security Council, *Resolution 678*, November 29, 1990, http://www.fas.org/news/un/iraq/sres/sres0678.htm.
25. United Nations Security Council, *Resolution 1441*, November 8, 2002, http://daccess-dds-ny.un.org/doc/UNDOC/GEN/N02/682/26/PDF/N0268226.pdf?OpenElement.
26. See Mary Ellen O'Connell, "The Myth of Preemptive Self-Defense," special issue: Task Force on Terrorism, *American Society of International Law* (August 2002): 5.
27. See note 23.
28. Nichols, "Just War, Not Prevention".
29. James Risen, "Iraq Said to Have Tried to Reach Last-Minute Deal to Avert War," *New York Times*, November 6, 2003. In November 2003, the international media discovered that Saddam Hussein had made a last minute effort to avoid the invasion by expressing his intention to submit to all American demands. That offer was rebuffed by the US.
30. Ken Adelman, "Cakewalk in Iraq," *Washington Post*, February 13, 2002. Assistant Defense Secretary Ken Adelman used the term "cakewalk" in this op-ed piece arguing in favor of the invasion.
31. Transcript, "Interview with Vice-President Dick Cheney," interview by Tim Russert, *Meet the Press*, NBC, March 16, 2003. Cheney stated that he believed the US would be "greeted as liberators."
32. Langan, "Is There a Just Cause for War Against Iraq?"

33. Carl Kaysen et al., *War with Iraq: Costs, Consequences, and Alternatives* (Cambridge, MA: American Academy of Arts & Sciences Committee on International Security Studies, 2002).
34. Ibid., 26.
35. Paul Rogers, Oxford Research Group, *Iraq: Consequences* (Oxford, UK: Parchment Ltd., 2002).

CHAPTER 10

The Sound of Freedom?
News Coverage of Public Debate over the F-35

by Andrew L. Roth

> *This conjunction of an immense military establishment and a large arms industry is new in the American experience. The total influence—economic, political, even spiritual—is felt in every city, every State house, every office of the Federal government. We recognize the imperative need for this development. Yet we must not fail to comprehend its grave implications. Our toil, resources and livelihood are all involved; so is the very structure of our society.*
> —PRESIDENT DWIGHT D. EISENHOWER, *January 17, 1961*

> *When a changed political reality becomes part of the very structure of news writing, then the story does not 'reflect' the new politics but becomes part of the new politics itself.*
> —MICHAEL SCHUDSON, *"The Politics of Narrative Form"*[1]

In his 1961 farewell address, President Eisenhower identified the United States' "military-industrial complex" and warned of its "total influence" and "grave implications" for American society. Fifty years later, the US spends $1.98 million *every minute* on defense, according to one estimate, and nearly 60 percent of the 2011 federal discretionary budget will go to military programs.[2] As a result of such budgetary decisions, the United States now expends more on its military than the *combined* defense budgets of the rest of the world's nations.[3]

The F-35 Joint Strike Fighter is one significant component of current US military expenditures. Describing the F-35 as "the backbone of the future tactical aircraft inventory for the Air Force, Navy, and Marine Corps, as well as our international partners," the Office of the Under Secretary of Defense (Comptroller) reports that the Fiscal Year (FY) 2010 budget allocated $10.8 billion for development and procurement of F-35 aircraft, and that the FY 2011 budget seeks another $10.7 billion for the F-35.[4]

This chapter considers what President Eisenhower described as the "total influence" of the military-industrial complex by examining in detail one specific aspect of the F-35 program, the US Air Force's Proposed Action "to bed down, or station, flight training squadrons at one or more installations to train pilots and personnel to safely and effectively operate F-35A aircraft."[5] The five candidate locations for F-35 training are the Arizona Air National Guard Base at Tucson International Airport; Boise Air Terminal Air Guard Station, also known as Gowen Field, in Idaho; Eglin Air Force Base in Florida; Holloman Air Force Base in New Mexico; and Luke Air Force Base in Arizona.[6]

By examining local newspaper coverage of the air force's decision-making process, this chapter analyzes public debate over the desirability of having the F-35 training mission in or near the community. Focusing on two of the candidate communities—Tucson, Arizona and Boise, Idaho—the chapter analyzes arguments made for and against basing the F-35 training mission in each of those communities. News articles, opinion pieces, and letters to the editor in each community's daily and weekly newspapers reveal *contests in rhetoric* and *clashes in values* that divide each community into competing factions, i.e., those who seek the introduction of the F-35 training mission as *desirable* for their community, and those who oppose its deployment as *destructive* of the community. The formation of competing publics—as "hawks" and "doves"[7]—within a community is a crucial, though often overlooked, aspect of what President Eisenhower meant when he described the military-industrial complex's "total influence" on American society.

At the same time, a close examination of local news also serves to identify how news coverage of this debate produces and reproduces boundaries that demarcate what issues are the subject of *legitimate controversy* and, thus, *debatable*. These typically tacit, taken-for-granted "parameters of the permissible" are another manifestation of the military-industrial complex's "total influence." By examining when and where journalists and community members invoke or tacitly accept official language and explanations, we gain an appreciation of the military-industrial complex's total and *hegemonic* influence.[8] Furthermore, by examining instances in which journalists and community members *withhold* their consent, by making explicit these taken-for-granted understandings and articulating alternatives from outside the official parameters of the permissible, we also identify strategies for contributing to the destabilization of the military-industrial complex's hegemony.[9]

DATA AND METHODS

The main data for this study come from two corporate-owned, daily newspapers—the *Arizona Daily Star* and the *Idaho Statesman*—and two "alternative" newsweeklies, the *Tucson Weekly* and the *Boise Weekly*.[10] I collected every news article, editorial, or letter to the editor on the F-35 published in these four newspapers between April 2009 and April 2010. During that time span, the *Daily Star* featured sixty-eight news items relating to the F-35 and the *Statesman* published forty items, while the *Tucson Weekly* and its Boise counterpart printed seven and four, respectively.[11] In addition to these four newspapers, I also examined the public involvement materials that were offered at the Tucson Scoping Open House Meetings held in March 2010 and are also available online.[12]

In order to understand the arguments made by both supporters of the proposed action and their opponents, I analyzed the *ideological themes* and *rhetorical devices* that give these texts their coherence. Like all texts, news items about the F-35 are not self-contained; instead, they are *polysemic*, marked by a multiplicity of possible meanings. Thus, for example, whereas supporters of the F-35 hear "the sound of freedom," opponents hear "noise pollution." Put in more general terms, the *meaning* of the jet's engine is subject to multiple, potentially conflicting interpretations.

The key themes analyzed in what follows were arrived at inductively. I read through the complete set of news items multiple times, initially identifying broad categories of argument such as "economics" or "quality of life." Subsequent readings served to refine these categories, in ways that should become evident in the analysis that follows. By proceeding from specific observations to broader generalizations, this method aims to identify both (1) major themes in the public arguments for and against the F-35 training mission and (2) underlying assumptions in the news coverage of this public debate.

In the air force's public involvement materials, the F-35 is described as "a cutting-edge, 5th-generation strike fighter" and the "premier strike aircraft through 2040." These descriptions frame the F-35 as *new, forward-looking*, and, in brief, *desirable*.

With few exceptions, print news coverage adopted the air force's own descriptions of the F-35. For example, a feature article in the *Tucson Weekly* quoted the air force's description of the F-35 as a replacement for aging "legacy aircraft" and as "the premier strike aircraft through 2040."[13] In an editorial published in the *Arizona Daily Star*, Governor Jan Brewer noted her official "proclamation recognizing the F-35 as the premiere fighter aircraft in the world, guaranteeing our nation's defense and continuing the proud heritage of military aviation in Arizona."[14] Similarly, the *Arizona Daily Star*[15] and the *Idaho Statesman*[16] described the F-35 as "the next-generation joint strike fighter." Another article described the F-35 as "the Air Force's multi-mission fighter for the future."[17]

However, not all coverage that invoked the military's official descriptions of the F-35 did so in order to encourage readers' support of the proposed action. In a smaller number of cases, coverage invokes an official description of the F-35 in order to contest it, as can be seen in this passage from an article in the *Boise Weekly*:

> A little FYI about the jet from a slick promotional website: It sports an advanced airframe and unsurpassed autonomic logistics, avionics, propulsion, firepower and stealth capabilities that, "will insure [sic] that the F-35 is the most affordable, lethal, supportive and survivable aircraft ever to be used," according to the Department of Defense.[18]

By attributing the description of the F-35 (as "affordable, lethal, supportive and survivable") to a third party (the Department of Defense) the journalist distances herself from it, and invites readers to recognize it as a partisan, rather than neutral, description of the aircraft.[19] The invitation to skepticism is underscored by the description of the quotation's source as "a slick promotional website."

Otherwise, oppositional descriptions of the F-35 itself typically focused on how loud it is. For example, one story in the *Idaho Statesman* begins, "By all accounts, the F-35 is a loud aircraft."[20] Similarly, an article in the *Arizona Daily Star* described the F-35 as "a new jet whose noise level spurred a lawsuit against the Air Force elsewhere."[21] The theme of the jet's loudness is analyzed in more detail below.

ECONOMIC ARGUMENTS

In both Boise and Tucson, advocates of basing the F-35 training mission in their communities invoked economic arguments to support their positions. For example, nearly every article in the Tucson newspapers cited the potential loss of 1,000 jobs and $280 million annually if Tucson did not secure the F-35 training mission. The Air National Guard unit stationed in Tucson currently trains pilots to fly the F-16, one of the aircraft the F-35 would replace. Thus, in describing a "battle for the hearts and minds" of the community over stationing the jets in Tucson, one article in the *Arizona Daily Star* reported, "At stake is the future of a military unit that brings $280 million a year to Tucson."[22] In an opinion piece published by the *Arizona Daily Star*, a prominent member of Tucson's business community, auto dealer Jim Click Jr., asserted:

> In these difficult economic times we should secure the future of one of our city's largest income-generators by letting decision makers know that we welcome the F-35 with open arms.[23]

Another article in the *Star* quoted a citizen who lives under the military air traffic route as saying, "To me this is about economic impact. . . . To lose 1,000 jobs in this horrid economy, there's no intelligence to that."[24]

Whereas economic arguments in support of the F-35 in Tucson focused on the potential loss of existing jobs, advocates in Boise focused on job creation. As in Tucson's coverage, nearly every article mentioned the number of jobs and the amount of money at stake in the decision of where to base the jets. For example, in an article on how the Idaho state lottery was lending its support to the F-35 campaign, the *Idaho Statesman* reported: "Basing the F-35 in Idaho would bring $1 billion a year in federal spending and 3,000 jobs to the state."[25] Similarly, an article in the *Boise Weekly* noted: "It's hard to ignore the economic boost that a jet squadron could bring Boise and Mountain Home. . . . The F-35s could bring an additional several hundred million dollars to the state and create about 3,000 jobs in the region, said Bibian Nertney, administrator for marketing and communications for the Idaho Department of Commerce."[26]

Opponents of basing the F-35 training mission in their communities countered these economic arguments in one of two ways: either they portrayed economics as the wrong basis for making the decision, or they contested the accuracy of the figures on jobs and money. Thus, for example, in Tucson, one letter to the editor urged community members to consider how the F-35's noise might impact the city's long-standing efforts to revitalize the downtown: "If you think it has taken a long time to reconstruct downtown Tucson, think about how long it will take the city to reconstruct midtown Tucson after it is taken down by the noise of the F-35."[27] Another letter emphasized impacts on public health and private property values as hidden costs: "In all of the unproven claims of positive economic benefits to the Tucson area that will come from basing F-35 jets at Tucson International Airport, I have seen no one address the very likely serious negative economic effects on property values, as well as mental and physical health."[28] An article in the *Tucson Weekly* quoted Marshall Vest, "a UA [University of Arizona] expert on the local economy," as putting the threatened job loss in broader perspective: "'We have somewhere in the neighborhood of 300,000 jobs in Pima County,' Vest said. 'So the loss of 1,000 jobs (if the F-16 mission is not replaced by the F-35) is a small portion of the overall picture.'"[29] More subtly, this article also raised the question of how the $280 million per year figure—cited frequently as a matter-of-fact measure of the Air National Guard unit's economic input into the local economy, based on its current F-16 training mission—was generated. Noting that the figure came from a 2008 report commissioned by former Governor Janet Napolitano, the *Tucson Weekly* reported that, "Repeated calls seeking further clarification from the consultants who prepared the study were not returned."[30]

In addition to contesting directly advocates' claims about the number of jobs or amount of money at stake, opponents of the F-35 mission also argued that economic interests distorted the terms of the debate, as can be seen in this quotation from a letter to the editor of the *Arizona Daily Star* by a retired US air force lieutenant colonel, who wrote: "The group that strongly supports the bed down of F-35s in Tucson is seduced by profit margins and personal monetary gain."[31] Numerous critics of basing the F-35 in Boise questioned the wisdom and ethics of making the local economy more dependent on military spending:

> "I feel that it's been taken for granted that Idahoans support this," said Michael Stanbulis, a member of the Idaho Peace Coalition. "This money can be better put toward economic activity that focuses on peaceful priorities. . . . [M]ilitary spending is not a good way to base an economy."[32]

A resident of Boise wrote to the *Statesman*, "Why should Americans pay out the $69 million per F-35 jet, when we're still cutting back on public education? What could the price of one jet do to improve basic education and living standards?"[33] For that matter, the editors of the *Statesman* repeatedly noted the "irony that some of the state's conservatives have set aside their skepticism about Uncle Sam in the interest of chasing a lucrative federal project."[34] Earlier, the *Statesman's* editors had noted the "disconnect" between Governor Butch Otter's criticism of a "federal-style, one-size-fits-all, nanny government . . . intent on spending us into recovery by mortgaging our children's future," on the one hand, and Governor Otter's enthusiasm for the F-35 as "one of Idaho's biggest economic development stories in years," on the other hand. The editors dryly observed: "It's funny how the talking points have a way of changing."[35]

Letters to the editor picked up on and amplified this criticism. For example, one Boise resident wrote,

> I urge all of your readers to call Otter's office and tell him that we do not want the federal government's money for the F-35. We want Otter and the rest of our Republican state politicians to keep their word when they tell us Idahoans that we do not want any stimulus monies. . . . It's time that we stand up and say enough is enough to wasteful spending.[36]

Both supporters and opponents of the air force's proposed F-35 training mission invoked economic arguments to advocate their positions. For the most part, then, the rhetorical contest over the economic value of the training mission took the form of a cost-benefit analysis. In that analysis, both advocates of the F-35 and journalists cited *official figures* on the economic benefits (in terms of jobs and dollars) of the F-35 training mission for the community, whereas opponents countered by raising concerns over *unspecified* costs (e.g., depreciation in property values, impacts on health) to the community. Figure 1 summarizes these findings.

FIGURE 1. ECONOMIC ARGUMENTS FOR AND AGAINST THE F-35 TRAINING MISSION

	Pro F-35	Con F-35
Jobs	Avoidance / of Loss (Tucson)	Small Impact on Overall Regional Employment
	Creation (Boise)	
Fiscal Impact	Positive	Negative
	Official Statistics (e.g., $280 million annually)	Unspecified Costs (e.g., threats to property values and health)
Rhetorical Form	Fact-based	Speculative

In the absence of official studies estimating the training missions' economic *costs*, as raised by opponents of the F-35, the resulting news coverage in both Boise and Tucson tended to favor advocates of the F-35, by portraying their arguments as *fact-based*, to the disadvantage of the F-35's opponents, whose economic counterarguments thus appeared relatively *speculative*.

POLITICAL ARGUMENTS

Advocates of basing the F-35 training mission in their communities frequently invoked patriotic arguments. While defending against the charge that their resistance was unpatriotic, opponents of the F-35 mission countered with arguments about quality of life, focusing especially on the F-35's noise. By contrast with economic arguments, which did not change significantly during the time period analyzed, political arguments for and against the F-35 training mission displayed dynamism, as each side modified its position to respond actively to the other side's counterarguments.

Noise Pollution and Quality of Life

Opponents of the F-35 took the initiative by arguing that noise pollution from the F-35s would destroy their community's quality of life. Thus, for example, the *Tucson Weekly* reported, "F-35 opponents fear the plane will dramatically degrade Tucson's quality of life. [Stanley] Feldman, a former chief justice of the Arizona Supreme Court, says of the F-35: 'It's going to destroy the integrity of the central city, and the quality of life in dozens of neighborhoods and across the University of Arizona.'"[37] According to a letter from a retired air force colonel, "[T]he Air Force has made a huge blunder in the designing of the new F-35 aircraft. It is too loud to be flown near any population center on the continent. . . . Tucsonans have not heard an aircraft this loud before, and will be appalled if a squadron of them starts flying here."[38] Similarly, the *Boise Weekly* quoted a local resident on the jets' noise impact: "The [F-35s] could really cause a lot of noise pollution around the airport."[39]

Both articles and opinion pieces characterized the jets' volume in terms of decibels (dB), a logarithmic measure of sound levels. The *Tucson Weekly* published a chart comparing maximum sound levels of the F-35 and the F-16C (the jet currently flown out of Tucson International Airport, due to be replaced by the F-35), at different altitudes, in decibels.[40] Thus, for instance, at an altitude of 500 feet, the F-35 measures 131 dB and the F-16C 104 dB; at 5,000 feet, the F-35 and F-16 measure 103 dB and 77 dB, respectively. Two points about decibels as a unit of measure are pertinent to these comparisons. First, as noted, decibels are a logarithmic measure, meaning that an increase of 10 dB represents a *doubling* of volume. Thus, to interpret the figures cited here, the F-35 is between *two* and *three times* louder than the F-16C.[41] Second, according to Department of Defense standards, sound levels above 65 dB are "generally not recommended for residential use"[42] and prolonged exposure to levels of 85 dB or above can cause hearing loss.[43]

In both Tucson and Boise, news coverage invoked the case of Valparaiso, Florida, near Eglin Air Force Base, the first base with operational F-35s. When the Environmental Impact Statement for the Eglin AFB F-35 mission indicated that the F-35s would put more than 70 percent of Valparaiso above the 65-decibel level, the city sued the air force. The suit was settled out of court in March 2010 when the air force agreed to establish a committee to address the noise issue. With knowledge of the Valparaiso case, Tucson residents called on the air force to conduct a test flyover by F-35s, so residents could experience their loudness. The *Arizona Daily Star* reported having received a message from a Pentagon official indicating that "no such testing would take place." An air force spokesman at the Pentagon explained, "The military has only a few of the new jets and can't spare them for such a test."[44] Opponents of basing the F-35 in Tucson reacted to this explanation with skepticism. "What are the decibel readings of the new F-35s, and why won't the Air Force do a flyover, or at least get us 'noise data' on them?" one letter to the editor questioned. "I have a strong feeling the decibels will be way above the range where hearing will be damaged for those of us on the ground."[45] As another resident argued, "We need to hear the jets for ourselves."[46]

The call to "hear for ourselves" invokes the importance of direct sensory experience as a basis for judging the F-35's impact on the community. In the absence of a flyover as one way of making the abstract decibel figures more sensible, Boise opponents of the F-35 mission compared the jet's sound to everyday noise sources. Thus, for example, a letter to the editor of the *Idaho Statesman* argued: "Independent sound level measurements taken near Eglin AFB . . . confirm consistent sound levels at takeoff from 90 decibels (dB) to 121 dB. 110 dB is the onset of physical ear pain, and 125 dB causes hearing loss. (Standing next to a jackhammer is a 100 dB noise level.)"[47] In another article, the *Statesman* quoted a Boise resident comparing the jet's noise, at an altitude of 1,000 feet, to standing next to a lawnmower.[48]

Mitigation

Advocates of the F-35 training mission countered by (1) arguing that the F-35's noise could be mitigated and, more forcefully, (2) *redefining the meaning* of the noise, as "the sound of freedom." Counterarguments that the jets' noise could be mitigated accept the *legitimacy* of the concern, while dismissing its *validity* as a basis for opposing the F-35 training mission. Thus, the *Tucson Weekly* quoted Tucson City Councilmember Richard Fimbres: "I was talking to an Air National Guardsman who assured me that they won't be revving up the F-35 when they take off or fly into TIA . . . and this will really decrease the noise impact."[49] The *Arizona Daily Star* noted that Arizona Senator John McCain said that limiting the use of afterburners would "turn down the volume some."[50] In Boise, a supporter wrote to the *Idaho Statesman's* editor to argue that "flight profiles such as take-off, landing, approach and departure routes can be tailored to mitigate local acoustical impacts."[51] Brigadier General Gary Sayler, commander of Idaho's Air National Guard, suggested that the air force might give residents money for noise-dampening insulation and windows, while Senator Jim Risch assured the *Statesman's* readers that, "With mitigation efforts and the type of aircraft, I'm convinced that [noise levels] will not be an issue."[52]

Opponents of the F-35 mission typically rejected supporters' noise mitigation arguments as inadequate. Thus, to take just one example, a former air traffic controller from both Davis-Monthan Air Force Base and Tucson International Airport said there was "no silver bullet to mitigate this thing. . . . There's not much the Air Force can do to mitigate (the noise) with the procedures we now have in place."[53]

"The Sound of Freedom"

By contrast, arguments that (re)defined the meaning of the F-35's noise as "the sound of freedom" not only contested the significance of the jets' noise but also served to identify F-35 supporters as "proud Americans," while calling into question opponents' patriotism. In an editorial published in the *Arizona Daily Star*, Tucson business leader Jim Click Jr. exemplified the patriotic arguments in support of the F-35 mission: "Tucson residents are proud Americans who wish to continue their support for our troops, who deserve the best tools and equipment to carry out their important work defending our way of life."[54] Click's formulation identifies F-35 supporters as "proud Americans" who support "our troops," with the unstated but obvious contrast that those who oppose the F-35 are neither proud Americans nor troop supporters. Opposition, in Click's formulation, threatens both "our troops" and "our way of life." Similarly, a letter to the *Arizona Daily Star's* editor addressed opponents of the F-35: "Quit complaining about the noise of the F-35. You only hear it for about 30 seconds or so. Do you realize these pilots are training to protect your freedom?"[55] Linking military jet noise to love of country, Governor Jan Brewer noted that she regularly heard "the roar" of jets from Luke Air Force Base and that she "loved" it:

> [W]henever I hear the sound of a jet overhead, I stop and think about what I am listening to—the sound of freedom, certainly. But I compare those sounds with the imagined sound of other jets—from an enemy country—flying overhead, and somehow the jets defending Arizona and the United States don't sound so loud after all.[56]

Letters to the editor adopted Brewer's phrasing and echoed her logic, as can be seen in this example, comparing Arizona's situation to Britain in World War II: "To me, the sound of our fighters is the sound of freedom. I thank God that they are our fighters and not those of an unfriendly force. Do you think that the British people complained about the sounds of Spitfires and Hurricanes? No, because they kept away the sounds of the ME-10-9s and DO-88s."[57] Additional letters invoked 9/11: "What about the decibels from the sirens of police and fire engines, the cries from people who were injured, the screaming and tears from people who lost loved ones? In comparison, the noise from the F-35 should be music to their ears."[58]

Boise advocates of the F-35 also invoked the sound of freedom. "For those who object to the sound of aircraft at Gowen Field," one letter to the editor argued, "I suggest they ponder the price of freedom. Jet noise is the sound of freedom."[59] Another letter characterized the sound of the F-15, F-16, A-10 "and, hopefully, the F-35" as "the sound of freedom" and admonished opponents, "Learn to love it, or leave it!"[60]

By redefining the F-35's noise as "the sound of freedom," supporters of the F-35 shifted the terms of debate, from the relatively objective standard of decibel measurements to patriotism. Opponents of the F-35 seized this opportunity to expand the terms of debate further, by escalating their critiques from the F-35 mission itself to US militarism more broadly. Although "sound of freedom" arguments threatened to degrade the F-35's opponents as "crybabies" or "un-American," they responded with the rhetorical equivalent of a judo wrestler's flip, adapting the "sound of . . ." format *against* the F-35's supporters. Thus, one Tucson resident argued, "When I hear the sound of a jet fighter passing overhead, I hear distant and meaningless war, death and destruction."[61] Another Tucson opponent of the F-35 mission wrote:

> Gov. Jan Brewer might hear "the sound of freedom" when military aircraft roar overhead, but pro-peace Arizonans hear instead the agonized screams of innocent victims of war. As for Brewer's imagined scenario of "jets from an enemy country" attacking the US, it is much more likely to become reality if the US continues on its present course of global military madness.[62]

Note how this example reverses the adversaries' roles: instead of opposing the F-35, this letter portrays its position as "pro-peace," contrasting it with the "global military madness." Additional letters contrasted the "sound of freedom" with "the sound of ever more bloat in the already over-bloated Pentagon budget"[63] and "the sound of an arrogant nation that still thinks force is the best defense from those who threaten us."[64]

To summarize, in debating the F-35 training mission's desirability for their local communities, advocates and opponents of the F-35 contested both the *measurement* and the *meaning* of the aircraft's loudness. When opponents argued that the sound of the F-35 would damage the community, advocates countered that steps could be taken to mitigate its volume. Official assessments of the F-35's loudness invoked decibels (dB) as an objective measure (e.g., the F-35 is 104 dBs loud at 500 feet altitude). Opponents sought to *make sense* of these objective but abstract measurements by comparing them to subjective but tangible experiences (e.g., "like standing next to a jackhammer").[65]

Even more dramatically, supporters of the F-35 claimed jet noise to be "the sound of freedom," a patriotic argument that opponents countered with brisk rhetorical revolutions, replacing "freedom" with a host of negative referents to redefine US military jet noise as the sound of "meaningless death," "innocent victims," and "an arrogant nation." Figure 2 summarizes the dynamic, escalating pattern of political arguments and counterarguments over time:

FIGURE 2. POLITICAL ARGUMENTS FOR AND AGAINST THE F-35 TRAINING MISSION

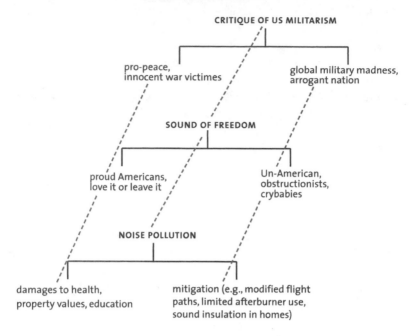

CONCLUSIONS

As should be clear from the preceding discussion, supporters of the F-35 training mission sought to establish their advocacy as both economically rational and patriotic; by contrast, opponents argued that the F-35 entailed unacknowledged economic costs and symbolized the excesses of "global military madness." In addition, each side portrayed the other's position in negative terms: F-35 advocates portrayed opponents as "not in my backyard" types or un-American, while the F-35's opponents depicted their adversaries as "seduced" by monetary gain and "military aggrandizement." For their part, local news media covered most aspects of the public debate over the F-35 as a matter of *legitimate political controversy*.[66]

What may be less obvious is how this news coverage incorporates fundamental understandings and assumptions that (intentionally or not) (1) favor those in support of the F-35 and, more generally, (2) promote identification of the nation and especially its citizens with the nation's economy and military. As Michael Schudson has argued, "The news story informs its readers about politics, but in a specific way. Its meaning lies in the instructions it tacitly gives about what to attend to, and how to attend, within the going concern of American political life."[67]

The deepest of these taken-for-granted understandings predates modern American journalism. We must look back to ancient Greece and the legacy of Socrates and Plato to appreciate our society's profound distrust of bodily and sensory experience in favor of an abstract, detached mode of thinking.[68] In this chapter, we have seen how news coverage of the F-35 debates privileges "objective" measures (such as economic statistics and decibel levels) and official accounts. By contrast, subjective alternatives that appeal to actual experience (e.g., "as loud as standing next to a jackhammer"), articulated by ordinary citizens, are not excluded altogether—but they are relegated to one domain of news coverage, the overtly partisan forum of letters to the editor. Subjective formulations based on sensory experience do not appear in so-called "hard" news stories where journalists adhere to the constraints of *depersonalization* and *balance* to achieve "objectivity."[69]

In the case of the air force and its proposed F-35 training mission, an immense network of institutions provides an ample supply of official experts and "objective" studies to assert the mission's military necessity and economic benefits. We have seen, for example, how the *Arizona Daily Star* repeatedly cited a figure of $280 million per year as a benefit to the community of the Air National Guard basing its 162nd Fighter Wing in Tucson. Only two journalists at the *Tucson Weekly* (Dave Devine and Molly McKasson) noted in print that the consultants who prepared this 2008 report for Arizona's governor were unavailable to clarify how the $280 million figure was determined. Otherwise, local news coverage took the figure for granted, as an indisputable fact in news coverage of the F-35 debate. Because no existing study assessed the potential economic costs (e.g., lowered property values and health impacts), the counterarguments of the F-35's opponents lacked equivalent "objective" status in news coverage of the debate. Whether intentionally or not, news coverage that uncritically repeated the $280 million per year figure lent support to advocates of the F-35 training mission.[70]

A division of content in the newspapers examined reproduces and reinforces the tacit privileging of official, "objective" evidence over subjective experience. The most powerful arguments against the F-35 training mission were those made in response to claims that the F-35 and other military jets are "the sound of freedom." As shown here, opponents of the F-35 countered "sound of freedom" arguments by identifying F-35 supporters' "patriotism" with nationalistic "arrogance" and "military madness." Two simple points underscore the significance of this finding: First, such arguments fell outside the officially defined "parameters of the permissible." Thus, for instance, in calling for "public involvement" as "a fundamental part" of its decision-making process, the air force invited "community-specific input" on: aircraft operations (including noise, safety, and air quality), natural resources (e.g., soils, surface and ground water), cultural and traditional resources, human resources (including environmental justice and protection of children), and infrastructure. Although this agenda includes many potential bases for strong opposition to the proposed F-35 training mission, its focus on one particular mission does not invite more comprehensive critiques of US militarism. Second, in news coverage of the public debate over the F-35 training mission, the most radical critiques of the proposed mission appear, with one exception, exclusively as letters to the editor. They are excluded from "hard" news coverage of the debate. The exception to this claim is the *Boise Weekly*, which did include quotations from peace activists questioning the United States' militarism in its "hard" news coverage. Notably, the *Boise Weekly* is the only independent newspaper examined in this study. Otherwise, the newspapers analyzed here relegated critiques that extended beyond the parameters of the permissible, by linking the specific F-35 training mission to more fundamental questions about the global role of the United States' military, to the most partisan section of the newspaper, the letters to the editor.

In 1961, when President Eisenhower warned of the "total influence" of the military-industrial complex on American society, he could not have anticipated the extent to which our increasingly concentrated and corporate news media would contribute to the military-industrial complex's scope and power. However, as analyzed in this chapter, local news coverage of the economic and political arguments mobilized by partisans in public debates over the basing of F-35 fighters near local communities shows the deep entrenchment of ideological beliefs about the necessity of the nation's military to our international security and economic prosperity. To oppose the basing of military aircraft that exceed federal guidelines for noise in your community is to risk being labeled un-American. The opposition between so-called "hawks" and "doves" is now embedded in the structure of US news reportage; it is one stock narrative form that journalists invoke to organize specific types of news stories. Among the industrial institutions that contribute to the military-industrial complex, we must include the corporate media.

Progressives seeking to undermine the hegemonic influence of the military-industrial complex must subject to constant scrutiny not only the official language and justifications of government and industry but also the forms and structure that journalists use to report on military matters. These journalistic conventions are another, underappreciated aspect of the military-industrial complex's total influence. By challenging them, we may more realistically hope to realize President Eisenhower's vision of a United States whose "leadership and prestige" will "depend, not merely upon our unmatched material progress, riches and military strength, but on how we use our power in the interests of world peace and human betterment."

ANDREW L. ROTH, PHD, is a sociologist with interests in news media, environment, and civil liberties. He was associate director of Project Censored between 2006 and 2008.

Notes

1. Michael Schudson, "The Politics of Narrative Form," in *The Power of News* (Cambridge, MA: Harvard University Press, 1995), 65.
2. The American Friends Service Committee calculated US defense expenditures per minute; see http://oneminuteforpeace.org/budget (accessed April 27, 2010). By contrast, the proposed 2011 budget allocates just 6 percent for health and human services and 4 percent for education.
3. See http://www.globalsecurity.org/military/world/spending.htm (accessed April 27, 2010); and Peter Phillips and Mickey Huff, "Truth Emergency: Inside the Military-Industrial Media Empire," in *Censored 2010: The Top 25 Censored Stories of 2008–09*, ed. Peter Phillips and Mickey Huff (New York: Seven Stories Press, 2009), 202.
4. See the US Department of Defense's Overview of its Fiscal Year 2011 Budget Request: http://comptroller.defense.gov/defbudget/fy2011/FY2011_Budget_Request_Overview _Book.pdf (accessed April 27, 2010).
5. The Department of Defense is developing three slightly different versions of the F-35 for the air force, marine corps, and navy, respectively. The F-35A is the air force version of the aircraft. "F-35A Training: Environmental Impact Statement." The quotation is from a hard copy document, made available at the air force's March 2010 Scoping Open House Meetings in Tucson, AZ. A slightly different version of this document is available electronically at http://www.f-35atrainingeis.com/resources/03%20F35A %20Poster%20PA%20and%20Alternatives%20-%202010-01-19%20-%20Final.pdf (accessed April 27, 2010).
6. The Air National Guard is the air force component of the National Guard. The air force distinguishes between training missions and "active operations" on the basis of "different and distinct requirements." See the air force's "F-35A Training Program Brochure," available online at http://www.f-35atrainingeis.com/PublicInvolve-

ment.html (accessed June 25, 2010). This chapter focuses on news coverage of the proposed F-35A training mission.

7. On the formation of competing constituencies around public problems, see, e.g. Murray Edelman, *Constructing the Political Spectacle* (Chicago: University of Chicago Press, 1988).

8. Drawing on the foundational work of Antonio Gramsci, Todd Gitlin provides a succinct definition of *hegemony* as "a ruling class's (or alliance's) domination of subordinate classes and groups through the elaboration and penetration of ideology (ideas and assumptions) into their common sense and everyday practice; it is the systematic (but not necessarily or even usually deliberate) engineering of mass consent to the established order." Todd Gitlin, *The Whole World Is Watching: Mass Media in the Making and Unmaking of the New Left* (Berkeley and London: University of California Press, 1980), 253.

9. "Because hegemony depends heavily on commonsense, taken-for-granted definitions, beliefs, and justifications, anything we can do to challenge these ways of seeing necessarily threatens to destabilize the status quo." Darnell M. Hunt, *Screening the Los Angeles "Riots": Race, Seeing, and Resistance* (Cambridge and New York: Cambridge University Press, 1997), 164.

10. The *Arizona Daily Star* and the *Idaho Statesman* are owned by Lee Enterprises and the McClatchy Company, respectively. Wick Communications owns the *Tucson Weekly*; the *Boise Weekly* is independent.

11. Though the two newsweeklies published far fewer items on the F-35, the articles that they did publish tended to be longer and more detailed than those found in the daily papers.

12. See http://www.f-35atrainingeis.com/PublicInvolvement.html (accessed April 26, 2010).

13. Dave Devine and Molly McKasson, "Stealth But Not Silent: What Impacts Would the F-35 Joint Strike Fighter Have on Tuscon?" *Tucson Weekly*, March 25, 2010.

14. Janice K. Brewer, "F-35 Fighter Would Enhance Bases' Local Economic Impacts," Gov. Janice K. Brewer Special to the Arizona Daily Star, *Arizona Daily Star*, December 8, 2009.

15. "McCain: Tucson, Glendale Finalists for F-35 Fighter," *Arizona Daily Star*, October 29, 2009.

16. Editorial, Our View, "The Feds: A Kindly Uncle—Or Nuisance of a Nanny?" *Idaho Statesman*, February 9, 2010; and Kevin Reichert, "Crapo: Politics Could Complicate Idaho's Bid for F-35 Projects," *Idaho Statesman*, February 15, 2010.

17. Andrew Taylor, Associated Press, "House Approves Defense Policy Bill," *Charlotte Observer*, October 9, 2009.

18. Carissa Wolf, "Did You Get Your F-35 Post Card?" *Boise Weekly*, April 5, 2010.

19. On third-party referred statements, see Steven Clayman and John Heritage, *The News Interview: Journalists and Public Figures on the Air* (Cambridge, UK and New York: Cambridge University Press, 2002), 152ff; and, more generally, Erving Goffman, "Footing," in *Forms of Talk* (Philadelphia: University of Pennsylvania Press, 1981), 124–159.

20. Kathleen Kreller, "Airport Neighbors Abuzz Over Noise Potential of F-35s," *Idaho Statesman*, March 16, 2010.

21. Carol Ann Alaimo, "McCain Calls Tucson Ideal for F-35," *Arizona Daily Star*, November 25, 2009.

22. Carol Ann Alaimo, "Decibel Level Jacks Up in Debate over Whether to Host F-35s," *Arizona Daily Star*, February 14, 2010.

23. Jim Click Jr., "F-35 Will Provide Vital Boost to Local Economy," *Arizona Daily Star,* January 22, 2010.

24. Carol Ann Alaimo, "Many at F-35 Forum Ask to Judge Noise With Flyby," *Arizona Daily Star,* March 2, 2010.

25. Associated Press, "Idaho Lottery Helping in Effort to Land F-35," April 11, 2010. The Idaho figures of $1 billion and 3,000 jobs are somewhat misleading in that they *combine two separate F-35 missions,* one for training (at Boise Air Terminal Air Guard Station, also referred to as Gowen Field) and one for active operations (at neighboring Mountain Home Air Force Base). Proponents of the F-35 training missing seldom made this distinction in citing these figures, however.

26. Carissa Wolf, "War Planes Over Boise: Can You Hear the Freedom?" *Boise Weekly,* April 7, 2010. Note a small but telling difference in language between these two examples. Whereas the *Idaho Statesman* presents the economic benefits as a certainty (". . . the F-35 *would* bring . . ."), the *Boise Weekly* and the source it quotes present those benefits as a possibility ("The F-35s *could* bring . . ."). I am grateful to Elizabeth Boyd for bringing this difference to my attention.

27. Jean de Jong, letter to the editor, *Arizona Daily Star,* April 2, 2010.

28. John Bieging, letter to the editor, *Arizona Daily Star,* February 12, 2010.

29. Devine and McKasson, "Stealth But Not Silent."

30. Ibid.

31. Jeff Latas, letter to the editor, *Arizona Daily Star,* February 23, 2010.

32. Wolf, "War Planes Over Boise."

33. Darrin Slack, letter to the editor, *Idaho Statesman,* March 3, 2010.

34. Editorial Board Position, "The F-35 Is a Good Fit for Idaho," *Idaho Statesman,* February 21, 2010.

35. Editorial, Our View, "The Feds: A Kindly Uncle."

36. Vincent DeWitt, letter to the editor, *Idaho Statesman,* February 19, 2009.

37. Dave Devine and Molly McKasson, "Flyover Future: The Air Force Holds Public Meetings As It Considers Locating a New Plane In Tucson," *Tucson Weekly,* February 25, 2010.

38. Robert Perkin, letter to the editor, *Arizona Daily Star,* January 23, 2010.

39. Wolf, "War Planes Over Boise."

40. Devine and McKasson, "Stealth But Not Silent."

41. Failure to understand decibels as a logarithmic unit of sound measurement may account for many advocates' claims that the F-35 is not much louder than other military jets. Without an understanding of logarithmic measures, for example, it *seems* that the F-35 is somewhere between 26 percent and 36 percent louder than the F-16C, depending on altitude. In fact, however, the differences summarized in the *Tucson Weekly*'s chart indicate that the F-35 is between 240 percent and 280 percent louder than the F-16C.

42. Quoted in Devine and McKasson, "Stealth But Not Silent."

43. National Institute on Deafness and Other Communication Disorders, "Noise-Induced Hearing Loss," http://www.nidcd.nih.gov/health/hearing/noise.asp#effects (accessed May 13, 2010).

44. Alaimo, "Many at F-35 Forum Ask to Judge Noise With Flyby."

45. Bob Publicover, letter to the editor, *Arizona Daily Star,* March 6, 2010.

46. Editorial, Our View, "The Only Way Tucsonans Can Decide if the Fighter Is Too Loud Is to Hear It," *Arizona Daily Star,* February 14, 2010.

47. Monty Mericle, letter to the editor, *Idaho Statesman,* March 31, 2010.

48. Kreller, Kathleen, "South Boise Residents Worry About Constant Annoyance and Lower Property Values if Gowen Field Lands the Air Force's New Jets," *Idaho Statesman*, March 16 2010.

49. Devine and McKasson, "Stealth But Not Silent."

50. Alaimo, "McCain Calls Tucson Ideal for F-35."

51. Gregory Drake, letter to the editor, *Idaho Statesman*, March 22, 2010.

52. Kreller, "Airport Neighbors Abuzz Over Noise Potential of F-35s."

53. Devine and McKasson, "Flyover Future."

54. Click Jr., "F-35 Will Provide Vital Boost to Local Economy."

55. Gene Ruffalo, letter to the editor, *Arizona Daily Star*, February 13, 2010.

56. Brewer, "F-35 Fighter Would Enhance Bases' Local Economic Impacts." In the same editorial, Governor Brewer characterized opponents of the F-35 in dismissive terms, as "obstructionists, professional naysayers, and habitual grumpy skeptics." A subsequent letter to the editor by a World War II navy veteran echoed Brewer: "To me, the people who complain about the noise are crybabies" (*Arizona Daily Star*, February 14, 2010).

57. Joseph Niehaus, letter to the editor, *Arizona Daily Star*, October 5, 2009.

58. Louis Romero Jr., letter to the editor, *Arizona Daily Star*, October 3, 2009.

59. Larry Woodard, letter to the editor, *Idaho Statesman*, March 27, 2010.

60. Steve Schott, letter to the editor, *Idaho Statesman*, November 20, 2009.

61. Robert Jacobson, Mailbag, *Tucson Weekly*, March 11, 2010.

62. Kim Mathews, letter to the editor, *Arizona Daily Star*, December 15, 2009.

63. Lois Putzier, letter to the editor, *Arizona Daily Star*, November 3, 2009.

64. Elwood Downey, letter to the editor, *Arizona Daily Star*, February 18, 2010.

65. David Abram writes, "To make sense is *to enliven the senses*" (emphasis original). In this usage, to make sense is "to renew and rejuvenate one's felt awareness of the world." See David Abram, *The Spell of the Sensuous* (New York: Random House, 1996), 265.

66. On *legitimate controversy* as one "sphere" of news coverage, see Daniel Hallin, *The "Uncensored War": The Media and Vietnam* (New York: Oxford University Press, 1986), 116ff; and Stuart Hall, "A World at One with Itself," in *The Manufacture of News*, ed. Stanley Cohen and Jock Young (Beverly Hills, CA: Sage, 1973), 85–94.

67. Schudson, *The Power of News*, 70.

68. See Abrams, *Spell of the Sensuous*, 94, 109.

69. See Robert Entman, "Objectivity, Slant, and Bias in the News," in *Democracy without Citizens* (New York: Oxford University Press, 1989), 30–38.

70. Another striking omission in news coverage, given proponents' focus on patriotic arguments, is that the Air National Guard's training mission in Tucson serves largely *foreign* pilots. Official air force literature available to the media and the public at the Scoping Open House Meetings held in Tucson indicated that "the 162nd Fighter Wing has trained pilots from more than 24 countries" to fly F-16s, the unit's existing aircraft that the F-35 would replace. The only mention of the unit's role in training foreign pilots was from a letter to the editor of the *Arizona Daily Star* from a veteran who questioned the jets' noise and in passing urged readers to "rethink the training of foreign pilots" at the Air National Guard base in Tucson (February 10, 2010).

Project Censored International
Building Media Democracy Worldwide

Project Censored is pleased to announce academic affiliations with colleges and universities in Germany, Italy, Spain, the Canary Islands, Ecuador, Chile, Scotland, Venezuela, Japan, Cuba, and Argentina. Our goal over the next few years is to link colleges and universities all over the globe in a frenzy of truth-telling. We believe that as corporate media consolidates worldwide and top-down information/propaganda increases, in service to a military-industrial-media empire, it becomes extremely important for truth and democracy movements to join forces.

Project Censored believes that colleges and universities have a role to play in building media democracy and in giving full transparency to what the powerful are doing in society. Universities are institutions founded on scientific, factual research and are tasked with sharing the results of this research with others, both within specific disciplines and outside of the academy. And, we are perhaps among the last semi-democratic and open-inquiry institutions left in the world. It falls to us to take a stand on truth and transparency by encouraging independent media and scholarship. We have both a public education role and a moral responsibility for training critical thinkers in society. Our job is to analyze the manipulations of the corporate media propaganda machine and to pull the covers off the powerful, thereby undermining hierarchy and exposing inconvenient truths.

Through shared investigative research, independent media validation, and critical news analysis, we can support democracy movements, equality building, and human betterment.

We welcome you to our first Project Censored International section, populated with scholars and communications professionals who see the broader, global implications for media democracy in action. Contributors include Peter Phillips and Mickey Huff, writing about Project

Censored's research methods and the global implications of university-level validation of independent news in fighting censorship; Dr. Concha Mateos of Spain, on the growing international problem of media control and propaganda; Dr. Rob Williams, on the significance of secession movements, new localism, and media freedom, using Vermont as a case study; David Mathison, on combating big media gatekeepers and sharing how to Be the Media; and the team at Index on Censorship from London, with a success story in which freedom of the press and the right to criticize the powerful prevailed. We hope these models of analysis are inspiring and help lay out proactive paths of democratic possibilities for the future.

—Peter Phillips and Mickey Huff

CHAPTER II

Colleges and Universities Validate Independent News and Challenge Censorship

by Peter Phillips and Mickey Huff

Project Censored has been a university media research program at Sonoma State University for the past thirty-five years. Annually, professors and students document the most important censored news stories that the corporate mainstream media in the United States failed to cover. In the beginning, Project Censored issued yearly press releases, widely covered by the alternative press, citing the under-covered and censored news stories. For the past seventeen years, Project Censored has published an annual yearbook, which since 1996 has been with Seven Stories Press in New York. Since 1998, the Project's Web site (www.projectcensored.org) has listed the most-censored stories, dating back to 1976 when the program was founded by Dr. Carl Jensen. In 1991, Project Censored moved under the legal authority of the nonprofit Media Freedom Foundation, Inc., though it has continued working with Sonoma State University students and professors as a community partner.

In 2008, Project Censored and the Media Freedom Foundation began involving other colleges and universities in the year-round research on important independent news stories that are censored or have very limited coverage in the corporate media. In the last two years, over thirty colleges and universities have participated (see Project Censored's *Censored 2010* for more details).[1]

This year—between March 2009 and March 2010—324 independent news stories were researched by students and professors from colleges throughout the United States and six other countries. To evaluate the amount of coverage these stories had in the corporate media, students used electronic newspaper databases, and faculty members who are experts in the topic validated the news stories for accuracy and importance. Validated Independent News stories (VINs) were posted on the Project Censored Media Freedom International site at www.mediafreedominternational.org.

Through the social networking Web sites Twitter and Facebook, the

VIN stories have been sent to thousands of people worldwide and have offered students the opportunity to publish important news stories daily online. The short-term goal, over the next few years, is to have thousands of students at hundreds of colleges validating and posting independent news stories year-round. Ultimately, from the annual VIN postings, the top twenty-five most censored stories for the *Censored* yearbooks would be voted on by all participating students and professors.

As corporate media globalizes, research and analysis of media failures and biases must globalize as well. Project Censored believes that corporate media is increasingly irrelevant to democracy and working people in the world, and that we need to tell our own news stories from the bottom up. What better project exists in support of media democracy than the act of universities and colleges worldwide supporting truth-telling and validating news stories and independent news sources?

Daily newspaper reading in the US has declined from 58 percent in 1993 to 34 percent in 2008. Among 18- to 24-year-olds, 34 percent in 2008 reported getting no news on a typical day, and only 15 percent of people under 25 read a daily newspaper. A total of 29 percent of people from all age groups reported getting news online daily, with 51 percent of 18- to 24-year olds reading news online.[2] Most people get all their news from corporate television, but now are increasingly getting news from the Internet. One of the biggest problems with the thousands of independent media sources on the Internet is that the abundance fosters a perception of inconsistent reliability. The public is often suspicious of the truthfulness and accuracy of news postings from non-corporate media sources. Over the past three decades, during hundreds of public presentations, audiences have frequently asked Project Censored staff, "What are the best sources for news and who do you trust?"

We now respond that corporate media is primarily in the entertainment business and frequently fails to critically cover important news stories that involve the powerful. Our goal is for young people to use trustworthy independent media as their primary sources of news and information. One way for that to happen is the widespread distribution of VINs researched at colleges and universities, to familiarize readers with trustworthy sources of online news. Thus, VIN stories and news sites can and will increasingly become the foundation of news for Internet-savvy young people, the core of local community radio and cable access news programs, and a basis for current event classroom discussions in schools and colleges.

In addition to the production of VIN content, the Project Censored and the Media Freedom Foundation Web site at www.censorednews.org hosts syndicated news feeds (RSS feeds) from some thirty primary independent news sources, encouraging students to read daily news online from trustworthy, non-corporate international sources like *Flashpoints*, *Democracy Now!*, *Christian Science Monitor*, Inter Press Service (IPS) news, *Guardian*, the BBC, and twenty-five other sources.

> *Colleges and universities are currently under attack across the country from corporately funded organizations. This is why it is so critical for students to become involved in organizations like Project Censored, because this is one of the few organizations that gives students a voice that reaches people across the nation. Project Censored and the Media Freedom Foundation inspire students to not only get involved with a variety of domestic and international issues but stay involved and actively fight to make a difference.*

—Sarah Maddox, Project Censored research intern and student, 2007–09

TRUTH EMERGENCY: KEEPING THE FACTS AT BAY

There is a growing need to broaden understanding of censorship in the US. The dictionary definition of censorship as direct government control of news is no longer adequate. The private corporate media in the US significantly under-covers, deliberately censors, and/or completely ignores numerous important news stories every year, even when based on university-quality research. It appears that certain topics are simply forbidden inside the mainstream corporate media today. To openly cover these news stories would stir up questions regarding "inconvenient truths" that many in the US power structure would rather avoid.

Some of these inconvenient truths that remain taboo for corporate media include civilian death rates in Iraq, ongoing torture by US forces, questions about 9/11, and election fraud in 2004.

Civilian death rates in Iraq

Researchers from Johns Hopkins University and Opinion Research Business (ORB), a professional survey company in Great Britain, report that the United States has been directly responsible for more than one million Iraqi deaths since the 2003 invasion. A 2006 Johns Hopkins study confirmed that US aerial bombing in civilian neighborhoods caused over a third of these deaths, and that over half of the deaths are directly attributable to US forces. In January 2008, ORB reported that "over 1,000,000 Iraqi citizens have died as a result of the conflict which started in 2003. . . . We now estimate that the death toll between March 2003 and August 2007 is likely to have been of the order of 1,033,000."[3] Iraqi civilian death levels in the summer of 2010 likely now exceed 1.3 million.[4]

John Tirman, executive director and principal research scientist at the Massachusetts Institute of Technology's Center for International Studies, wrote in the February 16, 2009, issue of the *Nation*:

> Several household surveys were conducted between 2004 and 2007. While there are differences among them, the range suggests a congruence of estimates. But none have been conducted for eighteen months, and the two most reliable surveys were completed in mid-2006. The higher of those found 650,000 "excess deaths" (mortality attributable to war); the other yielded 400,000. The war remained ferocious for twelve to fifteen months after those surveys were finished and then began to subside. Iraq Body Count, a London NGO [nongovernmental organization] that uses English-language press reports from Iraq to count civilian deaths, provides a means to update the 2006 estimates. While it is known to be an undercount, because press reports are incomplete and Baghdad-centric, IBC nonetheless provides useful trends, which are striking. Its estimates are nearing 100,000, more than double its June 2006 figure of 45,000. (It does not count nonviolent excess deaths—from health emergencies, for example—or insurgent deaths.) If this is an acceptable marker, a plausible estimate of total deaths can be calculated by doubling the totals of the 2006 household surveys, which used a much more reliable and sophisticated method for estimates that draws on long experience in epidemiology. So we have, at present, between 800,000 and 1.3 million "excess deaths" as we approach the six-year anniversary of this war.[5]

After Tirman's publication in the *Nation*, the Associated Press (AP) released a news story on April 23, 2009, claiming—in what seems to us at Project Censored to be deliberate disinformation—that only 87,215 civilians had died in Iraq since 2005, and about 110,000 since the US invasion.[6] Then on October 14, 2009, AP released a second story on Iraq War civilian deaths saying that "at least 85,000 people lost their lives from 2004–08 in [Iraq's] violence," according to the Human Rights Ministry in Iraq, the first official report by the Iraqi government on the death toll since the war began.[7]

Newspapers and television widely covered the AP numbers, but only a handful of outlets have addressed the one million number, leaving a huge information gap among the American people. For example, one of the few newspapers to regularly list civilian deaths in Iraq is the weekly "War Casualties" report from the *Washington Post*, which reported on June 27, 2009, that the Iraqi civilian death estimate was between 92,393 and 100,868.

A May 2010 article in *Survey Research Methods* questions some of the research methods used by ORB in its conflict deaths survey.[8] The article acknowledges that "all credible sources on conflict mortality since the 2003 invasion have shown a staggering level of human losses suffered by the people of Iraq," though examines whether "the ORB estimate is exceptionally high even within this universe of figures." But while the debate on methodology continues and ORB has yet to respond to the article, the corporate media continues to selectively use the lowest estimates of deaths available, as if such selectivity was sound journalism.

Ongoing torture by US forces

The information gaps in the corporate media are significant and have been particularly pervasive since September 11, 2001. Another distressing example is how on October 25, 2005, the American Civil Liberties Union (ACLU) posted to their Web site forty-four autopsy reports, acquired from American military sources, covering the deaths of civilians who died while in US military prisons in Iraq and Afghanistan from 2002 to 2004. The Department of Defense released the autopsy reports in response to a Freedom of Information Act request filed by the ACLU, the Center for Constitutional Rights, Physicians for Human Rights, Veterans for Common Sense, and Veterans For Peace.

The autopsy reports provided proof of widespread torture by US forces. Twenty-one of those deaths were listed as homicides. An overwhelming majority of the other twenty-three reports listed the cause of death as "arteriosclerotic cardiovascular disease" (heart attack). The documents show that detainees died during and after interrogations by Navy SEALs, military intelligence, and other government agencies. "These documents present irrefutable evidence that US operatives tortured detainees to death during interrogation," said Amrit Singh, an attorney with the ACLU. "The public has a right to know who authorized the use of torture techniques and why these deaths have been covered up."

One of the forty-four US military autopsy reports, for detainee DOD 003164, reads as follows:

[D]ied as a result of asphyxia (lack of oxygen to the brain) due to strangulation as evidenced by the recently fractured hyoid bone in the neck with soft tissue hemorrhage extending downwards to the level of the right thyroid cartilage.[9]

As Peter Phillips has summarized of the rest of the report:

Autopsy revealed bone fracture, rib fractures, contusions in mid abdomen, back and buttocks extending to the left flank, abrasions, lateral buttocks. Contusions, back of legs and knees; abrasions on knees, left fingers and encircling to left wrist. Lacerations and superficial cuts, right 4th and 5th fingers. Also, blunt force injuries, predominately recent contusions (bruises) on the torso and lower extremities. Abrasions on left wrist are consistent with use of restraints. No evidence of defense injuries or natural disease. Manner of death is homicide. Whitehorse Detainment Facility, Nasiriyah, Iraq.[10]

A press release by the ACLU announcing the deaths was immediately picked up by the Associated Press, making the story available to US corporate media nationwide. A thorough check of Nexis-Lexis and ProQuest library databases showed that at least 99 percent of the daily papers in the US—similar to the one million dead report—did not pick up the story, nor did AP ever conduct follow-up coverage on the issue.[11]

The Los Angeles Times covered the story on page A4 with a 635-word report headlined "Autopsies Support Abuse Allegations." Fewer than a dozen other daily newspapers actually covered the story: *Bangor Daily*

News, Maine, page 8; *Telegraph Herald*, Dubuque, Iowa, page 6; *Charleston Gazette*, West Virginia, page 5; *Advocate*, Baton Rouge, Louisiana, page 11; and a half dozen others. *The Pittsburgh Post-Gazette* and the *Seattle Times* buried the story inside general Iraq news articles. *USA Today* posted the story on their Web site. MSNBC posted the story on their Web site, but apparently did not consider it newsworthy enough to air on television. Somehow, over 1,600 newspaper editors decided, somewhat independently, not to cover the news story that widespread torture and homicides were occurring in Iraqi war zones at multiple US military sites. It appears that certain news stories are simply too hot for most US editors and newscasters to cover.

Election fraud in 2004

Other too-hot-to-handle stories are evident as well. Political analysts have long counted on exit polls as a reliable predictor of actual vote counts. The unusual discrepancy between exit poll data and the actual vote count in the 2004 election challenges that reliability. However, despite evidence of technological vulnerabilities in the voting system and a higher incidence of irregularities in swing states, this discrepancy was not scrutinized in the corporate media. They simply parroted the partisan declarations of "sour grapes" and "let's move on" instead of providing any meaningful analysis of a highly controversial election.

The official vote count for the 2004 election showed that George W. Bush won by three million votes. But exit polls projected a victory margin of five million votes for John Kerry. This eight-million-vote discrepancy is much greater than the margin of error: the overall error margin should statistically have been under 1 percent. But the official result deviated from the poll projections by more than 5 percent—a statistical impossibility.[12]

Questions about 9/11

As mentioned in the introduction to the Truth Emergency section of this volume, sometimes even new academic research goes largely unreported when the work contradicts a prevailing understanding of recent historical events. Any questioning of the official government report on 9/11 offers a prime example. A clear case of academic research that the media failed to report is the 2009 peer-reviewed journal article from *Open Chemical Physics Journal* entitled "Active Thermitic Material Discovered in Dust for the 9/11 World Trade Center Catastrophe." In the abstract, the authors write:

> We have discovered distinctive red/gray chips in all the samples. These red/gray chips show marked similarities in all four samples. . . . The properties of these chips were analyzed using optical microscopy, scanning electron microscopy (SEM), X-ray energy dispersive spectroscopy (XEDS), and differential scanning calorimetry (DSC). . . . The red portion of these chips is found to be an unreacted thermitic material and highly energetic.[13]

Thermite is a pyrotechnic composition of a metal powder and a metal oxide, which produces an aluminothermic reaction known as a thermite reaction; it could be used in controlled demolitions of buildings.

Project Censored has no idea how nanothermite chips got into the dust of the World Trade Center on 9/11. But more than 1,200 architects and engineers worldwide now support the call for a new investigation into the destruction of the twin towers and Building 7 at the World Trade Center complex on September 11, 2001.[14]

We strongly believe that there should not be any topics that cannot be openly addressed in a democratic media system, especially those deemed controversial. When corporate media refuses to address significant issues such as election fraud, torture, massive civilian deaths, and the official report on 9/11, red flags should go up for all scholars and researchers. University-level reviews of important news stories need to proceed in an open manner in order to speak truth to power in an honest and forthright way.

Tens of thousands of Americans engaged in various social justice issues constantly witness how corporate media marginalizes, denigrates, or simply ignores their concerns. Activist groups working on exposing issues have been systematically excluded from mainstream corporate news and the national conversation, leading to a genuine truth emergency in the country.

THE ROLE OF PUBLIC UNIVERSITIES IN BUILDING INVESTIGATIVE REPORTS ON MEDIA DEMOCRACY AND TRANSPARENCY OF THE POWERFUL

Public colleges and universities have a role to play in building media democracy and in giving full transparency to what the powerful are doing in society. Universities are institutions founded on scientific, factual research and tasked with sharing their results with others, both within specific disciplines and outside the academy. As corporate media continues on the path of entertainment and decreases support for investigative reporting, an opportunity for colleges and universities emerges to take on the responsibility of validating independent news and performing investigative research for publication in independent media news sources worldwide.

College professors do not always think about their research in terms of its public benefit; most are trained to write for academic journals in a style that is factual, but often too complex for mass public reading.

However, the role of universities in supporting public education is receiving new attention, as evidenced by disciplines that are more receptive to action research, liberation sociology, applied anthropology, comparative historical analysis, qualitative methods, community service involvement, and experiential learning. Certainly some aspects of these research styles are based on an understanding that the work is for human betterment and democracy building, rather than just theory and discipline expansion.

Investigative research asks: Why do inequalities persist in society? And who are the beneficiaries of these inequalities? In other words, investigative research identifies key deciders. Rarely do the powerful claim to be the primary decision makers, as George W. Bush declared in his famous quote, "I am the decider." But when we identify and examine the individuals behind significant decisions within powerful institutions in society, a heightened level of public awareness can emerge, pulling the covers off those behind the bureaucratic curtains, and exposing their self interests and unequal rewards.

In *Censored 2010*, undergraduate Project Censored student researcher Andrew Hobbs conducted an investigative research study analyzing the content of news stories on Venezuelan President Hugo Chávez and the conservative radio talk show host Rush Limbaugh.

In the study, Hobbs wrote:

The news from US networks is based on the presentations of partially factual stories framed inside socio-emotional story lines that juxtapose "evil" with patriotism and Christian fervor.

Two notorious, controversial modern figures will be examined here to explain what we mean by a hyperreality of knowinglessness. News coverage of Venezuelan President Hugo Chávez and right-wing radio personality Rush Limbaugh are unique examples, primarily because of their perceived opposing views and their unapparent similarities. But they are similar in that both should have little operable relevance to American policy, at least domestically, as one is an entertainer and the other is the leader of another country. They both are media personalities as well: Limbaugh claims an audience of 20 million a week, while Chávez hosts a telecast every Sunday through which he speaks to millions of people of Venezuela. Further, they are both strongly ideological in their pursuit of their beliefs, which seem diametrically opposed to each other.

Unfortunately, they both have ill-gotten relevance, ironically at least partially gleaned from the massive amount of attention turned to them by their press adversaries.[15]

Hobbs's chapter in *Censored 2010* was translated into Spanish, and Hugo Chávez commented on it on Venezuelan national television in December 2009.

Student research is one of the cornerstones of higher education. While a secondary source can often provide a digest, its tone is subject to coloration. Project Censored goes to the primary sources, does its own sociological research, and sharpens the ideas these student researchers present. Only with the support of the entire PC program could I have written "Hyperreality," and only through the rigorous approach fostered by PC could that piece have found its way to Hugo Chávez himself. The close involvement of students with primary news sources allows those students to expose, firsthand, the omissions and revisions of the mass media.
—Andrew Hobbs, philosophy major, Sonoma State University, 2009

In another investigative research study at Sonoma State University, sociology professor Andrew Roth focused on photographs appearing on the front pages of the *New York Times* and the *San Francisco Chronicle* during two periods, from March to December 2003, and from January 2006 to March 2007. Examining the data, Roth and his fellow researchers asked: How frequently do front-page news photographs depict war in Afghanistan or Iraq? And, to what extent do these photos portray the human cost of those wars?[16]

Based on content analysis of more than 6,000 front-page news photos spanning 1,389 days of coverage, researchers found that only 12.8 percent of the photos related in some way to the wars in Afghanistan and Iraq. A mere 3.3 percent of those front-page news photos represented war's most fundamental human cost, by depicting dead, injured, or missing humans. The study documented the enormous gap between the number of actual deaths in Afghanistan and Iraq during this time span—which numbered in the hundreds of thousands—and the number of deaths depicted visually, through front-page photographs: just forty-eight images of human death. Researchers concluded that the human cost of war is permitted only a small, marginal position on the front pages of US newspapers.

Student-centered investigative research makes use of social science research methods to conduct data collection and analysis of important socioeconomic issues for broad public dissemination—much like in-depth investigative reporting—with particular focus on releasing valuable information through independent media for public consumption in addition to, or instead of, publication in academic journals or presentations at scholarly conferences. This public commitment reminds us that investigative research is a democracy-building process, addressing the sociostructural circumstances of who decides, who wins, and who loses in society. Public investigative research in the social sciences asks the questions: Who are the people with the most power? Who makes the important decisions that affect our lives? How did these sociopolitical elites acquire their positions? What advantages do these individuals share and what impacts do these advantages have on others in society?

College and universities worldwide are invited to submit faculty-reviewed investigative research for publication on the Project Censored Web site at www.projectcensored.org/top-stories/articles/category/investigative-research.

STRATEGIES NEEDED TO ADDRESS A GLOBAL
TRUTH EMERGENCY

The Obama administration is maintaining the neoconservative agenda of US military domination of the world—albeit with perhaps a kinder, gentler face. Barack Obama's election brought a moment of hope for many. However, the new administration has not decreased military spending, nor reversed US military global dominance. Instead, Obama retained Bush's Secretary of Defense, Robert Gates, thus making Obama the first president from an opposing party in US history to keep in place the outgoing administration's secretary of defense/war. Additionally, Obama is expanding war in Afghanistan, making minimal long-range reductions in Iraq, and using drone attacks on civilian targets in multiple countries.

Universities and colleges are complex and diverse institutions; we have continuing disagreements, ongoing theoretical feuds, ego-based careerism, and an often-overwhelming aversion to controversy. Yet we face a global military-industrial-media complex so powerful, and so unrelenting in propagandizing its subjects with fear and misinformation, that we are perhaps among the last semi-democratic open scholarship institutions that remain. It falls to us to take a stand on truth and transparency by encouraging independent media and scholarship regarding the manipulations of the powerful. We have a public education role: the responsibility to both train critical thinkers in society and to expand public knowledge and awareness of inconvenient truths.

A commonality of purpose can help guide us in these endeavors: the principles espoused in the Universal Declaration of Human Rights offer the fundamental values that colleges and universities can openly share.[17] It is up to us scholars and student researchers to retain a belief in the Enlightenment, for we represent the institutions that can offer hope to people to unite and oppose the common oppressors manifested in a militarist and unresponsive government. Only when the public creates and controls its own information resources will it become armed with the power that knowledge gives to create a new and truly vibrant democratic society, promising—as well as delivering—liberty, peace, and prosperity to all.

HOW STUDENTS CAN GET INVOLVED: FINDING CENSORED NEWS STORIES

Several hundred independent news sources, both foreign and domestic, are listed at www.projectcensored.org/censorship/news-sources. Many of these sources have links to hundreds of other news sources; for example, scrolling down the home page at www.commondreams.org reveals links to hundreds of important news sites. The main Indymedia site at www.indymedia.org contains links to over 160 regional Indymedia Web sites around the world. Most sites offer syndicated (RSS) feeds for which students can sign up and receive current breaking stories by e-mail.

Project Censored's goal is to identify and validate important news stories about which people globally should be knowledgeable, but which have not been covered by the corporate mainstream news outlets. These news stories will be reviewed, researched, and vetted by university students in affiliated classes with the support of professors and community experts. The results will help build public trust in online independent new sources. This *is* media democracy in action.

We envision the day that Project Censored will no longer be needed, when instead of only seeing and hearing what the top-down corporate media want us to see and hear, we will have thousands of colleges and universities supporting the widespread review and validations of news from the bottom up. We have democracy to gain and truth to maintain. We need to *be* media democracy in action.

CURRENT PROJECT CENSORED AFFILIATE COLLEGES AND UNIVERSITIES

Sonoma State University, Diablo Valley College, San Francisco State University, University of San Francisco, Laney College, Ohlone College, Champlain College, Indian River State College, Santa Rosa Junior College, St. John's University, University of Oregon, Eastern Oregon University, Niagara University, DePaul University, DePauw University, University of Utah, Immaculata University, Marymount Manhattan College, Loyola College (Maryland), St. Cloud State University, Foothill College, State University of New York–Potsdam, Skyline College, Florida Atlantic University, Southwest Minnesota State University, California State University–Stanislaus, California State University–Northridge, Siena College, Muhlenberg College, University of Strathclyde (Glasgow), Complutense University of Madrid, University of Chile, University of Buenos Aires, Jacobs University (Germany), University of Siegen (Germany), TU Dortmund University (Germany), University of La Laguna (Canary Islands), CIESPAL (Ecuador)

PETER PHILLIPS is the former director of Project Censored; a professor of sociology at California State University–Sonoma; and the president of the Media Freedom Foundation.

MICKEY HUFF is the director of Project Censored; an associate professor of history at Diablo Valley College; and a member of the board of directors of the Media Freedom Foundation.

Thanks to NOLAN HIGDON, Project Censored intern, who helped with the research and citations for this article.

Notes

1. Peter Phillips, Mickey Huff, and Project Censored, *Censored 2010: The Top 25 Censored Stories of 2008–09* (New York: Seven Stories Press, 2009). For more information on the Project's college and university affiliate program, see www.projectcensored .org/about/affiliates-program and www.mediafreedominternational.org/an-invitation-to-colleges-and-universities.
2. Pew Research Center, "Audience Segments in a Changing News Environment: Key News Audiences Now Blend Online And Traditional Sources," 2008, http://people-press.org/reports/pdf/444.pdf.
3. Opinion Business Research, 2008, http://www.opinion.co.uk/Newsroom_details .aspx?NewsId=120.
4. Peter Phillips, Andrew Roth, and Project Censored, *Censored 2009: The Top 25 Censored Stories of 2007–08* (New York: Seven Stories Press, 2008), 20. This is censored story #1 for this volume, archived online at http://www.projectcensored.org/top-stories/articles/1-over-one-million-iraqi-deaths-caused-by-us-occupation. For the earlier casualty numbers, see Dr. Gideon Polya's article, http://www.countercurrents.org/iraq-polya070207.htm. Also see John Tirman's work listed in note 5.
5. John Tirman, "Bush's War Totals," *Nation*, February 16, 2009, http://www.then-ation.com/article/bushs-war-totals.
6. Associated Press, "Secret Tally Has 87,000 Iraqis Dead," April 23, 2009.
7. Rebecca Santana, "Iraq Government: 85,000 Iraqis Killed in 2004–08," Associated Press, October 14, 2009.
8. Michael Spagat and Joshua Dougherty, "Conflict Deaths in Iraq: A Methodological Critique of the ORB Survey Estimate," *Survey Research Methods* 4, no. 1 (2010): 3–15.
9. American Civil Liberties Union, "US Operatives Killed Detainees During Interrogations in Afghanistan and Iraq," October 24, 2005, http://www.aclu.org/human-rights-national-security/us-operatives-killed-detainees-during-interrogations-afghanistan-and-.
10. For more on this ACLU study, see http://www.aclu.org/intlhumanrights/ gen/21236prs20051024.html. Also see Peter Phillips, "A Study of Bias in The Associated Press," *Censored 2007: The Top 25 Censored Stories* (New York: Seven Stories

Press, 2006), 343–55, http://www.projectcensored.org/articles/story/a-study-of-bias-in-the-associated-press/.

11. Peter Phillips, "A Study of Bias."

12. Peter Phillips, "Another Year of Distorted Election Coverage," in *Censored 2006: The Top 25 Censored Stories* (New York: Seven Stories Press, 2005), 48; and Steve Freeman and Joel Bleifuss, *Was the 2004 Presidential Election Stolen?: Exit Polls, Election Fraud, and the Official Count* (New York: Seven Stories Press, 2006).

13. Niels H. Harrit et al., "Active Thermitic Material Discovered in Dust from the 9/11 World Trade Center Catastrophe," *Open Chemical Physics Journal* 2 (April 3, 2009): 7–31, http://www.bentham.org/open/tocpj/openaccess2.htm.

14. See the Architects and Engineers for 9/11 Truth Web site, http://www.ae911truth.org, for an updated count. As of July 1, 2010, 1,218 architectural and engineering professionals had signed the petition to demand of Congress a "truly independent investigation." Also see, Architects and Engineers for 9/11 Truth Press Conference, San Francisco, CA, February 19, 2010, http://www2.ae911truth.org/downloads/AE911Truth-Petition&Names.pdf. See the conference announcement video online at http://www.youtube.com/ae911truth#p/c/891B0945A34D98F7/0/R35O_QQP8Vw.

15. Andrew Hobbs and Peter Phillips, "The Hyperreality of a Failing Corporate Media System" in *Censored 2010: The Top 25 Censored Stories of 2008–09* (New York: Seven Stories Press, 2009), 251–59.

16. Andrew Roth et al., "Covering War's Victims: A Content Analysis of Iraq and Afghanistan War Photographs in the *New York Times* and *San Francisco Chronicle*," *Censored 2008: The Top 25 Censored Stories of 2006–07* (New York: Seven Stories Press, 2007), 253–71.

17. United Nations, Universal Declaration of Human Rights, 1948, http://www.un.org/en/documents/udhr/index.shtml.

CHAPTER 12

Commodity or Right
Laws that Regulate Communication in Spain and America

by Concha Mateos

> *Our media system is the direct result of government*
> *action—laws and regulatory policies—that established*
> *not just the playing field but also the winners of the game.*
> —ROBERT W. MCCHESNEY AND JOHN NICHOLS[1]

Media systems need to be controlled in order to be useful. The conflict between different broadcasters, whose transmission signals were interfering with each other, originated in the 1920s, and in 1927, the first laws in the United States were passed to license and regulate the media. This is how it all started: the political authority began governing the game of communication—supposedly in everyone's interests. But how is everyone's interest being protected a century later? Who is the law favoring?

The Organization of American States' Declaration of Principles on Freedom of Expression states:

ARTICLE 12. Monopolies or oligopolies in the ownership and control of the communication media should be subject to antitrust laws as they conspire against democracy by limiting the plurality and diversity which ensure the full exercise of people's right to information. . . . The concession of radio and television broadcast frequencies should take into account democratic criteria that provide equal opportunity of access for all individuals.

ARTICLE 13. The exercise of power and the use of public funds by the state, the granting of customs duty privileges, the arbitrary and discriminatory placement of official advertising and government loans, the concession of radio and television broadcast frequencies, among others, with the intent to put pressure on and punish or reward and provide privileges to social communicators and communications media because of the opinions they express threaten freedom of expression, and must be explicitly prohibited by law. The means of communication have the right to carry out their role in an independent manner. Direct or indirect pressures exerted upon journalists or other social communicators to stifle the dissemination of information are incompatible with freedom of expression.[2]

USA: POLICY IN FAVOR OF THE CONCENTRATION OF MEDIA POWER

The Federal Communications Commission (FCC) is the authority that regulates broadcasting in the United States. In each case, it must consider and prioritize the public interest, convenience, and necessity. These are some of the FCC's features:

▸ It is a pioneering entity.

▸ It is considered an independent government agency, with its own regulatory capacity and executive control, though its members are appointed by the president with the consent of the Senate.

▸ It has rarely regulated content.

▸ It has always operated under heavy and varied pressures from the US government, Congress, courts, lobbies, and, in the last decade, the public.

▸ Since the expansion of deregulatory policies in the 1980s, it has tended to reduce limitations on the concentration of media ownership, encouraging ever-higher levels of concentration.

The broadcasting reforms adopted by the FCC in 2003 are a paradigmatic example of how political power goes to help large corporations. News Corp./Fox, General Electric/NBC, Viacom/CBS, and Disney/ABC were accumulating other media companies and audiences at rates that exceeded limits previously set by regulatory standards, so the rules had to be amended or else the corporations would be illegal. The FCC thus changed the rules, allowing the percentage of national audience that one television network could target to increase from 35 percent to 45 percent. Additionally, the FCC permitted the co-ownership of a newspaper and a television network in the same market, and of more than two television stations.

The new rules prompted, for the first time in the US, an important social debate on these measures.[3] The Republican commissioners who controlled the FCC avoided public assemblies as much as possible, choosing instead to have hearings that featured pro-concentration corporate media presentations. However, a massive public outcry against further consolidation emerged from over 750,000 people, and more than 3 million messages were sent to the FCC.[4] The public reaction was particularly significant because the US is a country that has been accustomed, as media scholar Robert McChesney pointed out years before, to allowing the corporate domination of communication—assuming it to be a natural situation outside of political debate.[5]

Following the mobilization in 2003, McChesney and others recognized that a new social behavior toward media policy had emerged, as activists organized strategic protests around specific issues.[6] But it was not possible to stop the erosion of democracy, and the interests of the market were privileged over the protection of citizens' rights. The resistance, however, had an effect: it made visible the great distance between the political–corporate power structure and public citizen demands.

Vermont Senator Bernie Sanders, a critic of media monopolies, noted at the time, "It is not a coincidence that everything blew up the way it did this year. The American people know they are getting less information than they had before about decisions that are being made in their name, and they know that we are passing some critical points where, if we don't act, citizens are not going to have the information they need to function in a democracy."[7]

The Telecommunications Act of 1996, passed during the Clinton administration, left the door open for the FCC to continue allowing corporate media concentration. From that year on, FCC licensing regulations had to be reviewed every two years. As media scholar Juan Carlos Miguel de Bustos explained, this is a perverse mechanism that requires the FCC to perpetually seek evidence to prove the benefit of the rules adopted, leaving political power hampered with the permanent obligation to defend itself, or to succumb to the pressure.[8]

These are the peculiarities of the US system, which gradually become normalized as other countries take them as reference. On the other side of the Atlantic, the corporate model is expanding, eating away at the powerful concept of "public service" that was institutionalized in Europe between the creation of the first television station in the 1930s and just after the Second World War, and which was maintained throughout the last century.

SPAIN 2010: A LEGAL ARMOR TO PROTECT COMMUNICATIONS AS A BUSINESS

In Spain, there is a large gulf between communication policy and democracy. The dictator Francisco Franco died in 1975, and in 1978 the constitution currently in force was approved. At that time, public television was already twenty years old and had two unhealthy habits: it operated as a monopoly and was a propaganda tool for the government. The monopoly ended in the late 1980s, but the use of propaganda continued, leading to a 2003 court case that found public television guilty of manipulation of information.[9]

The last term of Spain's right-wing government was exemplary in its use of propaganda and its partisan control of the media system. In addition to the shameful sentence received by public television, the government blocked the decentralization of the licensing of radio; the creation of an independent audiovisual authority, which the public had demanded for thirty years; the legal framework for the development of local broadcasting and community media; and the operation of the newspaper, *Egunkaria*, which was unconstitutionally shut down—media censorship, which is against the law.[10]

Elections on March 14, 2004, removed the Popular Party from power and gave way to the victorious Socialist Party. The outgoing conservative president, José María Aznar, a promoter of Spain's participation in the 2003 invasion of Iraq, managed the social crisis in the worst way imaginable: he personally called the editors and foreign correspondents of the major newspapers to dictate headlines that would be acceptable.[11] He refused to answer key questions and promoted a presidential discourse to the media that contained lies. Amid this atmosphere of information suffocation, the new president, José Luis Rodríguez Zapatero, arrived with a stellar promise: to reform public media, and the media system in general—to pull it out of the propaganda pit. Among his first acts as the head of government, Zapatero appointed a board of socially and academically recognized experts to direct the reform. For the first time in the history of Spain, the government promoted a media policy designed by specialists in the field, not parties, and based on consultations with the public.

Shortly thereafter, Zapatero reversed course. The strides toward pluralism turned into actions promoting concentration; the reform of public service became a reduction of jobs; and the idea of a media advisory council—enlightened reason guiding policy decisions—was abandoned to give in to the pressure from media groups. The final developments in Spain's communication policy were already moving toward a neoliberal policy, with corporate control over reform, when two key regulatory actions in 2009 further contributed to the dismantling of antitrust policies and the weakening of public television.

First, the door was opened to greater concentration of media ownership in Spain with a royal decree in February 2009, which was reminiscent of the FCC reforms in the US in 2003. The decree repealed the limitation to owning more than 5 percent of media service providers, though to make it look as if pluralism had been protected, the percentage of the audience that the same media owner could accumulate was limited to 27 percent. A royal decree, promulgated by the government and constitutionally invoked in emergencies, ignores any kind of public participation in its development; right from this decree's opening words—"The major developed economies . . ."[12]—it was clear the issue was an economic one. Its urgency was justified by the economic conditions that "threaten[ed] the balance of television service," a threat that made it necessary, according to the law, to ensure the strength of companies.

While it *appears* that the law does not allow any operator to accumulate large audience shares, this is not really the case. The law simply stipulates that operators cannot merge when, within the previous twelve months of the merger, their audience share is larger than 27 percent. After a merger, the road is clear, and the market share that may be gained is no longer in the government's control.

As the possibility of accumulating power for private operators was extended, the same possibility for public operators was reduced: publicly owned providers could not reserve or be assigned more than 25 percent of the airwaves available for state television service through terrestrial stations, regardless of the audiences they manage to reach, and production tools were limited. For privately owned media, the production tools *appeared* to be limited, but only at the time of purchase; there were no conditions applied to the possibility of growth beyond purchase.

The second neoliberal blow was inflicted in August 2009, when the rules changed regarding the financing of public radio and television. Previously, public media were permitted to have 25 percent of their funding come through advertising, but the new law prohibited advertising, sponsorship, and teleshopping in the public sector. How do public corporations fill the gap in their funding? With contributions from private operators, which conveniently benefit from the elimination of competitors in their advertising markets. Public-access networks must contribute 3 percent of their income, restricted/pay networks 1.5 percent, and telecommunications operators 0.9 percent. Thus, the law was changed to garner easier profits for private operators.

Above all, this law has created a remarkable paradox because it has made public television dependent on the private: When it receives more funding from private operators, public television is able to deliver higher quality with greater resources, and as a result attract more viewers. But to receive more funding from private operators, public television needs to leave the audience to them so that they can earn more money through advertising. Therefore, if things go well for TVE (Spanish Television), they will also go wrong: if TVE attracts a large audience sector, contributions will be lower from those that ought to fund it and, therefore, TVE will lower its own income. The trap is perfect.[13]

Now suppose that, despite everything, Spanish public television were to do well—as it somehow managed to do for long periods during the Zapatero government. And suppose that, despite being unstable, it were to get enough money from its sources.[14] *Just in case* this were to occur, public operators were given even more restrictions, in the midst of all this deregulation, to further ensure that they would not be very good or very competitive. Besides the limit to not operate in more than 25 percent of the frequency spectrum, additional measures that reduce public media's potential for success and growth include an expenditure budget limited to €1,200 million in 2010–11, a limit to increasing that budget beyond 1 percent annually in the next triennium, and restrictions on programming for public television, which is neither permitted to spend more than 10 percent on sporting events of general interest nor allowed to premiere more than fifty-two major international film productions during prime time.

In summary, communications policy in Spain faced crippling intervention in the public sector while the private was afforded a great deal more freedom. Can you imagine applying a similar logic to public health care? Let's prevent the means to cure illness and to treat people properly in public hospitals because then patients might heal and leave the private health care businesses without clients! This sort of reasoning prevails when decisions are made by political parties that are pressured by corporations. When the experts and everyday citizens are consulted, a whole other approach succeeds.[15]

COMMODITY OR RIGHT: DEFENSE OR REDUCTION OF THE COLLECTIVE

What interests are behind the regulation of the media system? And who decides how it is regulated? These are the keys that allow us to distinguish the character of a law. Who is given the power to decide on the media?

The General Law on Audiovisual Communication in Spain, published on April 1, 2010, has put the finishing touch on deregulation, concentration, and strangulation of public media.[16] The law begins like this: "The audiovisual industry has become in recent years an area with increasing weight and importance for the economy." Once again, a law about communication designed to address an economic issue—communication treated as a commodity rather than a right. In countries like Spain and the United States, such propaganda has managed to make people accept the business priority as a natural state of things. But this is not the case in many other parts of the world. There are other possibilities.

LATIN AMERICA: A DECADE OF DEMOCRATIC RECONQUEST OF THE MEDIA SYSTEM

Restructuring public media and rethinking the management of media's private sectors are occurring in many countries.[17] Venezuela and Argentina have already made significant changes, and Uruguay has made particular advances on media policy, although Ecuador and Mexico have to date resisted pressures for reform. New frameworks for more participatory and less concentrated media systems are emerging, but resistance continues in the corporate sectors. The dominant corporate media, both national and international, tends to block information on the democratization of communication processes. Why? They feel harmed: their ability to become monopolies is limited. Audience participation relinquishes decision-making control over what programming should be, which media should be penalized, or who should be granted an operating license. And greater recognition of new media and community media means less audience share for corporate media.

On June 12, 2000, Venezuela passed the Telecommunications Act, updating a legal media framework that had not been updated for seventy years. The Ley Orgánica de Telecomunicaciones (LOTEL; Organic

Telecommunications Law) states in Article 7 that the broadcasting spectrum belongs to everyone. The LOTEL is still informed by the principles of free competition and economic freedom, giving licenses to private companies so that they can commercially exploit that spectrum with their own facilities, but the law does not say that the spectrum *belongs* to these companies—they can only use it. "The spectrum belongs to everyone," is noted again in the 2005 Law on Social Responsibility on Radio and Television, known as the Ley Resorte (Spring Law).[18] Because the spectrum belongs to everyone, so does the message. What are the implications of Venezuela's new way of conceiving the media system? Unlike in Spain and the US, citizens are encouraged to take over the message, in many ways.

By managing a medium. One direct way to take ownership of the spectrum is by directly managing a medium. For the first time in history, a country—Venezuela—has pushed through a state policy that recognizes, develops, and promotes community media.[19] In most other countries, this type of media has been limited by the force of the law or marginalized for not having the capacity to participate in economic auctions in which only the powerful manage to obtain licenses.[20] Other countries have followed Venezuela's lead, such as Uruguay, which adopted a regulation on community media in 2007.

By focusing on the local. Another way to take hold of the communal spectrum is by developing local programming that may then be transferred beyond the immediate public space to citizens through all channels, both public and private. Community media in particular must ensure such participation and transmit 70 percent of their own local productions.

By developing programs. Another strategy is to develop the content and become a national independent producer (NIP). By law all stations, public and private, must broadcast a percentage of content produced by NIPs. Public funds are available to finance these productions.

By deciding. One indirect way to participate is through decision-making organizations like the Comisión de Programación (Programming Committee), which establishes program guidelines. It has four voting members, one of whom is part of the government, while the other three represent operators providing radio and television services, producers, and users.

By allowing representation. Another indirect claim to the spectrum is by relegating authority to the state, which can occupy, on behalf of citizens, programming spaces at all stations. This last strategy, which says, "Communication is mine, but I leave it to someone else to look after it on my behalf," is the dominant model in Europe and in the United States.

In Spain, one change hailed as most democratizing, as supposed proof that the citizens decide for themselves, has been to have Parliament, rather than the government, represent the citizens and elect the president of the TVE corporation, who in turn elects the director of public media, who subsequently decides content. Oh, great progress in public participation! A little indirect, isn't it? All the opportunities that citizens have to participate in Spain's media system are highly indirect. Citizens have been granted the honor to have Parliament elect the audiovisual authority in their name. Let's look at the power of this authority:

▸ Licenses are granted by the government, not the authority.

▸ Rules, programming, and regulatory codes are set by radio and television stations themselves.

▸ The authority may, on behalf of the citizens, put sanctions on the media and sometimes also be consulted on matters of communication.

▸ The grand "democratizing" gesture of the new law: any citizen may request that the council admonish radio and television stations that broadcast programs considered improper.

This "democratizing advance" is ironic, just like the shameless US Republicans at the FCC who avoided public hearings prior to the FCC's 2003 broadcasting reforms.

Venezuela has been subjected to all sorts of criticism, but most of the critics ignore the two key collective entities that ensure implementation of the law—entities equivalent to the audiovisual authority or communications commissioner in other countries.

The Directorio de Responsabilidad Social (Board of Social Responsibility) is the executive body for communications policy, and is responsible for sanctions and budget management. It is composed of one representative with expertise in communication and information; one expert in education and sports; one with authority in the area of consumer and user protection; one from the Women's National Institute; one from the National Council for the Rights of Children and Adolescents; one religious representative; one from schools of social communication at national universities; and two community members. The group discusses and approves technical standards in accordance with the Ley Resorte; imposes sanctions and makes recommendations to grant or revoke radio and television licenses; and decides the allocation of resources from the Social Responsibility Fund, which serves especially in support of independent national production.

Venezuela also has the Consejo de Responsabilidad Social (Social Responsibility Council), an advisory body. On this council, community members at large have two representatives, while twenty-two other elected representatives each correspond to a sector: broadcasters, indigenous people, culture-related associations, and several others.

In this first decade of the twenty-first century, public media legislation in Argentina is in full force.[21] On October 10, 2009,[22] the Ley de Servicios de Comunicación Audiovisual (Law on Audiovisual Communication Services) was proclaimed.[23] Large media corporations were given one year to sell the percentages of their businesses necessary to avoid domination in the media. Companies that had grown too big are now in the process of divesting, de-monopolizing, and thinning their businesses.

In February 2010, the opposition failed in all its efforts to obstruct the law—during its public discussion, elaboration, approval, and enactment periods—and thus used the last recourse available: to block its implementation with a legal process. Two members of Parliament accused the law of having irregularities in its sanctions process. This was a strategy to extend the time corporations have to sell.

This Argentinean law has represented the viable adaptation of a media system to the political framework of democracy, and has been developed in a process of public debate that has never before occurred when setting a law on communication.[24] It was approved with more than two hundred modifications to the initial draft. The government has been the driving force behind setting the law, but it has also been very much a social initiative, as social organizations, unions, cooperatives, human rights organizations, universities, and opposition parties have participated in its definition and elaboration.

Convened by the Argentina Community Radio Forum (FARCO), the Coalition for Democratic Broadcasting formed in 2004; on August 21, 2004 , the coalition launched a proposal of twenty-one basic points necessary to ensure democratic broadcasting. Some critics have accused the government of building this coalition, but in fact, several parties of the center-left opposition have also supported the project in Parliament. Even sectors considered more radical have expressed support, such as the International Marxist Tendency, which spoke of Argentina's new audiovisual law as "liberating, democratic and revolutionary in Argentina."[25] Critical voices have spoken out against the law for various reasons, from both leftists and conservative big media allies. Criticism from the left is documented on the Web site BarricadaTV,[26] aimed at the "counter-informational revolutionary practice," a political and social praxis with the goal of transforming the unjust society in which we live.[27]

Listed below are the key demands made by the Coalition for Democratic Broadcasting on August 21, 2004. Progressive social organizations from other parts of the world have often demanded these same ideas:[28]

▸ Communication is a right rather than a business.

▸ It is necessary to set limits to concentration and monopolies.

▸ The spectrum represents the heritage of humanity and cannot be commercialized; the holders of licensees cannot trade them.

▸ License renewals must undergo public hearings.

▸ The three types of operators should be recognized equally: public, private with commercial aims, and nonprofit private operators.

▸ Thirty-three percent of the frequencies should be reserved for nonprofit operators.

▸ Public servants and members of the armed forces cannot receive licenses.

▸ Media and audiovisual arts workers, and citizens in general, should participate in the authority of law enforcement.

Corporate media has not been fond of many aspects of Argentina's new law because it involves control and limitations:

▸ It becomes more difficult to influence or manage the media authority because that authority is plural. The government holds a majority within it, but other organizations may join. The media will have to be publicly accountable.

▸ They have to divest and sell. Four focus groups control more than 80 percent of the business and content production (the newspaper *Clarín* holds 35 percent).

▸ Foreign capital cannot exceed 30 percent, though authorization to increase the percentage can be requested and the law respects preexisting international treaties. Some media is currently in the hands of transnational companies (Channel 9, FM Rock & Pop, etc.), and others have a large percentage of American capital in their budgets, such as *Clarín*.

▸ To obtain licenses, applicants have to prove the origin of funds needed for the investment required.

▸ The objectives of the services they provide—the promotion of federalism, regional integration, a priority to address the audience's media literacy, etc.—will be determined by law.

▸ Programming content (as in Venezuela and, to a much lesser extent, in Spain) is established as follows: Radio stations are required to transmit at least 70 percent national programming; 50 percent their own programming, which must include local news or information; and 20 percent educational, cultural, and public welfare programming. Television stations are required to transmit 60 percent national programming; 30 percent their own programming, which must include local news; and varying percentages (30 percent, 15 percent, and 10 percent) independent local programming, according to the size of their constituency.

▸ The government may intervene to limit the exclusive broadcasting and rebroadcasting rights of certain events of general interest.

▸ The distribution of official advertising will be regulated to prevent the favoring of "media friends."

As we can see, the new legal framework in Argentina is not intended as a gift to corporations, as it is in the US and Spain. In the absence of corporate favoritism, the dominant corporate media manipulated their coverage of the process of formulating the law.[29] *Clarín* never once provided favorable sources or published a single positive piece of information about the law. Additionally, the political arms of corporations continue to resort to legal tricks to boycott the parts of the law they do not like.[30]

Similar reasons explain the brakes put to new bills that had been approved in Ecuador and Mexico.

COMMUNITY COMMUNICATION AS DEMOCRATIZING FACTOR

A medium can be managed directly by the public sector for public purposes, by the private sector for private purposes, or by the private sector for public purposes. This latter framework is recognized as the "third sector of communication" and is often referred to as "community media," wherein an organized society manages communications to serve collective purposes without profit motives.

Three main elements allow us to recognize how community media contributes to the democratization of a media system. First, plurality becomes another distribution factor. Second, social interest drives expectations, not the imperative of economic benefit for the owner, providing benefits such as more culture, more social cohesion, etc. And third, participation is guided by organizations with democratic solvency, not economic solvency.

The first country in the Americas to develop a state policy with this profile was Venezuela. Community media organizations have also been recognized in other Latin American countries like Colombia, Ecuador, Bolivia, and Peru.

In Uruguay, in October 2005, several organizations presented a bill on community broadcasting.[31] In June 2007, a large majority of the Uruguayan Parliament approved a law that is considerably more progressive about community media than Spain. Some points the law covers:[32]

Spectrum reserve. The government will reserve "at least one third of the spectrum for each location in all analogue and digital frequency bands and for all forms of broadcast."

No coverage limitations. It is guaranteed that there will be no limitations to the power of stations, the radio coverage they can reach, or the number of stations by locality, because the law understands that the service they provide is defined by its public and social interest, not the scope of their transmission.

No limitations on economic development. As noted by the Asociación Mundial de Radios Comunitarias (AMARC; World Association of Community Broadcasters), the law has not confused the nonprofit model with an organization's ability to manage financial resources for its development. Media can "obtain resources from, among other sources, donations, solidarity contributions, sponsorships, advertising . . . which shall not be discriminated against."[33] To ensure that they maintain the nonprofit model, media groups are required to reinvest all of the obtained resources into their development as community communications services, which are controlled by periodic hearings.

Collective guidelines for social participation. A coalition of organizations drafted the guidelines for participation, with approved licenses granted (for the first time in Uruguay) via open public competition and after a public hearing. The Honorary Advisory Council for community broadcasting was created, comprised of governmental and nongovernmental members from universities and other research bodies, whose consent is mandatory to draw up regulations and implement licensing competitions and granting.

The Uruguayan community broadcasting law also has clear limits:

▸ The number of licenses that may be granted is controlled with measures taken to prevent granting among people with family ties.

▸ Programming must be mostly owner-produced, national, and independent.

▸ Stations may recruit staff, who may also be the license holders, but salaries higher than minimum wage are considered prohibited within the context of the nonprofit media model.

▸ Granted licenses cannot be sold, transferred, or rented.

Spain's 2010 General Law on Audiovisual Communication has legally recognized this community media sector, but has also put extra limitations on it: community media cannot be financed by advertising and annual budgets cannot exceed €100,000 (for television stations) and €50,000 (for radio stations)—a remarkable contrast to the freedom enjoyed by corporations within the same law.

In its valuation statement published about the Spanish law, the Unión Latina de Economía Politica de la Información, la Comunicación y la Cultura (ULEPICC; Latino Union of Political Economy of Information, Communication, and Culture), maintains that the law represents "a point of no return in the removal of the citizenship from the socialist communication policy and in its adaptation to the interests of communication business groups, . . . citizens' right to quality communication is little guaranteed . . . [and] it represents a separation from the basic criteria of the progressive tradition."[34]

When analyzing the legal framework of a whole country's media system, it is important to not become complacent with the ideal that community media exercises the "right to information and freedom of expression of the population of the Republic," as was stated in Article 4 of the 2007 Uruguayan law. Obviously, this is one of the purposes of community communication, but such a function is not assigned exclusively to community media, as if the rest of the media did not have the same obligation. This is the conceptual feature that differentiates the 2005 Venezuelan law, the Ley Resorte, from the other laws discussed here: the idea that all media, private or public, aspires to the same ideal of public service, with the same obligations and the same responsibilities. Hence the name of the law: on Social Responsibility on Radio and Television.

A country's social communication through radio and television is everybody's business, a public issue. Some entities may gain the privilege to do business by selling the public's attention, but when it comes to fundamental rights like communication, information, and freedom of expression, all media operators—public, private, and community—must be subject to public control. This public control requires the broad participation of all society—as long as we aim to call it democratic.

Notes

1. Robert W. McChesney and John Nichols, *Our Media, Not Theirs: The Democratic Struggle Against Corporate Media* (New York: Open Media/Seven Stories Press, 2002), 27.
2. "Declaration of Principles on Freedom of Expression," Inter-American Commission on Human Rights/Organization of American States, http://www.cidh.org/basicos/english/Basic21.Principles%20Freedom%20of%20Expression.htm.
3. Robert W. McChesney, *The Problem of the Media: U.S. Communication Politics in the 21st Century* (New York: Monthly Review Press, 2004).
4. Oswaldo León, "EEUU: Triunfo de los Monopolios Mediáticos" (Triumph of Media Monopolies), Agencia Latinoamericana de Informacíon (Latin American Information Agency), June 6, 2003, http://alainet.org/active/3844&lang=es; and Robert W. McChesney and John Nichols, "Up in Flames," *Nation*, November 17, 2003, http://www.thenation.com/doc/20031117/mcchesney.
5. Robert W. Mc Chesney, *Corporate Media and the Threat to Democracy* (New York: Open Media/Seven Stories Press, 1997), 8.
6. See McChesney, *The Problem of the Media*; and Fernando Tucho, "La Sociedad Civil ante el Sistema Mediático: El Movimiento de Reforma de los Medios en Estados Unidos" (Civil Society and Media System: The Media Reform Movement in the United States), *Zer* 20 (2006): 299–317, http://www.ehu.es/zer/zer20/zer20_18_tucho.pdf.
7. As quoted in McChesney and Nichols, "Up in Flames."
8. Juan Carlos Miguel de Bustos,"Caracterización de la Regulación de la FCC" (Characteristics of the FCC Regulation), *Zer* (2007): 119–137, http://www.ehu.es/zer/zer23/ZER23_miguel.pdf (accessed on April 27, 2010).
9. The first public television news programs were censured due to their biased treatment of the general strike against the government in May 2002. At the time, the director of public television was a government-appointed position. No one resigned after the sentencing.
10. The *Egunkaria* case is indeed one of direct censorship using the judiciary. On February 20, 2003, a court order by Judge Del Olmo shut down the newspaper *Egunkaria*, and the documents and belongings of several members of the board were confiscated. The board members were accused of belonging to the armed Basque separatist group Euskadi Ta Askatasuna (ETA) because of a police report that allegedly showed that the newspaper had acted under the ETA's orders. The newspaper's closing led to unemployed workers, the arrests of promoters and managers, financial losses, silenced voices, a public without a newspaper, a seven-year legal process, irreparable moral costs and damages. . . . The prosecution itself requested the dismissal, but two of the accusatory associations, who were backed by the incriminating and obsessive discourse of the right and the country's most reactionary media, insisted on carrying out the trial. On April 12, 2010, a ruling by the High Court terminated the trial and declared the innocence of all defendants, confirming that *Egunkaria* was not an instrument of ETA and that the closure of the newspaper had no direct constitutional authorization and lacked explicit

legal standards to authorize it. The newspaper *El Público* emphasized that a simple analysis of *Egunkaria*'s editorial line allowed them to "rule out that the paper was an instrument to commit crimes." The allegations were unable to prove "directly or indirectly" that *Egunkaria* was defending the principles of the terrorist group. Shocking and highly illustrative of the seriousness of the ruling power's obsessive, persecutory attitude is the story of Joan Mari Torrealdai, the newspaper's chairman of the board at the time of its closure, published by *El Público* before the conclusion of the trial: http://blogs.publico.es/dominiopublico/1768/desde-el-banquillo-de-los-acusados/.

11. Madrid's Atocha Station suffered a terrorist attack on March 11, 2004. The government withheld data of the police investigation that followed a trail from members of an Islamist group (who were eventually confirmed as the attackers), and instead attempted to impose the view that the attackers were from ETA. The idea of Islamist attackers did not suit the government at first for fear it would trigger the idea of retaliation for Spain having unlawfully participated in the invasion of Iraq.

12. Royal Legislative Decree 1/2009 on urgent measures in telecommunications matters, *Boletín Oficial del Estado* (Official Bulletin of the State), February 24, 2009, http://www.boe.es/boe/dias/2009/02/24/pdfs/BOE-A-2009-3022.pdf.

13. This copies the model used in France by Nicolas Sarkozy's conservative government.

14. Public television's income from private operators is supplemented with 80 percent of the state's airwave usage fee (out of maximum of €320 million) and an additional state subsidy.

15. The spirit of the advisory council for the reform of radio and television, which had encouraged the first steps of the socialist government in 2004, was buried; Zapatero had only been pretending to listen to society, albeit in an elitist way. But some council members were not afraid to question the quashing of their group. Enrique Bustamante, a council member writing on the elimination of advertising on public television in a paper on the counterreform, noted that in 2006, of the over eighty organizations and associations consulted by the council, none had asked for the end of advertising but for its control. The only exceptions were the groups Vocento, Telecinco, and Union de Televisiones Comerciales Asociadas (UTECA; Union of Associated Commercial Television Networks), which also demanded an end to subsidies—with the obvious intent of the predation and destruction of the public service. The advisory council had been an attempt to give voice to the social body in decisions beyond the parties and the industry, a voice beyond the political and economic power—a voice that was not heeded.

16. Law 7/2010 of March 31, *Boletín Oficial del Estado* (Official Bulletin of the State), April 1, 2010, http://boe.es/boe/dias/2010/04/01/pdfs/BOE-A-2010-5292.pdf.

17. Interview with Armand Mattelart, *Boletín Digital de Politicas de Comunicación* (Digital Bulletin of Communication Policies) 6 (July 2004), http://www.pyp-uba.com.ar/news6/news6.htm#2 (accessed on August 12, 2006).

18. Concha Mateos, "Del Saqueo a la Soberanía Mediática en Venezuela: La Vía de la Responsabilidad Social en los Medios" (From Plundering to Sovereignty in Venezuela: The Path of Social Responsibility in the Media), in t"Venezuela en Transición: La Experiencia Bolivariana de Gobierno" (Venezuela in Transition: The Bolivarian Government Experience), special issue, *Ágora: Revista de Ciencias Sociales* 13 (2005): 191–217.

19. As I explained in my 2005 *Ágora* piece, Article 200 of the LOTEL has reminded and demanded of the state, since 2000, that its duty is to "promote the existence of nonprofit radio stations and public-access channels, as means for pluralistic and transparent communication and action, of the communities organized in their respective fields." In other

words, the state has to "let go" for people to manage it, for the greater good. More media "owners," less concentration.

20. For instance, a 2001 report about Guatemala, in the round table summary on freedom of expression by the Organization of American States, cited the concern that "the Government will continue awarding concessions (of radio) based only on economic criteria that leave no access to the minority areas of the Guatemalan society, such as the indigenous people, youth and women."

21. Already in 1987, Argentina's former president Raúl Alfonsín had instructed the Council for the Consolidation of Democracy to draft a law on broadcasting. Renewal of the media system has been a long-blocked democratic demand and need. In a letter addressed to President Cristina Fernández de Kirchner in July 2008, the Coalition for Democratic Communication claimed that hundreds of projects submitted to senators and members of Parliament had not managed to get ahead. See "Carta de la Coalición por una Radiodifusión Democrática a la Presidenta de la Nación," Coalición por una Radiodifusión Democrática (Buenos Aires), July 2008, http://21puntos.blogspot.com/2008_08_01_archive.html.

22. The new law will replace the Broadcasting Law 22.285, which was signed by the dictator Jorge Videla.

23. "Servicios de Comunicación Audiovisual" (Audiovisual Communication Services), Law 26.522, *Boletín Oficial de la Republica Argentina* (Official Gazette of the Republic of Argentina), October 10, 2009, http://www.medios.gov.ar/images/stories/documentos/1010-ley.pdf.

24. "Las Frecuencias Nos Pertenecen a Todos" (The Frequencies Belong to Us All), *Página 12*, April 27, 2008, http://www.pagina12.com.ar/diario/elpais/1-103152-2008-04-27.html.

25. International Marxist Tendency, "Por una 'Ley de Medios' Emancipadora, Democrática y Revolucionaria en Argentina" (For an Emancipatory, Democratic and Revolutionary 'Media Law' in Argentina), *El Militante: Voz Socialista de los Trabajadores y la Juventud* (The Militant: The Voice of Socialist Workers and Youth), April 15, 2010, http://argentina.elmilitante.org/content/view/4696/60. This article allows you to read the whole of the International Declaration on the Communication signed by this political group, presented for public support. In it, they maintain their support for this law, which they consider a "step forward" even though it is not a "perfect law."

26. BarricadaTV, "Contrainformación," http://www.barricadatv.org/contrainformacion.html.

27. Barricada TV, "Imágenes en Lucha," http://www.barricadatv.org/quienes.html.

28. Available in full on Coalición por una Radiodifusión Democrática's Web sites, http://www.coalicion.org.ar/ and http://21puntos.blogspot.com.

29. The Media Observatory in Argentina conducted research on the coverage that the newspapers *Clarín*, *La Nación*, and *Página 12*—all published in Buenos Aires, with national circulation—gave to the parliamentary negotiation of the law. The two big corporate newspapers, *Clarín* and *La Nación*, showed manipulative treatment, always presenting the process negatively. The study is available at http://www.ciespal.net/mediaciones/images/obser1.leypercent2odepercent2omedios.informes. percent2or.pdf.

30. The application of the law was paralyzed at the time of closing the drafting of this text, in May 2010.

31. The Asociación Mundial de Radios Comunitarias (AMARC; World Association of Community Radio Broadcasters), the Uruguayan Press Association (APU), the Plenario Intersindical de Trabajadores y Convención Nacional Trabajadores (PIT-CNT; Intersyn-

dical Plenary of Workers and National Convention of Workers), the University of the Republic, human rights organizations like the Instituto de Estudios Legales y Sociales del Uruguay (IELSUR) and Instituto de Solidaridad y Desarrollo (ISODE), and the Federation of Housing Cooperatives (FUCVAM), as shown by AMARC at http://legislaciones.item.org.uy/index?q=node/255.

32. The full text of the law is available at http://legislaciones.amarc.org/URU_Proyecto _Ley_Radiodifusion_Comunitaria_05062007.pdf.

33. AMARC recognizes that this good practice has also been followed in laws in Colombia, Ecuador, Venezuela, and Peru, though it has not been recognized in Spain. Available at http://legislaciones.item.org.uy/index?q=node/255.

34. This document from the Latino Union of Political Economy of Information, Communication, and Culture, of academic character, was originally signed by twenty professors of Spanish universities and received the support of many others. The document is available at http://www.ulepicc.es/documentos/DeclaracionULEPICC.pdf.

Additional Sources

Bustamante, Enrique. "La contrarreforma audiovisual socialista." *Le Monde Diplomatique en Español* 172 (February 2010).

Cué, Carlos E. *¡Pásalo!: Los cuatro días de marzo que cambiaron el país*. Barcelona: Península, 2004.

Sáez Baeza, Chiara. "Tercer Sector de la Comunicación. Teoría y praxis de la televisión alternativa. Una mirada a los casos de España, Estados Unidos y Venezuela." PhD diss., Autonomous University of Barcelona, 2008. http://www.tesisenxarxa.net/TDX-1021109-003052/.

Segovia Alonso, Ana Isabel. "Repercusiones y Cambios de las Leyes de Propiedad de Medios de Comunicación: El Caso de Clear Channel Communications." *Zer* 16 (2004). http://www.ehu.es/zer/zer16/articulo_4.htm. Accessed April 28, 2010.

———. "Organismos de Regulación y Control de las Comunicaciones: El Caso de la FCC" (Communication Government Agencies: The Case of the FCC), *RLCS: Revista Latina de Comunicación Social* (Canary Islands, Spain) 64 (2004): 526–39. http://www.revistalatinacs.org/09/art/43_842_ULEPICC_15/52Segovia.html. Accessed April 22, 2010.

CHAPTER 13

Most Likely to Secede
US Empire, Vermont Secession, Citizen Journalism, and Media Democracy

by Rob Williams

> *You can't bloat a modest republic into a crapulent empire*
> *without sparking one hell of a centrifugal reaction.*
> —BILL KAUFFMAN, Bye Bye, Miss American Empire

> *The Gods of the Empire are not the Gods of Vermont.*
> —DENNIS STEELE, *2010 Vermont independent gubernatorial*
> *candidate*

> *Secession is every American's birth right.*
> —Vermont Commons: Voices of Independence
> *news journal*

THE "S" WORD INTRODUCED: HISTORY AND POLITICAL CULTURE

What's the dirtiest word in American politics? A few hints. It begins with an "s," and, in its verb form, sounds like "succeed." It is a word that even many well-educated Americans have trouble pronouncing, let alone spelling.

It is the founding principle of the United States as a political creation. With help from Benjamin Franklin, John Adams, and the first Continental Congress, Thomas Jefferson enshrined this key political concept as the first action verb—"dissolve"—in the 1776 Declaration of Independence.

It was a constitutionally legitimate and widely affirmed concept, publicly agreed upon by political leaders from both northern and southern states, during the first seventy years of the US republic.

Numerous new nineteenth-century American states, from Maine to Kentucky, employed it in hiving off from existing states.

Invented in the South, it was first championed as a regional movement by nineteenth-century New Englanders. Since President Abraham Lincoln's successful victory over the southern states in the so-called "Civil War," it has been largely forgotten.

The dirtiest word? Secession.[1]

A LITTLE REVISIONIST HISTORY IS USEFUL.

The eighteenth-century American "Revolution"—really, an English colonial struggle to secede from the British Empire and establish "free and independent states"—was built on it, and nineteenth-century northern and southern political leaders alike embraced it. The nineteenth-century New Englanders talked openly for decades about secession, in response to federal abuses of power involving war, militarism, territorial expansion, and immoral confiscation of escaped slaves. However, Lincoln's "War to Prevent Southern Secession" linked this legitimate nineteenth-century political concept of secession forever to the South, slavery, and racism, largely erasing it from our twentieth-century cultural and historical memory.

These days, the concept of secession is now deemed too radical, even treasonous, to be discussed in mainstream political, media, and news circles.

Until now.

Secession—the "s" word, the dirtiest word in US politics—is ready to reenter US political conversation as an old idea rediscovered. The next big thing. Which is funny. Because secession is about smallness. Decentralization. Devolution, not revolution. And there are signs that Americans of all stripes are interested.

"Secession is the next radical idea poised to enter mainstream discourse—or at least the realm of the conceivable," writes Bill Kauffman in his 2010 book, *Bye Bye, Miss American Empire: Neighborhood Patriots, Backcountry Rebels, and their Underdog Crusades to Redraw America's Political Map.* "The prospect of breaking away from a union once consecrated to liberty and justice but now degenerating into imperial putrefaction will only grow in appeal as we go marching with our Patriot Acts and National Security Strategies through Iraq, Iran, Afghanistan, and the frightful signposts on our road to nowhere."[2]

Secession's signposts, meanwhile, are popping up all over the United States.

▸ More than thirty of our fifty states in the US Empire are home to active secessionist organizations.[3]

▸ During the past five years, the country has witnessed three national conferences organized around secession—the first (Burlington, Vermont, in 2006) and the third (Manchester, New Hampshire, in 2008) both taking place in New England. The second, held in Tennessee, produced a document called the Chattanooga Declaration, which declared:

> The deepest questions of human liberty and government facing our time go beyond right and left, and in fact have made the old left-right split meaningless and dead.
>
> The privileges, monopolies, and powers that private corporations have won from government threaten everyone's health, prosperity, and liberty, and have already killed American self-government by the people.[4]

▸ In a July 2008 national Zogby poll, more than 20 percent of American adults agreed that "any state or region has the right to peaceably secede from the United States and become an independent republic."[5]

▸ Even venerable national newspapers and magazines of record—the *New York Times*, the *Wall Street Journal*, and *Time* among them—have begun covering the "secession story."

WHY SECESSION: THE US AS EMPIRE

Why nonviolent secession? Simply stated . . .

The United States is no longer a self-governing republic responsive to the needs and concerns of its citizens, but an uncontrollable empire governed by an unholy alliance of transnational corporations and a US government bought and paid for by the same.

Like blind men with the elephant, both liberal and conservative critics alike recognize portions of this troubling reality. Blue Staters rightly complain about Big Business and corporate personhood. Red Staters rightly bear witness to Big Government excess and intrusion into the lives of ordinary citizens.

In truth, they are both right. The twenty-first-century United States is governed by neither a republican form of government, nor organized around a capitalist form of economic life. Instead, "fascism" rules the day, as defined by Il Duce himself, good old Italian Benito Mussolini, who defined the term as "a monopolistic merger of Big Business and the power of the State." "This left-right thing has got to go," explains Ian Baldwin, publisher emeritus of *Vermont Commons: Voices of Independence.* "We're decentralists and we're up against a monster."[6]

Sightings of the monster-in-question, the United States of Empire, have been reported by Project Censored for decades now. On the domestic front, the news is deeply troubling. "Of all the western democracies, the United States stands near dead last in voter turnout, last in health care, last in education, highest in homicide rates, mortality, STDs among juveniles, youth pregnancy, abortion, and divorce," explains journalist Christopher Ketcham in a recent issue of *Good* magazine, summarizing his conversations with retired international businessman and Duke University economics professor emeritus Thomas Naylor, co-founder of secessionist think tank Second Vermont Republic. "The nation has trillions in deficits it can never repay, is beset by staggering income disparities, has destroyed its manufacturing base, and is the world's most egregious polluter and greediest consumer of fossil fuels." The nation is also inhabited by "some 40 million Americans living in poverty, tens of millions more in a category called 'near poverty,' and a permanent underclass trapped by a real unemployment rate of 17 percent."[7]

This depressing demographic data would be somewhat easier to confront if one assumed that the US government is at all interested in solving the myriad problems that bedevil its citizens. Or, that the current average size of US congressional districts—a whopping 647,000 citizens per representative, larger than the entire population of the state of Vermont—creates any sort of possibility for democratic discussion and representative government.

Instead, however, the evidence seems to indicate that Washington, DC, has allied itself with large corporations to strip away both decision-making control and resources from ordinary Americans in almost every conceivable way. Libraries' worth of books have been written on stupendous financial skullduggery and Wall Street's fleecing of Main Street, US war-making and arms dealing globally, multinational corporations' monopolistic control of our nation's food and energy supply, massive electoral fraud, and the impending bankruptcy of the US government, beholden to the Wall Street banksters, Goldman Sachs and their ilk, and the so-called Federal Reserve (which is neither).

To complicate matters even further, throw into this mix peak oil and global climate change, twin twenty-first-century sisters who are poised to clean planetary house and dramatically destabilize our world as we know it.

It is no wonder that the US, in the throes of what Yale historian Paul Kennedy calls "imperial overstretch," strives to maintain a policy of "full spectrum dominance" in an effort to control the world's remaining easily recoverable fossil fuel energy reserves.[8] Or that the US seeks to bolster what retired policy analyst Chalmers Johnson calls a global "empire of bases" (as many as 1,000, by best estimates) in more than 130 countries around the world—the best defense is a good offense.[9] Or that the US promotes what the former Wall Street financial analyst and regulator for Bush Sr., Catherine Austin Fitts, calls a "tapeworm economy," in which small groups of large corporations make obscene amounts of money by blowing up stuff (and people—"collateral damage"), rebuilding what they've destroyed with taxpayer and borrowed money paid to "contractors," and then privatizing once publicly held assets (e.g. oil, and much more).[10] Look no further than the now seven-year-old US invasion of Iraq as a case study in how the "tapeworm economy" works.[11]

In the face of what James Howard Kunstler called this "Long Emergency,"[12] what options do we as Americans, have? "The only ones I can envision are: denial, compliance, political reform, implosion, rebellion, and dissolution," writes the Second Vermont Republic's Thomas Naylor in his 2008 book, *Secession: How Vermont and All the Other States Can Save Themselves from the Empire*. In this passage below, Naylor briefly describes each of these options, and concludes that nonviolent secession "represents the only morally defensible response to the US Empire."

DENIAL: Most Americans—including our government, our politicians, corporate America, Wall Street, the Pentagon, and the media—are in complete denial of our perilous plight. In spite of all of our obvious problems, they seem oblivious to the cataclysmic risks we are facing. But, obviously denial does not solve problems, and it seems clear that these problems will not simply vanish or solve themselves. So we reject this option.

COMPLIANCE: Many armchair environmentalist, pacifist, democratic socialists, and simple-living adherents are all too aware of the risks facing the Empire, but feel completely powerless at the feet of corporate America and the US government to do anything about them. So they talk about how bad things are and they try to live their personal lives in positive ways, but in relation to our government they do nothing but naively hope for the best. For them the name of the game is compliance. Since that gets us nowhere, we reject this option, too.

REFORM: The real Pollyannas are liberal Democrats who believe that all we need do is elect the right Democrat president and all of our problems will be solved. They see political reform (such as campaign finance reform) as a panacea, failing to realize that, so long as the Congress is controlled by corporate America, there will never be any meaningful campaign finance reform. Since we have a single political party disguised as two, it matters not whether the president calls himself a Democrat or a Republican. The results will be the same. So, again, we reject this option.

IMPLOSION: When Soviet Leader Mikhail S. Gorbachev came to power in 1985, who could have imagined that the Soviet Union would soon implode and cease to exist? The United States seems to be well on its way to replicating the experience of its former archenemy in an American setting. So, do we want to sit by and wait for that to happen? Again we reject this option.

REBELLION: Just as armed rebellion gave birth to the United States in 1776, so too could some combination of stock market meltdown, economic depression, crippling unemployment, monetary crisis, skyrocketing crude oil prices, double-digit interest rates, soaring federal deficits and trade imbalances, curtailment of social services, repeated terrorist attacks, return of the military draft or environmental catastrophe precipitate a violent twenty-first century revolution against corporate America and the US Government. However, we also reject this option, because we are opposed to all forms of violence.[13]

There is, then, just one viable option: peaceful dissolution. Also called "secession."

SECESSION: WHY VERMONT?

First consider Vermont's political origins and culture. Vermont is the only state to exist prior to the creation of the United States as its own independent republic. Fourteen years, to be exact: from 1777 to 1791. "Only in Vermont was the concept of a state as self-constituted political community fully and radically tested," writes historian Peter Onuf in his book *The Origins of the Federal Republic*. "In this sense, Vermont was the only true American republic, for it alone has created itself."[14] (The Lone Star Republic of Texas and the Bear Flag Republic of California were both wrested from Spanish Mexico by force.) The state of Vermont, moreover, was front and center throughout nineteenth-century New England's secession conversations related to militarism, war, and expansion. Vermont was the first state to outlaw slavery within its borders, and Vermonters today still speak out against tyranny of all kinds—nuclear war, genetically modified seeds, the unlawful conscription of national guard troops by the US government for foreign invasions—every March during our annual town meeting day.

To outsiders, it would seem easy to pigeonhole tiny Vermont. The national, corporate, commercial "news" media think they have Vermont pegged as the bluest of Blue States, chock-full of "Obama-loving, latte-drinking, Prius-driving, Birkenstock-wearing, trust fund babies." It is true that we have more than our fair share of sometimes-smug Prius drivers on Vermont roads, and that 70 percent of the Vermont electorate voted for Mr. Obama in the 2008 presidential election (if electronic voting machines, which even tiny and independent-minded Vermont possesses in some of our towns, are to be believed). But it is also true that Vermont political trends are not so easily understood. To wit: we were the first state to bless civil unions for gay couples, *and*, as a state of hunters and farmers, we have the most open and progressive gun carry laws of any state in the country.

Rather than red versus blue, "radical" is our term of choice. "Arguably, Vermont is the most radical state in the Union, in terms of its commitment to human solidarity, sustainability, direct democracy, egalitarianism, political independence, and nonviolence," writes Thomas Naylor.[15] Culturally, historically, and politically, Vermont, with its commitment to "live and let live tolerance"—the promotion of individual rights balanced with an attention to the common good ("Freedom and

Unity" is our state's current motto)—is a natural starting place for considering any state's nonviolent secession. The word "radical" is simply defined as "getting to the root cause of a thing." And this thing called "the United States" is simply too big, too centralized, too corrupt, too inefficient, and too impossible to govern anymore. "If something is wrong, it is too big," wrote Leopold Kohr in his 1957 book, *The Breakdown of Nations.* "Instead of Union, let us have disunion now. Instead of fusing the small, let us dismember the big. Instead of creating fewer and larger states, let us create more and smaller ones."[16] If we heed Kohr's advice, Vermont can help reinvent the United States as the *Untied* States—decentralized, re-localized, with a "small is beautiful" paradigm.

Perhaps University of Vermont political science professor Frank Bryan and Vermont state representative and beekeeper Bill Mares said it best in their whimsical yet provocative 1987 book, *Out!: The Vermont Secession Book*:

> Vermonters can do it better themselves. We are better at education, welfare, building roads, catching crooks, dispensing justice, and helping farmers. We report our own news better. Vermonters know much more about what's happening in Vermont than Americans know about what's happening in America. We're better at democracy, too, much better. We can balance our budget! We've watched as Congress pitters and patters, dillies and dallies, postures, poses and primps. If that's America's idea of democracy, we want out![17]

"We report our own news better." It is to journalism, media, and democracy that we now turn.

SECESSION, JOURNALISM, MEDIA, AND DEMOCRACY

"Ideology of any sort . . . is a road without end that carries the enthusiast far from any place resembling home," author Bill Kauffman writes in *Bye Bye, Miss American Empire*. "A healthy secessionist movement must be founded in love: love of a particular place, its people (of all ethnicities and colors), its culture, its language and books and music and baseball teams, and yes, its beer and flowers and punk rock clubs."[18] And love of its journalism, as well.

The Vermont independence movement's statewide newspaper—*Vermont Commons: Voices of Independence*—quietly marked its fifth year in publication last spring. As the founding (Web) editor and now publisher, I've worked with our editorial board to co-create a particular set of values that may help reinvent journalism in this new century. Through an organic process shaped by experimentation, adaptability, and close monitoring of the larger "landscape of crisis" that has characterized the national news business, we've developed a set of principles I'd like to share here. In our more optimistic moments, we like to think that we are helping to pioneer a new and more sustainable model for twenty-first-century journalism, based on the following elements.

Principle #1: Provide news for people, not profit

We see *Vermont Commons* as a sort of nonprofit and homegrown "statewide multimedia coffeehouse," not as a commercially run, for-profit competitive entity. In an era marked by dramatic corporate media consolidation and the gutting of the print news business, we envision our news journal as provider of an essential public service for thinking Vermonters of all stripes. "Founded in 2005, *Vermont Commons: Voices of Independence* is a news journal by and for the citizens of Vermont," reads our Web site's introduction.

Principle #2: Be invitational

For more than a century, Americans have been told that "news" is something practiced by professionals who all must think alike (except on the op-ed page), while the rest of us poor citizen slobs can write a letter once every month to voice our ideas, questions, or concerns. We at *Vermont Commons* challenge this restrictive approach, and instead invite active participation from our readers. "We are a print and online forum for exploring the idea of Vermont independence—political, economic, social, and spiritual," explains our Web site. "We are unaffiliated with any other organization or media, and interested in all points of view. We welcome your writing, photos, thoughts, and participation." Our advice to aspiring twenty-first-century newspaper publishers: be invitational—early and often.

Principle #3: Focus on place and commons

In an era dominated by "placeless news" that is aggregated, packaged, and sold by everyone from Gannett to Google, *Vermont Commons* focuses on the goings-on within a single politically identifiable place—the once and future republic of Vermont—and its relationship with the rest of the world. We also adhere to a twin focus: 1) economic re-localization and the idea of "the Commons," and 2) political decentralization and Vermont independence. Our readers expect articles and commentary, in each of our print issues and on our Web site, that deal directly with these two themes, and we try not to disappoint.

Principle #4: Be civically minded and solutions-oriented

We seek out writers (with a focus on Vermont wordsmiths) and ask them to submit their work to us for publication as unpaid citizen journalists, chronicling solutions-oriented work being done by Vermonters across the state. Not all of our writers agree with our whole mission statement, and this, we hope, makes for interesting reading. We've also been fortunate in attracting nationally recognized writers to publish within our pages, as we are committed to providing lengthy and literate writing rather than dumbed-down "McNews."

Our Web site explains:

> *Vermont Commons: Voices of Independence* news journal and web site publish articles and opinion written by citizen journalists doing the good work required of us on a wide variety of fronts— energy, agriculture, local currency, education, land use, localvores, media and more—by writers as diverse as Frank Bryan, Hazel Henderson, John McClaughry, Robin McDermott, Bill McKibben, Kirkpatrick Sale, Catherine Austin Fitts, Peter Forbes, George Schenk and James Howard Kunstler. Some of our writers advocate nonviolent secession, others do not, while still others are on the fence. All of our writers, though, are fierce champions of localism and decentralization. These visionary thinkers are helping us imagine a more sustainable and self-reliant Vermont future into which we can invest our time, energy, and financial and spiritual resources.

Principle #5: Championing the paradox of fierce subjectivity and nonpartisanship

Our news journal makes no pretense towards objectivity, which, as many media scholars have pointed out, is often synonymous with Big Business/Empire. Instead, we've made a conscious decision to model *Vermont Commons: Voices of Independence* after the fiercely subjective nineteenth-century republican newspapers in the newly created United States.

We begin by articulating three central political tenets:

1. We at *Vermont Commons: Voices of Independence* believe that the United States is no longer a republic governed by its citizens, but an empire that is immoral and essentially ungovernable.

2. We believe that a sovereign state's right to nonviolently secede, first championed in the United States by the citizens of nineteenth-century New England, is a right that demands re-exploration in the twenty-first century.

3. We believe that a twenty-first-century Vermont, working in concert with our neighbors and the rest of the world, may be able to better feed, power, educate, and care for its citizens as an independent twenty-first-century commonwealth/republic than as one of fifty states within the US Empire. The endless "war on terror" being waged by the United States for geostrategic control of the world's remaining fossil fuel energy resources—"full spectrum dominance"—cannot and will not alter the emergent twenty-first-century reality of peak oil and climate change.

So begins *Vermont Commons*, with a clear, distinct, and subjective point of view. We also try and balance this viewpoint with a nonpartisan approach, seeing our news journal as a "big tent" for a variety of voices from a wide range of political perspectives—liberal, conservative, progressive, libertarian, and decentralist/mutualist among them.

Our Web site's mission statement captures all of these characteristics in a single sentence: *Vermont Commons* is "solutions-oriented, non-partisan, and interested in promoting ongoing and vigorous debate about a more sustainable future for the once and future republic of Vermont, and the world."

Principle #6: Blend old and new media tech apps

This is vital. *Vermont Commons* is committed to remaining a bimonthly print-based publication, because we believe that universal citizen access to a free print-based publication available for pickup in a wide variety of Vermont locations—bars, coffeehouses, gas stations, grocery stores, both for-profit and nonprofit businesses—is critical, and because we believe in the vitality of print news to generate public discussion and debate in what German sociologist and philosopher Jürgen Habermas once called "the public sphere."

We are not print dinosaurs, though. *Vermont Commons* has embraced the Internet and new social and digital media technologies as ways to provide up-to-the-minute news and commentary for our readers, reaching much wider audiences, both locally and globally. With this in mind, we employ more than one dozen volunteer bloggers (a roster that is growing), actively use new media technologies like RSS feeds, Facebook, Twitter, and YouTube, and offer our Web site visitors free access to each issue of our news journal in an easy-to-navigate digital e-reader format. In these ways, we hope to reach as many interested readers as possible with our "both/and" approach to distributing news and commentary.

Principle #7: Collaborative funding

Paying for a news journal, of course, is always a challenge. As a non-profit, we keep our costs low, leverage free media technologies and volunteer writers as best as we can, barter with supportive content providers, and pay three staff members—our editor, managing editor, and layout designer—fair but modest salaries on a "per issue" basis. We also rely on funding from multiple sources, including generous individuals, subscriptions, and advertising from Vermont-based businesses whose values match our own. Our immediate goal is to be 50 percent advertising-funded by the end of 2010, and to continue to grow our subscription base. We are also experimenting with a "co-op commons" model for subscribers that we hope will bear fruit in the months ahead.

CONCLUSION

We are under no illusions. The road ahead—for both the news business and the citizens of the United States of Empire—will be long and difficult. But we believe in the power of honest, regular, independent, accessible, and provocative news and commentary to shape citizen thought, feeling, and action over time.

The twenty-first-century world is shaping up to look little like the twentieth, and we need to prepare ourselves for the changes ahead. "Every empire, every too-big thing, fragments or shrinks according to its own unique character and to the age of history to which it belongs," explains *Wall Street Journal* writer Paul Starobin, author of *After America: Narratives for the Next Global Age*, in a recent editorial entitled "Divided We Stand." "America's return to its origins . . . could turn out to be an act of creative political destruction, with 'we the people' the better for it."[19]

Here in the Green Mountains, we're more interested in creation than in destruction. As of summer 2010, in addition to *Vermont Commons*, we now host a digital radio station called Free Vermont Radio; we are circulating a statement of principles focused on the re-localized production of finance, fuel, food, and other resources; and we are running (at least) ten candidates for statewide office, including our gubernatorial candidate, Dennis Steele, and our lieutenant gubernatorial candidate, Peter Garritano. While we don't pretend to have all the answers, the Vermont independence movement, full of questions, impulses, and entrepreneurial energy, is well underway.

Free Vermont! Long live the *Un*tied States.

ROB WILLIAMS, PHD, is a Vermont-based musician, historian, journalist, public speaker, and media/communications professor who teaches at Champlain College in the city of Burlington. The (Web) editor and publisher of the independent multimedia news journal *Vermont Commons: Voices of Independence* (www.vtcommons.org), Rob is also the founding president of the Action Coalition for Media Education (www.acmecoalition.org). In his other life, he is a yak herder and co-owner of Vermont Yak Company (www.vermontyak.com) in Vermont's Mad River Valley, a farm business raising grass-fed yaks for meat and agritourism, and he plays "music for happy brains" in an acoustic power band called Phineas Gage. For more information, or to contact him, visit www.robwilliamsmedia.com.

Notes

1. See Donald Livingston, "The New England Secession Tradition," *Vermont Commons: Voices of Independence*, May 2007, http://www.vtcommons.org/files/Livingston%20 PDF%20(9%20opt).pdf.

2. Bill Kauffman, *Bye Bye, Miss American Empire: Neighborhood Patriots, Backcountry Rebels, and their Underdog Crusades to Redraw America's Political Map* (White River Junction, Vermont: Chelsea Green, 2010), xv.

3. For a state-by-state list of secession organizations compiled by the Middlebury Institute, see http://middleburyinstitute.org/currentamericansecessionistgroups.html.

4. For the complete text of the Chattanooga Declaration, see http://middleburyinstitute.org/chattanoogadeclaration2007.html.

5. Christopher Ketcham, "The American Secessionist Streak," *Los Angeles Times*, September 10, 2008, http://www.latimes.com/news/opinion/commentary/la-oe-ketcham10-2008sep10,0,990090.story.

6. Kauffman, xx.

7. Christopher Ketcham, "Most Likely To Secede," *Good*, January 2008, http://www.good.is/post/most-likely-to-secede.

8. Paul Kennedy, *The Rise and Fall of the Great Powers: Economic Change and Military Conflict from 1500 to 2000* (New York: Vintage/Random House, 1987).

9. Chalmers Johnson, *The Sorrows of Empire: Militarism, Secrecy, and the End of the Republic* (New York: Henry Holt and Company, 2004).

10. Catherine Austin Fitts, "The American Tapeworm," Mapping the Real Deal, *Scoop*, April 30, 2003, http://www.scoop.co.nz/stories/HL0304/S00228.htm.

11. Visit http://www.vtcommons.org/essential-readings-sustainability-and-secession-2009 for the books and resources we think most useful in understanding the US as Empire.

12. James Howard Kunstler, *The Long Emergency: Surviving the Converging Catastrophes of the Twenty-first Century* (New York: Grove/Atlantic, 2005).

13. Thomas Naylor, *Secession: How Vermont and All the Other States Can Save Themselves from the Empire* (Port Townshend, Washington: Feral House, 2008), 43–44.

14. As quoted in Naylor, 47.

15. As quoted in Naylor, 47.

16. As quoted in Naylor, 97.

17. As quoted in Kauffman, 227.

18. Kauffman, xxix.

19. Paul Starobin, "Divided We Stand," *Wall Street Journal*, June 13, 2009, http://online.wsj.com/article/SB10001424052970204482304574219813708759806.html.

CHAPTER 14

Our Media Renaissance
Individual Empowerment and Community-owned Infrastructure

by David Mathison

OUR MEDIA RENAISSANCE: INDIVIDUAL EMPOWERMENT

If you have any message at all, in any form, that you want to convey to the world, you now have a platform to do so. If you have something to say, or sing, or film, or write, you have direct access to anyone who wants to hear, listen to, watch, or read it.

"*You*" means not only "you" the writer, musician, filmmaker, journalist, blogger, podcaster, or talk show host, but you the activist, publicist, religious leader, cartoonist, businessperson, politician, or virtually anyone else.

Your fans and supporters are never more than a click or two away, and they're ready to help you make history—or change it.

The following excerpts adapted from the book *Be the Media* tell you—in detail—how to reach these fans. You'll not only find everything you need to spread your message, but you'll be able to do so without traditional publishers, music labels, broadcast networks, commercial film studios, and similar behemoths.

Our main message? **You can do it.** And you can do it *by yourself,* with a little help from your friends.

THE AMERICAN DREAM, OR . . . DREAM ON?

The American dream—the belief that with talent, hard work, persistence, and perhaps a bit of luck, anyone can be successful—appears to be increasingly out of reach.

The gap between rich and poor Americans is wider than it has been since the Great Depression. The top 1 percent of Americans earns more income than the bottom 50 percent. The top 1 percent owns more wealth than the bottom 90 percent. Millions of Americans are working without a living wage or adequate health care. Their homes, pensions, and savings—all components of a traditional version of the American dream—are at risk under a trickle-down mentality that favors and rewards the wealthy few over the hardworking masses.

And what if the all-American dreamer happens to be an artist of any medium? Fat chance at quitting your day job, right? Or so it may have seemed lately. But take courage and read on.

These days, getting a deal from a major music label, book publisher, broadcast network, or movie studio lies far out of reach for more and more people. The major players in the entertainment industry mostly want bands that can move hundreds of thousands of CDs, authors who can sell tens of thousands of books, and filmmakers who can generate a hundred million dollars in ticket sales at the box office on opening night, plus DVDs later at retail and rental. They want artists who can be promoted with minimal development costs, a built-in audience hungry to buy whatever is offered, and an extensive platform—a roster of appearances on the *Today Show*, *Oprah*, and *Dr. Phil*, not to mention keynote speaking engagements, a newsletter, a popular Web site, and a well-read blog.

In other words, the biggies mostly want you only *after* you too have become a biggie in your own right.

Those "lucky" few who do secure a contract from a major player typically are not so lucky, after all. They are "rewarded" by giving up their rights, forking over most of the royalties, and ceding control over the marketing, publicity, and distribution of their creations, or even their very identity. Nor do they receive much money for advances, promotion, touring, and support.

So much for luck.

"AMERICAN IDOL" . . . THE SMALL PRINT

What this is really about is the American dream.
—SIMON COWELL, American Idol

A classic example of this expropriated version of the American dream is none other than the hugely popular show *American Idol*. Many consider winning *Idol* the ultimate sign of success. The show introduces the winner to an enormous audience of adoring fans, accompanied by international press coverage, an extensive distribution network, sub-stantial revenues, and the freedom to create more products.

But in his article "Slaves of Celebrity," journalist Eric Olsen argues that the *Idol* version of the American dream is an illusion:

> At first glance, [*Idol* winner Kelly] Clarkson would seem to have it made. . . . [But] Clarkson and the other finalists signed an unusually onerous contract with 19 Group . . . headed by British pop entrepreneur Simon Fuller. These young perform-ers are wrapped up for recording, management and merchandising under the most restrictive terms imaginable: *Their careers are literally not their own.*[1]

The one-sided terms in the contract from the first season revealed that Fuller and his company own the names, likenesses, and voices of *Idol* finalists, *forever*, anywhere in the cosmos:

> . . . I hereby grant to Producer the unconditional right through-out the universe in perpetuity to use, simulate or portray . . . my name, likeness . . . voice . . . personality, personal identifi-cation or personal experiences, my life story, biographical data, incidents, situations, and events. . . . I may reveal and/or relate . . . information about me of a personal, private, intimate, surprising, defamatory, disparaging, embarrassing or unfavor-able nature, that may be factual and/or fictional.[2]

American Idol is the fulfillment of a distorted version of the Ameri-can dream—a dream, that is, for the rich Australian-born Rupert Murdoch, head of Fox and News Corporation, the rich Briton Simon Fuller, and the rich Briton Simon Cowell, whose final five-year contract was worth $50 million—*every year*.

Idol is also fulfilling a dream for Freemantle Media, the company that produces the show. In 2007 alone, it earned $1.8 billion in revenues and $200 million *in profit*.

In an article titled "Idol Winners Aren't Singing All the Way to the Bank," Cox News Service's Rodney Ho wrote, "American Idol is a mon-strous moneymaker—for creator Simon Fuller, for the judges, for Fox. *Except, perhaps, for the once-unknown singers*" (emphasis added).

And, perhaps, except for the show's writers and producers. Employees of Freemantle Media filed more than $250,000 in claims with the California Labor Commission, which cited the company for wage and hour violations. Employees work 15–20 hour days with "mandatory 6-day workweeks, no benefits, no health insurance, or pension contribution."

The Writers Guild of America noted that writers "do not deserve to be cheated, abused and exploited . . . so that a few executives can rake in massive amounts of profits."

Such people and companies are not—mostly—playing illegally, just extremely well. If Simon Fuller, Simon Cowell, and Rupert Murdoch were to retire tomorrow, someone else would surely take their place. It's not the individuals or the corporations that are to blame; rather, it's the incentive and reward structure of the major label, publisher, and studio system that needs to change. And it *is* changing, thanks to the technological revolution, as well as to artists and transformed consumers, like us.

Meanwhile, the majors who rule this system and love their money-making stars have an unspoken message for independent musicians, writers, and filmmakers, not to mention new media creative people. It is this: "*You're on your own.*"

This leads us back to *our* major message: "Congratulations!" So you don't have a publisher wooing you, a record company knocking on your door, Hollywood begging to option your film. You may be much better off. If you are careful—that is, if you follow our advice—you'll maintain control over your content and keep most of the proceeds.

You will, however, need to do a great deal of work.

The good news? **You are not alone.** Keep reading. We'll tell you how to work the new (and ever-evolving) innovations, and be your own media.

REBOOTING THE AMERICAN DREAM

It's indisputable. Over the past few decades, the American dream has been hijacked little by little and more and more by winner-take-all pirates and their intermediaries, who turned it into a nightmare of a system that benefited only them and a few chosen "winners."

The effect of this cultural hijacking, on most entrepreneurs, artists, and society itself, has been unfair, unequal, and exploitative.

Then, just when it looked like most creative people might as well let their dream die, rescue arrived in the form of a technological and populist revolution.

This ongoing revolution—some, like our contributing author Douglas Rushkoff, consider it a renaissance—is right now rebooting the American dream. It is giving it new life. It is bringing back the traditional *all*-American dream, one that is fair and just and that provides equality and opportunity to any and all dreamers, not merely corporate executives.

Together we can wrest the dream back and not only reboot it, but also upgrade it, so that the rightful owners—the artists and their fans—can use it democratically and benefit equally from it.

After all, every one of us dreams.

But how does a dream become reality? *Be the Media* outlines three basic steps:

1. Cultivate a Core Audience: Create a direct relationship with your fans, thus cutting out the intermediaries. This enhances the bond between you and the fans, while also increasing both opportunities and profits.

2. Own Your Rights: Control your material so that you have the freedom to create new products and to "repurpose" existing products differently. Artists should avoid exploitative agreements that take all rights exclusively and in perpetuity (which are truly a pact with the devil).

3. Repurpose Your Work: Because you own the rights, you can constantly reconfigure your material and expertise into a range of progressively higher-value products and personalized experiences for your fans or your clientele.

A REPURPOSE-DRIVEN LIFE

Meet a leading light of repurposing, particularly in the field of publishing: Janet Switzer, the marketing guru behind some of the more successful publishing empires on the planet. She created no fewer than 327 new products for Jay Abraham, who had just a few products and a handful of special reports when they met. With Jack Canfield, she cowrote *The Success Principles,* which hit the best seller lists of the *New York Times* and *USA Today.* She helped build the megaempire for Jack Canfield and Mark Victor Hansen's *Chicken Soup for the Soul.*

Switzer has since published the *Instant Income* series and *Publishing Mavericks: How Experts Build Empires,* which teach people to package their expertise into new products and services at higher prices.

The visualization of this model is the Product Pricing Curve,[3] which can be used by virtually anyone with something to, well, emote. According to Switzer, "As the sophistication of your buyer increases on the left (from book buyers up to corporations), the products they will buy also get more elaborate along the bottom (from digital ezines to corporate contracts)."

WHERE ARE YOU ON THE PRODUCT PRICING CURVE?

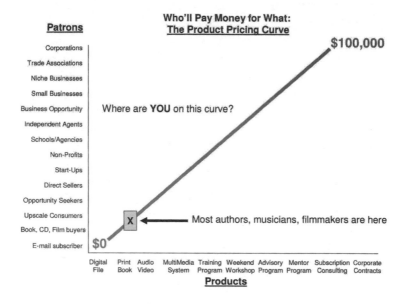

Most artists are in the lower-left corner of the Curve—blithely giving away digital samples and offering a single product: a $20 book, or CD, or DVD. Once the patron makes a purchase, even directly from you, the artist, there is nothing else to buy. Offering more products enables you to increase the potential lifetime value of each customer, which is worth vastly more than, say, a $20 book that will be read once.

Why is this important? As Switzer says, "Your book may never lead to a viable business model. Books are the lowest profit margined item in an information empire." The same can be said for sales of one-off songs, CDs, and DVDs.

Kevin Kelly agrees. Because multiple copies of *anything* have little or no value and are no longer the basis of wealth, he argues, "The key is to offer valuable intangibles that can not be reproduced at zero cost, and will thus be paid for. Such intangibles might include accessibility to the artist; authenticity; immediacy and priority access; patronage; curation; personalized products and experiences; support and guidance." (Think of the businesspeople, politicians, and journalists who get big money to consult or give keynote speeches; they know their way up the Curve.)

We all learn and experience things in different ways. Therefore, offering a variety of audio, video, and print products and live events will satisfy the unique needs of a larger audience, expand your opportunities and distribution outlets, and increase the likelihood of making sales that continue into your rosy future.

Media conglomerates know this well. They create multiple streams of income by selling products in various formats—print, audio, video, and digital products—as well as experiences such as conferences, concerts, and workshops. Why should conglomerates do all the conglomerating? By packaging your expertise into various media properties, you too can create multiple streams of income.

In *Be The Media*, we give examples of Product Pricing Curve scenarios for many different creative, activist, and political groups: authors, writers, Internet entrepreneurs, musicians, filmmakers, activists, and politicians.

To view these different scenarios, you can download the free introduction of *Be The Media* from www.BeTheMedia.com.

FAIR AND BALANCED

The *Idol* version of the American dream—the distorted, "winner-takes-all" model—is the ultimate version of an unfair system that continues to dominate the entertainment industry, as well as other areas of American life. The system relies on remote others' ownership and control of the creative output of some of our nation's most talented and beloved artists, as well as an upward redistribution of capital from hardworking consumers to a handful of already wealthy executives and corporations, which neither deserve it nor need it.

As *Be the Media* points out, however, the hijacked American dream, which too often lately has resembled a nightmare, is in the process of being rescued. The new, emerging model gives many, many artists and others the resources, freedom, and opportunity to succeed. Thanks to the participation and direct support of millions of people like you, unprecedented opportunities enable artists to control their own destiny.

The hope and promise of rebooting the American dream is to create a sustainable system that is more fair, balanced, and egalitarian; one that works for the people—from the bottom up—instead of enabling a few squillionaires to control the media (and the message) from the top down.

True, there are challenges and risks, and no guarantees of success. We face uncertain times in both the entertainment industry and the economy in general, making it even more critical for independents to repurpose their offerings to create multiple streams of income from diversified sources. Likewise, patrons should realize who benefits from every dollar they spend. Instead of supporting corporations and executives, a fan's hard-earned money should directly reward their favorite artists, so that those artists can keep a higher percentage of the revenues to grow, thrive, and prosper—and create more great products.

And creating the next great work of art is only the first step. If the distribution infrastructure remains choked by a few large corporations, we'll never be able to spread our message far and wide. Read on . . .

OUR MEDIA RENAISSANCE: COMMUNITY-OWNED INFRASTRUCTURE

We're all in this together.

We are living in a time unparalleled in the history of communication, a time that also means we face challenges and opportunities—all of possibly enormous consequence.

In the past, only a wealthy few had the resources to spread messages by publishing books, magazines, and newspapers, or by broadcasting radio and television shows, or by creating and distributing films. Today, inexpensive digital phones and computers—coupled with the Internet—have given rise to a wide, participatory renaissance among the global community. Today, almost anyone can create and distribute messages to people around the world, and can interact with them, too.

This new renaissance is comparable, in some ways, to what the philosopher Karl Jaspers called the "axial age," a period between 900 and 200 B.C.E. The incredible flourishing of human creativity in those years unleashed unprecedented changes in religion, thought, psychology, and philosophy. In four separate regions of the world, sages such as Gautama Buddha, Jeremiah, Muhammad, Confucius, Lao Tzu, and Socrates created religious traditions that continue to influence our spirituality today: Hinduism and Buddhism in India, monotheism in Israel, Confucianism and Daoism in China, and philosophical rationalism in Greece.

While the first axial age was considered a "renaissance of the individual," Karen Armstrong, in *The Great Transformation: The Beginning of Our Religious Traditions*, argues that currently the emphasis is changing back—or rather, forward—to a group effort.

> The old tribal ethic, which had developed a communal mentality to ensure the survival of the group, was being replaced by a new individualism. . . . The sages demanded that every single person become self-conscious, aware of what he was doing. . . . Today we are making another quantum leap forward. Our technology has created a global society, which is interconnected electronically, militarily, economically, and politically. *We now have to develop a global consciousness, because, whether we like it or not, we live in one world.*[4]

The individual who has taken the most stunning advantage of this renaissance of the community, as well as of the Internet's connective and collaborative power (and who understands why it must remain a public resource), is President Barack Obama. His presidential campaign was framed in terms of today's renaissance—we, the group; not me, the individual ("Yes we can" was his powerful mantra). He insisted that his candidacy was all about us, the American people, not about him, and he urged us to work beyond the divisiveness of "red" and "blue" states. This all-inclusiveness appealed to a global audience—including a global *wired-in* audience.

Obama engaged that wired-in audience through the Internet, just as Thomas Jefferson used newspapers to win the presidency in his time, Franklin Delano Roosevelt used the radio, and John F.Kennedy mastered television. Millions of true fans visited Obama's Web site, social networks, and YouTube channel, then virally accelerated his vision of unity and hope through their own networks and blogs and e-mails. The messaging was decentralized and participatory, versus the top-down, command-and-control style of his older adversaries.

His opponents, during both the Democratic primary and the general campaign, had neither the sophisticated tech-savvy staff nor the message that Obama's campaign, and the candidate himself, delivered: inclusion and participation. The concept of everyone working together is the touchstone of our current communal renaissance as well as of our shared history. Americans, despite the siren calls of "rugged individualism," have long united for common causes, such as the abolition of slavery, the advancement of civil rights, women's universal suffrage, and the protection of the environment. In the same way that our ancestors relied on family, friends, and neighbors to build barns, trails, roads, and schools, and to plant and harvest life-sustaining crops, so are many of us today working together to build not only a more perfect union, but a more perfect *world*.

The Internet, *if* applied and used democratically (think "affordable, open, and ubiquitous broadband") and imaginatively, can do more than connect, inform, entertain, and support us. It can also cut down enormously on energy consumption and toxic greenhouse gases. But note the word "if."

Who controls the renaissance?

Renaissances have a nasty tradition of being co-opted by powerful groups. As the Medicis controlled so much of the Italian art world, so do vast corporate interests in our time own and control the means of idea production and distribution. In virtually all aspects of media—newspapers, radio, television, and film—corporations dominate our spectrum. They create the messages, control the distribution infrastructure, and increasingly write the very rules of the game.

In the process, they privatize our communal rights to the public domain of knowledge. How? They freeload on our broadcast television and radio airwaves without paying rent, precisely like corporate welfare queens. They monopolize local rights of way for cable and phone access, in exchange for meager franchise fees. And now they are trying to get their mitts on the publicly funded Internet—the very heart and soul of our own renaissance.

Here are a few teeth-gnashing examples of the above. In 1994, despite the fact that the Internet was developed with billions of university, state, and federal tax dollars, the Federal Communications Commission (FCC) spinelessly allowed the Internet backbone to be turned over to private companies. That same year, the FCC started auctioning off control of some of our airwaves—let me be precise, our *public* airwaves—to the highest bidder, putting valuable wireless spectrum in the hands of a few wealthy corporations.

Then consider the dastardly 1996 Telecommunications Act, the mother of all media deregulations. It lifted restrictions on media ownership and deregulated the Baby Bells and cable television. The result: unprecedented ownership consolidation. Today, we are still paying the price. Five conglomerates now control most major media (Time Warner, Disney, Bertelsmann, Viacom, and News Corporation); in the telecommunications realm, Verizon, AT&T, and Qwest dominate; and two behemoths, Comcast and Time Warner, control over half the cable market.

Even more ominous: the phone and cable companies together control 98 percent of broadband Internet access. Game over! A single broadband provider can offer voice (telephone), video, and data (that is, high-speed Internet access)—a so-called "triple play" of services—to subscribers, all through one connection. Why is this ominous? For one example, acting entirely without legal authority, after 9/11 some of these "providers," at the government's behest, wiretapped millions of innocent Americans' phone calls and read their e-mails.

Feel that our renaissance is safe now? Need more ominous examples?

In 2000, corporations successfully lobbied Congress to extend copyright protection to works that had been created so long ago that they would have by then passed into the public domain. Congress obeyed, passing the heavily Disney-sponsored Sonny Bono Copyright Term Extension Act, derisively referred to as the "Mickey Mouse Protection Act." Not only does Disney own Mickey seemingly forever, but the rest of us cannot have access to works whose copyrights would have expired by now. Joichi Ito, the chief executive officer (CEO) of Creative Commons, said, "What was once part of common knowledge is becoming the property of corporations."

In another dastardly example of top-down control, since 2005 cable and phone companies have spent millions of lobbying dollars to kill net neutrality—the "first amendment" of the Internet. Maintaining the principle of "net neutrality" would have guaranteed to consumers the right to gain access to the content, applications, or devices of their choice, without restrictions or limitations. The telecom behemoths want to replace the previous "common carrier" model, which was in place until 2005, with tiered pricing. That would eliminate the level playing field (beloved by most) in which pauper or zillionaire alike has the same access to the Internet. Instead, tiered pricing would alter the ability of independent musicians, authors, bloggers, filmmakers, small businesses, and yes, politicians, to compete with those who can afford to pay higher prices to the gatekeepers of the virtual on-ramps. Tiered pricing has been defeated so far, thanks to the efforts of some of the activists discussed in *Be the Media*, but the corporations have not given up. In 2006, after the Democrats swept Congress, the conglomerates redeployed their army of lobbyists to battle in state legislatures.

As a result, over a dozen states have laws on the books—drafted by phone and cable company lobbyists—restricting municipalities from erecting their own broadband systems. Other corporate-inspired legislation moved local—that is, community—control over cable franchise negotiations to the state level.

The scary significance of corporate domination

One result? Our taxpayer-funded commonwealth has been redistributed (upwardly) to private companies. It's trickle-up economics, with a vengeance.

Another result is "redlining," the same word once used when banks redlined certain communities on a map—communities whose residents were not to be granted loans, typically for racial or class reasons. Today's modern version of redlining deploys broadband only to profitable areas, not to tens of millions of Americans who live in rural locations or areas of more modest income levels.

Voilà—a "digital divide," separating the interconnected "haves" from the isolated "have-nots."

The divide also *sub*divides people. Where broadband access does exist, download speeds are faster than uploads. Why? The corporations that control the flow see us as passive consumers of their products, not as creators, producers, and active participants in a democracy. Corporations hate competition, especially from the audience itself! Therefore they control the supply of bandwidth, products, and services to extract maximum profit. If you want to be ticked off even more, consider this: we American broadband subscribers get fewer choices at slower speeds and higher prices than do our counterparts in other Western nations.

My main point here, though, is that for our common global good, for our real and virtual community, for our very own renaissance, we must protect the infrastructure of the open Internet. As Eric Schmidt, CEO of

Google, has said, "Infrastructure is the foundation upon which wealth is created." This does not have to mean Google-istic wealth, but can simply mean making a living. Liberating technologies that enable podcasts, blogs, Web sites, and self-publishing mean little if our broadband provider limits or denies our ability to reach friends and fans across town or around the globe.

Internet infrastructure, after all, simply amounts to the latest kind of community infrastructure, one that everyone uses. Infrastructure means highways, levees, banking, courts, schools, hospitals, security, and clean air and water. Infrastructure allows all people to be productive and prosperous, not merely those who already have achieved that condition. In today's world, according to the InternetforEveryone.org coalition, broadband is a necessity, one that has fueled economic development, transformed communications, fostered free speech, unlocked new services and innovations, and engaged millions of people in civic participation.

It even helped elect a promising new Internet-savvy president.

The communications infrastructure, whatever big business says, is *not* a corporate birthright. It is ours. According to former FCC commissioner Jonathan Adelstein, "We've forgotten that the airwaves belong to the public and not to special interests. Fewer and fewer companies are consolidating control of the means of creating and distributing ideas. Ownership is the key to getting yourself heard."

Fights for universal access to critical infrastructure included, in their times, the distribution of electricity, telephones, radio, television, and cable and satellite TV. Universal access to broadband is only the most recent of these battles, and is the infrastructure battle of our generation.

According to Robert McChesney in the September 2008 issue of the *Monthly Review*:

> At key moments in U.S. history, there had been considerable debate over how to structure the media system, and it was never a foregone conclusion that the system should be turned over to powerful commercial interests. . . .
>
> But the policymaking process was corrupt and dominated by commercial interests. . . . So the television system was gift-wrapped and hand-delivered to Wall Street and Madison Avenue without a shred of public awareness and participation. The same thing happened with FM radio and cable and satellite television.
>
> Millions of Americans understand that there is nothing nat-

ural about the media system and they have a right and a responsibility to participate in policy deliberations.

Ultimately the battle over media is about whether people or corporations, public interest or private profit, should rule the realm of communication.[5]

The battle for controlling broadband—and for doing really interesting things with it—is not actually about the infrastructure itself, but rather about that infrastructure's ability to offer people a platform to distribute their own messages in an alternative manner to that of the dominant commercial media.

As futurist R. Buckminster Fuller once said, "We humans must comprehend the giants' games and game-playing equipment, rules and scoring systems."[6] Fortunately, some of us do comprehend. Among our numbers are activists, educators, bloggers, consumer advocates, and increasingly, everyday people who have been (and still are) reclaiming some of our own turf and making the tiny sliver of nonprofit, non-corporate media into something big, in its own little way.

In part two of my book, *Be the Media*, you can read about community newspapers and citizen journalists who enable the public, not corporations, to set the agenda for news coverage. You will find out how local, nonprofit radio, television, media centers, and news agencies provide people-powered broadcasting that is oriented to the community. You will thrill to learn how community broadband initiatives are cropping up around the country with ways to treat this vital infrastructure not like a private ATM but as a public utility, similar to the provision of gas, electricity, and water. And you will shout hosannas when you learn how "open source government" is enabling citizens to connect and engage with each other and their representatives, to solve problems collaboratively, to participate in government deliberations, and even to help shape legislation.

Their—or our—goal? To put decision-making processes and message-making power into the hands of the people, to ensure that this renaissance *of* and *for* the community will be controlled *by* the community.

> *Together we can be wiser than any of us can be alone.*
> —TOM ATLEE, *author of* The Tao of Democracy, *founder of Co-Intelligence Institute*

DAVID MATHISON is an internationally recognized media consultant, speaker, author, radio host, and hi-tech entrepreneur, with more than twenty-five years experience. His book, *Be the Media: How to Create and Accelerate Your Message . . . Your Way*, was featured in the *New York Times* after he sold over five thousand copies in eleven days via his Web site, Twitter, and Facebook. He has spoken from the United Nations to Columbia University, from Berlin to Cairo. He is host of an award-winning radio show whose guests have included author Seth Godin, singer Jill Sobule, Craigslist's Craig Newmark, and Wikipedia's Jimmy Wales. Mathison was previously vice president at Reuters, the world's largest news agency, where he pioneered online content syndication, and he was CEO of Kinecta Corporation (now part of Oracle), where he raised $30 million in under two years. Holding a masters degree from Columbia University, Mathison is currently founder and executive director of The HomeAThon Foundation, Ltd., a nonprofit organization whose mission is to help prevent homelessness. He serves on the board of directors for the Media Freedom Foundation and Speakers Without Borders.

Notes

1. Eric Olsen, "Slaves of Celebrity," *Salon*, September 18, 2002, http://dir.salon.com/ent/feature/2002/09/18/idol_contract/index.html (emphasis added).
2. Ibid.
3. The Product Pricing Curve is printed by permission in *Be the Media*, courtesy of Janet Switzer's *Publishing Mavericks*.
4. Karen Armstrong, *The Great Transformation: The Beginning of Our Religious Traditions* (New York: Alfred A. Knopf/Random House, 2006), 297 (emphasis added).
5. Robert W. McChesney, "The U.S. Media Reform Movement: Going Forward," *Monthly Review*, September 15, 2008, http://www.monthlyreview.org/080915mcchesney.php.
6. R. Buckminster Fuller, *Grunch of Giants* (New York: St. Martins Press, 1984). Text available online at http://www.american-buddha.com/grunch.giants.htm.

CHAPTER 15

Free Speech is Not for Sale
The Case of Simon Singh

by Padraig Reidy

The case of Simon Singh, the science writer sued by the British Chiropractic Association after he wrote that it "happily promoted" "bogus treatments" in an article for the *Guardian* newspaper in 2008—ironically pegged to Chiropractic Awareness Week—dominated the debate about free expression in the United Kingdom for much of 2009 and 2010. Index on Censorship was the only media outlet to cover every hearing in the case. Here we reproduce Index's reports on the court proceedings.

Eady Rules Against Singh in Chiropractic Defamation Case
May 7, 2009

The English High Court has ruled that science writer Simon Singh must show that the British Chiropractic Association (BCA) was deliberately dishonest in promoting chiropractic as a treatment for various children's ailments.

Mr Justice Eady ruled, with notes apparently written prior to today's preliminary hearing, that an article by Singh, published in the *Guardian* should be classified as a "statement" and added that by use of the word "bogus" Singh had inferred he believed the BCA had intent to convey dishonest claims to the British public.

In light of this ruling the matter may not go to trial. From Singh's standing he does not believe the BCA had intent to deceive and therefore cannot prove this.

Mr Justice Eady refused an appeal on the judgement but Index on Censorship has been told that Singh still will not stand down, and intends to pursue his defence by going to the court of appeals. If this is rejected he may then go to Strasbourg and appeal to the European Human Rights Commission.

Costs of £23,000, relating to the preliminary hearing, have been awarded to the BCA.

This first ruling on meaning seemed a disastrous setback for Singh's defense. In English libel law, the burden of proof lies entirely on the defendant. Singh insisted he had never meant to imply that the BCA was dishonest. Now it seemed he would have to defend a claim he had never actually made.

Simon Singh Refused Leave to Appeal
July 31, 2009

Science writer Simon Singh has been refused leave to appeal Mr Justice Eady's decision on meaning in Singh's legal battle with the British Chiropractic Association (BCA).

Singh is being sued for defamation by the BCA after he wrote an article for the *Guardian* questioning chiropractic's usefulness in treating childhood illnesses.

In an earlier hearing, Mr Justice Eady took Singh's use of the word "bogus" in describing chiropractic treatments as implying that the BCA deliberately offered remedies they knew to be false. Singh disputes this interpretation.

The refusal may mean that Singh will be allowed to make an "oral renewal" at the Court of Appeal.

The mood in Singh's camp was very low at this point. However, he was determined to carry on with the case, and went on to provide an "oral renewal" less than two weeks later.

Simon Singh to Attend Oral Hearing
August 10, 2009

Science writer Simon Singh is set [to] go to an oral hearing at the Court of Appeal later this year seeking permission to challenge an earlier decision by the court not to allow an appeal over a libel action, according to legal sources. This latest application will mean a new hearing by the Court of Appeal on October 14 over a piece published in the *Guardian* this April that was challenged by the British Chiropractic Association.

Simon Singh Wins Leave to Appeal in BCA Libel Case
October 14, 2009

A court ruling today affirmed science writer Simon Singh's right to free expression. It grants him leave to appeal Mr Justice

Eady's ruling against him in a libel action brought by the British Chiropractic Association, reports Padraig Reidy.

Popular science writer Simon Singh has been granted leave to appeal in the libel action brought against him by the British Chiropractic Association.

In a scathing rebuttal of Mr Justice Eady's previous judgement in the case, Lord Justice Laws said Eady had risked swinging the balance of rights too far in favour of the right to reputation and against the right to free expression. Lord Justice Laws described Eady's judgement, centred on Singh's use of the word "bogus" in an article published by the *Guardian* newspaper, as "legally erroneous."

Laws also pointed out that Eady's judgement had conflated two issues—the meaning of the phrases complained of, and the issue of whether the article was presented as fact or fair comment.

Laws said there was "no question" of the "good faith" of Singh in writing the article, as the matter was "clearly in the public interest."

Speaking after the judgement, Singh told Index on Censorship this was the "best possible result."

"But I try not to get my hopes up," he continued. "We have only won leave to appeal. Now we must convince the court of appeal on the issue of meaning. There is a long battle ahead. Reform of English libel laws, particularly the right to a public interest defence and a fairer costs structure, are vital."

The BCA was not represented at this morning's hearing.
Additional Reporting Síle Lane

This was the first chink of light for Simon. Lord Justice Laws's suggestion that the article had been written in "good faith" implied that Simon had not acted maliciously. While this is not a defense in England, it does lessen the case made by the BCA that Simon was accusing them of dishonesty. Simon's team spent the next few months compiling their appeal.

Judge "Baffled" by Simon Singh Chiropractic Case
February 23, 2010
The Lord Chief Justice expressed surprise today at the BCA's libel suit against Simon Singh.

England's most senior judge today said he was "baffled" by the British Chiropractic Association's (BCA) defamation suit against science writer Simon Singh.

Presiding at the appeal court in London today in a pre-trial hearing on the meaning of words in a 2008 article by Singh criticising chiropractic treatments, Lord Chief Justice Lord Judge said he was "troubled" by the "artificiality" of the case.

"The opportunities to put this right have not been taken," Lord Judge said. He continued: "At the end of this someone will pay an enormous amount of money, whether it be from Dr Singh's funds or the funds of BCA subscribers."

He went on to criticise the BCA's reluctance to publish evidence to back up claims that chiropractic treatments could treat childhood asthma and other ailments.

"I'm just baffled. If there is reliable evidence, why hasn't someone published it?"

However, Lord Judge stressed that his comments would not affect the judgement of the case before the Court of Appeal.

The Lord Chief Justice was presiding at a pre-trial appeal on meaning in the case of *BCA v Singh*. Singh is being sued by the organisation for comments in a 2008 article for the *Guardian* newspaper in which he criticised chiropractic and claimed the BCA promoted "bogus" treatments, despite there not being "a jot" of evidence of their effectiveness.

Judge is part of a panel which also includes the Master of the Rolls, Lord Neuberger, and Lord Justice Sedley—one of the most high-powered panels of judges ever to preside on a single case.

Adrienne Page QC, representing Simon Singh, said it was wrong of the BCA to claim that Singh implied it "knowingly" promoted treatments it knew to be ineffective.

"The least likely explanation [of the article] is that the BCA cynically and dishonestly engaged in peddling remedies it knew were of no value," Page told the court.

Representing the BCA, Heather Rogers QC said the organisation is a respectable one that takes its reputation seriously.

Rogers argued that the use of the word "bogus" suggested that the BCA knew some of the claims made for chiropractic to be false.

Lord Neuberger asked if it was not the case that Singh had outlined his interpretation of the word "bogus" in the original article, where he described how Professor of Complementary Medicine Edzard Ernst had been unable to find any evidence of the effectiveness of chiropractic in over 70 trials.

Rogers conceded that had Singh written that there was "no reliable evidence," the defamation suit might never have happened.

But Lord Justice Sedley suggested, "Isn't the first question as to whether something is evidence [is] that it is reliable?"

Earlier in the day, dozens of Singh's supporters had gathered outside the court to back the popular author's right to free expression.

A date has not been set for delivery of the judges' ruling.

The court was packed for this hearing in front of three of the most senior judges in the country. It seemed, for the first time, that the argument, essentially scientific in nature, was being grasped by the courts. Singh's supporters left the court feeling incredibly upbeat. They were right. . . .

Simon Singh Wins!
April 1, 2010

Simon Singh today scored a crucial victory in his libel defence against the British Chiropractic Association.

In a judgement handed down at 9:30 this morning, the Lord Chief Justice ruled that Singh's contention that the BCA promoted "bogus" treatments was "a statement of opinion, and one backed by reasons." Singh may now pursue a defence of "fair comment."

The judgement criticised the BCA, saying its action had created an "unhappy impression" that the case was "an endeavour by the BCA to silence one of its critics."

The judge added: "If that is where the current law of defamation takes us, we must apply it."

Addressing the effect of lengthy, costly libel trials on public debate and medicine, the judge commented: "It is now nearly two years since the publication of the offending article. It seems unlikely that anyone would dare repeat the opinions expressed by Dr Singh for fear of a writ. Accordingly this litigation has almost certainly had a chilling effect on public debate which might otherwise have assisted potential patients to make informed choices about the possible use of chiropractic."

Speaking outside the court, alongside MPs from all three major parties, Singh stressed that while he was pleased with the ruling, the case for libel reform remained. Singh's case could still potentially continue for another two years.

The BCA has issued a statement saying it is considering its position in the light of the ruling. Richard Brown, President of the BCA concludes:

> We are of course disappointed to lose the appeal, but this is not the end of the road and we are considering whether to seek permission to appeal to the Supreme Court and subsequently proceed to trial. Our original argument remains that our reputation has been damaged. To reiterate, the BCA brought this claim only to uphold its good name and protect its reputation, honesty and integrity.

The Simon Singh case represented a perfect storm. It coincided with the launch of Index on Censorship and English PEN's damning report on England's libel laws, "Free Speech is Not For Sale," and the rise of an increasingly vocal scientific and skeptical community in the UK. Over fifty thousand people signed a petition calling for libel reform. In March, the nation's best-known comics played a sold-out concert in support of the cause. In April, all three main political parties pledged their support for libel reform in the run-up to the general election. When the new Conservative/Liberal Democrat coalition announced its plan for government, libel reform was a key point of its civil liberties program.

PADRAIG REIDY is the news editor for Index on Censorship in London. For more information, please visit www.indexoncensorship.org.

Acknowledgments

Mickey Huff

This year is my first year as director of Project Censored, and *Censored 2011* is my first book as lead editor and coauthor, though I had the pleasure of co-editing with Dr. Peter Phillips for the *Censored 2010* volume and worked very closely with him on the *Censored 2009* book, which were great experiences (therefore my acknowledgements are lengthy). I have followed Project Censored since my undergraduate days in Ohio, when I bought the first full-length book by Project founder Dr. Carl Jensen at a local bookstore in 1993. I was very active against censorship in the arts, an active musician and composer, worked at the local historical society and art museum, and had just entered graduate school. I was a current events and news junkie, and I had a long-standing interest in combating censorship in the arts and literature. The book jumped off the shelf at me when I saw it. This is what I wanted to do, somehow, in some way.

I took many detours after that, finally moving to California in 1999. My life has never been the same since. I was a professional musician and the child of a working-class family that grew up outside of Pittsburgh, Pennsylvania, and somehow went west and realized a dream I did not fully understand, until things all fell into place.

Little did I know that soon after landing outside Berkeley, California, I would meet so many people that I now call colleagues, friends, and family. Of course, the most important of those people is my biggest supporter and partner, my wife Meg, mother of our daughter, without whom I would never have been able to do all the things I've been blessed to do over the past decade. Meg is a great inspiration, intellect, and editor of my work, and best friend. I owe most of what I have become since coming to California to her, for her patience and tolerance of my radical interests and occasionally manic ways. Thank you for helping me realize more fully who I am, and for raising the hope of the next generation.

Upon arriving in California, I also met another person who has proven to be the best mentor and professional supporter I have ever had—Dr. Peter Phillips. I have not worked as well in concert with anyone over my career as an academic and activist. I am pleased to call Peter a good friend. I met Peter in San Francisco at the Alternative Media Expo in 2001, where I met so many people I now call friends, which was just before I met my wife. The same year, I joined the faculty at Diablo Valley College, where I teach history and now call home base. That year turned out to be quite transformative for me in many ways, for the relationships I began developing then have proven the strongest I have known. Quite simply, I owe where I am now professionally to my wife, Meg, and to Peter. Sincerely, working with Peter, and the Project, has been a dream come true.

I thank Peter not only for believing in me, but for trusting me to lead what Carl Jensen started in 1976, and what he himself carried on and grew through this past year as the oldest media research group in the United States. I am humbled to be selected as director and will do my best in this important job of fighting censorship and maintaining a truly free press. I also thank all the board of directors of Project Censored's parent nonprofit, the Media Freedom Foundation (MFF), of which I'm also a member, for their faith and support of me as new director. To Carl, to Peter, to the MFF board, I give my utmost respect and appreciation and look forward to many productive years ahead combating the ongoing Truth Emergency we face.

I would like to thank many people who have contributed personally to who I am and how I got here, though I know I will forget some folks; please forgive me. Obviously my family, my late father, my mother, my sister Terri, my brother Chris, my late brother-in-law Eric, as well as extended family, especially Jeff and Sandra Huff; Chuck, Debbie, Anne, and Jaime Olescyski, along with Eric Pezzulo; Kate Boundy and Robert Sheffield, along with Ali, Brandon, Matt, Bruce, and Jan. I'd also like to thank Blake Bresnahan, Mark and Chris Boughter, Mike Orelli, Bob Cowan, Jim Tomon, Jon Reider, Kevin Glaz, Cody Wandel, Mike Masley (a.k.a. The Artist General), Alan Werner, Mihai Manilou, Barry Cleveland, Michael Slone, Jahni Misja, and Nate Mudd.

To the following people I give gratitude for their friendship and/or educational and professional support over the years, including Dr. John Ely, Dr. Paul Rea, Dr. Michael Parenti, Dr. Marc Sapir, Dr. Fred W. Viehe, Dr. Martin Berger, Dr. Louis Zona, Dr. Brenden Minogue, Dr. Janet Ore, Dirk Hermance, Jim and Joe Allgren, Dr. Martha Pallante, Dr. William Jenkins, Dr. J. C. Smith, and Dr. Andrew Roth.

From Diablo Valley College, where I teach history and critical thinking and advise the Students for a Democratic Society Club, I thank all my students and members of SDS, current and past, as well as Dr. Lyn Krause, Department Chair Greg Tilles, Dr. Matthew Powell, Dr. Manuel

Gonzalez, Dr. Bob Abele, Adam Bessie, Katie Graham, David Vela, Tiffany Higgins, Dr. Amer Araim, Dr. Dorrie Mazzone, Jacob VanVleet, Obed Vazquez, Hedy Wong, Dr. Jeremy Cloward, Terry Fournier, Rick Risborough, Dr. Lenore Gallin, Pam McNeilly, Dr. Andy Barlow, Dr. Steve Johnson, Bruce Lerro, Ed Trujillo, Glenn Appell, Bill Oye, Neal Skapura, Yukie Tokuyama, Jeff in Media Services, President Dr. Judy Walters, and my teaching assistants who helped considerably with this book, including Frances A. Capell, Nolan Higdon, Mike Smith, Kajal Shahali, Sy Cowie, Ryan Shehee, and Kira McDonough. Frankly, I thank all at DVC, where I have been welcomed with open arms for nearly a decade, for which I am grateful. Thank you for your support and sense of educational community.

I thank all the activists, musicians, and scholars in the Bay Area I have worked with, from anarchists to libertarians, greens and veterans groups, librarians and performance artists; from Berkeley and Sonoma, to Humboldt and Mendocino, from San Francisco to Santa Cruz, especially (though I know I'm forgetting some) Nora Barrows-Friedman, Dennis Bernstein, Bonnie Faulkner, Jim Hoffman, Vic Ashley, Dave Heller, Dave Harris, Ramsey Kannan and PM Press, AK Press, Jello Biafra and Alternative Tentacles, Richard Becker, Joan Berezin at Berkeley City College, Kip Waldo at Chabot College, Frank Runninghorse, all the local independent bookstores (everywhere), and Steve and all the folks at the Cheeseboard Collective for hanging our lecture signs and providing great food and community, as well as Cynthia, Stephen, and Bill at the Berkeley UU for hosting so many of our events, and to the Mount Diablo Peace and Justice Center. And thank you, Dr. Howard Zinn, for your vision and daring.

I thank all the contributors to this book: you make it what it is and it is an honor to work with each and every one of you. Some of you I know well, others only in print, but I appreciate all of you and hope to continue collaborating for a more just world in the future. And thank you, the reader, for your continued support in fighting censorship.

Peter Phillips

This past year, 2009, was my last as director of Project Censored. Since early 2010, Mickey Huff from Diablo Valley College has been director of Project Censored/Media Freedom International. Mickey Huff has proven to be a perfect fit to assume the role of director. He has been a longtime contributor to the yearbook, associate director of the Project for two years, and coauthor of *Censored 2010*. Mickey's work with Project Censored for the past several years makes him uniquely qualified to be the new director and lead author for *Censored 2011*. Thank you, Mickey, for taking on this important work.

I want to personally thank those close friends and intimates who have counseled and supported me through many years of Project Censored work. Most important is my wife Mary Lia, who as my trusted friend and life partner provides daily consultative support. The men in the Green Oaks breakfast group—Noel Byrne, Bob Butler, Bob Klose, Derrick West, Colin Godwin, Peter Tracy, and Bill Simon—are personal advisors and confidants who help with difficult decisions. A special thanks also to Carl Jensen, founder of Project Censored, and director for twenty years. His continued advice and support is critical to the Project.

Editors' Joint Acknowledgements

Project Censored is managed by Media Freedom Foundation, a nonprofit corporation based in Sonoma County, California, in cooperation with the Department of History at Diablo Valley College, the School of Arts and Humanities at Sonoma State University, and thirty other colleges and universities around the world. We are an investigative research and media analysis project dedicated to journalistic integrity and the freedom of information throughout the world.

A special thank you to Sonoma State University sociologist Elaine Wellin for long hours researching and writing sections of chapter 1 of this book. Your dedication is greatly appreciated.

Trish Boreta has returned as an editorial consultant to Project Censored after officially retiring from Sonoma State University this year, after ten years. Trish has continued her involvement as the primary editor of chapter 1. Her dedication and support are greatly appreciated.

A big thanks, as always, goes to the people at Seven Stories Press. They are not just a publishing house, but a top-of-the-line publisher on important cultural issues, who help edit our annual book in record time, and serve as advisors in the annual release process of the "Most Censored Stories." Publisher Dan Simon is dedicated to building democracy in America through knowledge and literature. He deserves full credit for assembling an excellent support crew including Jon Gilbert, Veronica Liu, Anna Lui, Theresa Noll, Ruth Weiner, Crystal Yakacki, John Thornton, Caitlin Thompson, Liz DeLong, and Silvia Stramenga.

Thanks also to the staff at Consortium Book Sales and Distribution, who will see to it that every independent bookstore, chain store, and wholesaler in the US are aware of *Censored 2011*. Thanks to Publishers Group Canada, our distributors in Canada, as well as Turnaround Publishers Services Ltd. in Great Britain and Palgrave Macmillan in Australia.

We especially thank Nuovi Mondi Media in Italy for translating and distributing the Censored yearbooks in Italian. Ernesto Carmona translates Project Censored stories into Spanish for *Argenpress* and for our Spanish-language publisher Timéli Ediciones Venezolana.

A big acknowledgement goes to Jodi Solomon Speakers Bureau in Boston for their longtime support in arranging speaking engagements at various colleges and universities nationwide. Proceeds from these appearances are a continuing financial supplement to Project Censored.

Thank you to Kristina Borjesson for all of her work going "Into the Buzzsaw"; she wrote an apt introduction to our *Censored 2011* edition.

Thanks also to the authors of the most censored stories for 2011, for without their often-unsupported efforts as investigative news reporters and writers, the stories presented in *Censored* would not be revealed.

Our guest writers this year include former Project Censored associate director Andy Roth, Fairness and Accuracy in Reporting's (FAIR) Peter Hart, Index on Censorship's Padraig Reidy, Frances A. Capell, Adam Bessie, Robert Abele, David Ray Griffin, Lance deHaven-Smith, Nora Barrows-Friedman, Rob Williams, Josette Canilao, Concha Mateos, David Mathison, Kenn Burrows, and the wonderful team at *Yes! Magazine*, led by Sarah van Gelder.

This year's book again features the cartoons of Khalil Bendib. We appreciate his continued support and talents, as his brilliant editorial work so enhances our content.

Our international judges, some of whom have been involved with the Project for thirty-four years, are among the top experts in the world concerned with First Amendment freedoms and media principles. We are honored to have them as the final voice in ranking the top twenty-five *Censored* stories. We welcome several new international judges to our roster this year.

An important thanks goes to our financial supporters, including the Sonoma State University Instructionally Related Activity Fund, the School of Social Sciences and the School of Art and Humanities at Sonoma State University, and the Social Science Division at Diablo Valley College. We offer a special thank you to Jordan Brody from Colorado: your support for our work is greatly appreciated. Continuing contributors to Project Censored include Elizabeth Sherif, Mark Swedlund and Deborah Dobish, Lynn and Leonard Riepenhoff, and thousands of individuals who purchase books and send us financial gifts each year. You are our financial base, the important few who continue to give year after year to this important student-run media research project.

This year we had over sixty-five faculty/community evaluators from two dozen universities and colleges assisting with our story assessment process. These expert volunteers read and rated the nominated stories for national importance, accuracy, and credibility. In April, they participated with over two hundred students from several colleges in selecting the final top 25 stories for 2009–10.

A big thank you to Adam Armstrong, our Web master and coordinator for the Project Censored Web sites including www.projectcensored.org, the PNN Daily News site at www.censorednews.org, the Project Censored daily blog at www.dailycensored.com, and the Media Freedom International validated news at www.mediafreedominternational.org.

Lastly, we want to thank our readers and supporters from all over the United States and the world. Hundreds of you nominated stories for consideration as the censored news story of the year. Thank you very much!

Project Censored Media Freedom Foundation Board
Dennis Bernstein, Cynthia Boaz, Kenn Burrows, Noel Byrne, Frances A. Capell, Gary Evans, Mickey Huff, Carl Jensen, Mary Lia, David Mathison, Miguel Molina, Peter Phillips, Bill Simon, Judith Volkart

Project Censored Consultants & Volunteers
Adam Armstrong: Web master
Trish Boreta: Editor
Ellaine Wellin: Editor
David Quintana: Intern
Derrick West: Financial Consultant

Participating Colleges and Universities, Faculty, and Students

Sonoma State University, California
Sociology of Media—Fall 2009
Instructor: Peter Phillips
Nohemi Ameral, Michaella Amanino, Greg Bernardi, Trinty Cambon, Danielle Caruso, Stephaine Constantine, Elisabeth Dembosz, Lauren Faulkner, Katrina Gargiulo, Marylou German, Joseph Hanley, Tyler Head, Eric Herbert, Kristin Laney, Casey Morse, Andrew Nassab, Daniel Nimoy, Joseph Parigi, Claire Prokop, Jameka Rothchild-Ballard, Steven Rutherford, Tony Sarganis, Gina Sarpy, Alma

Shaw, Ryan Stevens, Tracena Webster, Garret West, Ariana White, Chi Hang Yeung

Sonoma State University, California
Liberal Studies 320A—Fall 2009
Instructor: Ben Frymer
Amanda Olson, Nicole Jacobson, Scott Macky, Marissa Warfield, Jenni Schumann, Travis Hann, Bridget Grille, Megan Vosburgh, Kelsea Arnold, Jenna Stiver, Christina Risso, Mira Patel, Anne Cozza, Brittany Barret

Sonoma State University, California
Liberal Studies 304—Fall 2009
Instructor: Stephanie Dyer
Amanda Bruna, Meg Carlucci, Sharilyn Heinkel, Sterling Hellwege, Ashley Housley, Crystal Schreiner, Michelle Sewell, Dani Wright, Kelley Zaino

Sonoma State University, California
Political Sociology—Spring 2010
Instructor: Peter Phillips
Amelia Albertini, Molly Ashe, Ryan Borg, Danielle Caruso, Borrom Chim, Ian Cook, Jennifer DeLoach, Whiney Donnelly, Taylor Falbisaner, Katrina Gargiulo, Nicholas George, Kelsey Harris, Jenna Hornbuckle, Dana Johnson, Savannah Keen, Keven Knopf, Julie Lewis, Alma Delia Maciel, Shannon Molo, Brittany Morgan, Casey Morse, Alex Muxen, Jason Nelson, Kristy Nelson, Nicholas Nielsen, Sarah Payne, Lacy Perron, Ashlee Plouffe, Alina Schlabach, Fradley Shadoan, Rebecca Sullivan, Garret West

Sonoma State University, California
Liberal Studies 304—Spring 2010
Instructor: Stephanie Dyer
Amanda Bruna, Meg Carlucci, Sharilyn Heinkel, Sterling Hellwege, Ashley Housley, Crystal Schreiner, Michelle Sewell, Dani Wright, Kelley Zaino

Sonoma State University, California
Liberal Studies 308—Spring 2010
Instructor: Ben Frymer
Jessica Andrew, Christina Bailey, Brandon Brockmire, Alice Butcher, Kendall Daigle, Megan Dawson, Heidi Facciano, Lissonna Ferreira, Nicole Fletcher, Brittney Gates, Jason Giordano, Christina Harvey, Shawna Hettrich, Susana Huguet, Derek Hunter, Ashley Jackson-Lesti, Allyson Lewis, Thomas Macdonald, Christopher Marten, Anne Mcbride, Marissa Mendoza, Jessica Nelson, Mira Patel, Brittany Ross

Sonoma State University, California
Project Censored Interns for 2009–10
Instructors: Peter Phillips and Ben Frymer
Jennifer Donahue, Sarah Maddox, Andrew Hobbs, Natalie Gray, John Neylan,

Maria Tzouvelekis, Katie Barton, Jordan O'Halloran, Lily Rex, Tristan Theist, Nia Shimafra, Josette Canilao, Alexandra Hughes

Diablo Valley College, California
Project Censored Interns for 2009–10
Frances A. Capell, Nolan Higdon, Mike Smith, Sy Cowie, Kajal Shahali, Jenna Edmond, Elliot van Patten, Rane Stark, Ryan Shehee, Kira McDonough, the students in Critical Reasoning in History 122, the Students for a Democratic Society club, and the Project Censored Media Literacy Club, founded this year by Brian Donovan, plus everyone mentioned in Mickey Huff's acknowledgements above

DePauw University, Indiana
Media Culture & Society—Fall 2009
Faculty: Kevin Howley
Claire Apatoff, Joseph Bergfeld, Alex Burns, Delana Colvin, Shannon Cree, Lynn Demos, Colin Doran, Jillian Harbin, Michael Hemkens, Trisha Himmelein, Ryan Huffman, Erin Kielty, Anna Kung, John Rich, Leanne Schaub, Emily Schuler, Ryan Sever, Grover Simpson, Benjamin Solomon, Leighanne Steckbeck, Abigail Wilson, Steven Wojanis

Complutense University of Madrid, Spain
Faculty: Ana I. Segovia, associate professor, Department of Journalism
Student Researchers (PhD candidates): Dimitrina Jivkova, Joan Pedro, Luis Luján

Southwest Minnesota State University, Minnesota
Faculty: Teresa B. Henning, Vicki Brockman, Doug Simon, Joel Vargas
Student Researchers: Rebecca Albright, Mike McGovern, Christine Streff, Kurtis Szerlip, Kia Yang, Colleen Werner

University of La Laguna, Tenerife, Canary Islands, Spain
Faculty: José Manuel de-Pablos, José Pestano
Graduate Students: Alberto Ardevol-Abreu, Cruz Albertos Martínez-Arcos, Ciro Hernández

University of Buenos Aires, Argentina
Faculty: Silvia Lago Martinez, Gino Germani's Institute Reaserching team: researcher Andrea Pereyra, students Sheila Amado, Rafael de Bouza
Translation: Ariadna Umpierrez

Indian River State College, Florida
Faculty: Elliot Cohen
Student Researchers: Maritza Ahrens, Krystal Alexander, Mubiyna Casarez, Amber Davis, Keith Dingess, Brian Lorenzo, Christopher Lue, Rory T. Loveridge, Camille Mallory, Kelly Mastros, Wyatt Medina, David Murray, Amelia Rose Scherker, Cecele Senorine, Carolyn Zidor

DePaul University, Illinois
Faculty: Marla Donato
Student Researchers: Jody Lempa, Tina Shaerban, Katherine Tellez, Jillian Wolande

St. Cloud State University, Minnesota
Faculty: Julie Andrzejewski
Student Researchers: Nancy Shedrack Anwary, Cassie Barthel, Danielle Bennett, Kayla Beuning, Meghan Brandts, Bretta Diekmann, Rachel Dzuck, Alyssa Horton, Helen Kitilla, Molly Lipinski, Jordan Markwardt, Sarah Mulroy, Andrea Norton, Katie Nystrom, Amanda Peterson, Samantha West, Jessica Wiehr

Niagara University, New York
International Communication—Spring 2010
Professor: Brian Martin Murphy
Kaitlyn Bayne, Andrew Boser, Kaitlin Brennan, Vincent Brunetto, Chase Cedrone, Alexandra Cortese, Kelsey Cox, Amanda Defisher, Michael Desimone, Scott Erikson, Rianne Farrugia, Patrick Fetzer, Evan Giokas, Steven Gruhalla, Evan Jackson, Ken Lambert, Kristen McAuley, Frances McPhail, John Meszaros, Erin Mirando, Katelyn Oke, Olumatomilayo Omotosho, Mary Phelps, Matt Riley, Nicholas Sabato, Brittany Schottmiller, Shannor Sedor, Kristin Sito, Kathleen Smith, Daniel Stevens, Corey Swift, Alicia Wainwright, Daniel White, Alexandra Zimmerman

DePauw University, Indiana—Faculty Evaluators for 2009–10
Meryl Altman, English/Women's Studies
Jeremy Anderson, Philosophy
Russ Arnold, Religious Studies
Lynn Bedard, Biology
Christopher Bondy, Sociology
Rebeca Bordt, Sociology
Tim Cope, Geosciences
Bryan Hanson, Chemistry and Biochemistry
Mandy Henk, Coordinator of Access Services
Bryan Hanson, Chemistry and Biochemistry
Brian Howard, Computer Science
Jamie Knapp, Library and Information Sciences
Jeff McCall, Communications
Jo MacPhail, Reference Librarian
Rich Martoglio, Chemistry and Biochemistry
Clarissa Peterson, Political Science
Andrea Sununu, English
Eva Weisz, Education

Sonoma State University, California—Faculty Evaluators for 2009–10
Carlos Benito, Economics
Cynthia Boaz, Political Science

Suzel Bozada-Deas, Sociology
Kelly Bucy, Political Science
Noel Byrne, Sociology
Glenn Carter, Computer Science
Steven Cuellar, Economics
Laurie Dawson, Counseling
James Dean, Sociology
Stephanie Dyer, Liberal Studies
Mike Ezra, American Multicultural Studies
Ben Frymer, Liberal Studies
Robert Girling, Business
Myrna Goodman, Sociology
Keith Gouveia, Political Science
Diana Grant, Criminal Justice
Elizabeth Grayson-Slater, Business
Debora Hammond, Liberal Studies
Janet Hess, Liberal Studies
Shelia Katz, Sociology
Buzz Kellogg, Liberal Studies
Patricia Kim-Rajal, Chicano and Latino Studies
Heidi Lamoreaux, Liberal Studies
Elaine Leeder, Dean of Social Sciences; Sociology
Ron Lopez, Chicano and Latino Studies
Rick Luttmann, Mathamatics
Eric McGuckin, Anthropology
Mutombo M'Panya, Liberal Studies
Catherine Nelson, Political Science
Wendy Ostroff, Psychology
Ervand Peterson, Environmental Studies and Planning
James J. Preston, Sociology
Andrew Roth, Sociology
Rashmi Singh, American Multicultural Studies
Tony Spark, Geography
Cindy Stearns, Sociology
Rich Svendsen, Education
Francisco Vazquez, Liberal Studies
Sascha von Meier, Environmental Studies
Laura Watt, Environmental Studies and Planning
Elaine Wellin, Sociology
Tryon Woods, Criminal Justice
Carmen Works, Biology

Sonoma State University, California—Community Evaluators
Gary Evans, MD, Sonoma
Jimmy Dizmang, Computer Science, University of San Diego
Dorothy Owens, MD, Sonoma

Robin Takahashi, Ohlone College
Derrick West, Sonoma County Management

Project Censored 2009–10 International Judges

*Indicates having been a Project Censored judge since our founding in 1976

JULIE ANDRZEJEWSKI, professor of social responsibility, St. Cloud State University; author of five editions of the anthology, *Oppression and Social Justice: Critical Frameworks.*

ROBIN ANDERSEN, PHD, professor of communication and media studies, director of the MA program in Public Communications, director of the Peace and Justice Studies program, Fordham University. Author of the books *A Century of Media, A Century of War* (winner of the 2007 Alpha Sigma Nu Book Award), *Consumer Culture and TV Programming,* and *Critical Studies in Media Commercialism*; media criticisms for *EXTRA!*; and dozens of book chapters and journal articles. Co-editor of the two-volume *Battleground: The Media.* Member of the board of directors of FAIR and Deep Dish TV.

OLIVER BOYD-BARRETT, director of the School of Communication Studies, professor of journalism and telecommunications, Bowling Green State University; author of *The International New Agencies: the Globalization of News, Media in Global Context.*

KENN BURROWS, faculty member for the Institute for Holistic Health Studies, San Francisco State University; producer and director of the Future of Health Care annual conference.

ERNESTO CARMONA, Chilean journalist and writer; director of the Chilean Council of Journalists; executive secretary of the Investigation Commission on Attacks against Journalists, Latin American Federation of Journalists (CIAP-FELAP).

LIANE CLORFENE-CASTEN, co-founder and president of Chicago Media Watch; award-winning journalist with credits in national periodicals such as *E Magazine,* the *Nation, Mother Jones, Ms., Environmental Health Perspectives, In These Times,* and *Business Ethics*; author of *Breast Cancer: Poisons, Profits, and Prevention.*

ELLIOT COHEN, professor, Indian River State College; media ethicist and critic; coauthor of *The Last Days of Democracy: How Big Media and Power-Hungry Government Are Turning America Into a Dictatorship.*

JOSÉ MANUEL DE PABLOS, professor, University of La Laguna, Canary Islands, Spain; founder of the scientific journal *Revista Latina de Comunicación Social* and the Laboratory of Information Technologies and New Analysis of Communication (LATINA).

GEOFF DIVIDIAN, Milwaukee investigative journalist; editor of the online newspaper *Putman Pit* .

LENORE FOERSTEL, Women for Mutual Security; facilitator of the Progressive International Media Exchange (PRIME).

ROBERT HACKETT, professor, School of Communication, Simon Fraser University; co-director of News Watch Canada since 1993; author of *Democratizing Global Media: One World, Many Struggles* (co-edited with Yuezhi Zhao, 2005) and *Remaking Media: The Struggle to Democratize Public Communication* (with William K. Carroll, 2006).

KEVIN HOWLEY, associate professor of communication, DePauw University; editor of *Understand Community Media*; author of *Community Media: People, Places, and Communication Technologies.*

CARL JENSEN, professor emeritus of communication studies, Sonoma State University; founder and former director of Project Censored; author of *Censored: The News That Didn't Make the News and Why* (1990–1996) and *20 Years of Censored News* (1997).

NICHOLAS JOHNSON,* professor, College of Law, University of Iowa; former FCC commissioner (1966–73); author of *How to Talk Back to Your Television Set.*

CHARLES L. KLOTZER, editor and publisher emeritus, *St. Louis Journalism Review.*

NANCY KRANICH, past president of the American Library Association (ALA); senior research fellow, Free Expression Policy Project.

MARTIN LEE, investigative journalist, media critic, and author; co-founder of Fairness & Accuracy in Reporting (FAIR) in New York; former editor of *Extra!* magazine; author of *Acid Dreams: The Complete Social History of LSD—The CIA, the Sixties and Beyond.*

DENNIS LOO, associate professor of sociology at California State Polytechnic University–Pomona; co-editor of *Impeach the President: The Case Against Bush and Cheney* (Seven Stories Press, 2006).

PETER LUDES, professor of mass communication, Jacobs University–Bremen; founder in 1997 of the German initiative on news enlightenment, publishing the most neglected German news (Project Censored Germany).

WILLIAM LUTZ, professor of English, Rutgers University; former editor of the *Quarterly Review of Doublespeak;* author of *The New Doublespeak: Why No One Knows What Anyone's Saying Anymore* (1966).

SILVIA LAGO MARTINEZ, professor of sociology, University of Buenos Aires; co-director of Gino Germani Research Institute Program for Research on Information Society.

CONCHA MATEOS, faculty, Rey Juan Carlos University, Madrid; journalist for radio, television, and political organizations in Spain and Latin America; coordinator of Project Censored research in Europe and Latin America.

MARK CRISPIN MILLER, professor of media ecology, New York University; director of the Project on Media Ownership; author of several books on media and politics.

BRIAN MURPHY, associate professor of communications studies, Niagara University, specializing in media programming and management; investigation and reporting; media history and theory; and international communication.

JACK L. NELSON,* professor emeritus, Graduate School of Education, Rutgers University; author of sixteen books, including *Critical Issues in Education* (1996), and more than one hundred fifty articles.

PETER PHILLIPS, professor of sociology, Sonoma State University; director of Project Censored (1996–2009); president of Media Freedom Foundation; editor/co-editor of thirteen editions of *Censored*; co-editor of *Impeach the President: The Case Against Bush and Cheney* (Seven Stories Press, 2006).

ANA I. SEGOVIA, associate professor, Department of Journalism, Complutense University of Madrid, Spain.

NANCY SNOW, professor of public diplomacy and communications, Syracuse University; senior fellow, University of Southern California Center on Public Diplomacy; author of *Persuader-in-Chief* (Nimble Books), *Propaganda, Inc.* (Seven Stories), *Information War* (Seven Stories), *War, Media and Propaganda* (with Yahya Kamalipour), and the *Routledge Handbook of Public Diplomacy* (with Philip M. Taylor).

SHEILA RABB WEIDENFELD,* president of D.C. Productions, Ltd.; former press secretary to Betty Ford.

ROB WILLIAMS, co-president and board member, Action Coalition for Media Education (ACME); faculty, Champlain College.

Sonoma State University Supporting Staff and Offices
Eduardo Ochoa, Chief Academic Officer, and staff
Melinda Bernard, Vice Provost Academic Affairs
Elaine Leeder, Dean of School of Sciences, and staff
William Babula, Dean of School of Arts and Humanities
Barbara Butler and the SSU Library staff
Paula Hammett, Social Sciences Library Resources
Elisabeth Burch and faculty, Communications Studies
Susan Kashack, Jean Wasp, and staff, SSU Public Relations Office
Eric McGuckin and faculty, Hutchins School of Liberal Studies

How to Support Project Censored

NOMINATE A STORY

To nominate a *Censored* story, send us a copy of the article and include the name of the source publication, the date that the article appeared, and the page number. For news stories published on the Internet of which we should be aware, please forward the URL to mickey@project-censored.org and/or peter@projectcensored.org. The final deadline period for nominating a story for Most Censored Stories of the Year is March of each year.

Criteria for Project Censored news stories nominations

1. A censored news story contains information that the public has a right and a need to know, but to which the public has had limited access.

2. The news story is timely, ongoing, and has implications for a significant number of residents in the world.

3. The story has clearly defined concepts and is backed up with solid, verifiable documentation.

4. The news story has been publicly published, either electronically or in print, in a circulated newspaper, journal, magazine, newsletter, or similar publication from either a foreign or domestic source.

SUPPORT PROJECT CENSORED BY MAKING A FINANCIAL GIFT

Project Censored is supported by Media Freedom Foundation, a 501(c)3 nonprofit organization. We depend on tax-deductible donations and foundation grants to continue our work. To support our efforts for freedom of information send checks to the address below or call (707) 874-2695. Visa and Mastercard are accepted. Donations can be made online through our Web site at www.projectcensored.org. Please consider helping us fight news censorship.

Media Freedom Foundation
P.O. Box 571
Cotati, CA 94931
e-mail: mickey@projectcensored.org and/or peter@projectcensored.org

MEDIA FREEDOM FOUNDATION AND PROJECT CENSORED WEB SITES

Project Censored: www.projectcensored.org
Daily Independent News: www.censorednews.org
Validated Independent News: www.mediafreedominternational.org
Blog: www.dailycensored.com
In Spanish: www.proyectocensurado.org

A statement from Adam Armstrong, Web master for Project Censored, on the importance of new media technologies in combating censorship
As computers and mobile devices become more ingrained in everything we do, more and more media choices become available. And as the Big Media conglomerates try to stay valid in this ever-changing digital landscape, new technologies and services such as Twitter and Facebook (Project Censored uses both) become more important; in the last couple of years alone, we have seen demonstrations, rallies, and important news that was not found anywhere else but in these emerging technological arenas. This new way of sharing information has become so important that Big Media spend endless hours scouring the Internet trying to find relevant stories before you do. Some traditional media have even set up online systems to let users upload their own news as they see it.

At Project Censored, we know how important it is to keep the public informed of what the "real news" really is. That is why we have invested an ever-increasing amount of our time and money to ensure we are reaching as many people as possible within this new landscape. We are now reaching more people than ever, and we will continue to bring them unbiased, unfiltered, untampered news through all of our Web outlets. Please join us in this Validated Independent News revolution.

About the Editors

MICKEY HUFF is the new director of Project Censored, an associate professor of history at Diablo Valley College, and a member of the board of directors at the Media Freedom Foundation (MFF), which oversees Project Censored (www.projectcensored.org). He works closely with former Project Censored director Dr. Peter Phillips and helps coordinate the new Project Censored International College and Affiliates Program (www.mediafreedominternational.org).

Huff was associate director of Project Censored for two years prior to becoming director, during which time the organization received the 2008 PEN Oakland National Literary Censorship Award. He has taught courses in history and critical thinking at several colleges in the San Francisco Bay Area, and has been an adjunct lecturer in sociology at Sonoma State University, a visiting scholar for the academic library at the University of Nebraska–Lincoln, and the previous co-director of the alternative public opinion research agency, Retropoll (www.retropoll.org).

Huff has been interviewed for several documentaries and news programs throughout the country, including National Public Radio, Air America, Pacifica Radio Network, Republic Broadcasting, the Santa Rosa Press Democrat, No Lies Radio, and others, and has been published on numerous media and news Web sites including *Global Research, CounterPunch, Z Magazine, Buzzflash, Truthout, Dissident Voice,* and *Empire Report,* among others. In addition, Huff's work has been included in several academic journals and university publications. He teaches in US media history, sociology of media and censorship, propaganda studies, 9/11 and American Empire, and popular culture. At Berkeley City College, Huff designed the critical reasoning in history course titled "America, 9/11, and the War on Terror: Media Myth Making and the Propaganda of Historical Construction," and co-designed the history of US media class. He has also taught "American Popular Culture and Mass Media in Historical Perspectives."

Huff has co-organized and presented at numerous national conferences on media and recent historical events, including Truth Emergency and media reform issues (www.truthemergency.us), and recently spoke with Peter Phillips at the Understanding Deep Politics Conference in Santa Cruz, California. He has given public addresses at colleges, community halls, and bookstores across the US on media censorship and American historiography, and hosted the Modern Media Censorship lecture series at Sonoma State University in fall 2008. Most recently he was the organizer and host of the Empire, Power, and Propaganda lecture series in Berkeley, California, in spring 2010. The series is scheduled to resume in fall 2010.

With Seven Stories Press, Huff has been published in *Censored 2009: The Top 25 Censored Stories of 2007–08*, coauthoring the chapters "Media Reform Meets Truth Emergency" and "Deconstructing Deceit: 9/11, the Media, and Myth Information." He has written several articles with Peter Phillips on Truth Emergency, the military-industrial-media empire, and the impact of media censorship on peace and social justice movements in the US.

When he has time, he posts at Project Censored's blog, Daily Censored (www.dailycensored.com). Huff is also a musician and composer of over twenty years and lives with his family just outside Berkeley, California.

PETER PHILLIPS is a professor of sociology at Sonoma State University and recent past director of Project Censored. He teaches classes in media censorship, investigative sociology, sociology of power, political sociology, and sociology of media. With Seven Stories Press, he has published thirteen editions of the *Censored* yearbook, *Impeach the President: The Case Against Bush and Cheney* (2006, with Dennis Loo), and *Project Censored Guide to Independent Media and Activism* (2003).

In 2009, Phillips received the Union for Democratic Communications' Dallas Smythe Award, a national award given to researchers and activists who, through their research and/or production work, have made significant contributions to the study and practice of democratic communication.

Phillips writes op-ed pieces for independent media nationwide and has been published in dozens of publications, newspapers, and Web sites including *Common Dreams, Buzzflash, Dissident Voice, Global Research*, and Minuteman Media. He frequently speaks on media censorship and various sociopolitical issues on radio and TV talk shows, including National Public Radio's *Talk of the Nation*, Air America, Talk America, World Radio Network, and Flashpoints.

Phillips has completed several investigative research studies that are available at www.projectcensored.org, including "The Global Dominance

Group: 9/11 Pre-Warnings & Election Irregularities in Context," "A Study of Bias in the Associated Press," "Practices in Health Care and Disability Insurance: Deny Delay Diminish and Blame," "US Electromagnetic Weapons and Human Rights," "Building a Public Ivy: Diversity at Three California State Universities," and "The Left Progressive Media Inside the Propaganda Model."

Phillips earned a BA in social science in 1970 from Santa Clara University, and an MA in social science from California State University–Sacramento in 1974. He earned a second MA in sociology in 1991, and a PhD in sociology in 1994. His doctoral dissertation was entitled *A Relative Advantage: Sociology of the San Francisco Bohemian Club* (http://libweb.sonoma.edu/regional/faculty/Phillips/bohemianindex.htm).

Phillips is a fifth-generation Californian who grew up on a family-owned farm west of the Central Valley town of Lodi. Today he lives in rural Sonoma County with his wife, Mary Lia.

Index

GE. *See* General Electric
Gearhart, Chester, 282
Geithner, Timothy, 100, 102, 153, 155
Gelernt, Lee, 33
General Electric (GE), 94, 148, 213
General Law on Audiovisual Communication
  in Spain, 377
genetically modified organisms (GMOs), 47
Geneva Conventions, 83, 123, 126
genocide, 56
  in DRC, 85
  in Iraq, 83–84
Ghappour, Ahmed, 126
el Gharani, Mohammed, 127
Gillespie, Ed, 173
Gingrich, Newt, 173, 175–76
girder-failure theory, 276–77
Giuliani, Rudolph, 268
glaciers, 114
Glanz, James, 167, 270, 280
Glass-Steagall Act, 154
Global Investigative Journalism, 124
Glover, Henry, 150
GMOs. *See* genetically modified organisms
Goldberg, Jonah, 174–76
Goldman Sachs, 135, 155, 392
Goldstone, Richard, 147, 300, 312
Gombossy, George, 217
Goodman, Amy, 2
Google, 114–15, 117, 180
Gorbachev, Mikhail S., 394
Gott, Richard, 65
*The Grand Chessboard: American Primacy And
  Its Geostrategic Imperatives* (Brzezinski),
  153
Granholm, Jennifer, 110
Great Society, 247
*The Great Transformation: The Beginning of
  Our Religious Traditions* (Armstrong), 411
Greco, Emily Schwartz, 225
Green Line borders, 296, 309
Greenspan, Alan, 153
Greenwald, Glenn, 213, 215
*The Green Zone; the Environmental Costs of
  Militarism* (Sanders, Barry), 17
Griffin, David Ray, 73–74, 226, 267
Griffin, Phil, 213, 215
Griffiths, Jesse, 101
Ground Zero, 271
Guam
  Department of Defense, U.S. and, 22–23
  U.S. military in, 19, 21–24
Guantánamo Bay
  Bush, G. W. and, 82–83
  Obama and, 83–84, 123–27
Gulf Cooperation Council, 120
Gulf of Mexico oil spill, 98
  bioremediation and, 200–201
  propaganda and, 176–80
Gulf of Tonkin, 223, 233, 241, 281, 284
Gulf War, 318

Gupta, Sanjay, 3

H1N1 virus (swine flu), 60–63
Habeeb, Sameh, 308
Haig, Alexander, 257
Haiti, 63–67, 171
Haldeman, Bob, 254
Hale, Brian, 34
Hale, Robert, 154
Hamas, 82, 309, 311
  crimes against humanity by, 147
  Israel and, 298–99
Hamilton, Jesse, 194
Hampton, Cynthia, 163
Hansen, Mark Victor, 407
Hanway, Ed, 39
Harrit, Niels, 276, 282
Healing the Masses (Feinsilver), 66
health care, 9, 38–43, 70
Hedges, Chris, 11, 182
Heene, Falcon, 166–67
Heene, Richard, 166
Henderson, Hazel, 398
HEP. *See* Hour Exchange Portland
Hersh, Seymour, 122, 124
Hess, Michael, 268–69, 274
Heubert, Rob, 20
Hicks, David, 125
high crimes and misdemeanors, 244
high criminality, 231, 233, 258
High Seas Task Force (HSTF), 140
Hill, Paul T., 106
Himmelstein, David, 39
Hirpa, Haile, 46
Hiss, Alger, 252
Hitchens, Christopher, 316–22
Hitler, Adolf, 172–75
Ho, Rodney, 405
Hobbs, Andrew, 363–64
Hofnung, Daniel, 282
Hoover, J. Edgar, 252, 254
Hoover Institution, 174–75
Host Nation Trucking, 58
Hour Exchange Portland (HEP), 203
House Financial Services Committee, 136
House National Security Subcommittee, 59
Housing and Urban Affairs, 136
HSRC. *See* Human Sciences Research
  Council of South Africa
HSTF. *See* High Seas Task Force (HSTF)
Hudson, Michael, 13
Huff, Mickey, 3, 7, 353
Hu Jintao, 10
Humana Inc., 216
human intelligence (HUMINT), 37
human rights abuses, 53–56, 96
  in West Bank, 54–56
Human Rights Ministry, 359
Human Rights Watch, 123
Human Sciences Research Council of South
  Africa (HSRC), 54

Hume, Mick, 165
HUMINT. *See* human intelligence
Hunt, Dorothy, 256
Hunt, Howard, 254–55
Hunter, Michael, 150
Hunter, Rielle, 163
Hurricane Katrina, 106, 149
    race and, 149
Hussein, Saddam, 316–27
Huxley, Aldous, 160, 181, 182
hyperreality, 160, 173, 175

IAO. *See* Information Awareness Office
IBC. *See* Iraq Body Count
ICE. *See* Immigration and Customs
    Enforcement
ICMR. *See* Indian Council of Medical
    Research
ICRC. *See* International Committee of the
    Red Cross (ICRC)
illegal, unreported, and unregulated fleets
    (IUU), 140
illegal downloading, 28
IMF. *See* International Monetary Fund
Immediate Reaction Force (IRF), 124–25
Immigration and Customs Enforcement
    (ICE), 30–34
imminent threat, 324–25
imperial overstretch, 393
implosion, 268, 282
income disparity, 403–4
inconvenient truths, 357
independent media, 9
independent news, 355–57
Index on Censorship, 419–24
India
    Bhopal, 77–81
    biometric ID cards and, 116–18
    Centre for Science and the Environment
        in New Delhi, 79
    Mumbai, 118
Indian Council of Medical Research (ICMR),
    78
individual empowerment, media and, 403–
    16
IndyMedia, 28, 367
Information Awareness Office (IAO), 26
information dissemination, 8
Instant Income (Switzer), 407
Instant Response, 178
Institute for Policy Studies (IPS), 223, 225–
    26
Institute of Noetic Sciences, 208
intelligence-industrial complex, 251
Intelligent Optimists, 207
Intergovernmental Panel on Climate Change
    (IPCC), 113–14
Internal Revenue Service (IRS), 144
internal segregation, of Israel, 302
International Center for Leadership and
    Education, 107

International Committee of the Red Cross
    (ICRC), 64, 123
International Convention of the Suppression
    and Punishment of the Crime of
    Apartheid, 54
International Court of Justice, 50
International Criminal Court, 85–86
International Decade for the Eradication of
    Colonialism, 22
International Finance for Sustainability, 101
International Initiative to Prosecute U.S.
    Genocide in Iraq, 83
International Institute for Environment and
    Development, 46–47
international laws, 21–22, 82, 87, 324, 326
    violation of, 56, 293–98, 320–21
International Marxist Tendency, 380
International Monetary Fund (IMF), 11, 100
international monetary system, 13
International Security Assistance Force
    (ISAF), 59, 119
Internet, 114–16, 181
    infrastructure of, 414–15
    Obama and, 411–12
    privacy and, 24–29
InternetforEveryone.org, 415
iodine additives, 133
IPCC. *See* Intergovernmental Panel on
    Climate Change
IPS. *See* Institute for Policy Studies
Iran-Contra, 233–34, 241, 260, 281
    Bush, G. H. W. and, 253
    Bush, G. W. and, 257
    Gates and, 257
    Reagan and, 236
Iraq
    arguments for war, 315–29
    democracy in, 329
    genocide in, 83–84
    Spain and, 374
    U.S. invasion of, 315–29, 358
    war in, 18, 70, 86, 152, 225, 233, 258, 261,
        365
Iraq Body Count (IBC), 358
Iraq Oil Law, 97
IRF. *See* Immediate Reaction Force
iron triangles, 149, 247
IRS. *See* Internal Revenue Service
ISAF. *See* International Security Assistance
    Force
Islamic Movement of Uzbekistan, 37
Ismayil, Arafat Ahmed, 305
Israel
    apartheid in, 1, 295
    crimes against humanity by, 146
    discrimination and, 294, 302–5
    as disputed territory, 294
    Gaza and, 312
    Hamas and, 298–99
    internal segregation of, 302
    Naqab/Negev Desert, 304–5

Phillips, Peter, 3, 138, 168, 353, 360
photography, war and, 364–65
PhRMA. *See* Pharmaceutical Research and
   Manufacturers of America
Physicians for a National Health Program
   (www.pnhp.org), 41
Physicians for Human Rights, 359
Pinochet, Augusto, 82
placeless news, 398
Plame, Valerie, 257–58
Plant My Phone, 199
plastic bags, 198
ployamidoamine dendrimers (PAMAMs), 92
poaching, 141
Poindexter, John, 257
political-corporate power structure, 373
political criminality, 236, 243
political decentralization, 398
political hate speech, 173–74
political power, corporations and, 372
Politico, 177, 211
Pollack, Kenneth, 319
pollution
   by Chevron, 96
   Department of Defense, U.S. and, 18
   Gulf of Mexico oil spill, 98, 176–80,
      200–201
   in Israel, 300
   noise, 341–42
   toxic waste dumping, 140–41
   U.S. military and, 15–24
   water toxicity, 78–79
polychlorinated biphenyls (PCBs), 93
Popal, Ahmed Rate, 57–58
Popal, Rashid, 57
Popular Front for the Liberation of Palestine,
   309
Popular Party, 374
Portland, Maine, 203
Postman, Neil, 181
Postman, Said, 160–61
post-Soviet Russia, 14
Premier Wen Jiabao, 13
presidential debates, 151
Prince, Erik, 35
privacy, Internet and, 24–29
privatization, of education, 107, 112
pro-democracy uprisings, 14
Product Pricing Curve, 408–9
programming committee. *See* comisión de
   programación
Progress Energy, 141
progressive collapse, 278
Progressive Era, 247
Project on Emerging Nanotechnologies
   (PEN), 89, 92
Pronovost, Peter, 42
propaganda, 315
   Gulf of Mexico oil spill and, 176–80
   television as, 374
ProPublica, 150

psychological warfare, 255
PTPA. *See* Panama Trade Promotion
   Agreement
Public Citizen's Global Trade Watch, 100, 145
Public Radio International's *The World*, 33
public universities, 363–65
*Publishing Mavericks: How Experts Build
   Empires* (Switzer), 407

al-Qaeda, 35, 328
   9/11 and, 267, 279
   Obama and, 221
   in Pakistan, 37

race
   charter schools and, 102–3
   economic segregation and, 138
   Hurricane Katrina and, 149
   in schools, 137–39
Race to the Top, 106–7, 109–11
Rahmeh, Basem Abu, 56
Ramanathan, Usha, 118
RAND Corporation, 251
Rapp, Stephen, 86
Rather, Dan, 268, 285
Ratner, Michael, 83
Ratzkoff, Bathsheba, 1
Raytheon, 154
Reagan, Ronald, 242, 253, 257
   education and, 106
   Iran-Contra and, 236
redlining, 414
Red States, 391
Regional Council of Unrecognized Villages,
   304
regulation, of media, 371–87
Reich, Otto, 257
Reidy, Padraig, 421
Rejeski, David, 92
religious traditions, 411
renaissance
   control of, 412–13
   of individual, 411
   of media, 403, 407, 410–14
Renaissance 2010, 105
renewable energy, 200
Reno, Janet, 242
repurposing, 407–8
Rights of Persons with Disabilities, 132
Risch, Jim, 343
Ritter, Stacie, 39
RJ Lee Group, 275
Roadmap to Apartheid, 197
Robert Garrett Fund for the Treatment of
   Children, 43
Rogers, Desirée, 167
Rogers, Heather, 422
Ronald Reagan Ballistic Missile Defense Test
   Site, 23
Roosevelt, Franklin Delano, 411
Roper, Daniel, 120

in Arctic, 19–20
Blackwater and, 37
Chevron and, 97
education programs, 105
global empire of, 12
in Guam, 19, 21–24
in Israel, 307
military-industrial complex, 248–49
military-industrial-media empire, 221–27
mutual military assistance clause, 119
NATO and, 118–21, 141, 226
orders by Obama, 27
in Pakistan, 36, 222
in Palestine, 1
pollution and, 15–24
subsidizing of, 10
United Technologies, 148
Universal Declaration of Human Rights, 366
universal jurisdiction, 81–87
University of California-Los Angeles (UCLA), 103
UNSCOM. See United Nations Special Commission
UNSCR. See United Nations Security Council Resolution
UN Security Council, 326
US Agency for International Development, 69
US Alliance, 120
US Arms Trade Resource Center, 308
US Army and Marine Corps Counterinsurgency Center, 120
US Army European Command, 307
US Geological Survey (USGS), 221, 275
US Navy Arctic Roadmap, 19–20
US Training Center. See Blackwater
USAID. See United States Agency for International Development
USGS. See U.S. Geological Survey

Validated Independent News (VIN), 127, 355–57
Van Gelder, Sarah, 208
Venezuela, media and, 378–80, 382
Vermont
    Obama and, 395
    secession and, 392–401
Vermont Commons: Voices of Independence, 392, 397–401
Vest, Marshall, 338
Veterans for Common Sense, 359
Veterans for Peace, 359
Veterans Health Administration (VHA), 40–41
Vietnam War, 18, 69, 242, 261
VIN. See Validated Independent News
Visible Technologies, 27–28
Visscher, Marco, 209
Volcker, Paul, 153

Wallace, George

National Security Apparatus and, 252
    shooting of, 223, 235, 241, 256, 260–61
Wallach, Lori, 100
Wall Street, 135–36, 202, 394
    education and, 108–9
Walmartization, 108, 110
Walzer, Michael, 324–25
Wampi, 51
war
    in Afghanistan, 118–19, 365–66
    in Africa, 9
    in Cambodia, 233, 281
    economy of, 11
    in Iraq, 18, 70, 86, 152, 225, 233, 258, 261, 365
    in Laos, 233, 281
    in Latin America, 9
    in Middle East, 9
    in Pakistan, 34–37
    photography and, 364–65
    in Rwanda, 85
    Six-Day, 300
    on terror, 3, 328, 399
    in U.S., 9
    Vietnam, 18, 69, 242, 261
    against Yugoslavia, 119
War Casualties report, 359
war crimes
    in Gaza, 146–47
    by McChrystal, 122–24
Wardak, Abdul Rahim, 58
Wardak, Hamed, 58
war economy, 11
War Powers Act, 261
Warre, Earle, 242
Warren Commission, 237
Warsaw Pact, 119
War to Prevent Southern Secession, 390
Washington, George, 246
Washington Institute for Near East Policy (WINEP), 56
The Washington Teacher, 112
Watan Group, 57
water, 114
    Amazon and, 52–53
    Bhopal, India and, 77–81
    Israel and, 55–56
    toxicity, 78–79
Watergate, 223, 241
    as conspiracy theory, 232–34
    crimes of, 253–57
    Nixon and, 235–36, 254–57
    as SCAD, 260, 281
weapons of mass destruction (WMD), 225, 318, 323–24, 328
weapons proliferation, 305–11
"Web Providers Must Limit Internet's Carbon Footprint, Says Experts" (Johnson), 115
Webster, Daniel, 324
Weil, Danny, 106